M000248156

SECOND EDITION

STANDARD PRICE GUIDE TO

U.S. SCOUTING COLLECTIBLES

GEORGE CUHAJ

This Book Belongs To

Be Prepared

*Bookplate by Louise Cadwalader,
Cincinnati, OH, 1915.*

Published by

**krause
publications**

700 E. State Street • Iola, WI 54990-0001
Telephone: 715/445-2214

www.krause.com

Please call or write for our free catalog.
Our toll-free number to place an order or obtain a free catalog is 800-258-0929
or please use our regular business telephone 715-445-2214
for editorial comment and further information.

Library of Congress Catalog Number: 97-80596
ISBN: 0-87341-953-7

Printed in the United States of America

*Illustration on next page by Mel Kishner (1915–1991), who was a Milwaukee native and graduate of North
Division High School and the Milwaukee State Teachers College (now University of Wisconsin - Milwaukee.)
Professionally, he started working for The Journal in 1940, and in 1970 was appointed art director for The
Journal and Milwaukee Sentinel. He retired in 1978. In his private life, his painting earned national awards,
and he served four terms as president of the Wisconsin Painters and Sculptors organization. The father of four
children, his widow, Jane, kindly granted permission to use this illustration in the catalog.*

TABLE OF CONTENTS

THE BOY SCOUT

A popular print for framing from 1914, value $20.00 - $30.00.

PREFACE

Greetings and welcome to this second edition of *The Standard Price Guide to U.S. Scouting Collectibles.*

It has been my intent by publishing this work to assist members of the scout family and the general public in the range, variety, development and proper identification of items issued by the Boy Scout program in the United States and used on a national scope. These items would be those encountered by the enthusiast collector in the normal scope of developing a collection. These means may be by flea market, garage sale, estate auction, memorabilia dealer lists, antique mall booths or the conversation with members of the community.

Special enhancements to this second edition include brand new sections for merit badge pamphlets, philatelic covers and expanded coverage of uniforms, High Adventure Base items. Juvenile literature and series books have been grouped into an independent section regardless of the program covered. Finally, listings of Council Shoulder Patches (CSPs) Jamboree Shoulder Patches (JSPs) or Order of the Arrow Lodge Flaps are not included in this book as they are covered in very large specialized publications which are standards in their own right. To include them here would have made this work redundant. Should you require more information on a collecting specialty — eagle badges, rank patches, books, medallions, square knots — please consider purchasing the specialty volume for the area of interest. Titles of a number of quality resources are listed in the Reference Books section.

A bit about the author and his friends

I have been in scouting since age 8, when, in 1968, I joined the Cub Scout Pack meeting in the church next door to the apartment building. That institution served scouting in Astoria since 1928, and several members of the unit committee were active since the early 1940s. That was a great wealth of information which was shared with the younger troop members of unit history, trip antics, photographs and "stuff.' So begins the collector experience. As a youth, I earned the Eagle Scout Award, the Ad Altare Dei, and Pope Pius XII awards of my faith. I had the opportunity to hike the trails of Philmont, be the troop scribe of the Queens Council troop to the 1977 National Jamboree, and serve on the scout service corps the 1976 International Eucharistic Congress held in Philadelphia. As an adult, I stayed with the home unit, serving first as an assistant, then as scoutmaster for 13 years. During this time, I had an opportunity to be a summer camp staff member at Camp Aquehonga, Ten Mile River Scout Camps, and a member of the Brooklyn Diocese Catholic Committee on Scouting, and chapter advisor for Suanhacky Lodge's Tatanka Chapter. Later, I was awarded the Silver Beaver Award by the Queens Council and the Vigil Honor by Suanhacky Lodge #49. As part of my life-long interest in numismatics, I have organized the participation of the American Numismatic Association at the Coin Collecting Merit Badge Midway Booths at the National Jamborees of 1981, 1985, 1989, 1993, 1997, and 2001. Upon relocating to central Wisconsin, I have remained active first as a committee chairman, now as a scoutmaster. I have also worked with the district training staff and the Green Bay Diocese Catholic Committee on Scouting.

Professionally, I have been employed by the American Numismatic Society as its computer systems operator, chief usher at St. Patrick's Cathedral, catalog production manager for Stack's Rare Coins, and currently numismatic catalog production manager for Krause Publications, a nationally recognized employee-owned firm specializing in hobby publications.

Collecting, cataloging, and publishing have been both a profession and an avocation, and I credit the scout merit badge program for exposure to these fields. I feel very strongly that if one looks at the merit badges a scout earned, you could see traits of what he will become. For me, the first three merit badges were Stamp Collecting, Coin Collecting, and Railroading. A bit later, I earned Printing, Computers, and Photography. Stamp Collecting was first, as my father was a lifelong philatelist, and I learned by example. I took up coin collecting so as not to be in competition with him. Railroading was the family occupation, thus another natural choice. Printing, Computers and Photography came while a student at Brooklyn Technical High School. My career choices have been as a computer operator at a coin museum, and currently with database systems publishing catalogs for coin and paper money collectors.

Scouting Friends

Through numismatics, I met many collectors who had fond stories of their scouting experiences. Of many, I would like to single out four which I met as numismatists first, only later learning of their scouting experiences and collections.

In the mid-1970s, I was editor of a newsletter for the North Eastern Vecturists Association, a group of transportation token collectors. One member was Charles Rogers. Learning of my scout activities, Charles talked about camping at Camp Burton (now Alaire State Park, NJ) and experiences as Scoutmaster in Elizabeth, NJ. Charles shared with me a box of scout stuff, which included his 1928 tan uniform, full-square merit badges and a Camp Burton patch and postcard group — quite exciting, and my first acquisition of vintage scouting material.

About this time, I met Vincent Alones of the Long Island Coin Club. He and his wonderful wife Agnes were among the first advisors to a Young Numismatist program at New York area coin shows. They encouraged beginning collectors in getting a focus, but also in exhibiting and speaking. I got to know Vinnie best as a retired railroad man with the Long Island Rail Road, and later learned of his activities as a merit badge councilor with the Nassau County Council.

In the early 1980s, as systems operator at the American Numismatic Society (a coin museum in New York City), I met many visitors to the museum's collections. One of these was William Spengler. His visits would be frequent, but usually conversations never strayed far from coin topics. Upon my

William Spengler as a cub scout.

William Spengler and George Cuhaj.

mentioning my jamboree staff activities, Bill responded, "I did an Indian dance before Baden-Powell at the '37 World Jamboree." That remark broke the ice for several more boyhood stories about scouting activities. After my 1994 relocation to central Wisconsin and employment with Krause Publications, I would again work with Bill as a contributor to the *Standard Catalog of World Coins*. Over time, I learned that he was the first Cub Scout in the Valley Council to earn two gold and silver arrow points in the Wolf, Bear, and Lion program. Bill also was a staff member at Camp Gardner Dam and he signed up for the '35 National Jamboree but waited till '37 when he attended both the National and World events. It was at the latter jamboree that Bill did his Indian Dance for Baden-Powell and Queen Wilhelmina. (His troop photo is in the BSA's photo book of the 1937 Jamborees). In 1939, he earned the Eagle Scout Award. Most of the early Cub Scout and 1930s Boy Scout material illustrated in this second edition was carefully preserved by Bill.

Most recently, through my activities as treasurer (and a past president) of the American Medallic Sculpture Association, I have been able to meet and correspond with an international group of professional artists. One of these, Jeanne Stevens-Sollman, mentioned that her father was active in scouting. So, introductions were made, and it turns out that Ernest Stevens is an Eagle Scout and was an active camper at Rhode Island's Camp Yawgoog in the 1930s. He continued on as a unit leader and has lately become active in the camp's alumni association. A selection of his photos, cards, and patches has made a nice addition to this edition.

Ernest Stevens in 1938.

Ralph DeFalco and Kenneth Tremaine at summer camp.

I mention these experiences to share the collecting instinct. Folks with scouting backgrounds are everywhere; they each add to the program and take with them throughout life part of it.

In my scouting circles, I would like to acknowledge the friendships formed during my tenure in the Gateway District of Queens Council. Several fun-loving scout leaders have gone home, namely Oscar Howard (who would ring a doorbell with OH in Morse Code), George Stone (who would educate a generation of scouts in atomic energy and first aid — even after a leg amputation, he would be at camp in his motorized chair) and most recently Vito Vittelio (who was Mr. Registration at district events and training courses). Each one made a scout and scouter's experience broader.

The others whom I'd like to mention are still with us. Ralph DeFalco, John Pritchard, Brother Hugh Dymski OFM Conv., Roy Kramer, and Bruce Cobern who were participants in the Gateway District High Adventure Committee, a group who would organize 14 to 30-day touring trips in the summer. Camp-out travels with a school bus, a van and a trailer and two commercial cooking grills was a great experience.

Kenneth Tremaine, Kevin Dolce, Ron Newsam and Dennis Gaynor have been wonderful folks to do scouting with.

Denis Sackett and Mitch Morgenstern, as founders of the Jack Kohler Campership Association, deserve recognition. What started as a group of fun-loving ex-camp staffers who put together a fantastic party honoring Scouter John Kohler at his 50th anniversary in the program, now honors his memory with an association which is used as a fund-raising tool for assisting in sending needy scouts to camp. The next generation is in good hands, too, with the likes of Reidan Cruz, Frank Gaynor, John Ingoldsby, Harry Morales, Robert Petrillo, Franco Sagliocca, and Robert Soel.

Since my relocation to central Wisconsin, I've had the pleasure to be involved with a new fine group of volunteers in the Twin Lakes District of the Bay Lakes Council. I'll be looking forward to many years of training team work with the likes of Bob Burgdorf, Chris Angell, John Hielsberg, William Harris, and Wayne Youngblood.

I am sorry for any omissions. This is still a work in progress. Should you have information which you would like to see considered for future editions, I welcome your correspondence.

**George S. Cuhaj
P.O. Box 433
Iola, WI 54945**
Cuhajg@yahoo.com

DEDICATION

For Kenneth Michael Petrow, my cousin. Older by seven months, we grew up together on the same city block in Astoria, NY, attended the same church, grade school, and commuted to Brooklyn Technical High School on the subway for four years. We joined cub scouts the same year, but because Ken did not last in the program for long, there is just this one Christmas photo of us together in uniform. After high school, we continued our education at separate colleges; I remained single and he moved out of the city, married a wonderful lady, and started a family. We've kept in touch at family events, but several years ago, his life and family was forever changed with a challenge the magnitude of which I can only fathom. He is taking it in stride, and is doing what he can with his family. Ken wants to write a book, and I really hope that he will get it done to inspire others.

For Kevin Michalowski, one of my fellow employee-owners at Krause Publications. He has a keen sense of observation and a sometimes biting humor, and we struck up a friendship. Upon my return from an extended trip in 1998, I noticed that his hair style changed, to, like, nothing. Engaging him in some conversation, he brought up the trials and tribulations of chemotherapy, and life feelings. Awful is one of the few printable terms which come to mind. With a strong will, and family support, he has been cancer-free for some two years now. Kevin is continuing to enjoy time with his wife Jackie and his two kids. He has recently authored a book called *You Cook it! The Guy's Guide to Game Cookery*. I'm going to have to start hunting, so that I can make some use of that book.

For Jon Brecka. Jon was an enthusiastic and passionate collector of stuff, but mainly Hot Wheels®. He was a re-tread to the company, having been employed at KP before my arrival; and then after several years, returned, after I had joined the firm, this time with a wonderful wife, Shawn, and very young daughter. We would often have morning conversations about his most recent acquisitions, continuing knee surgery, or his newest photos of their daughter. Jon would go around acquiring items for his collection, and in the meantime would also buy things for others, which included my scouting or bowling or book collections. Jon was a most thoughtful fellow. Unfortunately, in December of 1999 on his way home during an early season rain-snow-ice storm, Jon's car was hit by a young driver who lost control and crossed the center-line. The accident placed Jon in a coma, from which he died in February 2000.

ACKNOWLEDGMENTS AND THANKS

Although I am the one ultimately responsible for this price guide, there have probably been hundreds of contributors who have assisted in this work in one way or another: perhaps by sharing a catalog, offering an item for sale, sending a letter, or having an item on display at a trade-o-ree or museum. To them I offer my thanks.

There are other I would like to publicly acknowledge by name for their assistance as fellow authors, collectors, and enthusiasts of scouting collectibles:

Doug Bearce	Kevin Doyle	Neil Larsen	William Spengler
Ken Beckman	Fred Duersch	Freddi Margolin	Dennis St. Jean
Gene Berman	Chuck Fisk	Tom Michael	Ernest Stevens
Bob Burgdorff	J.J. Goodwin	Dean Parks	Jim & Bea
Tom Casper	Dan Gould	Robert Petrillo	Stevenson
Bob Cylkowski	Terry Grove	John Pleasants	John Vacca
Ralph DeFalco	Jane Kishner	Mitch Reis	Mike Walton
Don DeYoung	David Kranz	Clark Robinson	Kelly Williams
Rudy Dioszegi	Josh Kunzman	Charles Rogers	

And these organizations:

American Numismatic Society, Troop 1, Flushing, Ottawa Scouting Museum, Milwaukee Heritage Museum, and the National Scout Museum.

A special thanks to my KP coworkers: database publising specialist Bonnie Tetzlaff, book designer Patsy Howell, color designer Jamie Martin, cover designer Mary Lou Marshall, editor Kris Manty, and photographers Ross Hubbard, Bob Best and Kris Kandler.

Troop photo from Camp Yawgoog, RI.

PRICE GUIDE USER'S MANUAL & SCOUTING TERMS

This price guide is organized into major sections based on the age-group divisions used within the scouting program — Cubs, Scouts, Explorers, Sea Scouts, Air Scouts, Lone Scouts, as well as special sections on the Order of the Arrow, National Jamborees, and High Adventure bases. Programs that have experienced name changes can be found within the major division, such as Sea Scouts — Sea Exploring; Explorer Scouts, Exploring, Venture. Juvenile literature and series books are presented in a special chapter.

Within each of the major-division groups, items of similar interest are listed together. For example,

all the Cub Scout program rank patches and awards are group together; handbooks, uniforms, position patches and program aids are similarly treated. An expanded index is included within each section. A full index appears at the back of the book. The specific listing titles are in larger type and bold for the major identification, and the variety identifications appear following in smaller type. On the line of the variety identification appear a years-of-use range, and then a reference and a price range of the item in commonly found grades. Items since 1970 are expected to be in mint condition.

A WORD ABOUT THE CROSS REFERENCES

In the past twenty years, specialists have developed detailed publications on specific areas of scouting collectibles. These specialists developed a numbering system, and these numbers have become a standard identification within the hobby, in auction listings, and on trade listings. The reference systems used in this book are listed at the beginning of the specific sections.

The listing sample to the right starts with the bold-face title of the book, then with three varieties. If a photograph was available, it would appear before the listing, or on a photo page very near to it. In this example the 'F' stands for the Bearce and Fisk book, *Collecting Boy Scout Literature*. The SM designation stands for Scoutmaster Handbooks. The numbers that follow are Bearce-Fisk variety numbers. Similar listings can be found for medallions, eagle medals, and rank badges.

BOY SCOUTS OF AMERICA, OFFICIAL HANDBOOK. BADEN-POWELL AND SETON, AUTHORS.

192 pgs, tan-yellow w/ brown imprint or green w/ light green imprint.	1910	F.001-005	1,400.- 2,500.
192 pgs, red leather-bound, gilt imprint.	1910	F.006	1,500. - 2,500.

BOY SCOUTS OF AMERICA, OFFICIAL MANUAL, OR HANDBOOK. SETON, AUTHOR.

192 pgs, cloth cover.	1910	F.007-009	1,250. - 1,750.

THE PRICE RANGE

In general, early scouting items, 1910-1945, are expected to have been used, but not abused. Handbook covers should be attached, but could be chipped or lightly folded. Full Square Merit Badges should still have a full square of material, but could have been sewn under a bit. They should not have been cut to a round shape, or worse yet, cut to the edge of the stitching. Early items, in new condition should command prices higher than that presented in this book. Items since 1970 are priced in mint condition. No marks in books, or needle holes in patches. Often, especially with lifetime collection groups, items form an ensemble, all rank patches are sewn on a cub uniform, merit badges and camp patches are on a sash. In many of these cases, the whole is worth more than the sum of the individual items.

In the open market (and the marketplace has been growing) and over time, you may be able to purchase items at less than the catalog range, more than the catalog ranges, and even within the catalog range. Supply, demand, and venue all play a part in the acquisition and disposal equation. Take your time, enjoy the subject matter. Welcome to the hobby. Expand your knowledge. Make new friends.

Young scout, cloth Turk's head neckerchief slide.

INSTANT IDENTIFICATION GUIDE

Program Areas:

Cub Scouts – Ranks (left); Position (right).

Exploring – CAW, Circle V, E. Ranks, Position.

Boy Scouts – Rank Patches.

 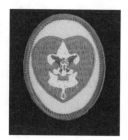 

Boy Scouts – Merit Badges.

Sea Scouts – Ranks.

Air Scout and Air Explorer – Rank Patches.

Boy Scouts – Youth Position (top);
Adult Position (bottom).

Lone Scouts.

INSTANT IDENTIFICATION GUIDE (CONT.)

Types of Patches:

Scoutmaster badges of the cut edge (left) and rolled-edge varieties.

Cut cloth, cut edge, rolled edge.

Types of Backing to Patches:

Rank patches have different backs which are collectible. The top two are both cut khaki cloth, one with a glue back and the second with a gauze backing. The bottom row illustrates twill cut edge badges with glue, gauze, and plastic backs.

Cloth back, glue back, plastic pack,
gauze back, gauze and glue back.

Types of Backing to Pins:

Locking C clasp (top);
safety pin, bent wire clasp, and clutch back (bottom).

Enamel / Coloring Styles:

JASM enamel (left); SPL painted bars (right).

SCOUTING ORGANIZATIONS AND TERMINOLOGY

Some quick references to program identification and dating of items

The National Council of the Boy Scouts of America was chartered in 1910, and had three offices in New York City. In 1953, the office was moved to North Brunswick, NJ, and in 1979 Irving, Texas.

Prior to 1953, the seal on BSA products reads Boy Scouts of America - National Council – New York City, around a First-Class emblem. After 1953, the seal reads Boy Scouts of America - National Council, around a Tenderfoot emblem.

The administrative level below the national office is called a region. From the 1940s through 1973, there were telve regions, more-or-less based on the boundaries of the Federal Reserve Banking System. In 1973, the telve regions were reduced to six, and in the mid-1990s reduced to the current four.

Under the region level is the local council. The council is made up of districts, which include cub packs, scout troops and venture crews.

The Order of the Arrow region divisions are called sections, with further divisions called areas. The local council division is a lodge, and operations on a district level occur as a chapter.

Many certificates in scouting, such as those for membership cards, charters, advancement cards, Silver Beaver Awards include signatures. Most of these signatures are printed facsimiles, of all or some of the following titled officers of the organization are used: President (head volunteer), chief scout executive (top professional), honorary president (U.S. president), national commissioner, chief scout, and honorary vice-presidents (all living past-presidents, and other famous figures). Some early eagle certificates include a real James E. West signature rather than a rubber-stamp version. Early Heroism Certificates have real Daniel Beard signatures. In addition to the above listing, later date certificates could have real or rubber-stamped signatures of council president, council, scout or district executives, council chairman, council commissioner and district chairman.

To assist with the dating of certificates, and their approximate time of use, following are the dates of service for president, chief scout executives, and honorary presidents.

Presidents of the Boy Scouts of America

Colin Livingston	1910-1925	Charles M. Pigott	1986-1988
James H. Storrow	*1925-1926	Harold S. Hook	1988-1990
Milton A. McRae	**1926	Richard H. Leet	1990-1992
Walter W. Head	1926-1931	John L. Clendenin	1992-1994
Mortimer L. Schiff*	1931	Norman R. Augustine	1994-1996
Walter W. Head	1931-1946	John W. Creighton, Jr.	1996-1998
Amory Houghton	1946-1951	Edward E. Whitacre, Jr.	1998-2000
John M. Schiff	1951-1956	Milton H. Ward	2000-
Kenneth K. Bechtel	1956-1959	*Died while in office	
Ellsworth H. Augustus	1959-1964	**Interim	
Thomas J. Watson, Jr.	1964-1968		
Irving J. Feist	1968-1971		
Norton Clapp	1971-1973	**Chief Scout Executives**	
Robert W. Reneker	1973-1975	James E. West	1911-1943
Arch Monson, Jr.	1975-1977	Elbert K. Fretwell	1943-1948
Downing B. Jenks	1977-1979	Arthur A. Schuck	1948-1960
John D. Murchison*	1979	Joseph A. Brunton, Jr.	1960-1967
Downing B. Jenks	1979-1980	Alden G. Barber	1967-1976
Thomas D. MacAvoy	1980-1982	Harvey L. Price	1976-1979
Edward C. Joullian III	1982-1984	J.L. Tarr	1979-1984
Sanford N. McDonnell	1984-1986	Ben H. Love	1985-1993
		Jere B. Ratcliffe	1993-2000
		Roy L. Williams	2000-

Presidents of the U.S. Serving as:

Honorary BSA President	Honorary BSA Vice-Pres.	
	Term in office	Year of death
Woodrow Wilson	1913-1921	1924
Warren G. Harding	1921-1923	—
Calvin Coolidge	1923-1929	1933
Herbert Hoover	1929-1933	1964
Franklin D. Roosevelt	1933-1945	—
Harry S Truman	1945-1953	1972
Dwight D. Eisenhower	1953-1961	1969
John F. Kennedy	1961-1963	—
Lyndon B. Johnson	1963-1969	1973
Richard M. Nixon	1969-1974	1994
Gerald R. Ford	1974-1977	
Jimmy Carter	1977-1981	
Ronald Reagan	1981-1989	
George Bush	1989-1993	
Bill Clinton	1993-2001	
George W. Bush	2001-	

The best thing on an 8th birthday—a Cub Scout uniform for the author!

CUB SCOUTS

The Cub Scout program went nationwide to join the Boy Scout program in 1930, but many troops had unofficial Junior Scouts or troop mascots—even the national supply division sold the *English Wolf Cub's Handbook* in the late 1920s. The Cub program is divided into age groups. When the program first began, a boy joined at nine, advancing to Wolf the first year. At ten, he became a Bear and at eleven a Lion. The Cubs wore knickers or shorts until 1947, when long pants were introduced. In 1949, when the Boy Scouts lowered the joining age to eleven, the Cub program lowered its to eight. In 1969, Webelos replaced Lion, and in 1982 a Tiger Cub program was introduced for seven-year-olds. Each group of eight or so Cubs was organized into dens, with a den mother (more recently den leader) in charge. A group of dens is organized into a cub pack, with a cubmaster as the unit leader.

RANK BADGES

BEAR PATCH

Felt.	1930-1940	3.00 - 5.00
Twill, cloth back.	1940-1975	1.00 - 2.00
Twill, plastic back.	1975	0.50 - 1.00

BOBCAT PATCH

Twill, plastic back.	1975	0.50 - 1.00

BOBCAT PIN

Clutch back.	1965	1.00 - 2.00
Safety pin back.	1957-1965	2.00 - 3.00

ARROW OF LIGHT

Blue bordered yellow arrow on khaki fine twill, cut edge border.	1965-1973	3.00 - 5.00
Blue bordered yellow arrow on khaki rough twill, cut edge border.	1940-1965	3.00 - 5.00
Blue bordered yellow arrow on khaki twill, plastic back.	1973	1.00 - 2.00

ARROW POINT

Gold, cloth back.	1930-1970	1.00 - 2.00
Gold, plastic back.	1970	0.25 - 0.50
Silver, cloth back.	1930-1970	1.00 - 2.00
Silver, plastic back.	1970	0.25 - 0.50

LION PATCH

Felt.	1930-1940	3.00 - 5.00
Twill, cloth back.	1930-1940	1.00 - 2.00

SPORTS BELT LOOP

Archery.	1985	0.25 - 0.50
Art.	1985	0.25 - 0.50
Badminton.	1985	0.25 - 0.50
Baseball.	1985	0.25 - 0.50
Basketball.	1985	0.25 - 0.50
BB Shooting.	1985	0.25 - 0.50
Bicycling.	1985	0.25 - 0.50
Bowling.	1985	0.25 - 0.50
Citizenship.	1985	0.25 - 0.50
Communicating.	1985	0.25 - 0.50
Fishing.	1985	0.25 - 0.50
Geography.	1985	0.25 - 0.50
Golf.	1985	0.25 - 0.50
Gymnastics.	1985	0.25 - 0.50
Heritages.	1985	0.25 - 0.50
Marbles.	1985	0.25 - 0.50
Mathematics.	1985	0.25 - 0.50
Music.	1985	0.25 - 0.50
Physical Fitness.	1985	0.25 - 0.50
Science.	1985	0.25 - 0.50
Skating.	1985	0.25 - 0.50
Skiing.	1985	0.25 - 0.50
Soccer.	1985	0.25 - 0.50
Softball.	1985	0.25 - 0.50
Swimming.	1985	0.25 - 0.50
Table Tennis.	1985	0.25 - 0.50
Tennis.	1985	0.25 - 0.50
Ultimate.	1985	0.25 - 0.50
Volleyball.	1985	0.25 - 0.50

SUMMERTIME PACK AWARD PIN

Clutch back.	1981	0.50 - 1.00

WEBELOS ACTIVITY BADGE, ENAMELED PIN

Aquanaut.	1990	0.50 - 0.75
Artist.	1990	0.50 - 0.75
Athlete.	1990	0.50 - 0.75
Citizen.	1990	0.50 - 0.75
Communicator.	1990	0.50 - 0.75
Craftsman.	1990	0.50 - 0.75
Engineer.	1990	0.50 - 0.75
Family Member.	1990	0.50 - 0.75
Fitness.	1990	0.50 - 0.75
Forester.	1990	0.50 - 0.75
Geologist.	1990	0.50 - 0.75
Handyman.	1990	0.50 - 0.75
Naturalist.	1990	0.50 - 0.75
Outdoorsman.	1990	0.50 - 0.75
Readyman.	1990	0.50 - 0.75
Scholar.	1990	0.50 - 0.75
Scientist.	1990	0.50 - 0.75
Showman.	1990	0.50 - 0.75
Sportsman.	1990	0.50 - 0.75
Traveler.	1990	0.50 - 0.75

WEBELOS ACTIVITY BADGE, NICKEL PIN

Aquanaut.	1967-1990	1.00 - 2.00
Artist.	1967-1990	1.00 - 2.00
Athlete.	1967-1990	1.00 - 2.00
Citizen.	1967-1990	1.00 - 2.00
Craftsman.	1967-1990	1.00 - 2.00
Engineer.	1967-1990	1.00 - 2.00
Forester.	1967-1990	1.00 - 2.00
Geologist.	1967-1990	1.00 - 2.00
Naturalist.	1967-1990	1.00 - 2.00
Outdoorsman.	1967-1990	1.00 - 2.00
Scholar.	1967-1990	1.00 - 2.00
Scientist.	1967-1990	1.00 - 2.00
Showman.	1967-1990	1.00 - 2.00
Sportsman.	1967-1990	1.00 - 2.00
Traveler.	1967-1990	1.00 - 2.00

WEBELOS COMPASS POINTS EMBLEM AND DEVICES

Pocket patch.	1985	1.00 - 2.00

WEBELOS PATCH

Twill, cloth back.	1969-1975	1.00 - 2.00
Twill, plastic back.	1975	0.50 - 1.00

WEBELOS TRI-COLOR

Locking pin, curved nameplate.	1967-1985	2.00 - 3.00
Pin, clutch back, straight nameplate.	1990	1.00 - 2.00

WOLF PATCH

Felt.	1930-1940	3.00 - 5.00
Twill, cloth back.	1940-1975	1.00 - 2.00
Twill, plastic back.	1975	0.50 - 1.00

HANDBOOKS

THE BOY'S CUBBOOK VOL. 1, WOLF

Drawing of Indian on board cover, 7 printings.	1930-1935	35.00 - 50.00

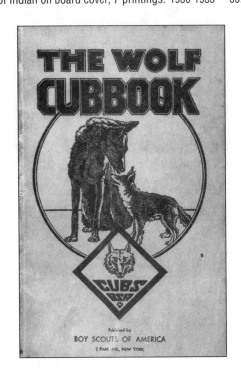

THE WOLF CUBBOOK
Wolf and cub on card cover, eight printings.	1936-1942	10.00 - 15.00
Wolf and cub on card cover, seven printings, w/ color plates.	1943-1946	10.00 - 15.00

WOLF BOOK
Red cover, eight printings.	1947-1954	5.00 - 10.00
Thirteen printings.	1954-1965	4.00 - 6.00
Twenty-four printings.	1967-1979	2.00 - 3.00

THE BOY'S CUBBOOK VOL. 2, BEAR
Drawing of Indian on board cover, nine printings.	1930-1937	35.00 - 50.00

THE BEAR CUBBOOK
Bear and cub on card cover, nine printings.	1937-1942	10.00 - 15.00
Bear and cub on card cover, seven printings w/ color plates.	1943-1947	10.00 - 15.00

BEAR BOOK
Blue cover, seven printings.	1948-1953	5.00 - 10.00
Thirteen printings.	1954-1965	4.00 - 6.00
Twenty-four printings.	1967-1979	2.00 - 3.00

THE BOY'S CUBBOOK VOL. 3, LION
Drawing of Indian on board cover, eight printings.	1930-1937	35.00 - 50.00

THE LION CUBBOOK
Lion and cub on card cover, seven printings.	1938-1942	10.00 - 15.00
Lion and cub on card cover, four printings, w/ color plates.	1943-1946	10.00 - 15.00

LION BOOK
Black cover, nine printings.	1947-1953	5.00 - 10.00

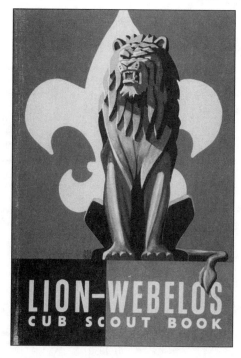

LION-WEBELOS BOOK
Fifteen printings.	1954-1965	4.00 - 6.00

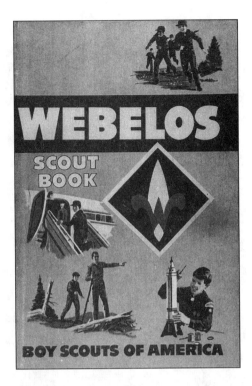

WEBELOS BOOK
Twenty-six printings including one in Spanish. 1967-1979   2.00 - 3.00

RESOURCE BOOKS

CASSETTES
Cub Scout Songtime.   (none)   5.00 - 7.50

CUB MASTER'S PACK BOOK
First edition, five printings.	1932-1939	10.00 - 15.00
Second edition, thirteen printings.	1943-1954	10.00 - 15.00
Third edition, thirteen printings.	1954-1966	10.00 - 15.00
Fourth edition, fifteen printings.	1967-1981	5.00 - 8.00

CUB SCOUT LEADER BOOK
Ten printings, three-ring binder format.   1982-1990   5.00 - 7.50

CUB SCOUT SONGBOOK
Twelve printings.   1947-1969   5.00 - 7.50

CUB SCOUT SPORT BOOK
Archery.	1985	1.00 - 2.00
Badminton.	1985	1.00 - 2.00
Baseball.	1985	1.00 - 2.00
Basketball.	1985	1.00 - 2.00
Bicycling.	1985	1.00 - 2.00
Bowling.	1985	1.00 - 2.00
Golf.	1985	1.00 - 2.00
Marbles.	1985	1.00 - 2.00
Physical Fitness.	1985	1.00 - 2.00
Skating.	1985	1.00 - 2.00
Skiing.	1985	1.00 - 2.00
Soccer.	1985	1.00 - 2.00
Softball.	1985	1.00 - 2.00
Swimming.	1985	1.00 - 2.00
Table Tennis.	1985	1.00 - 2.00
Ultimate.	1985	1.00 - 2.00
Volleyball.	1985	1.00 - 2.00

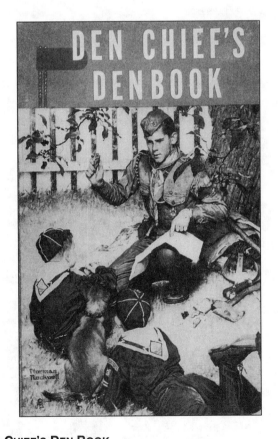

DEN CHIEF'S DEN BOOK
First edition, twelve printings.	1932-1941	5.00 - 7.50
Revised edition, twenty-five printings.	1942-1962	4.00 - 6.00
Revised edition, twenty-eight printings.	1965-1990	5.00 - 10.00

DEN LEADER COACH BOOK
Two printings.   1967-1968   5.00 - 7.50

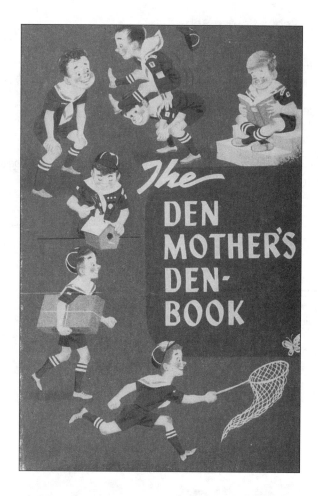

DEN LEADER'S BOOK
Nineteen printings.   1970-1988   4.00 - 6.00

DEN MOTHER'S DEN BOOK
First edition, eighteen printings.   1937-1950   5.00 - 7.50
Second edition, sixteen printings.   1951-1966   10.00 - 15.00
Third edition, three printings.   1967-1969   5.00 - 7.50

HOW BOOK OF CUB SCOUTING
Heavy fabric hardcover w/ red question mark,   1951-1966   10.00 - 15.00
  sixteen printings.

HOW BOOK OF CUBBING

Golden hardcover w/ large question mark, five printings.	1938-1942	10.00 - 15.00
Yellow hardcover w/ large question mark, seven printings.	1943-1949	10.00 - 15.00
Heavy fabric hardcover w/ green question mark, one printing.	1950	15.00 - 20.00

SLIDES & CASSETTE - CEREMONIES

The Cub Scout Trail.	1989	20.00 - 30.00

STAGING DEN AND PACK CEREMONIES

Twenty-six printings.	1953-1987	5.00 - 10.00

VIDEOS

The Big Bear Cub Scout Video.	1990	15.00 - 25.00
The Bobcat and Wolf Cub Scout Video.	1990	15.00 - 25.00
Webelos Scout Video.	1990	15.00 - 25.00
Cub Scout Jam - Revised.	1991	10.00 - 15.00
Ethics in Action.	1991	10.00 - 15.00
Tiger Cubs, Yeah!	1992	10.00 - 15.00
Cub Scouting: It's Not Just for Kids.	1993	10.00 - 15.00
Cub Scout Leader Basic Training.	1994	10.00 - 15.00
Webelos, Wow!	1994	10.00 - 15.00
The Five Cub Scout programs on one tape.	1996	12.50 - 17.50
The New Cub Scout Den Leader.	1996	7.50 - 12.50
The New Cubmaster.	1996	7.50 - 12.50
The New Tiger Cub Coach.	1996	7.50 - 12.50
The New Webelos Den Leader.	1996	7.50 - 12.50
The Pack Committee.	1996	7.50 - 12.50
Welcome to Tiger Cubs BSA.	1996	10.00 - 15.00

WEBELOS/DEN LEADER'S BOOK

Fifteen printings.	1967-1981	5.00 - 7.50

POSITION BADGES

ASSISTANT DENNER

One gold bar on blue twill cut cloth.	1930-1955	10.00 - 15.00
One gold bar on blue twill cut edge.	1955-1964	8.00 - 10.00
One gold bar on blue twill rolled edge, cloth back.	1965-1975	3.00 - 5.00
One gold bar on blue twill rolled edge, plastic back.	1975	1.00 - 2.00

DENNER

Two gold bars on blue twill cut cloth.	1930-1955	10.00 - 15.00
Two gold bars on blue twill cut edge.	1955-1964	8.00 - 10.00
Two gold bars on blue twill rolled edge, cloth back.	1965-1975	3.00 - 5.00
Two gold bars on blue twill rolled edge, plastic back.	1975	1.00 - 2.00

POSITION BADGES - ADULT

ASSISTANT CUBMASTER

Gold on blue twill, CUBS BSA below emblem, diamond-shaped patch.	1930-1940	15.00 - 20.00
Gold on blue twill, CUB SCOUTS BSA below emblem, diamond-shaped cut-edge patch.	1940-1964	10.00 - 15.00
Gold on blue twill, CUB SCOUTS BSA below emblem, diamond-shaped rolled-edge patch.	1965-1970	5.00 - 7.50
Solid blue embroidery, rolled edge.	1972-1989	2.00 - 3.00
Fully embroidered mylar thread, (trained leader).	1972-1989	3.00 - 5.00

Den mothers sporting sharp uniforms.

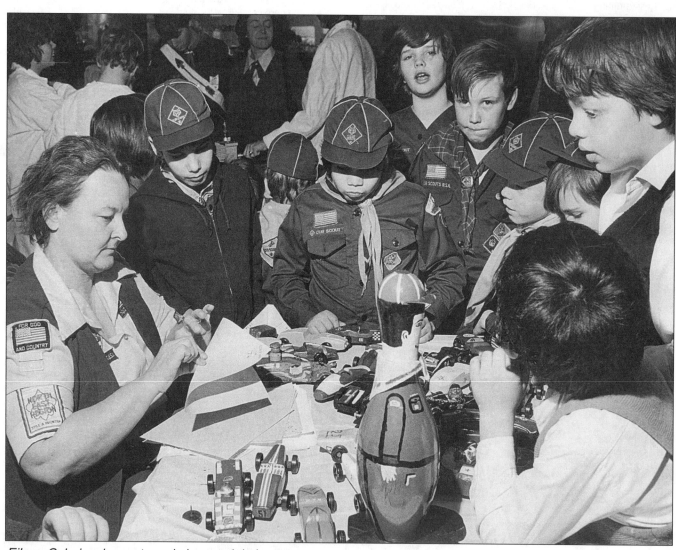

Eileen Cuhaj, cub scouts and pinewood derby cars.

TIGER CUB COACH
Orange twill, rolled edge.	1989	1.00 - 1.50

WEBELOS DEN LEADER
Solid blue embroidery, rolled edge.	1972-1989	2.00 - 3.00
Fully embroidered mylar thread, (trained leader).	1972-1989	3.00 - 5.00

UNIFORM SQUARE KNOTS

SQUARE KNOTS ON YELLOW TWILL
Cubmaster Award.	1988	5.00 - 7.50
Weblos Den Leader Award.	1988	5.00 - 7.50
Tiger Cub Coach Award.	1992	5.00 - 7.50

SQUARE KNOTS ON BLUE TWILL
Cub Scouter Award.	1988	5.00 - 7.50
Den Leader Award.	1988	5.00 - 7.50
Den Leader Coach Award.	1988	5.00 - 7.50

RELIGIOUS AWARDS - YOUTH

ALEPH
Jewish, lamp on open scroll.	1980	10.00 - 15.00

BISMILLAH
Islamic, Arabic calligraphy.	1980	10.00 - 15.00

CHI RHO
Eastern Orthodox, white cross with red orthodox cross within.	1980	10.00 - 15.00

DHARMA
Hindu, legend on diamond pendant.	1980	10.00 - 15.00

FAITH IN GOD
Church of Jesus Christ of Latter-day Saints (Mormon), father, mother and son before Salt Lake Temple.	1980	10.00 - 15.00

FRIENDS, THAT OF GOD
Religious Society of Friends (Quakers), The Light Shines on in the Dark legend around compass.	1980	10.00 - 15.00

GOD AND COUNTRY
First Church of Christ Scientist, red cross on white field.	1980	10.00 - 15.00

GOD AND COUNTRY, GOD AND FAMILY
Episcopal, red cross on white field, stars in blue 1st quadrant.	1967	10.00 - 15.00
Protestant, red cross on white field.	1967	10.00 - 15.00

GOD AND COUNTRY, GOD AND ME
Protestant, red cross on white field.	1980	10.00 - 15.00

GOD AND FAMILY
Lutheran, red cross on white field.	1967	10.00 - 15.00
The Salvation Army, Army emblem.	1980	10.00 - 15.00

GOD AND LIFE
The Salvation Army, Army emblem.	1980	10.00 - 15.00

JOYFUL SERVANT
Churches of Christ, cross and four hearts within white field.	1980	10.00 - 15.00

LIGHT OF CHRIST
Roman Catholic, youth with candle.	1980	10.00 - 15.00

ASSISTANT DEN LEADER
Solid blue embroidery, rolled edge.	1972-1989	2.00 - 3.00
Fully embroidered mylar thread, (trained leader).	1972-1989	3.00 - 5.00

ASSISTANT DEN MOTHER
Solid blue embroidery, rolled edge.	1972-1989	2.00 - 3.00

ASSISTANT WEBELOS DEN LEADER
Solid blue embroidery, rolled edge.	1972-1989	2.00 - 3.00

ASSISTANT WEBELOS LEADER
Fully embroidered mylar thread, (trained leader).	1972-1989	3.00 - 5.00

CUBMASTER
Silver on blue twill, CUBS BSA below emblem, diamond-shaped patch.	1930-1940	15.00 - 20.00
Silver on blue twill, CUB SCOUTS BSA below emblem, diamond-shaped cut-edge patch.	1940-1964	10.00 - 15.00
Silver on blue twill, CUB SCOUTS BSA below emblem, diamond-shaped rolled-edge patch.	1965-1970	5.00 - 7.50
Fully embroidered mylar thread, (trained leader).	1972-1989	3.00 - 5.00
Solid blue embroidery, rolled edge.	1972-1989	2.00 - 3.00

DEN LEADER COACH
On blue background.	1972-1989	2.00 - 3.00
Fully embroidered mylar thread, (trained leader).	1972-1989	3.00 - 5.00

DEN LEADER
Solid blue embroidery, rolled edge.	1972-1989	2.00 - 3.00
Fully embroidered mylar thread, (trained leader).	1972-1989	3.00 - 5.00

DEN MOTHER
Solid blue embroidery, rolled edge.	1972-1989	2.00 - 3.00

PACK COMMITTEE CHAIRMAN
Silver on green twill, CUBS BSA below emblem, diamond-shaped cut-edge patch.	1930-1955	15.00 - 20.00
Silver on green twill, CUB SCOUTS BSA below emblem, diamond-shaped cut-edge patch.	1955-1964	10.00 - 15.00
Silver on green twill, CUB SCOUTS BSA below emblem, diamond-shaped rolled-edge patch.	1965-1970	5.00 - 7.50

PACK COMMITTEE
Gold on green twill, CUBS BSA below emblem, diamond-shaped patch.	1930-1940	15.00 - 20.00
Gold on green twill, CUB SCOUTS BSA below emblem, diamond-shaped cut-edge patch.	1940-1964	10.00 - 15.00
Gold on green twill, CUB SCOUTS BSA below emblem, diamond-shaped rolled-edge patch.	1965-1970	5.00 - 7.50
Solid blue embroidery, rolled edge.	1972-1989	2.00 - 3.00

LOVE AND HELP
Unitarian Universalist, flame on pedestal, church steeple in background. 1980 10.00 - 15.00

LOVE FOR GOD
Meher Baba, pendant with Mastery in Service legend. 1980 10.00 - 15.00

LOVE OF GOD
Polish National Catholic Church, open book and cross in oval within cross. 1980 10.00 - 15.00

MACCABEE
Jewish, flame and Star of David in Menorah. 1980 10.00 - 15.00

METTA
Buddhist, ship's wheel. 1980 10.00 - 15.00

PARVULI DEI
Roman Catholic, Mary, Jesus and Joseph, Holy Spirit above. 1967 10.00 - 15.00

SAINT GEORGE
Eastern Orthodox, Saint George on horseback, slaying dragon. 1980 10.00 - 15.00

SILVER CREST
The Salvation Army, pendant and red/orange/blue ribbon bar. 1980 10.00 - 15.00

ST. GREGORY
Eastern Diocese of the Armenian Church of America, church building. 1980 10.00 - 15.00

UNITY OF MANKIND
Baha'l, globe. 1980 10.00 - 15.00

UNITY. GOD IN ME
Association of Unity Churches, flower bud. 1980 10.00 - 15.00

AWARD MEDALS

PINEWOOD DERBY MEDAL
Race car in red, white, or blue enamel disc hanging from red-white-blue ribbon. 1981 2.00 - 3.00
Race car in relief, copper, silvered or gilt pendant. 1970-1980 3.00 - 5.00

REGATTA MEDAL
Ship in red, white, or blue enamel disc hanging from red-white-blue ribbon. 1981 2.00 - 3.00
Ship in relief, copper, silvered or gilt pendant. 1970-1980 3.00 - 5.00

SPACE DERBY MEDAL
Space craft in red, white, or blue enamel disc hanging from red-white-blue ribbon. 1981 2.00 - 3.00
Space craft in relief, copper, silvered or gilt pendant. 1970-1980 3.00 - 5.00

MEMBERSHIP CARDS

Two fold. 1935-1955 10.00 - 15.00
Single card. 1953-1960 2.00 - 5.00

ADVANCEMENT CARDS

ARROW OF LIGHT CARD
Colored patch on yellow background. 1972-1989 0.50 - 1.00

BEAR CUB CARD
CUBS BSA at bottom of diamond-shaped card. 1930-1950 5.00 - 7.50
CUBS BSA on patch design flanked by orange color bar. 1945-1953 3.00 - 5.00
CUB SCOUTS BSA on patch design. 1953-1965 2.00 - 4.00
Colored patch on blue background. 1972-1989 0.50 - 1.00

BOBCAT CUB CARD
CUBS BSA on patch design flanked by orange color bar. 1945-1953 3.00 - 5.00
CUB SCOUTS BSA on patch design. 1953-1965 2.00 - 4.00
Colored patch on blue background. 1972-1989 0.50 - 1.00

LION CUB CARD

CUBS BSA at bottom of diamond-shaped card.	1930-1950	5.00 - 7.50
CUBS BSA on patch design flanked by orange color bar.	1945-1953	3.00 - 5.00
CUB SCOUTS BSA on patch design.	1953-1965	2.00 - 4.00

WEBELOS CARD

Arrow of Light patch design flanked by orange color bar.	1945-1953	3.00 - 5.00
Arrow of Light design.	1953-1965	2.00 - 4.00
Webelos badge patch on gray background.	1972-1989	0.50 - 1.00

WOLF CUB CARD

CUBS BSA at bottom of diamond-shaped card.	1930-1950	5.00 - 7.50
CUBS BSA on patch design flanked by orange color bar.	1945-1953	3.00 - 5.00
CUB SCOUTS BSA on patch design.	1953-1965	2.00 - 4.00
Colored patch on blue background.	1972-1989	0.50 - 1.00

UNIFORMS

BELT, WEB

CUB SCOUTS BSA on buckle emblem.	1940-1970	2.50 - 7.50
CUBS BSA on buckle emblem.	1930-1940	10.00 - 15.00

COUNCIL STRIP, BLUE AND YELLOW

New York City/Queens.	1945-1955	50.00 - 75.00

HAT, CUB

Blue w/ yellow front, baseball style.	1970	3.00 - 6.00
Blue with yellow stripes, CUB SCOUTS BSA on patch emblem.	1940-1970	10.00 - 15.00
Blue with yellow stripes, CUBS BSA on patch emblem.	1930-1940	15.00 - 20.00

HAT, WEBELOS

Blue, two-tone baseball style w/ Webelos patch.	1970	3.00 - 6.00

KNICKERS

Buckle below knee.	1930-1947	30.00 - 50.00

NECKERCHIEF

Webelos plaid with patch sewn on.	1970-1980	5.00 - 7.50
Yellow, with CUB SCOUTS BSA on emblem, triangle.	1940-1970	7.50 - 10.00
Yellow, with CUBS BSA on emblem, full square.	1930-1940	15.00 - 20.00
Yellow, with CUBS BSA on emblem, triangle.	1930-1940	12.50 - 17.50

NECKERCHIEF SLIDES, CLOTH "TURKS HEAD"

Blue and yellow.	1925-1953	10.00 - 15.00

PANTS, LONG

Blue, w/ fold over button down flap on pockets.	1947-1970	10.00 - 15.00

SHIRT, LONG SLEEVE

Blue, plain front pockets.	1970-1990	5.00 - 10.00
Blue, pleated pockets.	1947-1970	7.50 - 10.00

SHIRT, SHORT SLEEVE

Blue, plain front pockets.	1970-1990	5.00 - 10.00
Blue, pleated pockets.	1947-1970	10.00 - 15.00

SHORTS

Blue.	1930-1947	10.00 - 15.00

SHOULDER CORD, ASSISTANT DENNER
Single yellow cord with shoulder tab,   1970   5.00 - 7.50
  safety pin back.

SHOULDER CORD, DENNER
Two yellow cords with shoulder tab,   1970   5.00 - 7.50
  safety pin back.

SOCKS, KNEE
Blue with yellow tops.   1975   4.00 - 7.50

SOCKS, KNEE LENGTH
Blue, with elastic garters and yellow tabs.   1930-1975   10.00 - 15.00

STAR
Gold star w/ tenure number, clutch back pin,   1956   1.00 - 1.50
  yellow plastic disc.

STATE STRIP, BLUE AND YELLOW
ALA.	1945-1955	20.00 - 30.00
CALIF.	1945-1955	15.00 - 22.50
COLO.	1945-1955	20.00 - 30.00
CONN.	1945-1955	25.00 - 35.00
GA.	1945-1955	20.00 - 30.00
ILL.	1945-1955	15.00 - 25.00
IND.	1945-1955	15.00 - 25.00
IOWA.	1945-1955	20.00 - 30.00
MASS.	1945-1955	15.00 - 25.00
ME.	1945-1955	25.00 - 35.00
MICH.	1945-1955	20.00 - 30.00
MINN.	1945-1955	15.00 - 25.00
MO.	1945-1955	15.00 - 25.00
N.J.	1945-1955	20.00 - 30.00
N.Y.	1945-1955	15.00 - 25.00
OHIO.	1945-1955	20.00 - 30.00
PA.	1945-1955	15.00 - 25.00
TEXAS.	1945-1955	15.00 - 25.00
UTAH.	1945-1955	20.00 - 30.00
WASH.	1945-1955	15.00 - 25.00
WIS.	1945-1955	15.00 - 25.00

SWEATER
Blue, long sleeve, CUB SCOUTS BSA on strip.   1953-1975   25.00 - 40.00
Blue, long sleeve, CUBS BSA on strip.   1930-1953   50.00 - 75.00

UNIT NUMBER
Blue twill w/ yellow embroidery.   1950   1.00 - 1.50
Yellow felt rectangle w/ blue embroidery.   1930-1950   3.00 - 5.00

UNIFORMS - ADULT

BLAZER, BULLION-EMBROIDERED PROGRAM EMBLEM
Cub Scout emblem.   1971   15.00 - 20.00

BLOUSE
Yellow long sleve. CUB SCOUTS, B.S.A. strip.   1975-1985   10.00 - 15.00
Yellow short sleve. CUB SCOUTS, B.S.A. strip. 1975-1985   10.00 - 15.00

DEN MOTHER HAT
Metal emblem sewen on.   1965-1972   15.00 - 20.00

DRESS
Single piece, blue. CUB SCOUTS, B.S.A. strip. 1965-1975   25.00 - 35.00
Single piece, olive green. BOY SCOUTS OF   1980-1989   25.00 - 35.00
  AMERICA strip.

SCARF
Yellow and blue with cub emblem.   1980   15.00 - 20.00

PINS

BEAR RANK PIN
Bear w/CUBS BSA, paw below. Pinback.   1930-1953   10.00 - 15.00
Bear, CUB SCOUTS, BSA, paw print below   1953-1975   5.00 - 7.50
  locking pinback.
Bear, CUB SCOUTS, BSA,   1975-1990   2.00 - 5.00
  FDL below butterfly clasp pinback.
Bear, BEAR, FDL below butterfly clasp pinback. 1990   2.00 - 5.00

BOBCAT RANK PIN
Bobcat head. Pinback.   1930-1953   7.50 - 10.00
Bobcat head. Locking pinback.   1953-1975   7.50 - 10.00

LION RANK PIN
Lion w/CUBS BSA, paw below. Pinback.   1930-1953   10.00 - 15.00
Lion, CUB SCOUTS, BSA, paw print below.   1953-1969   5.00 - 7.50

WEBELOS RANK PIN
Webelos, CUB SCOUTS, BSA,   1975-1990   2.00 - 5.00
  FDL below butterfly clasp pinback.
Webelos, WEBELOS,   1990   2.00 - 5.00
  FDL below butterfly clasp pinback.

WOLF RANK PIN

Wolf w/CUBS BSA, paw below. Pinback.	1930-1953	10.00 - 15.00
Wolf, CUB SCOUTS, BSA, paw print below locking pinback.	1953-1975	5.00 - 7.50
Wolf, CUB SCOUTS, BSA, paw print below lockling pinback.	1953-1975	5.00 - 7.50
Wolf, CUB SCOUTS, BSA, FDL below butterfly clasp pinback.	1975-1990	2.00 - 5.00
Wolf, WOLF, FDL below butterfly clasp pinback.	1990	2.00 - 5.00

PINBACK BUTTONS

CUB SCOUT FACING

On red-white-blue, 7/8".	1940-1946	5.00 - 10.00
On red-white-blue, 1-1/4".	1940-1946	10.00 - 15.00
Red-white-blue background, 7/8" w/ fold tab.	1960-1965	5.00 - 7.50

ST. LOUIS COUNCIL CUBOREE

Scout and Indian seated at campfire, 1-3/4".	1941	10.00 - 15.00

A happy member of the program.

MEDALLIONS

Medallions are referenced to Rudy Dioszegi's book *Scouting Exonumnia Worldwide*.

AUDUBON DISTRICT CUB SCOUTS, NEW ORLEANS, LA, MARDI GRAS

39 mm, aluminum.	1969	Dio.1969.13a	1.00 - 2.00
39 mm, aluminum, blue color.	1969	Dio.1969.13b	1.00 - 2.00
39 mm, aluminum, golden color.	1969	Dio.1969.13c	1.00 - 2.00
39 mm, bronze.	1969	Dio.1969.13d	1.00 - 2.00
39 mm, .999 fine silver.	1969	Dio.1969.13e	20.00 - 25.00

AUDUBON DISTRICT CUB SCOUTS, NEW ORLEANS, LA

39 mm, aluminum, five rotation or edge varieties.	1971	Dio.1971.9a	1.00 - 2.00
39 mm, aluminum, blue color.	1971	Dio.1971.9b	1.00 - 2.00
39 mm, oxidized bronze.	1971	Dio.1971.9c	1.00 - 2.00
39 mm, bronze.	1971	Dio.1971.9d	1.00 - 2.00
39 mm, .999 fine silver.	1971	Dio.1971.9e	20.00 - 25.00
39 mm, aluminum.	1972	Dio.1972.13a	1.00 - 2.00
39 mm, aluminum, blue color.	1972	Dio.1972.13b	1.00 - 2.00
39 mm, bronze.	1972	Dio.1972.13c	1.00 - 2.00
39 mm, aluminum.	1973	Dio.1973.13a	1.00 - 2.00
39 mm, aluminum, blue color.	1973	Dio.1973.13b	1.00 - 2.00
39 mm, oxidized bronze.	1973	Dio.1973.13c	1.00 - 2.00
39 mm, bright bronze.	1973	Dio.1973.13d	1.00 - 2.00

AUDUBON DISTRICT, NEW ORLEANS, LA, CUB SCOUTS

39 mm, aluminum.	1968	Dio.1968.6a	1.00 - 2.00
39 mm, aluminum, blue color.	1968	Dio.1968.6b	1.00 - 2.00
39 mm, bronze.	1968	Dio.1968.6c	1.00 - 2.00
39 mm, .999 fine silver.	1968	Dio.1968.6d	20.00 - 25.00

CUB SCOUT PACK #73, MATER DOLOROSA SCHOOL, NEW ORLEANS, LA

40 mm, aluminum.	1969	Dio.1969.14a	1.00 - 2.00
40 mm, aluminum, blue color.	1969	Dio.1969.14b	1.00 - 2.00
40 mm, bronze.	1969	Dio.1969.14c	1.00 - 2.00
40 mm, .999 fine silver.	1969	Dio.1969.14d	20.00 - 25.00
40 mm, oxidized bronze.	1969	Dio.1969.14e	1.00 - 2.00

CUB SCOUT PACK #73, MATER DOLOROSA SCHOOL, NEW ORLEANS

40 mm, aluminum.	1968	Dio.1968.7a	1.00 - 2.00
40 mm, aluminum, golden color.	1968	Dio.1968.7b	1.00 - 2.00
40 mm, bronze.	1968	Dio.1968.7c	1.00 - 2.00
40 mm, .999 fine silver.	1968	Dio.1968.7d	20.00 - 25.00
40 mm, aluminum, blue color.	1968	Dio.1968.7e	1.00 - 2.00

CUB SCOUT PROMISE OFFICIAL MEDAL

32 mm, bronze, square.	1992	Dio.1992.6	2.00 - 3.00

CUB SCOUTS, 50TH ANNIVERSARY. CUB PROMISE REVERSE

33 mm, brass, square.	1980	Dio.1980.2	2.00 - 3.00

CUB SCOUTS, BSA, CUB PROMISE

32 mm, bronze, correct quotes.	1970	Dio.1970.1a	1.00 - 2.00
32 mm, bronze, inverted quotes.	1970	Dio.1970.1a1	1.00 - 2.00
32 mm, bronze, paw filled in.	1970	Dio.1970.1b	1.00 - 2.00

CUB SCOUTS, BSA. CUB PROMISE KEY CHAIN

Wolf w/ full ears, 31 mm, brass.	1950	Dio.1950.11a	3.00 - 4.00
Wolf w/ full ears, double thickness, 32 mm, brass.	1950	Dio.1950.11b	3.00 - 4.00
Wolf w/ pointed ears, 32 mm, brass.	1950	Dio.1950.11c	3.00 - 4.00

CUB SCOUTS, CUB PROMISE

Comma after "People" on reverse, 32 mm, bronze, square, not holed.	1972	Dio.1972.18a	1.00 - 2.00
No comma after "People" on reverse, 32 mm, bronze, square, not holed.	1972	Dio.1972.18b	1.00 - 2.00

CUBS BSA POCKET PIECE

31 mm, bright bronze, holed.	1935	Dio.1935.2	4.00 - 5.00

EI CUHAJ, GATEWAY DISTRICT, QUEENS COUNCIL, NY. PERSONAL TOKEN

42 mm, blue plastic, gold letting.	1985	Dio.1985.4	1.00 - 2.00

JOHNNY APPLESEED COUNCIL, OA. CATCH THAT PEPSI SPIRIT

Bobcat Badge, 38 mm, bronze, cast.	1982	Dio.1982.4	8.00 - 15.00
Wolf Badge, 38 mm, bronze, cast.	1982	Dio.1982.5	8.00 - 15.00
Bear Badge, 38 mm, bronze, cast.	1982	Dio.1982.6	8.00 - 15.00
Webelos Badge, 38 mm, bronze, cast.	1982	Dio.1982.7	8.00 - 15.00
Arrow of Light Award, 38 mm, bronze, cast.	1982	Dio.1982.9	8.00 - 15.00

NEW ORLEANS AREA COUNCIL, LA, POW WOW

39 mm, aluminum.	1975	Dio.1975.9a	1.00 - 2.00
39 mm, aluminum, golden color.	1975	Dio.1975.9b	1.00 - 2.00
39 mm, aluminum, purple.	1975	Dio.1975.9c	1.00 - 2.00

NEW ORLEANS AREA COUNCIL, POW WOW

39 mm, aluminum, bronze color.	1973	Dio.1973.16a	1.00 - 2.00
39 mm, aluminum.	1973	Dio.1973.16b	1.00 - 2.00
39 mm, blue aluminum.	1977	Dio.1977.5a	1.00 - 2.00
39 mm, red aluminum.	1977	Dio.1977.5b	1.00 - 2.00
39 mm, aluminum.	1977	Dio.1977.5c	1.00 - 2.00

NEW ORLEANS COUNCIL, LA, POW WOW

39 mm, aluminum.	1967	Dio.1967.8a	1.00 - 2.00
39 mm, aluminum, blue color.	1967	Dio.1967.8b	1.00 - 2.00
39 mm, bronze.	1967	Dio.1967.8c	1.00 - 2.00
39 mm, oxidized bronze.	1967	Dio.1967.8d	1.00 - 2.00
39 mm, bronze.	1968	Dio.1968.8a	1.00 - 2.00
39 mm, aluminum.	1968	Dio.1968.8b	1.00 - 2.00
39 mm, .999 fine silver.	1968	Dio.1968.8c	20.00 - 25.00
39 mm, aluminum, blue color.	1969	Dio.1969.15a	1.00 - 2.00
39 mm, aluminum, golden color.	1969	Dio.1969.15b	1.00 - 2.00
39 mm, bronze.	1969	Dio.1969.15c	1.00 - 2.00
39 mm, aluminum, green color.	1969	Dio.1969.15d	1.00 - 2.00
39 mm, aluminum.	1971	Dio.1971.10a	1.00 - 2.00
39 mm, aluminum, green color.	1971	Dio.1971.10b	20.00 - 25.00
39 mm, aluminum, red color.	1971	Dio.1971.10c	1.00 - 2.00
39 mm, oxidized bronze.	1971	Dio.1971.10d	1.00 - 2.00
39 mm, aluminum.	1972	Dio.1972.15a	1.00 - 2.00
39 mm, aluminum, purple color.	1972	Dio.1972.15b	1.00 - 2.00
39 mm, aluminum, copper color.	1972	Dio.1972.15c	1.00 - 2.00
39 mm, oxidized bronze.	1972	Dio.1972.15d	1.00 - 2.00

TIGER CUBS, OFFICIAL. PROGRAM EMBLEM. SEARCH, DISCOVER AND SHARE

31 mm, bronze, square.	1992	Dio.1992.5	2.00 - 3.00

CERTIFICATES

APPRECIATION	1972	0.50 - 1.00
ARROW OF LIGHT	1985	1.00 - 3.00

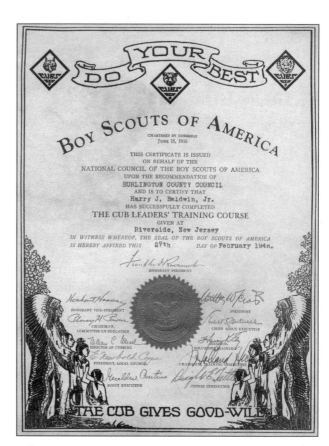

CUB LEADER'S TRAINING COURSE	1935-1953	10.00 - 15.00
PACK GRADUATION	1974	0.50 - 1.00
	1981	0.50 - 1.00
	1984	0.50 - 1.00
	1987	0.50 - 1.00
	1989	0.50 - 1.00
	1993	0.50 - 1.00
THANKS - DEN LEADER	1974	0.50 - 1.00
THANKS - DEN MOTHER	1970	1.00 - 2.00
TIGER CUBS, BSA, GRADUATE	1985	2.00 - 3.00

RECOGNITIONS - ADULT

CUB SCOUTER AWARD

Cub emblem medallion suspended from gold neck ribbon w/ blue stripe.	1985	15.00 - 20.00

CUBMASTER AWARD

Cub emblem medallion suspended from gold neck ribbon w/ two blue stripes.	1985	15.00 - 20.00

DEN LEADER AWARD

Cub emblem medallion suspended from blue neck ribbon w/ gold stripe.	1985	15.00 - 20.00

DEN LEADER COACH AWARD

Cub emblem medallion suspended from blue neck ribbon.	1985	15.00 - 20.00

DEN LEADER COACH TRAINING AWARD

Tenderfoot emblem on diamond-shaped background, gilt pendant on white ribbon w/ two thin green stripes.	1960-1970	5.00 - 7.50
Tenderfoot emblem on diamond-shaped background. 10 kt. GF on white ribbon w/ two thin green stripes.	1960-1970	10.00 - 15.00

DEN MOTHER'S TRAINING AWARD

Tenderfoot emblem on diamond-shaped background, 10 kt. GF pendant on white ribbon w/ one thin green stripe.	1960-1970	10.00 - 15.00
Tenderfoot emblem on diamond-shaped background, gilt pendant, white ribbon w/ one thin green stripe.	1960-1970	5.00 - 7.50

TIGER CUB COACH AWARD

Cub emblem medallion suspended from orange neck ribbon w/ black stripe.	1985	15.00 - 20.00

WEBELOS DEN LEADER AWARD

Cub emblem medallion suspended from gold neck ribbon.	1985	15.00 - 20.00

RECOGNITION ITEMS

TROPHY TOPS

Cub Scout standing with dog.	1985	10.00 - 15.00
Cub Scout giving sign. BSA on round base.	1989	20.00 - 25.00

SEALS & STICKERS

BEAR EMBLEM

Sheet of eight.	1985	0.50 - 1.00

CUB SCOUT STAMPS, B.S.A.

Head shot of Cub Scout, sheet of 100 stamps.	1955	5.00 - 7.50

CUB SCOUTS

Sheet of eight.	1985	0.50 - 1.00
Sheet of fifteen.	1990	0.50 - 1.00

TIGER CUBS

Sheet of fifteen.	1990	0.50 - 1.00

WEBELOS

Sheet of fifteen.	1990	0.50 - 1.00

WEBELOS EMBLEM

Sheet of eight.	1985	0.50 - 1.00

WOLF EMBLEM

Sheet of eight.	1985	0.50 - 1.00

UNIT EQUIPMENT

DEN FLAG

Number within diamond, yellow on blue background.	1940	5.00 - 7.50
Cub Scouts below logo, small number in corner.	1980	5.00 - 7.50

DEN FLAG - WEBELOS

Webelos emblem on blue background.	1970	5.00 - 7.50

FLAG POLE TOP

Wolf head within open diamond, CUBS BSA below.	1930-1940	40.00 - 60.00
Wolf head within open diamond, CUB SCOUTS BSA below.	1940	25.00 - 40.00
Cub Scout 50th Anniversary logo.	1980	50.00 - 75.00

PACK FLAG

Wool, yellow top, blue bottom, CUBS BSA on red diamond in ctr.	1930-1940	40.00 - 60.00
Wool, yellow top, blue bottom, CUB SCOUTS BSA on red diamond in ctr.	1940-1955	30.00 - 50.00
Cotton, yellow top, blue bottom, CUB SCOUTS BSA on red diamond in ctr.	1955-1970	20.00 - 40.00
Nylon, yellow top, blue bottom, CUB SCOUTS BSA on red diamond in ctr.	1970	25.00 - 35.00

MISCELLANEOUS STUFF

ACTIVITY CARDS
Pinewood Derby participant.	1980	0.25 - 0.50
Space Derby participant.	1980	0.25 - 0.50
Cub Scout Regatta participant.	1980	0.25 - 0.50

AUTO GRILLE MEDALLION
Cub Scout emblem, brass.	1990	20.00 - 30.00

AVON, BRUSH AND COMB SET
Plastic, blue, looks like pocket knife.	1975	7.50 - 12.50

CAKE TOP FIGURES
Cub Scout seated, legs crossed in front, plastic.	1955-1965	7.50 - 12.50
Cub Scout standing, hands at side, painted plaster.	1955-1965	5.00 - 7.50

CHARMS
Silvered bracelet, charms for Bobcat, Bear, Wolf, Webelo, Arrow of Light.	1975	10.00 - 15.00

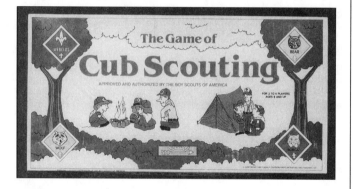

GAME
The Game of Cub Scouting, Cadaco Div., Rapid Mounting & Finishing Co.	1987	50.00 - 75.00

GREETING CARDS
To a Great Cub Scout, Cub helping little girl across street.	1965	2.00 - 3.00
Like a Good Cub Scout, Do Your Best!	1965	2.00 - 3.00

HANDKERCHIEF
Blue and yellow, Cub activities displayed.	1960-1975	3.00 - 5.00

KENNER DOLL
Cub Scout uniform on blond boy.	1974	35.00 - 50.00

NOTE PAPER
Cub Scout emblem in foil in upper corner, packet of 20 with envelopes.	1989	5.00 - 7.50
Cub Scout emblem in corners, full color border, packet of 50.	1998	7.50 - 12.50
Tiger, Cub and Akela emblems at top, blue lined, and border, packet of 20.	2000	5.00 - 7.50

PINEWOOD DERBY CAR
Thin body, detachable axles, solid thin wheels.	1955-1980	10.00 - 15.00
Thick body, fat wheels, cut out for driver.	1980-1993	5.00 - 7.50
Thick body, fat wheels, no cut out for driver.	1993	4.00 - 6.00

POSTERS
Cub Scout Circus, 11- 1/2" x 19".	1947	35.00 - 50.00
Cub Scout Pet Show, 11-1/2" x 19".	1947	35.00 - 50.00

PRESSED WOOD PLAQUE
Cub Promise, CUBS BSA on diamond patch.	1930-1950	15.00 - 20.00
Cub Law, CUBS BSA on diamond patch.	1930-1950	15.00 - 20.00
A Cub is Square, CUBS BSA on diamond patch.	1930-1950	15.00 - 20.00
Cub Scout Promise, CUB SCOUTS on diamond patch.	1950-1975	7.50 - 12.50
A Cub is Square, CUB SCOUTS BSA on diamond patch.	1950-1975	7.50 - 12.50
Cub Law, CUB SCOUTS on diamond patch.	1950-1975	7.50 - 12.50
A Cub Scout is Helpful, CUB SCOUTS BSA on diamond patch.	1975-1985	7.50 - 12.50

RADIO KIT
Crystal radio kit.	1940-1950	30.00 - 50.00

RECORD, 45
Akela Song Record Album for Cub Scouts, Nannette Guilford Corporation.	1954	15.00 - 20.00

RING
CUBS BSA on top, sterling.	1930-1945	15.00 - 20.00
CUB SCOUTS BSA on top, sterling.	1950-1975	7.50 - 12.50

SCOUT STATUE

Tom Clark's Gnome, gnome in pinewood derby car.	1992	75.00 - 100.00
Tom Clark's Gnomes, den leader.	1995	85.00 - 125.00

SCRAP BOOK

Cub Scout photo in lower corner.	1947	10.00 - 15.00

SHEET MUSIC

"Cub Scout March" by Prigge.		15.00 - 20.00

SWEATER CHAIN

Cub Scout emblem on white enamel background, gilt chain.	1965-1975	10.00 - 15.00

TIE BAR

Gilt with Cub Scout emblem in square at end.	1970	2.00 - 3.00

WALL PLAQUES

Wolf Cub Scout, shield shape, scroll below.	1947	10.00 - 15.00
Bear Cub Scout, shield shape, scroll below.	1947	10.00 - 15.00
Lion Cub Scout, shield shape, scroll below.	1947	10.00 - 15.00
Webelos Cub Scout, shield shape, scroll below.	1947	10.00 - 15.00
Den Chief Service, shield shape, scroll below.	1947	10.00 - 15.00
Den Mother Service, shield shape, scroll below.	1947	10.00 - 15.00

WATCH

Timex, blue plastic band, white dial.	1975	15.00 - 20.00

Cub scout pack, note the knee socks.

32

Dining hall KP (kitchen patrol) of the 1940s.

BOY SCOUTS

The Boy Scouts of America was founded in February 1910, based on the programs of Englishman Robert Baden-Powell's Boy Scouts, Ernest Thompson Seton's Woodcraft Indians (1902), and Daniel Carter Beard's Society of the Sons of Daniel Boone—later called Boy Pioneers (1905). William D. Boyce, a newspaper publisher from Chicago, financed the organization's beginnings, and with assistance from YMCA executive Edgar M. Robinson's New York office, scout troops were being formed throughout the nation. Seton and Beard were brought into the fold of the new organization, and by the fall of 1910, James E. West was hired for what was to be a 32-year run as the B.S.A.'s Chief Scout Executive. The headquarters moved out of the YMCA offices on 28th Street and took up home at 200 Fifth Avenue, New York City.

Early scouting opportunities for the "good turn" came available with a service corps at the 50th Anniversary Reunion of the Battle of Gettysburg and selling of Liberty Loan Bonds during World War I. By this time the scouting movement was a hit, because it educated youth in outdoor skills and leadership, and youth were exposed to many worthwhile professions due to the merit badge program. In the 1930s the National Office moved to 2 Park Avenue, and in 1953 to North Brunswick, New Jersey.

The scouting movement was at its height in the 1950s and early 1960s, with the advent of the baby boomers. The war in Vietnam affected scout membership, and the revision of the program in 1971 seemed to set it back even more. It took nearly 10 years, until the 1979 handbook revision by the master William "Green Bar Bill" Hillcourt, to set the program back on track. At this time the National Office moved to its current location in Irving, Texas.

Scouting has become a major part in the fabric of youth, and there are countless political leaders, sports and entertainment figures, CEOs, astronauts, and a former president of these United States (Gerald Ford) who have progressed through scouting to attain the Eagle Scout Award. Even for those who did not earn the Eagle Award, though, scouting has had a positive affect on the character of its members, and most can look back on good times and experiences when they were scouts. Scouts in the United States have had opportunities to become involved in a great number of programs to help them expand their horizons and learn that they are not alone in enjoying things that are special to the Boy Scout movement, including High Adventure opportunities like the Philmont Scout Ranch, the Charles M. Sommers Canoe Base, the Florida Sea Base, and National Jamborees.

Eagle scout, 1920.

RANK BADGES

References in the Rank Badges section are to Paul Meyer's book *Collecting Boy Scout Rank Badges*.

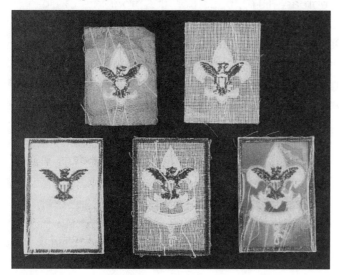

Rank patches have different backs, which are collectible varieties to some. The top two are both cut khaki cloth, one with a glue back and the second with a gauze backing. The bottom row illustrates twill cut edge badges with glue, gauze, and plastic backs.

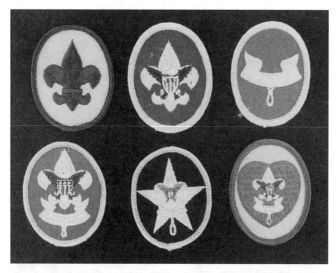

A group of 1972 oval badges: l. to r. (from top): Scout, Tenderfoot, Second-Class, First-Class, Star, and Life.

SCOUT

Oval rolled edge, brown on orange or gold background.	1972-1989	PM.01.01-3	1.00 - 2.00
Oval rolled edge, brown on tan background.	1989	PM.01.04	1.00 - 1.50

TENDERFOOT

Tan cloth, no ctr. line in short crown.	1921-1936	PM.02.01-2	30.00 - 40.00
Tan cloth, no ctr. line in tall crown.	1936-1937	PM.02.03	30.00 - 40.00
Tan cloth, ctr. line in tall crown.	1938-1942	PM.02.04-5A	20.00 - 30.00
Sand twill, ctr. line in tall crown.	1942-1945	PM.02.05B	20.00 - 30.00
Khaki cloth, ctr. line in tall crown.	1946-1954	PM.02.05c-6	10.00 - 15.00
Khaki cut edge, coarse twill.	1955-1964	PM.02.07A, 8A	5.00 - 7.50
Khaki cut edge, fine twill.	1965-1971	PM.02.07B, 8B	3.00 - 5.00
Oval rolled edge, brown background.	1972-1989	PM.02.09-11	1.00 - 2.00
Oval rolled edge, tan background.	1989	PM.02.12	1.00 - 1.50

Second-Class badges: Top row are fine tan twill with low and high scrolls; the bottom two are a cut khaki cloth and a cut edge khaki twill.

SECOND-CLASS

Tan cloth, high smile.	1913-1936	PM.03.01-4	40.00 - 60.00
Tan cloth, low smile.	1937-1942	PM.03.05A	30.00 - 40.00
Sand twill, low smile.	1942-1945	PM.03.05B	20.00 - 30.00
Khaki cloth.	1946-1954	PM.03.05C, 6	15.00 - 25.00
Khaki C/E, coarse twill.	1955-1964	PM.03.07A	5.00 - 10.00
Khaki cut edge, fine twill.	1965-1971	PM.03.07B	3.00 - 5.00
Oval rolled edge, green background.	1972-1989	PM.03.08-10	1.00 - 2.00
Oval rolled edge, tan background.	1989	PM.03.11	1.00 - 1.50

FIRST-CLASS

Tan cloth, short crown.	1913-1936	PM.04.01-3	150.00 - 200.00
Tan cloth, ctr. line in tall crown.	1937-1942	PM.04.04, 5A	40.00 - 60.00
Sand twill, ctr. line in tall crown.	1942-1945	PM.04.05B	40.00 - 60.00
Khaki cloth, ctr. line in tall crown.	1946-1954	PM.04.05C, 6	20.00 - 30.00
Khaki cut edge, coarse twill.	1955-1964	PM.04.07A, 8A	5.00 - 7.50
Khaki cut edge, fine twill.	1965-1971	PM.04.07B, 8B	2.00 - 5.00
Oval rolled edge, red background.	1972-1989	PM.04.09AB, 10	1.00 - 2.00
Oval rolled edge, tan background.	1989	PM.04.11	1.00 - 1.50

Short crown sand twill and cut edge khaki.

STAR SCOUT

Tan cloth, eagle head right, w/o hanging knot.	1913-1924	PM.05.01,3	75.00 - 125.00
Tan cloth, eagle head right, w/ hanging knot.	1913-1924	PM.05.02,4	75.00 - 125.00
Tan cloth, eagle head left.	1925-1942	PM.05.05A, 6A, 7A	40.00 - 60.00
Sand twill.	1942-1945	PM.05.07D	20.00 - 30.00
Khaki cloth.	1946-1954	PM.05.07E	15.00 - 20.00
Khaki cut edge, coarse twill.	1955-1964	PM.05.08A	7.50 - 10.00
Khaki cut edge, fine twill.	1965-1971	PM.05.08B	5.00 - 7.50
Oval rolled edge, purple background.	1972-1989	PM.05.09-11A	1.00 - 2.00
Oval rolled edge, tan background.	1989	PM.05.12	1.00 - 1.50

Life Scout badges. From top: a red knot variety, left a sand twill with the knot outside the heart, and right a khaki cut square, knot inside heart.

Life Scout badge of the 1960s.

LIFE SCOUT

Tan cloth, eagle head right, knot inside heart.	1913-1924	PM.06.01-2	150.00 - 225.00
Tan cloth, eagle head right, red hanging knot.	1913-1924	PM.06.03A,B. C.D-4	200.00 - 300.00
Tan cloth, eagle head left, gold hanging knot.	1925-1940	PM.06.05A	80.00 - 100.00
Tan cloth, no hanging knot.	1941-1942	PM.06.06A, 7A	40.00 - 60.00
Sand twill.	1942-1945	PM.06.07D	30.00 - 40.00
Khaki cloth.	1946-1954	PM.06.07E	20.00 - 30.00
Cut to heart shape.	1955-1971	PM.06.08A, 8B.	5.00 - 7.50
Oval rolled edge, orange background.	1972-1989	PM.06.09A-B	1.00 - 2.00
Oval rolled edge, tan background.	1989	PM.06.10	1.00 - 1.50

Eagle patch, first type, scroll extends into oval.

EAGLE SCOUT

Cut edge, tan or coffee cloth, scroll outline extends beyond oval.	1924-1932	PM.09.01a1	250.00 - 400.00
Cut edge, tan or coffee cloth, scroll outline inside oval, no knot beneath scroll.	1924-1932	PM.09.01a2	350.00 - 500.00
Cut edge, tan or coffee cloth, complete lettering, cotton or silk threads.	1932-1955	PM.09.02A	40.00 - 75.00
Cut edge sand (tan) twill cloth, fine weave, complete lettering around, cotton threads.	1933-1955	PM.09.02D	60.00 - 80.00
Cut edge khaki cloth, complete lettering around oval border, cotton threads.	1933-1955	PM.09.02E	40.00 - 60.00
Oval, red cloth, gray rolled edge, complete lettering. Small head, closed beak on eagle, thin knot, white gauze back.	1956-1972	PM.09.03A	15.00 - 25.00
Oval red cloth, gray rolled edge, complete lettering. Thick neck, closed beak on eagle, knot is thick circle, starched gauze back.	1956-1972	PM.09.03B	10.00 - 15.00
Oval red cloth, gray rolled edge, complete lettering. Open beak on eagle, white gauze or plastic back.	1956-1972	PM.09.03C	10.00 - 20.00
Oval fully embroidered background, gray rolled edge, no lettering. Eagle w/ 32 mm wingspan, tail feathers visible below perch, plain cloth or plastic back.	1972-1975	PM.09.04A	15.00 - 25.00
Oval fully embroidered gray rolled edge, no lettering. Eagle w/ 29 mm wingspan, no tail feathers visible, plain embroidered back.	1972-1975	PM.09.04B	15.00 - 25.00
Red cloth, white (silver) rolled edge, gray eagle and EAGLE SCOUT legend. Plastic back w/ or w/o gauze beneath. Three or more minor varieties.	1975-1985	PM.09.05A-C	5.00 - 10.00

Eagle Scout badges show (top) a khaki cut square, a 1960s rolled edge, and the 1973 no name oval, and (bottom) late 1970s silver thread rolled edge (with and without a Mylar edge), and a 1985 Mylar thread.

Oval red cloth, silver mylar rolled edge, eagle and complete lettering. Small eagle, flat scroll base.	1985-1986	PM.09.06	15.00 - 20.00
Oval red cloth, silver mylar edge, dark gray or silver gray eagle. Scroll curved, larger motto letters.	1987-1988	PM.09.07A-B	5.00 - 10.00
Oval red cloth, silver gray rolled edge, dark gray eagle.	1988	PM.09.08	5.00 - 10.00

ACHIEVEMENT AWARD #1

Gold legend on purple background.	1923-1950	150.00 - 250.00
Gold legend on red background.	1923-1950	150.00 - 250.00

ACHIEVEMENT AWARD #2

Gold legend on red background.	1923-1950	150.00 - 250.00
Gold lettering on purple background.	1923-1950	150.00 - 250.00

ACHIEVEMENT TENDERFOOT

Gold lettering on purple background.	1937-1950	150.00 - 250.00
Gold lettering on red background.	1937-1950	150.00 - 250.00

Small patches are added to the exterior of an oval rank patch in the Scouting for the Handicapped Program.

SCOUTING FOR THE HANDICAPPED PROGRAM

12 Ideals badge.	1972	10.00 - 15.00
Camping badge.	1972	1.00 - 1.50
Citizenship badge.	1972	1.00 - 1.50
Cooking badge.	1972	1.00 - 1.50
First Aid badge.	1972	1.00 - 1.50
Flag badge.	1972	1.00 - 1.50
Hiking badge.	1972	1.00 - 1.50
Knot Tying badge.	1972	1.00 - 1.50
Swimming badge.	1972	1.00 - 1.50
Symbols badge.	1972	1.00 - 1.50

Eagle scout, square merit badges on sash.

EAGLE SCOUT AWARD

Eagle Medals are referenced to Terry Grove's book *A Comprehensive Guide to the Eagle Scout Award.*

T.H. Foley (left); Dieges & Clust (right).

T.H. FOLEY, MAKER

1912-1915	THF.1-4	8,500. - 12,500.

DIEGES & CLUST, MAKER

1916-1920	D&C.1-3	300.00 - 450.00

ROB.1A   ROB.1B

ROBBINS CO., MAKER

Closed beak, deep notch on back where body tail feathers meet.	1920-1925	ROB.1A	200.00 - 300.00
Closed beak, where body and tail feathers meet on back form "W."	1925-1926	ROB.1B	250.00 - 400.00
Open beak, flat line notch on back where body meets tail feathers.	1926-1930	ROB.1C-D	100.00 - 150.00

ROB.1C   ROB.1D

ROB.1E   ROB.2A

Closed beak, BSA is high, A hangs over edge.	1930	ROB.1E	150.00 - 200.00
Finely engraded feathers, centered BSA. Back feathers form a body-ridge as V or a smooth transition.	1930-1933	ROB.2A-B	100.00 - 150.00
Closed beak, no BSA, full back.	1933-1954	ROB.3	75.00 - 150.00
Closed beak, no BSA, flat back.	1955-1969	ROB.4	75.00 - 150.00
Closed beak, BSA, feathered but flatter back.	1970-1978	ROB.5	75.00 - 100.00

ROB.3

ROB.4

ROB.5

STANGE CO., MAKER

Closed beak, no BSA, flat back.	1968-1971	STG.1	100.00 - 125.00
Closed beak, BSA, feathered but flatter back.	1971-1974	STG.2	75.00 - 100.00
Closed, thin beak, "mechanical, deco" look to the feathers. Usually a very long ribbon.	1974-1978	STG.3	75.00 - 100.00
Short, closed beak, BSA, feathered but flatter back. White stitched edge to ribbon.	1978-1980	STG.4	75.00 - 100.00
Silver-plated copper or sterling silver on special order. Short, closed beak, BSA, feathered but flatter back. White stitched edge to ribbon.	1980-1983	STG.5A	50.00 - 75.00
Silver-plated copper or sterling silver on special order. Short, closed beak, BSA, modified feather back. White stitched edge to ribbon.	1983-1986	STG.5B	50.00 - 75.00
Silver-plated copper or sterling silver on special order. Closed beak, BSA. S is not struck well and appears wider than B and A.	1986-1989	STG.5C	50.00 - 75.00
Silver-plated copper or sterling silver on special order. Closed beak, BSA of even thickness, feathered but flatter back.	1990	STG.5D	50.00 - 75.00

STG.1

STG.2

STG.3

STG.4

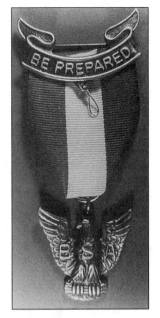

STG.5A   *STG.5B*   *STG.5C*   *STG.5D*

EAGLE SCOUT AWARD, STANGE CO., MAKER

Closed beak, feathered but flat back.	1995	STG.6	50.00 - 75.00

EAGLE SCOUT AWARD, CUSTOM FINE JEWELRY, MAKER

Closed beak, feathered but flat back. CFJ incuse in plain rectangle on back. Long stick pins. Non-silver.	1999	CFJ.1	100.00 - 125.00
Closed beak, feathered but flat back. CFJ raised in crisp plain rectangle on back. Laser engraved diework. Non-silver.	1999	CFJ.2	50.00 - 75.00

Closed beak, feathered but flat back. CFJ and .925 raised on back. Laser engraved diework. Sterling.	1999	CFJ.1	75.00 - 125.00
Closed beak, feathered but flat back. CFJ raised in irregular plain rectangle on back. Sterling, hallmarked on scroll. Recalled.	1999		150.00 - 200.00

Five eagle scouts from Northern New York state.

Youthful eagle scout, wide crimped merit badges on sash.

RANK & POSITION BADGES

TENDERFOOT

Scribe. Tenderfoot badge, gold-color thread, crossed quills on tan cloth.	1916-1925	500.00 - 700.00
Bugler. Tenderfoot badge, gold-color thread, bugle on tan cloth.	1917-1925	500.00 - 700.00
Patrol Leader. Silver-color thread, Tenderfoot badge on tan cloth.	1921-1925	700.00 - 900.00
Patrol Leader Scribe. Silver-color thread, Tenderfoot badge and crossed quills on tan cloth.	1916-1925	600.00 - 300.00
Patrol Leader Bugler. Silver-color thread Tenderfoot badge, bugle on tan cloth.	1917-1925	600.00 - 800.00

FIRST-CLASS

Scribe. Green First-Class badge, gold-color thread crossed quills on tan cloth.	1916-1925	400.00 - 550.00
Bugler. Green First-Class badge, gold-color thread bugle on tan cloth.	1917-1925	500.00 - 750.00
Patrol Leader. Silver-colored thread, First-Class badge on tan cloth.	1915-1925	300.00 - 450.00
Patrol Leader Scribe. Silver-color thread, First-Class badge, crossed quills on tan cloth.	1916-1925	600.00 - 800.00
Patrol Leader Bugler. Silver-color thread, First-Class badge, bugle on tan cloth.	1917-1925	400.00 - 450.00

SECOND-CLASS

Scribe. Second-Class badge, gold-color thread crossed quills on tan cloth.	1916-1925	500.00 - 700.00
Bugler. Second-Class badge, gold-color thread bugle on tan cloth.	1917-1925	600.00 - 800.00
Patrol Leader. Silver-colored thread, Second-Class badge on tan cloth.	1915-1925	400.00 - 550.00
Patrol Leader Scribe. Silver-color thread, Second-Class badge and crossed quills on tan cloth.	1916-1925	600.00 - 800.00
Patrol Leader Bugler. Silver-color thread, Second-Class badge, bugle on tan cloth.	1917-1925	600.00 - 800.00

POSITION BADGES

JUNIOR ASSISTANT SCOUTMASTER

Tan cloth, three green felt bars.	1926-1933	40.00 - 60.00
Tan cloth, three green felt bars, gold First-Class emblem w/short crown.	1934-1936	35.00 - 55.00
Tan cloth, three green bars, gold First-Class emblem w/tall crown.	1936-1942	30.00 - 45.00
Sand twill.	1942-1945	30.00 - 45.00
Khaki cloth.	1946	15.00 - 25.00
Round cut edge, brown Tenderfoot emblem, no legend.	1947-1951	7.50 - 15.00
Round cut edge, brown and gold Tenderfoot emblem, no legend.	1952-1958	5.00 - 10.00
Round cut edge, brown and gold design w/legend.	1959-1966	5.00 - 10.00
Round rolled edge, brown and gold design, First-Class emblem w/legend.	1967-1969	5.00 - 10.00
Round rolled edge, brown and gold design, Tenderfoot emblem w/title as: JR. ASST.	1970-1971	5.00 - 10.00
Round rolled edge, green background, Tenderfoot w/title as: JUNIOR ASSISTANT.	1972-1989	2.00 - 3.00
Round rolled edge, tan background, Tenderfoot emblem and title.	1989	1.00 - 2.00

SENIOR PATROL LEADER

Tan cloth, 2-1/2 white felt bars.	1910-1914	50.00 - 75.00
Tan cloth, 2-1/2 green felt bars.	1915-1933	50.00 - 75.00
Tan cloth, 2-1/2 green bars, First-Class emblem w/short crown.	1934-1936	50.00 - 75.00
Tan cloth, 2-1/2 green bars, gold First-Class emblem w/ tall crown.	1936-1942	40.00 - 65.00
Sand twill.	1942-1945	30.00 - 45.00
Khaki cloth.	1946-1954	20.00 - 30.00
Khaki cut edge, coarse twill.	1955-1964	7.50 - 10.00
Khaki cut edge, fine twill.	1965-1971	5.00 - 7.50
Round rolled edge, Tenderfoot emblem on green background, three bars and title.	1972-1989	2.00 - 3.00
Round rolled edge, First-Class emblem on tan background, three bars and title.	1989	1.00 - 2.00

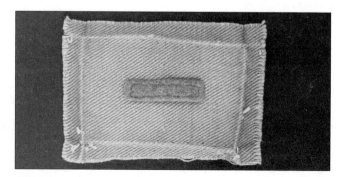

Assistant Patrol Leader patch in felt sewn on cut square tan cloth.

Assistant Patrol Leader patches in cut square khaki (l.), cut edge twill, coarse (top r.), and fine twill (bottom r.) varieties.

ASSISTANT SENIOR PATROL LEADER

Khaki cut edge, coarse twill, gold First-Class emblem, two green bars.	1959-1964	3.00 - 5.00
Khaki cut edge, fine twill.	1965-1971	3.00 - 5.00
Round rolled edge, Tenderfoot emblem on green background, 2-1/2 bars and title.	1972-1989	2.00 - 3.00
Round rolled edge, First-Class emblem on tan background, 2-1/2 bars and title.	1989	1.00 - 2.00

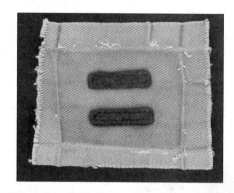

PATROL LEADER

Two white felt bars.	1910-1914	50.00 - 75.00
Tan cloth, two green felt bars.	1914-1933	30.00 - 40.00
Tan cloth, two green bars.	1934-1942	20.00 - 30.00
Sand twill, two embroidered green bars.	1942-1945	20.00 - 30.00
Khaki cloth.	1946-1954	10.00 - 15.00
Khaki cut edge, coarse twill, two embroidered green bars.	1955-1964	3.00 - 5.00
Khaki cut edge, fine twill, two embroidered green bars.	1965-1971	3.00 - 5.00
Round rolled edge. Tenderfoot on green background, two bars and title.	1972-1989	2.00 - 3.00
Round rolled edge, FDL on tan background w/two bars and title.	1989	1.00 - 2.00

ASSISTANT PATROL LEADER

One white felt bar.	1910-1914	50.00 - 75.00
Tan cloth, one green felt bar.	1914-1933	20.00 - 30.00
Tan cloth, one green bar.	1934-1942	15.00 - 25.00
Sand twill.	1942-1945	7.50 - 15.00
Khaki cloth.	1946-1954	5.00 - 10.00
Khaki cut edge, coarse twill.	1955-1964	3.00 - 5.00
Khaki cloth, fine twill.	1965-1971	1.50 - 2.00
Round rolled edge, green background. Tenderfoot w/one bar and legend.	1972-1989	1.50 - 2.00
Round rolled edge, tan background. FDL w/one bar and title.	1989	1.00 - 2.00

BSA LIFE GUARD

Scout Life Guard 3" blue twill, cut edge.	(none)	5.00 - 10.00

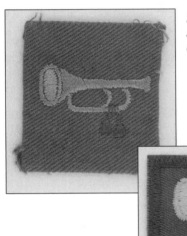

Bugler patches in cut square sand twill (left) and cut edge twill (below).

BUGLER

Tan cloth, bugle.	1926-1942	20.00 - 30.00
Sand twill.	1942-1945	15.00 - 25.00
Khaki cloth.	1946-1954	10.00 - 15.00
Khaki cut edge, coarse twill.	1955-1964	5.00 - 7.50
Khaki cut edge, fine twill.	1965-1971	5.00 - 7.50
Round rolled edge, green background, yellow border, gold bugle.	1972-1989	2.00 - 3.00
Round rolled edge, green background, red border, gold bugle. Error.	1980	65.00 - 85.00
Round rolled edge, tan background. FDL and bugle.	1989	1.00 - 2.00

CABIN BOY

Anchor on blue background within gold oval border. Tan cut cloth.	1924-1935	400.00 - 600.00
Anchor on blue background within gold oval border. Khaki cut cloth.	1935-1949	35.00 - 50.00

CHAPLAIN AIDE

Round rolled edge, green background, crozier and title.	1976-1989	2.00 - 3.00
Round rolled edge, tan background.	1989	1.00 - 2.00

DEN CHIEF

Round rolled edge, green background.	1972-1989	2.00 - 3.00
Round rolled edge, tan background. Cub Scout emblem and title.	1989	1.00 - 2.00

HISTORIAN

Round rolled edge, green background, FDL and open book.	1972-1989	2.00 - 3.00
Round rolled edge, tan background.	1989	1.00 - 2.00

INSTRUCTOR

Round rolled edge, khaki background, brown border, Tenderfoot emblem at ctr.	1962-1971	5.00 - 7.50
Round rolled edge, green background, yellow border.	1972-1989	3.00 - 5.00
Round rolled edge, tan background. Tenderfoot emblem and title.	1989	1.00 - 2.00

INTERPRETER STRIP

White lettering on tan cut edge cloth. Parle Francais.	1932-1935	50.00 - 75.00
White lettering on tan cut edge cloth. Habla Espano!.	1932-1935	50.00 - 75.00
White lettering on tan cut edge cloth. Sprecht Deutsch.	1932-1935	50.00 - 75.00
White lettering on tan cut edge cloth. Parlo Italiayno.	1932-1935	50.00 - 75.00

Red lettering on tan cut cloth. Parlo Italiano.	1936-1946	20.00 - 30.00
Red lettering on tan cut cloth. Parle Francais.	1936-1946	20.00 - 30.00
Red lettering on tan cut cloth. Parle Francais.	1936-1946	20.00 - 30.00
Red lettering on tan cut cloth. Habla Espanol.	1936-1946	20.00 - 30.00
Red lettering on tan cut cloth. Sprecht Deutsch.	1936-1946	20.00 - 30.00
Red lettering on khaki cut edge twill. "I Speak" Hebrew.	1946-1956	20.00 - 30.00

Red lettering on tan cut cloth. Parle Francais.	1946-1956	20.00 - 30.00
White lettering on red cut edge twill. Yugoslavian.	1957-1988	2.00 - 5.00
White lettering on red cut edge twill. Suomi.	1957-1988	2.00 - 5.00
White lettering on red cut edge twill. Signing.	1957-1988	2.00 - 5.00
White lettering on red cut edge twill. Mandarin.	1957-1988	2.00 - 5.00
White lettering on red cut edge twill. Vietnamese.	1957-1988	2.00 - 5.00
White lettering on red cut edge twill. Czech.	1957-1988	2.00 - 5.00
White lettering on red cut edge twill. Chinese.	1957-1988	2.00 - 5.00
White lettering on red cut edge twill. Thai.	1957-1988	2.00 - 5.00
White lettering on red cut edge twill. Tagakog.	1957-1988	2.00 - 5.00
White lettering on red cut edge twill. Svenska.	1957-1988	2.00 - 5.00
White lettering on red cut edge twill. Slovensky.	1957-1988	2.00 - 5.00
White lettering on red cut edge twill. Ellinka.	1957-1988	2.00 - 5.00
White lettering on red cut edge twill. Vlaamsch.	1957-1988	2.00 - 5.00
White lettering on red cut edge twill. Korean.	1957-1988	2.00 - 5.00
White lettering on red cut edge twill. Soumea.	1957-1988	2.00 - 5.00
White lettering on red cut edge twill. Norge.	1957-1988	2.00 - 5.00
White lettering on red cut edge twill. Ameslan.	1957-1988	2.00 - 5.00
White lettering on red cut edge twill. Japanese.	1957-1988	2.00 - 5.00
White lettering on red cut edge twill. Samoan.	1957-1988	2.00 - 5.00
White lettering on red cut edge twill. Samoa.	1957-1988	2.00 - 5.00
White lettering on red cut edge twill. PYCCKNN (Russian).	1957-1988	2.00 - 5.00
White lettering on red cut edge twill. Portugues.	1957-1988	2.00 - 5.00
White lettering on red cut edge twill. Polska.	1957-1988	2.00 - 5.00
White lettering on red cut edge twill. Pilpino.	1957-1988	2.00 - 5.00
White lettering on red cut edge twill. Dansk.	1957-1988	2.00 - 5.00
White lettering on red cut edge twill. Parla Italiano.	1957-1988	2.00 - 5.00
White lettering on red cut edge twill. Deutsch.	1957-1988	2.00 - 5.00
White lettering on red cut edge twill. Nederlands.	1957-1988	2.00 - 5.00
White lettering on red cut edge twill. Laotian.	1957-1988	2.00 - 5.00
White lettering on red cut edge twill. Swedish.	1957-1988	2.00 - 5.00
White lettering on red cut edge twill. Italiano.	1957-1988	2.00 - 5.00
White lettering on red cut edge twill. Hungarian.	1957-1988	2.00 - 5.00
White lettering on red cut edge twill. Hmong.	1957-1988	2.00 - 5.00
White lettering on red cut edge twill. Gaelic.	1957-1988	2.00 - 5.00
White lettering on red cut edge twill. Filipino.	1957-1988	2.00 - 5.00
White lettering on red cut edge twill. Portuguese.	1957-1988	2.00 - 5.00
White lettering on red cut edge twill. Philippine.	1957-1988	2.00 - 5.00
White lettering on red cut edge twill. Japanese	1957-1988	2.00 - 5.00
White lettering on red cut edge twill. Cambodian.	1957-1988	2.00 - 5.00
White lettering on red cut edge twill. Iranian	1957-1988	2.00 - 5.00
White lettering on red cut edge twill. Portugues.	1957-1988	2.00 - 5.00
White lettering on red cut edge twill. Polish.	1957-1988	2.00 - 5.00
White lettering on red cut edge twill. Philippino.	1957-1988	2.00 - 5.00
White lettering on red cut edge twill. Philipine.	1957-1988	2.00 - 5.00
White lettering on red cut edge twill. Norsk.	1957-1988	2.00 - 5.00
White lettering on red cut edge twill. Netherlands.	1957-1988	2.00 - 5.00
White lettering on red cut edge twill. Latviski.	1957-1988	2.00 - 5.00
White lettering on red cut edge twill. Latinam.	1957-1988	2.00 - 5.00
White lettering on red cut edge twill. Serbian.	1957-1988	2.00 - 5.00
White lettering on red cut edge twill. Kurdish.	1957-1988	2.00 - 5.00
White lettering on red cut edge twill. Benzala.	1957-1988	2.00 - 5.00
White lettering on red cut edge twill. Bulgarian	1957-1988	2.00 - 5.00
White lettering on red cut edge twill. Cesky.	1957-1988	2.00 - 5.00
White lettering on red cut edge twill. Creole.	1957-1988	2.00 - 5.00
White lettering on red cut edge twill. Czechylovaki.	1957-1988	2.00 - 5.00

White lettering on red cut edge twill. Espanol.	1957-1988	2.00 - 5.00
White lettering on red cut edge twill. Bengali.	1957-1988	2.00 - 5.00
White lettering on red cut edge twill. Francais.	1957-1988	2.00 - 5.00
White lettering on red cut edge twill. Hablo Espanol.	1957-1988	2.00 - 5.00
White lettering on red cut edge twill. Hindi.	1957-1988	2.00 - 5.00
White lettering on red cut edge twill. Hollandsch.	1957-1988	2.00 - 5.00
White lettering on red cut edge twill. Icelandic.	1957-1988	2.00 - 5.00
White lettering on red cut edge twill. Dutch.	1957-1988	2.00 - 5.00
Red lettering on tan cut edge twill. Plastic back. Arabic	1989	1.00 - 2.00
Red lettering on tan cut edge twill. Plastic back. Vietnamese.	1989	1.00 - 2.00
Red lettering on tan cut edge twill. Plastic back. Ellinkia.	1989	1.00 - 2.00
Red lettering on tan cut edge twill. Plastic back. Polish.	1989	1.00 - 2.00
Red lettering on tan cut edge twill. Plastic back. Espanol.	1989	1.00 - 2.00
Red lettering on tan cut edge twill. Plastic back. Lithuanian.	1989	1.00 - 2.00
Red lettering on tan cut edge twill. Plastic back. Filipino.	1989	1.00 - 2.00
Red lettering on tan cut edge twill. Plastic back. Sverige.	1989	1.00 - 2.00
Red lettering on tan cut edge twill. Plastic back. Srpski.	1989	1.00 - 2.00
Red lettering on tan cut edge twill. Plastic back. Pyccku.	1989	1.00 - 2.00
Red lettering on tan cut edge twill. Plastic back. Nederlands.	1989	1.00 - 2.00
Red lettering on tan cut edge twill. Plastic back. Italiano.	1989	1.00 - 2.00
Red lettering on tan cut edge twill. Plastic back. Korean.	1989	1.00 - 2.00
Red lettering on tan cut edge twill. Plastic back. Hungarian.	1989	1.00 - 2.00
Red lettering on tan cut edge twill. Plastic back. Hebrew.	1989	1.00 - 2.00
Red lettering on tan cut edge twill. Plastic back. Greek.	1989	1.00 - 2.00
Red lettering on tan cut edge twill. Plastic back. Chinese.	1989	1.00 - 2.00
Red lettering on tan cut edge twill. Plastic back. Finnish.	1989	1.00 - 2.00
Red lettering on tan cut edge twill. Plastic back. Dutch.	1989	1.00 - 2.00

Red lettering on tan cut edge twill. Plastic back. Farsi.	1989	1.00 - 2.00
Red lettering on tan cut edge twill. Plastic back. Francais.	1989	1.00 - 2.00
Red lettering on tan cut edge twill. Plastic back. Gujrati.	1989	1.00 - 2.00
Red lettering on tan cut edge twill. Plastic back. Hrvatski.	1989	1.00 - 2.00
Red lettering on tan cut edge twill. Plastic back. Indonesian.	1989	1.00 - 2.00
Red lettering on tan cut edge twill. Plastic back. Japanese.	1989	1.00 - 2.00
Red lettering on tan cut edge twill. Plastic back. Magyar.	1989	1.00 - 2.00
Red lettering on tan cut edge twill. Plastic back. Persian.	1989	1.00 - 2.00
Red lettering on tan cut edge twill. Plastic back. Portuguese.	1989	1.00 - 2.00
Red lettering on tan cut edge twill. Plastic back. Romanian.	1989	1.00 - 2.00
Red lettering on tan cut edge twill. Plastic back. Signing.	1989	1.00 - 2.00
Red lettering on tan cut edge twill. Plastic back. Deutsch.	1989	1.00 - 2.00

LEADERSHIP CORPS

Tall keystone shape, rolled edge, red twill background, lamp of knowledge.	1972-1982	2.00 - 3.00
Round. Rolled edge, red twill background.	1982-Prs	7.50 - 10.00

LIBRARIAN

Tan cloth, Tenderfoot emblem on open book.	1936-1942	30.00 - 45.00
Sand twill.	1942-1945	30.00 - 45.00
Khaki cloth.	1946-1954	10.00 - 20.00
Khaki cut edge, coarse twill.	1955-1964	5.00 - 10.00
Khaki cut edge, fine twill.	1965-1971	5.00 - 10.00
Round rolled edge, green background, three books.	1972-1989	0.00 - 0.00
Round rolled edge, tan background, FDL and three books.	1989	1.00 - 2.00

LIFE SAVING SCOUT

Senior 4" x 2" vertical diamond white twill.		10.00 - 15.00
LSS Junior 2" circle white twill cut edge.		5.00 - 7.50

MUSICIAN

Tan cloth. Short crown Tenderfoot emblem on lyre.	1923-1936	40.00 - 60.00
Tan cloth. Tenderfoot emblem w/tall crown on lyre.	1937-1942	40.00 - 60.00
Round dark green twill w/rolled edge (for regional and national bands).	1938-1951	150.00 - 225.00
Sand twill.	1942-1945	30.00 - 45.00
Khaki cloth.	1946-1954	20.00 - 30.00
Khaki cut edge, coarse twill.	1955-1964	5.00 - 10.00
Khaki cut edge, fine twill.	1965-1971	5.00 - 10.00
Round rolled edge, green background, red border, music notes.	1972-1989	2.00 - 3.00
Round rolled edge, tan background. FDL and music note.	1989	1.00 - 2.00

Quartermaster patches in cut square khaki (top) and cut edge twill (right).

QUARTERMASTER

Tan cloth, key and wagon wheel.	1923-1942	30.00 - 40.00
Sand twill.	1942-1945	25.00 - 35.00
Khaki cloth.	1946-1954	20.00 - 30.00
Khaki cut edge, coarse twill.	1955-1964	5.00 - 10.00
Khaki cut edge, fine background.	1965-1971	5.00 - 10.00
Round rolled edge, green background, backpack.	1972-1989	2.00 - 3.00
Round rolled edge, tan background. FDL and backpack.	1989	1.00 - 2.00

SCRIBE

Tan cloth, two crossed quills.	1926-1942	35.00 - 45.00
Sand twill.	1942-1945	30.00 - 40.00
Khaki cloth.	1946-1951	20.00 - 30.00
Khaki cloth. Tenderfoot emblem w/two crossed quills.	1952-1954	20.00 - 30.00
Khaki cut edge, coarse twill.	1955-1964	5.00 - 10.00
Khaki cut edge, fine twill.	1965-1971	5.00 - 10.00
Round cut edge, green background, one quill and title.	1972-1989	2.00 - 3.00
Round rolled edge, tan background, FDL w/one quill and title.	1989	1.00 - 2.00

TROOP GUIDE

Round rolled edge, red background. First-Class emblem w/title as: GUIDE.	1988-1989	2.00 - 3.00
Round rolled edge, tan background. First-Class emblem w/title as: TROOP GUIDE.	1989	1.00 - 2.00

VENTURE CREW CHIEF

Tan rolled edge.	1989	1.00 - 2.00

ADVANCEMENT CARDS

Early style advancement cards. This group is from the late 1920s and early 1930s.

EAGLE PALM CARD. BRONZE, SILVER, OR GOLD

Pocket size, National Council New York City seal.	1945-1953	7.50 - 10.00
Badge in circle, line flanking, National Council on seal.	1953-1968	3.00 - 6.00
Badge at top, National Council on yellow seal.	1960-1968	3.00 - 5.00
Badge at top, BE PREPARED on yellow seal.	1968-1972	2.50 - 5.00
Medal design w/ yellow seal.	1972-1989	4.00 - 6.00

EAGLE SCOUT CARD

200 Fifth Avenue address.	1920-1930	10.00 - 15.00
2 Park Avenue address.	1930-1945	10.00 - 15.00
Pocket size, National Council New York City seal.	1945-1953	7.50 - 10.00
Badge in circle, line flanking, National Council on seal.	1953-1968	3.00 - 6.00
Badge at top, National Council on yellow seal.	1960-1968	4.00 - 6.00
Badge at top, BE PREPARED on yellow seal.	1968-1972	2.50 - 5.00
Medal design w/ yellow seal.	1972-1989	4.00 - 6.00

FIRST CLASS CARD

200 Fifth Avenue address.	1920-1930	5.00 - 7.50
2 Park Avenue address.	1930-1945	5.00 - 7.50
Pocket size, National Council New York City seal.	1945-1953	3.00 - 5.00
Badge in circle, line flanking, National Council on seal.	1953-1968	2.00 - 4.00
Badge at top, National Council on yellow seal.	1960-1968	1.00 - 2.00
Badge at top, BE PREPARED on yellow seal.	1968-1972	1.00 - 2.00
Colored background patch, green border.	1972-1989	0.50 - 1.00

LIFE SCOUT CARD

200 Fifth Avenue address.	1920-1930	7.50 - 12.50
2 Park Avenue address.	1930-1945	7.50 - 12.50
Pocket size, National Council New York City seal.	1945-1953	5.00 - 7.50
Badge in circle, line flanking, National Council on seal.	1953-1968	2.00 - 4.00
Badge at top, National Council on yellow seal.	1960-1968	1.00 - 2.00
Badge at top, BE PREPARED on yellow seal.	1968-1972	1.00 - 2.00
Colored background patch, green border.	1972-1989	0.50 - 1.00

MERIT BADGE CARD

200 Fifth Avenue address.	1920-1930	5.00 - 7.50
2 Park Avenue address.	1930-1945	5.00 - 7.50
Badge in circle, line flanking, National Council on seal.	1953-1968	2.00 - 4.00
Badge at top, National Council on yellow seal.	1960-1968	1.00 - 2.00
Badge at top, BE PREPARED on yellow seal.	1968-1972	1.00 - 2.00
Red stripes at top and bottom w/ rank badges in blue.	1972-1989	0.50 - 1.00

SECOND CLASS CARD

200 Fifth Avenue address.	1920-1930	5.00 - 7.50
2 Park Avenue address.	1930-1945	5.00 - 7.50
Pocket size, National Council New York City seal.	1945-1953	3.00 - 5.00
Badge in circle, line flanking, National Council on seal.	1953-1968	2.00 - 4.00
Badge at top, National Council on yellow seal.	1960-1968	1.00 - 2.00
Badge at top, BE PREPARED on yellow seal.	1968-1972	1.00 - 2.00
Colored background patch, green border.	1972-1989	0.50 - 1.00

STAR SCOUT CARD

200 Fifth Avenue address.	1920-1930	7.50 - 12.50
2 Park Avenue address.	1930-1945	7.50 - 12.50
Pocket size, National Council New York City seal.	1945-1953	5.00 - 7.50
Badge in circle, line flanking, National Council on seal.	1953-1968	2.00 - 4.00
Badge at top, National Council on yellow seal.	1960-1968	1.00 - 2.00
Badge at top, BE PREPARED on yellow seal.	1968-1972	1.00 - 2.00
Colored background patch, green border.	1972-1989	0.50 - 1.00

TENDERFOOT CARD

200 Fifth Avenue address.	1920-1930	5.00 - 7.50
2 Park Avenue address.	1930-1945	5.00 - 7.50
Pocket size, National Council New York City seal.	1945-1953	3.00 - 5.00
Badge in circle, line flanking, National Council on seal.	1953-1968	2.00 - 4.00
Badge at top, National Council on yellow seal.	1960-1968	1.00 - 2.00
Badge at top, BE PREPARED on yellow seal.	1968-1972	1.00 - 2.00
Colored background patch, green border.	1972-1989	0.50 - 1.00

Advancement cards of the 1960s (top), from the 1970s (bottom).

Neighborhood Commissioner square cut khaki.

Neighborhood Commissioner and District Executive patches.

Scoutmaster cut edge.

IDENTIFYING UNIT DISTRICT & COUNCIL LEVEL POSITION INSIGNIA, 1913-1970

LARGE FIRST CLASS DESIGN (77 mm)

	Badge outline	Eagle	Background	
Scout Commissioner	dark blue	brown	dark blue	1913-1916
Deputy Scout Comm.	powder blue	brown	powder blue	1913-1916
Deputy Scout Comm.	dark blue	brown	dark blue	1916-1919
Asst. Deputy Comm.	powder blue	brown	powder blue	1916-1919
Troop/Council Comm.	white	brown	white	1914-1919
National Committee	purple	brown	purple	1911-1919
National Committee	purple	brown	purple	1920-1928
Local Councilman	silver	silver	blue	1920-1928
Scout Master	green	brown	green	1911-1919
Scout Master	silver	silver	brown	1920-1928
Asst. Scout Master	gold	gold	brown	1920-1928
Asst. Scout Master	red	brown	red	1911-1938

Scoutmaster rolled edge.

FIRST CLASS DESIGN ENCIRCLED BY A WREATH

	Wreath	1st Class background	Eagle	1st Class badge outline	
Scout Commissioner	yellow	blue	brown	blue	1916-1919
Scout/Council Comm.	silver	blue	silver	silver	1920-1969
Asst. Council Comm.	silver	blue	gold	silver	1966-1069
Deputy Scout Comm.	gold	blue	silver	silver	1920-1931
Field/District Comm.	gold	blue	silver	silver	1931-1969
Asst. Deputy Comm.	gold	blue	gold	silver	1920-1931
Asst. Field/Dist. Comm.	gold	blue	gold	silver	1931-1969
Neighborhood Comm.	gold	blue	gold	gold	1933-1969
Scout Executive	yellow	white	yellow	white	1917-1919
Scout Executive	silver	red	silver	silver	1920-1969
Asst. Scout Executive	gold	red	silver	silver	1920-1969
Field/District Exec.	gold	red	gold	silver	1920-1969
Asst. Field/Dist. Exec.	gold	red	gold	gold	1931-1969
Layman	none	blue	gold	gold	1928-1969
Council President	gold	blue	brown	gold 2 hands	1966-1969
Council Past President	gold	blue	brown	gold 1 hand	1966-1969

Silver is actually white in many early badges: A Scout Executive badge is described as silver, yet every badge pre-1950s I have observed is actually white.

Coloration will apply to lapel pins and collar pins, as well as badges. Dates apply only to badges. All badges from 1970 have the position title embroidered in the design.

POSITION BADGES - ADULT

AMBASSADOR

Tenderfoot emblem on fully embroidered purple, rolled edge.	1989	5.00 - 10.00

AREA COMMITTEE

Tenderfoot emblem on dark green twill, rolled edge.	1973	10.00 - 15.00

AREA PRESIDENT

Tenderfoot emblem on dark green twill, rolled edge.	1973	10.00 - 15.00

ASSISTANT CHIEF SCOUT EXECUTIVE

Khaki, cut cloth.	1943-1956	250.00 - 300.00
Khaki cut edge, solid wreath.	1956-1967	175.00 - 225.00
Khaki, rolled edge.	1967-1972	40.00 - 60.00
Tenderfoot emblem on maroon twill, titled, gray rolled edge.	1973	75.00 - 100.00

ASSISTANT COUNCIL COMMISSIONER

First-Class emblem in white w/yellow eagle and white wreath on blue twill, rolled edge.	1968-1970	10.00 - 15.00
Tenderfoot emblem on light blue twill, rolled edge.	1970-1973	5.00 - 7.50
Tenderfoot emblem on red twill, rolled edge.	1972-1989	2.50 - 5.00
Tenderfoot emblem on red twill, rolled edge.	1973	5.00 - 7.50

ASSISTANT DEPUTY SCOUT COMMISSIONER

First-Class emblem, light blue behind eagle.	1911	1,000. - 1,500.
Tan cloth, light blue First-Class emblem, brown eagle.	1915-1920	1,000. - 1,500.
Tan cloth, blue First-Class emblem w/ silver border, gold eagle, and fine wreath.	1921-1938	400.00 - 800.00

ASSISTANT DISTRICT SCOUT EXECUTIVE

Fine wreath, khaki cut cloth.	1938-1956	100.00 - 125.00
Solid wreath, khaki cut edge.	1956-1967	8.50 - 12.50
Solid wreath, khaki rolled edge.	1967-1972	8.50 - 12.50
Tenderfoot emblem, solid wreath, titled, rolled edge.	1973	15.00 - 20.00

ASSISTANT DISTRICT (FIELD) EXECUTIVE STAFF

Tan cloth, red First-Class emblem w/ gold border, eagle, and fine wreath.	1926-1938	150.00 - 300.00

ASSISTANT DISTRICT COMMISSIONER

First-Class emblem in yellow on red background, full wreath, khaki-cut cloth.	1943-1956	20.00 - 30.00
First-Class emblem in yellow on red background, solid wreath, khaki cut edge.	1956-1967	7.50 - 10.00
First-Class emblem, solid wreath, khaki rolled edge.	1967-1970	7.50 - 10.00
Tenderfoot emblem on light blue twill, rolled edge.	1970-1973	5.00 - 7.50
Tenderfoot on red twill, rolled edge.	1973	2.50 - 5.00

ASSISTANT RANGER

First-Class emblem in yellow w/yellow eagle and background. Khaki cut edge.	1956-1967	30.00 - 40.00
Tenderfoot emblem in yellow on red twill rolled edge, white title.	1967-1970	7.50 - 10.00
Tenderfoot emblem on red twill, rolled edge.	1972	2.50 - 5.00
Tenderfoot emblem in yellow on red twill rolled edge, yellow title.	1975	5.00 - 7.50

ASSISTANT SCOUT EXECUTIVE

Tan cloth, red First-Class emblem w/ silver border and eagle, fine gold wreath.	1921-1938	150.00 - 250.00
Full wreath on khaki cloth.	1943-1956	30.00 - 45.00

ASSISTANT SCOUTMASTER - VENTURE

Tan rolled edge.	1989	1.00 - 1.50

Assistant Scoutmaster Patch on square cut wool. Note that there is no central split line in the short crown of the FDL.

ASSISTANT SCOUTMASTER

Tan cloth, red First-Class emblem, brown eagle.	1911-1920	200.00 - 300.00
First-Class badge, red behind eagle.	1911	350.00 - 450.00
Tan cloth, green First-Class emblem, gold border, and eagle.	1921-1934	75.00 - 100.00
First-Class badge, red behind eagle, khaki cut cloth.	1934	60.00 - 80.00
First-Class emblem in yellow outline on green cut edge twill.	1938-1966	10.00 - 15.00
First-Class emblem in yellow outline on green rolled edge twill.	1966-1972	7.50 - 10.00
Tenderfoot emblem, fully embroidered green mylar thread (trained leader).	1972-1989	15.00 - 20.00
Tenderfoot emblem on green twill, rolled edge.	1972-1989	2.50 - 5.00
Tenderfoot emblem on tan twill, rolled edge.	1989	2.50 - 5.00

BLAZER SCOUT LEADER
Tenderfoot emblem in ctr.   1989   7.50 - 10.00

CHAPLAIN
First-Class emblem and crook, within circle, 1931-1940 80.00 - 100.00
  cut tan cloth.
First-Class emblem and crook, within circle, 1940-1966 80.00 - 100.00
  cut khaki cloth.
First-Class emblem and crook, within circle, 1967-1972 25.00 - 35.00
  rolled edge.
Crook, CHAPLAIN, and Tenderfoot emblem in 1968-1972 10.00 - 15.00
  vertical oval, rolled edge.
Tenderfoot emblem and Crook on white twill, 1973   5.00 - 7.50
  dark blue rolled edge border.

CHARTERED ORGANIZATION REPRESENTATIVE
Tenderfoot emblem on tan twill, rolled edge. 1989   2.50 - 5.00

CHIEF SCOUT EXECUTIVE
Tan cloth, purple First-Class emblem   1921-1923 4,000. - 6,000.
  w/ silver border, eagle, and fine wreath.
Tan cloth, silver First-Class emblem   1923-1938 2,000. - 3,000.
  w/ silver border, eagle, and fine wreath.
  Red-white-blue behind emblem.
First-Class on white background,   1943-1956 250.00 - 500.00
  w/ white eagle and wreath,
  red-white-blue center. Khaki cut cloth.
First-Class on white background, w/ white   1956-1969 150.00 - 250.00
  eagle and wreath, red-white-blue center.
  Red-white-blue scroll, khaki cut edge.
First-Class on white background, w/ white   1959-1967 125.00 - 175.00
  eagle and wreath, red-white-blue center,
  blue twill scroll, khaki cut edge.
First-Class on white background, w/white eagle 1967-1970 100.00 - 150.00
  and wreath, red-white-blue center,
  blue twill scroll, khaki rolled edge.
Tenderfoot emblem on red twill, rolled edge. 1970-1973 30.00 - 50.00
Tenderfoot emblem on maroon twill,   1973   50.00 - 75.00
  rolled edge.

CHIEF SCOUT
First-Class emblem in white, w/ brown eagle, 1943-1956 500.00 - 750.00
  white wreath, khaki cut cloth.
First-Class emblem in white, w/ brown eagle, 1956-1967 150.00 - 250.00
  white wreath, khaki cut edge.

COUNCIL COMMISSIONER
First-Class emblem in full wreath on khaki cloth 1943-1956 25.00 - 35.00
  cut.
First-Class emblem in solid wreath,   1956-1967 20.00 - 30.00
  khaki cut edge.
First-Class emblem in solid wreath,   1967-1970 15.00 - 20.00
  khaki rolled edge.
Tenderfoot emblem on light blue twill,   1970-1973 7.50 - 12.50
  rolled edge.
Tenderfoot emblem on red twill, rolled edge. 1973   7.50 - 12.50

COUNCIL COMMITTEE
Tenderfoot emblem on light blue twill,   1973   5.00 - 7.50
  rolled edge.

COUNCIL EXECUTIVE BOARD
Tenderfoot emblem on light blue twill,   1973   5.00 - 7.50
  rolled edge.

COUNCIL EXECUTIVE STAFF
Tenderfoot emblem on red twill, rolled edge. 1973   7.50 - 10.00

COUNCIL EXECUTIVE
Tenderfoot emblem on red twill, rolled edge. 1973   7.50 - 10.00

COUNCIL PAST PRESIDENT
First-Class emblem w/yellow background,   1956-1967 50.00 - 75.00
  eagle and wreath. Hands point down.
  Khaki cut edge.

First-Class emblem w/yellow background,   1967-1968 50.00 - 75.00
  eagle and wreath. Hands point down.
  Khaki rolled edge.
First-Class emblem w/brown eagle,   1968-1970 40.00 - 60.00
  yellow background and wreath.
  Hands point down. Khaki rolled edge.
Tenderfoot emblem in white on   1970-1973 10.00 - 15.00
  light blue twill, rolled edge.
Tenderfoot emblem in yellow on   1973   10.00 - 15.00
  light blue twill, rolled edge.
Tenderfoot emblem on light blue twill,   1973   10.00 - 15.00
  rolled edge.

COUNCIL PRESIDENT
First-Class emblem, yellow eagle and wreath, 1956-1967 75.00 - 100.00
  blue center. Hands pointed out.
  Khaki cut edge.
First-Class emblem, yellow eagle and wreath, 1967-1968 50.00 - 75.00
  blue center. Hands pointed out.
  Khaki rolled edge.
First-Class emblem, brown eagle and yellow   1968-1970 40.00 - 60.00
  wreath, blue center. Hands pointed out.
  Khaki rolled edge.
Tenderfoot emblem in white on light blue twill, 1970-1973 30.00 - 40.00
  rolled edge.
Tenderfoot emblem in yellow on light blue twill, 1973   10.00 - 15.00
  rolled edge.
Tenderfoot emblem on light blue twill,   1973   5.00 - 7.50
  rolled edge.

COUNCIL VICE PRESIDENT
Tenderfoot emblem on light blue twill,   1973   7.50 - 10.00
  rolled edge.

DEPUTY CHIEF SCOUT EXECUTIVE
Tan cloth, purple First-Class emblem   1920-1923 2,000. - 3,000.
  w/silver border, eagle, and fine silver wreath.
Tan cloth, silver First-Class emblem   1923-1938 1,000. - 1,500.
  w/silver border, eagle, and fine silver
  wreath. Red-white-blue behind emblem.
Silver First-Class emblem w/silver border,   1943-1956 250.00 - 300.00
  eagle, and fine silver wreath. Red-white-blue
  behind emblem, khaki cut cloth.
Silver First-Class emblem w/ silver border, 1956-1967 100.00 - 150.00
  eagle, and fine gold wreath. Red-white-blue
  behind emblem, khaki cut edge.

DEPUTY SCOUT COMMISSIONER
First-Class emblem w/dark blue background.   1910   1,000. - 1,500.
Tan cloth, dark blue First-Class emblem,   1915-1920 250.00 - 400.00
  brown eagle.
Tan cloth, light blue First-Class emblem   1921-1938 100.00 - 200.00
  w/silver border, eagle, and fine gold wreath.

DISTRICT (FIELD SCOUT) EXECUTIVE
Tan cloth, red First-Class emblem w/silver   1926-1938 100.00 - 200.00
  border and gold eagle, fine gold wreath.

DISTRICT CHAIRMAN

Tenderfoot emblem on light blue twill, rolled edge.	1973	2.50 - 5.00

DISTRICT COMMISSIONER

Full wreath, khaki cloth cut.	1943-1956	30.00 - 45.00
Solid wreath, khaki cut edge.	1956-1967	10.00 - 15.00
Solid wreath, khaki rolled edge.	1967-1970	7.50 - 12.50
Tenderfoot emblem on light blue twill, title in yellow. Rolled edge.	1970-1973	5.00 - 7.50
Tenderfoot emblem on red twill, rolled edge.	1973	2.50 - 5.00

DISTRICT COMMITTEE

Tenderfoot emblem on light blue twill, title in yellow. Rolled edge.	1970-1973	5.00 - 7.50
Tenderfoot emblem on light blue twill, white title, rolled edge.	1970-1973	3.00 - 4.00

DISTRICT EXECUTIVE STAFF

Tenderfoot emblem on maroon twill, rolled edge.	1973	5.00 - 7.50

DISTRICT EXECUTIVE

Fine wreath, khaki cloth cut.	1943-1956	30.00 - 40.00
Solid wreath, khaki cut edge.	1956-1967	15.00 - 25.00
Solid wreath, khaki rolled edge.	1967-1970	10.00 - 15.00
Tenderfoot emblem on maroon twill.	1973	5.00 - 7.50
Tenderfoot emblem on maroon twill, rolled edge.	1973	5.00 - 7.50

EMPLOYEE

First-Class emblem in bronze w/red background on tan cut cloth.	1926-1940	150.00 - 200.00
First-Class emblem in bronze w/red background on khaki cut cloth.	1940-1956	100.00 - 140.00
First-Class emblem in yellow w/red background on khaki cut edge.	1956-1967	50.00 - 80.00
Tenderfoot emblem on red twill, rolled edge.	1967-1970	30.00 - 40.00
Tenderfoot emblem on red twill, white title, rolled edge.	1970-1975	20.00 - 25.00
Tenderfoot emblem on red twill, yellow title, rolled edge.	1975	5.00 - 7.50

INSTITUTIONAL REPRESENTATIVE

Tenderfoot emblem on light blue twill, rolled edge.	1972-1975	2.50 - 5.00

INTERNATIONAL COMMISSIONER

First-Class emblem in yellow wreath, brown eagle, green center, khaki cut cloth.	1943-1956	400.00 - 500.00
First-Class emblem in yellow wreath, brown eagle, green center, khaki cut edge.	1956-1958	80.00 - 100.00
First-Class emblem on white background, brown eagle, white wreath, khaki cut edge.	1958-1967	50.00 - 75.00
First-Class emblem on white background, eagle, red-white-blue center to wreath. Khaki rolled edge.	1967-1970	50.00 - 75.00

INTERNATIONAL REPRESENTATIVE

Tenderfoot emblem on fully embroidered purple, rolled edge.	1989	5.00 - 10.00

INTERNATIONAL SCOUT COMMISSIONER

First-Class emblem at ctr. of starburst, eight clasped hands at 3, 6, 9, and 12 o'clock, Golden eagle behind.	1931-1943	1,500. - 2,000.

LADY SCOUTER

Tenderfoot emblem in blue outline on cream square.	1968	10.00 - 15.00
Tenderfoot emblem in yellow outline on navy square.	1968-1970	10.00 - 15.00
Tenderfoot emblem in blue on white square.	1970-1972	10.00 - 15.00

LAYMAN

First-Class emblem w/yellow outline and blue background, tan cut cloth.	1929-1932	150.00 - 200.00
First-Class emblem, yellow eagle and background, on khaki cut cloth.	1932-1938	100.00 - 150.00
First-Class emblem, yellow eagle and background, on round khaki cloth.	1938-1943	100.00 - 150.00
First-Class emblem, yellow eagle and background on blue twill.	1943-1956	50.00 - 100.00
First-Class emblem, yellow eagle and background on khaki cut edge.	1956-1967	10.00 - 15.00
First-Class emblem, yellow eagle and background on khaki rolled edge.	1967-1972	7.50 - 10.00

LOCAL COUNCIL

Tan cloth, blue First-Class emblem, silver border, and eagle.	1921-1928	0.00 - 0.00

LOCAL COUNCILMAN

First-Class emblem, white background, tan cut cloth.	1921-1928	600.00 - 800.00
First-Class emblem in blue, white outline, rolled edge.	1970-1973	50.00 - 75.00

NATIONAL COMMITTEE

Tan cloth, purple First-Class emblem, brown eagle.	1911-1920	2,000. - 3,000.
Tan cloth, purple First-Class emblem, silver border, and eagle.	1921-1930	400.00 - 600.00
Tenderfoot emblem on purple twill, rolled edge.	1973-1980	15.00 - 20.00

NATIONAL EXECUTIVE BOARD, BSA

Tenderfoot emblem within wreath.	1973	75.00 - 100.00

NATIONAL EXECUTIVE BOARD

First-Class emblem on arrowhead, all within circle. Khaki cut cloth.	1943-1956	250.00 - 350.00
First-Class emblem on arrowhead, all within circle. Khaki cut edge.	1956-1967	200.00 - 250.00
First-Class emblem on arrowhead, khaki twill, gold rolled edge.	1967-1968	80.00 - 100.00
First-Class emblem on arrowhead, khaki twill, purple rolled edge.	1968-1970	80.00 - 100.00
Tenderfoot emblem in white on purple twill, rolled edge.	1970-1973	5.00 - 10.00
Tenderfoot emblem in yellow on purple twill, rolled edge.	1973-1980	15.00 - 20.00
Tenderfoot emblem on fully embroidered purple, rolled edge.	1980	5.00 - 10.00

NATIONAL EXECUTIVE STAFF
Tenderfoot emblem on red-white-blue center on maroon twill, rolled edge.   1973   10.00 - 15.00

NATIONAL FIELD SCOUT COMMISSIONER
Tan cloth, silver First-Class emblem w/silver border, eagle, and fine gold wreath. Dark blue behind emblem.   1921-1938   600.00 - 800.00

NATIONAL PARTNER REPRESENTATIVE
Tenderfoot emblem on purple twill, title at top, rolled edge.   1970-1973   60.00 - 80.00

Tenderfoot emblem on purple twill within wreath, title split between top and bottom, rolled edge.   1973   10.00 - 15.00

NATIONAL PAST PRESIDENT
First-Class emblem on arrowhead, hand below, gavel and ax behind.   1931-1932   1,000. - 1,500.

First-Class emblem on arrowhead, star below, gavel and ax behind.   1932-1943   350.00 - 500.00

Tenderfoot emblem in white on purple twill, rolled edge.   1970-1973   80.00 - 100.00

Tenderfoot emblem in yellow on purple twill, rolled edge.   1973   75.00 - 100.00

NATIONAL PRESIDENT
First-Class emblem on arrowhead, two hands below, crossed gavel and ax.   1931-1932   600.00 - 750.00

First-Class emblem on arrowhead, two stars flanking, crossed gavel and ax. Brown eagle.   1932-1943   400.00 - 600.00

First-Class emblem on arrowhead, two stars flanking, crossed gavel and ax. Gold eagle.   1943-1958   400.00 - 600.00

First-Class emblem in white w/ white eagle and wreath, khaki cut edge.   1958-1959   150.00 - 250.00

First-Class emblem in white w/ brown eagle and white wreath, khaki cut edge.   1959-1968   100.00 - 175.00

Tenderfoot emblem in white on purple twill, rolled edge.   1970-1972   80.00 - 100.00

Tenderfoot emblem in yellow on purple twill, rolled edge.   1973   50.00 - 75.00

NATIONAL SCOUT COMMISSIONER
First-Class emblem w/yellow background and wreath, white eagle and powerhorn. Tan cut cloth.   1915-1923   2,000. - 3,000.

First-Class emblem w/yellow background and wreath, white eagle and powerhorn. Tan cut cloth.   1923-1937   700.00 - 900.00

First-Class emblem w/white background, wreath, eagle and powerhorn. Tan cut cloth.   1937-1940   600.00 - 800.00

First-Class emblem in yellow w/yellow background, wreath, eagle and powerhorn. Khaki cut cloth.   1940-1956   500.00 - 750.00

First-Class emblem in white w/white background, wreath, eagle and powerhorn. Khaki cut edge.   1956-1958   400.00 - 500.00

NATIONAL STAFF
Tan cloth, silver First-Class emblem w/silver border, gold eagle, and fine wreath. Red-white-blue behind emblem.   1931-1938   300.00 - 400.00

First-Class emblem on red-white-blue background, wreath. khaki cut cloth.   1940-1946   150.00 - 200.00

First-Class emblem on red-white-blue background, wreath, khaki cut edge.   1956-1967   30.00 - 45.00

First-Class emblem on red-white-blue background, wreath, rolled edge.   1967-1970   30.00 - 40.00

Tenderfoot emblem in yellow on red twill w/blue in wreath, rolled edge.   1970   5.00 - 10.00

NATIONAL VICE PRESIDENT
Tenderfoot emblem in white on purple twill, rolled edge.   1970-1972   10.00 - 15.00

Tenderfoot emblem on fully embroidered purple, rolled edge.   1980   10.00 - 15.00

NEIGHBORHOOD COMMISSIONER
Tan cloth, blue First-Class emblem w/gold border, eagle, and fine wreath.   1932-1938   40.00 - 60.00

Full wreath, khaki cut cloth.   1943-1956   30.00 - 40.00

First-Class emblem w/yellow eagle and blue background on khaki cut edge.   1956-1967   20.00 - 25.00

First-Class emblem w/yellow eagle and blue background on khaki rolled edge.   1967-1970   10.00 - 15.00

Tenderfoot emblem on blue twill, rolled edge.   1970-1972   5.00 - 10.00

PARAPROFESSIONAL
Tenderfoot emblem on red twill, rolled edge.   1970   2.00 - 3.00

PHYSICIAN

Caduceus behind First-Class emblem in circle, khaki cut cloth.	1931-1956	100.00 - 125.00
Caduceus (yellow) behind First-Class emblem in circle, cut edge.	1956-1958	60.00 - 80.00
Caduceus (red) behind First-Class emblem in circle, khaki cut edge.	1958-1966	40.00 - 50.00
Caduceus behind First-Class emblem on yellow twill. Rolled edge.	1967-1970	10.00 - 15.00
Caduceus behind Tenderfoot emblem in circle, PHYSICIAN, rolled edge.	1970-1972	20.00 - 30.00
Tenderfoot emblem and Caduceus on white twill, dark blue rolled edge.	1973	5.00 - 7.50

PRIMARY LEADER

Tenderfoot emblem on green twill, rolled edge.	1975-1989	5.00 - 7.50

RANGER

First-Class emblem with red background and yellow outline. Khaki cut cloth.	1947-1956	40.00 - 60.00
First-Class emblem with yellow background and outline. Khaki cut edge.	1956-1967	30.00 - 40.00
First-Class emblem with yellow background and outline. Khaki rolled edge.	1967-1970	20.00 - 30.00
Tenderfoot emblem w/white title on red twill, rolled edge.	1970-1975	10.00 - 15.00
Tenderfoot emblem on red twill, rolled edge.	1973	2.50 - 5.00
Tenderfoot emblem w/yellow title on red twill, rolled edge.	1975	5.00 - 10.00

REGION COMMITTEE

Tenderfoot emblem on wine twill, rolled edge.	1973	10.00 - 15.00

REGION PRESIDENT

Tenderfoot emblem on wine twill, rolled edge.	1973	10.00 - 15.00

REGIONAL SCOUT EXECUTIVE

Tan cloth, gold First-Class emblem w/gold border, eagle, and fine wreath. Red-white-blue behind emblem.	1921-1938	400.00 - 600.00

SCOUT COMMISSIONER

Tan cloth, fine yellow wreath, dark blue First-Class emblem, brown eagle.	1915-1920	300.00 - 500.00
Tan cloth, blue First-Class emblem w/ silver border, eagle, and fine wreath.	1921-1938	250.00 - 400.00

SCOUT EXECUTIVE

Tan cloth, fine yellow wreath, white First-Class emblem, yellow eagle.	1915-1920	400.00 - 600.00
Tan cloth, red First-Class emblem w/silver border and eagle, fine silver wreath.	1921-1938	300.00 - 400.00
Wreath, khaki cut cloth.	1943-1956	30.00 - 40.00
Khaki cut edge.	1956-1967	20.00 - 30.00
Khaki rolled edge.	1967-1970	15.00 - 25.00
Tenderfoot emblem in white on maroon twill, rolled edge.	1970-1973	10.00 - 15.00
Tenderfoot emblem in yellow on maroon twill, rolled edge.	1973	5.00 - 7.50

SCOUTING COORDINATOR

Tenderfoot emblem on light blue twill, rolled edge.	1975	5.00 - 7.50

Scoutmaster badges of the cut edge (left) and rolled edge varieties.

SCOUTMASTER

Green First -Class emblem, white stars and motto, 77 mm long.	1910	300.00 - 400.00
Tan cloth, green First-Class emblem, brown eagle.	1911-1920	150.00 - 200.00
Tan cloth, green First-Class emblem, silver border, and eagle.	1921-1938	100.00 - 150.00
White outline First-Class badge within white circle, cut edge green twill.	1938-1967	25.00 - 35.00
White outline First-Class badge within white circle, rolled edge green twill.	1967-1970	20.00 - 25.00
White outline First-Class badge within white circle, SCOUTMASTER title, rolled edge.	1970-1972	10.00 - 15.00
Tenderfoot emblem on green twill, rolled edge.	1972-1989	2.50 - 5.00
Tenderfoot emblem on fully embroidered green mylar thread (trained leader).	1972-1989	15.00 - 20.00
Tenderfoot emblem on tan twill, rolled edge.	1989	2.50 - 5.00

SPECIAL NATIONAL FIELD SCOUT COMMISSIONER

Tan cloth, purple First-Class emblem w/silver border, eagle, and fine gold wreath. Red-white-blue behind emblem.	1920-1923	1,000. - 1,500.
Silver First-Class emblem within wreath, tan cut cloth.	1923-1938	400.00 - 600.00
Silver First-Class emblem, brown eagle, all within wreath, tan cut cloth.	1923-1938	400.00 - 600.00
First-Class emblem on blue background, red-white-blue center of yellow wreath, khaki cut cloth.	1940-1956	40.00 - 55.00
First-Class emblem in white w/ white eagle on purple center, khaki cut edge.	1956-1961	40.00 - 55.00
First-Class emblem in white w/ brown eagle on purple center, khaki cut edge.	1961-1967	50.00 - 75.00
First-Class emblem in white w/ white eagle on purple center, khaki rolled edge.	1967-1970	20.00 - 30.00

SPONSOR COORDINATOR
Tenderfoot emblem on light blue twill, rolled edge.	1973-1989	2.50 - 5.00

TROOP COMMITTEE
Tan cloth, blue First-Class emblem, gold border, and eagle.	1921-1938	300.00 - 450.00
First-Class emblem in blue on blue twill rolled edge, yellow title.	1970-1972	5.00 - 8.00
Tenderfoot emblem on green twill, rolled edge.	1973-1989	2.50 - 5.00
Tenderfoot emblem on tan twill, rolled edge.	1989	2.50 - 5.00

TROOP COMMISSIONER
Tenderfoot emblem on blue background, yellow border.	1975	5.00 - 7.50
Tenderfoot emblem on blue background, silver mylar border.	1975-1989	7.50 - 10.00

TROOP COMMITTEE CHAIRMAN
Tenderfoot emblem on green twill, rolled edge.	1973-1989	2.50 - 5.00
Tenderfoot emblem on tan twill, rolled edge.	1989	2.50 - 5.00

TROOP COMMITTEE OR LOCAL COUNCIL COMMITTEE
Tan cloth, white Firs--Class emblem, brown eagle.	1911-1920	750.00 - 1,000.

UNIT COMMISSIONER
Tenderfoot emblem on red twill, rolled edge white border.	1973-1975	5.00 - 7.50
Tenderfoot emblem on red twill, rolled edge silver mylar border.	1975-1989	5.00 - 7.50
Tenderfoot emblem on red twill, yellow rolled edge.	1975-1989	2.00 - 3.00

WOMEN'S RESERVE
Tenderfoot emblem on white twill, dark blue rolled edge.	1973-1989	7.50 - 10.00

Adult position badges of the 1970s.

AWARD MEDALS

CONTEST MEDAL. OCTAGONAL PENDANT, REGULAR RIBBON AND DRAPE BEHIND.

Plain center, laurel wreath. Red-white-blue ribbon, pendant in gold, silver, or bronze.	1914-1920	300.00 - 400.00

CONTEST MEDAL. OCTAGONAL PENDANT, REGULAR RIBBON.

Plain center, laurel wreath. Red-white-blue ribbon, pendant in gold, silver, or bronze.	1921-1928	60.00 - 80.00

CONTEST MEDAL. SCALLOPED PENDANT, REGULAR RIBBON AND DRAPE BEHIND.

Female striding, facing forward, outstretched arms. Solid ribbon, pendant in gold, silver, or bronze.	1914-1920	300.00 - 400.00
First Aid, female striding, w/ eagle and shield, white enamel cross. Red-white-blue ribbon, pendant in gold, silver, or bronze.	1914-1920	400.00 - 550.00
Plain center, laurel wreath. Red-white-blue ribbon, pendant in gold, silver, or bronze.	1914-1920	300.00 - 400.00
Signal flags within wreath. Red-white-blue ribbon, pendant in gold, silver, or bronze.	1914-1920	300.00 - 400.00
Swimming. Red-white-blue ribbon, pendant in gold, silver, or bronze.	1914-1920	300.00 - 400.00
Tenderfoot emblem in ctr. Red-white-blue ribbon, pendant in gold, silver, or bronze.	1914-1920	300.00 - 400.00
Track runner at start. Red-white-blue ribbon, pendant in gold, silver, or bronze.	1914-1920	300.00 - 400.00
Track runner w/ palm branch. Red-white-blue ribbon, pendant in gold, silver, or bronze.	1914-1920	300.00 - 400.00
Tug of war contest. Red-white-blue ribbon, pendant in gold, silver, or bronze.	1914-1920	300.00 - 400.00

CONTEST MEDAL. SCALLOPED PENDANT, REGULAR RIBBON.

Female striding forward, arms outstretched. Red-white-blue ribbon, pendant in gold, silver, or bronze.	1921-1928	200.00 - 300.00
First Aid, female striding w/ eagle and shield, enamel white cross. Red-white-blue ribbon, pendant in gold, silver, or bronze.	1921-1928	250.00 - 400.00
Plain ctr., laurel wreath. Red-white-blue ribbon, pendant in gold, silver, or bronze.	1921-1928	250.00 - 400.00
Signal flags within laurel wreath. Red-white-blue ribbon, pendant in gold, silver, or bronze.	1921-1928	300.00 - 400.00
Swimming. Red-white-blue ribbon, pendant in gold, silver, or bronze.	1921-1928	200.00 - 300.00
Tenderfoot emblem. Red-white-blue ribbon, pendant in gold, silver, or bronze.	1921-1928	250.00 - 400.00
Track runner and laurel branch. Red-white-blue ribbon, pendant in gold, silver, or bronze.	1921-1928	200.00 - 300.00

Track runner at start. Red-white-blue ribbon, pendant in gold, silver, or bronze.	1921-1928	200.00 - 300.00
Tug of war contest. Red-white-blue ribbon, pendant in gold, silver, or bronze.	1921-1928	200.00 - 300.00

OCTAGONAL PENDANT IN GOLD, SILVER, OR BRONZE. REGULAR RED-WHITE-BLUE RIBBON.

Archery.	1928-1932	150.00 - 200.00
Bridge Building.	1928-1932	100.00 - 200.00
Bugling.	1928-1932	100.00 - 200.00
Camping.	1928-1932	100.00 - 200.00
Canoeing.	1928-1932	100.00 - 200.00
Cooking.	1928-1932	100.00 - 200.00
Field.	1928-1932	100.00 - 200.00
Fire Making.	1928-1932	100.00 - 200.00
First Aid.	1928-1932	100.00 - 200.00
First Class emblem within wreath.	1928-1932	100.00 - 200.00
Handicraft.	1928-1932	100.00 - 200.00
Knife & Ax Work.	1928-1932	100.00 - 200.00
Knot Tying.	1928-1932	150.00 - 200.00
Plain within laurel wreath.	1928-1932	100.00 - 200.00
Signaling.	1928-1932	150.00 - 200.00
Tent Pitching.	1928-1932	150.00 - 200.00
Tower Building.	1928-1932	150.00 - 200.00
Track.	1928-1932	100.00 - 200.00
Wall Scaling.	1928-1932	150.00 - 200.00

Contest Medals: Knot Tying (left) and Fire Building.

OCTAGONAL PENDANT IN GOLD, SILVER, OR BRONZE. REGULAR SOLID BLUE RIBBON.

Archery.	1933-1954	75.00 - 125.00
Bridge Building.	1933-1954	75.00 - 125.00
Bugling.	1933-1954	75.00 - 125.00
Camping.	1933-1954	75.00 - 125.00
Canoeing.	1933-1954	75.00 - 125.00
Cooking.	1933-1954	75.00 - 125.00
Field.	1933-1954	75.00 - 125.00
Fire Making.	1933-1954	75.00 - 125.00
First Aid.	1933-1954	75.00 - 125.00
First Class emblem within wreath.	1933-1954	75.00 - 125.00
Handicraft.	1933-1954	75.00 - 125.00
Knife & Ax Work.	1933-1954	75.00 - 125.00
Knot Tying.	1933-1954	75.00 - 125.00
Plain within wreath.	1933-1954	75.00 - 125.00
Signaling.	1933-1954	75.00 - 125.00
Signaling.	1933-1954	75.00 - 125.00

Swimming.	1933-1954	75.00 - 125.00
Tent Pitching.	1933-1954	75.00 - 125.00
Tower Building.	1933-1954	75.00 - 125.00
Track.	1933-1954	75.00 - 125.00
Wall Scaling.	1933-1954	75.00 - 125.00
Wall Scaling.	1933-1954	75.00 - 125.00

*General Contest Medal,
Tenderfoot emblem.*

*General Contest Medal,
First-Class emblem.*

CONTEST MEDAL. OCTAGONAL PENDANT.

Tenderfoot emblem in ctr. in gold, silver or bronze colored metal; red/white ribbon. Locking clasp back, finely pebbled detail in design.	1953-1970	10.00 - 15.00
Tenderfoot emblem in ctr. in gold, silver or bronze colored metal; red/white ribbon. Locking clasp back, roughly pebbled detail in design.	1970-1985	5.00 - 10.00
Tenderfoot emblem in ctr. in gold, silver or bronze colored metal; red/white ribbon. Open clasp back, roughly pebbled detail in design.	1985	5.00 - 7.50

Troop 16, Queens Council gathers around NYC Mayor Ed Koch after Medal of Merit presentation to Salvatore Bonamico.

HEROISM AND SPECIAL AWARD MEDALS

CERTIFICATE FOR HEROISM

Large illuminated style parchment, often signed by Daniel C. Beard.	1911-1940	2,500. - 4,000.

HARMON FOUNDATION SCHOLARSHIP

Small Eagle on 'H' in circle, lapel stud.	1927-1931	750.00 - 1,250.

HEROISM AWARD MEDAL

Type I reads "FOR MERITORIOUS ACTION." Gilt silver, red enamel. Red-white-red ribbon.	1979-1989	300.00 - 400.00
Type II reads "FOR HEROISM." Gilt silver, red enamel. Red-white-red ribbon.	1989-1999	200.00 - 250.00

HONOR MEDAL

Type I. Gold w/tri-colored enameled ctr. Red ribbon.	1925-1960	1,250. - 1,500.
Type II. Gilt silver w/tri-colored enamel ctr.	1960	500.00 - 750.00

HONOR MEDAL W/ CROSSED PALMS

Type I. Gold w/ tri-colored enameled ctr. Red ribbon.	1925-1960	1,500. - 1,750.
Type II. Gilt silver w/tri-colored enameled ctr. Red ribbon.	1960	300.00 - 500.00

LIFESAVING GOLD AWARD

Maltese cross w/ Tenderfoot badge suspended from BE PREPARED scroll, white ribbon drape. Hallmark of Degist & Clust, NY.	1915-1925	10,000. - 13,000.

James A. Hannan presents Scout John Flory of Wauwatosa, WI, a Heroism Certificate in 1930.

LIFESAVING SILVER AWARD

Maltese cross w/ Tenderfoot emblem suspended from BE PREPARED scroll, blue ribbon drape. Hallmark of Degist & Clust, NY.   1915-1925   6,000. - 8,000.

LIFESAVING BRONZE AWARD

Maltese cross w/ Tenderfoot emblem suspended from BE PREPARED scroll, red ribbon drape. Hallmark of Degist & Clust, NY.   1915-1925   4,000. - 5,000.

Maltese Cross w/ Tenderfoot emblem, suspended with chain links from BE PREPARED scroll, red ribbon drape. T.H. Foley Hallmark.   1911-1915   9,000. - 12,500.

MEDAL OF MERIT

Type I. Gilt silver w/ blue enamel, gold-blue-gold ribbon.   1946-1989   300.00 - 500.00

Type II. Gilt silver w/red enamel, gold-blue-gold ribbon.   1925-1999   175.00 - 225.00

WILLIAM T. HORNADAY AWARD

Bronze medal, green ribbon, legend.	1979	250.00 - 400.00
Gold medal, green ribbon, no legend.	1951-1975	4,000. - 6,000.
Gold medal.	1979	1,000. - 1,500.
Gold pin bar, no legend.	1951-1975	750.00 - 1,000.
Gold pin bar.	1914-1950	3,000. - 4,500.
Legend: FOR SERVICE TO WILD LIFE.		
Silver medal, green ribbon, legend.	1978	750.00 - 1,000.
Silver medal, green ribbon, no legend.	1976-1977	1,000. - 1,500.
Silver pin bar, no legend.	1976-1977	250.00 - 400.00

Troop 34, Waupaca, WI (c. 1936).

MEMBERSHIP CARDS

The earliest style of membership cards were multiple pages held together by a corner rivet.

POCKET CARD, RIVET CORNER

Four pages, square ctr. to flags.	1913	150.00 - 200.00
Four pages, square ctr. to flags.	1914	125.00 - 175.00
Four pages, square ctr. to flags.	1915	100.00 - 150.00
Four pages, square ctr. to flags.	1916	100.00 - 150.00
Four pages, square ctr. to flags.	1917	75.00 - 125.00
Four-page rivet corner, square ctr. to flags.	1918-1919	75.00 - 125.00

POCKET CARD. 4 PAGE, RIVET CORNER

Diagonal semaphore flags, correct letter.	1917-1920	40.00 - 75.00

POCKET CARD

Two copper links holding pages together, square ctr. to flags.	1918-1919	75.00 - 125.00

ADULT POCKET CARD, RIVET CORNER

Pocket Card. 4 page rivet corner. Morse flags corrected.	1917	75.00 - 125.00
Pocket Card. 4 page rivet corner. Morse flags corrected. Horizontal format.	1918	75.00 - 125.00
Pocket Card. 4 page rivet corner. Morse flags corrected. Vertical format.	1918	75.00 - 125.00

Pocket Card. 4 page rivet corner. Morse flags reversed.	1915	100.00 - 140.00
Pocket Card. 4 page rivet corner. Morse flags reversed.	1916	100.00 - 140.00
Pocket Card. 4 page rivet corner. Morse flags reversed.	1917	75.00 - 125.00
Pocket Card. 4 page, ring binding. Morse flags corrected. Vertical format.	1918	75.00 - 125.00
Pocket Card. 4 page, rivet corner. Morse flags corrected. Vertical format.	1919	75.00 - 125.00
Tri-fold. Vertical format to adult tenure info.	1919-1927	25.00 - 40.00

Two membership cards: 1928-1927 (top) and 1928-1940.

The tri-fold membership cards came with three distinct graphics in the centerfold.

TRI-FOLD CARD

Cub, Boy Scout and Sea Scout walking left, Loyalty, Patriotism, Service in tan bordered scenes.	1939-1943	10.00 - 20.00
Scout signaling, 2 Park Avenue address, Loyalty, Patriotism, Service in gray bordered scenes.	1930-1940	10.00 - 20.00
Scout signaling, 200 Fifth Avenue address, Loyalty, Patriotism, Chivalry below flag, rope border to design scenes.	1921-1930	20.00 - 30.00

The third and final tri-fold card is a Rockwell design, which was changed into a bi-fold card format during World War II (shown here).

BI-FOLD CARD

Cub, Boy Scout and Sea Scout walking left.	1944-1948	10.00 - 15.00
Flag exterior; Cub, Tenderfoot and Explorer E emblems inside.	1983-1984	0.50 - 1.00
Flag exterior; Diamond Jubilee emblem inside.	1985-1986	0.50 - 1.00

Membership cards from the 1950s and 1960s became single cards, some with nice graphics.

SINGLE CARD

Bicentennial motif.	1975-1977	0.50 - 1.00
Cub, Boy Scout and Explorer walking forward, Liberty Bell in background, forward on Liberty's Team legend.	1952-1956	5.00 - 7.50
Cub, Boy Scout and Sea Scout walking left, red banner at bottom.	1946-1949	5.00 - 7.50
Cub, Explorer and Scout looking upward, Washington in prayer in background.	1957-1960	4.00 - 6.00
First-Class emblem and patrol hiking.	1965-1972	2.00 - 4.00
Leader and Scout looking up at tablet w/ Oath, Law and Cub Promise.	1955-1958	4.00 - 6.00
Modernized Tenderfoot emblem.	1990	0.25 - 0.50
Scout leader and boy within archway on top, olive-black color.	1942-1945	5.00 - 7.50
Scout Oath and Tenderfoot emblem on blue background, 50th Anniversary emblem added.	1960	3.00 - 5.00
Scout Oath and Tenderfoot emblem on blue background.	1959-1965	3.00 - 4.00
Scouting the Better Life slogan.	1981-1983	0.50 - 1.00
Scouting's 70th, Cub Scouts' 50th anniversaries.	1979-1981	0.50 - 1.00
Tenderfoot emblem on green background.	1972-1976	0.50 - 1.00
Tenderfoot emblem on red background.	1986-1990	0.50 - 1.00

Using the same design as the membership card, an 8-1/2" x 10-1/2" certificate was available to adults for framing, value $10.00 - $15.00. This example is from 1933.

HANDBOOKS

Handbooks are referenced to Doug Bearce and Chuck Fisk's book, *Collecting Boy Scout Literature: A Collector's Guide to Boy Scout Fiction and Non-Fiction.*

BOY SCOUTS OF AMERICA, OFFICIAL HANDBOOK. BADEN-POWELL AND SETON, AUTHORS.

192 pgs, tan-yellow w/ brown imprint or green w/ light green imprint.	1910	F.001-005	1,400.- 2,500.
192 pgs, red leather-bound, gilt imprint.	1910	F.006	1,500. - 2,500.

BOY SCOUTS OF AMERICA, OFFICIAL MANUAL, OR HANDBOOK. SETON, AUTHOR.

192 pgs, cloth cover.	1910	F.007-009	1,250. - 1,750.

BOY SCOUTS OF AMERICA HANDBOOK FOR BOYS. SCOUT STRIDING, RAISING HAT IN AIR.

320 or 400 pages, olive-drab or maroon cover. Proof copy, first edition.	1911	F.010-012	1,250. - 1,750.
404 pgs, olive-drab or maroon cover. Second edition, 1-5 printing. Some marked Fourth Edition.	1911-1913	F.013-019	250.00 - 400.00
416 pgs, maroon cover. Fourth edition.	1913-1914	F.020-021	250.00 - 400.00
440 pgs, maroon cover.	1914	F.022-023	125.00 - 250.00

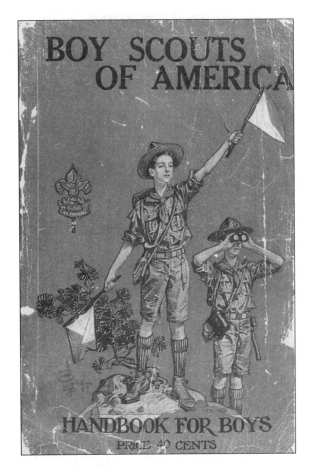

BOY SCOUTS OF AMERICA, HANDBOOK FOR BOYS. SCOUT SINGLING AND ONE RECEIVING.

472 pgs, light gray cover. Morse code (square center) signal flags, no knot on First Class badge. Eleventh and twelfth edition.	1914-1915	F.024-025	100.00 - 250.00
464 pgs, light gray cover. Morse code (square center) signal flags, no knot on First Class badge. Thirteenth edition.	1915-1916	F.026-027	100.00 - 200.00
498 pgs,. red or green cover. Scout signals letter "L," knot on First Class badge. Fourteenth through eighteenth edition.	1916-1918	F.028-032	100.00 - 200.00
496 pgs, pale green cover. Eighteenth edition, reprint and nineteenth edition.	1918	F.032-033	100.00 - 200.00
496 pgs, pale green cover. Twentieth and Twenty-first edition.	1919	F.034-035	40.00 - 75.00
492 pgs, pale green cover. Twenty-second edition.	1920	F.036	40.00 - 75.00
488 pgs, pale green cover. Twenty-third edition.	1921	F.037	40.00 - 75.00
488 pgs, pale green cover. Signal flags corrected to Semaphore type. Updated uniforms. Twenty-fourth edition.	1921	F.038	40.00 - 75.00
512 pgs, olive-green cover. Twenty-fifth through Thirty-seventh edition.	1922-1927	F.039-051	40.00 - 75.00

HANDBOOK FOR BOYS, BOY SCOUTS OF AMERICA.
SCOUT PROFILE LEFT, BACKGROUND W/ HISTORIC FIGURES.

Conquistador at far right. 636 pgs.	1927	F.052	15.00 - 35.00
Conquistador at left, 638 pgs.	1927-1928	F.053-057	15.00 - 35.00
Lindbergh profile at far right, 646 pgs.	1928-1930	F.058-064	10.00 - 30.00
650 pgs.	1930-1931	F.065-066	10.00 - 25.00
646 pgs.	1931	F.067	10.00 - 25.00
650 pgs.	1932	F.068-069	10.00 - 25.00
658 pgs.	1933-1935	F.070-075	10.00 - 25.00
660 pgs.	1936	F.076-077	10.00 - 25.00
668 pgs.	1936-1938	F.078-082	10.00 - 25.00
676 pgs.	1938-1940	F.083-085	10.00 - 25.00

HANDBOOK FOR BOYS, BOY SCOUTS OF AMERICA.
CUB SCOUT, BOY SCOUT, AND SEA EXPLORER LEFT.

680 pgs, some printings with 8- or 16-page color insert.	1940-1943	F.086-089	12.50 - 30.00
570 pgs, plus 6 in b/w. Size reduction.	1944-1946	F.090-092	10.00 - 20.00

HANDBOOK FOR BOYS, BOY SCOUTS OF AMERICA.
5 SCOUTS HIKING IN WOODS.

566 pgs, fifth edition. 1-2 printing.	1948-1949	F.093-094	10.00 - 20.00

HANDBOOK FOR BOYS, BOY SCOUTS OF AMERICA.
3 SCOUTS AROUND CAMPFIRE, INDIAN FIGURE IN SMOKE.

564 pgs, fifth edition. 3-4 printing.	1950-1951	F.095-096	7.50 - 15.00
568 pgs, fifth edition. 5-12 printing, some 10th editions have special 4-pg. commemorative for 15-millionth Handbook copy.	1952-1958	F.097-104	7.50 - 15.00

BOY SCOUT HANDBOOK, BOY SCOUTS OF AMERICA.
SCOUT STRIDING RIGHT, CAMP SCENE IN BACKGROUND.

480 pgs, sixth edition, 1-6 printing.	1959-1963	F.105-110	7.50 - 15.00
439 pgs, special printing for use in Ryuku Islands and Okinawa.	1963	F.109a	15.00 - 25.00
470 pgs, ads replaced w/ 24-pg. supplement of revised requirements.	1965	F.111	7.50 - 20.00

SCOUT HANDBOOK, BOY SCOUTS OF AMERICA. DUAL GREEN,
DRAWING OF SCOUTS LOOKING THRU TELESCOPE AT MOON.

480 pgs, eighth edition, 1-3 printing.	1972-1975	F.119-121	5.00 - 7.50

BOY SCOUT HANDBOOK, BOY SCOUTS OF AMERICA,
3 SCOUTS HIKING, CAMP SCENES IN BACKGROUND.

448 pgs, seventh edition, 1-7 printing.	1965-1971	F.112-118	2.50 - 10.00
Features "orientalized" for use in Ryuku Islands.	1966	F.113a	2.50 - 10.00

SCOUT HANDBOOK, BOY SCOUTS OF AMERICA.
WHITE COVER W/ CROWD SCENE OF ACTIVE SCOUTS.

480 pgs, eighth edition, 4-5 printing.	1976-1977	F.122-123	10.00 - 20.00

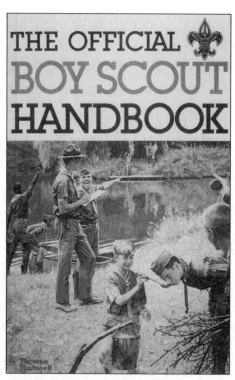

OFFICIAL BOY SCOUT HANDBOOK.
 SCENE OF SCOUTS CAMPING BY LAKE.

576 pgs, ninth edition, 1-12   1979-1989 F.124-135   3.00 - 7.50
 printings. First and second
 printings have either a black or
 blue and red cover title. Second
 printing also includes some
 w/ Simon and Schuster name
 on spine.

BOY SCOUT HANDBOOK, BOY SCOUTS OF AMERICA.
 PHOTOS OF SCOUT HIKING, BALD EAGLE AND LEAF.

Photo hardcover.	1997	20.00 - 30.00
Hardcover, leather binding.	1997	50.00 - 75.00
Regular cover.	1997	5.00 - 7.50

BOY SCOUT HANDBOOK, BOY SCOUTS OF AMERICA.
 PHOTOS OF SCOUT RAPPELLING, CAMPING, AND RAFTING.

662 pgs, tenth edition,   1990-1997 F.136-143   3.00 - 7.50
 1-7 printings. Black or green
 Child Abuse Parents Guide
 tear-out in front.

HANDBOOKS - LEADERS

For additional information on handbooks, consult Doug Bearce and Chuck Fisk's book, *Collecting Scout Literature*.

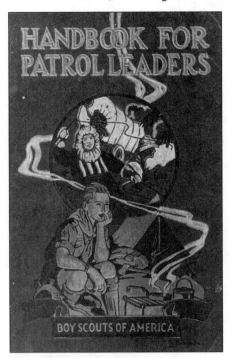

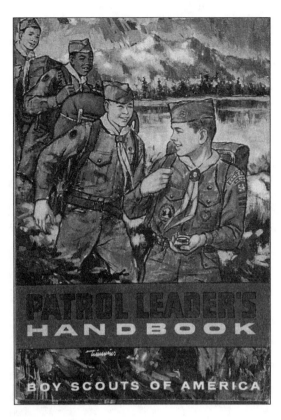

HANDBOOK FOR PATROL LEADERS

1st-4th printings, 399 or 408 pgs. Scout by campfire on cover, dark green background.	1929-1933	20.00 - 30.00
5th-12th printings, 562-598 pgs. Scout by campfire on cover, silver background.	1935-1943	15.00 - 25.00
13th-18th printings, 444 pgs. Scout by campfire on cover, silver background.	1944-1949	10.00 - 15.00
19th-34th printings, 376-392 pgs. Hiking scout w/patrol flag on cover.	1950-1965	7.50 - 12.50

PATROL LEADER'S HANDBOOK

Second edition, 4 printings, 217 pgs. Patrol hiking in wilderness on cover.	1967-1970	5.00 - 7.50

PATROL AND TROOP LEADERSHIP

Seven printings, 128 pgs. Patrol group seated w/ one standing, on dual green cover.	1972-1979	5.00 - 7.50

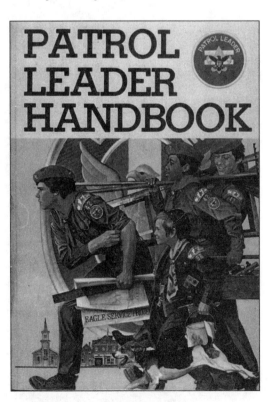

OFFICIAL PATROL LEADER'S HANDBOOK

Third edition, 9 printings, 204 pgs. Action painting and patrol leader insignia on cover.	1980-1988	5.00 - 7.50

SCOUT FIELD BOOK

First edition, 1st-14th printings,   1944-1959   15.00 - 25.00
540 or 552 pgs.

FIELDBOOK FOR BOYS AND MEN

Second edition, five printings, 656 pgs.   1967-1972   5.00 - 10.00

FIELDBOOK

Second edition, title change, 6th-14th   1973-1983   5.00 - 10.00
   printings, 656 pgs. Two-tone green cover.
Third edition, 630 pgs. High adventure   1984   5.00 - 7.50
   scenes on cover.

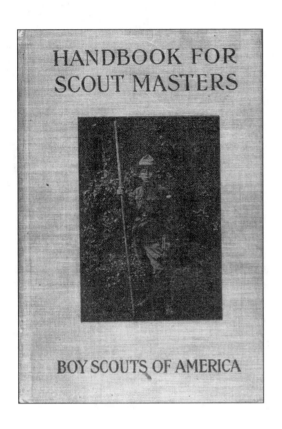

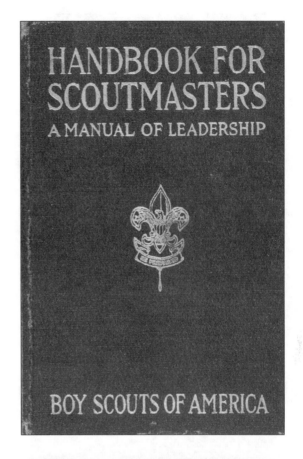

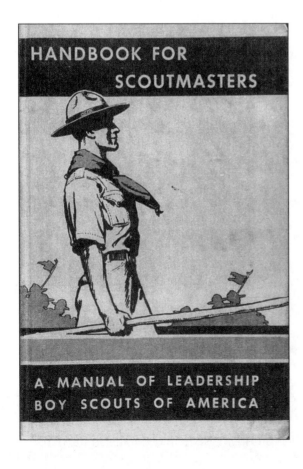

HANDBOOK FOR SCOUTMASTERS

1st-3rd proof editions, 203 or 161 pgs.	1912-1912	150.00 - 200.00
Fifth edition, 1st-6th printings, 509 or 510 pgs.	1959-1964	10.00 - 15.00
Fifth edition, 7th-11th printings, 542 pgs.	1965-1970	10.00 - 15.00
First edition, 344, 352 or 404 pgs, plus ads. Nine printings.	1913-1919	125.00 - 175.00
Fourth edition, 11 printings, 512 pgs.	1947-1957	20.00 - 30.00
Second edition, 10th-15th printings, 676 pgs.	1926-1930	75.00 - 100.00
Second edition, 16th-19th printings, 628 pgs.	1932-1935	60.00 - 80.00
Second edition, 1st printing, 608 pgs.	1920-1920	100.00 - 135.00
Second edition, 3rd-6th printings, 632 pgs.	1922-1924	75.00 - 100.00
Second edition, 7th-9th printings, 668 pgs.	1924-1926	75.00 - 100.00
Second edition, second printing, 615 pgs, plus maps.	1920-1921	90.00 - 120.00
Seventh edition, 9 printings, 368 pgs.	1981-1990	5.00 - 10.00
Sixth edition, 9 printings, 382 pgs.	1972-1980	5.00 - 7.50
Third edition, Vol. 1, 13 printings, 501 or 498 pgs.	1936-1945	40.00 - 60.00
Third edition, Vol. 2, 11 printings, between 1,142 and 1,164 pgs.	1937-1945	40.00 - 60.00

HOW BOOK OF SCOUTING

First edition, 5 printings, 420 pgs.	1927-1931	15.00 - 25.00
Second edition, 2 printings, 512 pgs.	1934-1935	15.00 - 25.00
Third edition, 2 printings, 627 pgs.	1938-1941	10.00 - 20.00

REQUIREMENT MANUAL

Annual, various month and year printings.	1960-1970	3.00 - 4.00
Dual year dates on cover.	1979-1998	2.00 - 3.00
Single year dates on cover.	1971-1979	2.00 - 3.00

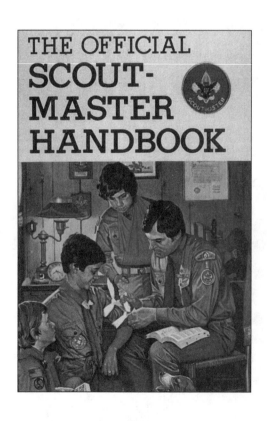

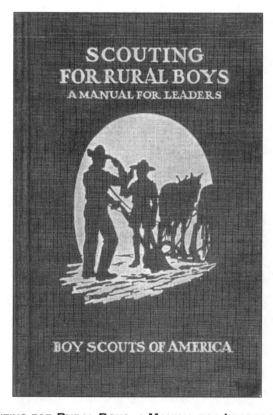

SCOUTING FOR RURAL BOYS, A MANUAL FOR LEADERS

1938	25.00 - 35.00

SCOUTING FOR THE DEAF

| | 1970 | 5.00 - 7.50 |

SCOUTING FOR THE MENTALLY HANDICAPPED

| | 1967 | 5.00 - 7.50 |

SCOUTING FOR THE PHYSICALLY HANDICAPPED
Two printings, 96 pgs.

| | 1971-1979 | 5.00 - 7.50 |

SWIMMING AND WATER SAFETY

| Second edition. | 1927 | 20.00 - 30.00 |
| Third edition, three printings. | 1931-1936 | 20.00 - 30.00 |

SWIMMING, WATER SPORTS AND SAFETY
Fourth edition.

| | 1938 | 20.00 - 30.00 |

WATER SAFETY PROGRAM, EVERY SCOUT A SWIMMER
First edition.

| | 1924 | 25.00 - 35.00 |

WINTER CAMPING
Proof edition and 1st edition.

| | 1927 | 25.00 - 35.00 |

William "Green Bar Bill" Hillcourt, author of the first Patrol Leader Handbook and several editions of the Scout Handbook and Fieldbook. In the 1980s, he was very popular on the autograph circuit.

RESOURCE BOOKS

ANNUAL REPORT

1910 BSA published.	1910	50.00 - 75.00
1911 BSA published.	1911	50.00 - 75.00
1912 BSA published.	1912	50.00 - 75.00
1914 BSA published.	1914	50.00 - 75.00
1915 BSA published.	1915	50.00 - 75.00
1916 BSA published.	1916	50.00 - 75.00
1917 BSA published.	1917	40.00 - 60.00
1918 BSA published.	1918	40.00 - 60.00
1919 BSA published.	1919	40.00 - 60.00
1920 BSA published.	1920	40.00 - 60.00
1921 BSA published.	1921	40.00 - 60.00
1921 U.S. Gov't Printing Office.	1921	30.00 - 40.00
1922 BSA published.	1922	40.00 - 60.00
1922 U.S. Gov't Printing Office.	1922	30.00 - 40.00
1923 U.S. Gov't Printing Office.	1923	30.00 - 40.00
1924 U.S. Gov't Printing Office.	1924	30.00 - 40.00
1925 U.S. Gov't Printing Office.	1925	25.00 - 35.00
1926 U.S. Gov't Printing Office.	1926	25.00 - 35.00
1927 U.S. Gov't Printing Office.	1927	25.00 - 35.00
1928 U.S. Gov't Printing Office.	1928	25.00 - 35.00
1929 U.S. Gov't Printing Office.	1929	25.00 - 35.00
1930 U.S. Gov't Printing Office.	1930	20.00 - 30.00
1931 U.S. Gov't Printing Office.	1931	20.00 - 30.00
1932 U.S. Gov't Printing Office.	1932	20.00 - 30.00
1933 U.S. Gov't Printing Office.	1933	20.00 - 30.00
1934 U.S. Gov't Printing Office.	1934	20.00 - 30.00
1935 U.S. Gov't Printing Office.	1935	20.00 - 30.00
1936 U.S. Gov't Printing Office.	1936	20.00 - 30.00
1937 U.S. Gov't Printing Office.	1937	20.00 - 30.00
1938 U.S. Gov't Printing Office.	1938	20.00 - 30.00
1939 U.S. Gov't Printing Office.	1939	20.00 - 30.00
1940 U.S. Gov't Printing Office.	1940	20.00 - 30.00
1941 U.S. Gov't Printing Office.	1941	15.00 - 20.00
1942 U.S. Gov't Printing Office.	1942	15.00 - 20.00
1943 U.S. Gov't Printing Office.	1943	15.00 - 20.00
1944 U.S. Gov't Printing Office.	1944	15.00 - 20.00
1945 U.S. Gov't Printing Office.	1945	15.00 - 20.00
1946 U.S. Gov't Printing Office.	1946	15.00 - 20.00
1947 U.S. Gov't Printing Office.	1947	15.00 - 20.00
1948 U.S. Gov't Printing Office.	1948	15.00 - 20.00
1949 U.S. Gov't Printing Office.	1949	15.00 - 20.00
1950 U.S. Gov't Printing Office.	1950	12.50 - 17.50
1951 U.S. Gov't Printing Office.	1951	12.50 - 17.50
1952 U.S. Gov't Printing Office.	1952	12.50 - 17.50
1953 U.S. Gov't Printing Office.	1953	12.50 - 17.50
1954 U.S. Gov't Printing Office.	1954	12.50 - 17.50
1955 U.S. Gov't Printing Office.	1955	12.50 - 17.50
1956 U.S. Gov't Printing Office.	1956	12.50 - 17.50
1957 U.S. Gov't Printing Office.	1957	12.50 - 17.50
1958 U.S. Gov't Printing Office.	1958	12.50 - 17.50
1959 U.S. Gov't Printing Office.	1959	12.50 - 17.50
1960 U.S. Gov't Printing Office.	1960	10.00 - 15.00
1961 U.S. Gov't Printing Office.	1961	10.00 - 15.00
1962 U.S. Gov't Printing Office.	1962	10.00 - 15.00
1963 U.S. Gov't Printing Office.	1963	10.00 - 15.00
1964 U.S. Gov't Printing Office.	1964	10.00 - 15.00
1965 U.S. Gov't Printing Office.	1965	10.00 - 15.00
1966 U.S. Gov't Printing Office.	1966	7.50 - 12.50
1967 U.S. Gov't Printing Office.	1967	7.50 - 12.50
1968 U.S. Gov't Printing Office.	1968	7.50 - 12.50
1969 U.S. Gov't Scrinting Office.	1969	7.50 - 12.50
1970 U.S. Gov't Printing Office.	1970	7.50 - 12.50
1971 U.S. Gov't Printing Office.	1971	7.50 - 12.50
1972 U.S. Gov't Printing Office.	1972	7.50 - 12.50
1973 U.S. Gov't Printing Office.	1973	7.50 - 12.50
1974 U.S. Gov't Printing Office.	1974	7.50 - 12.50
1975 U.S. Gov't Printing Office.	1975	7.50 - 12.50
1976 U.S. Gov't Printing Office.	1976	5.00 - 7.50
1977 U.S. Gov't Printing Office.	1977	5.00 - 7.50
1978 U.S. Gov't Printing Office.	1978	5.00 - 7.50
1979 U.S. Gov't Printing Office.	1979	5.00 - 7.50
1980 U.S. Gov't Printing Office.	1980	5.00 - 7.50
1981 U.S. Gov't Printing Office.	1981	5.00 - 7.50
1982 U.S. Gov't Printing Office.	1982	5.00 - 7.50
1983 U.S. Gov't Printing Office.	1983	5.00 - 7.50
1984 U.S. Gov't Printing Office.	1984	5.00 - 7.50
1985 U.S. Gov't Printing Office.	1985	5.00 - 7.50
1986 U.S. Gov't Printing Office.	1986	5.00 - 7.50
1987 U.S. Gov't Printing Office.	1987	5.00 - 7.50
1988 U.S. Gov't Printing Office.	1988	5.00 - 7.50
1989 U.S. Gov't Printing Office.	1989	5.00 - 7.50
1990 U.S. Gov't Printing Office.	1990	5.00 - 7.50
1991 U.S. Gov't Printing Office.	1991	5.00 - 7.50
1992 U.S. Gov't Printing Office.	1992	5.00 - 7.50
1993 U.S. Gov't Printing Office.	1993	5.00 - 7.50
1994 U.S. Gov't Printing Office.	1994	5.00 - 7.50
1995 U.S. Gov't Printing Office.	1995	5.00 - 7.50
1996 U.S. Gov't Printing Office.	1996	5.00 - 7.50
1997 U.S. Gov't Printing Office.	1997	5.00 - 7.50

BOY SCOUT DIARY

1913.	1913	200.00 - 275.00
1914.	1914	200.00 - 275.00
1915.	1915	150.00 - 225.00
1916.	1916	150.00 - 225.00
1917.	1917	100.00 - 150.00
1918.	1918	100.00 - 150.00
1919.	1919	100.00 - 150.00
1920.	1920	50.00 - 75.00
1921.	1921	50.00 - 75.00
1922.	1922	50.00 - 75.00
1923.	1923	30.00 - 50.00
1924.	1924	30.00 - 50.00
1925.	1925	20.00 - 35.00
1926.	1926	30.00 - 50.00
1927.	1927	20.00 - 30.00
1928.	1928	20.00 - 30.00
1929.	1929	20.00 - 30.00
1930.	1930	20.00 - 30.00
1931.	1931	20.00 - 30.00

1932.	1932	15.00 - 25.00
1933.	1933	15.00 - 25.00
1934.	1934	15.00 - 25.00
1935.	1935	10.00 - 15.00
1936.	1936	10.00 - 15.00
1937.	1937	10.00 - 15.00
1938.	1938	10.00 - 15.00
1939.	1939	10.00 - 15.00
1940.	1940	10.00 - 15.00
1941.	1941	10.00 - 15.00
1942.	1942	15.00 - 25.00
1943.	1943	15.00 - 25.00
1944.	1944	15.00 - 25.00
1945.	1945	20.00 - 35.00
1946.	1946	20.00 - 35.00
1947.	1947	20.00 - 35.00
1948.	1948	20.00 - 35.00
1949.	1949	20.00 - 35.00
1950.	1950	20.00 - 35.00
1951.	1951	20.00 - 35.00
1952.	1952	20.00 - 35.00
1953.	1953	20.00 - 35.00
1954.	1954	20.00 - 35.00
1955.	1955	20.00 - 35.00
1956.	1956	20.00 - 35.00
1957.	1957	20.00 - 35.00
1958.	1958	20.00 - 35.00
1959	1959	20.00 - 35.00

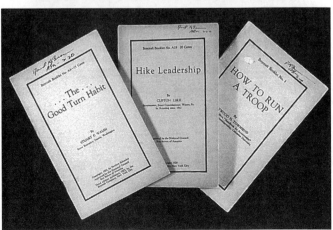

BOYCRAFT BOOKLETS FOR SCOUT LEADERS

Building Troop Spirit.	1923-1926	10.00 - 15.00
Camp Fire Talks on the Scout Law.	1926	10.00 - 15.00
Camp Fires and Camp Cookery.		10.00 - 15.00
Discipline Without Demerits.	1922-1926	10.00 - 15.00
First Aid Made Easy.		10.00 - 15.00
The Good Turn Habit.	1922-1926	10.00 - 15.00
Helpbook for Boy Scouts.	1926	10.00 - 15.00
Hike Leadership.	1926	10.00 - 15.00
Hints on the Scout Tests.	1927	10.00 - 15.00
How to Run a Patrol.	1922-1926	10.00 - 15.00
How to Run a Troop.	1924	10.00 - 15.00
Identification of Trees.		10.00 - 15.00
The Job of the Troop Committee.	1926	10.00 - 15.00
Nature Games.		10.00 - 15.00
Nature Notebook for Scouts.		25.00 - 40.00
Patrol Leader's Record Book.		10.00 - 15.00
Starting the Troop Right.	1922-1926	10.00 - 15.00
Treasure Island Songbook.		10.00 - 15.00
Troop Ceremonies.	1926	10.00 - 15.00
The Troop Headquarters.		10.00 - 15.00
Troop Stunts.	1925	10.00 - 15.00
The Whys and Hows of Scouting.	1925	10.00 - 15.00

BOYS' LIFE - PEDRO BOOKS

Ahead of their Time, G.P. Putnam's Sons.	1968	3.00 - 7.50
Baseball as We Played It, G.P. Putnam's Sons.	1969	3.00 - 7.50
Best Jokes from Boys' Life, G.P. Putnam's Sons.	1970	3.00 - 7.50
Best of Boys Life 1, G.P. Putnam's Sons.	1968	3.00 - 7.50
Great Crime Busters, Alan Hynd, G.P. Putnam's Sons.	1967	3.00 - 7.50
Great True Adventures, G.P. Putnam's Sons.	1968	3.00 - 7.50
Pedro's Tall Tales, G.P. Putnam's Sons.	1967	3.00 - 7.50
Time Machine to the Rescue, Donald Keith, G.P. Putnam's Sons.	1967	3.00 - 7.50

BOYS' LIFE EDITORS

Boys' Life Adventure Stories, Nelson.	1950	3.00 - 10.00
Boys' Life Book of Scout Stories, Doubleday.	1953	3.00 - 10.00
Boys' Life Dog Stories. Nelson.	1949	3.00 - 10.00
The Boys' Life Treasury, Simon & Schuster.	1958	3.00 - 10.00

BOYS' LIFE REPRINT BOOKLETS

Be A Second-Class Scout.	1973	2.00 - 3.00
Be First-Class.	1973	2.00 - 3.00
Bill of Rights.	1973	2.00 - 3.00
Boats and Canoes.	1973	2.00 - 3.00
Cooking Skills and Menus.	1973	2.00 - 3.00
Craftsman Activity Badge Helps.	1973	2.00 - 3.00
First Aid Skills.	1973	2.00 - 3.00
Fishing.	1973	2.00 - 3.00
Forester Activity Badge Helps.	1973	2.00 - 3.00
Fun With Tools.	1973	2.00 - 3.00
Handicraft.	1973	2.00 - 3.00
Hiking and Camping Equipment.	1973	2.00 - 3.00
Indian Lore.	1973	2.00 - 3.00
Law and Justice.	1973	2.00 - 3.00
Litepac Camping Equipment.	1973	2.00 - 3.00
Model Railroading.	1973	2.00 - 3.00
Naturalist Activity Badge Helps.	1973	2.00 - 3.00
Nature Hobbies and Activities.	1973	2.00 - 3.00
Our Heritage of Freedom.	1973	2.00 - 3.00
Outdoorsman Activity Badge Helps.	1973	2.00 - 3.00
Patrol Activities.	1973	2.00 - 3.00
Pioneering.	1973	2.00 - 3.00
Scoutcraft Skills.	1973	2.00 - 3.00
Shore-Wave Listening.	1973	2.00 - 3.00
Showman Activity Badge Helps.	1973	2.00 - 3.00

Slides of the Month.	1973	2.00 - 3.00
Sports Tips.	1973	2.00 - 3.00
Stamp Collecting.	1973	2.00 - 3.00
Stunts & Skits.	1973	2.00 - 3.00
Swimming and Waterfront Activities.	1973	2.00 - 3.00
Toughen Up.	1973	2.00 - 3.00
Webelos Scout Helps.	1973	2.00 - 3.00
Winter Activities.	1973	2.00 - 3.00

BULLETINS

293,000 Boys Aid the Nation.	1917-1925	10.00 - 15.00
A Message to Garcia.	1917-1925	10.00 - 15.00
Address by Dr. Charles W. Eliot.	1917-1925	10.00 - 15.00
Army and Navy Athletic Handbook.	1917-1925	10.00 - 15.00
B.S. of A. and Girl Scouts.	1917-1925	10.00 - 15.00
The Boy Scout Movement and the Public Schools.	1917-1925	10.00 - 15.00
Boy Scout Scheme in Nutshell.	1917-1925	10.00 - 15.00
Boy Scout Training Under Catholic Leadership.	1917-1925	10.00 - 15.00
The Boy Scouts and My Boy.	1917-1925	10.00 - 15.00
The Boy Scouts and the Church.	1917-1925	10.00 - 15.00
The Boy Scouts and Wesley Intermediate Bible-Classes.	1917-1925	10.00 - 15.00
Boy Scouts of America Drill Manual.	1917-1925	10.00 - 15.00
Boy Scouts of Girard.	1917-1925	10.00 - 15.00
The Boy Scouts.	1917-1925	10.00 - 15.00
The Boy.	1917-1925	10.00 - 15.00
Customs and Drill Manual.	1917-1925	10.00 - 15.00
General Information.	1917-1925	10.00 - 15.00
How the Boy Scouts of America Stand on National Prepardness.	1917-1925	10.00 - 15.00
How to Save.	1917-1925	10.00 - 15.00
Is the Church Caring for its Scouts?	1917-1925	10.00 - 15.00
The Largest Boys' Club in the World.	1917-1925	10.00 - 15.00
Making Men of Them.	1917-1925	10.00 - 15.00
Membership Circular.	1917-1925	10.00 - 15.00

Military Training Pamphlet #1.	1917-1925	10.00 - 15.00
Minimum Standards for Lone Troop Camps.	1917-1925	10.00 - 15.00
Mortimer L. Schiff Address, 1915.	1917-1925	10.00 - 15.00
Our Boys and the Boy Scout Movements.	1917-1925	10.00 - 15.00
Pedagogical Interpretations and Applications of the Methods of Boy Scout Education.	1917-1925	10.00 - 15.00
Practical Patriotism.	1917-1925	10.00 - 15.00
The Psychology of Scouting.	1917-1925	10.00 - 15.00
Reprint of War Department Circular No.168. March's order for decommissioned men to give service to scouting.	1917-1925	10.00 - 15.00
Resolution Passed by Washington Convention, G.A.R.	1917-1925	10.00 - 15.00
Roosevelt Appeals for Scoutmasters.	1917-1925	10.00 - 15.00
Rope and its Uses.	1917-1925	10.00 - 15.00
Rotary Club No. 3.	1917-1925	10.00 - 15.00
Scout Helps - First-Class.	1917-1925	10.00 - 15.00
Scout Helps - Second-Class.	1917-1925	10.00 - 15.00
Scouting Education.	1917-1925	10.00 - 15.00
The Scoutmaster.	1917-1925	10.00 - 15.00
Sea Scouts of the Boy Scouts of America.	1917-1925	10.00 - 15.00
Trained for Citizenship: The Boy Scout.	1917-1925	10.00 - 15.00
The Troop Committee.	1917-1925	10.00 - 15.00
What Boy Scouts Do.	1917-1925	10.00 - 15.00
What Scouts Do?	1917-1925	10.00 - 15.00

CASSETTES

Bugle Calls.		5.00 - 7.50
Scouting Along with Burl Ives.		5.00 - 7.50
The Voice of Lord Baden-Powell.		5.00 - 7.50

COMPACT DISCS

StockShots5: Jamboree.	1997	17.50 - 25.00
StockShots6: The Venturing Experience.	1998	17.50 - 25.00
StockShots7: Boy Scouts.	1999	17.50 - 25.00

EASTMAN KODAK CO.

Proof Positive, A Kodak Story for Boys.	1912	15.00 - 20.00

FLIERS & FOLDERS

Can You Name Them?	1929	7.50 - 12.50
Development.	1929	7.50 - 12.50
Dividends of Scouting.	1929	7.50 - 12.50
Fourteen Reasons Why.	1929	7.50 - 12.50
Give Him a Chance.	1929	7.50 - 12.50
High Adventure.	1929	7.50 - 12.50
I Am a First-Class Scout.	1929	7.50 - 12.50
If He Lives on a Farm, He Needs Scouting.	1929	7.50 - 12.50
I'm a Second-Class Scout.	1929	7.50 - 12.50
Let's Go Camping This Winter.	1929	7.50 - 12.50
Merit Badge Counselors.	1929	7.50 - 12.50
Now I am a Tenderfoot Scout.	1929	7.50 - 12.50
Our Troop Committee.	1929	7.50 - 12.50
The Scout Uniform.	1929	7.50 - 12.50
Scouting Around the World.	1929	7.50 - 12.50
Sea Scouting.	1929	7.50 - 12.50
Send Him to Camp.	1929	7.50 - 12.50
To Parents.	1929	7.50 - 12.50
The Twelfth Scout Law.	1929	7.50 - 12.50
What is a Boy Scout?	1929	7.50 - 12.50
What Is He Reading?	1929	7.50 - 12.50
What is Scouting?	1929	7.50 - 12.50
What We Are Aiming At.?	1929	7.50 - 12.50
Why Mention the Boy Scouts.	1929	7.50 - 12.50
Won't You Be Our Scoutmaster?	1929	7.50 - 12.50

SCOUT AND CAMPFIRE PLAYS SERIES

Boy Scout Hero, Puller, Edwin, Dennison.	1916	15.00 - 25.00

SCOUT TESTAMENTS AND BIBLES

Bible for Scouts and Scoutmasters. Khaki cloth binding, 4 x 6.	1915-1925	25.00 - 35.00
Bible for Scouts and Scoutmasters. Suede leather binding, 4 x 6.	1915-1925	35.00 - 60.00
Boy Scout Bible. Khaki cloth binding, twelve maps, 5-3/4 x 3-5/8.	1915-1925	40.00 - 60.00
Boy Scout Bible. Khaki leather binding, twelve maps, 5-3/4 x 3-5/8.	1915-1925	50.00 - 75.00
Catholic Prayer Book. Cloth binding, 2-1/2 x 4-1/2.	1915-1925	10.00 - 15.00
Catholic Prayer Book. Leather binding, 2-1/2 x 4-1/2.	1915-1925	15.00 - 20.00
Pocket Bible. Khaki cloth, button fastener, 2-3/4 x 3-3/4.	1915-1925	30.00 - 45.00
Pocket Testament. Khaki cloth, thin paper, color illustrations, 2-1/2 x 3-3/4.	1915-1925	20.00 - 30.00
The Scout Laws. A course for Bible study.	1915-1925	5.00 - 10.00
Scout Testament. Khaki cloth binding, 4-1/2 x 2-5/8.	1915-1925	20.00 - 30.00
Scout Testament. Khaki leather binding, 4-1/2 x 2-5/8.	1915-1925	20.00 - 30.00
Scoutmaster's Testament. Khaki cloth binding, 4 x 6.	1915-1925	25.00 - 35.00
Scoutmaster's Testament. Khaki cloth binding, two make, 5-3/4 x 3-5/8.	1915-1925	30.00 - 45.00
Scouts' Pocket Testament. Khaki suede leather binding, 2-1/4 x 4.	1915-1925	40.00 - 60.00
Scouts' Pocket Testament. Khaki cloth binding, 2-1/4 x 4.	1915-1925	20.00 - 30.00

SERVICE LIBRARY - HANDICRAFTS GROUP

Craftstrip Braiding Projects.	1940	15.00 - 25.00
Leathercraft Methods Booklet.	1940	15.00 - 25.00
Metalcraft Methods Booklet.	1940	15.00 - 25.00
The Pine Tree Patrol.	1930	15.00 - 25.00

SERVICE LIBRARY - PLAYS GROUP

A Strenuous Afternoon.	1931	10.00 - 20.00
After Dark - A Boy Scout Comedy.	1931	10.00 - 20.00
Be Prepared.		10.00 - 20.00
Calling Jack's Bluff.		10.00 - 20.00
Coming Clean - A Boy Scout Comedy.	1931	10.00 - 20.00
Father Ex-Officio.		10.00 - 20.00
The Fourth Musketeer.	1939	10.00 - 20.00
Jambomania.		10.00 - 20.00
Joe's Capture.	1937	10.00 - 20.00
Kid's Awakening.		10.00 - 20.00
The Missing Link.		10.00 - 20.00
The Scout Circus.	1934	10.00 - 20.00
Scout Entertainments.		10.00 - 20.00
Scout Plays.	1931	10.00 - 20.00
Scouts in Camp.		10.00 - 20.00
Twice a Scout.	1949	10.00 - 20.00
The Upper Trail.		10.00 - 20.00

SERVICE LIBRARY - SERIES A

The Adventures of a District Commissioner.	1933	15.00 - 25.00
Celebrating Anniversary Week.	1928	15.00 - 25.00
Constitution and By-laws of the B.S.A.	1933	20.00 - 35.00
Publicity.	1928	15.00 - 25.00
Standard Local Council Constitution and By-Laws and District Committee By-Laws.	1933	15.00 - 25.00
The Uniform, Badges and Insignia.	1929	15.00 - 25.00
Uniform, Badges and Insignia.	1933	15.00 - 25.00
Vacation Programs.	1929	15.00 - 25.00

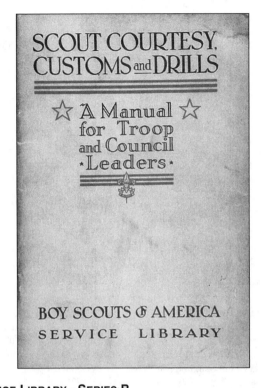

SERVICE LIBRARY - SERIES B

A Manual of Customs and Drills for Boy Scouts.	1929	15.00 - 25.00
After Dark - A Boy Scout Comedy.	1931	15.00 - 25.00
Bird Homes and How to Build Them.	1928	15.00 - 25.00
Cal Ruggles, Troop Committeeman.	1930	15.00 - 25.00
Coming Clean - A Boy Scout Comedy.	1931	15.00 - 25.00
First-Class Helps.	1931	15.00 - 25.00
General Information Bulletin.	1927	15.00 - 25.00
The Good Turn Test.	1928	15.00 - 25.00
How to Organize a Troop of Boy Scouts.	1929	15.00 - 25.00
Indian Handicraft.	1930	15.00 - 25.00
Investiture Ceremonies.	1928	15.00 - 25.00
Knifecraft.	1929	15.00 - 25.00
Meeting Rooms for Troop & Patrol.	1931	15.00 - 25.00
Model Airplanes.	1929	15.00 - 25.00
The Patrol Method.	1930	15.00 - 25.00
Pets.	1930	15.00 - 25.00
The Practice of the Oath and Law.	1928	15.00 - 25.00
Projects in Leather.	1930	15.00 - 25.00
Requirements for the First-Class Scout.	1929	15.00 - 25.00
Requirements for the Second-Class Scout.	1929	15.00 - 25.00
Requirements for the Tenderfoot Scout.	1929	15.00 - 25.00
Scout Courtesy, Customs and Drills.	1942	15.00 - 25.00
Scout Plays.	1931	15.00 - 25.00
Scouting with a Neckerchief.	1927	15.00 - 25.00
The Scoutmaster and His Troop.	1929	15.00 - 25.00
The Scoutmasters' First Six Weeks.	1930	15.00 - 25.00
Second-Class Helps.	1930	15.00 - 25.00
Tenderfoot Helps.	1931	15.00 - 25.00
The Troop Committee.	1929	15.00 - 25.00
Troop Meeting Rooms.	1930	15.00 - 25.00
Troop Spirit.	1930	15.00 - 25.00
Troop Stunts.	1931	15.00 - 25.00
The Yucca Patrol Idea.	1930	15.00 - 25.00

SERVICE LIBRARY - SERIES D

Archery.	1929	15.00 - 25.00
Boat Building and Canoe Repair.		15.00 - 25.00
Boat Building, Canoe Repair and Paddle Making.	1940	15.00 - 25.00
The Boy Scout Bird Record Book for Home, Camp and Hike.	1930	15.00 - 25.00
Camp Buildings and Scout Shelters.	1929	15.00 - 25.00
Camp Fire Helps.	1930	15.00 - 25.00
Camp Fires and Camp Cookery.		15.00 - 25.00
Camp Fires and Cooking.	1935	15.00 - 25.00
Commissary, Cooking Gear & Food Cost Accounting.	1938	15.00 - 25.00
How to Spin a Rope.	1930	15.00 - 25.00
Kites (and Kite Flying).	1931	15.00 - 25.00
Making Nature Collections.		15.00 - 25.00
Minimum Standards for Boy Scout Camps.	1928	15.00 - 25.00
Nature Collections.	1929	15.00 - 25.00
Totem Poles.	1929	15.00 - 25.00

SERVICE LIBRARY - SERIES F

The Boy Scout Scheme.	1929	15.00 - 25.00
The Father and Son Idea and Scouting.	1928	15.00 - 25.00
The Heart of a Boy.	1928	15.00 - 25.00
Meeting that Secret Hazard.	1928	15.00 - 25.00
Scouting Education.	1927	15.00 - 25.00
Scouting in Relation to the Schools.	1927	15.00 - 25.00
Service Clubs and Scouting.	1929	15.00 - 25.00
True Stories of Real Scouts.	1931	15.00 - 25.00
Your Home, Your Boy and Scouting.		15.00 - 25.00

SERVICE LIBRARY - SERIES NOT ASSIGNED

Canoeing.	1931	15.00 - 25.00
The Rally Book.	1931	15.00 - 25.00
The Troop Program and Scout Tenure. Division of Program.	1934	15.00 - 25.00

SLIDES

Rockwell Paintings.	1976	17.50 - 25.00
StockShots2: The Historical Collection.	1992	27.50 - 32.50
StockShots4: The Outdoor Collection.	1995	27.50 - 32.50

SLIDES & CASSETTE - CEREMONIES

85 Years of Tradition.	1995	30.00 - 40.00
America the Beautiful.	1995	30.00 - 40.00
America.	1985	20.00 - 30.00
The American's Creed.	1991	20.00 - 30.00
Campfire Stories.	1993	20.00 - 30.00
Character Counts.	1995	30.00 - 40.00
Check out the Boy Scouts.	1995	30.00 - 40.00
COPE: The Fun and Challenge Begin.	1993	20.00 - 30.00
Delivering the Promise.	1995	30.00 - 40.00
Forever Young.	1986	20.00 - 30.00
The Future is You.	1991	20.00 - 30.00
God Bless the U.S.A.	1986	20.00 - 30.00
I Volunteer.	1992	20.00 - 30.00
Joe Csatari: The Tradition Continues.	1991	20.00 - 30.00
On My Honor.	1985	20.00 - 30.00
Pass It On.	1995	30.00 - 40.00
Pledge of Allegiance.	1995	30.00 - 40.00
The Rock Climb.	1993	20.00 - 30.00
Salute to Leaders.	1995	30.00 - 40.00
Scouters' Porch.	1995	30.00 - 40.00
Scoutin' U.S.A.	1986	20.00 - 30.00
The Star Spangled Banner. 20 slides.	1988	20.00 - 30.00
The Star Spangled Banner. 61 slides.	1988	30.00 - 40.00
The Trail to Eagle.	1991	20.00 - 30.00
Urban Opening.	1995	30.00 - 40.00

THE BOY SCOUTS' YEARBOOK

1915 Mathiews, Franklin K., D. Appleton & Co.	1915	40.00 - 75.00
1916 Mathiews, Franklin K., D. Appleton & Co.	1916	40.00 - 75.00
1917 Mathiews, Franklin K., D. Appleton & Co.	1917	40.00 - 75.00
1918 Mathiews, Franklin K., D. Appleton & Co.	1918	40.00 - 75.00
1919 Mathiews, Franklin K., D. Appleton & Co.	1919	30.00 - 50.00
1920 Mathiews, Franklin K., D. Appleton & Co.	1920	30.00 - 50.00
1921 Mathiews, Franklin K., D. Appleton & Co.	1921	30.00 - 50.00
1922 Mathiews, Franklin K., D. Appleton & Co.	1922	30.00 - 50.00
1923 Mathiews, Franklin K., D. Appleton & Co.	1923	20.00 - 40.00
1924 Mathiews, Franklin K., D. Appleton & Co.	1924	20.00 - 40.00
1925 Mathiews, Franklin K., D. Appleton & Co.	1925	20.00 - 40.00
1926 Mathiews, Franklin K., D. Appleton & Co.	1926	15.00 - 30.00
1927 Mathiews, Franklin K., D. Appleton & Co.	1927	15.00 - 30.00
1928 Mathiews, Franklin K., D. Appleton & Co.	1928	15.00 - 30.00
1929 Mathiews, Franklin K., D. Appleton & Co.	1929	15.00 - 30.00
1930 Mathiews, Franklin K., D. Appleton & Co.	1930	15.00 - 30.00
1931 Mathiews, Franklin K., D. Appleton & Co.	1931	15.00 - 30.00
1932 Mathiews, Franklin K., D. Appleton & Co.	1932	10.00 - 25.00
1933 Ghost and Mystery Stories, Mathiews, Franklin K., D. Appleton & Co.	1933	10.00 - 25.00
1934 Stories of Brave Boys and Fearless Men, Mathiews, Franklin K., D. Appleton & Co.	1934	10.00 - 25.00
1935 Stories About Dogs, Mathiews, Franklin K., D. Appleton & Co.	1935	10.00 - 25.00
1936 Sports Stories, Mathiews, Franklin K., D. Appleton & Co.	1936	10.00 - 25.00
1937 Stories of Daring and Danger, Mathiews, Franklin K., D. Appleton & Co.	1937	10.00 - 25.00
1938 Fun and Fiction, Mathiews, Franklin K., D. Appleton & Co.	1938	10.00 - 25.00
1939 Stories of Daring and Danger, Mathiews, Franklin K., D. Appleton & Co.	1939	10.00 - 25.00
1940 Wild Animal Stories, Mathiews, Franklin K., D. Appleton & Co.	1940	10.00 - 25.00
1941 Patriotic Stories, Mathiews, Franklin K., D. Appleton & Co.	1941	10.00 - 25.00
1942 Stories of Boy Heroes, Mathiews, Franklin K., D. Appleton & Co.	1942	10.00 - 25.00
1943 Stories of Adventure Fliers, Mathiews, Franklin K., D. Appleton & Co.	1943	10.00 - 25.00
1944 Stories of Boy Scout Courageous, Mathiews, Franklin K., D. Appleton & Co.	1944	10.00 - 25.00
1945 Stories Boys Like Best, Mathiews, Franklin K., D. Appleton & Co.	1945	10.00 - 25.00

THE BOYS' LIFE LIBRARY BOOKS

The Boys' Life Book of World War II Stories, Random House.	1965	3.00 - 7.50
The Boys' Life Book of Baseball Stories, Random House.	1964	3.00 - 7.50
The Boys' Life Book of Baseball Stories, Windward Books paperback, original cover.	1964	1.00 - 4.00
The Boys' Life Book of Baseball Stories, Windward Books, paperback, silver cover.	1964	1.00 - 4.00
The Boys' Life Book of Basketball Stories, Random House.	1966	3.00 - 7.50
The Boys' Life Book of Flying Stories, Random House.	1964	3.00 - 7.50
The Boys' Life Book of Football Stories, Random House.	1963	3.00 - 7.50
The Boys' Life Book of Football Stories, Windward Books, paperback, silver cover.	1963	2.00 - 4.00
The Boys' Life Book of Football Stories, Windward Books, paperback, regular cover.	1963	2.00 - 4.00
The Boys' Life Book of Horse Stories, Random House.	1963	3.00 - 7.50
The Boys' Life Book of Mystery Stories, Random House.	1963	3.00 - 7.50
The Boys' Life Book of Outer Space Stories, Random House.	1964	3.00 - 7.50
Mutiny in the Time Machine, Donald Keith, Random House.	1963	3.00 - 7.50

THE CONSERVATION HANDBOOK

	1992	7.50 - 12.50

VIDEOS

A Road Worth Traveling: The Big Picture of How to Start a New Scout Unit.	1997	12.50 - 17.50
A time to tell.	1989	10.00 - 20.00
An American Passage.	1983	12.50 - 17.50
The Barbecue: Working with the Troop Committee.	1988	10.00 - 15.00
Boy Scout Advancement.	1989	15.00 - 20.00
Boy Scout Recruiting.	1992	10.00 - 15.00
Boy Scout Summer Camp: Making it Happen.	1990	12.50 - 17.50
Cold-Weather Camping.	1988	20.00 - 25.00
First-Class Scout Advancement.	1989	20.00 - 30.00
It Happened to Me.	1991	17.50 - 22.50
The Outdoor Program.	1987	7.50 - 12.50
The Outdoor Program.	1990	7.50 - 12.50
Safe Swim Defense...It Works!	1998	12.50 - 17.50
Safety Afloat.	1989	12.50 - 17.50
Scouting in Rural America.	1988	12.50 - 17.50
Scouting Safety...Begins with Leadership.	1998	12.50 - 17.50
Second-Class Scout Advancement.	1989	20.00 - 30.00
Selecting Quality Leader.	1995	17.50 - 25.00
Tenderfoot Advancement.	1989	20.00 - 30.00
The Troop Meeting.	1987	7.50 - 12.50
The Troop Meeting.	1990	7.50 - 12.50
Troop Organization.	1987	7.50 - 12.50
Troop Organization.	1990	7.50 - 12.50
Troop Program Planning.	1991	17.50 - 25.00
Unit Commissioner's Orientation: Helping Units Succeed.	1999	12.50 - 17.50
Unit Problem-Solving for Commissioners.	1997	12.50 - 17.50
Varsity Scout Leader Fast Start.	1989	12.50 - 17.50
Youth Protection Training for Adult Leaders.	1988	30.00 - 40.00
Youth Protection Training for Adult Leaders.	1990	30.00 - 40.00
Youth Protection Training for Adult Leaders.	1998	30.00 - 40.00
Youth Protection: Boy Scout and Cub Scout Leader Training Module.	1988	10.00 - 20.00
Youth Protection: Personal Safety Awareness.	1998	12.50 - 17.50

VIDEOS - CEREMONIES

1910 Society: Giving for the Future.	1998	10.00 - 15.00
1997 Report to the Nation.	1998	10.00 - 15.00
85 Years of Tradition.	1995	17.50 - 22.50
America the Beautiful.	1995	17.50 - 22.50
American Scout.	1998	10.00 - 15.00
Character Counts!	1995	17.50 - 22.50
Delivering the Promise.	1995	17.50 - 22.50
Pass It On.	1995	17.50 - 22.50
Pledge of Allegiance.	1995	17.50 - 22.50
Salute to Leaders.	1995	17.50 - 22.50
Scouters' Porch.	1995	17.50 - 22.50
Scoutin' U.S.A.	1986	10.00 - 15.00
The Star Spangled Banner.	1988	17.50 - 22.50
Urban Opening.	1995	17.50 - 22.50
Wisdon Tapes: Strong Leaders.	1999	10.00 - 15.00
Wisdon Tapes: Strong Values.	1998	10.00 - 15.00

VIDEOS - RELATIONSHIPS DIVISION

American Legion and Scouting.	1994	10.00 - 15.00
Baptists and Scouting: Building Values Together.	1996	10.00 - 15.00
Elks and Scouting.	1994	10.00 - 15.00
Moose and Scouting.	1995	10.00 - 15.00
Pope John Paul II Visit to the U.S. and Scouts in Central Park.	1996	10.00 - 15.00
Presbyterians and Scouting...Building Values Together.	1997	10.00 - 15.00
The Salvation Army and Scouting.	1996	10.00 - 15.00
Scouting and the Eastern Catholic Church.	1996	10.00 - 15.00
Scouting in the Catholic Church.	1998	10.00 - 15.00
Scouting in the LDS Church.	1999	10.00 - 15.00
Scouting Ministry in the United Methodist Church.	1998	10.00 - 15.00
Scouting: It Works for Your Youth.	1998	10.00 - 15.00

VIDEOS - SCOUTREACH

Hispanic Opportunity.	1988	10.00 - 15.00
Hispanic Visions: Beyond the Street.	1994	10.00 - 15.00
La Familia de Scouts.	1988	10.00 - 15.00
National Urban Leaders Testimonials.	1999	10.00 - 15.00
Preserving a Tradition: Scouting for Indo-Chinese Families.	1990	10.00 - 15.00
Pro 2 Pro: Urban Emphasis.	1994	10.00 - 15.00
Rainbow Visions: Operation First-Class.	1995	10.00 - 15.00
Recruiting Urban Unit Leaders.	1996	10.00 - 15.00
Scouting in the Chinese-American Community.	1997	10.00 - 15.00
Scouting in the Korean Community.	1999	10.00 - 15.00
Scouting in the Vietnamese Community.	1997	10.00 - 15.00
Visions: Scouting in Urban Communities.	1993	10.00 - 15.00
Working With Public Housing, Parks and Recreation.	1996	10.00 - 15.00

RELIGIOUS AWARDS - YOUTH

Scout Religious Medals.

AD ALTARE DEI

Roman Catholic, Cross, ribbon of yellow-white-yellow with r-w-b-w-r in center. Back of cross with raised info.	1940-1970	20.00 - 30.00
Roman Catholic, Cross, ribbon of yellow-white-yellow with r-w-b-w-r in center. Back of cross plain.	1970	10.00 - 20.00

ALPHA AND OMEGA

Eastern Orthodox, White cross, orthodox cross in red at ctr. lt. blue ribbon with six thin white stripes.	1980	25.00 - 40.00

ARARAT

Eastern Diocese of the Armenian Church of America, Cross, purple ribbon.	1980	15.00 - 25.00

COMPASSIONATE FATHER

Meher Baba, Mastery in Service on pendant, rainbow ribbon.	1980	20.00 - 30.00

ETERNAL LIGHT, NER TAMID

Jewish, Lighted flame, blue/white ribbon.	1953	15.00 - 25.00

FRIENDS, SPIRIT OF TRUTH

Religious Society of Friends (Quakers), The Light Shines on in the Dark, legend on compass. Red/white/blue/red/ ribbon.	1967	20.00 - 30.00

GOD AND CHURCH

Lutheran, Lutheran heart emblem on white field, red ribbon.	1975	10.00 - 20.00

GOD AND COUNTRY

Baptist, Cross and open book in blue circle on white field, blue ribbon.	1967	10.00 - 20.00
First Church of Christ Scientist, Red cross in white field, blue ribbon.	1967	10.00 - 20.00
The Salvation Army, Army logo, blue ribbon.	1967	10.00 - 20.00
Moravian, Blue enamel on bar, white enamel behind lamb with banner, red/white repeated ribbon.	1980	20.00 - 30.00

GOD AND COUNTRY, (BOG I OJCZYZNA)

Polish National Catholic Church, Red enamel on bar, red/white/red ribbon, Open book and cross at ctr of cross.	1980	15.00 - 25.00

GOD AND COUNTRY, GOD AND CHURCH

Protestant, Red cross on white field, blue ribbon	1953	10.00 - 20.00
Methodist, Cross and flame on white field, blue ribbon.	1967	10.00 - 20.00
Episcopal, Red cross on white field, stars in blue 1st quadrant, red ribbon.	1967	10.00 - 20.00
Presbyterian, Dove, two flames flanking priestly vestment, blue ribbon.	1967	10.00 - 20.00
Christian Church (Disciples of Christ), Red chalice with cross in white field, blue ribbon.	1980	10.00 - 20.00

GOD AND COUNTRY, GOD AND LIFE

Episcopal, Red cross on white field, stars in blue 1st quadrant, red ribbon.	1967	10.00 - 20.00
Protestant, Red cross on white field, dark green ribbon.	1967	10.00 - 20.00

GOD IS GREAT

Islamic Council of Scouters, Crescent in World Scouting knot, white ribbon.	1980	40.00 - 60.00

GOOD LIFE

Zoroastrian, Flame pyre, white ribbon.	1980	25.00 - 40.00

GOOD SERVANT

Churches of Christ, Cross and four hearts, red ribbon.	1980	10.00 - 20.00

IN THE NAME OF GOD

Islamic, Crescents and tracery, green ribbon.	1975	35.00 - 50.00

LIGHT IS LIFE

Eastern Rite, Catholic, Greek letters on cross, blue ribbon.	1980	25.00 - 40.00

LIVING FAITH

Lutheran, P and Cross on white enamel pendant, red ribbon.	1980	10.00 - 20.00

ON MY HONOR

Church of Jesus Christ of Later-day Saints, FDL and Angel, green and yellow ribbon.	1967	15.00 - 25.00

PIUS XII

Roman Catholic, Yellow/white ribbon, Crossed keys and papla tiara.	1967	10.00 - 20.00

PRO DEO ET PATRIA

Lutheran, Red cross on white field, blue ribbon.	1953	20.00 - 30.00

RELIGION IN LIFE

Unitarian Universalist, Flame on pedestal, white enamel globe around, blue ribbon.	1980	10.00 - 20.00

SANGHA

Buddhist, Ship's wheel, rainbow ribbon.	1980	20.00 - 30.00

ST. MESORIB

Armenian Apostolic Church of America, Western Prelacy, red, blue, orange ribbon, figure and legend.	1980	20.00 - 30.00

THE NEW CHURCH, A NEW CHRISTIANITY, OPEN WORD

General Church of the New Jerusalem, Open book, white/red ribbon.	1980	10.00 - 20.00

UNITY OF MANKIND

Baha'l, Enameled blue and green globe, green/ white/ green ribbon.	1980	20.00 - 30.00

UNITY, LIGHT OF GOD

Association of Unity Churches, Flower head enameled, blue/yellow/blue ribbon.	1980	15.00 - 25.00

WORLD COMMUNITY, (LIAHONA - COMPASS)
Reorganized Church of Jesus Christ of Later-   1980   20.00 - 30.00
day Saints, Peace and family within purple
enameled cross and globe. Purple/orange/
purple ribbon.

*A Scout is Reverent is the title of this 1930 stained-glass
window in the Catholic Chapel at Camp Kernochan, Ten
Mile River Scout Camps, G.N.Y.C.*

RELIGIOUS AWARDS - ADULT

BISHOP ZIELINSKI AWARD
Polish National Catholic Church, open book   1980   50.00 - 75.00
with cross in ctr. on red-white-red neck
ribbon.

DAVID ZEISBERGER AWARD
Moravian Church in America, lamb with   1980   50.00 - 75.00
banner, red-white-blue ribbon. Legend: Our
Lamb Has Conquered, Let Us Follow Him.

DISTINGUISHED YOUTH SERVICE AWARD
Association of Unity Churches, sunburst,   1980   50.00 - 75.00
enameled, blue-yellow-blue neck ribbon.

FAITHFUL SERVANT AWARD
Churches of Christ, cross and four hearts, red   1980   50.00 - 75.00
neck ribbon.

FRIENDS AWARD
Religious Society of Friends (Quakers),   1980   50.00 - 75.00
compass, red-white-blue-red-blue-white-red
neck ribbon. Legend: The Light Shines on in
the Dark.

GOD AND SERVICE AWARD
Presbyterian, vestment flanked by flames, dove   1980   50.00 - 75.00
above, pale blue neck ribbon. Legend: Life-
Family-Church.
Protestant, red cross on white field, blue neck   1980   50.00 - 75.00
ribbon. Legend: Life-Family-Church.
United Methodist, flame and cross, white-red-   1980   50.00 - 75.00
white neck ribbon. Legend: Life-Family-
Church.

LAMB
Lutheran, lamb, cross on hill, red neck ribbon.   1980   50.00 - 75.00

PROPHET ELIAS AWARD
Eastern Orthodox, white cross with red   1980   50.00 - 75.00
orthodox cross within. Light blue neck ribbon
with six thin white stripes.

RELIGION AND YOUTH AWARD
Unitarian Universalist Association, flame on   1980   50.00 - 75.00
lamp, white field, blue neck ribbon.

SCOUTERS AWARD
The Salvation Army, emblem on red-orange-   1980   50.00 - 75.00
blue neck ribbon.

SHOFAR
Jewish, Shofar horn and lamp, multi-stripe   1980   50.00 - 75.00
blue-white neck ribbon.

ST. GEORGE
Episcopal, St. George slaying dragon, within   1980   50.00 - 75.00
cross, red neck ribbon.
Roman Catholic, St. George slaying dragon,   1980   50.00 - 75.00
yellow neck ribbon with green-red-white-
blue-green thin stripes.

UNIFORMS

Tenderfoot scout with four bellow pocket coat and belt, breeches, and Army duck leggings.

BELT

Olive-drab web, black steel buckle, First-Class emblem.	1911-1930	10.00 - 15.00

BREECHES

Knee length, ties at ends. Heavy olive-drab material.	1911-1930	40.00 - 60.00
Knee length, ties at ends. Light olive-drab material.	1911-1930	30.00 - 50.00

CAMPAIGN HAT

Summer weight, olive drab, leather-reinforced brown band.	1911-1930	40.00 - 60.00
Thin olive-drab felt, leather or silk hat band. Various makers.	1911-1930	40.00 - 60.00

COAT

High collar, four expandable 'bellow' pockets, light olive-drab material.	1911-1930	125.00 - 175.00
High collar, four pockets, heavy olive-drab material.	1911-1930	75.00 - 125.00
High collar.	1910-1921	125.00 - 175.00
Open collar, often found w/ rank, merit badges and troop insignia on sleeves. No inside pocket for membership card.	1920-1923	100.00 - 150.00
Open collar, often found w/ rank, merit badges and troop insignia on sleeves. Inside pocket for membership card.	1923-1928	100.00 - 150.00
Open collar, w/o insignia.	1928-1941	75.00 - 125.00

1911-1920 BSA Copper Collar Monogram.

1911-1920 Unit Collar Number.

COLLAR BRASS

BSA, screw post or crude fold pins.	1912-1920	40.00 - 60.00
Unit numerals: 1, 2, 3, 4, 5, 6, 7, 8, 0. Screw post.	1912-1920	20.00 - 30.00

COMMUNITY STRIP. KHAKI AND RED.

Various town names.	1945-1955	7.50 - 15.00

Community and State Strips in khaki with red embroidery or red with white embroidery. Council Shoulder Strip in red with white embroidery.

COUNCIL STRIP. KHAKI AND RED.

New York City/Brooklyn.	1945-1955	12.50 - 17.50
New York City/Manhattan.	1945-1955	12.50 - 17.50
New York City/Queens.	1945-1955	12.50 - 17.50
New York City/Staten Island.	1945-1955	15.00 - 20.00
New York City/The Bronx.	1945-1955	12.50 - 17.50

KNICKERS

Knee length, buckles at ends. Olive-drab material.	1911-1930	100.00 - 150.00

LANYARDS

Blue.	1930-1953	10.00 - 15.00
Gold.	1930-1953	10.00 - 15.00
Green & white.	1930-1953	20.00 - 30.00
Khaki.	1930-1953	10.00 - 15.00
Red, white & blue.	1930-1953	10.00 - 15.00
Red.	1930-1953	10.00 - 15.00
White.	1930-1953	10.00 - 15.00

LEGGINGS

Army 'duck' material, roll.	1911-1930	15.00 - 20.00

MERIT BADGE SASH

False sleeve for coat.	1916-1925	100.00 - 150.00
Narrow khaki (two across).	1946-1979	7.50 - 12.50
Narrow tan (two across).	1924-1945	5.00 - 10.00
Wide dark green (two across).	1972-1979	5.00 - 10.00
Wide khaki (three across).	1946-1979	5.00 - 10.00
Wide olive (three across).	1980	5.00 - 10.00
Wide tan (three across).	1924-1945	5.00 - 10.00

Top: Neckerchief, Full Square, with small National Headquarters emblem. Bottom: Full Square with BSA and Tenderfoot emblem in contrasting colors.

NECKERCHIEF

Full Square. Combination of two colors, 28" x 32", First-Class Badge within circle. 14 available.	1926-1931	5.00 - 7.50
Full Square. Combination of two colors, 28" x 32", First-Class Badge. 14 available.	1924-1926	7.50 - 12.50
Full Square. Combination of two colors, 30" x 30", Tenderfoot Badge within diamond. 14 colors available.	1932	5.00 - 7.50
Full Square. Combination of two colors, 32" x 32", Tenderfoot Badge within diamond. 16 colors available.	1933-1947	4.00 - 7.50
Full Square. Solid color, 28" x 32", First-Class Badge within circle, 17 colors available.	1926-1931	5.00 - 7.50
Full Square. Solid color, 28", w/Official Badge 11" x 6-1/2", 8 colors available.	1914-1915	20.00 - 25.00
Full Square. Solid color, 30" x 30", Tenderfoot Badge within diamond, 13 colors available.	1932	5.00 - 7.50
Full Square. Solid color, 32" x 32", Tenderfoot Badge within diamond, 15 colors available.	1933-1947	4.00 - 7.50
Full Square. Solid color, Merceen, 28", small Official Badge, 18 colors available.	1916-1918	15.00 - 25.00
Full Square. Solid color, Pongee, 28" x 32", small Official Badge, 16 colors available.	1919-1920	15.00 - 20.00
Full Square. Solid color, Soisette, 28" x 32", small Official Badge, 16 colors available.	1921-1926	10.00 - 15.00
Kente Cloth.	1997	10.00 - 15.00
Triangular. Combination of two colors, Tenderfoot Badge within diamond.	1947	2.00 - 5.00
Triangular. Embroidered Tenderfoot Badge.	1972	5.00 - 7.50
Triangular. Solid color, Tenderfoot Badge within diamond.	1947	2.00 - 5.00

NECKERCHIEF SLIDE

Metal stamped braided "Turks head" thin one piece loop.	1991	0.50 - 1.00
Metal stamped braided "Turks head" two thick back flaps.	1945-1975	3.00 - 5.00

NECKERCHIEF SLIDES, CLOTH "TURKS HEAD"

Black.	1925-1953	2.50 - 7.50
Blue-orange, Special for Scout Service Corps members, NY World's Fair.	1939-1940	30.00 - 40.00
Brown.	1925-1953	2.50 - 7.50
Gold	1925-1953	2.50 - 7.50
Gray.	1925-1953	2.50 - 7.50
Green.	1925-1953	2.50 - 7.50
Khaki.	1925-1953	2.50 - 7.50
Orange.	1925-1953	2.50 - 7.50
Purple.	1925-1953	2.50 - 7.50
Red (professionals).	1925-1953	10.00 - 15.00
Red, white & blue.	1925-1953	10.00 - 15.00
Royal Blue.	1925-1953	2.50 - 7.50
White.	1925-1953	2.50 - 7.50
Yellow.	1925-1953	2.50 - 7.50

PANTS

Khaki long with red piping around front pocket flaps.	1946-1971	5.00 - 7.50
Khaki long with regular pockets.	1972-1979	5.00 - 7.50
Olive drab long, w/ regular pockets only.	1990-1998	5.00 - 7.50
Olive drab with large cargo pockets.	1980-1989	5.00 - 7.50

PANTS, SHORT

Heavy olive-drab material.	1911-1930	20.00 - 35.00
Heavy olive-drab material. Woolen.	1911-1930	20.00 - 35.00
Light olive-drab material.	1911-1930	20.00 - 35.00

PROGRAM STRIP

BOY SCOUTS of AMERICA in red on one line. Khaki cloth.	1946-1971	3.00 - 5.00
BOY SCOUTS OF AMERICA in red on one line. Tan cloth.	1920-1921	150.00 - 200.00
BOY SCOUTS of AMERICA in red on one line. Tan cloth.	1922-1945	20.00 - 40.00
BOY SCOUTS OF AMERICA in red on two lines. Tan cloth.	1918-1919	200.00 - 300.00
BOY SCOUTS of AMERICA in red. Tan khaki cloth.	1980	3.00 - 5.00
SCOUT B.S.A. in red. Dark green cloth.	1972-1979	3.00 - 5.00
SCOUT B.S.A. in red. Khaki cloth.	1972-1979	3.00 - 5.00

PUTTEES

Leather. Buckle strap around calf.	1911-1930	75.00 - 125.00

RECRUITER STRIP

Recruiter and Boypower/Manpower logo.	1972-1975	0.50 - 1.50
Recruiter and compass.	1965-1970	0.50 - 1.50
Recruiter and rocket.	1960-1970	0.50 - 1.50
Recruiter and scouts marching w/flags.	1960-1970	1.50 - 2.50
Recruiter and three portraits.	1970-1975	0.50 - 1.50
Recruiter and Wonderful World of Scouting logo.	1975-1980	0.50 - 1.50
Recruiter in border.	1961	0.50 - 1.50
Recruiter in border.	1962	0.50 - 1.50
Recruiter in border.	1963	0.50 - 1.50
Recruiter, I helped the Odds.	1971	0.50 - 1.50
Scout recruiter, cowboy on horse.	1950-1960	2.50 - 5.00

SERVICE STAR

Gold star screwback on gray felt (three years).	1932-1936	2.00 - 4.00
Gold star screwback on green felt (one year).	1923-1946	2.00 - 4.00
Gold star screwback on purple felt (10 years).	1932-1946	2.00 - 4.00
Gold star screwback on red felt (five years).	1932-1946	2.00 - 4.00
Gold star w/ tenure number, clutch back on green plastic disc.	1956	1.00 - 2.00
Gold star w/ tenure number, screwback on green felt.	1947-1955	2.00 - 4.00
Silver star screwback on red felt (five years).	1923-1931	2.00 - 4.00

SERVICE STRIPE

Gold, 1/8" wide (five years).	1921-1924	15.00 - 25.00
Green 1/8" wide (one year).	1920-1924	15.00 - 25.00
Green 3/8" wide (one year).	1913-1919	15.00 - 25.00
Red 1/8" wide (three years).	1920-1924	15.00 - 25.00
Red 3/8" wide (three years).	1913-1919	15.00 - 25.00

SHIRT

Heavy olive-drab material, winter weight, long sleeve.	1911-1930	20.00 - 30.00
Heavy olive-drab material, woolen, long sleeve.	1911-1930	20.00 - 30.00
Khaki long sleeves, pleated pocket.	1946-1965	5.00 - 7.50
Khaki short sleeves, pleated pocket.	1946-1965	5.00 - 7.50
Light olive-drab material, summer weight, long sleeve.	1911-1930	20.00 - 30.00
Tan khaki long sleeves with epaulets.	1980	5.00 - 10.00
Tan khaki short sleeves with epaulets.	1980	5.00 - 10.00

SHOES

International Shoe Company, Brown Oxford. Plain sole.	1953-1965	45.00 - 55.00

STATE STRIP. KHAKI AND RED

ALA.	1945-1955	5.00 - 7.50
ALASKA.	1945-1955	30.00 - 40.00
ARIZ.	1945-1955	5.00 - 7.50
ARK.	1945-1955	7.50 - 12.50
CALIF.	1945-1955	5.00 - 7.50
COLO.	1945-1955	5.00 - 7.50
CONN.	1945-1955	5.00 - 7.50
DEL.	1945-1955	20.00 - 25.00
FLA.	1945-1955	5.00 - 7.50
GA.	1945-1955	5.00 - 7.50
IDAHO.	1945-1955	12.50 - 17.50
ILL.	1945-1955	5.00 - 7.50
IND.	1945-1955	5.00 - 7.50
IOWA.	1945-1955	5.00 - 7.50
KANS.	1945-1955	5.00 - 7.50
KY.	1945-1955	5.00 - 7.50
LA.	1945-1955	5.00 - 7.50
MASS.	1945-1955	5.00 - 7.50
MD.	1945-1955	5.00 - 7.50
ME.	1945-1955	50.00 - 75.00
MICH.	1945-1955	5.00 - 7.50
MINN.	1945-1955	5.00 - 7.50
MISS.	1945-1955	17.50 - 25.00
MO.	1945-1955	5.00 - 7.50
MONT.	1945-1955	30.00 - 40.00
N. DAK.	1945-1955	7.50 - 12.50
N. MEX.	1945-1955	7.50 - 12.50
N.C.	1945-1955	5.00 - 7.50
N.H.	1945-1955	17.50 - 25.00
N.J.	1945-1955	5.00 - 7.50
N.Y.	1945-1955	5.00 - 7.50
N.Y.C.	1945-1955	80.00 - 110.00
NEB.	1945-1955	5.00 - 7.50
NEV.	1945-1955	30.00 - 40.00
OHIO.	1945-1955	5.00 - 7.50
OKLA.	1945-1955	5.00 - 7.50
ORE.	1945-1955	5.00 - 7.50
PA.	1945-1955	5.00 - 7.50
R.I.	1945-1955	5.00 - 7.50
S. DAK.	1945-1955	7.50 - 12.50
S.C.	1945-1955	30.00 - 40.00
T.H. (Territory of Hawaii).	1945-1955	500.00 - 650.00
TENN.	1945-1955	5.00 - 7.50
TEXAS.	1945-1955	5.00 - 7.50
UTAH.	1945-1955	5.00 - 7.50
VA.	1945-1955	5.00 - 7.50
VT.	1945-1955	17.50 - 25.00
W. VA.	1945-1955	5.00 - 7.50
WASH.	1945-1955	5.00 - 7.50
WIS.	1945-1955	5.00 - 7.50
WYO.	1945-1955	10.00 - 15.00

STOCKINGS

Knee length green cotton.	1911-1930	10.00 - 15.00

UNIT NUMBER

Red cut edge twill, white embroidered numeral.	1992	0.25 - 0.35
Red felt square, white embroidered numeral. Single-, two- or three-digit combinations. Gauze backing.	1927-1952	2.00 - 4.00
Red square screen printed on white felt square, white numeral.	1915-1926	20.00 - 25.00
Red square, white numeral, fully embroidered.	1953-1992	0.50 - 1.00

First Class Scout John Flory of Wauwatosa, WI, 1927.

PATROL RIBBONS

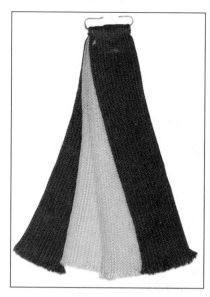

4-1/2" LONG

Black and brown. Raccoon.	1926-1928	125.00 - 150.00
Black and brown. Seal.	1926-1928	125.00 - 150.00
Black and khaki. Bat.	1926-1928	125.00 - 150.00
Black and white. Horse.	1926-1928	125.00 - 150.00
Black and white. Crow.	1926-1928	125.00 - 150.00
Black. Raven.	1926-1928	125.00 - 150.00
Blue and gray. Wood Pigeon.	1926-1928	125.00 - 150.00
Blue and white. Stork.	1926-1928	125.00 - 150.00
Blue and yellow. Beaver.	1926-1928	125.00 - 150.00
Blue. Owl.	1926-1928	125.00 - 150.00
Brown and green. Pine Tree.	1926-1928	125.00 - 150.00
Brown and red. Bear.	1926-1928	125.00 - 150.00
Brown and white. Otter.	1926-1928	125.00 - 150.00
Brown. Ram.	1926-1928	125.00 - 150.00
Gray and black. Jackal.	1926-1928	125.00 - 150.00
Gray and brown. Cat.	1926-1928	125.00 - 150.00
Gray and green. Alligator.	1926-1928	125.00 - 150.00
Gray and pink. Wild Boar.	1926-1928	125.00 - 150.00
Gray and violet. Pelican.	1926-1928	125.00 - 150.00
Gray. Cuckoo.	1926-1928	125.00 - 150.00
Gray. Sea Gull.	1926-1928	125.00 - 150.00
Green and black. Eagle.	1926-1928	125.00 - 150.00
Green and black. Hawk.	1926-1928	125.00 - 150.00
Green and violet. Woodpecker.	1926-1928	125.00 - 150.00
Green and white. Peewit.	1926-1928	125.00 - 150.00
Green. Curlew.	1926-1928	125.00 - 150.00
Khaki and blue. Swallow.	1926-1928	125.00 - 150.00
Khaki and green. Antelope.	1926-1928	125.00 - 150.00
Khaki and orange. Rhinoceros.	1926-1928	125.00 - 150.00
Khaki and red. Black Bear.	1926-1928	125.00 - 150.00
Orange and black. Cobra.	1926-1928	125.00 - 150.00
Orange. Hound.	1926-1928	125.00 - 150.00
Pink and black. Hippo.	1926-1928	125.00 - 150.00
Red and gray. Kangaroo.	1926-1928	125.00 - 150.00
Red and white. Buffalo.	1926-1928	125.00 - 150.00
Red, white and blue. Flying Eagle.	1926-1928	125.00 - 150.00
Violet and black. Stag.	1926-1928	125.00 - 150.00
Violet. Tiger.	1926-1928	125.00 - 150.00
White and blue. Elephant.	1926-1928	125.00 - 150.00
White and gray. Moose.	1926-1928	125.00 - 150.00
White and khaki. Bobwhite.	1926-1928	125.00 - 150.00
White and pink. Rattlesnake.	1926-1928	125.00 - 150.00
Yellow and black. Wolf.	1926-1928	125.00 - 150.00
Yellow and brown. Hyena.	1926-1928	125.00 - 150.00

Yellow and red. Lion.	1926-1928	125.00 - 150.00
Yellow. Panther.	1926-1928	125.00 - 150.00

5-1/2" LONG

Black and brown. Raccoon.	1911-1916	125.00 - 150.00
Black and brown. Seal.	1911-1916	125.00 - 150.00
Black and khaki. Bat.	1911-1916	125.00 - 150.00
Black and white. Crow.	1911-1916	125.00 - 150.00
Black and white. Horse.	1911-1916	125.00 - 150.00
Black. Raven.	1911-1916	125.00 - 150.00
Blue and gray. Wood Pigeon.	1911-1916	125.00 - 150.00
Blue and white. Stork.	1911-1916	125.00 - 150.00
Blue and yellow. Beaver.	1911-1916	125.00 - 150.00
Blue. Owl.	1911-1916	125.00 - 150.00
Brown and green. Pine Tree.	1911-1916	125.00 - 150.00
Brown and red. Bear.	1911-1916	125.00 - 150.00
Brown and White. Otter.	1911-1916	125.00 - 150.00
Brown. Ram.	1911-1916	125.00 - 150.00
Gray and black. Jackal.	1911-1916	125.00 - 150.00
Gray and brown. Cat.	1911-1916	125.00 - 150.00
Gray and green. Alligator.	1911-1916	125.00 - 150.00
Gray and pink. Wild Boar.	1911-1916	125.00 - 150.00
Gray and violet. Pelican.	1911-1916	125.00 - 150.00
Gray. Cuckoo.	1911-1916	125.00 - 150.00
Gray. Sea Gull.	1911-1916	125.00 - 150.00
Green and black. Eagle.	1911-1916	125.00 - 150.00
Green and black. Hawk.	1911-1916	125.00 - 150.00
Green and blue. Peacock.	1911-1916	125.00 - 150.00
Green and violet. Woodpecker.	1911-1916	125.00 - 150.00
Green and white. Peewit.	1911-1916	125.00 - 150.00
Green. Curlew.	1911-1916	125.00 - 150.00
Khaki and blue. Swallow.	1911-1916	125.00 - 150.00
Khaki and green. Antelope.	1911-1916	125.00 - 150.00
Khaki and orange. Rhinoceros.	1911-1916	125.00 - 150.00
Khaki and red. Black Bear.	1911-1916	125.00 - 150.00
Orange and black. Cobra.	1911-1916	125.00 - 150.00
Orange. Hound.	1911-1916	125.00 - 150.00
Pink and black. Hippo.	1911-1916	125.00 - 150.00
Red and gray. Kangaroo.	1911-1916	125.00 - 150.00
Red and white. Buffalo.	1911-1916	125.00 - 150.00
Red, white and blue. Flying Eagle.	1911-1916	125.00 - 150.00
Violet and black. Stag.	1911-1916	125.00 - 150.00
Violet. Tiger.	1911-1916	125.00 - 150.00
White and blue. Elephant.	1911-1916	125.00 - 150.00
White and gray. Moose.	1911-1916	125.00 - 150.00
White and khaki. Bobwhite.	1911-1916	125.00 - 150.00
White and pink. Rattlesnake.	1911-1916	125.00 - 150.00
Yellow and black. Wolf.	1911-1916	125.00 - 150.00
Yellow and brown. Hyena.	1911-1916	125.00 - 150.00
Yellow and green. Fox.	1911-1916	125.00 - 150.00
Yellow and red. Lion.	1911-1916	125.00 - 150.00
Yellow. Panther.	1911-1916	125.00 - 150.00

5" LONG

Black and brown. Raccoon.	1917-1926	125.00 - 150.00
Black and brown. Seal.	1917-1926	125.00 - 150.00
Black and khaki. Bat.	1917-1926	125.00 - 150.00
Black and white. Horse.	1917-1926	125.00 - 150.00
Black and white. Crow.	1917-1926	125.00 - 150.00
Black. Raven.	1917-1926	125.00 - 150.00
Blue and gray. Wood Pigeon.	1917-1926	125.00 - 150.00
Blue and white. Stork.	1917-1926	125.00 - 150.00
Blue and yellow. Beaver.	1917-1926	125.00 - 150.00
Blue. Owl.	1917-1926	125.00 - 150.00
Brown and green. Pine Tree.	1917-1926	125.00 - 150.00
Brown and red. Bear.	1917-1926	125.00 - 150.00
Brown and white. Otter.	1917-1926	125.00 - 150.00
Brown. Ram.	1917-1926	125.00 - 150.00

Gray and black. Jackal.	1917-1926	125.00 - 150.00
Gray and brown. Cat.	1917-1926	125.00 - 150.00
Gray and green. Alligator.	1917-1926	125.00 - 150.00
Gray and pink. Wild Boar.	1917-1926	125.00 - 150.00
Gray and violet. Pelican.	1917-1926	125.00 - 150.00
Gray. Cuckoo.	1917-1926	125.00 - 150.00
Gray. Sea Gull.	1917-1926	125.00 - 150.00
Green and black. Eagle.	1917-1926	125.00 - 150.00
Green and black. Hawk.	1917-1926	125.00 - 150.00
Green and blue. Peacock.	1917-1926	125.00 - 150.00
Green and violet. Woodpecker.	1917-1926	125.00 - 150.00
Green and white. Peewit.	1917-1926	125.00 - 150.00
Green. Curlew.	1917-1926	125.00 - 150.00
Khaki and blue. Swallow.	1917-1926	125.00 - 150.00
Khaki and green. Antelope.	1917-1926	125.00 - 150.00
Khaki and orange. Rhinoceros.	1917-1926	125.00 - 150.00
Khaki and red. Black Bear.	1917-1926	125.00 - 150.00
Orange and black. Cobra.	1917-1926	125.00 - 150.00
Orange. Hound.	1917-1926	125.00 - 150.00
Pink and black. Hippo.	1917-1926	125.00 - 150.00
Red and gray. Kangaroo.	1917-1926	125.00 - 150.00
Red and white. Buffalo.	1917-1926	125.00 - 150.00
Red, white and blue. Eagle.	1917-1926	125.00 - 150.00
Violet. Tiger.	1917-1926	125.00 - 150.00
White and blue. Elephant.	1917-1926	125.00 - 150.00
White and gray. Moose.	1917-1926	125.00 - 150.00
White and khaki. Bobwhite.	1917-1926	125.00 - 150.00
White and pink. Rattlesnake.	1917-1926	125.00 - 150.00
Yellow and black. Wolf.	1917-1926	125.00 - 150.00
Yellow and brown. Hyena.	1917-1926	125.00 - 150.00
Yellow and green. Fox.	1917-1926	125.00 - 150.00
Yellow and red. Lion.	1917-1926	125.00 - 150.00
Yellow. Panther.	1917-1926	125.00 - 150.00

PATROL PATCHES

Patrol medallion varieties include a square felt, a round felt w/o BSA (top), a round felt w/ BSA (bottom l.), and red twill (bottom r.).

AEROPLANE
Round felt, black image and cut edge.	1927-1933	75.00 - 125.00
Round felt, BSA below black image, cut edge.	1933-1953	5.00 - 10.00

ALLIGATOR
Round felt, black image and cut edge.	1927-1933	75.00 - 125.00
Round felt, BSA below black image, cut edge.	1933-1953	5.00 - 10.00
Round twill, BSA below black image, cut edge.	1953-1971	2.00 - 5.00
Round collared twill, colored image and rolled edge. Two varieties.	1972-1989	1.00 - 2.00
Round tan twill and rolled edge, colored image.	1989	1.00 - 2.00

AMERICAN BISON
Square felt, silk-screened design and border.	1926-1928	400.00 - 600.00
Round felt, black image and cut edge.	1927-1933	75.00 - 125.00
Round felt, BSA below black image, cut edge.	1933-1953	5.00 - 10.00
Round twill, BSA below black image, cut edge.	1953-1971	2.00 - 5.00
Round collared twill, colored image and rolled edge. Five varieties.	1972-1989	1.00 - 2.00
Round tan twill and rolled edge, colored image.	1989	1.00 - 2.00

ANTELOPE
Square felt, silk-screened design and border.	1926-1928	400.00 - 600.00
Round felt, black image and cut edge.	1927-1933	75.00 - 125.00
Round felt, BSA below black image, cut edge.	1933-1953	5.00 - 10.00
Round twill, BSA below black image, cut edge.	1953-1971	2.00 - 5.00
Round collared twill, colored image and rolled edge. Three varieties.	1972-1989	1.00 - 2.00
Round tan twill and rolled edge, colored image.	1989	1.00 - 2.00

BADGER
Square felt, silk-screened design and border.	1926-1928	400.00 - 600.00
Round felt, black image and cut edge.	1927-1933	75.00 - 125.00
Round felt, BSA below black image, cut edge.	1933-1953	5.00 - 10.00
Round twill, BSA below black image, cut edge.	1953-1971	2.00 - 5.00
Round collared twill, colored image and rolled edge. Two varieties.	1972-1989	1.00 - 2.00
Round tan twill and rolled edge, colored image. Two varieties.	1989	1.00 - 2.00

1923 Eagle scout Leo Merchie with patrol ribbon and merit badges on sleeve.

BAT

Square felt, silk-screened design and border.	1926-1928	400.00 - 600.00
Round felt, black image and cut edge.	1927-1933	75.00 - 125.00
Round felt, BSA below black image, cut edge.	1933-1953	5.00 - 10.00
Round twill, BSA below black image, cut edge.	1953-1971	2.00 - 5.00
Round collared twill, colored image and rolled edge. Two varieties	1972-1989	1.00 - 2.00
Round tan twill and rolled edge, colored image.	1989	1.00 - 2.00

BEAR

Square felt, silk-screened design and border.	1926-1928	400.00 - 600.00
Round felt, black image and cut edge.	1927-1933	75.00 - 125.00
Round felt, BSA below black image, cut edge.	1933-1953	5.00 - 10.00
Round twill, BSA below black image, cut edge.	1953-1971	2.00 - 5.00
Round collard twill, colored image and rolled edge. Three varieties	1972-1989	1.00 - 2.00
Round tan twill and rolled edge, colored image.	1989	1.00 - 2.00

BEAVER

Square felt, silk-screened design and border.	1926-1928	400.00 - 600.00
Round felt, black image and cut edge.	1927-1933	75.00 - 125.00
Round felt, BSA below black image, cut edge.	1933-1953	5.00 - 10.00
Round twill, BSA below black image, cut edge.	1953-1971	2.00 - 5.00
Round collard twill, colored image and rolled edge. Two varieties	1972-1989	1.00 - 2.00
Round tan twill and rolled edge, colored image.	1989	1.00 - 2.00

BLACK BEAR

Square felt, silk-screened design and border.	1926-1928	400.00 - 600.00
Round felt, black image and cut edge.	1927-1933	75.00 - 125.00
Round felt, BSA below black image, cut edge.	1933-1953	5.00 - 10.00
Round twill, BSA below black image, cut edge.	1953-1971	2.00 - 5.00

BLANK

Round felt, black cut edge.	1927-1933	75.00 - 125.00
Round felt, BSA below black image, cut edge.	1933-1953	5.00 - 10.00
Round twill, BSA below black image, cut edge.	1953-1971	2.00 - 5.00
Round collard twill, colored image and rolled edge.	1972-1989	1.00 - 2.00
Round tan twill and rolled edge, colored image.	1989	1.00 - 2.00

BLAZING ARROW

Round felt, black image and cut edge.	1927-1933	75.00 - 125.00
Round felt, BSA below black image, cut edge.	1933-1953	5.00 - 10.00
Round twill, BSA below black image, cut edge.	1953-1971	2.00 - 5.00
Round collard twill, colored image and rolled edge. Two varieties.	1972-1989	1.00 - 2.00
Round tan twill and rolled edge, colored image.	1989	1.00 - 2.00

BOBCAT

Round felt, black image and cut edge.	1927-1933	75.00 - 125.00
Round felt, BSA below black image, cut edge.	1933-1953	5.00 - 10.00
Round twill, BSA below black image, cut edge.	1953-1971	2.00 - 5.00
Round collard twill, colored image and rolled edge. Two varieties.	1972-1989	1.00 - 2.00
Round tan twill and rolled edge, colored image.	1989	1.00 - 2.00

BOBWHITE

Square felt, silk-screened design and border.	1926-1928	400.00 - 600.00
Round felt, black image and cut edge.	1927-1933	75.00 - 125.00
Round felt, BSA below black image, cut edge.	1933-1953	5.00 - 10.00
Round twill, BSA below black image, cut edge.	1953-1971	2.00 - 5.00
Round collard twill, colored image and rolled edge. Three varieties	1972-1989	1.00 - 2.00
Round tan twill and rolled edge, colored image.	1989	1.00 - 2.00

BUFFALO

Square felt, silk-screened design and border.	1926-1928	400.00 - 600.00
Round felt, black image and cut edge.	1927-1933	75.00 - 125.00
Round felt, BSA below black image, cut edge.	1933-1953	5.00 - 10.00
Round twill, BSA below black image, cut edge.	1953-1971	2.00 - 5.00
Round twill, BSA below black image, cut edge.	1953-1971	2.00 - 5.00

BULL

Square felt, silk-screened design and border.	1926-1928	400.00 - 600.00
Round felt, black image and cut edge.	1927-1933	75.00 - 125.00
Round felt, BSA below black image, cut edge.	1933-1953	5.00 - 10.00

CAT

Square felt, silk-screened design and border.	1926-1928	400.00 - 600.00
Round felt, black image and cut edge.	1927-1933	75.00 - 125.00
Round felt, BSA below black image, cut edge.	1933-1953	5.00 - 10.00
Round twill, BSA below black image, cut edge.	1953-1971	2.00 - 5.00

COBRA

Square felt, silk-screened design and border.	1926-1928	400.00 - 600.00
Round felt, black image and cut edge.	1927-1933	75.00 - 125.00
Round felt, BSA below black image, cut edge.	1933-1953	5.00 - 10.00
Round twill, BSA below black image, cut edge.	1953-1971	2.00 - 5.00
Round collard twill, colored image and rolled edge.	1972-1989	1.00 - 2.00
Round tan twill and rolled edge, colored image.	1989	1.00 - 2.00

CONDOR

Round felt, black image and cut edge.	1927-1933	75.00 - 125.00
Round felt, BSA below black image, cut edge.	1933-1953	5.00 - 10.00
Round twill, BSA below black image, cut edge.	1953-1971	2.00 - 5.00

COVERED WAGON

Round felt, black image and cut edge.	1927-1933	75.00 - 125.00
Round felt, BSA below black image, cut edge.	1933-1953	5.00 - 10.00
Round twill, BSA below black image, cut edge.	1953-1971	2.00 - 5.00

CROW

Round felt, black image and cut edge.	1927-1933	75.00 - 125.00
Round felt, BSA below black image, cut edge.	1933-1953	5.00 - 10.00
Round twill, BSA below black image, cut edge.	1953-1971	2.00 - 5.00

CUCKOO

Round felt, black image and cut edge.	1927-1933	75.00 - 125.00
Round felt, BSA below black image, cut edge.	1933-1953	5.00 - 10.00
Round twill, BSA below black image, cut edge.	1953-1971	2.00 - 5.00

CURLEU

Round felt, black image and cut edge.	1927-1933	75.00 - 125.00
Round felt, BSA below black image, cut edge.	1933-1953	5.00 - 10.00
Round twill, BSA below black image, cut edge.	1953-1971	2.00 - 5.00

DAN BEARD

Square felt, silk-screened design and border.	1926-1928	400.00 - 600.00
Round felt, black image and cut edge.	1927-1933	75.00 - 125.00
Round felt, BSA below black image, cut edge.	1933-1953	5.00 - 10.00
Round twill, BSA below black image, cut edge.	1953-1971	2.00 - 5.00

DRAGON

Round tan twill and rolled edge, colored image.	1989	1.00 - 2.00

DUCK

Round felt, black image and cut edge.	1927-1933	75.00 - 125.00
Round felt, BSA below black image, cut edge.	1933-1953	5.00 - 10.00
Round twill, BSA below black image, cut edge.	1953-1971	2.00 - 5.00

EAGLE

Square felt, silk-screened design and border.	1926-1928	400.00 - 600.00
Round felt, black image and cut edge.	1927-1933	75.00 - 125.00
Round felt, BSA below black image, cut edge.	1933-1953	5.00 - 10.00
Round twill, BSA below black image, cut edge.	1953-1971	2.00 - 5.00
Round collard twill, colored image and rolled edge. Two varieties	1972-1989	1.00 - 2.00
Round tan twill and rolled edge, colored image.	1989	1.00 - 2.00

ELEPHANT

Square felt, silk-screened design and border.	1926-1928	400.00 - 600.00
Round felt, black image and cut edge.	1927-1933	75.00 - 125.00
Round felt, BSA below black image, cut edge.	1933-1953	5.00 - 10.00

FLYING EAGLE

Square felt, silk-screened design and border.	1926-1928	400.00 - 600.00
Round felt, black image and cut edge.	1927-1933	75.00 - 125.00
Round felt, BSA below black image, cut edge.	1933-1953	5.00 - 10.00
Round twill, BSA below black image, cut edge.	1953-1971	2.00 - 5.00
Round collard twill, colored image and rolled edge. Three varieties	1972-1989	1.00 - 2.00
Round tan twill and rolled edge, colored image.	1989	1.00 - 2.00

FOX

Square felt, silk-screened design and border.	1926-1928	400.00 - 600.00
Round felt, black image and cut edge.	1927-1933	75.00 - 125.00
Round felt, BSA below black image, cut edge.	1933-1953	5.00 - 10.00
Round twill, BSA below black image, cut edge.	1953-1971	2.00 - 5.00
Round collard twill, colored image and rolled edge. Three varieties	1972-1989	1.00 - 2.00
Round tan twill and rolled edge, colored image.	1989	1.00 - 2.00

FROG

Round collard twill, colored image and rolled edge. Five varieties	1972-1989	1.00 - 2.00
Round tan twill and rolled edge, colored image. Two varieties.	1989	1.00 - 2.00

FRONTIERSMAN

Round felt, BSA below black image, cut edge.	1933-1953	5.00 - 10.00
Round twill, BSA below black image, cut edge.	1953-1971	2.00 - 5.00
Round collard twill, colored image and rolled edge. Three varieties.	1972-1989	1.00 - 2.00
Round tan twill and rolled edge, colored image.	1989	1.00 - 2.00

HAWK

Square felt, silk-screened design and border.	1926-1928	400.00 - 600.00
Round felt, black image and cut edge.	1927-1933	75.00 - 125.00
Round felt, BSA below black image, cut edge.	1933-1953	5.00 - 10.00
Round twill, BSA below black image, cut edge.	1953-1971	2.00 - 5.00
Round collard twill, colored image and rolled edge. Two varieties.	1972-1989	1.00 - 2.00
Round tan twill and rolled edge, colored image.	1989	1.00 - 2.00

HIPPO

Square felt, silk-screened design and border.	1926-1928	400.00 - 600.00
Round felt, black image and cut edge.	1927-1933	75.00 - 125.00
Round felt, BSA below black image, cut edge.	1933-1953	5.00 - 10.00

HORSE

Square felt, silk-screened design and border.	1926-1928	400.00 - 600.00
Round felt, black image and cut edge.	1927-1933	75.00 - 125.00
Round felt, BSA below black image, cut edge.	1933-1953	5.00 - 10.00
Round twill, BSA below black image, cut edge.	1953-1971	2.00 - 5.00

HOUND

Square felt, silk-screened design and border.	1926-1928	400.00 - 600.00
Round felt, black image and cut edge.	1927-1933	75.00 - 125.00
Round felt, BSA below black image, cut edge.	1933-1953	5.00 - 10.00
Round twill, BSA below black image, cut edge.	1953-1971	2.00 - 5.00

HYENA

Square felt, silk-screened design and border.	1926-1928	400.00 - 600.00
Round felt, black image and cut edge.	1927-1933	75.00 - 125.00
Round felt, BSA below black image, cut edge.	1933-1953	5.00 - 10.00

INDIAN

Round felt, black image and cut edge.	1927-1933	75.00 - 125.00
Round felt, BSA below black image, cut edge.	1933-1953	5.00 - 10.00
Round twill, BSA below black image, cut edge.	1953-1971	2.00 - 5.00
Round collard twill, colored image and rolled edge. Three varieties.	1972-1989	1.00 - 2.00
Round tan twill and rolled edge, colored image.	1989	1.00 - 2.00

JACKAL

Square felt, silk-screened design and border.	1926-1928	400.00 - 600.00
Round felt, black image and cut edge.	1927-1933	75.00 - 125.00
Round felt, BSA below black image, cut edge.	1933-1953	5.00 - 10.00

KANGAROO

Square felt, silk-screened design and border.	1926-1928	400.00 - 600.00
Round felt, black image and cut edge.	1927-1933	75.00 - 125.00
Round felt, BSA below black image, cut edge.	1933-1953	5.00 - 10.00

LARK

Square felt, silk-screened design and border.	1926-1928	400.00 - 600.00
Round felt, black image and cut edge.	1927-1933	75.00 - 125.00
Round felt, BSA below black image, cut edge.	1933-1953	5.00 - 10.00

LIBERTY

Round collard twill, colored image and rolled edge. Three varieties.	1972-1989	1.00 - 2.00
Round tan twill and rolled edge, colored image.	1989	1.00 - 2.00

LIGHTNING

Round tan twill and rolled edge, colored image.	1989	1.00 - 2.00

LION

Square felt, silk-screened design and border.	1926-1928	400.00 - 600.00
Round felt, black image and cut edge.	1927-1933	75.00 - 125.00
Round felt, BSA below black image, cut edge.	1933-1953	5.00 - 10.00
Round twill, BSA below black image, cut edge.	1953-1971	2.00 - 5.00

LONGHORN

Square felt, silk-screened design and border.	1926-1928	400.00 - 600.00
Round felt, black image and cut edge.	1927-1933	75.00 - 125.00
Round felt, BSA below black image, cut edge.	1933-1953	5.00 - 10.00
Round twill, BSA below black image, cut edge.	1953-1971	2.00 - 5.00

MONGOOSE

Square felt, silk-screened design and border.	1926-1928	400.00 - 600.00
Round felt, black image and cut edge.	1927-1933	75.00 - 125.00
Round felt, BSA below black image, cut edge.	1933-1953	5.00 - 10.00

MOOSE

Square felt, silk-screened design and border.	1926-1928	400.00 - 600.00
Round felt, black image and cut edge.	1927-1933	75.00 - 125.00
Round felt, BSA below black image, cut edge.	1933-1953	5.00 - 10.00
Round twill, BSA below black image, cut edge.	1953-1971	2.00 - 5.00
Round collard twill, colored image and rolled edge.	1972-1989	1.00 - 2.00
Round tan twill and rolled edge, colored image.	1989	1.00 - 2.00

OTTER

Square felt, silk-screened design and border.	1926-1928	400.00 - 600.00
Round felt, black image and cut edge.	1927-1933	75.00 - 125.00
Round felt, BSA below black image, cut edge.	1933-1953	5.00 - 10.00
Round twill, BSA below black image, cut edge.	1953-1971	2.00 - 5.00

OWL

Square felt, silk-screened design and border.	1926-1928	400.00 - 600.00
Round felt, black image and cut edge.	1927-1933	75.00 - 125.00
Round felt, BSA below black image, cut edge.	1933-1953	5.00 - 10.00
Round felt, BSA below black image, cut edge.	1933-1953	5.00 - 10.00
Round twill, BSA below black image, cut edge.	1953-1971	2.00 - 5.00
Round collard twill, colored image and rolled edge. Two varieties.	1972-1989	1.00 - 2.00
Round tan twill and rolled edge, colored image.	1989	1.00 - 2.00

PANTHER

Square felt, silk-screened design and border.	1926-1928	400.00 - 600.00
Round felt, black image and cut edge.	1927-1933	75.00 - 125.00
Round felt, BSA below black image, cut edge.	1933-1953	5.00 - 10.00
Round twill, BSA below black image, cut edge.	1953-1971	2.00 - 5.00
Round collard twill, colored image and rolled edge. Two varieties.	1972-1989	1.00 - 2.00
Round tan twill and rolled edge, colored image. Four varieties.	1989	1.00 - 2.00

PAUL BUNYAN

Round felt, BSA below black image, cut edge.	1933-1953	5.00 - 10.00
Round twill, BSA below black image, cut edge.	1953-1971	2.00 - 5.00

PEACOCK
Square felt, silk-screened design and border.	1926-1928	400.00 - 600.00
Round felt, black image and cut edge.	1927-1933	75.00 - 125.00
Round felt, BSA below black image, cut edge.	1933-1953	5.00 - 10.00

PEDRO
Round twill, BSA below black image, cut edge.	1953-1971	2.00 - 5.00
Round collard twill, colored image and rolled edge. Four varieties.	1972-1989	1.00 - 2.00
Round tan twill and rolled edge, colored image.	1989	1.00 - 2.00

PEEWIT
Square felt, silk-screened design and border.	1926-1928	400.00 - 600.00
Round felt, black image and cut edge.	1927-1933	75.00 - 125.00
Round felt, BSA below black image, cut edge.	1933-1953	5.00 - 10.00

PELICAN
Square felt, silk-screened design and border.	1926-1928	400.00 - 600.00
Round felt, black image and cut edge.	1927-1933	75.00 - 125.00
Round felt, BSA below black image, cut edge.	1933-1953	5.00 - 10.00
Round twill, BSA below black image, cut edge.	1953-1971	2.00 - 5.00

PENGUIN
Round felt, black image and cut edge.	1927-1933	75.00 - 125.00
Round felt, BSA below black image, cut edge.	1933-1953	5.00 - 10.00

PHEASANT
Round collard twill, colored image and rolled edge. Three varieties.	1972-1989	1.00 - 2.00
Round tan twill and rolled edge, colored image.	1989	1.00 - 2.00

PINE TREE
Square felt, silk-screened design and border.	1926-1928	400.00 - 600.00
Round felt, black image and cut edge.	1927-1933	75.00 - 125.00
Round felt, BSA below black image, cut edge.	1933-1953	5.00 - 10.00
Round twill, BSA below black image, cut edge.	1953-1971	2.00 - 5.00
Round collard twill, colored image and rolled edge. Two varieties.	1972-1989	1.00 - 2.00
Round tan twill and rolled edge, colored image.	1989	1.00 - 2.00

PORCUPINE
Round felt, BSA below black image, cut edge.	1933-1953	5.00 - 10.00
Round twill, BSA below black image, cut edge.	1953-1971	2.00 - 5.00

RACCOON
Square felt, silk-screened design and border.	1926-1928	400.00 - 600.00
Round felt, black image and cut edge.	1927-1933	75.00 - 125.00
Round felt, BSA below black image, cut edge.	1933-1953	5.00 - 10.00
Round twill, BSA below black image, cut edge.	1953-1971	2.00 - 5.00
Round collard twill, colored image and rolled edge. Two varieties.	1972-1989	1.00 - 2.00
Round tan twill and rolled edge, colored image.	1989	1.00 - 2.00

RAM
Square felt, silk-screened design and border.	1926-1928	400.00 - 600.00
Round felt, black image and cut edge.	1927-1933	75.00 - 125.00
Round felt, BSA below black image, cut edge.	1933-1953	5.00 - 10.00
Round twill, BSA below black image, cut edge.	1953-1971	2.00 - 5.00
Round collard twill, colored image and rolled edge. Three varieties	1972-1989	1.00 - 2.00
Round tan twill and rolled edge, colored image.	1989	1.00 - 2.00

RATTLESNAKE
Square felt, silk-screened design and border.	1926-1928	400.00 - 600.00
Round felt, black image and cut edge.	1927-1933	75.00 - 125.00
Round felt, BSA below black image, cut edge.	1933-1953	5.00 - 10.00
Round twill, BSA below black image, cut edge.	1953-1971	2.00 - 5.00
Round collard twill, colored image and rolled edge. Two varieties.	1972-1989	1.00 - 2.00
Round tan twill and rolled edge, colored image.	1989	1.00 - 2.00

RAVEN
Square felt, silk-screened design and border.	1926-1928	400.00 - 600.00

Round felt, black image and cut edge.	1927-1933	75.00 - 125.00
Round felt, BSA below black image, cut edge.	1933-1953	5.00 - 10.00
Round twill, BSA below black image, cut edge.	1953-1971	2.00 - 5.00
Round collard twill, colored image and rolled edge. Two varieties.	1972-1989	1.00 - 2.00
Round tan twill and rolled edge, colored image.	1989	1.00 - 2.00

RHINO
Square felt, silk-screened design and border.	1926-1928	400.00 - 600.00
Round felt, black image and cut edge.	1927-1933	75.00 - 125.00
Round felt, BSA below black image, cut edge.	1933-1953	5.00 - 10.00

ROADRUNNER
Round twill, BSA below black image, cut edge.	1953-1971	2.00 - 5.00
Round collard twill, colored image and rolled edge. Three varieties.	1972-1989	1.00 - 2.00
Round tan twill and rolled edge, colored image. Two varieties.	1989	1.00 - 2.00

ROCKET
Round felt, BSA below black image, cut edge.	1933-1953	5.00 - 10.00
Round twill, BSA below black image, cut edge.	1953-1971	2.00 - 5.00

SCORPION
Round tan twill and rolled edge, colored image.	1989	1.00 - 2.00

SEA GULL
Round felt, BSA below black image, cut edge.	1933-1953	5.00 - 10.00
Round twill, BSA below black image, cut edge.	1953-1971	2.00 - 5.00

SEAL
Square felt, silk-screened design and border.	1926-1928	400.00 - 600.00
Round felt, black image and cut edge.	1927-1933	75.00 - 125.00
Round felt, BSA below black image, cut edge.	1933-1953	5.00 - 10.00

SHARK
Round tan twill and rolled edge, colored image.	1989	1.00 - 2.00

SQUIRREL
Round felt, BSA below black image, cut edge.	1933-1953	5.00 - 10.00
Round twill, BSA below black image, cut edge.	1953-1971	2.00 - 5.00

STAG
Square felt, silk-screened design and border.	1926-1928	400.00 - 600.00
Round felt, black image and cut edge.	1927-1933	75.00 - 125.00
Round felt, BSA below black image, cut edge.	1933-1953	5.00 - 10.00
Round collard twill, colored image and rolled edge.	1972-1989	1.00 - 2.00
Round tan twill and rolled edge, colored image.	1989	1.00 - 2.00

STORK
Square felt, silk-screened design and border.	1926-1928	400.00 - 600.00
Round felt, black image and cut edge.	1927-1933	75.00 - 125.00
Round felt, BSA below black image, cut edge.	1933-1953	5.00 - 10.00

SWALLOW
Square felt, silk-screened design and border.	1926-1928	400.00 - 600.00
Round felt, black image and cut edge.	1927-1933	75.00 - 125.00
Round felt, BSA below black image, cut edge.	1933-1953	5.00 - 10.00

TIGER
Square felt, silk-screened design and border.	1926-1928	400.00 - 600.00
Round felt, black image and cut edge.	1927-1933	75.00 - 125.00
Round felt, BSA below black image, cut edge.	1933-1953	5.00 - 10.00
Round twill, BSA below black image, cut edge.	1953-1971	2.00 - 5.00
Round collard twill, colored image and rolled edge.	1972-1989	1.00 - 2.00
Round tan twill and rolled edge, colored image.	1989	1.00 - 2.00

VIKING
Round collard twill, colored image and rolled edge. Two varieties.	1972-1989	1.00 - 2.00
Round tan twill and rolled edge, colored image.	1989	1.00 - 2.00

WHIPPOORWILL

Square felt, silk-screened design and border.	1926-1928	400.00 - 600.00
Round felt, black image and cut edge.	1927-1933	75.00 - 125.00
Round felt, BSA below black image, cut edge.	1933-1953	5.00 - 10.00
Round twill, BSA below black image, cut edge.	1953-1971	2.00 - 5.00

WILD BOAR

Square felt, silk-screened design and border.	1926-1928	400.00 - 600.00
Round felt, black image and cut edge.	1927-1933	75.00 - 125.00
Round felt, BSA below black image, cut edge.	1933-1953	5.00 - 10.00

WOLF

Square felt, silk-screened design and border.	1926-1928	400.00 - 600.00
Round felt, black image and cut edge.	1927-1933	75.00 - 125.00
Round felt, BSA below black image, cut edge.	1933-1953	5.00 - 10.00
Round twill, BSA below black image, cut edge.	1953-1971	2.00 - 5.00
Round collard twill, colored image and rolled edge. Three varieties	1972-1989	1.00 - 2.00
Round tan twill and rolled edge, colored image.	1989	1.00 - 2.00

WOLVERINE

Round felt, black image and cut edge.	1927-1933	75.00 - 125.00
Round felt, BSA below black image, cut edge.	1933-1953	5.00 - 10.00
Round twill, BSA below black image, cut edge.	1953-1971	2.00 - 5.00
Round tan twill and rolled edge, colored image.	1989	1.00 - 2.00

WOOD PIGEON

Square felt, silk-screened design and border.	1926-1928	400.00 - 600.00
Round felt, black image and cut edge.	1927-1933	75.00 - 125.00
Round felt, BSA below black image, cut edge.	1933-1953	5.00 - 10.00

WOODPECKER

Square felt, silk-screened design and border.	1926-1928	400.00 - 600.00
Round felt, black image and cut edge.	1927-1933	75.00 - 125.00
Round felt, BSA below black image, cut edge.	1933-1953	5.00 - 10.00
Round twill, BSA below black image, cut edge.	1953-1971	2.00 - 5.00

PRIVATE ISSUE, COMMERCIALLY PRODUCED TWO COLOR FELT

Heart.	1925-1930	20.00 - 30.00
Star.	1925-1930	20.00 - 30.00
Pine Tree.	1925-1930	20.00 - 30.00

MERIT BADGE PAMPHLETS, LISTINGS BY BADGE

Until 1915, when separate pamphlets made an appearance, merit badge requirements were printed in the *Scout Handbook*. There have been nine major types of covers with several minor varieties in the early types and numerous printing dates in the later issues of these pamphlets.

The first type is the "White Cover." The first variety (1a) and the interior were printed on the same weight paper stock. Its title is "BE PREPARED for Merit Badge Examinations," and there is a line drawing of a scene, which includes the badge design and name. The second variety (1b) of the White Covers has an ornate frame design around the requirements and a line illustration below. Both "White Cover" varieties were issue concurrently, from roughly 1918–1922.

The second major type of pamphlet cover is the "Brown or Tan Cover." Above a large colored illustration there is the title of the badge, and below there is a First-Class emblem, Merit Badge Series, and the National Office name and address. There are four varieties of the type, which are easy to distinguish by the phrasing of the national address. The first (2a) has "200 Fifth Ave. New York City" on two lines (1925–1928). The second variety (2b) has "Two Park/Avenue New York City" on two lines (1928–1939, but some into the mid-1940s); this is the most common brown-covered pamphlet. The third variety (2c) has "Two Park/Avenue New York, N.Y." on two lines (1936–1939); this is the hardest brown-covered pamphlet to find. The fourth variety (2d) has "Two Park Avenue, New York, N.Y." on one line (1937–1939).

The third major type (3) of pamphlet is the "Standing Scout Cover." A uniformed scout (in color) stands to the left of a vertical red stripe. Sometimes this is called the "vertical red and white." It was in use from 1939–1944. Value 7.50 - 12.50 each.

The fourth type (4) is the "Red & White Cover." Used from 1944–1952, the design has the badge name and design in black on the white top half, and a red bottom area with the National Office information. There are two collectible varieties based on the thickness of the cover stock. A heavy cardboard stock was used in 1944 and 1945, then it was changed to a lighter weight and coated card stock.

The fifth type (5) is the "Photo Red Covers," in use from 1949–1966. This is the most common of all pamphlet cover designs, due to its long use and use during scouting's membership peak. The top half has a photo of a scout doing something relating to the badge, and the lower portion remained red as in the fourth type. Changes appear in some photos in later printings.

The sixth type (6) is the "Full Photo Cover" in use from 1966–1971. There is no red stripe, the badge name appears at the top, and a line drawing of the badge appears in a red circle in the lower right corner. Changes appear in some photos in later printings. Value 1.00 - 3.00 each.

The seventh type (7) is the "Green Stripe Top," which made its introduction with the "improved" scouting program of 1971–1979. The badge name in black outlined letters appears on a light green background above a full photo. Changes appear in some photos in later printings.

The eighth type (8) is the "Red Stripe Top," which was introduced in 1980. It has the merit badge name within a red stripe at the top and a full photo. Changes appear in some photos in later printings.

The ninth type (blue) is for Air Scout program and was introduced in 1940 and used until 1949. The covers are blue.

Serious collectors of merit badge pamphlets wishing additional information should consider Joseph Price's detailed *Kahuna Katalog of Merit Badge Pamphlets.*

AERODYNAMICS	Blue.
AERONAUTICS	Blue.
AGRIBUSINESS	8.
AGRICULTURE	1a, b; 2a, b, c, d; 3, 4, 5, 6, 7.
AIRPLANE DESIGN	Blue, 4.
AIRPLANE STRUCTURE	Blue, 4.
AMERICAN BUSINESS	6, 7, 8.
AMERICAN CULTURES	8.
AMERICAN HERITAGE	7, 8.
AMERICAN LABOR	8.
ANGLING	1a, b; 2a, b, c, d; 3, 4.
ANIMAL INDUSTRY	2a, b, c, d; 3, 4, 5, 6, 7.
ANIMAL SCIENCE	7, 8.
ARCHERY	1a, b; 2a, b, c, d; 3, 4, 5, 6, 7, 8.
ARCHITECTURE	1a, b; 2a, b, c, d; 3, 4, 5, 6, 7, 8.
ART	1a, b; 2a, b, c, d; 3, 4, 5, 6, 7, 8.
ASTRONOMY	1a, b; 2a, b, c, d; 3, 4, 5, 6, 7, 8.
ATHLETICS	1a, b; 2a, b, c, d; 3, 4, 5, 6, 7, 8.
ATOMIC ENERGY	5, 6, 7, 8, special yellow cover edition.
AUTOMOBILING	1a, b; 2a, b, c, d; 3, 4, 5.
AUTOMOTIVE SAFETY	5, 6, 7.
AVIATION	1a, b; 2a, b, c, d; 3, 5, 6, 7, 8.
BACKPACKING	8.
BASKETRY	2a, b, c, d; 3, 4, 5, 6, 7, 8.
BEE KEEPING	1, 2a, b, c, d; 4, 5, 6, 7, 8.
BEEF PRODUCTION	2a, b, c, d; 4, 5, 6, 7.
BIRD STUDY (ORNITHOLOGY)	1a, b; 2a, b, c, d; 3, 4, 5, 6, 7, 8.
BLACKSMITHING	1a, b; 2a, b, c, d; 3, 4.
BOOKBINDING	2a, b, c, d; 3, 4, 5, 6, 7, 8.
BOTANY	1a, b; 2a, b, c, d; 3, 4, 5, 6, 7, 8.
BUSINESS	1a, b; 2a, b, c, d; 3, 4, 5.
CAMPING	1a, b; 2a, b, c, d; 3, 4, 5, 6, 7, 8.
CANOEING	2a, b, c, d; 3, 4, 5, 6, 7, 8.
CARPENTRY	1a, b; 2a, b, c, d; 3, 4.
CEMENT WORK	1a, b; 2a, b, c, d; 3, 4, 5.
CHEMISTRY	2a, b, c, d; 3, 4, 5, 6, 7, 8.
CITIZENSHIP	6.
CITIZENSHIP IN THE COMMUNITY	7, 8.
CITIZENSHIP IN THE NATION	7, 8.
CITIZENSHIP IN THE WORLD	7, 8.
CITRUS FRUIT CULTURE	2a, b, c, d.
CIVICS	1a, b; 2a, b, c, d; 3, 4.
COIN COLLECTING	2a, b, c, d; 4, 5, 6, 7, 8.
COLONIAL PHILADELPHIA	Special council pamphlet.
COMMUNICATIONS	6, 7, 8.
COMPUTERS	6, 7, 8.
CONSERVATION	1a, b; 2a, b, c, d; 3, 4.
CONSERVATION OF NATURAL RESOURCES	6.
CONSUMER BUYING	7, 8.
COOKING	1a, b; 2a, b, c, d; 3, 4, 5, 6, 7, 8.
CORN FARMING	2a, b, c, d; 3, 4, 5, 6, 7.
COTTON FARMING	2a, b, c, d; 4, 5, 6, 7.
CRAFTSMANSHIP - BASKETRY	1, 2a, b, c, d.
CRAFTSMANSHIP - BOOKBINDING	1, 2a, b, c, d.
CRAFTSMANSHIP - CEMENT	1, 2a, b, c, d.
CRAFTSMANSHIP - LEATHER	1, 2a, b, c, d.
CRAFTSMANSHIP - METAL	1, 2a, b, c, d.
CRAFTSMANSHIP - POTTERY	1, 2a, b, c, d.
CRAFTSMANSHIP - WOOD	1, 2a, b, c, d.
CRAFTSMANSHIP - WOOD CARVING	1, 2a, b, c, d.
CYCLING	1a, b; 2a, b, c, d; 3, 4, 5, 6, 7, 8.
DAIRYING	1a, b; 2a, b, c, d; 3, 4, 5, 6, 7.
DENTISTRY	7, 8.
DOG CARE	2a, b, c, d; 3, 4, 5, 6, 7, 8.
DRAFTING	5, 6, 7, 8.
DRAMATICS	2a, b, c, d; 4, 5.
ELECTRICITY	1a, b; 2a, b, c, d; 3, 4, 5, 6, 7, 8.
ELECTRONICS	5, 6, 7, 8.
EMERGENCY PREPAREDNESS	7, 8.
ENERGY	7, 8.
ENGINEERING	6, 7, 8.
ENVIRONMENTAL SCIENCE	7, 8.
FARM & RANCH MANAGEMENT	8.
FARM ARRANGEMENTS	5, 6, 7.
FARM HOME AND ITS PLANNING	2a, b, c, d; 4.

FARM LAYOUT AND BUILDING ARRANGEMENT	2a, b, c, d; 4, 5.
FARM MECHANICS	2a, b, c, d; 4, 5, 6, 7, 8.
FARM RECORDS	5, 6, 7.
FARM RECORDS & BOOKKEEPING	2a, b, c, d; 4, 5.
FINGERPRINTING	2a, b, c, d; 3, 4, 5, 6, 7, 8, special Jamboree printing.
FIREMANSHIP	1a, b; 2a, b, c, d; 3, 4, 5, 6, 7, 8.
FIRST AID	1a, b; 2a, b, c, d; 3, 4, 5, 6, 7, 8.
FIRST AID TO ANIMALS	1a, b; 2a, b, c, d; 3, 4, 5, 6.
FISH & WILDLIFE MANAGEMENT	7, 8.
FISHING	4, 5, 6, 7, 8.
FOOD SYSTEMS	7, 8.
FORAGE CROPS	5, 6, 7.
FORESTRY	1a, b; 2a, b, c, d; 3, 4, 5, 6, 7, 8.
FOUNDRY PRACTICE	2a, b, c, d; 4.
FRUIT AND NUT GROWING	5, 6, 7.
FRUIT CULTURE	2a, b, c, d; 4.
GARDENING	1a, b; 2a, b, c, d; 3, 4, 5, 6, 7, 8.
GENEALOGY	7, 8.
GENERAL SCIENCE	7, 8.
GEOLOGY	5, 6, 7, 8.
GOLF	7, 8.
GRAPHIC ARTS	8.
GRASSES, LEGUMES & FORAGE CROPS	2a, b, c, d; 4, 5.
HANDICAPPED AWARENESS	8.
HANDICRAFT	6, 7, 8.
HIKING	1a, b; 2a, b, c, d; 3, 4, 5, 6, 7, 8.
HOG & PORK PRODUCTION	2a, b, c, d; 4, 5.
HOG PRODUCTION	5, 6, 7.
HOME REPAIRS	3, 4, 5, 6, 7, 8.
HORSEMANSHIP	1a, b; 2a, b, c, d; 3, 4, 5, 6, 7, 8.
INDIAN LORE	2a, b, c, d; 3, 4, 5, 6, 7, 8.
INSECT LIFE	2a, b, c, d; 4, 5, 6, 7, 8.
INSECT STUDY	8.
INTERPRETING	1a, b; 2a, b, c, d; 4.
JOURNALISM	2a, b, c, d; 3, 4, 5, 6, 7, 8.
LANDSCAPE ARCHITECTURE	6, 7, 8.
LANDSCAPE GARDENING	2a, b, c, d; 3, 4, 5.
LANDSCAPING	5.
LAW	7, 8.
LEATHERCRAFT	2a, b, c, d; 3, 4.
LEATHERWORK	2a, b, c, d; 3, 4, 5, 6, 7, 8.
LEATHERWORKING	1a, b; 2a, b, c, d.
LIFESAVING	1a, b; 2a, b, c, d; 3, 4, 5, 6, 7, 8.
MACHINERY	1a, b; 2a, b, c, d; 3, 4, 5, 6, 7, 8.
MAMMAL STUDY	8.
MAMMALS	6, 7, 8.
MARKSMANSHIP	1a, b; 2a, b, c, d; 3, 4, 5.
MASONRY	1a, b; 2a, b, c, d; 3, 4, 5, 6, 7, 8.
MECHANICAL DRAWING	2a, b, c, d; 4, 5.
METAL WORK	1a, b; 2a, b, c, d; 3, 4, 5, 6, 7, 8.
METALLURGY	6.
METALS ENGINEERING	7, 8.
MINING	1a, b; 2a, b, c, d.
MODEL DESIGN & BUILDING	5, 6, 7, 8.
MOTORBOATING	5, 6, 7, 8.
MUSIC & BUGLING	1a, b; 2a, b, c, d; 3, 4, 5, 6, 7, 8.
NATURE	5, 6, 7, 8.
NUT CULTURE	2a, b, c, d; 4.
OCEANOGRAPHY	5, 6, 7, 8.
ORIENTEERING	7, 8.
PAINTING	1a, b; 2a, b, c, d; 3, 4, 5, 6, 7, 8.
PATHFINDING	1a, b; 2a, b, c, d; 3, 4, 5.
PERSONAL FINANCES	5, 6.
PERSONAL FITNESS	5, 6, 7, 8.
PERSONAL HEALTH	1a, b; 2a, b, c, d; 3, 4.
PERSONAL MANAGEMENT	7, 8.
PETS	5, 6, 7, 8.
PHOTOGRAPHY	1a, b; 2a, b, c, d; 3, 4, 5, 6, 7, 8.
PHYSICAL DEVELOPMENT	1a, b; 2a, b, c, d; 3, 4.
PIGEON RAISING	2a, b, c, d; 3, 4, 5, 6, 7.
PIONEERING	1a, b; 2a, b, c, d; 3, 4, 5, 6, 7, 8.
PLANT SCIENCE	7, 8.
PLUMBING	1a, b; 2a, b, c, d; 3, 4, 5, 6, 7, 8.
POTTERY	2a, b, c, d; 3, 4, 5, 6, 7, 8.
POULTRY KEEPING	1a, b; 2a, b, c, d; 3, 4, 5, 6, 7.
PRINTING	1a, b; 2a, b, c, d; 3, 4, 5, 6, 7, 8.
PRINTING COMMUNICATION	8.
PUBLIC HEALTH	1a, b; 2a, b, c, d; 3, 4, 5, 6, 7, 8.
PUBLIC SPEAKING	2a, b, c, d; 4, 5, 6, 7, 8.
PULP & PAPER	7, 8.

RABBIT RAISING	4, 5, 6, 7, 8.
RADIO	1a, b; 2a, b, c, d; 3, 4, 5, 6, 7, 8.
RAILROADING	5, 6, 7, 8, special AAR edition.
READING	2a, b, c, d; 3, 4, 5, 6, 7, 8.
REPTILE STUDY	2, b, c, d; 4, 5, 6, 7, 8.
RIFLE & SHOTGUN SHOOTING	6, 7, 8.
RIFLE SHOOTING	8.
ROCKS & MINERALS	2a, b, c, d; 3, 4.
ROWING	2a, b, c, d; 3, 4, 5, 6, 7, 8.
SAFETY	2a, b, c, d; 3, 4, 5, 6, 7, 8.
SAFETY FIRST	1a, b; 2a, b, c, d.
SALESMANSHIP	2a, b, c, d; 4, 5, 6, 7, 8.
SCHOLARSHIP	1a, b; 2a, b, c, d; 3, 4, 5, 6, 7, 8.
SCULPTURE	1a, b; 2a, b, c, d; 4, 5, 6, 7, 8.
SEAMANSHIP	1a, b; 2a, b, c, d; 3, 4, 5.
SHEEP FARMING	2a, b, c, d; 4, 5, 6, 7.
SHOTGUN SHOOTING	8.
SIGNALING	1a, b; 2a, b, c, d; 3, 4, 5, 6, 7, 8.
SKATING	7, 8.
SKIING	2a, b, c, d; 3, 4, 5, 6, 7, 8.
SMALL BOAT SAILING	6, 7, 8.
SMALL GRAINS	5, 6, 7.
SMALL GRAINS & CEREAL FOODS	3, 4, 5.
SOIL & WATER CONSERVATION	5, 6, 7, 8.
SOIL MANAGEMENT	2a, b, c, d; 3, 4.
SPACE EXPLORATION	6, 7, 8.
SPORTS	7, 8.
STALKING	1a, b; 2a, b, c, d; 3, 4.
STAMP COLLECTING	2a, b, c, d; 3, 4, 5, 6, 7, 8.
SURVEYING	1a, b; 2a, b, c, d; 3, 4, 5, 6, 7, 8.
SWIMMING	1a, b; 2a, b, c, d; 3, 4, 5, 6, 7, 8.
TAXIDERMY	1a, b; 2a, b, c, d; 3, 4.
TEXTILES	2a, b, c, d; 3, 4, 5, 6, 7, 8.
THEATER	6, 7, 8.
TRAFFIC SAFETY	7, 8.
TRUCK TRANSPORTATION	7, 8.
VETERINARY SCIENCE	7, 8.
WATER SKIING	6, 7, 8.
WEATHER	2a, b, c, d; 3, 4, 5, 6, 7, 8.
WHITEWATER	8.
WILDERNESS SURVIVAL	7, 8.

WILDLIFE MANAGEMENT	5, 6, special 1953 Jamboree issue.
WIRELESS	1a, b.
WOOD TURNING	2a, b, c, d; 3, 4.
WOOD WORK	2a, b, c, d; 3, 4, 5, 6, 7, 8.
WOODCARVING	2a, b, c, d; 3, 4, 5, 6, 7, 8.
ZOOLOGY	2a, b, c, d; 3, 4, 5, 6.

Eagle scout with narro crimped merit badges.

MERIT BADGE PAMPHLETS, BY TYPE

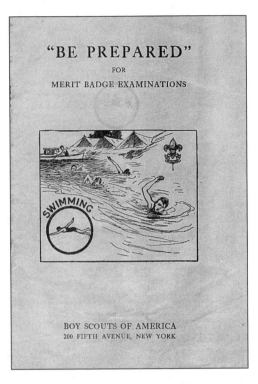

WHITE COVER, "BE PREPARED" FOR MERIT BADGE EXAMINATIONS TITLE, ILLUSTRATION BELOW

Agriculture.	1918-1922	75.00 - 100.00
Angling.	1918-1922	75.00 - 100.00
Archery.	1918-1922	75.00 - 100.00
Architecture.	1918-1922	75.00 - 100.00
Art.	1918-1922	75.00 - 100.00
Astronomy.	1918-1922	75.00 - 100.00
Athletics.	1918-1922	75.00 - 100.00
Aviation.	1918-1922	75.00 - 100.00
Bee Keeping.	1918-1922	75.00 - 100.00
Bird Study.	1918-1922	75.00 - 100.00
Blacksmithing.	1918-1922	75.00 - 100.00
Botany.	1918-1922	75.00 - 100.00
Business.	1918-1922	75.00 - 100.00
Camping.	1918-1922	75.00 - 100.00
Carpentry.	1918-1922	75.00 - 100.00
Cement Work.	1918-1922	75.00 - 100.00
Cooking.	1918-1922	75.00 - 100.00
Craftsmanship - Basketry.	1918-1922	75.00 - 100.00
Craftsmanship - Bookbinding.	1918-1922	75.00 - 100.00
Craftsmanship - Cement.	1918-1922	75.00 - 100.00
Craftsmanship - Leather.	1918-1922	75.00 - 100.00
Craftsmanship - Metal.	1918-1922	75.00 - 100.00
Craftsmanship - Pottery.	1918-1922	75.00 - 100.00
Craftsmanship - Wood Carving.	1918-1922	75.00 - 100.00
Craftsmanship - Wood.	1918-1922	75.00 - 100.00
Cycling.	1918-1922	75.00 - 100.00
Dairying.	1918-1922	75.00 - 100.00
Electricity.	1918-1922	75.00 - 100.00
Firemanship.	1918-1922	75.00 - 100.00
First Aid to Animals.	1918-1922	75.00 - 100.00
First Aid.	1918-1922	75.00 - 100.00
Forestry.	1918-1922	75.00 - 100.00
Gardening.	1918-1922	75.00 - 100.00
Hiking.	1918-1922	75.00 - 100.00
Horsemanship.	1918-1922	75.00 - 100.00

Interperting.	1918-1922	75.00 - 100.00
Leatherwork.	1918-1922	75.00 - 100.00
Machinery.	1918-1922	75.00 - 100.00
Marksmanship.	1918-1922	75.00 - 100.00
Metal Work.	1918-1922	75.00 - 100.00
Mining.	1918-1922	75.00 - 100.00
Music & Bugling.	1918-1922	75.00 - 100.00
Ornithology.	1918-1922	75.00 - 100.00
Painting.	1918-1922	75.00 - 100.00
Pathfinding.	1918-1922	75.00 - 100.00
Personal Health.	1918-1922	75.00 - 100.00
Photography.	1918-1922	75.00 - 100.00
Physical Development.	1918-1922	75.00 - 100.00
Pioneering.	1918-1922	75.00 - 100.00
Plumbing.	1918-1922	75.00 - 100.00
Poultry Keeping.	1918-1922	75.00 - 100.00
Printing.	1918-1922	75.00 - 100.00
Public Health.	1918-1922	75.00 - 100.00
Radio.	1918-1922	75.00 - 100.00
Safety First.	1918-1922	75.00 - 100.00
Scholarship.	1918-1922	75.00 - 100.00
Sculpture.	1918-1922	75.00 - 100.00
Seamanship.	1918-1922	75.00 - 100.00
Signaling.	1918-1922	75.00 - 100.00
Stalking.	1918-1922	75.00 - 100.00
Swimming.	1918-1922	75.00 - 100.00
Taxidermy.	1918-1922	75.00 - 100.00
Wireless.	1918-1922	75.00 - 100.00

WHITE COVER, BADGE TITLE AND REQUIREMENTS CENTERED, ILLUSTRATION BELOW

Agriculture.	1918-1922	75.00 - 100.00
Angling.	1918-1922	75.00 - 100.00
Archery.	1918-1922	75.00 - 100.00
Architecture.	1918-1922	75.00 - 100.00
Art.	1918-1922	75.00 - 100.00
Astronomy.	1918-1922	75.00 - 90.00
Automobiling.	1918-1922	75.00 - 100.00
Aviation.	1918-1922	75.00 - 100.00
Bee Keeping.	1918-1922	75.00 - 100.00

Blacksmithing.	1918-1922	75.00 - 100.00
Botany.	1918-1922	75.00 - 100.00
Business.	1918-1922	75.00 - 100.00
Camping.	1918-1922	75.00 - 100.00
Carpentry.	1918-1922	75.00 - 100.00
Cement Work.	1918-1922	75.00 - 100.00
Civics.	1918-1922	75.00 - 100.00
Conservation.	1918-1922	75.00 - 100.00
Cooking.	1918-1922	75.00 - 100.00
Craftsmanship - Basketry.	1918-1922	75.00 - 100.00
Craftsmanship - Bookbinding.	1918-1922	75.00 - 100.00
Craftsmanship - Cement.	1918-1922	75.00 - 100.00
Craftsmanship - Leather.	1918-1922	75.00 - 100.00
Craftsmanship - Metal.	1918-1922	75.00 - 100.00
Craftsmanship - Pottery.	1918-1922	75.00 - 100.00
Craftsmanship - Wood Carving.	1918-1922	75.00 - 100.00
Craftsmanship - Wood.	1918-1922	75.00 - 100.00
Cycling.	1918-1922	75.00 - 100.00
Dairying.	1918-1922	75.00 - 100.00
Electricity.	1918-1922	75.00 - 100.00
Firemanship.	1918-1922	75.00 - 100.00
First Aid to Animals.	1918-1922	75.00 - 100.00
First Aid.	1918-1922	75.00 - 100.00
Forestry.	1918-1922	75.00 - 100.00
Gardening.	1918-1922	75.00 - 100.00
Hiking.	1918-1922	75.00 - 100.00
Horsemanship.	1918-1922	75.00 - 100.00
Interpreting.	1918-1922	75.00 - 100.00
Leatherwork.	1918-1922	75.00 - 100.00
Lifesaving.	1918-1922	75.00 - 100.00
Machinery.	1918-1922	75.00 - 100.00
Marksmanship.	1918-1922	75.00 - 100.00
Masonry.	1918-1922	75.00 - 100.00
Metal Work.	1918-1922	75.00 - 100.00
Mining.	1918-1922	75.00 - 100.00
Music & Bugling.	1918-1922	75.00 - 100.00
Ornithology.	1918-1922	75.00 - 100.00
Painting.	1918-1922	75.00 - 100.00
Pathfinding.	1918-1922	75.00 - 100.00
Personal Health.	1918-1922	75.00 - 100.00
Photogrpahy.	1918-1922	75.00 - 100.00
Physical Development.	1918-1922	75.00 - 100.00
Pioneering.	1918-1922	75.00 - 100.00
Plumbing.	1918-1922	75.00 - 100.00
Poultry Keeping.	1918-1922	75.00 - 100.00
Printing.	1918-1922	75.00 - 100.00
Public Health.	1918-1922	75.00 - 100.00
Radio.	1918-1922	75.00 - 100.00
Safety First.	1918-1922	75.00 - 100.00
Scholarship.	1918-1922	75.00 - 100.00
Sculpture.	1918-1922	75.00 - 100.00
Seamanship.	1918-1922	75.00 - 100.00
Signaling.	1918-1922	75.00 - 100.00
Stalking.	1918-1922	75.00 - 100.00
Surveying.	1918-1922	75.00 - 100.00
Swimming.	1918-1922	75.00 - 100.00
Taxidermy.	1918-1922	75.00 - 100.00
Wireless.	1918-1922	75.00 - 100.00

AIR SCOUT BLUE COVER

Aerodynamics.	1940-1949	35.00 - 50.00
Aeronautics.	1940-1949	35.00 - 50.00
Airplane Design.	1940-1949	35.00 - 50.00
Airplane Structure.	1940-1949	35.00 - 50.00

BROWN COVER, BADGE TITLE AND ILLUSTRATION, ADDRESS AS 200 FIFTH AVENUE, NEW YORK CITY

Agriculture.	1925-1928	8.50 - 12.50
Angling.	1925-1928	8.50 - 12.50
Animal Industry.	1925-1928	8.50 - 12.50
Archery.	1925-1928	8.50 - 12.50
Architecture.	1925-1928	8.50 - 12.50
Art.	1925-1928	8.50 - 12.50
Astronomy.	1925-1928	8.50 - 12.50
Athletics.	1925-1928	8.50 - 12.50
Automobiling.	1925-1928	8.50 - 12.50
Aviation.	1925-1928	8.50 - 12.50
Basketry.	1925-1928	8.50 - 12.50
Bee Keeping.	1925-1928	8.50 - 12.50
Beef Production.	1925-1928	8.50 - 12.50
Bird Study.	1925-1928	8.50 - 12.50
Blacksmithing.	1925-1928	8.50 - 12.50
Bookbinding.	1925-1928	8.50 - 12.50
Botany.	1925-1928	8.50 - 12.50
Business.	1925-1928	8.50 - 12.50
Camping.	1925-1928	8.50 - 12.50
Canoeing.	1925-1928	8.50 - 12.50
Carpentry.	1925-1928	8.50 - 12.50
Cement Work.	1925-1928	8.50 - 12.50
Chemistry.	1925-1928	8.50 - 12.50
Citrus Fruit Culture.	1925-1928	8.50 - 12.50
Civics.	1925-1928	8.50 - 12.50
Conservation.	1925-1928	8.50 - 12.50
Cooking.	1925-1928	8.50 - 12.50
Corn Farming.	1925-1928	8.50 - 12.50
Cotton Farming.	1925-1928	8.50 - 12.50
Craftsmanship - Basketry.	1925-1928	8.50 - 12.50
Craftsmanship - Cement.	1925-1928	8.50 - 12.50
Craftsmanship - Leather.	1925-1928	8.50 - 12.50
Craftsmanship - Metal.	1925-1928	8.50 - 12.50
Craftsmanship - Pottery.	1925-1928	8.50 - 12.50
Craftsmanship - Wood Carving.	1925-1928	8.50 - 12.50
Craftsmanship - Wood.	1925-1928	8.50 - 12.50
Cycling.	1925-1928	8.50 - 12.50
Dairying.	1925-1928	8.50 - 12.50
Dog Care.	1925-1928	8.50 - 12.50
Dramatics.	1925-1928	8.50 - 12.50

Electricity.	1925-1928	8.50 - 12.50
Farm Home and Its Planning.	1925-1928	8.50 - 12.50
Farm Mechanics.	1925-1928	8.50 - 12.50
Farm Records & Bookkeeping.	1925-1928	8.50 - 12.50
Fingerprinting.	1925-1928	8.50 - 12.50
Firemanship.	1925-1928	8.50 - 12.50
First Aid to Animals.	1925-1928	8.50 - 12.50
First Aid.	1925-1928	8.50 - 12.50
Forestry.	1925-1928	8.50 - 12.50
Gardening.	1925-1928	8.50 - 12.50
Grasses, Legumes & Forage Crops.	1925-1928	8.50 - 12.50
Hiking.	1925-1928	8.50 - 12.50
Hog & Pork Production.	1925-1928	8.50 - 12.50
Horsemanship.	1925-1928	8.50 - 12.50
Indian Lore.	1925-1928	8.50 - 12.50
Insect Life.	1925-1928	8.50 - 12.50
Interpreting.	1925-1928	8.50 - 12.50
Journalism.	1925-1928	8.50 - 12.50
Landscape Gardening.	1925-1928	8.50 - 12.50
Larm Layout and Building Arrangement.	1925-1928	8.50 - 12.50
Leathercraft.	1925-1928	8.50 - 12.50
Leatherworking.	1925-1928	8.50 - 12.50
Lifesaving.	1925-1928	8.50 - 12.50
Machinery.	1925-1928	8.50 - 12.50
Marksmanship.	1925-1928	8.50 - 12.50
Masonry.	1925-1928	8.50 - 12.50
Mechanical Drawing.	1925-1928	8.50 - 12.50
Metal Work.	1925-1928	8.50 - 12.50
Mining.	1925-1928	8.50 - 12.50
Music & Bugling.	1925-1928	8.50 - 12.50
Nut Culture.	1925-1928	8.50 - 12.50
Painting.	1925-1928	8.50 - 12.50
Pathfinding.	1925-1928	8.50 - 12.50
Personal Health.	1925-1928	8.50 - 12.50
Photography.	1925-1928	8.50 - 12.50
Physical Development.	1925-1928	8.50 - 12.50
Pigeon Raising.	1925-1928	8.50 - 12.50
Pioneering.	1925-1928	8.50 - 12.50
Plumbing.	1925-1928	8.50 - 12.50
Pottery.	1925-1928	8.50 - 12.50
Poultry Keeping.	1925-1928	8.50 - 12.50
Printing.	1925-1928	8.50 - 12.50
Public Health.	1925-1928	8.50 - 12.50
Public Speaking.	1925-1928	8.50 - 12.50
Radio.	1925-1928	8.50 - 12.50
Reading.	1925-1928	8.50 - 12.50
Reptile Study.	1925-1928	8.50 - 12.50
Rocks & Minerals.	1925-1928	8.50 - 12.50
Rowing.	1925-1928	8.50 - 12.50
Safety First.	1925-1928	8.50 - 12.50
Safety.	1925-1928	8.50 - 12.50
Salesmanship.	1925-1928	8.50 - 12.50
Scholarship.	1925-1928	8.50 - 12.50
Sculpture.	1925-1928	8.50 - 12.50
Seamanship.	1925-1928	8.50 - 12.50
Sheep Farming.	1925-1928	8.50 - 12.50
Signaling.	1925-1928	8.50 - 12.50
Skiing.	1925-1928	8.50 - 12.50
Soil Management.	1925-1928	8.50 - 12.50
Stalking.	1925-1928	8.50 - 12.50
Stamp Collecting.	1925-1928	8.50 - 12.50
Surveying.	1925-1928	8.50 - 12.50
Swimming.	1925-1928	8.50 - 12.50
Taxidermy.	1925-1928	8.50 - 12.50
Textiles.	1925-1928	8.50 - 12.50
Weather.	1925-1928	8.50 - 12.50
Wood Turning.	1925-1928	8.50 - 12.50

Wood Work.	1925-1928	8.50 - 12.50
Woodcarving.	1925-1928	8.50 - 12.50
Zoology.	1925-1928	8.50 - 12.50

BROWN COVER, BADGE TITLE AND ILLUSTRATION, ADDRESS AS TWO PARK AVENUE, NEW YORK CITY ON TWO LINES

Agriculture.	1928-1939	5.00 - 10.00
Angling.	1928-1939	5.00 - 10.00
Animal Industry.	1928-1939	5.00 - 10.00
Archery.	1928-1939	5.00 - 10.00
Architecture.	1928-1939	5.00 - 10.00
Art.	1928-1939	5.00 - 10.00
Astronomy.	1928-1939	5.00 - 10.00
Athletics.	1928-1939	5.00 - 10.00
Automobiling.	1928-1939	5.00 - 10.00
Aviation.	1928-1939	5.00 - 10.00
Basketry.	1928-1939	5.00 - 10.00
Bee Keeping.	1928-1939	5.00 - 10.00
Bee Production.	1928-1939	5.00 - 10.00
Bird Study.	1928-1939	5.00 - 10.00
Blacksmithing.	1928-1939	5.00 - 10.00
Bookbinding.	1928-1939	5.00 - 10.00
Business.	1928-1939	5.00 - 10.00
Camping.	1928-1939	5.00 - 10.00
Canoeing.	1928-1939	5.00 - 10.00
Carpentry.	1928-1939	5.00 - 10.00
Cement Work.	1928-1939	5.00 - 10.00
Chemistry.	1928-1939	5.00 - 10.00
Citrus Fruit Culture.	1928-1939	5.00 - 10.00
Civics.	1928-1939	5.00 - 10.00
Coin Collecting.	1928-1939	5.00 - 10.00
Conservation.	1928-1939	5.00 - 10.00
Cooking.	1928-1939	5.00 - 10.00
Corn Farming.	1928-1939	5.00 - 10.00
Cotton Farming.	1928-1939	5.00 - 10.00
Craftsmanship - Basketry.	1928-1939	5.00 - 10.00
Craftsmanship - Bookbinding.	1928-1939	5.00 - 10.00
Craftsmanship - Cement.	1928-1939	5.00 - 10.00
Craftsmanship - Leather.	1928-1939	5.00 - 10.00
Craftsmanship - Metal.	1928-1939	5.00 - 10.00
Craftsmanship - Pottery.	1928-1939	5.00 - 10.00
Craftsmanship - Wood Carving.	1928-1939	5.00 - 10.00

Craftsmanship - Wood.	1928-1939	5.00 - 10.00
Cycling.	1928-1939	5.00 - 10.00
Dairying.	1928-1939	5.00 - 10.00
Dog Care.	1928-1939	5.00 - 10.00
Dramatics.	1928-1939	5.00 - 10.00
Electricity.	1928-1939	5.00 - 10.00
Farm Home and its Planning.	1928-1939	5.00 - 10.00
Farm Layout and Building Arrangement.	1928-1939	5.00 - 10.00
Farm Mechanics.	1928-1939	5.00 - 10.00
Farm Records & Bookkeeping.	1928-1939	5.00 - 10.00
Fingerprinting.	1928-1939	5.00 - 10.00
Firemanship.	1928-1939	5.00 - 10.00
First Aid to Animals.	1928-1939	5.00 - 10.00
First Aid.	1928-1939	5.00 - 10.00
Forestry.	1928-1939	5.00 - 10.00
Foundry Practice.	1928-1939	5.00 - 10.00
Fruit Culture.	1928-1939	5.00 - 10.00
Gardening.	1928-1939	5.00 - 10.00
Grasses, Legumes & Forrage Crops.	1928-1939	5.00 - 10.00
Hiking.	1928-1939	5.00 - 10.00
Hog & Pork Production.	1928-1939	5.00 - 10.00
Horsemanship.	1928-1939	5.00 - 10.00
Indian Lore.	1928-1939	5.00 - 10.00
Insect Life.	1928-1939	5.00 - 10.00
Interpreting.	1928-1939	5.00 - 10.00
Journalism.	1928-1939	5.00 - 10.00
Landscape Gardening.	1928-1939	5.00 - 10.00
Leathercraft.	1928-1939	5.00 - 10.00
Leatherwork.	1928-1939	5.00 - 10.00
Leatherworking.	1928-1939	5.00 - 10.00
Lifesaving.	1928-1939	5.00 - 10.00
Machinery.	1928-1939	5.00 - 10.00
Marksmanship.	1928-1939	5.00 - 10.00
Masonry.	1928-1939	5.00 - 10.00
Mechanical Drawing.	1928-1939	5.00 - 10.00
Metal Work.	1928-1939	5.00 - 10.00
Mining.	1928-1939	5.00 - 10.00
Music & Bugling.	1928-1939	5.00 - 10.00
Nut Culture.	1928-1939	5.00 - 10.00
Painting.	1928-1939	5.00 - 10.00
Pathfinding.	1928-1939	5.00 - 10.00
Personal Health.	1928-1939	5.00 - 10.00
Photography.	1928-1939	5.00 - 10.00
Physical Development.	1928-1939	5.00 - 10.00
Pigeon Raising.	1928-1939	5.00 - 10.00
Pioneering.	1928-1939	5.00 - 10.00
Plumbing.	1928-1939	5.00 - 10.00
Pottery.	1928-1939	5.00 - 10.00
Poultry Keeping.	1928-1939	5.00 - 10.00
Printing.	1928-1939	5.00 - 10.00
Public Health.	1928-1939	5.00 - 10.00
Public Speaking.	1928-1939	5.00 - 10.00
Radio.	1928-1939	5.00 - 10.00
Reading.	1928-1939	5.00 - 10.00
Reptile Study.	1928-1939	5.00 - 10.00
Rocks & Minerals.	1928-1939	5.00 - 10.00
Rowing.	1928-1939	5.00 - 10.00
Safety First.	1928-1939	5.00 - 10.00
Safety.	1928-1939	5.00 - 10.00
Salesmanship.	1928-1939	5.00 - 10.00
Scholarship.	1928-1939	5.00 - 10.00
Sculpture.	1928-1939	5.00 - 10.00
Seamanship.	1928-1939	5.00 - 10.00
Sheep Farming.	1928-1939	5.00 - 10.00
Signaling.	1928-1939	5.00 - 10.00
Skiing.	1928-1939	5.00 - 10.00
Soil Management.	1928-1939	5.00 - 10.00

Stalking.	1928-1939	5.00 - 10.00
Stamp Collecting.	1928-1939	5.00 - 10.00
Surveying.	1928-1939	5.00 - 10.00
Swimming.	1928-1939	5.00 - 10.00
Taxidermy.	1928-1939	5.00 - 10.00
Textiles.	1928-1939	5.00 - 10.00
Weather.	1928-1939	5.00 - 10.00
Wood Turning.	1928-1939	5.00 - 10.00
Wood Work.	1928-1939	5.00 - 10.00
Woodcarving.	1928-1939	5.00 - 10.00
Zoology.	1928-1939	5.00 - 10.00

BROWN COVER, BADGE TITLE AND ILLUSTRATION, ADDRESS AS TWO PARK AVENUE, NEW YORK, N.Y. ON ONE LINE

Agriculture.	1937-1939	7.50 - 12.50
Angling.	1937-1939	7.50 - 12.50
Animal Industry.	1937-1939	7.50 - 12.50
Archery.	1937-1939	7.50 - 12.50
Architecture.	1937-1939	7.50 - 12.50
Art.	1937-1939	7.50 - 12.50
Astronomy.	1937-1939	7.50 - 12.50
Athletics.	1937-1939	7.50 - 12.50
Automobiling.	1937-1939	7.50 - 12.50
Aviation.	1937-1939	7.50 - 12.50
Basketry.	1937-1939	7.50 - 12.50
Bee Keeping.	1937-1939	7.50 - 12.50
Beef Production.	1937-1939	7.50 - 12.50
Bird Study.	1937-1939	7.50 - 12.50
Blacksmithing.	1937-1939	7.50 - 12.50
Bookbinding.	1937-1939	7.50 - 12.50
Botany.	1937-1939	7.50 - 12.50
Business.	1937-1939	7.50 - 12.50
Camping.	1937-1939	7.50 - 12.50
Canoeing.	1937-1939	7.50 - 12.50
Carpentry.	1937-1939	7.50 - 12.50
Cement Work.	1937-1939	7.50 - 12.50
Chemistry.	1937-1939	7.50 - 12.50
Citrus Fruit Culture.	1937-1939	7.50 - 12.50
Civics.	1937-1939	7.50 - 12.50
Coin Collecting.	1937-1939	7.50 - 12.50
Conservation.	1937-1939	7.50 - 12.50
Cooking.	1937-1939	7.50 - 12.50
Corn Farming.	1937-1939	7.50 - 12.50

Cotton Farming.	1937-1939	7.50 - 12.50
Cycling.	1937-1939	7.50 - 12.50
Dairying.	1937-1939	7.50 - 12.50
Dog Care.	1937-1939	7.50 - 12.50
Dramatics.	1937-1939	7.50 - 12.50
Electricity.	1937-1939	7.50 - 12.50
Farm Home and its Planning.	1937-1939	7.50 - 12.50
Farm Layout and Building Arrangement.	1937-1939	7.50 - 12.50
Farm Mechanics.	1937-1939	7.50 - 12.50
Farm Records & Bookkeeping.	1937-1939	7.50 - 12.50
Fingerprinting.	1937-1939	7.50 - 12.50
Firemanship.	1937-1939	7.50 - 12.50
First Aid to Animals.	1937-1939	7.50 - 12.50
First Aid.	1937-1939	7.50 - 12.50
Forestry.	1937-1939	7.50 - 12.50
Foundry Practice.	1937-1939	7.50 - 12.50
Fruit Culture.	1937-1939	7.50 - 12.50
Gardening.	1937-1939	7.50 - 12.50
Grasses, Legumes & Forage Crops.	1937-1939	7.50 - 12.50
Hiking.	1937-1939	7.50 - 12.50
Hog & Pork Production.	1937-1939	7.50 - 12.50
Horsemanship.	1937-1939	7.50 - 12.50
Indian Lore.	1937-1939	7.50 - 12.50
Insect Life.	1937-1939	7.50 - 12.50
Interpreting.	1937-1939	7.50 - 12.50
Journalism.	1937-1939	7.50 - 12.50
Landscape Gardening.	1937-1939	7.50 - 12.50
Leathercraft.	1937-1939	7.50 - 12.50
Leatherwork.	1937-1939	7.50 - 12.50
Leatherworking.	1937-1939	7.50 - 12.50
Lifesaving.	1937-1939	7.50 - 12.50
Machinery.	1937-1939	7.50 - 12.50
Marksmanship.	1937-1939	7.50 - 12.50
Masonry.	1937-1939	7.50 - 12.50
Mechanical Drawing.	1937-1939	7.50 - 12.50
Metal Work.	1937-1939	7.50 - 12.50
Mining.	1937-1939	7.50 - 12.50
Music & Bugling.	1937-1939	7.50 - 12.50
Painting.	1937-1939	7.50 - 12.50
Pathfinding.	1937-1939	7.50 - 12.50
Personal Health.	1937-1939	7.50 - 12.50
Photography.	1937-1939	7.50 - 12.50
Physical Development.	1937-1939	7.50 - 12.50
Pigeon Raising.	1937-1939	7.50 - 12.50
Pioneering.	1937-1939	7.50 - 12.50
Plumbing.	1937-1939	7.50 - 12.50
Pottery.	1937-1939	7.50 - 12.50
Poultry Keeping.	1937-1939	7.50 - 12.50
Printing.	1937-1939	7.50 - 12.50
Public Health.	1937-1939	7.50 - 12.50
Public Speaking.	1937-1939	7.50 - 12.50
Radio.	1937-1939	7.50 - 12.50
Reading.	1937-1939	7.50 - 12.50
Reptile Study.	1937-1939	7.50 - 12.50
Rocks & Minerals.	1937-1939	7.50 - 12.50
Rowing.	1937-1939	7.50 - 12.50
Safety.	1937-1939	7.50 - 12.50
Safety.	1937-1939	7.50 - 12.50
Salesmanship.	1937-1939	7.50 - 12.50
Scholarship.	1937-1939	7.50 - 12.50
Sculpture.	1937-1939	7.50 - 12.50
Seamanship.	1937-1939	7.50 - 12.50
Sheep Farming.	1937-1939	7.50 - 12.50
Signaling.	1937-1939	7.50 - 12.50
Skiing.	1937-1939	7.50 - 12.50
Soil Management.	1937-1939	7.50 - 12.50
Stalking.	1937-1939	7.50 - 12.50

Stamp Collecting.	1937-1939	7.50 - 12.50
Surveying.	1937-1939	7.50 - 12.50
Swimming.	1937-1939	7.50 - 12.50
Taxidermy.	1937-1939	7.50 - 12.50
Textiles.	1937-1939	7.50 - 12.50
Weather.	1937-1939	7.50 - 12.50
Wood Turning.	1937-1939	7.50 - 12.50
Wood Work.	1937-1939	7.50 - 12.50
Woodcarving.	1937-1939	7.50 - 12.50
Zoology.	1937-1939	7.50 - 12.50

BROWN COVER, BADGE TITLE AND ILLUSTRATION, ADDRESS AS TWO PARK AVENUE, NEW YORK, N.Y. ON TWO LINES

Agriculture.	1936-1939	15.00 - 20.00
Angling.	1936-1939	15.00 - 20.00
Animal Industry.	1936-1939	15.00 - 20.00
Archery.	1936-1939	15.00 - 20.00
Architecture.	1936-1939	15.00 - 20.00
Art.	1936-1939	15.00 - 20.00
Astronomy.	1936-1939	15.00 - 20.00
Athletics.	1936-1939	15.00 - 20.00
Automobiling.	1936-1939	15.00 - 20.00
Aviation.	1936-1939	15.00 - 20.00
Basketry.	1936-1939	15.00 - 20.00
Bee Keeping.	1936-1939	15.00 - 20.00
Bird Study.	1936-1939	15.00 - 20.00
Blacksmithing.	1936-1939	15.00 - 20.00
Bookbinding.	1936-1939	15.00 - 20.00
Botany.	1936-1939	15.00 - 20.00
Business.	1936-1939	15.00 - 20.00
Camping.	1936-1939	15.00 - 20.00
Canoeing.	1936-1939	15.00 - 20.00
Carpentry.	1936-1939	15.00 - 20.00
Cement Work.	1936-1939	15.00 - 20.00
Chemistry.	1936-1939	15.00 - 20.00
Citrus Fruit Culture.	1936-1939	15.00 - 20.00
Civics.	1936-1939	15.00 - 20.00
Coin Collecting.	1936-1939	15.00 - 20.00
Conservation.	1936-1939	15.00 - 20.00
Cooking.	1936-1939	15.00 - 20.00
Corn Farming.	1936-1939	15.00 - 20.00
Cotton Farming.	1936-1939	15.00 - 20.00

Cycling.	1936-1939	15.00 - 20.00
Dairying.	1936-1939	15.00 - 20.00
Dog Care.	1936-1939	15.00 - 20.00
Dramatics.	1936-1939	15.00 - 20.00
Electricity.	1936-1939	15.00 - 20.00
Farm Home and its Planning.	1936-1939	15.00 - 20.00
Farm Layout and Building Arrangement.	1936-1939	15.00 - 20.00
Farm Mechanics.	1936-1939	15.00 - 20.00
Farm Records & Bookkeeping.	1936-1939	15.00 - 20.00
Fingerprinting.	1936-1939	15.00 - 20.00
Firemanship.	1936-1939	15.00 - 20.00
First Aid to Animals.	1936-1939	15.00 - 20.00
First Aid.	1936-1939	15.00 - 20.00
Forestry.	1936-1939	15.00 - 20.00
Foundry Practice.	1936-1939	15.00 - 20.00
Fruit Culture.	1936-1939	15.00 - 20.00
Gardening.	1936-1939	15.00 - 20.00
Grasses, Legumes & Forrage Crops.	1936-1939	15.00 - 20.00
Hiking.	1936-1939	15.00 - 20.00
Hog & Pork Production.	1936-1939	15.00 - 20.00
Horsemanship.	1936-1939	15.00 - 20.00
Indian Lore.	1936-1939	15.00 - 20.00
insect Study.	1936-1939	15.00 - 20.00
Interpreting.	1936-1939	15.00 - 20.00
Journalism.	1936-1939	15.00 - 20.00
Landscape Gardening.	1936-1939	15.00 - 20.00
Leathercraft.	1936-1939	15.00 - 20.00
Leatherwork.	1936-1939	15.00 - 20.00
Lifesaving.	1936-1939	15.00 - 20.00
Machinery.	1936-1939	15.00 - 20.00
Marksmanship.	1936-1939	15.00 - 20.00
Masonry.	1936-1939	15.00 - 20.00
Mechanical Drawing.	1936-1939	15.00 - 20.00
Metal Work.	1936-1939	15.00 - 20.00
Mining.	1936-1939	15.00 - 20.00
Music & Bugling.	1936-1939	15.00 - 20.00
Painting.	1936-1939	15.00 - 20.00
Pathfinding.	1936-1939	15.00 - 20.00
Personal Health.	1936-1939	15.00 - 20.00
Photography.	1936-1939	15.00 - 20.00
Pigeon Raising.	1936-1939	15.00 - 20.00
Pioneering.	1936-1939	15.00 - 20.00
Plumbing.	1936-1939	15.00 - 20.00
Pottery.	1936-1939	15.00 - 20.00
Poultry Keeping.	1936-1939	15.00 - 20.00
Printing.	1936-1939	15.00 - 20.00
Public Health.	1936-1939	15.00 - 20.00
Public Speaking.	1936-1939	15.00 - 20.00
Radio.	1936-1939	15.00 - 20.00
Reading.	1936-1939	15.00 - 20.00
Reptile Study.	1936-1939	15.00 - 20.00
Rocks & Minerals.	1936-1939	15.00 - 20.00
Rowing.	1936-1939	15.00 - 20.00
Safety.	1936-1939	15.00 - 20.00
Salesmanship.	1936-1939	15.00 - 20.00
Scholarship.	1936-1939	15.00 - 20.00
Sculpture.	1936-1939	15.00 - 20.00
Seamanship.	1936-1939	15.00 - 20.00
Sheep Farming.	1936-1939	15.00 - 20.00
Signaling.	1936-1939	15.00 - 20.00
Skiing.	1936-1939	15.00 - 20.00
Soil Management.	1936-1939	15.00 - 20.00
Stalking.	1936-1939	15.00 - 20.00
Stamp Collecting.	1936-1939	15.00 - 20.00
Surveying.	1936-1939	15.00 - 20.00
Swimming.	1936-1939	15.00 - 20.00
Taxidermy.	1936-1939	15.00 - 20.00

Textiles.	1936-1939	15.00 - 20.00
Weather.	1936-1939	15.00 - 20.00
Wood Turning.	1936-1939	15.00 - 20.00
Wood Work.	1936-1939	15.00 - 20.00
Woodcarving.	1936-1939	15.00 - 20.00
Zoology.	1936-1939	15.00 - 20.00

STANDING SCOUT COVER, W/ OR W/O WAR INFORMATION

Agriculture.	1939-1944	12.50 - 17.50
Angling.	1939-1944	12.50 - 17.50
Animal Industry.	1939-1944	12.50 - 17.50
Archery.	1939-1944	12.50 - 17.50
Architecture.	1939-1944	12.50 - 17.50
Art.	1939-1944	12.50 - 17.50
Astronomy.	1939-1944	12.50 - 17.50
Athletics.	1939-1944	12.50 - 17.50
Automobiling.	1939-1944	12.50 - 17.50
Aviation.	1939-1944	12.50 - 17.50
Basketry.	1939-1944	12.50 - 17.50
Bird Study.	1939-1944	12.50 - 17.50
Blacksmithing.	1939-1944	12.50 - 17.50
Bookbinding.	1939-1944	12.50 - 17.50
Botany.	1939-1944	12.50 - 17.50
Business.	1939-1944	12.50 - 17.50
Camping.	1939-1944	12.50 - 17.50
Canoeing.	1939-1944	12.50 - 17.50
Carpentry.	1939-1944	12.50 - 17.50
Cement Work.	1939-1944	12.50 - 17.50
Chemistry.	1939-1944	12.50 - 17.50
Civics.	1939-1944	12.50 - 17.50
Conservation.	1939-1944	12.50 - 17.50
Cooking.	1939-1944	12.50 - 17.50
Corn Farming.	1939-1944	12.50 - 17.50
Cyclying.	1939-1944	12.50 - 17.50
Dairying.	1939-1944	12.50 - 17.50
Dog Care.	1939-1944	12.50 - 17.50
Electricity.	1939-1944	12.50 - 17.50
Fingerprinting.	1939-1944	12.50 - 17.50

Firemanship.	1939-1944	12.50 - 17.50
First Aid to Animals.	1939-1944	12.50 - 17.50
First Aid.	1939-1944	12.50 - 17.50
Forestry.	1939-1944	12.50 - 17.50
Gardening.	1939-1944	12.50 - 17.50
Hiking.	1939-1944	12.50 - 17.50
Home Repairs.	1939-1944	12.50 - 17.50
Horsemanship.	1939-1944	12.50 - 17.50
Indian Lore.	1939-1944	12.50 - 17.50
Journalism.	1939-1944	12.50 - 17.50
Landscape Gardening.	1939-1944	12.50 - 17.50
Leathercraft.	1939-1944	12.50 - 17.50
Leatherwork.	1939-1944	12.50 - 17.50
Lifesaving.	1939-1944	12.50 - 17.50
Machinery.	1939-1944	12.50 - 17.50
Marksmanship.	1939-1944	12.50 - 17.50
Masonry.	1939-1944	12.50 - 17.50
Metal Work.	1939-1944	12.50 - 17.50
Music & Bugling.	1939-1944	12.50 - 17.50
Painting.	1939-1944	12.50 - 17.50
Pathfinding.	1939-1944	12.50 - 17.50
Personal Health.	1939-1944	12.50 - 17.50
Photography.	1939-1944	12.50 - 17.50
Physical Development.	1939-1944	12.50 - 17.50
Pigeon Raising.	1939-1944	12.50 - 17.50
Pioneering.	1939-1944	12.50 - 17.50
Plumbing.	1939-1944	12.50 - 17.50
Pottery.	1939-1944	12.50 - 17.50
Poultry Keeping.	1939-1944	12.50 - 17.50
Printing.	1939-1944	12.50 - 17.50
Public Health.	1939-1944	12.50 - 17.50
Radio.	1939-1944	12.50 - 17.50
Reading.	1939-1944	12.50 - 17.50
Rocks & Minerals.	1939-1944	12.50 - 17.50
Rowing.	1939-1944	12.50 - 17.50
Safety.	1939-1944	12.50 - 17.50
Scholarship.	1939-1944	12.50 - 17.50
Seamanship.	1939-1944	12.50 - 17.50
Signaling.	1939-1944	12.50 - 17.50
Skiing.	1939-1944	12.50 - 17.50
Small Grains & Cereal Foods.	1939-1944	12.50 - 17.50
Soil Management.	1939-1944	12.50 - 17.50
Stalking.	1939-1944	12.50 - 17.50
Stamp Collecting.	1939-1944	12.50 - 17.50
Surveying.	1939-1944	12.50 - 17.50
Swimming.	1939-1944	12.50 - 17.50
Taxidermy.	1939-1944	12.50 - 17.50
Textiles.	1939-1944	12.50 - 17.50
Weather.	1939-1944	12.50 - 17.50
Wood Turning.	1939-1944	12.50 - 17.50
Wood Work.	1939-1944	12.50 - 17.50
Wood Work.	1939-1944	12.50 - 17.50
Woodcarving.	1939-1944	12.50 - 17.50
Zoology.	1939-1944	12.50 - 17.50

RED & WHITE COVERS

Agriculture.	1944-1952	3.50 - 7.50
Airplane Design.	1944-1952	3.50 - 7.50
Airplane Structure.	1944-1952	3.50 - 7.50
Angling.	1944-1952	3.50 - 7.50
Animal Industry.	1944-1952	3.50 - 7.50
Archery.	1944-1952	3.50 - 7.50
Architecture.	1944-1952	3.50 - 7.50
Art.	1944-1952	3.50 - 7.50
Astronomy.	1944-1952	3.50 - 7.50
Athletics.	1944-1952	3.50 - 7.50
Automobiling.	1944-1952	3.50 - 7.50
Aviation.	1944-1952	3.50 - 7.50
Basketry.	1944-1952	3.50 - 7.50
Bee Keeping.	1944-1952	3.50 - 7.50
Beef Production.	1944-1952	3.50 - 7.50
Bird Study.	1944-1952	3.50 - 7.50
Blacksmithing.	1944-1952	3.50 - 7.50
Bookbinding.	1944-1952	3.50 - 7.50
Botany.	1944-1952	3.50 - 7.50
Business.	1944-1952	3.50 - 7.50
Camping.	1944-1952	3.50 - 7.50
Canoeing.	1944-1952	3.50 - 7.50
Carpentry.	1944-1952	3.50 - 7.50
Cement Work.	1944-1952	3.50 - 7.50
Civics.	1944-1952	3.50 - 7.50
Coin Collecting.	1944-1952	3.50 - 7.50
Conservation.	1944-1952	3.50 - 7.50
Cooking.	1944-1952	3.50 - 7.50
Corn Farming.	1944-1952	3.50 - 7.50
Cotton Farming.	1944-1952	3.50 - 7.50
Cycling.	1944-1952	3.50 - 7.50
Dairying.	1944-1952	3.50 - 7.50
Dog Care.	1944-1952	3.50 - 7.50
Dramatics.	1944-1952	3.50 - 7.50
Electricity.	1944-1952	3.50 - 7.50
Farm Home and its Planning.	1944-1952	3.50 - 7.50
Farm Layout and Building Arrangement.	1944-1952	3.50 - 7.50
Farm Mechanics.	1944-1952	3.50 - 7.50
Farm Records & Bookkeeping.	1944-1952	3.50 - 7.50
Fingerprinting.	1944-1952	3.50 - 7.50

Firemanship.	1944-1952	3.50 - 7.50
First Aid to Animals.	1944-1952	3.50 - 7.50
First Aid.	1944-1952	3.50 - 7.50
Fishing.	1944-1952	3.50 - 7.50
Forestry.	1944-1952	3.50 - 7.50
Foundry Practice.	1944-1952	3.50 - 7.50
Fruit Culture.	1944-1952	3.50 - 7.50
Gardening.	1944-1952	3.50 - 7.50
Grasses, Legumes & Forrage Crops.	1944-1952	3.50 - 7.50
Hiking.	1944-1952	3.50 - 7.50
Hog & Pork Production.	1944-1952	3.50 - 7.50
Home Repairs.	1944-1952	3.50 - 7.50
Horsemanship.	1944-1952	3.50 - 7.50
Indian Lore.	1944-1952	3.50 - 7.50
Insect Life.	1944-1952	3.50 - 7.50
Interpreting.	1944-1952	3.50 - 7.50
Journalism	1944-1952	3.50 - 7.50
Landscape Gardening.	1944-1952	3.50 - 7.50
Leathercraft.	1944-1952	3.50 - 7.50
Leatherworking.	1944-1952	3.50 - 7.50
Lifesaving.	1944-1952	3.50 - 7.50
Machinery.	1944-1952	3.50 - 7.50
Marksmanship.	1944-1952	3.50 - 7.50
Masonry.	1944-1952	3.50 - 7.50
Mechanical Drawing.	1944-1952	3.50 - 7.50
Metal Work.	1944-1952	3.50 - 7.50
Music & Bugling.	1944-1952	3.50 - 7.50
Nut Culture.	1944-1952	3.50 - 7.50
Painting.	1944-1952	3.50 - 7.50
Pathfinding.	1944-1952	3.50 - 7.50
Personal Health.	1944-1952	3.50 - 7.50
Photography.	1944-1952	3.50 - 7.50
Physical Development.	1944-1952	3.50 - 7.50
Pigeon Raising.	1944-1952	3.50 - 7.50
Pioneering.	1944-1952	3.50 - 7.50
Plumbing.	1944-1952	3.50 - 7.50
Pottery.	1944-1952	3.50 - 7.50
Poultry Keeping.	1944-1952	3.50 - 7.50
Printing.	1944-1952	3.50 - 7.50
Public Health.	1944-1952	3.50 - 7.50
Public Speaking.	1944-1952	3.50 - 7.50
Rabbit Raising.	1944-1952	3.50 - 7.50
Radio.	1944-1952	3.50 - 7.50
Reading.	1944-1952	3.50 - 7.50
Reptile Study.	1944-1952	3.50 - 7.50
Rocks & Minerals.	1944-1952	3.50 - 7.50
Rowing.	1944-1952	3.50 - 7.50
Safety.	1944-1952	3.50 - 7.50
Salesmanship.	1944-1952	3.50 - 7.50
Scholarship.	1944-1952	3.50 - 7.50
Sculpture.	1944-1952	3.50 - 7.50
Seamanship.	1944-1952	3.50 - 7.50
Sheep Farming.	1944-1952	3.50 - 7.50
Signaling.	1944-1952	3.50 - 7.50
Skiing.	1944-1952	3.50 - 7.50
Small Grains & Cereal Foods.	1944-1952	3.50 - 7.50
Soil Management.	1944-1952	3.50 - 7.50
Stalking.	1944-1952	3.50 - 7.50
Stamp Collecting.	1944-1952	3.50 - 7.50
Surveying.	1944-1952	3.50 - 7.50
Surveying.	1944-1952	3.50 - 7.50
Swimming.	1944-1952	3.50 - 7.50
Taxidermy.	1944-1952	3.50 - 7.50
Textiles.	1944-1952	3.50 - 7.50
Weather.	1944-1952	3.50 - 7.50
Wood Turning.	1944-1952	3.50 - 7.50
Wood Work.	1944-1952	3.50 - 7.50

Woodcarving.	1944-1952	3.50 - 7.50
Zoology.	1944-1952	3.50 - 7.50

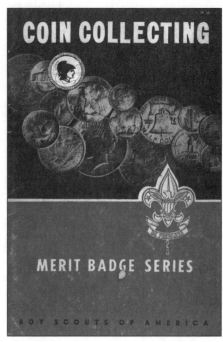

PHOTO TOP, RED BOTTOM COVER

Agriculture.	1949-1966	2.00 - 3.50
Animal Industry.	1949-1966	2.00 - 3.50
Archery.	1949-1966	2.00 - 3.50
Architecture.	1949-1966	2.00 - 3.50
Art.	1949-1966	2.00 - 3.50
Astronomy.	1949-1966	2.00 - 3.50
Athletics.	1949-1966	2.00 - 3.50
Atomic Energy.	1949-1966	2.00 - 3.50
Automobiling.	1949-1966	2.00 - 3.50
Automotive Safety.	1949-1966	2.00 - 3.50
Aviation.	1949-1966	2.00 - 3.50
Basketry.	1949-1966	2.00 - 3.50
Bee Keeping.	1949-1966	2.00 - 3.50
Beef Production.	1949-1966	2.00 - 3.50
Bird Study.	1949-1966	2.00 - 3.50
Bookbinding.	1949-1966	2.00 - 3.50
Botany.	1949-1966	2.00 - 3.50
Business.	1949-1966	2.00 - 3.50
Camping.	1949-1966	2.00 - 3.50
Canoeing.	1949-1966	2.00 - 3.50
Cement Work.	1949-1966	2.00 - 3.50
Citizenship.	1949-1966	2.00 - 3.50
Coin Collecting.	1949-1966	2.00 - 3.50
Cooking.	1949-1966	2.00 - 3.50
Corn Farming.	1949-1966	2.00 - 3.50
Cotton Farming.	1949-1966	2.00 - 3.50
Cycling.	1949-1966	2.00 - 3.50
Dairying.	1949-1966	2.00 - 3.50
Dog Care.	1949-1966	2.00 - 3.50
Drafting.	1949-1966	2.00 - 3.50
Dramatics.	1949-1966	2.00 - 3.50
Electricity.	1949-1966	2.00 - 3.50
Electronics.	1949-1966	2.00 - 3.50
Farm Arrangements.	1949-1966	2.00 - 3.50
Farm Home and its Planning.	1949-1966	2.00 - 3.50
Farm Layout and Building Arrangement.	1949-1966	2.00 - 3.50
Farm Mechanics.	1949-1966	2.00 - 3.50
Farm Records.	1949-1966	2.00 - 3.50
Farm Recrods & Bookkeeping.	1949-1966	2.00 - 3.50

Fingerprinting.	1949-1966	2.00 - 3.50
Firemanship.	1949-1966	2.00 - 3.50
First Aid to Animals.	1949-1966	2.00 - 3.50
First Aid.	1949-1966	2.00 - 3.50
Fishing.	1949-1966	2.00 - 3.50
Forage Crops.	1949-1966	2.00 - 3.50
Forestry.	1949-1966	2.00 - 3.50
Fruit and Nut Growing.	1949-1966	2.00 - 3.50
Gardening.	1949-1966	2.00 - 3.50
Geology.	1949-1966	2.00 - 3.50
Grasses, Legumes & Forage Crops.	1949-1966	2.00 - 3.50
Hiking.	1949-1966	2.00 - 3.50
Hog & Pork Production.	1949-1966	2.00 - 3.50
Hog Production.	1949-1966	2.00 - 3.50
Home Repairs.	1949-1966	2.00 - 3.50
Horsemanship.	1949-1966	2.00 - 3.50
Indian Lore.	1949-1966	2.00 - 3.50
Insect Life.	1949-1966	2.00 - 3.50
Journalism.	1949-1966	2.00 - 3.50
Landscape Gardening.	1949-1966	2.00 - 3.50
Landscaping.	1949-1966	2.00 - 3.50
Leatherwork.	1949-1966	2.00 - 3.50
Lifesaving.	1949-1966	2.00 - 3.50
Machinery.	1949-1966	2.00 - 3.50
Marksmanship.	1949-1966	2.00 - 3.50
Masonry.	1949-1966	2.00 - 3.50
Mechanical Drawing.	1949-1966	2.00 - 3.50
Metal Work.	1949-1966	2.00 - 3.50
Model Design & Building.	1949-1966	2.00 - 3.50
Motorboating.	1949-1966	2.00 - 3.50
Music & Bugling.	1949-1966	2.00 - 3.50
Nature.	1949-1966	2.00 - 3.50
Oceanography.	1949-1966	2.00 - 3.50
Painting.	1949-1966	2.00 - 3.50
Pathfinding.	1949-1966	2.00 - 3.50
Personal Finances.	1949-1966	2.00 - 3.50
Personal Fitness.	1949-1966	2.00 - 3.50
Pets.	1949-1966	2.00 - 3.50
Photography.	1949-1966	2.00 - 3.50
Pigeon Raising.	1949-1966	2.00 - 3.50
Pioneering.	1949-1966	2.00 - 3.50
Plumbing.	1949-1966	2.00 - 3.50
Pottery.	1949-1966	2.00 - 3.50
Poultry Keeping.	1949-1966	2.00 - 3.50
Printing.	1949-1966	2.00 - 3.50
Public Health.	1949-1966	2.00 - 3.50
Public Speaking.	1949-1966	2.00 - 3.50
Rabbit Raising.	1949-1966	2.00 - 3.50
Radio.	1949-1966	2.00 - 3.50
Radio.	1949-1966	2.00 - 3.50
Railroading.	1949-1966	2.00 - 3.50
Reading.	1949-1966	2.00 - 3.50
Reptile Study.	1949-1966	2.00 - 3.50
Rowing.	1949-1966	2.00 - 3.50
Safety.	1949-1966	2.00 - 3.50
Salesmanship.	1949-1966	2.00 - 3.50
Scholarship.	1949-1966	2.00 - 3.50
Sculpture.	1949-1966	2.00 - 3.50
Seamanship.	1949-1966	2.00 - 3.50
Sheep Farming.	1949-1966	2.00 - 3.50
Signaling.	1949-1966	2.00 - 3.50
Skiing.	1949-1966	2.00 - 3.50
Small Grains & Cereal Foods.	1949-1966	2.00 - 3.50
Small Grains.	1949-1966	2.00 - 3.50
Soil & Water Conservation.	1949-1966	2.00 - 3.50
Stamp Collecting.	1949-1966	2.00 - 3.50
Surveying.	1949-1966	2.00 - 3.50

Swimming.	1949-1966	2.00 - 3.50
Textiles.	1949-1966	2.00 - 3.50
Weather.	1949-1966	2.00 - 3.50
Wildlife Management.	1949-1966	2.00 - 3.50
Wood Work.	1949-1966	2.00 - 3.50
Woodcarving.	1949-1966	2.00 - 3.50
Zoology.	1949-1966	2.00 - 3.50

FULL PHOTO COVER

Agriculture.	1966-1971	1.50 - 2.50
American Business.	1966-1971	1.50 - 2.50
Animal Industry.	1966-1971	1.50 - 2.50
Archery.	1966-1971	1.50 - 2.50
Architecture.	1966-1971	1.50 - 2.50
Art.	1966-1971	1.50 - 2.50
Astronomy.	1966-1971	1.50 - 2.50
Athletics.	1966-1971	1.50 - 2.50
Atomic Energy.	1966-1971	1.50 - 2.50
Automotive Safety.	1966-1971	1.50 - 2.50
Aviation.	1966-1971	1.50 - 2.50
Basketry.	1966-1971	1.50 - 2.50
Bee Keeping.	1966-1971	1.50 - 2.50
Beef Production.	1966-1971	1.50 - 2.50
Bird Study.	1966-1971	1.50 - 2.50
Bookbinding.	1966-1971	1.50 - 2.50
Botany.	1966-1971	1.50 - 2.50
Camping.	1966-1971	1.50 - 2.50
Canoeing.	1966-1971	1.50 - 2.50
Chemistry.	1966-1971	1.50 - 2.50
Citizenship in the Home.	1966-1971	1.50 - 2.50
Coin Collecting.	1966-1971	1.50 - 2.50
Communications.	1966-1971	1.50 - 2.50
Computers.	1966-1971	1.50 - 2.50
Conservation of Natural Resources.	1966-1971	1.50 - 2.50
Cooking.	1966-1971	1.50 - 2.50
Corn Farming.	1966-1971	1.50 - 2.50
Cotton Farming.	1966-1971	1.50 - 2.50
Cycling.	1966-1971	1.50 - 2.50
Dairying.	1966-1971	1.50 - 2.50
Dog Care.	1966-1971	1.50 - 2.50
Drafting.	1966-1971	1.50 - 2.50
Electricity.	1966-1971	1.50 - 2.50

Electronics.	1966-1971	1.50 - 2.50
Engineering.	1966-1971	1.50 - 2.50
Farm Arrangements.	1966-1971	1.50 - 2.50
Farm Mechanics.	1966-1971	1.50 - 2.50
Farm Records.	1966-1971	1.50 - 2.50
Fingerprinting.	1966-1971	1.50 - 2.50
Firemanship.	1966-1971	1.50 - 2.50
First Aid to Animals.	1966-1971	1.50 - 2.50
First Aid.	1966-1971	1.50 - 2.50
Fishing.	1966-1971	1.50 - 2.50
Forestry.	1966-1971	1.50 - 2.50
Forrage Crops.	1966-1971	1.50 - 2.50
Fruit and Nut Growing.	1966-1971	1.50 - 2.50
Gardening.	1966-1971	1.50 - 2.50
Geology.	1966-1971	1.50 - 2.50
Handicraft.	1966-1971	1.50 - 2.50
Hiking.	1966-1971	1.50 - 2.50
Hog Production.	1966-1971	1.50 - 2.50
Home Repairs.	1966-1971	1.50 - 2.50
Horsemanship.	1966-1971	1.50 - 2.50
Indian Lore.	1966-1971	1.50 - 2.50
Insect Life.	1966-1971	1.50 - 2.50
Journalism.	1966-1971	1.50 - 2.50
Landscape Architecture.	1966-1971	1.50 - 2.50
Leatherwork.	1966-1971	1.50 - 2.50
Lifesaving.	1966-1971	1.50 - 2.50
Machinery.	1966-1971	1.50 - 2.50
Mammals.	1966-1971	1.50 - 2.50
Masonry.	1966-1971	1.50 - 2.50
Metal Work.	1966-1971	1.50 - 2.50
Metallurgy.	1966-1971	1.50 - 2.50
Model Design & Building.	1966-1971	1.50 - 2.50
Motorboating.	1966-1971	1.50 - 2.50
Music & Bugling.	1966-1971	1.50 - 2.50
Nature.	1966-1971	1.50 - 2.50
Oceanography.	1966-1971	1.50 - 2.50
Painting.	1966-1971	1.50 - 2.50
Personal Finances.	1966-1971	1.50 - 2.50
Personal Fitness.	1966-1971	1.50 - 2.50
Pets.	1966-1971	1.50 - 2.50
Photography.	1966-1971	1.50 - 2.50
Pigeon Raising.	1966-1971	1.50 - 2.50
Pioneering.	1966-1971	1.50 - 2.50
Plumbing.	1966-1971	1.50 - 2.50
Pottery.	1966-1971	1.50 - 2.50
Poultry Keeping.	1966-1971	1.50 - 2.50
Printing.	1966-1971	1.50 - 2.50
Public Health.	1966-1971	1.50 - 2.50
Public Speaking.	1966-1971	1.50 - 2.50
Rabbit Raising.	1966-1971	1.50 - 2.50
Radio.	1966-1971	1.50 - 2.50
Railroading.	1966-1971	1.50 - 2.50
Reading.	1966-1971	1.50 - 2.50
Reading.	1966-1971	1.50 - 2.50
Reptile Study.	1966-1971	1.50 - 2.50
Rifle & Shotgun Shooting.	1966-1971	1.50 - 2.50
Rowing.	1966-1971	1.50 - 2.50
Safety.	1966-1971	1.50 - 2.50
Salesmanship.	1966-1971	1.50 - 2.50
Scholarship.	1966-1971	1.50 - 2.50
Sculpture.	1966-1971	1.50 - 2.50
Sheep Farming.	1966-1971	1.50 - 2.50
Signaling.	1966-1971	1.50 - 2.50
Skiing.	1966-1971	1.50 - 2.50
Small Boat Sailing.	1966-1971	1.50 - 2.50
Small Grains.	1966-1971	1.50 - 2.50
Soil & Water Conservation.	1966-1971	1.50 - 2.50

Space Exploration.	1966-1971	1.50 - 2.50
Stamp Collecting.	1966-1971	1.50 - 2.50
Surveying.	1966-1971	1.50 - 2.50
Swimming.	1966-1971	1.50 - 2.50
Textiles.	1966-1971	1.50 - 2.50
Theater.	1966-1971	1.50 - 2.50
Water Skiing.	1966-1971	1.50 - 2.50
Weather.	1966-1971	1.50 - 2.50
Wildlife Management.	1966-1971	1.50 - 2.50
Wood Work.	1966-1971	1.50 - 2.50
Woodcarving.	1966-1971	1.50 - 2.50
World Brotherhood.	1966-1971	1.50 - 2.50
Zoology.	1966-1971	1.50 - 2.50

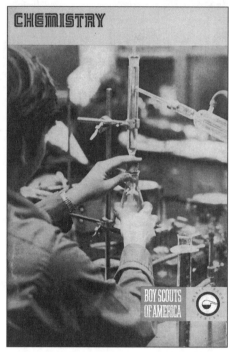

GREEN STRIPE TOP, FULL PHOTO COVER

Agriculture.	1971-1979	1.00 - 2.00
American Business.	1971-1979	1.00 - 2.00
American Heritage.	1971-1979	1.00 - 2.00
Animal Industry.	1971-1979	1.00 - 2.00
Animal Science.	1971-1979	1.00 - 2.00
Archery.	1971-1979	1.00 - 2.00
Architecture.	1971-1979	1.00 - 2.00
Art.	1971-1979	1.00 - 2.00
Astronomy.	1971-1979	1.00 - 2.00
Atomic Energy.	1971-1979	1.00 - 2.00
Automotive Safety.	1971-1979	1.00 - 2.00
Aviation.	1971-1979	1.00 - 2.00
Basketry.	1971-1979	1.00 - 2.00
Bee Keeping.	1971-1979	1.00 - 2.00
Beef Production.	1971-1979	1.00 - 2.00
Bird Study.	1971-1979	1.00 - 2.00
Bookbinding.	1971-1979	1.00 - 2.00
Botany.	1971-1979	1.00 - 2.00
Camping.	1971-1979	1.00 - 2.00
Canoeing.	1971-1979	1.00 - 2.00
Chemistry.	1971-1979	1.00 - 2.00
Citizenship in the Community.	1971-1979	1.00 - 2.00
Citizenship in the Nation.	1971-1979	1.00 - 2.00
Citizenship in the World.	1971-1979	1.00 - 2.00
Coin Collecting.	1971-1979	1.00 - 2.00
Communications.	1971-1979	1.00 - 2.00
Consumer Buying.	1971-1979	1.00 - 2.00

Cooking.	1971-1979	1.00 - 2.00
Corn Farming.	1971-1979	1.00 - 2.00
Cotton Farming.	1971-1979	1.00 - 2.00
Cycling.	1971-1979	1.00 - 2.00
Dairying.	1971-1979	1.00 - 2.00
Dentistry.	1971-1979	1.00 - 2.00
Dog Care.	1971-1979	1.00 - 2.00
Drafting.	1971-1979	1.00 - 2.00
Electricity.	1971-1979	1.00 - 2.00
Electronics.	1971-1979	1.00 - 2.00
Emergency Prepardness.	1971-1979	1.00 - 2.00
Energy.	1971-1979	1.00 - 2.00
Engineering.	1971-1979	1.00 - 2.00
Environmental Science.	1971-1979	1.00 - 2.00
Farm Arrangements.	1971-1979	1.00 - 2.00
Farm Mechanics.	1971-1979	1.00 - 2.00
Farm Records.	1971-1979	1.00 - 2.00
Fingerprinting.	1971-1979	1.00 - 2.00
Firemanship.	1971-1979	1.00 - 2.00
First Aid.	1971-1979	1.00 - 2.00
Fish & Wildlife Management.	1971-1979	1.00 - 2.00
Fishing.	1971-1979	1.00 - 2.00
Food Systems.	1971-1979	1.00 - 2.00
Forestry.	1971-1979	1.00 - 2.00
Forrage Crops.	1971-1979	1.00 - 2.00
Fruit and Nut Growing.	1971-1979	1.00 - 2.00
Gardening.	1971-1979	1.00 - 2.00
Genealogy.	1971-1979	1.00 - 2.00
General Science.	1971-1979	1.00 - 2.00
Geology.	1971-1979	1.00 - 2.00
Golf.	1971-1979	1.00 - 2.00
Handicraft.	1971-1979	1.00 - 2.00
Hiking.	1971-1979	1.00 - 2.00
Hog Production.	1971-1979	1.00 - 2.00
Home Repairs.	1971-1979	1.00 - 2.00
Horsemanship.	1971-1979	1.00 - 2.00
Indian Lore.	1971-1979	1.00 - 2.00
Insect Life.	1971-1979	1.00 - 2.00
Journalism.	1971-1979	1.00 - 2.00
Landscape Architecture.	1971-1979	1.00 - 2.00
Law.	1971-1979	1.00 - 2.00
Leatherwork.	1971-1979	1.00 - 2.00
Lifesaving.	1971-1979	1.00 - 2.00
Machinery.	1971-1979	1.00 - 2.00
Mammals.	1971-1979	1.00 - 2.00
Masonry.	1971-1979	1.00 - 2.00
Metal Work.	1971-1979	1.00 - 2.00
Metals Engineering.	1971-1979	1.00 - 2.00
Model Design & Building.	1971-1979	1.00 - 2.00
Motorboating.	1971-1979	1.00 - 2.00
Music & Bugling.	1971-1979	1.00 - 2.00
Nature.	1971-1979	1.00 - 2.00
Oceanography.	1971-1979	1.00 - 2.00
Orienteering.	1971-1979	1.00 - 2.00
Painting.	1971-1979	1.00 - 2.00
Personal Fitness.	1971-1979	1.00 - 2.00
Personal Management.	1971-1979	1.00 - 2.00
Pets.	1971-1979	1.00 - 2.00
Photography.	1971-1979	1.00 - 2.00
Pigeon Raising.	1971-1979	1.00 - 2.00
Pioneering.	1971-1979	1.00 - 2.00
Plant Science.	1971-1979	1.00 - 2.00
Plumbing.	1971-1979	1.00 - 2.00
Poetry.	1971-1979	1.00 - 2.00
Poultry Keeping.	1971-1979	1.00 - 2.00
Printing.	1971-1979	1.00 - 2.00
Public Health.	1971-1979	1.00 - 2.00

Public Speaking.	1971-1979	1.00 - 2.00
Pulp & Paper.	1971-1979	1.00 - 2.00
Rabbit Raising.	1971-1979	1.00 - 2.00
Radio.	1971-1979	1.00 - 2.00
Railroading.	1971-1979	1.00 - 2.00
Reading.	1971-1979	1.00 - 2.00
Reptile Study.	1971-1979	1.00 - 2.00
Rifle & Shotgun Shooting.	1971-1979	1.00 - 2.00
Rowing.	1971-1979	1.00 - 2.00
Safety.	1971-1979	1.00 - 2.00
Salesmanship.	1971-1979	1.00 - 2.00
Scholarship.	1971-1979	1.00 - 2.00
Sculpture.	1971-1979	1.00 - 2.00
Sheep Farming.	1971-1979	1.00 - 2.00
Signaling.	1971-1979	1.00 - 2.00
Skating.	1971-1979	1.00 - 2.00
Skiing.	1971-1979	1.00 - 2.00
Small Boat Sailing.	1971-1979	1.00 - 2.00
Small Grains.	1971-1979	1.00 - 2.00
Soil & Water Conservation.	1971-1979	1.00 - 2.00
Space Exploration.	1971-1979	1.00 - 2.00
Sports.	1971-1979	1.00 - 2.00
Stamp Collecting.	1971-1979	1.00 - 2.00
Surveying.	1971-1979	1.00 - 2.00
Swimming.	1971-1979	1.00 - 2.00
Textiles.	1971-1979	1.00 - 2.00
Theater.	1971-1979	1.00 - 2.00
Traffic Safety.	1971-1979	1.00 - 2.00
Truck Transportation.	1971-1979	1.00 - 2.00
Veterinary Science.	1971-1979	1.00 - 2.00
Water Skiing.	1971-1979	1.00 - 2.00
Weather.	1971-1979	1.00 - 2.00
Wilderness Survival.	1971-1979	1.00 - 2.00
Wood Carving.	1971-1979	1.00 - 2.00
Wood Work.	1971-1979	1.00 - 2.00

RED STRIPE TOP, FULL PHOTO COVER

American Business.	1980	1.00 - 2.00
American Cultures.	1980	1.00 - 2.00
American Heritage.	1980	1.00 - 2.00
American Labor.	1980	1.00 - 2.00
Animal Science.	1980	1.00 - 2.00
Archery.	1980	1.00 - 2.00
Architecture.	1980	1.00 - 2.00

Art.	1980	1.00 - 2.00	Music & Bugling.	1980	1.00 - 2.00
Astronomy.	1980	1.00 - 2.00	Nature.	1980	1.00 - 2.00
Athletics.	1980	1.00 - 2.00	Oceanography.	1980	1.00 - 2.00
Aviation.	1980	1.00 - 2.00	Orienteering.	1980	1.00 - 2.00
Backpacking.	1980	1.00 - 2.00	Painting.	1980	1.00 - 2.00
Basketry.	1980	1.00 - 2.00	Personal Fitness.	1980	1.00 - 2.00
Bee Keeping.	1980	1.00 - 2.00	Personal Management.	1980	1.00 - 2.00
Bird Study.	1980	1.00 - 2.00	Pets.	1980	1.00 - 2.00
Bookbinding.	1980	1.00 - 2.00	Photography.	1980	1.00 - 2.00
Botany.	1980	1.00 - 2.00	Pioneering.	1980	1.00 - 2.00
Camping.	1980	1.00 - 2.00	Plant Science.	1980	1.00 - 2.00
Canoeing.	1980	1.00 - 2.00	Plumbing.	1980	1.00 - 2.00
Chemistry.	1980	1.00 - 2.00	Pottery.	1980	1.00 - 2.00
Citizenship in the Community.	1980	1.00 - 2.00	Printing Communication.	1980	1.00 - 2.00
Citizenship in the Nation.	1980	1.00 - 2.00	Printing.	1980	1.00 - 2.00
Citizenship in the World.	1980	1.00 - 2.00	Public Health.	1980	1.00 - 2.00
Coin Collecting.	1980	1.00 - 2.00	Public Speaking.	1980	1.00 - 2.00
Communications.	1980	1.00 - 2.00	Pult & Paper.	1980	1.00 - 2.00
Computers.	1980	1.00 - 2.00	Rabbit Raising.	1980	1.00 - 2.00
Consumer Buying.	1980	1.00 - 2.00	Radio.	1980	1.00 - 2.00
Cooking.	1980	1.00 - 2.00	Railroading.	1980	1.00 - 2.00
Cycling.	1980	1.00 - 2.00	Reading.	1980	1.00 - 2.00
Dentistry.	1980	1.00 - 2.00	Reptile Study.	1980	1.00 - 2.00
Dog Care.	1980	1.00 - 2.00	Rifle & Shotgun Shooting.	1980	1.00 - 2.00
Drafting.	1980	1.00 - 2.00	Rifle Shooting.	1980	1.00 - 2.00
Electricity.	1980	1.00 - 2.00	Rowing.	1980	1.00 - 2.00
Electronics.	1980	1.00 - 2.00	Safety.	1980	1.00 - 2.00
Emergency Prepardness.	1980	1.00 - 2.00	Salesmanship.	1980	1.00 - 2.00
Energy.	1980	1.00 - 2.00	Scholarship.	1980	1.00 - 2.00
Engineering.	1980	1.00 - 2.00	Sculpture.	1980	1.00 - 2.00
Environmental Science.	1980	1.00 - 2.00	Shotgun Shooting.	1980	1.00 - 2.00
Farm & Ranch Management.	1980	1.00 - 2.00	Signaling.	1980	1.00 - 2.00
Farm Mechanics.	1980	1.00 - 2.00	Skating.	1980	1.00 - 2.00
Fingerprinting.	1980	1.00 - 2.00	Skiing.	1980	1.00 - 2.00
Firemanship.	1980	1.00 - 2.00	Small Boat Sailing.	1980	1.00 - 2.00
First Aid.	1980	1.00 - 2.00	Soil & Water Conservation.	1980	1.00 - 2.00
Fish & Wildlife Management.	1980	1.00 - 2.00	Space Exploration.	1980	1.00 - 2.00
Fishing.	1980	1.00 - 2.00	Sports.	1980	1.00 - 2.00
Food Systems.	1980	1.00 - 2.00	Stamp Collecting.	1980	1.00 - 2.00
Food Systems.	1980	1.00 - 2.00	Surveying.	1980	1.00 - 2.00
Forestry.	1980	1.00 - 2.00	Swimming.	1980	1.00 - 2.00
Gardening.	1980	1.00 - 2.00	Textiles.	1980	1.00 - 2.00
Genealogy.	1980	1.00 - 2.00	Theater.	1980	1.00 - 2.00
General Science.	1980	1.00 - 2.00	Traffic Safety.	1980	1.00 - 2.00
Geology.	1980	1.00 - 2.00	Truck Transportation.	1980	1.00 - 2.00
Golf.	1980	1.00 - 2.00	Veterinary Science.	1980	1.00 - 2.00
Graphic Arts.	1980	1.00 - 2.00	Water Skiing.	1980	1.00 - 2.00
Handicapped Awareness.	1980	1.00 - 2.00	Weather.	1980	1.00 - 2.00
Handicraft.	1980	1.00 - 2.00	Whitewater.	1980	1.00 - 2.00
Hiking.	1980	1.00 - 2.00	Wilderness Survival.	1980	1.00 - 2.00
Home Repairs.	1980	1.00 - 2.00	Wood Work.	1980	1.00 - 2.00
Horsemanship.	1980	1.00 - 2.00	Woodcarving.	1980	1.00 - 2.00
Indian Lore.	1980	1.00 - 2.00			
Insect Life.	1980	1.00 - 2.00			
Insect Study.	1980	1.00 - 2.00			
Journalism.	1980	1.00 - 2.00			
Landscape Architecture.	1980	1.00 - 2.00			
Law.	1980	1.00 - 2.00			
Leatherwork.	1980	1.00 - 2.00			
Lifesaving.	1980	1.00 - 2.00			
Machinery.	1980	1.00 - 2.00			
Mammal Study.	1980	1.00 - 2.00			
Masonry.	1980	1.00 - 2.00			
Metal Work.	1980	1.00 - 2.00			
Metals Engineering.	1980	1.00 - 2.00			
Model Design & Building.	1980	1.00 - 2.00			
Motorboating.	1980	1.00 - 2.00			

Eagle Scouts all — Brothers John, Karsten, and Curtis Flory, wearing their sashes which include square cut merit badges and Wisconsin's Indian Mound Reservation Patches of the late 1920s.

MERIT BADGES

Merit badges come in nine major styles. Dating badges by their manufacture versus their dates of use has been a problematic item for some, and not of concern to others. The date of distribution at the council service center to a unit could be several years after a particular design was changed and in use in other areas of the country. This listing is based on those developed by Fred Duersch and John Pleasants and published in the Spring 1996 issue of the *Journal of the American Scouting Historical Society*.

Full square

The first is full square tan twill, in use from 1911–1933. The size varies from 1-1/2" to 3" square, with the larger size the scarcer. Some of these were sewn on the sash in a square format, others were tucked under, and still others were trimmed round and tucked under.

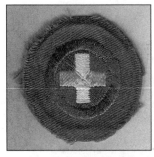

Wide Border Crimped

Second is a tan twill wide border crimped edge. This 1934–1935 type was the first circular design, with a 1/4" area from the exterior of the green ring to the material crimp (assisting in sewing the badge on a sash in a neat circle.) This is one of the most difficult types to find.

Third is a coarse tan twill narrow border crimped edge. This 1936–1942 type is a circular design with a 1/8" area from the exterior of the green ring to the material crimp.

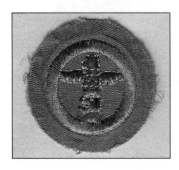

Fine Twill

Fourth is a fine tan twill narrow border crimped edge. This 1942–1946 type is probably the most difficult to find behind the second type. The material was changed from a coarse twill to fine twill due to the war effort.

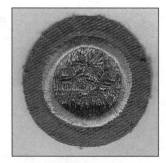

*Khaki Narrow
Border Crimped*

Fifth is a khaki twill narrow border crimped edge. In use from 1947–1960, it is one of the more common varieties.

Khaki Rolled Edge

Sixth is the khaki twill rolled edge. Issued from 1961–1968, these have a cloth (gauze) backing.

Seventh is a fully-embroidered cloth back, rolled edge of green or white. (1961–1971).

Eighth is a fully-embroidered plastic back, rolled edge of green or white (1972–present)

Plastic Back

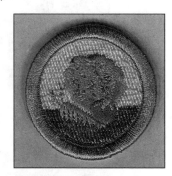

Computer Generated

Ninth is a computer generated design, plastic back (1993-1996), which is distinguished by a wide or narrow tan circle on the back, usually larger in diameter than a rolled edge, which is flat. They were often issued in individual packages.

Fred Duersch, Jr. has privately published *Merit Badge Field Guide*.

The prices in this section have been developed with assistance from John Pleasants and the staff at Brush Creek Trading Co.

Eagle scout with merit badges on sleeve, senior patrol pin on hat and an unofficial bugle.

MERIT BADGES

AERODYNAMICS
Tan rough twill, narrow crimped.	1942-1946	125.00 - 200.00
Khaki twill, narrow crimped. For blue border issue, see Air Scout Program listing.	1947-1952	325.00 - 425.00

AERONAUTICS
Tan rough twill, narrow crimped.	1942-1946	140.00 - 180.00
Khaki twill, narrow crimped. Formerly and then later Aviation. For blue border issue, see Air Scout Program listing.	1947-1952	200.00 - 275.00

AGRIBUSINESS
Fully embroidered, plastic back. Formerly Farm Records.	1987-1995	0.50 - 1.00

AGRICULTURE
Cut square (four varieties).	1911-1933	40.00 - 60.00
Tan, wide crimped.	1934-1935	100.00 - 140.00
Tan rough twill, narrow crimped.	1936-1942	7.50 - 12.50
Tan fine twill, narrow crimped.	1942-1946	40.00 - 75.00
Khaki twill, narrow crimped.	1947-1960	3.00 - 5.00
Khaki twill, rolled edge.	1961-1968	0.50 - 1.00
Fully embroidered, cloth back.	1969-1971	1.00 - 3.00
Fully embroidered, plastic back. Merged into plant science.	1972-1975	0.50 - 1.00

AIRPLANE DESIGN
Tan rough twill, narrow crimped.	1942-1946	150.00 - 200.00
Khaki twill, narrow crimped. For blue border issue, see Air Scout Program listing.	1947-1952	550.00 - 650.00

AIRPLANE STRUCTURE
Tan fine twill, narrow crimped.	1942-1946	325.00 - 375.00
Tan rough twill, narrow crimped.	1942-1946	140.00 - 180.00
Khaki twill, narrow crimped. For blue border issue, see Air Scout Program listing.	1947-1952	325.00 - 375.00

AMERICAN BUSINESS
Fully embroidered, cloth back.	1967-1971	1.00 - 3.00
Fully embroidered, plastic back.	1972-1993	0.50 - 1.00
Computer stitched, bagged.	1993	0.50 - 1.00

AMERICAN CULTURES
Fully embroidered, cloth back, (error).	1979	90.00 - 120.00
Fully embroidered, plastic back.	1979	0.50 - 1.00

AMERICAN HERITAGE
Fully embroidered, plastic back.	1975-1993	0.50 - 1.00
Computer stitched, bagged.	1993	0.50 - 1.00

AMERICAN LABOR
Fully embroidered, plastic back.	1987-1993	0.50 - 1.00
Computer stitched, bagged.	1993	0.50 - 1.00

ANGLING
Cut square (two varieties).	1911-1933	75.00 - 125.00
Tan, wide crimped.	1934-1935	100.00 - 150.00
Tan rough twill, narrow crimped.	1936-1942	7.50 - 15.00
Tan fine twill, narrow crimped.	1942-1946	80.00 - 120.00
Khaki twill, narrow crimped. Became fishing.	1947-1951	2.50 - 5.00

ANIMAL INDUSTRY
Cut square (horse head).	1928-1933	20.00 - 30.00
Tan, wide crimped.	1934-1935	25.00 - 40.00
Tan rough twill, narrow crimped.	1936-1942	5.00 - 10.00
Tan fine twill, narrow crimped.	1942-1946	10.00 - 17.50
Khaki twill, narrow crimped.	1947-1960	3.00 - 7.50
Khaki twill, rolled edge.	1961-1968	0.50 - 1.00
Fully embroidered, cloth back (horse galloping).	1969-1971	1.00 - 3.00
Fully embroidered, plastic back. Merged into animal science.	1972-1975	0.50 - 1.00

ANIMAL SCIENCE
Fully embroidered, plastic back (cow head right).	1975-1993	0.50 - 1.00
Computer stitched, bagged. Formerly animal industry.	1993	0.50 - 1.00

ARCHAEOLOGY
Fully embroidered, plastic back.	1997	0.50 - 1.00

ARCHERY
Cut square (two varieties).	1914-1933	250.00 - 325.00
Tan, wide crimped.	1934-1935	250.00 - 325.00
Tan rough twill, narrow crimped.	1936-1942	12.50 - 20.00
Tan fine twill, narrow crimped.	1942-1946	30.00 - 50.00
Khaki twill, narrow crimped.	1947-1960	2.50 - 5.00
Khaki twill, rolled edge (bow and arrow vertical).	1961-1968	0.50 - 1.00
Fully embroidered, cloth back (bow and arrow diagonal).	1969-1971	1.00 - 3.00
Fully embroidered, plastic back.	1972	0.50 - 1.00

ARCHITECTURE
Cut square (four varieties).	1911-1933	100.00 - 140.00
Tan, wide crimped.	1934-1935	150.00 - 200.00
Tan rough twill, narrow crimped.	1936-1942	12.50 - 20.00
Tan fine twill, narrow crimped.	1942-1946	20.00 - 30.00
Khaki twill, narrow crimped.	1947-1960	3.00 - 7.50
Khaki twill, rolled edge.	1961-1968	0.50 - 1.00
Fully embroidered, cloth back.	1969-1971	1.00 - 3.00
Fully embroidered, plastic back.	1972-1993	0.50 - 1.00
Computer stitched, bagged.	1993	0.50 - 1.00

ART
Cut square (six varieties).	1911-1933	60.00 - 90.00
Tan, wide crimped.	1934-1935	80.00 - 120.00
Tan rough twill, narrow crimped.	1936-1942	5.00 - 10.00
Tan fine twill, narrow crimped.	1942-1946	20.00 - 40.00
Khaki twill, narrow crimped.	1947-1960	3.00 - 5.00
Khaki twill, rolled edge.	1961-1968	0.50 - 1.00
Fully embroidered, cloth back.	1969-1971	1.00 - 3.00
Fully embroidered, plastic back.	1972	0.50 - 1.00

ASTRONOMY
Cut square (two varieties).	1911-1933	140.00 - 180.00
Tan, wide crimped.	1934-1935	80.00 - 125.00
Tan rough twill, narrow crimped.	1936-1942	12.50 - 20.00
Tan fine twill, narrow crimped.	1942-1946	15.00 - 25.00
Khaki twill, narrow crimped (star).	1947-1958	5.00 - 10.00
Khaki twill, narrow crimped (Saturn).	1959-1960	5.00 - 10.00
Fully embroidered, cloth back.	1961-1971	1.00 - 3.00
Fully embroidered, plastic back.	1972	0.50 - 1.00

ATHLETICS
Cut square (six varieties).	1911-1933	5.00 - 12.50
Tan, wide crimped.	1934-1935	5.00 - 10.00
Tan rough twill, narrow crimped.	1936-1942	3.00 - 7.50
Tan fine twill, narrow crimped.	1942-1946	5.00 - 10.00
Khaki twill, narrow crimped.	1947-1960	1.00 - 3.00
Khaki twill, rolled edge.	1961-1968	0.50 - 1.00
Fully embroidered, cloth back.	1969-1971	1.00 - 3.00
Fully embroidered, plastic back.	1972	0.50 - 1.00

ATOMIC ENERGY
Fully embroidered, cloth back (w/o nucleus).	1963	50.00 - 75.00
Fully embroidered, cloth back (w/ nucleus).	1964-1971	1.00 - 3.00
Fully embroidered, plastic back.	1972-1993	0.50 - 1.00
Computer stitched, bagged.	1993	0.50 - 1.00

AUTO MECHANICS
Fully embroidered, plastic back.	1992	0.50 - 1.00

AUTOMOBILING
Cut square (12-spoke wheel, two varieties).	1911-1915	175.00 - 225.00
Cut square (9-spoke wheel, three varieties).	1915-1933	7.50 - 15.00
Tan, wide crimped.	1934-1935	15.00 - 25.00
Tan rough twill, narrow crimped, (wheel).	1936-1942	5.00 - 10.00
Tan fine twill, narrow crimped.	1942-1946	20.00 - 30.00
Tan rough twill, narrow crimped, (car)	1943-1946	10.00 - 17.50
Khaki twill, narrow crimped. Became automotive safety.	1947-1961	3.00 - 5.00

AUTOMOTIVE SAFETY
Khaki twill, rolled edge.	1962-1968	0.50 - 1.00
Fully embroidered, cloth back. Formerly automobiling, became traffic safety.	1969-1971	1.00 - 3.00

AVIATION
Cut square (biplane, w/ or w/o tail wing).	1911-1933	225.00 - 275.00
Tan, wide crimped.	1934-1935	250.00 - 325.00
Tan rough twill, narrow crimped.	1936-1939	100.00 - 150.00
Tan rough twill, narrow crimped, (propeller airplane).	1940-1941	800. - 1,100.
Khaki twill, narrow crimped, (jet).	1952-1960	7.50 - 15.00
Khaki twill, rolled edge.	1957-1960	7.50 - 15.00
Fully embroidered, cloth back, (no pilot in jet).	1961-1971	1.00 - 3.00
Fully embroidered, cloth back, (pilot in jet).	1961-1971	1.00 - 3.00
Fully embroidered, plastic back. Became aeronautics 1942-52.	1972	0.50 - 1.00

BACKPACKING
Fully embroidered, plastic back.	1982	0.50 - 1.00

BASKETRY
Cut square (basket w/handle).	1928-1933	20.00 - 35.00
Tan, wide crimped.	1934-1935	7.50 - 12.50
Tan rough twill, narrow crimped.	1936-1942	5.00 - 10.00
Tan fine twill, narrow crimped.	1942-1946	10.00 - 17.50
Khaki twill, narrow crimped.	1947-1960	1.00 - 3.00
Khaki twill, rolled edge.	1961-1968	0.50 - 1.00
Fully embroidered, cloth back (basket).	1969-1971	1.00 - 3.00
Fully embroidered, plastic back.	1972	0.50 - 1.00

BEE FARMING
Cut square (center grove in wings, blob at end of feet). Became beekeeping.	1911-1913	175.00 - 225.00

BEEF PRODUCTION
Cut square (white horns up).	1928-1929	325.00 - 375.00
Cut square (no horns).	1929-1933	800. - 1,100.
Tan, wide crimped.	1934-1935	300.00 - 375.00
Tan rough twill, narrow crimped.	1936-1942	10.00 - 20.00
Tan fine twill, narrow crimped.	1942-1946	15.00 - 25.00
Khaki twill, narrow crimped.	1947-1960	3.00 - 5.00
Khaki twill, rolled edge.	1961-1968	0.50 - 1.00
Fully embroidered, cloth back.	1969-1971	1.00 - 3.00
Fully embroidered, plastic back.	1972-1975	0.50 - 1.00

BEEKEEPING
Cut square (two varieties).	1914-1934	175.00 - 225.00
Tan, wide crimped.	1934-1935	350.00 - 425.00
Tan rough twill, narrow crimped (black bee, four legs).	1936-1939	275.00 - 325.00
Tan rough twill, narrow crimped (black bee, six legs).	1940-1946	75.00 - 125.00
Tan fine twill, narrow crimped.	1942-1946	175.00 - 225.00
Khaki twill, narrow crimped.	1947-1960	225.00 - 275.00
Khaki twill, narrow crimped (top view bee).	1952-1956	30.00 - 50.00
Khaki twill, narrow crimped (side view bee).	1957-1960	10.00 - 20.00
Fully embroidered, cloth back.	1961-1971	1.00 - 3.00
Fully embroidered, cloth back, silver border (error).	1969-1971	50.00 - 75.00
Fully embroidered, plastic back. Formerly bee farming.	1972-1995	0.50 - 1.00

BIRD STUDY
Cut square (two varieties).	1914-1933	7.50 - 15.00
Tan, wide crimped.	1934-1935	7.50 - 12.50
Tan rough twill, narrow crimped.	1936-1942	3.00 - 7.50
Tan fine twill, narrow crimped.	1942-1946	5.00 - 10.00
Khaki twill, narrow crimped.	1947-1960	1.00 - 3.00
Khaki twill, rolled edge.	1961-1968	0.50 - 1.00
Fully embroidered, cloth back (bird on branch).	1969-1971	1.00 - 3.00
Fully embroidered, plastic back. Formerly ornithology.	1972	0.50 - 1.00

BLACKSMITHING
Cut square (three varieties).	1911-1933	200.00 - 275.00
Tan, wide crimped.	1934-1935	200.00 - 275.00
Tan rough twill, narrow crimped.	1936-1942	40.00 - 60.00
Tan fine twill, narrow crimped.	1942-1946	125.00 - 175.00
Khaki twill, narrow crimped.	1947-1952	175.00 - 225.00

BOOKBINDING
Cut square.	1927-1933	5.00 - 12.50
Tan, wide crimped.	1934-1935	7.50 - 12.50
Tan rough twill, narrow crimped.	1936-1942	5.00 - 10.00
Tan fine twill, narrow crimped.	1942-1946	20.00 - 30.00
Khaki twill, narrow crimped.	1947-1960	3.00 - 5.00
Khaki twill, rolled edge (w/o bookmark).	1961-1966	0.50 - 1.00
Khaki twill, rolled edge (w/ bookmark).	1966-1968	3.00 - 7.50
Fully embroidered, cloth back.	1969-1971	1.00 - 3.00
Fully embroidered, plastic back.	1972-1987	0.50 - 1.00

BOTANY
Cut square.	1921-1933	60.00 - 90.00
Tan, wide crimped.	1934-1935	75.00 - 125.00
Tan rough twill, narrow crimped.	1936-1942	7.50 - 15.00
Tan fine twill, narrow crimped.	1942-1946	75.00 - 125.00
Khaki twill, narrow crimped.	1947-1960	5.00 - 10.00
Khaki twill, rolled edge.	1961-1968	0.50 - 1.00
Fully embroidered, cloth back.	1969-1971	1.00 - 3.00
Fully embroidered, plastic back.	1972-1995	0.50 - 1.00

BUGLING
Cut square (six varieties).	1911-1933	60.00 - 90.00
Tan, wide crimped.	1934-1935	60.00 - 90.00
Tan rough twill, narrow crimped.	1936-1942	5.00 - 12.50
Tan fine twill, narrow crimped.	1942-1946	80.00 - 125.00
Khaki twill, narrow crimped.	1947-1960	3.00 - 5.00
Khaki twill, rolled edge.	1961-1968	0.50 - 1.00
Fully embroidered, cloth back.	1969-1971	1.00 - 3.00
Fully embroidered, plastic back.	1972	0.50 - 1.00

BUSINESS
Cut square (three varieties).	1911-1933	80.00 - 125.00
Tan, wide crimped.	1934-1935	60.00 - 90.00
Tan rough twill, narrow crimped.	1936-1942	12.50 - 20.00
Tan fine twill, narrow crimped.	1942-1946	80.00 - 125.00
Khaki twill, narrow crimped.	1947-1960	3.00 - 5.00
Khaki twill, rolled edge. Became American business.	1961-1966	0.50 - 1.00

CAMPING
Cut square (four varieties).	1911-1933	3.00 - 10.00
Tan, wide crimped.	1934-1935	7.50 - 12.50
Tan rough twill, narrow crimped.	1936-1942	3.00 - 7.50
Tan fine twill, narrow crimped.	1942-1946	5.00 - 10.00
Khaki twill, narrow crimped.	1947-1960	1.00 - 3.00
Khaki twill, rolled edge.	1961-1968	0.50 - 1.00
Fully embroidered, cloth back, silver border.	1969-1971	1.00 - 3.00
Fully embroidered, plastic back, green border.	1972	0.50 - 1.00
Fully embroidered, plastic back, silver border.	1972	0.50 - 1.00

CANOEING

Cut square.	1927-1933	80.00 - 125.00
Tan, wide crimped.	1934-1935	80.00 - 125.00
Tan rough twill, narrow crimped.	1936-1942	7.50 - 15.00
Tan fine twill, narrow crimped.	1942-1946	25.00 - 40.00
Khaki twill, narrow crimped.	1947-1960	3.00 - 5.00
Khaki twill, rolled edge.	1961-1968	0.50 - 1.00
Fully embroidered, cloth back.	1969-1971	1.00 - 3.00
Fully embroidered, plastic back.	1972	0.50 - 1.00

CARPENTRY

Cut square (plane, eight varieties).	1911-1933	5.00 - 12.50
Tan, wide crimped.	1934-1935	5.00 - 10.00
Tan rough twill, narrow crimped.	1936-1942	3.00 - 7.50
Tan fine twill, narrow crimped.	1942-1946	5.00 - 10.00
Khaki twill, narrow crimped.	1947-1952	1.00 - 3.00
Merged into woodwork.		

CEMENT WORK

Cut square.	1927-1933	200.00 - 275.00
Tan, wide crimped.	1934-1935	200.00 - 275.00
Tan rough twill, narrow crimped.	1936-1942	30.00 - 50.00
Tan fine twill, narrow crimped.	1942-1946	200.00 - 275.00
Khaki twill, narrow crimped.	1947-1952	20.00 - 45.00

CHEMISTRY

Cut square (three varieties).	1911-1933	40.00 - 60.00
Tan, wide crimped.	1934-1935	12.50 - 20.00
Tan rough twill, narrow crimped.	1936-1942	5.00 - 10.00
Tan fine twill, narrow crimped.	1942-1946	40.00 - 60.00
Khaki twill, narrow crimped.	1947-1960	3.00 - 5.00
Khaki twill, rolled edge.	1961-1968	0.50 - 1.00
Fully embroidered, cloth back.	1969-1971	1.00 - 3.00
Fully embroidered, plastic back.	1972-1992	0.50 - 1.00
Computer stitched, bagged.	1993	0.50 - 1.00

CINEMATOGRAPHY

Fully embroidered, plastic back.	1989-1993	0.50 - 1.00
Computer stitched, bagged.	1993	0.50 - 1.00

CITIZENSHIP

Khaki twill, narrow crimped. Formerly civics, divided into the citizenship series.	1947-1951	1.00 - 3.00

CITIZENSHIP IN THE COMMUNITY

Khaki twill, narrow crimped.	1952-1960	1.00 - 3.00
Fully embroidered, cloth back, green border.	1961-1969	1.00 - 3.00
Fully embroidered, cloth back, silver border.	1969-1971	1.00 - 3.00
Fully embroidered, plastic back, silver border.	1972	0.50 - 1.00

CITIZENSHIP IN THE HOME

Khaki twill, narrow crimped.	1952-1960	1.00 - 3.00
Fully embroidered, cloth back.	1961-1971	1.00 - 3.00
Fully embroidered, plastic back.	1972-1972	0.50 - 1.00

CITIZENSHIP IN THE NATION

Khaki twill, narrow crimped.	1952-1960	1.00 - 3.00
Fully embroidered, cloth back, blue-white-red stripes, green border.	1961-1969	1.00 - 3.00
Fully embroidered, cloth back, blue-white-red stripes, silver border.	1969-1971	1.00 - 3.00
Fully embroidered, cloth back, red-white-blue stripes, large bell, silver border.	1969-1971	1.00 - 3.00
Fully embroidered, cloth back, red-white-blue stripes, small bell, silver border.	1969-1971	1.00 - 3.00
Fully embroidered, plastic back, blue-white-red, silver border.	1972-1975	0.50 - 1.00
Fully embroidered, plastic back, red-white-blue, small bell, silver border.	1976-1992	0.50 - 1.00
Fully embroidered, plastic back, red-white-blue, large bell, silver border.	1992	0.50 - 1.00

CITIZENSHIP IN THE WORLD

Fully embroidered, plastic back, silver border.	1972	0.50 - 1.00
Formerly world brotherhood.		

CITRUS FRUIT CULTURE

Cut square.	1931-1933	2,000. - 2,250.
Tan, wide crimped.	1934-1935	350.00 - 450.00
Tan rough twill, narrow crimped.	1936-1942	90.00 - 120.00
Tan fine twill, narrow crimped.	1942-1946	250.00 - 325.00
Khaki twill, narrow crimped.	1947-1954	200.00 - 275.00
Merged into fruit and nut growing.		

CIVICS

Cut square (four varieties).	1911-1933	5.00 - 10.00
Cut square (reversed colors on staff).	1911-1920	10.00 - 20.00
Tan, wide crimped.	1934-1935	5.00 - 10.00
Tan rough twill, narrow crimped.	1936-1942	3.00 - 7.50
Tan fine twill, narrow crimped.	1942-1946	5.00 - 10.00
Divided into the citizenship series.		

CLIMBING

Computer stitched, bagged.	1997	0.50 - 1.00

COIN COLLECTING

Tan rough twill, narrow crimped.	1938-1942	15.00 - 25.00
Tan fine twill, narrow crimped.	1942-1946	20.00 - 30.00
Khaki twill, narrow crimped.	1947-1960	3.00 - 5.00
Khaki twill, rolled edge (ancient coin).	1961-1968	0.50 - 1.00
Fully embroidered, cloth back (Washington quarter).	1969-1971	1.00 - 3.00
Fully embroidered, plastic back (white LIBERTY).	1972	100.00 - 140.00
Fully embroidered, plastic back (black LIBERTY).	1973-1992	0.50 - 1.00
Fully embroidered, plastic back (black ring around coin).	1992	0.50 - 1.00

COLLECTIONS

Fully embroidered, plastic back.	1992	0.50 - 1.00

COLONIAL PHILADELPHIA

Fully embroidered, cloth back (error).	1975	75.00 - 100.00
Fully embroidered, plastic back w/ green or yellow border.	1975	20.00 - 30.00

COMMUNICATIONS

Fully embroidered, cloth back.	1965-1971	1.00 - 3.00
Fully embroidered, plastic back, green border (satellite).	1972	80.00 - 110.00
Fully embroidered, plastic back, silver border (satellite).	1972-1973	0.50 - 1.00
Fully embroidered, plastic back, silver border (three views).	1973	0.50 - 1.00

COMPUTERS

Fully embroidered, cloth back.	1967-1971	1.00 - 3.00
Fully embroidered, plastic back (punch card and tape reel).	1972-1984	0.50 - 1.00
Fully embroidered, plastic back (personal computer).	1984	0.50 - 1.00

CONSERVATION

Cut square (eight varieties).	1911-1933	20.00 - 35.00
Tan, wide crimped.	1934-1935	12.50 - 20.00
Tan rough twill, narrow crimped.	1936-1942	7.50 - 12.50
Tan fine twill, narrow crimped.	1942-1946	12.50 - 20.00
Khaki twill, narrow crimped.	1947-1952	3.00 - 5.00
Became wildlife management.		

CONSERVATION OF NATURAL RESOURCES

Fully embroidered, cloth back, green border.	1966-1969	1.00 - 3.00
Fully embroidered, cloth back, silver border.	1969-1971	1.00 - 3.00
Fully embroidered, plastic back, green border.	1972-1974	3.00 - 5.00
Fully embroidered, plastic back, silver border.	1972-1974	3.00 - 5.00

SQUARE MERIT BADGE DESIGNS

From the collection of John Pleasants and Kelly Williams

AGRICULTURE

ANGLING

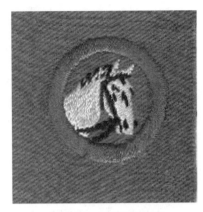

ANIMAL INDUSTRY

ARCHERY

ARCHITECTURE

ART

ASTRONOMY

ATHLETICS

AUTOMOBILING

SQUARE MERIT BADGE DESIGNS

AVIATION

BASKETRY

BEE KEEPING

*BEEF PRODUCTION
NO HORNS*

BEEF PRODUCTION - HORNS

BIRD STUDY

BOOK BINDING

BOTANY

BUGLING

SQUARE MERIT BADGE DESIGNS

BUSINESS

CAMPING

CANOEING

CARPENTRY

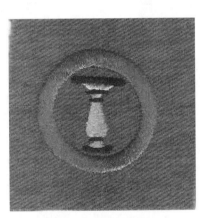

CEMENT WORK

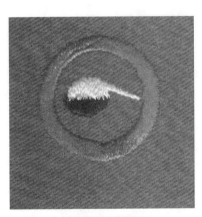

CHEMISTRY

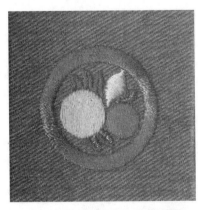

CITRUS FRUIT CULTURE

CIVICS - REVERSED COLORS

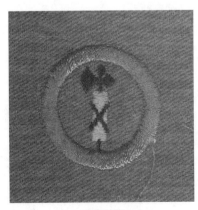

CIVICS

SQUARE MERIT BADGE DESIGNS

CONSERVATION

COOKING

CORN FARMING

COTTON FARMING

CRAFTSMANSHIP

CYCLING

DAIRYING

DRAMATICS

ELECTRICITY

SQUARE MERIT BADGE DESIGNS

FARM HOME

FARM LAYOUT

FARM MECHANICS

FARM RECORDS

FIREMANSHIP

FIRST AID TO ANIMALS

FIRST AID

FORESTRY

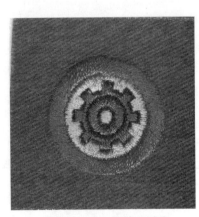

FOUNDRY SERVICE

SQUARE MERIT BADGE DESIGNS

FRUIT CULTURE

GARDENING

HANDICRAFT

HIKING

HOG PRODUCTION

HOME REPAIRS

HORSEMANSHIP

INDIAN LORE

INSECT LIFE - APHID

SQUARE MERIT BADGE DESIGNS

INSECT LIFE - SPIDER

INTERPRETING

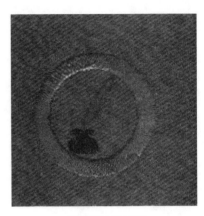

JOURNALISM

LANDSCAPE GARDENING

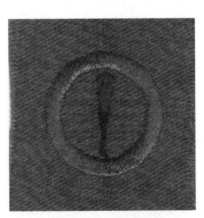

LEATHER WORKING

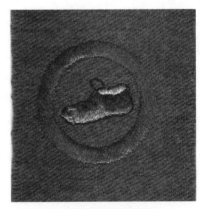

LEATHERCRAFT

LIFE SAVING

MACHINERY

MARKSMANSHIP

SQUARE MERIT BADGE DESIGNS

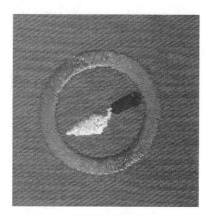

MASONRY

METALWORK

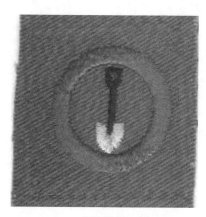

MINING

MUSIC

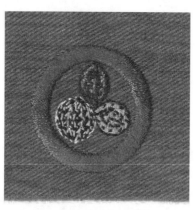

NUT CULTURE

PAINTING

PERSONAL HEALTH

PHOTOGRAPHY

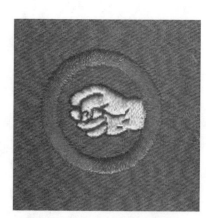

PHYSICAL DEVELOPMENT

SQUARE MERIT BADGE DESIGNS

PIGEON RAISING

PIONEERING

PLUMBING

POTTERY

PRINTING

PUBLIC HEALTH

PUBLIC SPEAKING

RADIO

READING

SQUARE MERIT BADGE DESIGNS

REPTILE STUDY

ROWING

SAFETY

SALESMANSHIP

SCHOLARSHIP

SCULPTURE

SEAMANSHIP

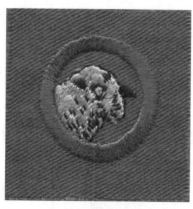

SHEEP FARMING

SIGNALING

SQUARE MERIT BADGE DESIGNS

SOIL MANAGEMENT

STALKING

STAMP COLLECTING

SURVEYING

SWIMMING

TAXIDERMY

TEXTILES

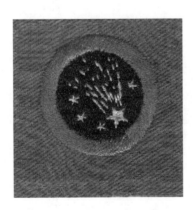

WEATHER - COMET

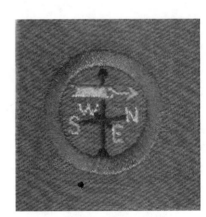

WEATHER - WEATHERVANE

SQUARE MERIT BADGE DESIGNS

WOOD CARVING

WOOD TURNING

WOODWORK

ZOOLOGY

CONSUMER BUYING
Fully embroidered, plastic back.	1975-1995	0.50 - 1.00

COOKING
Cut square (five varieties).	1911-1933	3.00 - 10.00
Tan, wide crimped.	1934-1935	5.00 - 10.00
Tan rough twill, narrow crimped.	1936-1942	3.00 - 7.50
Tan fine twill, narrow crimped.	1942-1946	5.00 - 10.00
Khaki twill, narrow crimped.	1947-1960	1.00 - 3.00
Khaki twill, rolled edge.	1961-1968	0.50 - 1.00
Fully embroidered, cloth back, silver border.	1969-1971	1.00 - 3.00
Fully embroidered, plastic back, green border.	1972	0.50 - 1.00
Fully embroidered, plastic back, silver border.	1972	0.50 - 1.00

CORN FARMING
Cut square.	1928-1933	250.00 - 325.00
Tan, wide crimped.	1934-1935	175.00 - 225.00
Tan rough twill, narrow crimped.	1936-1942	10.00 - 17.50
Tan fine twill, narrow crimped.	1942-1946	140.00 - 175.00
Khaki twill, narrow crimped.	1947-1960	5.00 - 10.00
Khaki twill, rolled edge.	1961-1968	0.50 - 1.00
Fully embroidered, cloth back.	1969-1971	1.00 - 3.00
Fully embroidered, plastic back.	1972-1975	0.50 - 1.00
Merged into plant science.		

COTTON FARMING
Cut square.	1931-1933	1,800. - 2,200.
Tan, wide crimped.	1934-1935	450.00 - 550.00
Tan rough twill, narrow crimped.	1936-1942	25.00 - 40.00
Tan fine twill, narrow crimped.	1942-1946	100.00 - 140.00
Khaki twill, narrow crimped.	1947-1960	10.00 - 15.00
Khaki twill, rolled edge.	1961-1968	0.50 - 1.00
Fully embroidered, cloth back.	1969-1971	0.50 - 1.00
Fully embroidered, plastic back.	1972-1975	0.50 - 1.00
Merged into plant science.		

CRAFTSMANSHIP
Cut square (dividers, three varieties). Split into basketry, bookbinding, cement, leather, metal, pottery, wood, wood carving.	1911-1925	5.00 - 15.00

CRIME PREVENTION
Fully embroidered, plastic back.	1996	0.50 - 1.00

CYCLING
Cut square (three varieties).	1911-1933	3.00 - 10.00
Tan, wide crimped.	1934-1935	12.50 - 20.00
Tan rough twill, narrow crimped.	1936-1942	5.00 - 10.00
Tan fine twill, narrow crimped.	1942-1946	10.00 - 15.00
Khaki twill, narrow crimped.	1947-1960	3.00 - 5.00
Khaki twill, rolled edge.	1961-1968	0.50 - 1.00
Fully embroidered, cloth back (wheel).	1969-1971	1.00 - 3.00
Fully embroidered, plastic back (bicycle).	1972-1974	0.50 - 1.00
Fully embroidered, plastic back (bicycle in triangle).	1975-1999	0.50 - 1.00

DAIRYING
Cut square (three varieties).	1911-1933	80.00 - 120.00
Tan, wide crimped.	1934-1935	80.00 - 120.00
Tan rough twill, narrow crimped.	1936-1942	7.50 - 12.50
Tan fine twill, narrow crimped.	1942-1946	20.00 - 30.00
Khaki twill, narrow crimped.	1947-1960	3.00 - 5.00
Khaki twill, rolled edge (churn).	1961-1968	0.50 - 1.00
Fully embroidered, cloth back (milk bottle).	1969-1971	1.00 - 3.00
Fully embroidered, plastic back.	1972-1975	0.50 - 1.00
Merged into animal science.		

DENTISTRY
Fully embroidered, plastic back.	1975-1993	0.50 - 1.00
Computer stitched, bagged.	1993	0.50 - 1.00

DISABILITY AWARENESS
Computer stitched, bagged.	1994	0.50 - 1.00
Formerly handicapped awareness.		

DOG CARE
Tan rough twill, narrow crimped.	1938-1942	7.50 - 12.50
Tan fine twill, narrow crimped.	1942-1946	20.00 - 30.00
Khaki twill, narrow crimped.	1947-1960	3.00 - 5.00
Khaki twill, rolled edge.	1961-1968	0.50 - 1.00
Fully embroidered, cloth back.	1969-1971	1.00 - 3.00
Fully embroidered, plastic back.	1972	0.50 - 1.00

DRAFTING
Khaki twill, rolled edge.	1965-1968	0.50 - 1.00
Fully embroidered, cloth back.	1969-1971	1.00 - 3.00
Fully embroidered, plastic back.	1972	0.50 - 1.00
Formerly mechanical drawing.		

DRAMATICS
Cut square.	1932-1933	2,300. - 2,600.
Tan, wide crimped.	1934-1935	175.00 - 225.00
Tan rough twill, narrow crimped.	1936-1942	15.00 - 25.00
Tan fine twill, narrow crimped.	1942-1946	30.00 - 40.00
Khaki twill, narrow crimped.	1947-1960	5.00 - 10.00
Fully embroidered, cloth back. Became theater.	1961-1966	1.00 - 3.00

ELECTRICITY
Cut square (four varieties).	1911-1933	3.00 - 12.50
Tan, wide crimped.	1934-1935	7.50 - 12.50
Tan rough twill, narrow crimped.	1936-1942	3.00 - 7.50
Tan fine twill, narrow crimped.	1942-1946	10.00 - 15.00
Khaki twill, narrow crimped.	1947-1960	1.00 - 3.00
Khaki twill, rolled edge (small hand).	1961-1962	30.00 - 50.00
Khaki twill, rolled edge (large hand as a blob).	1962-1963	30.00 - 60.00
Fully embroidered, cloth back (large hand w/ fingers.).	1964-1971	1.00 - 3.00
Fully embroidered, plastic back.	1972	0.50 - 1.00

ELECTRONICS
Fully embroidered, cloth back.	1963-1971	1.00 - 3.00
Fully embroidered, plastic back.	1972-1993	0.50 - 1.00
Computer stitched, bagged.	1993	0.50 - 1.00

EMERGENCY PREPAREDNESS
Fully embroidered, plastic back, red cross, silver border.	1972-1979	0.50 - 1.00
Fully embroidered, plastic back, green cross, silver border.	1979	0.50 - 1.00
Fully embroidered, plastic back, silver border (error, gold cross).	1997	10.00 - 15.00

ENERGY
Fully embroidered, plastic back.	1976-1993	0.50 - 1.00
Computer stitched, bagged.	1993	0.50 - 1.00

ENGINEERING
Fully embroidered, cloth back.	1967-1971	1.00 - 3.00
Fully embroidered, plastic back.	1972	0.50 - 1.00

ENTREPRENEURSHIP
Fully embroidered, plastic back.	1998	0.50 - 1.00

ENVIRONMENTAL SCIENCE
Fully embroidered, plastic back, silver border.	1972	0.50 - 1.00
Formerly wildlife management and zoology.		

FAMILY LIFE
Fully embroidered, plastic back, green border (large and small people).	1992	2.00 - 3.00
Fully embroidered, plastic back, silver border (large and small people).	1992	0.50 - 1.00

FARM & RANCH MANAGEMENT
Fully embroidered, plastic back. Formerly farm arrangement and farm records. — 1974-1987 — 0.50 - 1.00

FARM ARRANGEMENT
Khaki twill, narrow crimped. — 1959-1960 — 7.50 - 12.50
Fully embroidered, cloth back (small buildings). — 1961-1962 — 1.00 - 3.00
Fully embroidered, cloth back (large buildings). — 1963-1971 — 1.00 - 3.00
Fully embroidered, plastic back. Merged into farm & ranch management. — 1972-1973 — 1.00 - 3.00

FARM HOME & ITS PLANNING
Cut square. — 1928-1933 — 40.00 - 60.00
Tan, wide crimped. — 1934-1935 — 40.00 - 60.00
Tan rough twill, narrow crimped. — 1936-1942 — 7.50 - 15.00
Tan fine twill, narrow crimped. — 1942-1946 — 40.00 - 60.00
Khaki twill, narrow crimped. Merged into farm arrangement. — 1947-1958 — 5.00 - 10.00

FARM LAYOUT & BUILDING ARRANGEMENT
Cut square (picket or rail fence varieties). — 1928-1933 — 50.00 - 75.00
Tan, wide crimped. — 1934-1935 — 20.00 - 30.00
Tan rough twill, narrow crimped. — 1936-1942 — 7.50 - 15.00
Tan fine twill, narrow crimped. — 1942-1946 — 20.00 - 30.00
Khaki twill, narrow crimped. Merged into farm arrangement. — 1947-1958 — 5.00 - 10.00

FARM MECHANICS
Cut square (hoe). — 1928-1933 — 100.00 - 140.00
Tan, wide crimped. — 1934-1935 — 125.00 - 175.00
Tan rough twill, narrow crimped. — 1936-1942 — 15.00 - 25.00
Tan fine twill, narrow crimped. — 1942-1946 — 40.00 - 60.00
Khaki twill, narrow crimped. — 1947-1960 — 3.00 - 5.00
Khaki twill, rolled edge. — 1961-1968 — 0.50 - 1.00
Fully embroidered, cloth back (tractor). — 1969-1971 — 1.00 - 3.00
Fully embroidered, plastic back. — 1972-1993 — 0.50 - 1.00
Computer stitched, bagged. — 1993 — 0.50 - 1.00

FARM RECORDS
Khaki twill, narrow crimped. — 1959-1960 — 0.00 - 0.00
Khaki twill, rolled edge. — 1961-1968 — 0.50 - 1.00
Fully embroidered, cloth back. — 1969-1971 — 1.00 - 3.00
Fully embroidered, plastic back. Merged on farm & ranch management. — 1972-1978 — 0.50 - 1.00

FARM RECORDS & BOOKKEEPING
Cut square. — 1928-1933 — 125.00 - 175.00
Tan, wide crimped. — 1934-1935 — 125.00 - 175.00
Tan fine twill, narrow crimped. — 1942-1946 — 20.00 - 30.00
Khaki twill, narrow crimped. Changed to farm records. — 1947-1958 — 5.00 - 10.00

FINGERPRINTING
Tan rough twill, narrow crimped. — 1938-1942 — 10.00 - 15.00
Tan fine twill, narrow crimped. — 1942-1946 — 20.00 - 30.00
Khaki twill, narrow crimped. — 1947-1960 — 5.00 - 10.00
Fully embroidered, cloth back. — 1961-1971 — 1.00 - 3.00
Fully embroidered, plastic back. — 1972 — 0.50 - 1.00

FIRE SAFETY
Fully embroidered, plastic back. Formerly firemanship. — 1995 — 0.50 - 1.00

FIREMANSHIP
Cut square (five varieties). — 1911-1933 — 3.00 - 12.50
Tan, wide crimped. — 1934-1935 — 3.00 - 7.50
Tan rough twill, narrow crimped. — 1936-1942 — 3.00 - 7.50
Tan fine twill, narrow crimped. — 1942-1946 — 5.00 - 10.00
Khaki twill, narrow crimped. — 1947-1960 — 1.00 - 3.00
Khaki twill, rolled edge. — 1961-1968 — 0.50 - 1.00
Fully embroidered, cloth back. — 1969-1971 — 1.00 - 3.00
Fully embroidered, plastic back. Changed to fire safety. — 1972-1994 — 0.50 - 1.00

FIRST AID
Cut square (four varieties). — 1911-1933 — 3.00 - 7.50
Tan, wide crimped. — 1934-1935 — 3.00 - 7.50
Tan rough twill, narrow crimped. — 1936-1942 — 3.00 - 7.50
Tan fine twill, narrow crimped. — 1942-1946 — 5.00 - 10.00
Khaki twill, narrow crimped. — 1947-1960 — 1.00 - 3.00
Fully embroidered, cloth back, green border. — 1961-1969 — 1.00 - 3.00
Fully embroidered, cloth back, silver border. — 1969-1971 — 1.00 - 3.00
Fully embroidered, plastic back, silver border. — 1972 — 0.50 - 1.00

FIRST AID TO ANIMALS
Cut square (three varieties). — 1911-1933 — 4.00 - 15.00
Tan, wide crimped. — 1934-1935 — 5.00 - 10.00
Tan rough twill, narrow crimped. — 1936-1942 — 5.00 - 10.00
Tan fine twill, narrow crimped. — 1942-1946 — 10.00 - 15.00
Khaki twill, narrow crimped. — 1947-1960 — 3.00 - 5.00
Khaki twill, rolled edge. — 1961-1968 — 0.50 - 1.00
Fully embroidered, cloth back. — 1969-1971 — 1.00 - 3.00
Fully embroidered, plastic back, green border. — 1972 — 0.50 - 1.00
Fully embroidered, plastic back, silver border (error). Became veterinary science. — 1972 — 1.00 - 3.00

FISH & WILDLIFE MANAGEMENT
Fully embroidered, plastic back. Formerly wildlife management. — 1972 — 0.50 - 1.00

FISHING
Khaki twill, narrow crimped. — 1952-1960 — 0.00 - 0.00
Khaki twill, rolled edge. — 1961-1968 — 0.50 - 1.00
Fully embroidered, cloth back (fish jumping). — 1969-1971 — 1.00 - 3.00
Fully embroidered, plastic back. Formerly angling. — 1972 — 0.50 - 1.00

FOOD SYSTEMS
Fully embroidered, cloth back (error). — 1978-1979 — 10.00 - 15.00
Fully embroidered, plastic back. Merged into plant science. — 1978-1987 — 0.50 - 1.00

FORAGE CROPS
Khaki twill, narrow crimped. — 1959-1960 — 0.00 - 0.00
Fully embroidered, cloth back. — 1961-1971 — 1.00 - 3.00
Fully embroidered, plastic back. Formerly grasses, legumes & forage crops; merged into plant science. — 1972-1975 — 0.50 - 1.00

FORESTRY
Cut square (four varieties). — 1912-1933 — 40.00 - 65.00
Tan, wide crimped. — 1934-1935 — 12.50 - 20.00
Tan rough twill, narrow crimped. — 1936-1942 — 7.50 - 12.50
Tan fine twill, narrow crimped. — 1942-1946 — 12.50 - 20.00
Khaki twill, narrow crimped. — 1947-1960 — 3.00 - 5.00
Khaki twill, rolled edge (bud). — 1961-1968 — 0.50 - 1.00
Fully embroidered, cloth back (tree). — 1969-1971 — 1.00 - 3.00
Fully embroidered, plastic back. — 1972 — 0.50 - 1.00

FOUNDRY PRACTICE
Cut square. — 1923-1933 — 225.00 - 275.00
Tan, wide crimped. — 1934-1935 — 225.00 - 275.00
Tan rough twill, narrow crimped. — 1936-1942 — 60.00 - 90.00
Tan fine twill, narrow crimped. — 1942-1946 — 100.00 - 140.00
Khaki twill, narrow crimped. — 1947-1952 — 80.00 - 120.00

FRUIT & NUT GROWING
Khaki twill, narrow crimped. — 1953-1960 — 10.00 - 20.00
Fully embroidered, cloth back. — 1961-1971 — 1.00 - 3.00
Fully embroidered, plastic back. Formerly fruit culture; merged into plant science. — 1972-1975 — 0.50 - 1.00

FRUIT CULTURE

Cut square.	1928-1933	1,000. - 1,350.
Tan, wide crimped.	1934-1935	225.00 - 275.00
Tan rough twill, narrow crimped.	1936-1942	90.00 - 120.00
Tan fine twill, narrow crimped.	1942-1946	100.00 - 150.00
Khaki twill, narrow crimped.	1947-1954	100.00 - 175.00
Merged into fruit & nut growing.		

GARDENING

Cut square (tan corn, four varieties).	1911-1933	150.00 - 200.00
Cut square (white corn, two varieties).	1911-1933	60.00 - 90.00
Cut square (yellow corn).	1911-1933	60.00 - 90.00
Tan, wide crimped.	1934-1935	40.00 - 60.00
Tan rough twill, narrow crimped (vegetables).	1936-1942	12.50 - 20.00
Tan rough twill, narrow crimped (yellow corn).	1936-1939	15.00 - 25.00
Tan fine twill, narrow crimped.	1940-1946	20.00 - 30.00
Khaki twill, narrow crimped.	1947-1960	5.00 - 10.00
Fully embroidered, cloth back.	1961-1971	1.00 - 3.00
Khaki twill, rolled edge.	1961-1968	0.50 - 1.00
Fully embroidered, plastic back.	1972	0.50 - 1.00
Computer stitched, bagged.	1993	0.50 - 1.00

GENEALOGY

Fully embroidered, plastic back.	1972	0.50 - 1.00

GENERAL SCIENCE

Fully embroidered, plastic back.	1972-1993	0.50 - 1.00
Computer stitched, bagged.	1993-1995	0.50 - 1.00

GEOLOGY

Khaki twill, narrow crimped.	1953-1960	5.00 - 10.00
Fully embroidered, cloth back.	1961-1971	1.00 - 3.00
Fully embroidered, plastic back.	1972	0.50 - 1.00
Formerly rocks & minerals.		

GOLF

Fully embroidered, plastic back.	1976-1993	0.50 - 1.00
Computer stitched, bagged.	1993	0.50 - 1.00

GRAPHIC ARTS

Fully embroidered, plastic back.	1987	0.50 - 1.00
Formerly printing.		

GRASSES, LEGUMES & FORAGE CROPS

Tan rough twill, narrow crimped.	1938-1942	25.00 - 40.00
Tan fine twill, narrow crimped.	1942-1946	35.00 - 50.00
Khaki twill, narrow crimped.	1947-1958	7.50 - 15.00
Changed to forage crops.		

HANDICAPPED (HANDICAP) AWARENESS

Fully embroidered, plastic back.	1980-1993	0.50 - 1.00
Changed to disability awareness.		

HANDICRAFT

Cut square.	1911-1933	3.00 - 7.50
Tan, wide crimped.	1934-1935	3.00 - 7.50
Tan rough twill, narrow crimped.	1936-1942	3.00 - 7.50
Tan fine twill, narrow crimped.	1942	5.00 - 10.00
Became home repairs.		

HIKING

Cut square.	1921-1933	30.00 - 50.00
Tan, wide crimped.	1934-1935	50.00 - 75.00
Tan rough twill, narrow crimped.	1936-1942	7.50 - 12.50
Tan fine twill, narrow crimped.	1942-1946	40.00 - 60.00
Khaki twill, narrow crimped.	1947-1960	1.00 - 3.00
Khaki twill, rolled edge (shoe).	1961-1968	0.50 - 1.00
Fully embroidered, cloth back (scout hiking).	1969-1971	1.00 - 3.00
Fully embroidered, plastic back.	1972	0.50 - 1.00

HOG & PORK PRODUCTION

Cut square.	1928-1933	225.00 - 275.00
Tan, wide crimped.	1934-1935	175.00 - 225.00
Tan rough twill, narrow crimped.	1936-1942	12.50 - 20.00
Tan fine twill, narrow crimped.	1942-1946	125.00 - 175.00
Khaki twill, narrow crimped.	1947-1958	3.00 - 5.00
Changed to hog production.		

HOG PRODUCTION

Khaki twill, narrow crimped.	1959-1960	0.00 - 0.00
Khaki twill, rolled edge.	1961-1968	0.50 - 1.00
Fully embroidered, cloth back.	1969-1971	1.00 - 3.00
Fully embroidered, plastic back.	1972-1975	0.50 - 1.00
Formerly hog & pork production; merged into animal science.		

HOME REPAIRS

Tan rough twill, narrow crimped.	1943-1946	1.00 - 3.00
Khaki twill, narrow crimped.	1947-1960	1.00 - 3.00
Khaki twill, rolled edge.	1961-1968	0.50 - 1.00
Fully embroidered, cloth back.	1969-1971	1.00 - 3.00
Fully embroidered, plastic back.	1972	0.50 - 1.00
Formerly handicraft.		

HORSEMANSHIP

Cut square.	1911-1933	40.00 - 60.00
Tan, wide crimped.	1934-1935	50.00 - 75.00
Tan rough twill, narrow crimped.	1936-1942	7.50 - 12.50
Tan fine twill, narrow crimped.	1942-1946	50.00 - 75.00
Khaki twill, narrow crimped.	1947-1960	5.00 - 10.00
Khaki twill, rolled edge (horseshoe).	1961-1968	0.50 - 1.00
Fully embroidered, cloth back (saddle).	1969-1971	1.00 - 3.00
Fully embroidered, plastic back.	1972	0.50 - 1.00

INDIAN LORE

Cut square.	1931-1933	400.00 - 550.00
Tan, wide crimped.	1934-1935	100.00 - 140.00
Tan rough twill, narrow crimped.	1936-1942	10.00 - 15.00
Tan fine twill, narrow crimped.	1942-1946	20.00 - 30.00
Khaki twill, narrow crimped.	1947-1960	3.00 - 5.00
Khaki twill, rolled edge (arrowpoint).	1961-1968	0.50 - 1.00
Fully embroidered, cloth back (headdress).	1969-1971	1.00 - 3.00
Fully embroidered, plastic back.	1972	0.50 - 1.00

INSECT LIFE

Cut square (spider on web).	1923-1924	2,250. - 2,750.
Cut square (aphid on twig).	1924-1933	450.00 - 550.00
Tan, wide crimped.	1934-1935	450.00 - 550.00
Tan rough twill, narrow crimped.	1936-1942	12.50 - 20.00
Tan fine twill, narrow crimped.	1942-1946	30.00 - 45.00
Khaki twill, narrow crimped.	1947-1960	3.00 - 5.00
Khaki twill, rolled edge.	1961-1968	0.50 - 1.00
Fully embroidered, cloth back.	1969-1971	1.00 - 3.00
Fully embroidered, plastic back.	1972-1984	0.50 - 1.00
Changed to insect study.		

INSECT STUDY

Fully embroidered, plastic back.	1985	0.50 - 1.00

INTERPRETING

Cut square (four varieties).	1911-1933	100.00 - 140.00
Tan, wide crimped.	1934-1935	100.00 - 140.00
Tan rough twill, narrow crimped.	1936-1942	25.00 - 40.00
Tan fine twill, narrow crimped.	1942-1946	80.00 - 120.00
Khaki twill, narrow crimped. Changed to interpreter's strips.	1947-1952	100.00 - 120.00

INVENTION

Cut square. None known to exist in collections; only 10 earned.	1911-1915	

ROUND MERIT BADGE DESIGNS

AGRICULTURE

AMERICAN BUSINESS

AMERICAN CULTURES

AMERICAN HERITAGE

AMERICAN LABOR

ANIMAL SCIENCE

ARCHERY

ARCHITECTURE

ART

ASTRONOMY

ATHLETICS

ATOMIC ENERGY

AUTO MECHANICS

AUTOMOTIVE SAFETY

AVIATION

BACKPACKING

ROUND MERIT BADGE DESIGNS

BASKETRY

BEEKEEPING

BEEF PRODUCTION

BIRD STUDY

BOOK BINDING

BOTANY

BUGLING

CAMPING

CANOEING

CHEMISTRY

CINEMATOGRAPHY

*CITIZENSHIP
IN THE COMMUNITY*

*CITIZENSHIP
IN THE NATION*

*CITIZENSHIP
IN THE WORLD*

COIN COLLECTING

COLLECTIONS

ROUND MERIT BADGE DESIGNS

COMMUNICATIONS

*COMPUTERS
(OLD DESIGN)*

COMPUTERS

CONSUMER BUYING

COOKING

COTTON FARMING

CYCLING (OLD)

CYCLING

DAIRYING

DENTISTRY

*DISABILITIES
AWARENESS*

DOG CARE

DRAFTING

ELECTRICITY

ELECTRONICS

*EMERGENCY
PREPAREDNESS
red or green cross*

ROUND MERIT BADGE DESIGNS

ENERGY

ENGINEERING

ENVIRONMENTAL SCIENCE

FAMILY LIFE

FARM ARRANGEMENT

FARM MECHANICS

FARM RECORDS

FINGERPRINTING

FIRE SAFETY

FIRST AID

FISH AND WILDLIFE MANAGEMENT

FISHING

FORESTRY

FORRAGE CROPS

FRUIT AND NUT GROWING

GARDENING

ROUND MERIT BADGE DESIGNS

GENEALOGY

GENERAL SCIENCE

GEOLOGY

GOLF

GRAPHIC ARTS

HIKING

HOG PRODUCTION

HOME REPAIRS

HORSEMANSHIP

INDIAN LORE

INSECT STUDY

JOURNALISM (OLD)

JOURNALISM (NEW)

LANDSCAPE ARCHITECTURE

LAW

LEATHERWORK

ROUND MERIT BADGE DESIGNS

LIFESAVING

MACHINERY

MAMMAL STUDY

MASONRY

MEDICINE

METAL WORKS

METALS ENGINEERING

*MODEL DESIGN
AND BUILDING*

MOTORBOATING

MUSIC

NATURE

OCEANOGRAPHY

ORIENTEERING

PAINTING

PERSONAL FINANCES

PERSONAL FITNESS

ROUND MERIT BADGE DESIGNS

PERSONAL
MANAGEMENT

PETS

PHOTOGRAPHY

PIGEON RAISING

PIONEERING

PLANT SCIENCE

PLUMBING

POTTERY

POULTRY KEEPING

PRINTING

PUBLIC HEALTH

PUBLIC SPEAKING

PULP & PAPER

RABBIT RAISING

RADIO

RAILROADING

ROUND MERIT BADGE DESIGNS

READING

REPTILE STUDY

REPTILE AND AMPHIBIAN STUDY

RIFLE SHOOTING

RIFLE AND SHOTGUN SHOOTING

ROWING

SAFETY

SALESMANSHIP

SCHOLARSHIP

SCULPTURE

SHEEP FARMING

SHOTGUN SHOOTING

SIGNALING

SKATING

SKIING

SMALL BOAT SAILING

ROUND MERIT BADGE DESIGNS

SMALL GRAINS

SNOW SPORTS

SOIL & WATER

SPACE EXPLORATION

SPORTS

STAMP COLLECTING

SURVEYING

SWIMMING

TEXTILE

THEATER

TRAFFIC SAFETY

TRUCK TRANSPORTATION

VETERINARY MEDICINE

WATER SKIING

WEATHER

WHITEWATER

ROUND MERIT BADGE DESIGNS

WILDERNESS SURVIVAL

WOODCARVING

WOODWORK

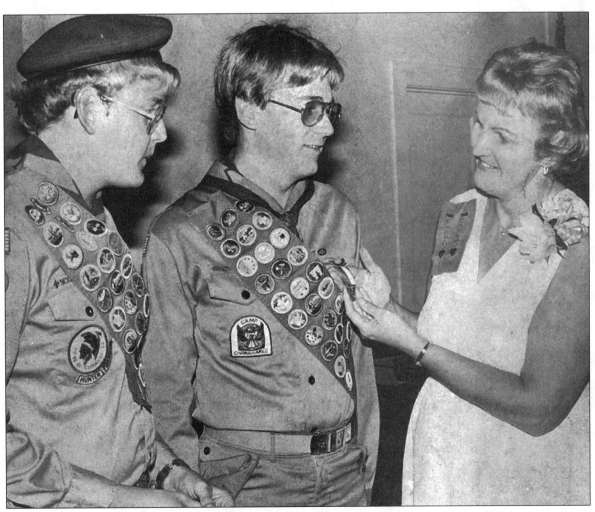

Brothers Dean and Dale Parks receive their eagle medals from their mom, Margaret Parks, who proudly sports a double "mother pin" ribbon.

JOURNALISM

Cut square.	1927-1933	125.00 - 175.00
Tan, wide crimped.	1934-1935	40.00 - 60.00
Tan rough twill, narrow crimped.	1936-1942	7.50 - 12.50
Tan fine twill, narrow crimped.	1942-1946	15.00 - 25.00
Khaki twill, narrow crimped.	1947-1960	5.00 - 10.00
Khaki twill, rolled edge (inkwell & quill).	1961-1968	0.50 - 1.00
Fully embroidered, cloth back (typewriter J-key).	1969-1971	1.00 - 3.00
Fully embroidered, plastic back.	1972-1976	0.50 - 1.00
Fully embroidered, cloth back, (error) (microphone).	1976	40.00 - 60.00
Fully embroidered, plastic back.	1976-1992	0.50 - 1.00
Computer stitched, bagged.	1993	0.50 - 1.00

LANDSCAPE ARCHITECTURE

Fully embroidered, cloth back (fountain and sun dial).	1967-1969	1.00 - 3.00
Fully embroidered, cloth back (pine tree).	1969-1971	1.00 - 3.00
Fully embroidered, plastic back.	1972-1993	0.50 - 1.00
Computer stitched, bagged. Formerly landscaping.	1993	0.50 - 1.00

LANDSCAPE GARDENING

Cut square.	1930-1933	400.00 - 500.00
Tan, wide crimped.	1934-1935	125.00 - 175.00
Tan rough twill, narrow crimped.	1936-1942	20.00 - 30.00
Tan fine twill, narrow crimped.	1942-1946	100.00 - 140.00
Khaki twill, narrow crimped.	1947-1958	5.00 - 10.00

LANDSCAPING

Khaki twill, narrow crimped.	1959-1960	5.00 - 10.00
Khaki twill, rolled edge. Formerly landscape gardening, became landscape architecture.	1961-1966	3.00 - 5.00

LAW

Fully embroidered, plastic back.	1974	0.50 - 1.00

LEATHERCRAFT

Cut square (shoe).	1927-1933	3.00 - 7.50
Tan, wide crimped.	1934-1935	7.50 - 12.50
Tan rough twill, narrow crimped.	1936-1942	3.00 - 7.50
Tan fine twill, narrow crimped.	1942-1946	10.00 - 15.00
Khaki twill, narrow crimped. Merged into leatherwork.	1947-1952	0.00 - 0.00

LEATHERWORK

Khaki twill, narrow crimped.	1947-1952	3.00 - 5.00
Khaki twill, narrow crimped (shoe).	1953-1960	3.00 - 5.00
Fully embroidered, cloth back.	1961-1971	1.00 - 3.00
Khaki twill, rolled edge.	1961-1968	0.50 - 1.00
Fully embroidered, plastic back. Formerly leather working and leather craft.	1972	0.50 - 1.00

LEATHERWORKING

Cut square (awl, four varieties).	1911-1933	25.00 - 40.00

LEATHERWORKING/ LEATHERWORK

Tan, wide crimped.	1934-1935	80.00 - 120.00
Tan rough twill, narrow crimped.	1936-1942	10.00 - 15.00
Tan fine twill, narrow crimped. Merged into leatherwork.	1942-1946	12.50 - 17.50

LIFESAVING

Cut square (all white buoy).	1911-1920	25.00 - 40.00
Cut square (white and green buoy).	1915-1933	3.00 - 7.50
Tan, wide crimped.	1934-1935	5.00 - 10.00
Tan rough twill, narrow crimped.	1936-1942	3.00 - 7.50
Tan fine twill, narrow crimped.	1942-1946	5.00 - 10.00
Khaki twill, narrow crimped.	1947-1960	1.00 - 3.00
Khaki twill, rolled edge.	1961-1968	0.50 - 1.00
Fully embroidered, cloth back, silver border.	1969-1971	1.00 - 3.00
Fully embroidered, plastic back, silver border.	1972	0.50 - 1.00

MACHINERY

Cut square (three varieties).	1912-1933	20.00 - 30.00
Tan, wide crimped.	1934-1935	20.00 - 35.00
Tan rough twill, narrow crimped.	1936-1942	5.00 - 10.00
Tan fine twill, narrow crimped.	1942-1946	10.00 - 15.00
Khaki twill, narrow crimped.	1947-1960	3.00 - 5.00
Khaki twill, rolled edge.	1961-1968	0.50 - 1.00
Fully embroidered, cloth back.	1969-1971	1.00 - 3.00
Fully embroidered, plastic back.	1972-1993	0.50 - 1.00

MAMMAL STUDY

Fully embroidered, plastic back. Formerly mammals.	1985	0.00 - 0.00

MAMMALS

Fully embroidered, plastic back. Became mammal study.	1972-1985	0.50 - 1.00

MARKSMANSHIP

Cut square.	1911-1933	20.00 - 35.00
Tan, wide crimped.	1934-1935	12.50 - 20.00
Tan rough twill, narrow crimped.	1936-1942	7.50 - 15.00
Tan fine twill, narrow crimped.	1942-1946	12.50 - 20.00
Khaki twill, narrow crimped.	1947-1960	3.00 - 5.00
Fully embroidered, cloth back. Became rifle and shotgun shooting.	1961-1966	1.00 - 3.00

MASONRY

Cut square (three varieties).	1911-1933	35.00 - 55.00
Tan, wide crimped.	1934-1935	25.00 - 45.00
Tan rough twill, narrow crimped.	1936-1942	5.00 - 12.50
Tan fine twill, narrow crimped.	1942-1946	12.50 - 20.00
Khaki twill, narrow crimped.	1947-1960	3.00 - 5.00
Khaki twill, rolled edge.	1961-1968	0.50 - 1.00
Fully embroidered, cloth back.	1969-1971	1.00 - 3.00
Fully embroidered, plastic back.	1972-1995	0.50 - 1.00

MECHANICAL DRAWING

Cut square.	1933	1,100. - 1,350.
Tan, wide crimped.	1934-1935	100.00 - 140.00
Tan rough twill, narrow crimped.	1936-1942	5.00 - 10.00
Tan fine twill, narrow crimped.	1942-1946	10.00 - 15.00
Khaki twill, narrow crimped.	1947-1960	3.00 - 5.00
Khaki twill, rolled edge Changed to drafting.	1961-1964	0.50 - 1.00

MEDICINE

Fully embroidered, plastic back.	1992	0.50 - 1.00

METALLURGY

Fully embroidered, cloth back. Became medals engineering.	1965-1971	1.00 - 3.00

METALS ENGINEERING

Fully embroidered, plastic back.	1972-1993	0.50 - 1.00
Computer stitched, bagged. Formerly metallurgy.	1993-1995	0.50 - 1.00

METALWORK

Cut square.	1927-1933	10.00 - 17.50
Tan, wide crimped.	1934-1935	7.50 - 12.50
Tan rough twill, narrow crimped.	1936-1942	3.00 - 7.50
Tan fine twill, narrow crimped.	1942-1946	7.50 - 12.50
Khaki twill, narrow crimped.	1947-1960	1.00 - 3.00
Khaki twill, rolled edge.	1961-1968	0.50 - 1.00
Fully embroidered, cloth back.	1969-1971	1.00 - 3.00
Fully embroidered, plastic back.	1972	0.50 - 1.00

MINING

Cut square (three varieties).	1911-1933	225.00 - 275.00
Tan, wide crimped.	1934-1935	275.00 - 350.00
Tan rough twill, narrow crimped.	1936-1947	800.00 - 1,100.

MODEL DESIGN & BUILDING
Fully embroidered, cloth back.	1963-1971	1.00 - 3.00
Fully embroidered, plastic back.	1972	0.50 - 1.00

MOTORBOATING
Fully embroidered, cloth back.	1961-1971	1.00 - 3.00
Fully embroidered, plastic back.	1972	0.50 - 1.00

MUSIC
Cut square (three varieties).	1911-1933	15.00 - 30.00
Tan, wide crimped.	1934-1935	7.50 - 12.50
Tan rough twill, narrow crimped.	1936-1942	2.50 - 7.50
Tan fine twill, narrow crimped.	1942-1946	7.50 - 12.50
Khaki twill, narrow crimped.	1947-1960	3.00 - 5.00
Khaki twill, rolled edge.	1961-1968	0.50 - 1.00
Fully embroidered, cloth back.	1969-1971	1.00 - 3.00
Fully embroidered, plastic back.	1972	0.50 - 1.00

NATURE
Khaki twill, narrow crimped.	1952-1960	1.00 - 3.00
Fully embroidered, cloth back, green border.	1961-1969	1.00 - 3.00
Fully embroidered, cloth back, silver border.	1969-1971	1.00 - 3.00
Fully embroidered, plastic back, green border.	1972	0.50 - 1.00
Fully embroidered, plastic back, silver border.	1972	0.50 - 1.00

NUT CULTURE
Cut square.	1928-1933	2,000. - 2,400.
Tan, wide crimped.	1934-1935	400.00 - 500.00
Tan rough twill, narrow crimped.	1936-1942	225.00 - 275.00
Tan fine twill, narrow crimped.	1942-1946	325.00 - 375.00
Khaki twill, narrow crimped.	1947-1954	225.00 - 275.00
Merged into fruit & nut growing.		

OCEANOGRAPHY
Fully embroidered, cloth back.	1964-1971	1.00 - 3.00
Fully embroidered, plastic back.	1972	0.50 - 1.00

ORIENTEERING
Fully embroidered, plastic back.	1973	0.50 - 1.00

ORNITHOLOGY
Cut square. Became bird study.	1911-1913	0.00 - 0.00

PAINTING
Cut square (narrow brush).	1911-1933	15.00 - 25.00
Cut square (wide brush).	1911-1920	175.00 - 225.00
Tan, wide crimped.	1934-1935	12.50 - 20.00
Tan rough twill, narrow crimped.	1936-1942	5.00 - 10.00
Tan fine twill, narrow crimped.	1942-1946	12.50 - 17.50
Khaki twill, narrow crimped.	1947-1960	3.00 - 5.00
Khaki twill, rolled edge.	1961-1968	0.50 - 1.00
Fully embroidered, cloth back.	1969-1971	1.00 - 3.00
Fully embroidered, plastic back.	1972	0.50 - 1.00

PATHFINDING
Cut square (five feathers).	1911-1933	3.00 - 10.00
Cut square (four feathers, three varieties).	1911-1933	3.00 - 10.00
Cut square (six feathers, five varieties).	1911-1933	3.00 - 10.00
Tan, wide crimped.	1934-1935	5.00 - 10.00
Tan rough twill, narrow crimped.	1936-1942	3.00 - 7.50
Tan fine twill, narrow crimped.	1942-1946	7.50 - 12.50
Khaki twill, narrow crimped.	1947-1952	1.00 - 3.00

PERSONAL FINANCES
Fully embroidered, cloth back.	1962-1971	1.00 - 3.00
Fully embroidered, plastic back.	1972	0.50 - 1.00
Became personal management.		

PERSONAL FITNESS
Khaki twill, narrow crimped.	1952-1960	0.00 - 0.00
Khaki twill, rolled edge.	1961-1968	0.50 - 1.00
Fully embroidered, cloth back, silver border.	1969-1971	1.00 - 3.00
Fully embroidered, plastic back, silver border.	1972	0.50 - 1.00

PERSONAL HEALTH
Cut square.	1911-1933	3.00 - 10.00
Tan, wide crimped.	1934-1935	3.00 - 7.50
Tan rough twill, narrow crimped.	1936-1942	3.00 - 7.50
Tan fine twill, narrow crimped.	1942-1946	5.00 - 10.00
Khaki twill, narrow crimped.	1947-1951	1.00 - 3.00
Merged into personal fitness.		

PERSONAL MANAGEMENT
Fully embroidered, plastic back, silver border. Formerly personal finances.	1972	0.50 - 1.00

PETS
Khaki twill, narrow crimped.	1958-1960	7.50 - 12.50
Khaki twill, rolled edge.	1961-1968	0.50 - 1.00
Fully embroidered, cloth back.	1969-1971	1.00 - 3.00
Fully embroidered, plastic back, silver border.	1972	0.50 - 1.00

PHOTOGRAPHY
Cut square.	1911-1933	30.00 - 45.00
Tan, wide crimped.	1934-1935	40.00 - 60.00
Tan rough twill, narrow crimped.	1936-1942	12.50 - 20.00
Tan fine twill, narrow crimped.	1942-1946	80.00 - 120.00
Khaki twill, narrow crimped (tripod camera).	1947-1953	7.50 - 15.00
Khaki twill, narrow crimped (camera).	1954-1960	5.00 - 10.00
Fully embroidered, cloth back.	1961-1971	1.00 - 3.00
Fully embroidered, plastic back.	1972	0.50 - 1.00
Computer stitched, bagged.	1993	0.50 - 1.00

PHYSICAL DEVELOPMENT
Cut square (straight extended thumb, three varieties).	1914-1920	275.00 - 350.00
Cut square (regular bent thumb, two varieties).	1920-1933	15.00 - 25.00
Tan, wide crimped.	1934-1935	7.50 - 12.50
Tan rough twill, narrow crimped.	1936-1942	3.00 - 7.50
Tan fine twill, narrow crimped.	1942-1946	10.00 - 17.50
Khaki twill, narrow crimped.	1947-1952	5.00 - 10.00
Merged into personal health which later became personal fitness.		

PIGEON RAISING
Cut square.	1933	3,500. - 4,500.
Tan, wide crimped.	1934-1935	250.00 - 325.00
Tan rough twill, narrow crimped.	1936-1942	10.00 - 17.50
Tan fine twill, narrow crimped.	1942-1946	100.00 - 140.00
Khaki twill, narrow crimped.	1947-1960	5.00 - 10.00
Khaki twill, rolled edge.	1961-1968	0.50 - 1.00
Fully embroidered, cloth back.	1969-1971	1.00 - 3.00
Fully embroidered, plastic back.	1972-1980	0.50 - 1.00
Merged into bird study.		

PIONEERING
Cut square (four varieties).	1911-1933	3.00 - 10.00
Tan, wide crimped.	1934-1935	5.00 - 10.00
Tan rough twill, narrow crimped.	1936-1942	3.00 - 7.50
Tan fine twill, narrow crimped.	1942-1946	5.00 - 10.00
Khaki twill, narrow crimped.	1947-1960	1.00 - 3.00
Khaki twill, rolled edge.	1961-1968	0.50 - 1.00
Fully embroidered, cloth back (signal tower).	1969-1971	1.00 - 3.00
Fully embroidered, plastic back.	1972	0.50 - 1.00

PLANT SCIENCE
Fully embroidered, plastic back.	1974	0.50 - 1.00

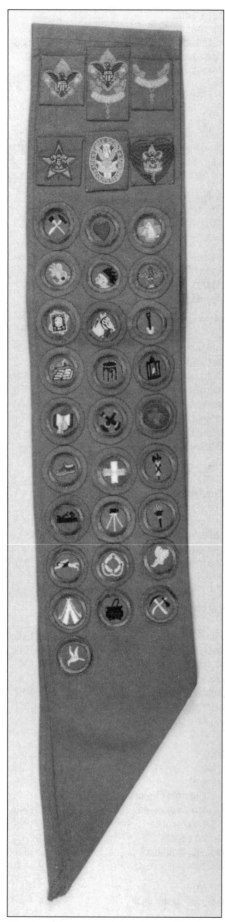

Sash with many wide crimped badges.

PLUMBING

Cut square (two varieties).	1912-1933	20.00 - 35.00
Tan, wide crimped.	1934-1935	12.50 - 20.00
Tan rough twill, narrow crimped.	1936-1942	5.00 - 10.00
Tan fine twill, narrow crimped.	1942-1946	12.50 - 17.50
Khaki twill, narrow crimped.	1947-1960	3.00 - 5.00
Khaki twill, rolled edge.	1961-1968	0.50 - 1.00
Fully embroidered, cloth back.	1969-1971	1.00 - 3.00
Fully embroidered, plastic back.	1972-1993	0.50 - 1.00
Computer stitched, bagged.	1993	0.50 - 1.00

POTTERY

Cut square.	1927-1933	275.00 - 325.00
Tan, wide crimped.	1934-1935	175.00 - 225.00
Tan rough twill, narrow crimped.	1936-1942	20.00 - 35.00
Tan fine twill, narrow crimped.	1942-1946	40.00 - 60.00
Khaki twill, narrow crimped.	1947-1960	5.00 - 10.00
Khaki twill, rolled edge.	1961-1968	0.50 - 1.00
Fully embroidered, cloth back.	1969-1971	1.00 - 3.00
Fully embroidered, plastic back.	1972	0.50 - 1.00

POULTRY FARMING

Cut square.	1911-1913	100.00 - 140.00

POULTRY KEEPING

Cut square (four varieties).	1914-1933	100.00 - 140.00
Tan, wide crimped.	1934-1935	175.00 - 225.00
Tan rough twill, narrow crimped.	1936-1942	7.50 - 15.00
Tan fine twill, narrow crimped.	1942-1946	100.00 - 140.00
Khaki twill, narrow crimped.	1947-1960	5.00 - 10.00
Khaki twill, rolled edge.	1961-1968	0.50 - 1.00
Fully embroidered, cloth back.	1969-1971	1.00 - 3.00
Fully embroidered, plastic back.	1972-1975	0.50 - 1.00
Merged into animal science.		

PRINTING

Cut square (two varieties).	1911-1933	25.00 - 40.00
Tan, wide crimped.	1934-1935	15.00 - 30.00
Tan rough twill, narrow crimped.	1936-1942	10.00 - 15.00
Tan fine twill, narrow crimped.	1942-1946	15.00 - 25.00
Khaki twill, narrow crimped.	1947-1960	3.00 - 5.00
Khaki twill, rolled edge.	1961-1968	0.50 - 1.00
Fully embroidered, cloth back.	1969-1971	1.00 - 3.00
Fully embroidered, plastic back.	1972-1981	0.50 - 1.00
Changed to printing communication.		

PRINTING COMMUNICATION

Fully embroidered, plastic back.	1982-1989	0.50 - 1.00
Formerly printing; became graphic arts.		

PUBLIC HEALTH

Cut square (four varieties).	1911-1933	3.00 - 10.00
Tan, wide crimped.	1934-1935	3.00 - 7.50
Tan rough twill, narrow crimped.	1936-1942	3.00 - 7.50
Tan fine twill, narrow crimped.	1942-1946	5.00 - 10.00
Khaki twill, narrow crimped.	1947-1960	1.00 - 3.00
Khaki twill, rolled edge.	1961-1968	0.50 - 1.00
Fully embroidered, cloth back.	1969-1971	1.00 - 3.00
Fully embroidered, plastic back.	1972	0.50 - 1.00
Computer stitched, bagged.	1993	0.50 - 1.00

PUBLIC SPEAKING

Cut square.	1932-1933	350.00 - 450.00
Tan, wide crimped.	1934-1935	100.00 - 140.00
Tan rough twill, narrow crimped.	1936-1942	10.00 - 15.00
Tan fine twill, narrow crimped.	1942-1946	100.00 - 140.00
Khaki twill, narrow crimped.	1947-1960	3.00 - 5.00
Khaki twill, rolled edge.	1961-1968	0.50 - 1.00
Fully embroidered, cloth back.	1969-1971	1.00 - 3.00
Fully embroidered, plastic back.	1972-1992	0.50 - 1.00
Computer stitched, bagged.	1993	0.50 - 1.00

PULP & PAPER
Fully embroidered, plastic back.   1972   0.50 - 1.00

RABBIT RAISING
Tan fine twill, narrow crimped.	1943-1946	15.00 - 25.00
Khaki twill, narrow crimped.	1947-1960	5.00 - 10.00
Khaki twill, rolled edge.	1961-1968	0.50 - 1.00
Fully embroidered, cloth back.	1969-1971	1.00 - 3.00
Fully embroidered, plastic back.	1972-1993	0.50 - 1.00

RADIO
Cut square. Formerly wireless.	1923-1933	100.00 - 140.00
Tan, wide crimped.	1934-1935	60.00 - 90.00
Tan rough twill, narrow crimped.	1936-1942	12.50 - 17.50
Tan fine twill, narrow crimped.	1942-1946	40.00 - 60.00
Khaki twill, narrow crimped.	1947-1960	5.00 - 10.00
Khaki twill, rolled edge.	1961-1968	0.50 - 1.00
Fully embroidered, cloth back.	1969-1971	1.00 - 3.00
Fully embroidered, plastic back.	1972	0.50 - 1.00

RAILROADING
Khaki twill, narrow crimped.	1952-1960	5.00 - 10.00
Fully embroidered, cloth back.	1961-1971	1.00 - 3.00
Fully embroidered, plastic back.	1972	0.50 - 1.00

READING
Cut square.	1929-1933	10.00 - 17.50
Tan, wide crimped.	1934-1935	5.00 - 10.00
Tan rough twill, narrow crimped.	1936-1942	3.00 - 7.50
Tan fine twill, narrow crimped.	1942-1946	5.00 - 10.00
Khaki twill, narrow crimped.	1947-1960	1.00 - 3.00
Khaki twill, rolled edge.	1961-1968	0.50 - 1.00
Fully embroidered, cloth back.	1969-1971	1.00 - 3.00
Fully embroidered, plastic back.	1972	0.50 - 1.00

REPTILE & AMPHIBIAN STUDY
Fully embroidered, plastic back.   1994   0.50 - 1.00
  Formerly reptile study.

REPTILE STUDY
Cut square.	1926-1933	20.00 - 35.00
Tan, wide crimped.	1934-1935	10.00 - 17.50
Tan rough twill, narrow crimped.	1936-1942	5.00 - 10.00
Tan fine twill, narrow crimped.	1942-1946	12.50 - 20.00
Khaki twill, narrow crimped.	1947-1960	3.00 - 5.00
Khaki twill, rolled edge.	1961-1968	0.50 - 1.00
Fully embroidered, cloth back.	1969-1971	1.00 - 3.00
Fully embroidered, plastic back.	1972-1993	0.50 - 1.00

  Changed to reptile & amphibian study.

RIFLE & SHOTGUN SHOOTING
Fully embroidered, cloth back.	1967-1971	0.00 - 0.00
Fully embroidered, plastic back.	1972-1987	0.50 - 1.00

  Formerly marksmanship;
  split into rifle shooting or shotgun shooting.

RIFLE SHOOTING
Fully embroidered, plastic back.   1988   0.50 - 1.00
  Formerly part of rifle and shotgun shooting.

ROCKS & MINERALS
Tan rough twill, narrow crimped.	1937-1942	40.00 - 75.00
Tan fine twill, narrow crimped.	1942-1946	75.00 - 100.00
Khaki twill, narrow crimped.	1947-1953	30.00 - 50.00

  Formerly mining; became geology.

ROWING
Cut square.	1933-1933	1,300. - 1,700.
Tan, wide crimped.	1934-1935	12.50 - 20.00
Tan rough twill, narrow crimped.	1936-1942	5.00 - 10.00
Tan fine twill, narrow crimped.	1942-1946	10.00 - 15.00
Khaki twill, narrow crimped (swim suit and white skin).	1947-1957	1.00 - 3.00
Khaki twill, narrow crimped (swim trunks and flesh skin).	1958-1960	3.00 - 5.00
Khaki twill, rolled edge.	1961-1968	0.50 - 1.00
Fully embroidered, cloth back.	1969-1971	1.00 - 3.00
Fully embroidered, plastic back.	1972	0.50 - 1.00

SAFETY
Cut square (white cross and green ring).	1927-1933	60.00 - 90.00
Tan, wide crimped.	1934-1935	3.00 - 7.50
Tan rough twill, narrow crimped.	1936-1942	3.00 - 7.50
Tan fine twill, narrow crimped.	1942-1946	5.00 - 10.00
Khaki twill, narrow crimped.	1947-1960	1.00 - 3.00
Fully embroidered, cloth back, green border.	1961-1969	1.00 - 3.00
Fully embroidered, cloth back, silver border.	1969-1971	1.00 - 3.00
Fully embroidered, plastic back, silver border.	1972	0.50 - 1.00

  Formerly safety first.

SAFETY FIRST
Cut square (green cross and ring,   1916-1926   30.00 - 50.00
  four varieties). Changed to safety.

SALESMANSHIP
Cut square (dashed line).	1927-1933	225.00 - 275.00
Tan, wide crimped.	1934-1935	100.00 - 140.00
Tan rough twill, narrow crimped.	1936-1942	10.00 - 20.00
Tan fine twill, narrow crimped.	1942-1946	10.00 - 17.50
Khaki twill, narrow crimped.	1947-1960	5.00 - 10.00
Khaki twill, rolled edge.	1961-1968	0.50 - 1.00
Fully embroidered, cloth back (SALE sign).	1969-1971	1.00 - 3.00
Fully embroidered, plastic back.	1972	0.50 - 1.00

SCHOLARSHIP
Cut square (five varieties).	1911-1933	5.00 - 15.00
Tan, wide crimped.	1934-1935	7.50 - 12.50
Tan rough twill, narrow crimped.	1936-1942	3.00 - 7.50
Tan fine twill, narrow crimped.	1942-1946	15.00 - 25.00
Khaki twill, narrow crimped.	1947-1960	1.00 - 3.00
Khaki twill, rolled edge.	1961-1968	0.50 - 1.00
Fully embroidered, cloth back.	1969-1971	1.00 - 3.00
Fully embroidered, plastic back.	1972	0.50 - 1.00

SCULPTURE
Cut square (three varieties).	1911-1933	550.00 - 650.00
Tan, wide crimped.	1934-1935	175.00 - 225.00
Tan rough twill, narrow crimped.	1936-1942	30.00 - 50.00
Tan fine twill, narrow crimped.	1942-1946	125.00 - 175.00
Khaki twill, narrow crimped.	1947-1960	5.00 - 10.00
Khaki twill, rolled edge.	1961-1968	0.50 - 1.00
Fully embroidered, cloth back.	1969-1971	1.00 - 3.00
Fully embroidered, plastic back.	1972	0.50 - 1.00

SEAMANSHIP
Cut square (angled bar to red anchor).	1911-1933	2,300. - 2,700.
Cut square (straight bar to black anchor).	1911-1920	225.00 - 275.00
Cut square (straight bar to red anchor).	1911-1920	700.00 - 800.00
Tan, wide crimped.	1934-1935	175.00 - 225.00
Tan rough twill, narrow crimped.	1936-1942	10.00 - 17.50
Tan fine twill, narrow crimped.	1942-1946	125.00 - 175.00
Khaki twill, narrow crimped.	1947-1960	12.50 - 20.00
Khaki twill, rolled edge.	1961-1964	0.50 - 1.00

  Became small boat sailing.

Sash with rank pins and narrow crimped badges.

SHEEP FARMING

Cut square (two varieties).	1928-1933	650.00 - 800.00
Tan, wide crimped.	1934-1935	125.00 - 175.00
Tan rough twill, narrow crimped.	1936-1942	30.00 - 50.00
Tan fine twill, narrow crimped.	1942-1946	125.00 - 175.00
Khaki twill, narrow crimped.	1947-1960	5.00 - 10.00
Khaki twill, rolled edge.	1961-1968	0.50 - 1.00
Fully embroidered, cloth back.	1969-1971	1.00 - 3.00
Fully embroidered, plastic back. Merged into animal science.	1972-1975	0.50 - 1.00

SHOTGUN SHOOTING

Fully embroidered, plastic back.	1988	0.50 - 1.00
Formerly part of rifle and shotgun shooting.		

SIGNALING

Cut square (red flag on left, reversed color).	1911-1920	400.00 - 550.00
Cut square (white flag on left, correct color).	1911-1933	30.00 - 50.00
Tan, wide crimped.	1934-1935	25.00 - 40.00
Tan rough twill, narrow crimped.	1936-1942	12.50 - 20.00
Tan fine twill, narrow crimped.	1942-1946	15.00 - 25.00
Khaki twill, narrow crimped.	1947-1960	5.00 - 10.00
Khaki twill, rolled edge.	1961-1968	0.50 - 1.00
Fully embroidered, cloth back.	1969-1971	1.00 - 3.00
Fully embroidered, plastic back.	1972-1992	0.50 - 1.00

SKATING

Fully embroidered, plastic back.	1972-1993	0.50 - 1.00
Computer stitched, bagged.	1993	0.00 - 0.00

SKIING

Tan rough twill, narrow crimped.	1938-1942	80.00 - 125.00
Tan fine twill, narrow crimped.	1942-1946	40.00 - 60.00
Khaki twill, narrow crimped.	1947-1960	5.00 - 10.00
Fully embroidered, cloth back.	1961-1971	1.00 - 3.00
Fully embroidered, plastic back (brown skis).	1972-1979	0.50 - 1.00
Fully embroidered, plastic back (blue skis).	1980	0.50 - 1.00

SMALL BOAT SAILING

Fully embroidered, cloth back.	1964-1971	1.00 - 3.00
Fully embroidered, plastic back.	1972	0.50 - 1.00
Formerly Seamanship.		

SMALL GRAINS

Khaki twill, narrow crimped.	1959-1960	0.00 - 0.00
Fully embroidered, cloth back.	1961-1971	1.00 - 3.00
Fully embroidered, plastic back.	1972-1975	0.50 - 1.00
Formerly small grains and cereal foods; merged into plant science.		

SMALL GRAINS & CEREAL FOODS

Tan rough twill, narrow crimped.	1941-1942	25.00 - 50.00
Tan fine twill, narrow crimped.	1942-1946	40.00 - 60.00
Khaki twill, narrow crimped.	1947-1958	5.00 - 10.00
Became small grains.		

SOIL & WATER CONSERVATION

Khaki twill, narrow crimped.	1952-1960	3.00 - 5.00
Fully embroidered, cloth back (vertical crop rows).	1961-1969	1.00 - 3.00
Fully embroidered, cloth back (horizontal crop rows).	1970-1971	3.00 - 5.00
Fully embroidered, plastic back.	1972	0.50 - 1.00
Formerly soil management.		

SOIL MANAGEMENT

Cut square.	1928-1933	325.00 - 375.00
Tan, wide crimped.	1934-1935	175.00 - 225.00
Tan rough twill, narrow crimped.	1936-1942	60.00 - 90.00
Tan fine twill, narrow crimped.	1942-1946	150.00 - 200.00
Khaki twill, narrow crimped.	1947-1952	125.00 - 175.00
Became soil and water conservation.		

SPACE EXPLORATION

Fully embroidered, cloth back.	1965-1971	1.00 - 3.00
Fully embroidered, plastic back.	1972	0.50 - 1.00

SPORTS

Fully embroidered, plastic back, silver border.	1972	0.50 - 1.00

STALKING

Cut square (leaf). Unknown.	1911-1913	0.00 - 0.00
Cut square (cougar, three varieties).	1913-1933	225.00 - 275.00
Tan, wide crimped.	1934-1935	225.00 - 275.00
Tan rough twill, narrow crimped.	1936-1942	60.00 - 90.00
Tan fine twill, narrow crimped.	1942-1946	225.00 - 275.00
Khaki twill, narrow crimped.	1947-1952	100.00 - 140.00

STAMP COLLECTING

Cut square.	1931-1933	60.00 - 90.00
Tan, wide crimped.	1934-1935	12.50 - 20.00
Tan rough twill, narrow crimped.	1936-1942	7.50 - 15.00
Tan fine twill, narrow crimped.	1942-1946	10.00 - 20.00
Khaki twill, narrow crimped.	1947-1960	3.00 - 5.00
Khaki twill, rolled edge.	1961-1968	0.50 - 1.00
Fully embroidered, cloth back.	1969-1971	1.00 - 3.00
Fully embroidered, plastic back.	1972-1993	0.50 - 1.00
Computer stitched, bagged.	1993	0.50 - 1.00

SURVEYING

Cut square (three legs).	1911-1920	125.00 - 175.00
Cut square (two legs).	1920-1933	325.00 - 375.00
Tan, wide crimped.	1934-1935	35.00 - 50.00
Tan rough twill, narrow crimped.	1936-1942	7.50 - 12.50
Tan fine twill, narrow crimped.	1942-1946	15.00 - 25.00
Khaki twill, narrow crimped.	1947-1960	3.00 - 5.00
Khaki twill, rolled edge.	1961-1968	0.50 - 1.00
Fully embroidered, cloth back.	1969-1971	1.00 - 3.00
Fully embroidered, plastic back.	1972	0.50 - 1.00

SWIMMING

Cut square (three varieties).	1911-1933	3.00 - 7.50
Tan, wide crimped.	1934-1935	3.00 - 7.50
Tan rough twill, narrow crimped.	1936-1942	3.00 - 7.50
Tan fine twill, narrow crimped.	1942-1946	40.00 - 60.00
Khaki twill, narrow crimped (swim suit and white skin).	1947-1957	3.00 - 5.00
Khaki twill, narrow crimped (swim trunks and flesh skin).	1958-1960	1.00 - 3.00
Khaki twill, rolled edge.	1961-1968	0.50 - 1.00
Fully embroidered, cloth back, silver border.	1969-1971	1.00 - 3.00
Fully embroidered, plastic back, silver border.	1972	0.50 - 1.00

TAXIDERMY

Cut square (three varieties).	1911-1933	325.00 - 375.00
Tan, wide crimped.	1934-1935	325.00 - 375.00
Tan rough twill, narrow crimped.	1936-1942	100.00 - 140.00
Tan fine twill, narrow crimped.	1942-1946	175.00 - 225.00
Khaki twill, narrow crimped.	1947-1953	175.00 - 225.00

TEXTILE

Fully embroidered, plastic back. Formerly textiles.	1973	0.50 - 1.00

TEXTILES

Cut square.	1924-1933	100.00 - 140.00
Tan, wide crimped.	1934-1935	25.00 - 40.00
Tan rough twill, narrow crimped.	1936-1942	7.50 - 15.00
Tan fine twill, narrow crimped.	1942-1946	20.00 - 30.00
Khaki twill, narrow crimped.	1947-1960	5.00 - 10.00
Khaki twill, rolled edge.	1961-1968	0.50 - 1.00
Fully embroidered, cloth back. Became textile.	1969-1971	1.00 - 3.00

THEATER

Fully embroidered, cloth back.	1967-1971	0.00 - 0.00
Khaki twill, rolled edge.	1967-1968	0.50 - 1.00
Fully embroidered, plastic back. Formerly dramatics.	1972	0.50 - 1.00

TRAFFIC SAFETY

Fully embroidered, plastic back.	1975-1992	0.50 - 1.00
Computer stitched, bagged. Formerly automotive safety.	1993	0.50 - 1.00

TRUCK TRANSPORTATION

Fully embroidered, plastic back.	1972	0.50 - 1.00

VETERINARY MEDICINE

Computer stitched, bagged. Formerly veterinary science.	1995	0.00 - 0.00

VETERINARY SCIENCE

Fully embroidered, plastic back. Formerly first aid to animals; became veterinary medicine.	1973-1993	0.50 - 1.00
Computer stitched, bagged. Became veterinary medicine.	1993-1995	0.00 - 0.00

WATER SKIING

Fully embroidered, cloth back.	1969-1971	1.00 - 3.00
Fully embroidered, plastic back (w/o life vest).	1972-1995	0.50 - 1.00
Fully embroidered, plastic back (w/ life vest).	1996	0.00 - 0.00

WEATHER

Cut square (comet).	1927-1929	500.00 - 600.00
Cut square (weather vane).	1929-1933	100.00 - 140.00
Tan, wide crimped.	1934-1935	80.00 - 125.00
Tan rough twill, narrow crimped.	1936-1942	7.50 - 15.00
Tan fine twill, narrow crimped.	1942-1946	60.00 - 90.00
Khaki twill, narrow crimped.	1947-1960	3.00 - 5.00
Khaki twill, rolled edge.	1961-1968	0.50 - 1.00
Fully embroidered, cloth back.	1969-1971	1.00 - 3.00
Fully embroidered, plastic back.	1972	0.50 - 1.00

WHITEWATER

Fully embroidered, plastic back, black border (error).	1987	20.00 - 35.00
Fully embroidered, plastic back, green border.	1987-1993	0.50 - 1.00
Computer stitched, bagged.	1993	0.50 - 1.00

WILDERNESS SURVIVAL

Fully embroidered, plastic back.	1973	0.50 - 1.00

WILDLIFE MANAGEMENT

Khaki twill, narrow crimped.	1952-1960	3.00 - 5.00
Fully embroidered, cloth back. Became fish and wildlife management.	1961-1971	1.00 - 3.00

WIRELESS

Cut square. Became radio.	1918-1922	100.00 - 140.00

WOOD CARVING

Cut square.	1927-1933	3.00 - 7.50
Tan, wide crimped.	1934-1935	7.50 - 12.50
Tan rough twill, narrow crimped.	1936-1942	3.00 - 7.50
Tan fine twill, narrow crimped.	1942-1946	5.00 - 10.00
Khaki twill, narrow crimped.	1947-1960	1.00 - 3.00
Khaki twill, rolled edge.	1961-1968	0.50 - 1.00
Fully embroidered, cloth back.	1969-1971	1.00 - 3.00
Fully embroidered, plastic back.	1972	0.50 - 1.00

WOOD TURNING

Cut square.	1930-1933	100.00 - 140.00
Tan, wide crimped.	1934-1935	60.00 - 90.00
Tan rough twill, narrow crimped.	1936-1942	12.50 - 20.00
Tan fine twill, narrow crimped.	1942-1946	60.00 - 90.00
Khaki twill, narrow crimped. Merged into woodwork.	1947-1952	3.00 - 5.00

Sash of the fully embroidered variety.

WOODWORK

Cut square.	1927-1933	3.00 - 7.50
Tan, wide crimped.	1934-1935	5.00 - 10.00
Tan rough twill, narrow crimped.	1936-1942	3.00 - 7.50
Tan fine twill, narrow crimped.	1942-1946	5.00 - 10.00
Khaki twill, narrow crimped (seat).	1947-1952	3.00 - 5.00
Khaki twill, narrow crimped (plane).	1953-1960	3.00 - 5.00
Khaki twill, rolled edge.	1961-1968	0.50 - 1.00
Khaki twill, rolled edge.	1961-1968	1.00 - 3.00
Fully embroidered, cloth back (hammer and square).	1969-1971	1.00 - 3.00
Fully embroidered, plastic back. Formerly carpentry, wood turning and wood work.	1972	0.50 - 1.00

WORLD BROTHERHOOD

Khaki twill, narrow crimped.	1952-1960	3.00 - 5.00
Fully embroidered, cloth back (world map).	1961-1968	1.00 - 3.00
Fully embroidered, cloth back (scout sign).	1969-1971	1.00 - 3.00
Fully embroidered, plastic back. Became citizenship in the world.	1972	0.50 - 1.00

ZOOLOGY

Cut square.	1930-1933	225.00 - 275.00
Tan, wide crimped.	1934-1935	60.00 - 90.00
Tan rough twill, narrow crimped.	1936-1942	10.00 - 20.00
Tan fine twill, narrow crimped.	1942-1946	80.00 - 125.00
Khaki twill, narrow crimped.	1947-1960	5.00 - 10.00
Khaki twill, rolled edge.	1961-1968	0.50 - 1.00
Fully embroidered, cloth back.	1969-1971	1.00 - 3.00
Fully embroidered, plastic back. Merged into environmental science.	1972	0.50 - 1.00

Until the 1950s, adults could also earn Eagle. Note the modified sash of four rows across.

Left, a merit badge sash with narrow crimped edge khaki badges, c. 1950. Right, a dark green leadership corps/explorer sash with plastic back badges from 1977.

HAT OR COLLAR DEVICES

ASSISTANT DEPUTY COMMISSIONER
First-Class emblem in silver, gold eagle, blue   1920-1938   75.00 - 100.00
  enamel background, gold wreath 23-25 mm.

ASSISTANT DEPUTY SCOUT COMMISSIONER
First-Class emblem with light blue enamel   1917-1919   400.00 - 600.00
  40 mm.

ASSISTANT SCOUTMASTER
First-Class emblem with red enamel. 40 mm.   1917-1919   200.00 - 250.00
First-Class emblem in gold with green enamel. 1920-1938   10.00 - 15.00
  23-25 mm.
First-Class emblem in gold on green enameled 1950-1967   15.00 - 25.00
  circle. Double clutch pin back.
First-Class emblem in gold on green enameled 1950-1967   15.00 - 25.00
  circle. Vertical safety pin back.

CHAPLAIN
First-Class emblem and crook on blue and   1950-1967   60.00 - 80.00
  white circle. Double clutch pin back.

DEPUTY COMMISSIONER
First-Class emblem in silver, silver eagle, blue 1920-1938 75.00 - 100.00
  enamel background, gold wreath. 23-25 mm.

DEPUTY SCOUT COMMISSIONER
First-Class emblem with dark blue enamel.   1917-1919   400.00 - 600.00
  40 mm.

EAGLE SCOUT
Silver, R.W.B. enamel w/o BSA on eagle.   150.00 - 200.00
Silver, B.W.R. enamel w/o BSA on eagle.   250.00 - 300.00
Silver, R.W.B. enamel / BSA on eagle.   150.00 - 200.00

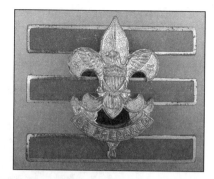

JUNIOR ASSISTANT SCOUTMASTER
First-Class emblem in gold on three green   1926-1938   25.00 - 35.00
  enameled bars. Screw back.

LAYMAN
First-Class emblem with white enamel. 40 mm. 1917-1919 250.00 - 300.00
First-Class emblem in gold on blue enameled   1950-1967 10.00 - 17.50
  circle.

LOCAL COUNCIL COMMITTEE
First-Class emblem in silver with blue enamel. 1920-1938 40.00 - 60.00
  23-25 mm.

NATIONAL COMMITTEE
First-Class emblem with purple enamel.   1917-1919 1,000. - 1,500.
  40 mm.
First-Class emblem on white enamel swastika.   1920-1925 500.00 - 7.50
First-Class emblem on silver arrowhead.   1930-1945 150.00 - 200.00
First-Class emblem on silver arrowhead in   1950-1967 75.00 - 125.00
  circle.

NATIONAL COUNCIL COMMITTEE
First-Class emblem in silver w/ purple   1920-1938 75.00 - 100.00
  background. 23-25 mm.

NATIONAL COUNCIL STAFF
First-Class emblem on red-white-blue   1950-1967 80.00 - 100.00
  background in wreath with ribbon.

NATIONAL EXECUTIVE BOARD
First-Class emblem on silver arrowhead   1950-1967 300.00 - 400.00
  in circle.

NATIONAL PAST PRESIDENT
First-Class emblem on silver arrowhead   1950-1967 400.00 - 600.00
  in circle.

PHYSICIAN
First-Class emblem and caduceus on blue and   1950-1967 150.00 - 200.00
  white circle. Double clutch pin back.

SCOUT COMMISSIONER
First-Class emblem in dark blue enamel in gold 1917-1919 600.00 - 800.00
  wreath. Screw back w/ bent tabs; 35 mm.
First-Class emblem in silver, silver eagle,   1920-1938 75.00 - 100.00
  blue enamel background, silver wreath.
  23-25 mm.

SCOUT EXECUTIVE

First-Class emblem in white enamel in gold wreath. Screw back w/ bent tabs on back; 35 mm.   1917-1919   400.00 - 500.00

SCOUTMASTER

First-Class emblem with green enamel. 40 mm.   1917-1919   200.00 - 250.00

First-Class emblem in silver with green enamel. 23-25 mm.   1920-1938   10.00 - 15.00

First-Class emblem in silver on green enamel circle. Double clutch pin back.   1950-1967   15.00 - 25.00

First-Class emblem in silver on green enamel circle. Vertical safety pin back.   1950-1967   15.00 - 25.00

SENIOR PATROL LEADER

First-Class emblem in silver on 2-1/2 green enameled bars. Screw back.   1921-1933   25.00 - 35.00

First-Class emblem in gold on 2-1/2 green enameled bars.   1933-1938   15.00 - 25.00

SPECIAL NATIONAL FIELD SCOUT COMMISSIONER

First-Class emblem in wreath with ribbon.   1950-1967   600.00 - 750.00

TROOP COMMITTEE

First-Class emblem in gold with blue enamel. 23-25 mm.   1920-1938   40.00 - 60.00

The circular Tenderfoot emblem for the Australian style hat, and the new First Class pin for the Campaign hat.

UNIVERSAL HAT EMBLEM

First-Class Emblem with clutch back pins (for campaign hat).   1996   5.00 - 7.50

Tenderfoot emblem in circle (for Australian style hat).   1996   5.00 - 7.50

Scouts display a bus subway advertisement to vice-president Spiro Agnew.

UNIFORMS - ADULT

1918 leader uniforms.

BLAZER

Blue with gilt buttons, Hart, Shapner & Marx.	1971	60.00 - 75.00
Green with gilt buttons.	1971	60.00 - 75.00

Queens Council Scout Executive Dennis St. Jean addresses a Gateway District Dinner. Note the bullion pocket patch and striped tie.

BLAZER BULLION EMBLEM

Tenderfoot embroidered emblem, clasp back pin attachment.	1971	10.00 - 15.00

BREECHES

Olive-drab cotton, laced below the knee.	1911-1930	40.00 - 60.00
Olive-drab wool, laced below the knee.	1911-1930	50.00 - 75.00

COAT

Lightweight olive-drab cotton, four pockets, no belt.	1911-1930	50.00 - 75.00
Norfolk design, two front pockets, belt.	1910-1920	250.00 - 325.00
Open collar, four pockets, belt.	1921-1945	75.00 - 125.00
Special grade olive-drab wool.	1911-1930	100.00 - 150.00

COLLAR BRASS

BSA, screw posts, floret or hexagon fasteners.	1912-1928	60.00 - 80.00
Unit numerals, screw post: 1, 2, 3, 4, 5, 6, 7, 8, 0.	1912-1928	25.00 - 40.00

JACKET

Open collar, no belt.	1945-1970	60.00 - 75.00

KNICKERS

Lightweight olive-drab cotton, buckle below knee.	1911-1930	30.00 - 50.00

NORFOLK COAT

Quality olive-drab cotton cloth, double pleats, belt.	1911-1930	150.00 - 200.00

SERVICE STAR

Gold star w/tenure number, clutch back with blue plastic disc.	1956	2.00 - 4.00
Gold star w/tenure number, screw back with blue felt.	1947-1955	2.00 - 4.00

TROUSERS

Full-length olive-drab cotton.	1911-1930	40.00 - 60.00

UNIFORM RIBBON BARS

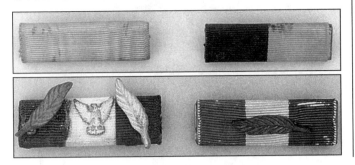

UNIFORM SQUARE KNOTS

Colors	Award Name
Black on white in black border	Professional Training Award
Black and white in red border	Whitney M. Young Jr. Award
Blue and red in blue border	Ace Award, Air Scouts
Blue and red on white	Silver Anchor Award, Sea Explorers
Blue and red on blue	Silver Anchor Award, Sea Explorers
Blue and white	Silver Beaver Award
Blue and white on blue	Silver Beaver Award, Sea Explorers
Blue and white on white	Silver Beaver Award, Sea Explorers
Blue and white on dark green	Silver Beaver Award, Explorers
Blue and yellow	Medal of Merit
Blue and yellow on blue	Cub Scouter Award
Blue and yellow on blue	Den Leader Coach Training Award
Blue on blue	Den Leader Coach Award
Blue on blue	Quartermaster Award, Sea Exploring
Blue on red-white	George Meany Award
Blue on yellow	Cubmaster Award
Blue on white-red	George Meany Award, colors reversed
Blue on white	Quartermaster Award, Sea Exploring
Blue-green-white	William T. Hornaday Award
Green and red in yellow border	Arrow of Light, Cub Scouts
Dark blue and white	Skipper's Key, Sea Scouts
Dark green and black	Bronze Wolf
Dark green and olive in green border	Ranger Award, Explorers
Green and gold in red border	James E. West Award
Green and gold in red border	
Green and white	Scouter's Key
Green and white on dark green	Scouter's Key, Explorers
Green and white on white	Scouter's Key, Sea Explorers
Green and whtie on blue	Scouter's Key, Sea Explorers
Green	Scouter's Training Award
Green on dark green	Scouter's Training Award, Explorers
Green on white	Scouter's Training Award, Sea Exploring
Green on blue	Scouter's Training Award, Sea Exploring
Gold mylar on white	Sea Explorer Memorial Award
Gold on yellow	Webelos Den Leader Award
Gold and white	Silver Antelope Award
Light blue and dark blue on blue	Sea Explorer Leader Training Award
Purple on gray, silver mylar bdr.	Religious Award, adult
Red and white	Silver Buffalo Award
Red on white	Heroism Award
Red	Honor Medal
Red-white-blue	Eagle Scout Award
Red-white-blue on dark green	Eagle Scout Award, Explorers
Red-white-blue on white	Eagle Scout Award, Sea Explorers
Red-white-blue on dark blue	Eagle Scout Award, Sea Explorers
Red-white-blue on lt. blue	Eagle Scout Awards, Air Explorers
Red and black in red border on yellow	Tiger Cub Coach Award
Red and green in yellow border	Arrow of Light error
Red and yellow on dark green	Silver Award, Explorers
Silver mylar on purple	Religious Award, youth
Silver on red-white-blue	Explorer Achievement Award
Silver on red-white-blue	Explorer Gold Award
Silver on red	Explorer Service Team Award
Silver on red	Distinguished Commissioner Service Award
Silver overhand knot on blue	District Award of Merit
Three stars silver mylar and red stripes	Silver World Award
Trident (one, two or three)	Sea Badge, Sea Explorers
White	Scoutmaster Award of Merit
White on blue in dk. blue border	NSF Antarctic Service
White on blue	Quartermaster Award, Sea Exploring
White on red	OA Distinguished Service
Yellow in yellow border on dk. blue	Spurgeon Award, Explorers
Yellow on blue	Den Leader Award
Yellow on blue	Den Mother Award

RIBBON BAR

Silver Buffalo, red/white/red, 1-3/8" x 1/4".	1934-1946	100.00 - 150.00
Silver Beaver, blue/white/blue, 1-3/8" x 1/4".	1934-1946	100.00 - 150.00
Silver Antelope, yellow/white/yellow, 1-3/8" x 1/4".	1934-1946	100.00 - 150.00
Eagle Scout, red/white/blue, 1-3/8" x 1/4".	1934-1940	50.00 - 85.00
Honor Medal, red, 1-3/8" x 1/4".	1934-1946	100.00 - 150.00
Eagle Scout, red/white/blue w/eagle miniature, 1-3/8" x 1/4".	1940-1946	50.00 - 85.00

OVERHAND KNOT ON BLUE TWILL

District Award of Merit.	1973-1979	10.00 - 15.00
District Award of Merit.	1980	5.00 - 7.50

SQUARE KNOT, BLUE TWILL

Ace Award, red knot in blue frame.	1950-1954	250.00 - 300.00

SQUARE KNOT, GRAY TWILL

Religious Award, adult.	1973	5.00 - 7.50

SQUARE KNOT, PURPLE TWILL

Religious Award, youth.	1973	5.00 - 7.50

SQUARE KNOT, SOLID EMBROIDERY

Professional Training Award.	1982	20.00 - 25.00
George Meany Award.	1987	20.00 - 25.00

SQUARE KNOT, SOLID EMBROIDERY

Silver World Award.	1982	75.00 - 100.00

SQUARE KNOTS ON KHAKI TWILL CLOTH

Quartermaster Medal.	1946	250.00 - 300.00
Scouter's Key Award.	1946-1979	10.00 - 15.00
Scouter's Training Award.	1946-1979	10.00 - 15.00
Silver Antelope.	1946-1979	25.00 - 40.00
Silver Beaver Award.	1946-1979	15.00 - 20.00
Silver Buffalo Award.	1946-1979	75.00 - 100.00
Eagle Scout Award.	1947-1979	10.00 - 15.00
Honor Medal.	1947-1979	100.00 - 150.00
Ranger Award.	1950-1955	250.00 - 300.00
Medal of Merit.	1953-1979	100.00 - 150.00
Arrow of Light.	1979	10.00 - 15.00

SQUARE KNOTS ON RED TWILL

Distinguished Commissioner Service.	1989	20.00 - 25.00

SQUARE KNOTS ON TAN TWILL CLOTH

Medal of Merit.	1980	75.00 - 100.00
Scouter's Key.	1980	5.00 - 7.50
Scouter's Training Award.	1980	5.00 - 7.50
Silver Antelope.	1980	20.00 - 30.00
Eagle Scout Award.	1980	5.00 - 7.50
Silver Beaver.	1980	10.00 - 15.00
Silver Buffalo.	1980	50.00 - 75.00
Honor Medal.	1980	100.00 - 150.00
Arrow of Light, correct green/red colors.	1980	5.00 - 7.50
Scoutmaster Award of Merit.	1987	25.00 - 35.00
Whitney M. Young Jr. Award.	1989	50.00 - 75.00
Arrow of Light, reversed colors, red/green.	1989	15.00 - 20.00
William T. Hornaday Award.	1990	75.00 - 100.00
James E. West Award (Currently Heritage Society).	1993-2000	15.00 - 20.00
Heritage Society (formerly James E. West).	2000	15.00 - 20.00

RECOGNITIONS - ADULT

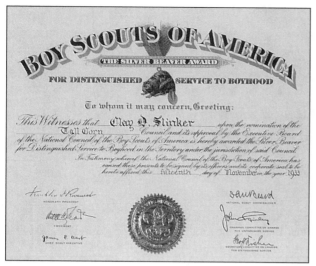

CERTIFICATES

District Award of Merit.	1970-	5.00 - 7.50
Five-Year Training Award.	1940-1953	15.00 - 25.00
Two weeks in camp seal label plain.		
Five-Year Training Award.	1935-1940	20.00 - 30.00
Two weeks in camp seal label overset.		
Scouter's Key.	1970-	5.00 - 10.00
Scouter's Training Award.	1953-	5.00 - 10.00
Scoutmaster's Key.	1953-	5.00 - 10.00
Silver Antelope.	1980-	75.00 - 125.00
Silver Antelope.	1960-1980	100.00 - 150.00
Silver Antelope.	1940-1960	150.00 - 250.00
Silver Antelope. Unawarded.	1970-	15.00 - 30.00
Silver Beaver.	1990-	7.50 - 15.00
Silver Beaver.	1930-1940	60.00 - 80.00
Silver Beaver.	1940-1950	40.00 - 50.00
Silver Beaver.	1950-1960	30.00 - 40.00
Silver Beaver.	1970-1990	15.00 - 25.00
Silver Beaver. Unawarded.	1970-	10.00 - 20.00
Silver Beaver.	1960-1970	20.00 - 30.00
Silver Buffalo.	1926-1940	250.00 - 400.00
Silver Buffalo.	1960-1980	100.00 - 250.00
Silver Buffalo.	1940-1960	200.00 - 400.00
Silver Buffalo.	1980-	75.00 - 150.00
Silver Buffalo. Unawarded.	1970-	20.00 - 30.00
Silver Fawn.	1970-1974	200.00 - 300.00

Brother Hugh Dymski OFM Conv. proudly displays his Silver Beaver Award with Kenneth Tremaine.

CHIEF SCOUT EXECUTIVE WINNER'S CIRCLE AWARDS

Belt buckle, CSE's Emblem on mottled background. Sterling.	1994	100.00 - 140.00
Belt buckle, CSE's Emblem on smooth background. Sterling. Prototype.	1994	150.00 - 200.00
Box, CSE's Emblem in pewter mounted on wooden box.	2000	75.00 - 100.00
Letter opener, CSE's Emblem in pewter.	2000	25.00 - 40.00

DISTINGUISHED COMMISSIONER AWARD

Bronze medallion on wood plaque.	1980	15.00 - 25.00

DISTINGUISHED EAGLE SCOUT AWARD

Type I, 14kt. gold eagle pendant on red-white-blue neck ribbon.	1969-1980	300.00 - 400.00
Type II, gold-plated eagle pendant on red-white-blue neck ribbon.	1980	150.00 - 200.00

DISTRICT AWARD OF MERIT

Pewter emblem on wood plaque.	1973	15.00 - 25.00

SCOUTER'S KEY AWARD

First-Class emblem on key background 10 kt. GF on green ribbon w/ one thick white stripe.	1960-1970	15.00 - 20.00
Tenderfoot emblem on key background. 10 kt. GF on green ribbon w/ one thick white stripe.	1960-1970	10.00 - 15.00
Tenderfoot emblem on key background. Gilt pendant on green ribbon w/ two thin white stripes.	1960-1970	5.00 - 7.50

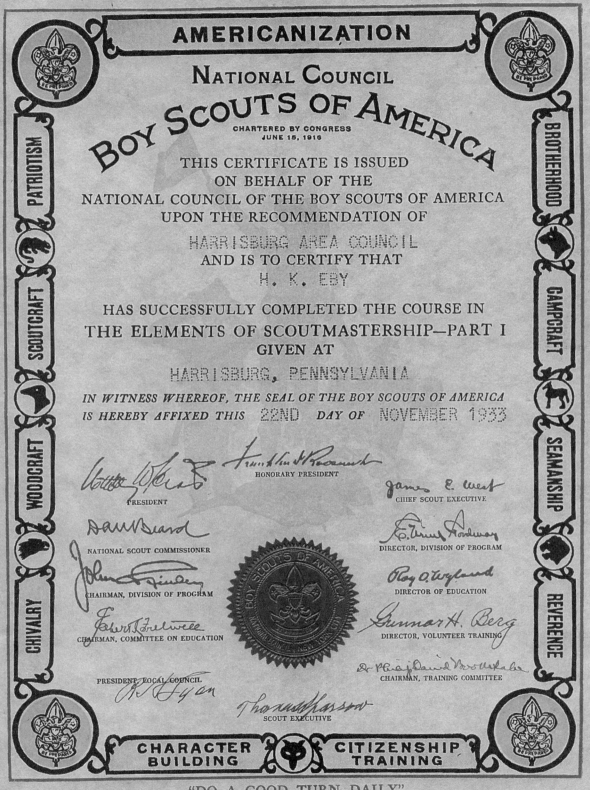

SCOUTER'S TRAINING AWARD

First-Class emblem on a background. 10 kt. GF on green ribbon w/ one thin white stripe.	1960-1970	15.00 - 20.00
Tenderfoot emblem on a background. 10 kt. GF on green ribbon w/ one thin white stripe.	1960-1970	10.00 - 15.00
Tenderfoot emblem on A background. 10 kt. GF on solid green ribbon.	1960-1970	10.00 - 15.00
Tenderfoot emblem on A background. Gilt pendant on green ribbon w/ one thin white stripe.	1960-1970	5.00 - 7.50

SILVER ANTELOPE AWARD

Type I, silver pendant on gold-white-gold neck ribbon.	1955	200.00 - 250.00
Type II, silver pendant on gold-white-gold neck ribbon.	1971	125.00 - 175.00
Type III, rhodium pendant on gold-white-gold neck ribbon.	1980	100.00 - 150.00

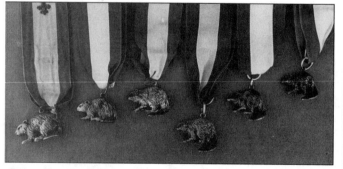

Silver Beaver Award, six major varieties, 1935-1995.

SILVER BEAVER AWARD

Type I, very large silver beaver on blue-white-blue pocket ribbon silver w/ FDL emblem pin.	1931-1933	350.00 - 400.00
Type II, very large silver beaver on blue-white-blue neck ribbon silver w/ FDL emblem pin.	1933-1938	250.00 - 350.00
Type III, medium silver beaver on blue-white-blue neck ribbon.	1940-1950	200.00 - 250.00
Type IV, medium silver beaver on blue-white-blue neck ribbon.	1950-1960	150.00 - 200.00
Type V, medium silver beaver on blue-white-blue neck ribbon.	1960-1971	125.00 - 175.00
Type VI, small silver beaver on blue-white-blue snap back neck ribbon.	1971-1980	125.00 - 175.00
Type VII, small rhodium beaver on blue-white-blue snap back neck ribbon.	1980	100.00 - 150.00

SILVER BUFFALO AWARD

Type 1, large silver pendant on red-white-red neck ribbon.	1925	800.00 - 1,000.
Type II, small silver pendant on red-white-red-neck ribbon.	1955	400.00 - 600.00
Type III, small rhodium pendant on red-white-red neck ribbon.	1980	200.00 - 250.00

SILVER FAWN

Small silver pendant on thin green-white neck ribbon.	1971-1974	300.00 - 400.00

SILVER WORLD

Red-white ribbon.	250.00 - 400.00

VETERAN PATCHES

V. First-Class emblem, BS above V below.	1924-1995	10.00 - 15.00
X. First-Class emblem, X behind.	1925-1945	10.00 - 15.00
XV. First-Class emblem, XV behind.	1925-1945	15.00 - 25.00
XX. First-Class emblem, XX behind.	1930-1945	15.00 - 25.00
XXV. First-Class emblem, XXV behind.	1935-1945	15.00 - 25.00
XXX. First-Class emblem, XXX behind.	1940-1945	20.00 - 30.00

VETERAN PIN

05 year, BS and V with First-Class emblem at ctr. 14 kt. gold and enamel.	1916-1940	30.00 - 50.00
05 year, BS and V with First-Class emblem at ctr. 10 kt. gold and enamel.	1916-1940	25.00 - 40.00
05 year, BS and V with First-Class emblem at ctr. 10 kt. GF and enamel.	1916-1940	15.00 - 20.00
05 year, Tenderfoot emblem in blue border, five below.	1972-2000	5.00 - 10.00
05 year, Tenderfoot emblem, five above.	1940-1971	10.00 - 15.00
10 year, First-Class emblem on XX in enamel circle. 14 kt. GF.	1916-1940	15.00 - 25.00
10 year, First-Class emblem on XX in enamel circle. 14 kt. gold.	1916-1940	30.00 - 50.00
10-year, Tenderfoot emblem in blue border, 10 below.	1972-2000	5.00 - 10.00
10-year, Tenderfoot emblem, 10 above.	1940-1971	10.00 - 15.00
15-year, First-Class emblem on XV in circle.	1925-1940	15.00 - 25.00
15-year, Tenderfoot emblem in blue border, 15 below.	1972-2000	5.00 - 10.00
15-year, Tenderfoot emblem, 15 above.	1940-1971	10.00 - 15.00
20-year, First-Class emblem on XX in circle.	1935	15.00 - 25.00
20-year, Tenderfoot emblem in blue border, 20 below.	1972-2000	5.00 - 10.00
20-year, Tenderfoot emblem, 20 above.	1940-1971	10.00 - 15.00
25-Year, First-Class emblem on XXV in circle.	1935-1940	15.00 - 25.00
25-year, Tenderfoot emblem in blue border, 25 below.	1972-2000	5.00 - 10.00
25-year, Tenderfoot emblem, 25 above.	1940-1971	10.00 - 15.00
30-year, First-Class emblem on XXX in circle.	1935-1940	20.00 - 30.00
30-year, Tenderfoot emblem in blue border, 30 below.	1972-2000	5.00 - 10.00
30-year, Tenderfoot emblem, 30 above.	1940-1971	10.00 - 15.00
40-year, Tenderfoot emblem in blue border, 40 below.	1972-2000	5.00 - 10.00
40-year, Tenderfoot emblem, 40 above.	1950-1971	10.00 - 15.00
50-year, Tenderfoot emblem and large 50.	1960-2000	30.00 - 40.00
75-year, Tenderfoot emblem and large 75.	1985-2000	30.00 - 40.00

CERTIFICATES

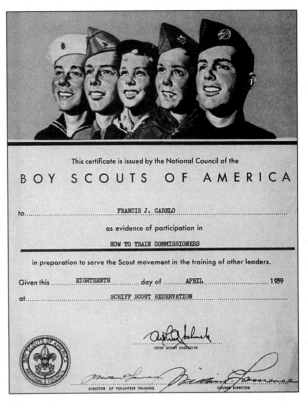

APPRECIATION

	1972	0.50 - 1.00
	1974	0.50 - 1.00

APPRECIATION CERTIFICATES, GENERAL USE

Blue foil, 8" x 10".	1990	1.00 - 2.50
Gold foil, 5" x 7".	1990	1.00 - 2.50
Gold foil, 8" x 10".	1990	1.00 - 2.50
Green foil, 8" x 10".	1990	1.00 - 2.50
Red foil, 8" x 10".	1990	1.00 - 2.50
Silver foil, 8" x 10".	1990	1.00 - 2.50

ASSISTANT SENIOR PATROL LEADER

	1972	0.50 - 1.00
	1986	0.50 - 1.00

ASSISTANT SENIOR PATROL LEADER'S WARRANT

	1966	1.00 - 2.00

ASSOCIATE MEMBER

Scout Law flanking central area, multicolor.	1920	100.00 - 125.00

CERTIFICATE OF APPRECIATION

		0.50 - 1.00
	1973	0.50 - 1.00

COMMENDATION

	1985	1.00 - 2.00

COMMISSIONER'S RIGHT WAY

	1975	3.00 - 5.00

COUNCIL PRESIDENT

	1955-1965	25.00 - 35.00

DEN CHIEF

	1973	0.50 - 1.00

DEN CHIEF'S WARRANT

	1968	1.00 - 2.00

FIVE YEAR TRAINING PROGRAM
Legend and nine circles for foil seals.   1930-1940   15.00 - 25.00

IN APPRECIATION

	1978	0.50 - 1.00
	1979	0.50 - 1.00
	1984	0.50 - 1.00
	1990	0.50 - 1.00
Vertical format.	1990	1.00 - 2.50

INSTRUCTOR

1972	0.50 - 1.00

JUNIOR ASSISTANT SCOUTMASTER

1972	0.50 - 1.00
1985	0.50 - 1.00

JUNIOR ASSISTANT SCOUTMASTER'S WARRANT

1959	1.00 - 2.00

JUNIOR LEADER'S CERTIFICATE OF TRAINING

1965-1975	1.00 - 2.00

LEADERSHIP CORPS

1972	0.50 - 1.00

LIBRARIAN
12/72 printing.   1972   0.50 - 1.00
6/72 printing   1972   0.50 - 1.00

PATROL LEADER

1972	0.50 - 1.00
1985	0.50 - 1.00

PATROL LEADER'S WARRANT

1967	1.00 - 2.00

QUARTERMASTER

1972	0.50 - 1.00

SCOUTER'S WIFE AWARD
Horizontal format, foil-embossed Tenderfoot   1990   1.00 - 2.50
emblem.

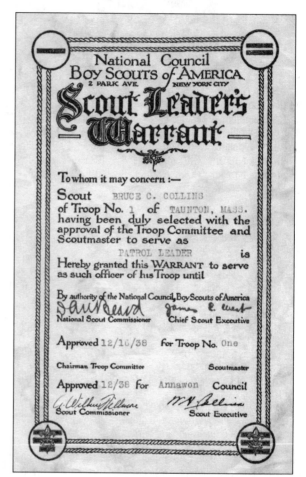

SCOUT LEADER'S WARRANT

	1930-1940	15.00 - 25.00

SENIOR PATROL LEADER

1972	0.50 - 1.00
1985	0.50 - 1.00

SENIOR PATROL LEADER'S WARRANT

1967	1.00 - 2.00

THANKS - DEN CHIEF

1966	1.00 - 2.00

TROOP JUNIOR LEADER

1985	0.50 - 1.00

TROOP JUNIOR LEADER CERTIFICATE

1985	0.50 - 1.00

TROOP LEADER'S CERTIFICATE

1978	0.50 - 1.00
1980	0.50 - 1.00

UNIFORM INSPECTION UNIT AWARD

1970	1.00 - 2.00

WARRANT OFFICER

1967	1.00 - 2.00

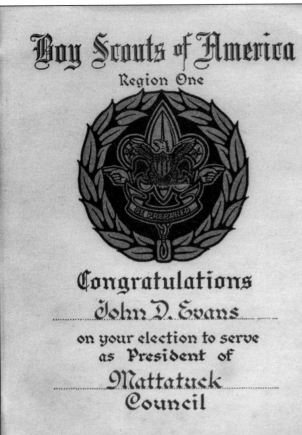

Boy Scouts of America
Region One

Congratulations

John D. Evans

on your election to serve
as President of

Mattatuck
Council

This Certificate is issued by the National Council of the

BOY SCOUTS OF AMERICA

to........FRANCIS J. CARELLO........

as evidence of his participation in

ROUNDTABLES

in preparation to serve the Scout Movement in the Training of other Leaders.

Given this........4-5........ day of ....DECEMBER........ 1954

at........SCHIFF SCOUT RESERVATION........

PRESIDENT

DIRECTOR OF VOLUNTEER TRAINING

CHIEF SCOUT EXECUTIVE

COURSE DIRECTOR

Council President certificates (above) were often customized by hand. Training certificates (right) undergo many changes.

PERSONAL EQUIPMENT

Cooking a meal in Rhode Island.

BACKPACKS

Bedding Roll and Carryall.	1925-1935	25.00 - 35.00
Haversack, tie down top flap.	1925-1953	20.00 - 30.00
Haversack, web shoulder straps, full length cover buckle close.	1925-1930	30.00 - 40.00
Camp-o-sack. Tie-down bottom flap, top flap with double strap close.	1929-1953	25.00 - 35.00
Duffle bag, 10 x 30.	1930-1953	30.00 - 40.00
Duffle bag, 21 x 33.	1930-1953	30.00 - 40.00
Rover Pack (like a duffle bag but with straps).	1930-1953	35.00 - 45.00
Haversack, four side eyelits, tie down top flap.	1935-1953	20.00 - 30.00
Hike Bag, top flap, cloth strap	1935-1953	20.00 - 30.00
Pack Board, aluminum frame, double cloth strap top.	1935-1953	35.00 - 45.00
Yucca Pack, six side eyelets, double strap top flap, single tie large flap.	1935-1953	20.00 - 30.00
Camper pack, fits on aluminum frame, two side one back pocket, double strap top.	1960-1975	35.00 - 45.00
Day Hike Musette, single strap top, rounded bottom.	1960-1975	15.00 - 25.00
Duffle bag, end tie.	1960-1975	25.00 - 35.00
Duffle bag, full length zipper.	1960-1975	25.00 - 35.00
Alpinsac shoulder bag, tie top.	1965-1970	15.00 - 20.00
Duffle bag, nylon, full zipper, 13 x 30.	1975-1980	20.00 - 30.00
Horizon I, nylon, four side pockets, one back pocket, large top flap.	1975-1985	35.00 - 45.00
Horizon I, nylon, two side pockets, one back pocket, large top flap.	1975-1980	25.00 - 35.00
Rayado pack, nylon, two side pockets, large top flap.	1975-1980	20.00 - 30.00
Yucca Ranger pack. Nylon, back pocket, double tie top flap.	1975-1980	20.00 - 30.00
Horizon I, nylon, four side pockets, one back pocket, large top flap. Flag design.	1976	75.00 - 100.00
Black Bull Horizon. Nylon.	1995	35.00 - 50.00
Black Bull Jr., Nylon.	1995	35.00 - 50.00
Camper backpack, Nylon, two side, one back zipper pockets, top flap.	1995	20.00 - 35.00
Duffle bag. Nylon, full zipper, 20 x 10.	1995	15.00 - 25.00
Organizer pack, large oval back zipper, top zipper.	1995	15.00 - 25.00
Yucca Ranger, Nylon, zipper back pocket, double tie top flap.	1995	15.00 - 25.00

BLANKET

Wool, First-Class, HQ NYC emblem.	1930-1953	60.00 - 85.00
Wool, First-Class emblem, BSA in circle.	1930-1953	60.00 - 85.00
Wool, tenderfoot emblem.	1965-1970	40.00 - 60.00

BOMB AND NAIL CLIPPER

Plastic comb, metal nail clipper and sleeve, Tenderfoot emblem on sleeve.	1965	1.00 - 2.00

CANTEEN

Polyethylene, 2-liter. Tenderfoot emblem on canvas cover.	1989	10.00 - 12.50

COMB

Plastic comb and sleeve, Tenderfoot emblem on sleeve.	1965	0.50 - 1.00

FLINT AND STEEL KIT

Flint, steel, tinder and case.	1985	4.00 - 7.50

HEATAB STOVE

Fold-up aluminum. Tenderfoot emblem.	1960	3.50 - 7.50

HOT SPARK FIRE STARTER

Scraper bar with tenderfoot emblem.	1975	1.00 - 2.50

LAUNDY BAG

Tenderfoot emblem on white nylon.	1990	5.00 - 7.50

MAGNIFIER

Tenderfoot emblem, fold out plastic magnifier.	1985	2.00 - 3.00

MATCH SAFE

First-Class emblem on metal top.	1930-1953	5.00 - 7.50
Tenderfoot emblem on metal top.	1953-1985	4.00 - 6.00
Tenderfoot emblem on plastic top.	1985	1.50 - 3.00

SOAP HOLDER

tenderfoot emblem on white plastic, rope hanger.	1985	1.50 - 2.50

SPORT SAW

Folding, plastic handle, 5-1/4 inch blade.	1985	10.00 - 15.00

SPORTGLASSES

Pop-up Tasco enlargement glasses.	1985	7.50 - 10.00

TENTS

Dan Beard tent, 9 x 7.	1933-1953	50.00 - 75.00

TOOTHBRUSH

Folding, plastic case.	1965	1.00 - 1.50

WOODZIG SAW

Folding, wooden handle, 11-1/2 inch blade.	1985	7.50 - 10.00

ZIPPER THERMOMETER

Tenderfoot emblem and thermometer.	1985	2.50 - 4.00

KNIVES

After the handbook and a uniform, most scouts want a knife. At first, many think it is cool to have a knife, but use it before proper training and care for the tool can be instilled. Finger carving becomes one of the immediate projects, soon followed by realistic first aid. If one is scarred by scouting, this is the quickest way. A scout knife is intended to be used, therefore very few of the pre-1960 issues exist with clean blades and etching. Collector editions and premium knives did not come along until the mid-1980s, with the 75th anniversary of the program. Those knives were never really intended for use, and always should be collected in the original box.

CAMILLUS CUTLERY CO.

First-Class emblem in shield-shaped shield, 3-5/8" black handle, two-piece can opener, line on bolsters.	1946-1949	CC.1	275.00 - 325.00
First-Class emblem in shield-shaped shield, 3-5/8" pearl handle, two-piece can opener, line on bolsters.	1949-1953	CC.1A	150.00 - 200.00
First-Class emblem in shield-shaped shield, 3-5/8" black handle, one-piece can opener, line on bolsters.	1950-1953	CC.2	50.00 - 75.00
First-Class emblem in shield-shaped shield, 3-5/8" black handle, one-piece can opener, short screwdriver, line on bolsters, removable shackle.	1954	CC.3	275.00 - 325.00
First-Class emblem in shield-shaped shield, 3-5/8" black handle, match nail nick.	1947-1969	CW.1	100.00 - 150.00
First-Class emblem in shield-shaped shield, 3-5/8" black handle, match nail nick, removable shackle.	1947-1969	CW.1A	100.00 - 150.00
First-Class emblem in shield-shaped shield, 3-5/8" brown handle, match nail nick.	1947-1969	CW.1B	100.00 - 150.00
Tenderfoot emblem in round shield, black handle.	1965-1970	CW.3	60.00 - 80.00
Tenderfoot emblem in round shield, brown handle.	1965-1970	CW.3A	40.00 - 60.00
Tenderfoot emblem in round shield, brown handle, w/ shackle.	1970-1979	CW.3B	25.00 - 40.00
Tenderfoot emblem in round shield, 3-5/8" stag handle.	1985-1989	CW.W3C	25.00 - 40.00
Tenderfoot emblem in round shield, 3-5/8" white handle.	1980-1984	CW.W3D	20.00 - 35.00
Eagle emblem on red-white-blue handle, 2-1/4", spear, file, and scissors.	1987-1990	E.1	25.00 - 40.00

CATTARAUGUS CUTLERY CO.

First-Class emblem in octagon shield, 3-7/16" bone handle, four blades, w/ shackle.	1933-1940	CAC.2	275.00 - 325.00
First-Class emblem in octagon shield, 3-7/16" bone handle, three blades, no shackle.	1933-1940	CAC.3	275.00 - 325.00
First-Class emblem in octagon shield, 3-7/16" bone handle, three blades, w/ shackle.	1933-1940	CAC.4	275.00 - 325.00
First-Class emblem in octagon shield, 3-7/16" bone handle, four blades, no shackle.	1933-1940	CC.1	275.00 - 325.00

IMPERIAL KNIFE CO.

First-Class emblem on shield, 3-3/4" black handle, large can opener, long screwdriver.	1949-1955	I.1	40.00 - 75.00
First-Class emblem on shield, 3-3/4" pearl handle, large can opener, long screwdriver.	1949-1955	I.2	40.00 - 75.00
First-Class emblem in plastic shield, 3-3/4" black handle, large can opener, long screwdriver.	1955-1958	I.3	20.00 - 25.00
First-Class emblem in plastic shield, 3-3/4" black handle, can opener, short screwdriver.	1958-1962	I.3A	20.00 - 25.00
First-Class emblem on shield, 3-1/2" rosewood handle, five-blade deluxe.	1952-1962	I.4	20.00 - 25.00
First-Class emblem on shield, 3-1/2" pearl handle, five-blade deluxe.	1952-1962	I.4A	20.00 - 25.00
First-Class emblem on circle, 3-1/2" stag handle, five-blade deluxe.	1963-1970	I.4B	20.00 - 25.00
First-Class emblem on circle, 3-1/2" smooth plastic handle, simulated wood.	1962-1963	I.4C	25.00 - 35.00
First-Class emblem carved, 3-3/4", reddish brown handle.	1958-1962	I.5	20.00 - 25.00
Tenderfoot emblem stamped on black handle, 3-3/4", utility knife.	1973-1979	I.6	15.00 - 20.00
Tenderfoot emblem stamped on white handle, 3-3/4", utility knife.	1980-1981	I.6A	15.00 - 20.00
Tenderfoot emblem stamped on brown handle, 3-3/4", utility knife.	1982-1985	I.6B	15.00 - 20.00
Tenderfoot emblem stamped on red handle, 3-3/4", utility knife.	1986-1989	I.6C	15.00 - 20.00
First-Class emblem in plastic shield, 3-5/8" black handle, long puff on main blade.	1963-1969	IW.2	25.00 - 35.00

IMPERIAL KNIFE CO. - FRONTIER

Tenderfoot emblem stamped on white handle, 2-7/8", blade etched, clip and pen on same end.	1982-1985	IF.1	17.50 - 22.50
Tenderfoot emblem stamped on white handle, 2-7/8", blade not etched, clip and pen on opposite ends.	1981	IF.1A	17.50 - 22.50

IMPERIAL KNIFE CO. - KINGSTON

No shield, stainless handle, main blade etched, shackle stamped KINGSTON.	1945-1947	IK.2	45.00 - 60.00

KEEN KUTTER MFG. CO.

Name etched on handle, 3-3/8", spear and pen blades, for Boys' Life subscriptions.	1916-1921	KK.1	300.00 - 350.00

LANDERS, FRARY AND CLARK

First-Class emblem in flat-top shield, 3-3/4" black composition handle, lines on bolster.	1931-1939	LFC.1	130.00 - 160.00
First-Class emblem in flat-top shield, 3-3/8" black composition handle, no lines on bolster.	1931-1939	LFC.2	130.00 - 160.00
First-Class emblem in flat-top shield, 3-3/8" black composition handle, spear and screwdriver/caplifter.	1931-1933	LFC.3	130.00 - 160.00
First-Class emblem in flat-top shield, 3-3/8" black composition handle, three blades, no shackle.	1934-1939	LFC.4	130.00 - 160.00

Scout knives are identified by the shield on the handle. Shown are: Remington (acorn shield), Camillus Cutlery (shield; two examples), Ulster (round), and Imperial (stamped emblem).

NEW YORK KNIFE CO.

BE PREPARED on plaque, 3-5/8" bone handle, punch blade w/ pat. date of 6.10.02, very large shackle.	1911-1916	NYK.1	225.00 - 275.00
BE PREPARED on plaque, 3-5/8" bone handle, punch blade w/ pat. #, removable shackle.	1917-1922	NYK.1A	275.00 - 325.00
BE PREPARED on plaque, 3-1/2" ebony handle, sheepfoot and pen blade, very large shackle.	1911-1916	NYK.2	275.00 - 325.00
BE PREPARED on plaque, 3-1/2" ebony handle, two blades, removable shackle.	1917-1922	NYK.2A	225.00 - 325.00
First-Class emblem in oval shield, 3-1/2" bone handle, two blades, removable shackle.	1917-1922	NYK.2B	275.00 - 325.00
BE PREPARED on plaque, 3-5/8" bone handle, clip and implement blade.	1920-1925	NYK.3	275.00 - 325.00
First-Class emblem in oval shield, 3-5/8" bone handle, punch blade w/ pat. #, removable shackle.	1923-1926	NYK.4	225.00 - 275.00
First-Class emblem in oval shield, 3-5/8" bone handle, screwdriver/ wirescraper, canopener/caplifter, spiral punch w/ pat. #1,171,422.	1926-1931	NYK.5	225.00 - 275.00
First-Class emblem in oval shield, 3-5/8" bone handle, screwdriver/ wire scraper, can opener/caplifter, spear.	1926-1931	NYK.5A	225.00 - 275.00
First-Class emblem in oval shield, 3-5/8" pearl shell handle, screwdriver/wire scraper, can opener/caplifter, spiral punch w/ pat. #1,171,422.	1926-1931	NYK.5B	450.00 - 550.00
First-Class emblem in oval shield, 3-3/8" bone handle, screwdriver/ wire scraper, can opener/caplifter, spiral punch w/ pat. #1,171,422.	1926-1931	NYK.6	175.00 - 225.00
First-Class emblem in oval shield, 3-3/8" bone handle, screwdriver/ wire scraper, can opener/caplifter, spear.	1926-1931	NYK.6A	175.00 - 225.00
First-Class emblem in oval shield, 3-3/8" bone handle, clip and punch blade.	1926-1931	NYK.7	175.00 - 225.00

PAL BLADE CO.

First-Class emblem in circle, 3-3/4" bone handle, two-piece can opener.	1940-1942	PB.1	50.00 - 75.00
First-Class emblem in circle, 3-1/2" bone handle, no belt shackle.	1940-1942	PB.2	60.00 - 80.00
First-Class emblem in circle, 3-3/4" black plastic handle, one-piece can opener.	1942	PB.3	50.00 - 75.00

REMINGTON

First-Class emblem in Acorn shield, 3-3/4" bone handle, can opener/ stubby screwdriver.	1923-1924	R.1	275.00 - 325.00
First-Class emblem in Acorn shield, 3-3/4" bone handle, two-piece can opener w/ lift tab.	1924-1926	R.1A	275.00 - 325.00
First-Class emblem in Acorn shield, 3-3/4" bone handle, second shield engraved, "The Remington Award for Heroism."	1924-1932	R.1B	400.00 - 500.00
First-Class emblem in Acorn shield, 3-3/8" bone handle, can opener.	1923-1924	R.2	275.00 - 325.00
First-Class emblem in Acorn shield, 3-3/8" bone handle, two-piece can opener w/ lift tab.	1924-1926	R.2A	275.00 - 325.00
First-Class emblem in cut out shield, 3-3/4" bone handle, long screwdriver.	1927	R.3	275.00 - 325.00
First-Class emblem in round shield, 3-3/4" bone handle, long screwdriver, vertical lift tab on can opener.	1929-1932	R.4	150.00 - 200.00
First-Class emblem in round shield, 3-3/4" bone handle, long screwdriver, parallel lift tab on can opener.	1933-1935	R.4A	150.00 - 200.00
First-Class emblem in round shield, 3-3/4" bone handle, parallel lift tab on can opener, plain bolster.	1935-1939	R.4B	150.00 - 200.00
First-Class emblem in round shield, 3-3/8" bone handle, pinched bolster, vertical lift tab on can opener.	1929-1932	R.5	150.00 - 200.00
First-Class emblem in round shield, 3-3/8" bone handle, smooth bolster, parallel lift tab on can opener.	1933-1939	R.5A	150.00 - 200.00
First-Class emblem in round shield, 3-3/8" bone handle, three blades, no shackle.	1928-1932	R.6	150.00 - 200.00
First-Class emblem in round shield, 3-1/2" bone handle, three blades, screwdriver w/ main blade, removable shackle.	1934-1939	R.7	250.00 - 300.00
First-Class emblem in round shield, 3-1/2" bone handle, three blades, can opener w/ main blade, removable shackle.	1934-1939	R.7A	250.00 - 300.00

SCHRADE CO.

Tenderfoot emblem stamped on stainless handle, 2-7/8", spear and file blade.	1970-1978	S.2	17.50 - 22.50
Tenderfoot emblem in round shield, 3-5/8" Delrin stag handle, long pull.	1973	SW.4	17.50 - 22.50

SCHRADE WALDEN

First-Class emblem on oval shield, 2-3/4" Delrin stag handle, clip and pen blade.	1962-1972	S.1	17.50 - 22.50

ULSTER KNIFE CO.

First-Class emblem in shield-shaped shield, 3-5/8" bone handle, short screwdriver, one-piece can opener, long nail nick.	1923-1926	U.1	20.00 - 30.00
First-Class emblem in shield-shaped shield, 3-5/8" pearl shell handle, short screwdriver, one-piece can opener, long nail nick.	1926-1928	U.1A	17.50 - 22.50
First-Class emblem in shield-shaped shield, 3-3/8" bone handle, short screwdriver, one-piece can opener, long nail nick.	1923-1926	U.2	17.50 - 22.50
First-Class emblem in shield-shaped shield, 3-5/8" bone handle, long screwdriver, short nail nick, three-piece can opener.	1927-1940	U.3	17.50 - 22.50
First-Class emblem in shield-shaped shield, 3-3/8" bone handle, long screwdriver, short nail nick, three-piece can opener.	1927-1940	U.4	10.00 - 17.50
First-Class emblem in shield-shaped shield, 3-3/8" bone handle, long screwdriver, three-piece can opener.	1934-1940	U.5	10.00 - 17.50
First-Class emblem in shield-shaped shield, 3-3/8" bone handle, long screwdriver, three-piece can opener, removable shackle..	1934-1940	U.5A	10.00 - 17.50
First-Class emblem in shield-shaped shield, 3-1/2" bone handle, spear and pen blades.	1923-1931	U.6	10.00 - 17.50

ULSTER, U.S.A.

Tenderfoot emblem in round shield, 3-3/4" brown handle.	1962-1979	U.1	60.00 - 80.00
Tenderfoot emblem in round shield, 3-3/4" white handle.	1962-1979	U.1A	17.50 - 22.50
Tenderfoot emblem in round shield, 3-3/4" stag handle.	1983-1985	U.1B	15.00 - 25.00
Tenderfoot emblem in round shield, 3-3/4" stag grooved handle, stainless blades.	1966-1976	U.2	15.00 - 25.00
Tenderfoot emblem in round shield, 3-3/4" stag handle, five- blade deluxe, no shackle.	1976-1979	U.3	15.00 - 25.00
Tenderfoot emblem in round shield, 3-3/4" ivory handle, five-blade deluxe, no shackle.	1980-1981	U.3A	20.00 - 35.00
Tenderfoot emblem in round shield, 3-3/4" white handle, five-blade deluxe, no shackle.	1982-1983	U.3B	20.00 - 30.00
Tenderfoot emblem in round shield, 3-3/4" smooth white handle, five-blade deluxe, no shackle.	1984-1985	U.3C	20.00 - 30.00
Tenderfoot emblem in round shield, 3-3/4" black handle, five-blade deluxe, stamped Camillus.	1986-1987	UC.4	20.00 - 30.00

VICTORINOX

Tenderfoot and Swiss emblem stamped on red handle, 3-1/2", 14 tools (eight blades), Huntsman.	1987-1989	V.1	45.00 - 55.00
Tenderfoot and Swiss emblem stamped on red handle, 3-1/4", 12 tools (six blades), Tinker.	1987-1989	V.2	25.00 - 35.00
Tenderfoot and Swiss emblem stamped on red handle, 2-1/4", five tools (three blades),-Classic.	1987-1989	V.3	20.00 - 25.00

WENGER

Tenderfoot and Swiss emblem stamped on red handle, 3-3/8", nine tools, Young Hunter.	1982-1986	W.1	30.00 - 40.00
Tenderfoot and Swiss emblem stamped on red handle, 3-3/8", seven tools, Scout Special.	1982-1986	W.2	25.00 - 35.00
Tenderfoot and Swiss emblem stamped on red handle, 2-1/2", five tools, Viceroy.	1982-1986	W.3	15.00 - 20.00

Ernest Stevens sports his "Kit Carson" combination short knife and ax on a belt sheath.

AXES AND SHEATH KNIVES

Ax

Description	Years	Value
Plumb. Head with nail slot. Small First Class emblem. Hickory handle.	1911-1929	40.00 - 60.00
Keen Kutter. Head w/o nail pull.	1917-1925	100.00 - 150.00
Collins. Head w/nail slot, First Class emblem on head. Wood handle with green end.	1923-1938	40.00 - 60.00
Plumb. Head w/o nail slot. Small First Class emblem. 27" handle.	1928-1940	50.00 - 75.00
Plumb. Head with nail slot. First Class emblem in seal. Red hickory handle.	1930-1940	40.00 - 60.00
Plumb. Head w/o nail slot. First Class emblem in seal.	1933-1944	40.00 - 60.00
Bridgeport. Head w/nail slot, single piece handle. First Class emblem in head, 1" area before handle thins out from head.	1934-1948	40.00 - 60.00
Vaughn and Bushnell. Head w/o nail slot, 13" cream hickory handle, red end. First Class emblem on handle.	1934-1940	100.00 - 125.00
Vaughn and Bushnell. Head w/o nail slot, 28" hickory handle, red end.	1934-1940	100.00 - 125.00
Collins. Head w/o nail slot, First Class emblem in head, 28" hickory handle.	1938-1950	75.00 - 100.00
Collins. Head w/nail slot, tool steel, black rustproofed. First Class emblem on head. Hickory handle with green end.	1939-1942	100.00 - 125.00
Plumb. Head w/o nail slot, steel handle w/leaf springs. Wood outer hand grip.	1940-1943	100.00 - 150.00
Vaughn and Bushnell. Head w/nail slot, single piece head and 13" handle. First Class seal on head.	1940-1942	100.00 - 125.00
Plumb. Head w/o nail slot, carbon steel. 15" hickory handle, red bottom w/leather tie.	1947-1953	50.00 - 75.00
Bridgeport. Head w/nail slot, single piece handle. First Class emblem in head, 1/2" area before handle thins out from head.	1948-1960	40.00 - 60.00
True Temper. Head w/o nail pull. Forged steel head bonded to steel shaft. Shock-absorbant handle. First Class emblem on head.	1957-1966	60.00 - 75.00
Bridgeport. Head w/nail slot, single piece handle. Neoprene grips.	1960-1965	40.00 - 60.00
Plumb. Head w/o nail slot, carbon steel. Permabond head.	1960-1975	40.00 - 60.00
Plumb. Head w/o nail slot, carbon steel. 24" hickory handle.	1964-1975	50.00 - 75.00
Bridgeport. Head w/nail slot, single piece handle. Tenderfoot emblem in head, Neoprene grips.	1967-1970	40.00 - 60.00
True Temper. Head w/o nail pull. Forged steel head bonded to steel shaft. Shock-absorbant handle. Tenderfoot emblem on head.	1967-1982	60.00 - 75.00
True Temper. Head w/o nail pull. Forged steel, 14" handle.	1975-1995	40.00 - 60.00
Plumb. Head w/o nail slot, steel. Permabond head to 13" handle.	1983-1998	40.00 - 60.00
Plumb. Head w/o nail slot, 28" hickory handle.	1985	75.00 - 100.00

Sheath Knife

Description	Years	Value
Marbles. Woodcraft, 4-1/2" blade, curved top, handle w/o finger groves. Five rivets to sheath.	1933-1940	50.00 - 75.00
Remington, 4-1/2" blade, curved top, handle w/finger groves. Seven rivets to sheath.	1933-1939	50.00 - 75.00
Remington, 4-1/2" blade, curved top, handle w/o finger groves. Seven rivets to sheath.	1933-1939	50.00 - 75.00
Remington, 4" blade, straight top, handle w/finger groves. Five rivets to sheath.	1933-1939	50.00 - 75.00
Remington, 4" blade, straight top, handle w/o finger groves. Five rivets to sheath.	1933-1939	50.00 - 75.00
Marbles. Sport, 4" blade, straight top, handle w/o finger groves. Five rivets to sheath.	1935-1940	50.00 - 75.00
Union Cutlery, 3-1/2" blade, straight top, handle w/finger groves. Four rivets to sheath.	1937-1940	75.00 - 100.00
Union Cutlery, 5" blade, straight top, handle w/finger groves. Five rivets to sheath.	1937-1948	50.00 - 75.00
Pal Blade Co., 4-3/4" blade, straight top, blood grove, smooth handle. Five rivets to sheath.	1940-1942	125.00 - 150.00
Pal Blade Co., 4-3/4" blade, straight top, smooth handle, aluminum end-cap. Five rivets to sheath.	1940-1942	100.00 - 125.00
Pal Blade Co., 4-3/4" blade, straight top, smooth handle, wood end-cap. Five rivets to sheath.	1940-1942	100.00 - 125.00
Pal Blade Co., 4" blade, straight top, smooth handle. Five rivets to sheath.	1940-1942	100.00 - 125.00
Cardinal Cutlery, 4" blade, straight top, smooth handle. Five rivets to sheath.	1945-1948	75.00 - 100.00
Cardinal Cutlery, 5" blade, straight top, smooth handle. Five rivets to sheath.	1945-1948	75.00 - 100.00
Marbles. Mohawk, 4" blade, straight top, handle w/o finger groves. Five rivets to sheath.	1947-1960	50.00 - 75.00
Western States Cutlery, 4-1/2" blade, straight top, smooth handle. Four rivets to sheath.	1948-1951	125.00 - 150.00
Western States Cutlery, 5" blade, straight top, large blood grove, smooth handle. Five rivets to sheath.	1948-1951	125.00 - 150.00
Western Boulder, 4-1/2" blade, straight top, smooth handle. 5 rivets to sheath, First Class emblem on snap.	1951-1960	75.00 - 100.00
Western Boulder, 5" blade, straight top, large blood grove, smooth handle. Five rivets to sheath.	1951-1955	75.00 - 100.00
Western Boulder, 4" blade, straight top thin blade, smooth handle. Four rivets to sheath, First Class emblem on snap.	1955-1960	75.00 - 100.00
Western Boulder, 4-1/2" blade, straight top, smooth handle. Five rivets to sheath, Tenderfoot emblem on snap.	1960-1970	75.00 - 100.00
Western Boulder, 4" blade, straight top thin blade, smooth handle. Four rivets to sheath, Tenderfoot emblem on snap, rope and knot design stamped.	1960-1970	75.00 - 100.00
Western Boulder, 3-1/2" blade, curved top blade, delrin handle. Four rivets to sheath, Tenderfoot emblem on snap.	1971-1979	75.00 - 100.00
Western Boulder, 4-1/2" blade, curved top blade, delrin handle. Five rivets to sheath, Tenderfoot emblem on snap.	1971-1974	75.00 - 100.00
Camillus Cutlery, 3-1/2" blade, curved top thin blade, white delrin handle. Two rivets to sheath.	1980-1984	75.00 - 100.00

Sheath Knife and Ax Combination - Kit Carson Kit

Description	Years	Value
Display box and leather belt wear sheath.	1940-1984	225.00 - 275.00
Leather belt wear sheath.	1940-1984	175.00 - 225.00

UNIT EQUIPMENT

FORTY KNOTS

Knot display card, red and white ropes to tie knots.	1975	1.00 - 2.50

TENTS

Hike Tent, 7 x 5.	1920-1953	15.00 - 25.00
Pinetree Tent, 7 x 5.	1920-1953	15.00 - 25.00
Baker Tent, 7 x 7.	1930-1953	35.00 - 50.00
Featherweight Shelter Tent, 8 x 5.	1930-1953	30.00 - 40.00
Forester's Tent, 7 x 7.	1930-1953	25.00 - 35.00
Half-pyramid Tent, 9 x 9.	1930-1953	20.00 - 30.00
Hickory Tent. 11 x 6.	1930-1953	35.00 - 45.00
Indian Tepee. 16 ft. diameter.	1930-1953	150.00 - 200.00
Pup Tent, 7 x 5.	1930-1953	20.00 - 30.00
Rover Tent, 6 x 4.	1930-1953	25.00 - 35.00
Shelter Tent, 8 x 5.	1930-1953	25.00 - 35.00
Tramper Tent, 6 x 4.	1930-1953	25.00 - 35.00
Two-boy Tent/fly.	1930-1953	20.00 - 30.00
Wall Tent, 10 x 12.	1930-1953	25.00 - 35.00
Camper Tent, 7 x 9.	1960-1975	25.00 - 35.00
Miner's Tent, 7 x 7.	1960-1975	25.00 - 35.00
Overnighter Tent, 4 x 7.	1960-1975	25.00 - 35.00
Voyageur, 7 x 8, w/ floor.	1960-1975	45.00 - 55.00
Voyageur, 7 x 8, w/o floor.	1960-1975	35.00 - 45.00
Adventurer I, Nylon, 7 x 8.	1985-1995	50.00 - 75.00
Adventurer II, Nylon, 5 x 8.	1985-1995	50.00 - 75.00
Companion, 5 x 7.	1985-1995	45.00 - 55.00
Dome Tent, 7 x 9.	1985-1995	50.00 - 75.00
Free Spirit I, 7 x 8. Nylon.	1985-1995	50.00 - 75.00
Free Spirit II, 5 x 7. Nylon.	1985-1995	50.00 - 75.00
Philmont Backpacker. 5 x 7.	1985-1995	45.00 - 55.00
Wall Tent, Lodge, 12 x 16.	1995	100.00 - 150.00
Wall Tent, Square, 9 x 9.	1995	75.00 - 125.00
Wall Tent, Staff, 10 x 12.	1995	100.00 - 150.00
Wall Tent, Standard, 7 x 9.	1995	75.00 - 125.00
Wall Tent, Wide, 9 x 7.	1995	75.00 - 125.00

TROOP CHARTER

Scout Law within rope border, large V underprint in ctr. Five-year tenured unit.	1925-1945	15.00 - 20.00
Scout Law within rope border, large X underprint in ctr. 10-year tenured unit.	1925-1945	20.00 - 30.00
Scout Law within rope border, large XV underprint in ctr. 15-year tenured unit.	1925-1945	20.00 - 30.00
Scout Law within rope border, large XX underprint in ctr. 20-year tenured unit	1925-1945	25.00 - 35.00
Scout Law within rope border, large XXV underprint in ctr. 25-year tenured unit	1925-1945	25.00 - 35.00
Scout Law within rope border, large XXX underprint in ctr. 30-year tenured unit	1925-1945	30.00 - 40.00
Scout Law within rope border, no underprint in ctr.	1925-1945	15.00 - 20.00
White, First-Class emblem within red-white-blue ribbon at top. Statue of Liberty in blue at left corner, National Seal in right corner.	1946-1950	15.00 - 20.00
White, First-Class emblem within red-white-blue ribbon at top. National Seal at bottom center.	1950-1965	10.00 - 15.00

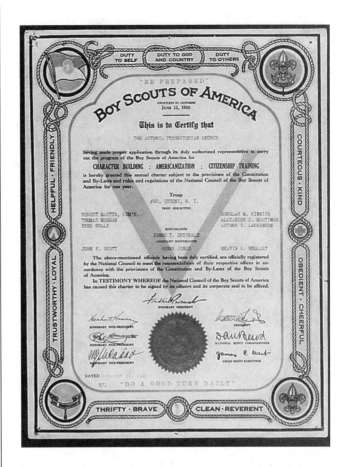

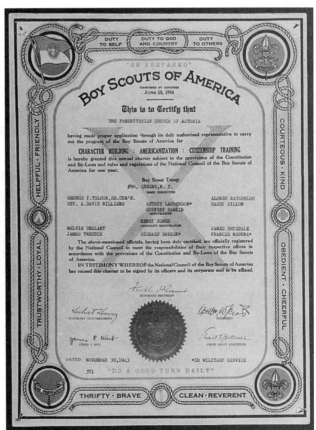

Troop Charters. In the pre-1945 design, the tenure of a unit was included as a large underprint in the central area.

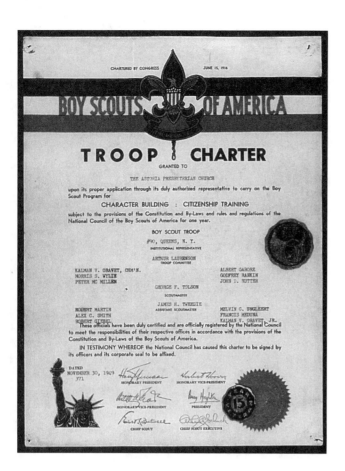

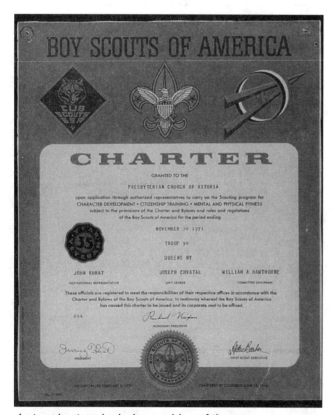

Later charters include graphics of the era.

Central image of a cotton troop flag

TROOP FLAG

First-Class emblem at left ctr, red top, white bottom, 22" x 36".	1911-1930	50.00 - 75.00
First-Class emblem at ctr, white top, red bottom, wool, pennant end.	1920-1935	50.00 - 75.00
First-Class emblem at ctr, white top, red bottom, wool, square end.	1925-1950	40.00 - 60.00
First-Class emblem at ctr, white top, red bottom, square end, cotton.	1950-1970	20.00 - 40.00
First-Class emblem at ctr. white top, red bottom, nylon.	1970	15.00 - 30.00

TROOP MEETING SIGN

First-Class Emblem, gilt and white on blue field, pulp backing.	1920-1953	40.00 - 60.00
First-Class Emblem, imitation gold leaf and white on blue field, w/o pult backing.	1920-1953	40.00 - 60.00

WATER BAG

Canvas, 2 gallon. First-Class, HQ NYC seal.	1930-1953	25.00 - 35.00
Canvas, 2 gallon. First-Class, National Council emblem.	1953-1970	15.00 - 20.00

MISCELLANEOUS STUFF

AQUATIC SCHOOL, BSA

Tenderfoot emblem within lifering, crossed oars behind, 4" circle.	1945-1955	10.00 - 15.00

AUTO GRILLE MEDALLION

Tenderfoot emblem to apply to car grille. Brass.	1990	25.00 - 30.00

AUTO RADIATOR CAP

First-Class emblem.	1920-1930	100.00 - 150.00

BANDANAS

Animal Tracks, 21" square.	1998	5.00 - 7.50
Constellations, 21" square.	1998	5.00 - 7.50
First Aid, 21" square.	1998	5.00 - 7.50
Forty Knots, 21" square.	1998	5.00 - 7.50

BANK

Celluloid pocket bank. A scout is Thrifty, Save money and pay your own way. Tenderfoot emblem in center.	1917-1925	50.00 - 75.00
Scout and shield with red-white-blue stripes, lithographed tin.	1920	20.00 - 30.00
Scout standing w/ staff, two-part cast iron, painted.	1920	40.00 - 75.00
Scout standing, hands on waist, cast iron, painted.	1920	40.00 - 60.00
Scouts in camp, boy w/ flag, mechanical, cast iron, painted. (Reproductions exist, $50.)	1920	500.00 - 2,000.
First-Class emblem supported on wide base, FDL on back with coin slot.	1953	25.00 - 40.00
Scout Bust wearing overseas cap, slot in back.	1953	15.00 - 25.00

BIRDHOUSE

Wax-treated paperboard. First-Class emblem.	1955	5.00 - 7.50
Wax-treated paperboard. Tenderfoot emblem, green and tan.	1963	5.00 - 7.50

BLOTTERS, BROWN & BIGELOW

Scout Law Series. A illustration, explanation and advertisement.	1923	15.00 - 20.00
America's future lies in its youth!	1940s	10.00 - 15.00
Onward…For God and My Country	1950s	15.00 - 20.00

*A 1923 ink blotter by Brown & Bigelow from its
Scout Law series. Vertical and horizontal formats
used the same illustration.*

BOOKMARK

First-Class emblem at ctr.	1950-1960	5.00 - 7.50
Tenderfoot emblem at ctr, green enamel background.	1960-1970	2.00 - 3.00

BSA CELEBRATION BANNER

Red, blue, green yellow squares around black FDL.	1997	20.00 - 30.00

CAMERA

Seneca 2A Box Scout, or Scout Camera.	1915	50.00 - 75.00
Agfa Ansco Boy Scout Memo Camera.	1929	40.00 - 60.00
Kodak, Boy Scout. Olive green bellows, case, and leather belt pouch.	1929-1934	125.00 - 200.00
Kodak, Boy Scout Brownie, 120 film.	1932	100.00 - 125.00
Kodak, Boy Scout Brownie, 620 film.	1933-1934	30.00 - 50.00
Kodak, Boy Scout Black bellows, olive green case, and leather belt pouch.	1934-1940	100.00 - 150.00
Herco Scout 120.	1950-1955	30.00 - 50.00
Herco Imperial 620 Reflex.	1955-1960	20.00 - 30.00
Official Camera, 620 film.	1960-1963	10.00 - 15.00
Official three-way, 127 film.	1960-1963	10.00 - 15.00
Official flash camera, round attachment, 127 film.	1961-1963	10.00 - 15.00
Official flash camera, square attachment, 127 film.	1963-1965	10.00 - 15.00
Lark Flash, built in, 127 film.	1964-1966	10.00 - 15.00
Cubex IV, 127 film.	1966-1968	5.00 - 10.00
Instant load, 126 cartridge.	1969-1971	5.00 - 10.00

CAMPFIRE MARSHMALLOW TIN

Tent, scouts around campfire.	(none)	25.00 - 35.00

COLLECTOR'S CAP

1995.	1995	15.00 - 20.00
1996.	1996	15.00 - 20.00
1997.	1997	15.00 - 20.00
1998.	1998	15.00 - 20.00
1999.	1999	15.00 - 20.00
2000.	2000	15.00 - 20.00

CONTEST CUP

First-Class emblem atop 10" high cup w/ wide bottom and fluted top, silverplate.	1920-1935	50.00 - 75.00
First-Class emblem atop 10" high cup, thin base, silverplate.	1920-1935	50.00 - 75.00

CONTEST PLAQUE

Fancy brass w/ First-Class emblem at top, 9" x 10".	1920-1935	75.00 - 100.00
Ornate brass w/ First-Class emblem in bottom border, 9" x 10".	1920-1935	75.00 - 100.00
Shield shape w/ scout on signal tower and First-Class emblem, 9" x 10".	1920-1935	100.00 - 125.00

CUFF LINKS

First-Class emblem in oval, enameled silver, pair.	1915-1925	150.00 - 200.00
First-Class emblem in oval, silver, pair.	1915-1925	125.00 - 175.00
Second-Class emblem in oval, enameled silver, pair.	1915-1925	125.00 - 175.00
Second-Class emblem in oval, silver, pair.	1915-1925	125.00 - 175.00
Second-Class emblem in oval, silver, pair.	1915-1925	125.00 - 175.00
Tenderfoot emblem in oval, enameled silver, pair.	1915-1925	125.00 - 175.00
Tenderfoot emblem in oval, silver, pair.	1915-1925	125.00 - 175.00
Tenderfoot emblem in faux mother-of-pearl rectangle.	1960	17.50 - 25.00
Tenderfoot emblem on black enamel rectangle.	1960	10.00 - 15.00
Tenderfoot emblem on rectangle, horizontal lines on background.	1960-1970	10.00 - 15.00
Tenderfoot emblem 'floating' within oval.	1975-1985	10.00 - 15.00

CUP, COLLAPSIBLE

First-Class emblem on top, brass, nickel-plated.	1911-1930	30.00 - 45.00
Tenderfoot emblem on top, brass, nickel-plated.	1930-1950	15.00 - 20.00
Tenderfoot emblem on cover, aluminum.	1950-1970	5.00 - 7.50
Tenderfoot emblem on cover, plastic.	1960-1980	3.00 - 7.50

DESK

Folding child's room desk. Compartments for papers, books, pencils, and roll top signs of scouts in various activities.	1915-1925	500.00 - 750.00

FIGURINE. GROSSMAN, ROCKWELL'S

A Scout is Helpful.	1985	35.00 - 50.00
Can't Wait.	1985	25.00 - 40.00
Good Turn (first).	1985	35.00 - 50.00
Good Turn (second).	1985	35.00 - 50.00
Physically Strong.	1985	35.00 - 50.00
Scout Memories.	1985	35.00 - 50.00

FIRST AID KIT

Bauer & Black, rounded corners and green, orange top, (if no contents, deduct 50%).	1932	40.00 - 60.00
Bauer & Black, rectangular corners and green, orange top, (if no contents, deduct 50%).	1935	40.00 - 60.00
Johnson & Johnson, rectangular, green and red, (if no contents, deduct 50%).	1938	30.00 - 50.00
Johnson & Johnson, square, removable top, (if no contents, deduct 50%).	1945	25.00 - 35.00
Johnson & Johnson, square, flip top, (if no contents, deduct 50%).	1955	20.00 - 40.00
Johnson & Johnson, curved plastic, (if no contents, deduct 50%).	1965	10.00 - 15.00

GAME

The Game of Boy Scouts, Parker Brothers.	1912	40.00 - 60.00
Cracker Jack, Snap, 12 cards, 1" x 3".	1915-1925	100.00 - 125.00
American Boys, a game. Milton Bradley.	1920	75.00 - 100.00
Boy Scout 10 pins (bowling).	1920	40.00 - 60.00
Boy Scout 5 pins (bowling).	1920	30.00 - 50.00
Boy Scouts in Camp, cardboard figures on wood blocks.	1920	75.00 - 100.00
Snap in Cracker Jack, cards.	1920	100.00 - 150.00
Sunny Andy Kiddie Kampers, tin litho.	1920	80.00 - 120.00
Target Ball (marble shoot).	1920	40.00 - 60.00
Game of Scouting, Parker Brothers.	1926	40.00 - 60.00
The Boy Scout Progress Game.	1926	60.00 - 90.00
Boy Scout Game, card pick to do action.	1930	30.00 - 40.00
Mickey Mouse - The Scout. Cut out figures from Post Toasties Box.	1939	40.00 - 60.00
Scout Mania, booklet and tape.	1985	10.00 - 15.00
Scouting Trails	1987	10.00 - 17.50

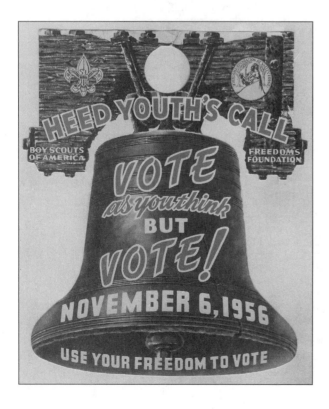

GET OUT THE VOTE! DOOR HANGER

Liberty Bell shape.	1952-1956	10.00 - 15.00

GRAVE MARKER

Tenderfoot emblem above palm on square area for name and dates, cast bronze.	1930-1940	250.00 - 300.00

GREETING CARDS

Various themes.	1960-1967	2.00 - 3.00

HIKING STAFF EMBLEMS

BSA 50 Miler.	1990	4.00 - 6.00
BSA High Adventure.	1990	4.00 - 6.00
Eagle and Flag.	1990	4.00 - 6.00
Eagle Badge.	1990	4.00 - 6.00
First-Class Badge.	1990	4.00 - 6.00
Historic Trails Award.	1990	4.00 - 6.00
International Logo.	1990	4.00 - 6.00
Junior Leader Training.	1990	4.00 - 6.00
Life Badge.	1990	4.00 - 6.00
National Camping School.	1990	4.00 - 6.00
National Eagle Scout Association.	1990	4.00 - 6.00
Order of the Arrow, Brotherhood Arrow.	1990	4.00 - 6.00
Order of the Arrow, MGM Indian Logo.	1990	4.00 - 6.00
Order of the Arrow, Ordeal Arrow.	1990	4.00 - 6.00
Order of the Arrow, Vigil Arrow.	1990	4.00 - 6.00
Order of the Arrow, Vigil Triangle.	1990	4.00 - 6.00
Scout Badge.	1990	4.00 - 6.00
Second-Class Badge.	1990	4.00 - 6.00
Silver Beaver.	1990	4.00 - 6.00
Star Badge.	1990	4.00 - 6.00
Tenderfoot Badge.	1990	4.00 - 6.00
Tenderfoot emblem on red, Be Prepared below.	1990	4.00 - 6.00
Wood Badge beads and axe-in-log.	1990	4.00 - 6.00
Wood Badge - Antelope.	1995	4.00 - 6.00
Wood Badge - Bear.	1995	4.00 - 6.00
Wood Badge - Beaver.	1995	4.00 - 6.00
Wood Badge - Bobwhite.	1995	4.00 - 6.00
Wood Badge - Buffalo.	1995	4.00 - 6.00
Wood Badge - Eagle.	1995	4.00 - 6.00
Wood Badge - Fox.	1995	4.00 - 6.00
Wood Badge - Owl.	1995	4.00 - 6.00
Arrow of Light Badge.	1998	4.00 - 6.00
Bear Badge.	1998	4.00 - 6.00
Bobcat Badge.	1998	4.00 - 6.00
Patrol Emblem - Cobra.	1998	4.00 - 6.00
Patrol Emblem - Dragon.	1998	4.00 - 6.00
Patrol Emblem - Eagle (head).	1998	4.00 - 6.00
Patrol Emblem - Flaming Arrow.	1998	4.00 - 6.00
Patrol Emblem - Flying Eagle.	1998	4.00 - 6.00
Patrol Emblem - Indian Chief.	1998	4.00 - 6.00

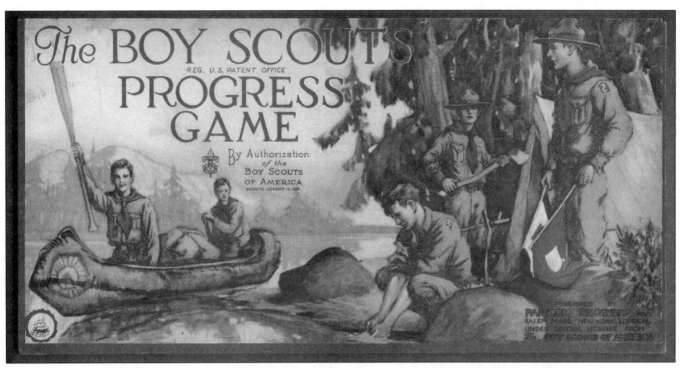

Game board for the 1924 Parker Brothers "The Boy Scouts' Progress Game."

Winchester rifles 1985 tribute lithograph, painted by J. Csatari, value $75.00 - $100.00.

Patrol Emblem - Panther.	1998	4.00 - 6.00
Patrol Emblem - Scorpion.	1998	4.00 - 6.00
Patrol Emblem - Shark.	1998	4.00 - 6.00
Patrol Emblem - Wolverine.	1998	4.00 - 6.00
Tiger Cubs.	1998	4.00 - 6.00
Wolf Badge.	1998	4.00 - 6.00
High Advenure HA logo.	1999	4.00 - 6.00
Venture emblem.	1999	4.00 - 6.00
Webelos badge.	1999	4.00 - 6.00

KENNER'S BOB SCOUT DOLL
In uniform w/ box.	1975	55.00 - 75.00

KENNER'S STEVE SCOUT DOLL
In uniform w/ box, CSP decal card, discount coupon booklet.	1975	45.00 - 60.00

KENNER'S STEVE SCOUT EXTRAS
Fire Fighter Gear.	1975	5.00 - 7.50
Metal Detector Gear.	1975	5.00 - 7.50

LAPEL PIN, CLIP ON
First-Class emblem in oval, silver.	1915-1925	60.00 - 80.00
Second-Class emblem in oval, silver.	1915-1925	100.00 - 125.00
Tenderfoot emblem in oval, silver.	1915-1925	125.00 - 150.00

LAPEL PIN, LONG PIN
First-Class emblem in oval, silver.	1915-1925	60.00 - 80.00
Second-Class emblem in oval, silver.	1915-1925	100.00 - 125.00
Tenderfoot emblem in oval, silver.	1915-1925	125.00 - 150.00

LARIAT
20-foot length, in box.	1928	75.00 - 100.00

LIGHT BULB
First-Class emblem in filament.	1935-1940	125.00 - 150.00

MORSE FLAGS
Red-white square, 24" muslin.	1911-1930	15.00 - 20.00

NOTE CARDS
Eagle Card, Eagle badge flanked by large scout law, blue/gray.	1970	0.50 - 1.00
Eagle Card, Eagle badge flanked by scout law, white background.	1970	0.50 - 1.00
Eagle Scout medal, white background. Scout law above.	1970	0.50 - 1.00
Tenderfoot emblem, foil embossed, plain.	1970	0.50 - 1.00
Tenderfoot emblem, foil embossed, Thank You inscribed.	1970	0.50 - 1.00
Tenderfoot emblem in foil, Best Wishes printed.	1989	0.00 - 0.00
Tenderfoot emblem in foil, Congratulations printed.	1989	0.50 - 1.00
Tenderfoot emblem in foil, You're Invited printed.	1989	0.50 - 1.00
Eagle Scout medal, white background. Congratulations above.	1990	0.50 - 1.00
Scout Law as frame, photo of scout in outdoors.	1997	0.50 - 1.00
Scout Oath as frame, photo of scout in outdoors.	1997	0.50 - 1.00
Tenderfoot emblem above Congratulations! on plain card, 4 x 5-1/2.	2001	1.00 - 2.00
Tenderfoot emblem above Thank You! on plain card, 4 x 5-1/2.	2001	1.00 - 2.00
Tenderfoot emblem on plain card, 4 x 5-1/2.	2001	1.00 - 2.00

NOTE PAPER
Box of 24 sheets and envelopes, First-Class emblem.	1920-1930	20.00 - 30.00
Box of 24 sheets and envelopes, Second-Class emblem.	1920-1930	20.00 - 30.00
Box of 24 sheets and envelopes, Tenderfoot emblem.	1920-1930	20.00 - 30.00
First class emblem flanked by two oval scenes. 24 sheets and envelopes in box.	1935	25.00 - 35.00
Tenderfoot embelm at top. In brown folder.	1985	10.00 - 15.00
Tenderfoot emblem in foil in upper corner. Packet of 20 with envelopes.	1989	5.00 - 7.50
FDL in corners, full color border. Packet of 50.	1998	7.50 - 12.50
Hiking scene at top, camp scene at bottom, full color border. Packet of 50.	1998	7.50 - 12.50
Merit Badge photo border, Tenderfoot emblem in ctr. Packet of 20.	2000	5.00 - 7.50

PATROL FLAG
Red emblem silk-screened on both sides of white muslin, 11" x 27", 47 different available.	1911-1930	50.00 - 75.00
Red silk screen emblem on white cotton, two ties, and seam for pole insert.	1930-1940	20.00 - 30.00
Red silk screen emblem on white cotton, two ties at end.	1940-1950	15.00 - 25.00
White cotton with black emblem on red twill disc, two ties.	1950-1972	10.00 - 20.00
White cotton pennant with red twill circle, black embroidered animal or figure, B.S.A. below.	1955-1972	7.50 - 15.00
White cotton with black emblem on yellow twill disc., two ties.	1972	7.50 - 12.50
White cotton with yellow twill circle, black embroidered animal or figure, B.S.A. below.	1972-1989	3.00 - 7.50

PENCIL BOX TIN
Wallace Pencil Co. multi-color camp scene.	1930-1940	30.00 - 50.00

PENNANT

First-Class emblem, BE PREPARED, 12" x 24" felt.	1911-1930	25.00 - 30.00
First-Class emblem, BE PREPARED, 9" x 18" felt.	1911-1930	15.00 - 20.00
Be Prepared, seal at wide end, 9" x 18", silk-screened.	1920-1940	7.50 - 15.00
Be Prepared, seal at wide end, 12" x 24", silk-screened.	1920-1940	10.00 - 20.00
Boy Scouts of America, no seal, 15" x 36", silk-screened.	1920-1940	10.00 - 20.00
Boy Scouts, seal at wide end, 15" x 36", red felt, white letters and seal.	1920-1940	20.00 - 30.00
Boy Scouts, seal at wide end, white lettering, red wood, 18" x 42".	1920-1940	25.00 - 35.00
Boy Scouts, seal at wide end, white on blue felt, 15" x 36".	1920-1940	20.00 - 30.00
Boy Scouts, stitched seal, felt letters, 15" x 36".	1920-1940	20.00 - 30.00
Do a Good Turn Daily, seal at wide end, 15" x 36", silk-screened.	1920-1940	10.00 - 20.00

PICTURES

Charles A. Lindbergh, 10 x 12".	1927-1940	30.00 - 50.00
Dan Beard, 12 x 13".	1927-1940	30.00 - 50.00
Executive Board Members, 11 x 14".	1927-1940	30.00 - 50.00
James E. West, w/o printed autograph, 10 x 12".	1927-1940	30.00 - 50.00
James E. West, w/ printed autograph, 10 x 12".	1927-1940	30.00 - 50.00
Rockwell's A Red Cross Man in the Making, 8-1/2 x 11.	1927-1940	20.00 - 30.00
Rockwell's Handbook Cover, paper, laminated, 10 x 12".	1927-1940	30.00 - 50.00
Rockwell's Handbook Cover, printed on canvas, 16 x 22.	1927-1940	50.00 - 75.00
Rockwell's Scouting Makes Real Men Out of Real Boys, 8-1/2 x 11.	1927-1940	20.00 - 30.00
Rockwell's Straight Talk From the Scoutmaster, 8-1/2 x 11.	1927-1940	20.00 - 30.00
Rockwell's The Daily Good Turn, 8-1/2 x 11.	1927-1940	20.00 - 30.00

PLAQUES, LAMINATED

Official badges and insignia.	1940-1953	20.00 - 30.00
Official badges and insignia.	1953-1965	15.00 - 25.00
In Appreciation for Interest and Services to the Youth of our Community. Explorer, Scout and Cub giving sign standing before Scout Oath and Liberty Bell.	1955	7.50 - 12.50
In Appreciation. Cub, Scout and Explorer, flag background. For your interest in and Service to the Youth of our Community.	1957	7.50 - 12.50
In Appreciation. Cub, Scout and Explorer. Onward for God and My Country Program.	1958	7.50 - 12.50
In Appreciation. Cub, Scout and Explorer, star and r-w-b background. Onward for God and My Country program.	1959	7.50 - 12.50
In Grateful recognition. 1910 scout passing scroll to 1960 scout and cub.	1960	7.50 - 12.50

Laminated plaque, above, identifies scout badges of the 1940s, and below, a 1960s recognition plaque.

Street car or bus weekly passes often honored Scout Week, or scout camps. Generally $5.00 - 7.50 each.

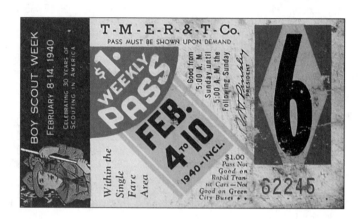

PLATE, GORHAM CHINA, ROCKWELL'S

A Scout is Loyal.	1980	40.00 - 60.00
Beyond the Easel.	1980	50.00 - 75.00
Campfire Story.	1980	40.00 - 60.00
Good Sign.	1980	40.00 - 60.00
Our Heritage.	1980	40.00 - 60.00
Pointing the Way.	1980	40.00 - 60.00
The Scoutmaster.	1980	60.00 - 80.00

PLATE, GROSSMAN CHINA, ROCKWELL'S

Can't Wait.	1980	40.00 - 60.00
Young Doctor.	1980	40.00 - 60.00

POSTERS

Boy Scout Creed, by Ludvig S. Dale, 6" x 7".	1923-1930	15.00 - 25.00
John Glenn, 13" x 19".	1961-1965	15.00 - 20.00
The Merits of Scouting Black Background, 119 merit badges.	1980	2.50 - 5.00
The Merits of Scouting White Background, 120 merit badges.	1985	2.50 - 5.00
The Merits of Scouting White Background, 119 merit badges.	1989	2.50 - 5.00
Outdoor Code. Silhouette of Scouts Hiking.	1990	2.50 - 5.00
The Merits of Scouting. Black Background, 124 merit badges.	1993	2.50 - 5.00
Merits of Scouting Black Background, 123 merit badges.	1995	2.50 - 5.00
Scout Law surrounds photo of scout.	1997	20.00 - 25.00
Scout Oath surrounds photo of scout.	1997	20.00 - 25.00
It's Great to be a Scout. Scout waving hat in outdoor scene, 16 x 22.	1928	45.00 - 60.00
Rockwell head. Character Development, Americanization, Citizenship Training, 18 x 25.	1928	45.00 - 60.00
Scout Oath and Law with insignia in border, 13 x 33.	1928	25.00 - 40.00
Scout Oath and Law. Merit Badges and insignia around border, 22 x 45-1/2.	1928	60.00 - 80.00
Scout Standing, saluting. Decalcomania poster, 7-1/4 x 14-1/2.	1928	25.00 - 35.00
Scouts of Today, Men of leadership tomorrow, 13-1/2 x 19-1/2.	1928	45.00 - 60.00
The Badge of Better Boyhood. First-Class emblem, 24-1/2 x 18-1/4.	1928	45.00 - 60.00

POSTERS, CORTE SCOPE PHOTO ENLARGEMENTS, SET OF 25 PRINTS, 7 x 9

Backwoods Cooking.	1927-1935	150.00 - 200.00
Care and Use of Axe and Knife.	1927-1935	150.00 - 200.00
Fire Lighting and Fire Building.	1927-1935	150.00 - 200.00
Hiking, Packing and Trailing.	1927-1935	150.00 - 200.00
How to Handle a Canoe.	1927-1935	150.00 - 200.00
Knots and Their Uses.	1927-1935	150.00 - 200.00
Lifesaving.	1927-1935	150.00 - 200.00
Miscellaneous Activities.	1927-1935	150.00 - 200.00
Signaling.	1927-1935	150.00 - 200.00
Swimming.	1927-1935	150.00 - 200.00
Use of Neckerchief for First Aid.	1927-1935	150.00 - 200.00

POSTERS, SCOUTING SCENES, 11x14

01. A Barbecue in Camp.	1917-1922	10.00 - 15.00
02. A Lecture in Camp.	1917-1922	10.00 - 15.00
03. Around the Camp Fire.	1917-1922	10.00 - 15.00
04. Artificial Respiration.	1917-1922	10.00 - 15.00
05. A scout is cheerful.	1917-1922	10.00 - 15.00
06. A scout rally.	1917-1922	10.00 - 15.00
07. Back from a swim.	1917-1922	10.00 - 15.00
08. Bugling.	1917-1922	10.00 - 15.00
09. Coat Staff Stretcher.	1917-1922	10.00 - 15.00
10. Conservation.	1917-1922	10.00 - 15.00
11. Field Wireless Outfit.	1917-1922	10.00 - 15.00
12. Fireman's Lift.	1917-1922	10.00 - 15.00
13. First Aid Contests.	1917-1922	10.00 - 15.00
14. In the Hands of His Friends.	1917-1922	10.00 - 15.00
15. Knot Tying.	1917-1922	10.00 - 15.00
16. Leaders of the Scout Movement.	1917-1922	10.00 - 15.00
17. Mapmaking.	1917-1922	10.00 - 15.00
18. Mess Line at Camp Hunter.	1917-1922	10.00 - 15.00
19. No Expensive Equipment.	1917-1922	10.00 - 15.00
20. No Matches.	1917-1922	10.00 - 15.00
21. Overcoming Difficulties.	1917-1922	10.00 - 15.00
22. Patience Rewarded.	1917-1922	10.00 - 15.00
23. Putting up Shelter.	1917-1922	10.00 - 15.00
24. Scout Plan of Practical Education.	1917-1922	10.00 - 15.00
25. Shoulder to Shoulder.	1917-1922	10.00 - 15.00
26. Signaling.	1917-1922	10.00 - 15.00
27. Signaling Tower.	1917-1922	10.00 - 15.00
28. Spearing a Sturgeon.	1917-1922	10.00 - 15.00
29. Stalking Without a Gun.	1917-1922	10.00 - 15.00
30. Stuffing Mattresses.	1917-1922	10.00 - 15.00
31. Supper for Eight.	1917-1922	10.00 - 15.00
32. Swimming Exercises.	1917-1922	10.00 - 15.00

168

Frameable posters were available in the 1960s, value $10.00 - $15.00.

33. The Three Man Lift.	1917-1922	10.00 - 15.00
34. Their First Attempt.	1917-1922	10.00 - 15.00
35. Thrifty and Handy.	1917-1922	10.00 - 15.00
36. To Get the Lay of the Land.	1917-1922	10.00 - 15.00
37. Treatment for Fracture.	1917-1922	10.00 - 15.00
38. Use of the Labor.	1917-1922	10.00 - 15.00
39. Washing Dishes in Camp.	1917-1922	10.00 - 15.00
40. Wig Wag.	1917-1922	10.00 - 15.00
Full set of 40.	1917-1922	300.00 - 500.00

POSTERS, SCOUTING SCENES, 8 x 10

01. Proper measures for sanitation.	1917-1922	10.00 - 15.00
02. This beats digging bait all hollow.	1917-1922	10.00 - 15.00
03. Every boy can tie a knot.	1917-1922	10.00 - 15.00
04. Colonel Roosevelt reviews Boy Scouts.	1917-1922	10.00 - 15.00
05. Boy Scout Band.	1917-1922	10.00 - 15.00
06. A Scout is a good climber.	1917-1922	10.00 - 15.00
07. Colonel Roosevelt addressing Scouts.	1917-1922	10.00 - 15.00
08. A Trek Cart bridge.	1917-1922	10.00 - 15.00
09. Scouts starting for their War Gardens.	1917-1922	10.00 - 15.00
10. Each Scout does his share.	1917-1922	10.00 - 15.00
11. Winter camp and hike.	1917-1922	10.00 - 15.00
12. A model Scout camp.	1917-1922	10.00 - 15.00
13. First hike of the season.	1917-1922	10.00 - 15.00
14. Stories around the camp fire.	1917-1922	10.00 - 15.00
15. Mail from home.	1917-1922	10.00 - 15.00
16. Scouts at home in the woods.	1917-1922	10.00 - 15.00
17. Stories by old comrads.	1917-1922	10.00 - 15.00
18. A good Scout up a tree.	1917-1922	10.00 - 15.00
19. When dinner is ready.	1917-1922	10.00 - 15.00
20. Business before pleasure.	1917-1922	10.00 - 15.00
21. All ready for the hike.	1917-1922	10.00 - 15.00
22. Scouts visiting Washington.	1917-1922	10.00 - 15.00
23. At the Service of other people at all times.	1917-1922	10.00 - 15.00
24. Whittling their way to a merit badge.	1917-1922	10.00 - 15.00
25. The mecca of all true Scouts.	1917-1922	10.00 - 15.00
26. We pledge allegiance to our Flag.	1917-1922	10.00 - 15.00
27. Starting a fire without matches.	1917-1922	10.00 - 15.00
28. A big Scout encampment.	1917-1922	10.00 - 15.00
29. What do you say, fellows - all in?	1917-1922	10.00 - 15.00
30. Scouts making the correct sign.	1917-1922	10.00 - 15.00
31. Pretty good bunch of fellows.	1917-1922	10.00 - 15.00
32. The battle in the woods.	1917-1922	10.00 - 15.00
33. A scout is clean.	1917-1922	10.00 - 15.00
34. Mapmaking a fascinating study.	1917-1922	10.00 - 15.00
35. Practical value of Scout Stunts.	1917-1922	10.00 - 15.00
36. A scout is brave.	1917-1922	10.00 - 15.00
37. Making camp dies get a man dirty.	1917-1922	10.00 - 15.00
38. When Scouting depends on bare good nature.	1917-1922	10.00 - 15.00
39 He has learned the clover hitch.	1917-1922	10.00 - 15.00
40. Helping the Nation.	1917-1922	10.00 - 15.00

RECORD

Scouting Along with Burl Ives, Columbia Special Products, CSP 347.	1960	20.00 - 30.00
Scouting Breaks the Sound Barrier, Nanette Guilford Corp SAAB-320.	1965	15.00 - 25.00

RECORD, 33.3

President Kennedy's message and John Glenn Salute	1962	15.00 - 25.00
Eagle Records: The Scout March Explorer March, size of a 45.	1960	10.00 - 15.00

REFLECTIVE SIGN FOR COMMUNITY USE

18", Tenderfoot Emblem.	1990	25.00 - 35.00
30", Tenderfoot Emblem.	1990	60.00 - 80.00

First Class ring.   *Early Eagle Scout ring.*

RING

First-Class emblem enclosed in oval top, spiral design on sides. 10 kt. gold.	1916-1920	100.00 - 150.00
First-Class emblem enclosed in oval top, spiral design on sides. Gold filled.	1916-1920	50.00 - 75.00
First-Class emblem enclosed in oval top, spiral design on sides. Sterling silver.	1916-1920	40.00 - 60.00
First -Class emblem enclosed in oval top, vertical double loop knot on sides. Sterling silver.	1921-1928	40.00 - 60.00
First-Class emblem enclosed in oval top, vertical double loop knot on sides. 10 kt. gold.	1921-1928	100.00 - 150.00
First-Class emblem enclosed in oval top. Vertical double loop knot on sides. Gold filled.	1921-1928	60.00 - 75.00
Eagle-Scout design on red-white-blue oval field, vertical double loop knot on side. Sterling silver.	1925-1932	60.00 - 90.00
First-Class emblem raised in oval top, overhand knot on sides. 10 kt. gold.	1929-1938	100.00 - 150.00
First-Class emblem raised in oval top, overhand knot on sides. Gold filled.	1929-1949	60.00 - 75.00
First-Class emblem raised in oval top, overhand knot on sides. Sterling Silver.	1929-1949	40.00 - 60.00
Eagle Scout design on red-white-blue oval field, vertical double loop knot on side. 10 kt. white gold.	1930-1932	150.00 - 200.00
Eagle-Scout design on red-white-blue oval field, overhand knot on side. 10 kt. white gold.	1933-1940	150.00 - 200.00
Eagle-Scout design on red-white-blue oval field, overhand knot on side. Sterling silver.	1933-1940	70.00 - 90.00
Eagle-Scout design on red-white-blue oval set on rectangular top, ribbed edges, blank sides. Sterling silver.	1937-1957	40.00 - 60.00
Life emblem raised on black square. Sterling silver.	1937-1947	20.00 - 25.00
Star emblem raised on black square. Sterling silver.	1937-1947	15.00 - 20.00
Tenderfoot emblem raised on black square (large emblem). Sterling silver.	1937-1947	10.00 - 15.00
Tenderfoot emblem raised on black square (small emblem). Sterling silver.	1937-1947	10.00 - 15.00
Eagle-Scout design on red-white-blue oval field, overhand knot on side, rope is continuous. 10 kt. gold.	1941-1947	125.00 - 175.00
Eagle-Scout design on red-white-blue oval field, overhand knot on side, rope is continuous. 14 kt. gold.	1941-1947	250.00 - 300.00
Eagle-Scout design on red-white-blue oval field, overhand knot on side, rope is continuous. Sterling silver.	1941-1947	70.00 - 90.00
First-Class emblem raised in rectangle top, plain sides. Sterling silver.	1950-1965	10.00 - 15.00
Tenderfoot emblem raised on rectangle top. Sterling silver.	1965-1979	10.00 - 15.00

SCOUT LAW STATUE, SCOUTING BRONZES
01. Trustworthy.	1990	250.00 - 300.00
02. Loyal.	1990	250.00 - 300.00
03. Helpful.	1990	250.00 - 300.00
04. Friendly.	1990	250.00 - 300.00
05. Courteous.	1990	250.00 - 300.00
06. Kind.	1990	250.00 - 300.00
07. Obedient.	1990	250.00 - 300.00
09. Thrifty.	1990	250.00 - 300.00
10. Brave.	1990	250.00 - 300.00
11. Clean.	1990	250.00 - 300.00
12. Reverent.	1990	250.00 - 300.00

SCOUT LIFE GUARD
Blue twill rectangle, crossed oars and lifering.   7.50 - 12.50

SCOUT OATH ILLUMINATED POSTER
Scout Oath within simulated illuminated frame. 1950-1960   15.00 - 20.00

The McKennzie 11" version first introduced in 1930s.

Daniel C. Beard statue by Scouting Bronzes.

SCOUT STATUE
Tom Clark's Gnome Hiking with canteen and walking stick. 9 inches tall.   1990   75.00 - 100.00

SCOUT STATUE BY R. TAIT MCKENZIE
11" base metal-plated bronze, silver, or copper. Scout law on base. Wood or plastic Bakelite base.	1930-2000	40.00 - 60.00
17" plaster composition, ivory (white) bronze or copper finishes.	1914-1928	300.00 - 400.00

SCOUT STATUE, SCOUTING BRONZES
Daniel Carter Beard.	1990	400.00 - 500.00
Lady Olive Baden-Powell.	1990	400.00 - 500.00
Lord R.S.S. Baden-Powell.	1990	400.00 - 500.00
William Hillcourt.	1990	400.00 - 500.00
Baden-Powell bust on pedestal.	1994	175.00 - 250.00

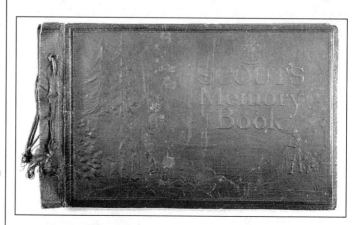

SCOUT'S MEMORY BOOK
Kodak photo album, leatherette, 7-1/2" x 12" or 12" by 7-1/2".   1920-1930   75.00 - 125.00

The Modern Art Foundry in the Steinway section of Queens, New York, is where the life-size statue of R. Tait McKenzie is cast.

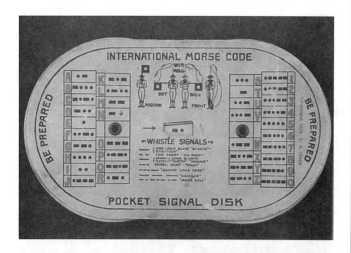

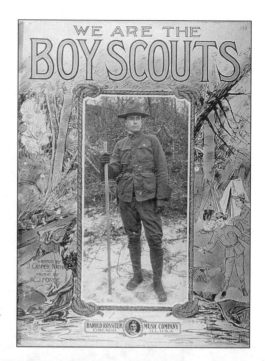

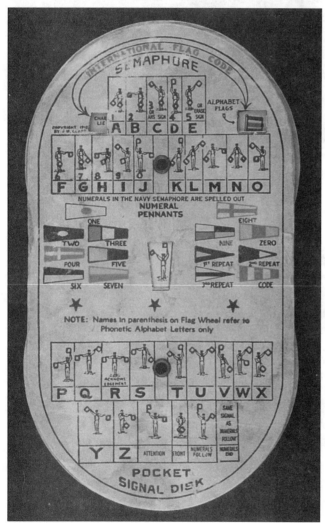

The Pocket Semaphore disc includes helpful graphics on two rotating discs.

SEMAPHORE AND MORSE SIGNAL POCKET DISC
Rotating discs with openings   1916-1930   30.00 - 50.00
  for letter and code.

SEMAPHORE SIGNAL FLAGS
Red-white diagonal 18" square, muslin.   1911-1930   15.00 - 20.00

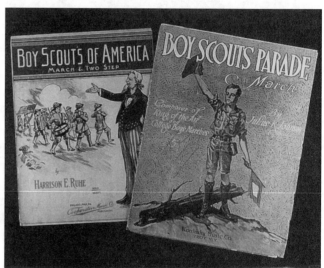

Sheet music scores include contemporary graphics.

SHEET MUSIC

"Boy Scouts March" by Kvelve.		15.00 - 20.00
"Boy Scouts on Parade" by Powell		15.00 - 20.00
"Carry On" by Schneider and Smalle.		15.00 - 20.00
"March of the Boy Scouts" by Wright.		15.00 - 20.00
"Our Country Forever" dedicated to the BS. By Bowen.		15.00 - 20.00
"Red, White and Blue" (USBS) by Irving and Harrington.		15.00 - 20.00
"Scouts of the South" by Vandevere.		15.00 - 20.00
"Scouts on Parade" by Dunn.		15.00 - 20.00
"The Boy Scouts of America" by Robinson.		15.00 - 20.00
"The Boy Scouts of the U.S.A." by Morgan and Oakley.		15.00 - 20.00
"The Scouts" by Vandevere		15.00 - 20.00
"We Are the Boy Scouts" by Nathan.		
"The Boy Scouts March" by Herman.	1911	20.00 - 30.00
"A Good Turn" by Murphy.	1912	20.00 - 30.00
"March of the Boy Scouts" by Martin.	1912	20.00 - 30.00
"March of the Boy Scouts" by Grant-Schaefer.	1913	20.00 - 30.00

"Be a Good Scout" by Murphy.	1914	20.00 - 30.00
"The Boy Scout's Dream" by James.	1915	20.00 - 30.00
"Boy Scouts of America - A March" by Sousa.	1916	20.00 - 30.00
"Boy Scouts on Parade" by Johnson.	1917	20.00 - 30.00
"Follow Old Glory," American Jr. Boy Scouts.	1917	20.00 - 30.00
"Boy Scouts on Parade" by Martin.	1920	20.00 - 30.00
"Boy Scouts" by Hopkins.	1920	20.00 - 30.00
"Off to Camp" by Anthony.	1921	20.00 - 30.00
"A Day with the Boy Scouts" by Rovanger.	1928	20.00 - 30.00
"At a Boy Scout Camp" by Gaul.	1930	10.00 - 15.00
"Boy Scouts March" by Heltman.	1930	20.00 - 30.00
"Youth Pastimes" by Rolfe.	1930	10.00 - 15.00
"Let's All Be Good Scouts Together" by Penner-Raynor.	1938	20.00 - 30.00
"If He's a Scout" by Waring.	1940	10.00 - 15.00
"Tough-up, Buckle-down."	1944	5.00 - 10.00
"Tomorrow America."	1949	10.00 - 15.00
"The Boy Scout Anthem" by Wright-Mitchell.	1954	10.00 - 15.00
"Be Prepared," dedicated to BSA by Sterns.	1955	5.00 - 10.00
"Onward for God and Country" by Waring-Dolph.	1955	10.00 - 15.00

SHOE
General Shoe Corporation, brown, compass on heel, sole plain.	1940	40.00 - 60.00

SIGNAL SET
Morse listing on wooden base.	1916-1930	35.00 - 50.00
Morse listing on plastic base.	1955-1970	5.00 - 10.00

SIGNALER
M.M Fleron & Sons, maker, metal, pair.	1935-1953	50.00 - 75.00

TAPES
Give a Little Love. Ben Vereen.	1989	7.50 - 10.00

TEDDY BEAR
9" stuffed bear, GNYC CSP. Tan and green uniform with neckerchief.	1985	17.50 - 25.00

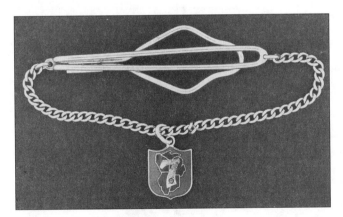

Tie chain from Region 7.

TIE CHAIN
Various events, regions, and councils.	1940-1955	5.00 - 15.00

TIE CLIP
Various events, councils, positions.	1950-1970	5.00 - 7.50

TYPEWRITER
Remington - Remie Scout Model.	1950	40.00 - 60.00

VALENTINE
Various themes.	1920-1935	10.00 - 15.00

WALL PLAQUES
Attendance Award and emblem, shield shape, scroll below.	1947	10.00 - 15.00
Award and tenderfoot emblem, shield shape, scroll below.	1947	10.00 - 15.00
First-Class Scout and emblem, shield shape, scroll below.	1947	10.00 - 15.00
Second-Class Scout and emblem, shield shape, scroll below.	1947	10.00 - 15.00
Tenderfoot Scout and emblem, shield shape, scroll below.	1947	10.00 - 15.00

WATCH FOB

Scout Signaling.	1911-1920	75.00 - 100.00
Scout standing with rifle.	1911-1920	60.00 - 90.00
Scout with cross rifles.	1911-1920	60.00 - 90.00
First-Class emblem, gilt.	1915-1925	250.00 - 350.00
First-Class patrol leader, silver.	1915-1925	350.00 - 500.00
Second-Class patrol leader, silver.	1915-1925	350.00 - 500.00
Second-Class emblem, gilt.	1915-1925	250.00 - 350.00
Tenderfoot emblem, gilt.	1915-1925	500.00 - 600.00
Tenderfoot patrol leader, silver.	1915-1925	600.00 - 750.00

WATCH FOB - LEADER

Assistant deputy scout commissioner, light blue ribbon.	1915-1925	350.00 - 200.00
Assistant scoutmaster.	1915-1925	350.00 - 500.00
Scout commissioner, dark blue ribbon.	1915-1925	350.00 - 500.00
Scoutmaster, green ribbon.	1915-1925	350.00 - 500.00
Troop committee, local council committee, white ribbon.	1915-1925	350.00 - 500.00

WATCH, POCKET

Radiolite.	1919-1925	100.00 - 150.00
Reliance, seven-jewel.	1919-1925	100.00 - 150.00
Waterbury, lite.	1919-1925	100.00 - 150.00
Ingersoll.	1934-1940	100.00 - 150.00
Seven Seas.	1941-1950	50.00 - 100.00
Shipmate.	1941-1950	50.00 - 100.00

WATCH, POCKET. INGERSOL

Hands read: A SCOUT IS. and BE PREPARED. Between numbers are 12 law points. Camp scene at ctr., second hand is First-Class emblem.	1920	300.00 - 350.00

WATCH, WRIST

Daynite, nickel-plated.	1919-1925	100.00 - 150.00
Daynite, silver.	1919-1925	150.00 - 200.00
Midget radiolite, Army strap.	1919-1925	100.00 - 150.00
Headquarters, NYC, First-Class emblem on face.	1930	125.00 - 150.00
Elgin.	1934-1940	100.00 - 150.00
Ingersoll.	1934-1940	100.00 - 150.00
New Haven.	1934-1940	100.00 - 150.00
Sun watch.	1934-1940	75.00 - 100.00
Imperial.	1941-1950	50.00 - 100.00
Elgin.	1944-1950	50.00 - 100.00
New Haven.	1944-1950	50.00 - 100.00
Timex, shock-proof.	1955-1965	20.00 - 30.00

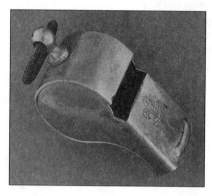

WHISTLE

Long and round, First-Class emblem and BOY SCOUTS OF AMERICA stamped. Brass w/ ring for lanyard.	1911-1930	20.00 - 30.00
Conventional type, nickel-plated brass, First-Class emblem by lip.	1930-1940	10.00 - 15.00

Troop band from Rockford, IL.

WOOD COMPOSITION (PRESSED)

Bookends, rounded shield shape w/ First-Class emblem.	1930-1950	20.00 - 30.00
First-Class emblem in shield.	1930-1950	10.00 - 15.00
Paperweight, Scout and Washington.	1930-1950	10.00 - 15.00
Scout Oath, Scout profile left.	1930-1950	10.00 - 15.00
Tie rack, First-Class emblem in shield, camp scene in background. Metal bar or simulated wood bar to hold ties.	1930-1950	20.00 - 30.00
Trinket box, Scout and Washington stg. law points flanking.	1930-1950	15.00 - 25.00

WOOL BLANKET

Green, black HQ NYC seal in ctr., 6" x 5" feet.	1925	50.00 - 75.00

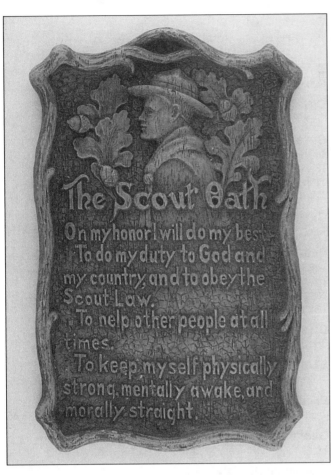

Pressed wood, and later wood composition, plaques, book ends, tie racks, and trinket boxes come in a variety of designs and were made from the 1930s through the 1960s.

RECOGNITION ITEMS

AFGHANS

BSA 1910, Tenderfoot emblem in center.	1999	35.00 - 45.00
Cub Scout emblem.	1999	35.00 - 45.00
Eagle Scout emblem.	1999	35.00 - 45.00
Order of the Arrow, Arrowhead logo.	1999	35.00 - 45.00
Woodbadge, Troop 1.	1999	35.00 - 45.00
Guiding Hand, adapted from Rockwell calendar.	2000	55.00 - 65.00
Tenderfoot emblem in circle, Boy Scouts of America around, custom lettering, green and gold.	2000	40.00 - 50.00
Tenderfoot emblem in circle, Boy Scouts of America around, custom lettering, red and gold.	2000	40.00 - 50.00
Tommy Tenderfoot, Scout Law border.	2000	40.00 - 50.00
Character Counts logo.	2001	40.00 - 50.00
Cub Scout Badges.	2001	55.00 - 65.00
I Will Do My Best.	2001	55.00 - 65.00
The Adventure Trail.	2001	55.00 - 65.00

BABY SPOON

Floral scroll, engraved bowl.	1995	17.50 - 22.50

BABY'S CUP

Pewter, engraveable, 2-1/2" by 2-5/8".	1993	25.00 - 35.00

BREAD TRAY

Scout Oath, cast metal.	1995	40.00 - 55.00

CANVAS CALENDAR PRINTS, FRAMED

High Adventure.	1990	250.00 - 300.00
The Patrol Leader.	1990	250.00 - 300.00
The Scoutmaster, by Csatari.	1990	225.00 - 275.00

CARVED HALL KNIFE SET

Contemporary knife set, chrome handles.	1995	50.00 - 60.00
Traditional knife set, wood handles.	1995	60.00 - 75.00

CARVELL HALL CARVING SET

Knife, slicer and fork.	2000	100.00 - 125.00

CARVELL HALL LETTER OPENER

Stainless steel, tenderfoot emblem engraved, walnut base.	1995	15.00 - 25.00

CARVELL HALL STEAK KNIVES

Set of six.	2000	100.00 - 125.00

CHISEL TOWER AWARD

Lucite, logo etched.	2000	65.00 - 80.00

COBALT COASTER

Tenderfoot emblem and gilt stripes.	1995	7.50 - 10.00

COBALT MUG

Tenderfoot emblem and gilt stripes.	1995	17.50 - 22.50

COFFEE MUG W/GLASS INSERT

4" with handle.	1995	30.00 - 40.00

CONTESSA TROPHY BOWL

Crystal, 9" diameter, various logo etchings available.	1993	75.00 - 100.00

CONTESSA TROPHY VASE

Crystal, 4-3/4" by 7".	1995	75.00 - 100.00

CRYSTAL ARROWHEAD

Black, 6-3/4".	1992	35.00 - 45.00
Clear, 6-3/4".	1992	30.00 - 40.00

CRYSTAL BLOCK

Tenderfoot emblem etched on 3" x 4" block.	1992	25.00 - 35.00

CRYSTAL BOX

3-3/8" x 3-3/8" box, etched.	1995	17.50 - 27.50
4-3/4" x 3-1/2" x 2-1/2" logo etched.	1997	50.00 - 60.00

CRYSTAL CANDY DISH

Octagonal with cover, etched.	1995	17.50 - 27.50

CRYSTAL CHRISTMAS ORNAMENT

Tenderfoot emblem and 1993 etched.	1993	10.00 - 15.00
Tenderfoot emblem and 1995.	1995	10.00 - 15.00

CRYSTAL HEXAGONAL DESK CLOCK

Quartz movement, 4" across.	1997	25.00 - 40.00

CRYSTAL ICEBERG

Tenderfoot emblem etched, walnut base, 4-3/4".	1992	35.00 - 50.00

CRYSTAL ICEBERG AND BASE

Iceberg with logo, black base, 4" x 8" overall.	1997	65.00 - 80.00

CRYSTAL PICTURE FRAME

10" x 7" curved.	1997	40.00 - 50.00

CRYSTAL TROPHY CUP

Tenderfoot emblem etched, 8".	1992	50.00 - 75.00
10" height, etched.	1995	100.00 - 130.00
11" height, etched.	1995	150.00 - 175.00
9" height, etched.	1995	100.00 - 130.00

CRYSTAL VASE

Tenderfoot emblem etched, 10".	1992	75.00 - 100.00

DESK SET

One pen and various emblems.	1985	15.00 - 25.00
Tenderfoot emblem on wood base, two pens.	1985	35.00 - 40.00
Various emblems and slant-tip engraved plate.	1985	10.00 - 15.00
Tenderfoot emblem laser etched, one pen.	1990	27.50 - 35.00

DIANTHUS VASE

Crystal, 6" x 7".	1997	40.00 - 60.00

EAGLE SCOUT RELIEF KNIT SWEATER

White cotton, Eagle Scout emblem in center.	1990	35.00 - 45.00

EXECUTIVE WATER SET

Pitcher and glasses.	1995	35.00 - 50.00

GEORGE WASHINGTON CAMP CUP

Tenderfoot emblem, pewter, 2-3/4" by 3-3/16".	1992	35.00 - 45.00

HAMMERED PLATE

Tenderfoot emblem on hand-hammered bronze plate.	1985	40.00 - 60.00
Tenderfoot emblem on hand-hammered aluminum plate.	1993	25.00 - 35.00

HITCHCOCK STABLE STOOL

Hardwood.	1995	125.00 - 175.00

HITCHCOCK'S CAPTAIN'S CHAIR

Tenderfoot emblem on back, hardwood, ebony finish.	1993	325.00 - 375.00

JADE CRYSTAL FLEUR-DE-LIS

Tenderfoot emblem etched on fleur-de-lis, 7-1/2" tall.	1993	125.00 - 150.00

JAFFA CRYSTAL PAPERWEIGHT

Tenderfoot emblem etched, 3-1/2".	1992	22.50 - 30.00

JAFFA CRYSTAL VASE

Tenderfoot emblem etched, 9-1/2" tall.	1993	35.00 - 45.00

JEFFERSON CUP

Tenderfoot emblem on pewter cup.	1985	15.00 - 20.00

LEATHER CARRY-ALL
22" x 8-1/2" square. — 1996 — 120.00 - 140.00

LINCOLN WALL CLOCK
13" x 22-1/2", cherry wood cabinet, quartz clock. — 1997 — 275.00 - 325.00

LOVING CUP
Pewter, 5-3/4". — 1995 — 85.00 - 105.00

LUCITE PAPERWEIGHTS
Cub Scout emblem embedded. — 1992 — 15.00 - 20.00
Eagle Scout emblem embedded. — 1992 — 15.00 - 20.00
Tenderfoot emblem embedded. — 1992 — 15.00 - 20.00

LUCITE THERMOMETER
Tenderfoot emblem etched, 3-5/16" tall. — 1992 — 20.00 - 25.00

MARBLE CERAMIC MUGS
Etched with logo choice, 11 oz. blue, black, maroon or green. — 1997 — 12.50 - 17.50

MARBLE PYRAMID CLOCK
Tenderfoot emblem, 3-1/2". — 1995 — 65.00 - 85.00

McKENZIE STATUE, RECTANGLE BASE
Statue is 4-1/2" tall, gilt pewter. — 1992 — 50.00 - 60.00

McKENZIE STATUE, ROUND BASE, MOUNTED ON SQUARE WOOD, TWO TENDERFOOT EMBLEMS IN CORNERS
Statue is 10-1/2" tall, silver plated. — 1992 — 75.00 - 100.00
Statue is 17" tall, green colored plaster. — 1992 — 250.00 - 300.00

NAMBE BUTTERFLY BOWL
7" diameter. — 1996 — 80.00 - 100.00

NAMBE EAGLE
Eagle perched, 9-1/2" tall, black marble base. — 1993 — 225.00 - 275.00

NAMBE JEFFERSON CLOCK
Clock set into metal. — 1997 — 100.00 - 125.00

NAMBE PLATES
Tenderfoot emblem in center of 11" square plate. — 1995 — 100.00 - 125.00
Tenderfoot emblem in center of 9" square plate. — 1995 — 75.00 - 100.00

NAMBE SANTA FE BOWL
5-3/4" diameter. — 1998 — 90.00 - 115.00

NAMBE TRI-CORNERED BOWL
9" diameter. — 1996 — 110.00 - 135.00

PAPERWEIGHTS
Thank You, inset with various emblems. — 1993 — 10.00 - 15.00
Be Prepared. — 1995 — 12.50 - 17.50
On My Honor. — 1995 — 12.50 - 17.50
Once an Eagle, Always an Eagle. — 1995 — 12.50 - 17.50

PAUL REVERE BOWL
Tenderfoot emblem engraved, 6" in diameter. — 1992 — 50.00 - 75.00

PEWTER COASTER SET OF FOUR
Engraveable logos, 4-1/2" diameter. — 1996 — 60.00 - 80.00

POLO CUP
Pewter, tenderfoot emblem, 8 oz. — 1993 — 20.00 - 30.00

PORCELAIN STATUETTE
Can't Wait, adapted from Rockwell calendar, 9-1/2" tall. — 1995 — 100.00 - 130.00
Scoutmaster, adapted from Rockwell calendar, 13" tall. — 1996 — 180.00 - 225.00

SCOUTER'S EXECUTIVE MUG
Pedestalled pewter mug, ceramic liner. — 1990 — 30.00 - 40.00

SCOUTING-CLASSICS
Bugle. — 2000 — 90.00 - 110.00
Classic literature kit, membership card, Scouting equipment number, and others. — 2000 — 20.00 - 25.00
Cub Scout baby ensemble, hat and neckerchief. — 2000 — 20.00 - 25.00
Flashlight, retro. — 2000 — 10.00 - 15.00
Handbook for Boys reprint. — 2000 — 12.50 - 15.00
Memorabilia box. — 2000 — 25.00 - 35.00
Semaphore code flags, red and yellow. — 2000 — 20.00 - 25.00
Wood badge patrol emblems, set of eight. — 2000 — 10.00 - 15.00
Yucca backpack. — 2000 — 30.00 - 35.00
Canteen. — 2001 — 20.00 - 25.00
Duffel bag. — 2001 — 30.00 - 40.00
Neckerchiefs, full square, 28", six different available. — 2001 — 17.50 - 22.50
Skill awards in box set. — 2001 — 25.00 - 27.50
WWI weapon for liberty poster, 18" x 24". — 2001 — 5.00 - 7.50

SCOUTING SEAL GLASS DISCS
5" glass disc, gold-plated Tenderfoot emblem seal, walnut base. — 1992 — 40.00 - 60.00
7" glass disc, gold-plated Tenderfoot emblem seal, walnut base. — 1992 — 75.00 - 90.00
9" glass disc, gold-plated Tenderfoot emblem seal, walnut base. — 1992 — 100.00 - 125.00

SENTINEL PORCELAIN EAGLE
Bald Eagle head, mounted on walnut base, 9-3/4". — 1993 — 60.00 - 90.00

SIMULATED GRANITE SCULPTURES
Boy Scout sign, 7-1/2" tall. — 1997 — 50.00 - 65.00
Cub Scout sign, 7" tall. — 1997 — 50.00 - 65.00

SMOKED GLASS PLAQUE
Various emblems available to be etched with specific message, 5" x 7" beveled edges. — 1993 — 25.00 - 35.00

SNOW GLOBE
Winter Camping Scene. — 1996 — 40.00 - 50.00
Eagle Ceremony. — 1997 — 40.00 - 50.00
The Scoutmaster. — 1998 — 40.00 - 50.00
Guiding Hand. — 2000 — 40.00 - 50.00

TANKARD
Tenderfoot emblem on pewter tankard. — 1985 — 25.00 - 30.00

TEMPERATURE GAUGE DESK SET
Temperature gauge set on wood square, horizontal area for placement of various emblems. — 1985 — 35.00 - 45.00

TOWER AWARD
Cherry wood, slant top. — 1995 — 22.50 - 30.00

TREE SLAB PLAQUE
Tenderfoot emblem laser etched onto tree cross section, 6" diameter. — 1992 — 25.00 - 35.00

TROPHY TOPS
Eagle Scout emblem. — 1985 — 10.00 - 15.00
Tenderfoot emblem. — 1985 — 7.50 - 10.00
Scout hiking, BSA on round base. — 1989 — 20.00 - 25.00
Scout saluting, BSA on round base. — 1989 — 20.00 - 25.00
Scout standing at attention wearing merit-badge sash, BSA on round base. — 1989 — 20.00 - 25.00

VAL SAINT LAMBERT CRYSTAL LANDING EAGLE
Eagle landing, with walnut base. — 1993 — 500.00 - 550.00
Eagle landing, without base, 9-1/2" tall. — 1993 — 425.00 - 475.00

VALET BOX
Scout oath, cast metal. — 1995 — 60.00 - 75.00

Mahogany, pewter Tenderfoot emblem and plate, 5-1/2" x 7-1/2".   1999   45.00 - 55.00

W. BRITAIN BSA SCOUT FIGURES
Boy Scout pair, one holding American or unit flag.   1997   40.00 - 60.00
Cub Scout pair, one saluting, one with flag.   1997   40.00 - 60.00

WATER GLOBE
Tomorrow's leader.   1999   40.00 - 55.00

WATERFORD ACCENT TRAY
7-3/4" x 5-3/4", with stand.   1997   125.00 - 150.00

WATERFORD COLONNADE CLOCK
7-1/2" x 3-1/2" tall.   1998   35.00 - 45.00

WATERFORD CRYSTAL BOWL
8" engraved, with walnut stand.   1995   200.00 - 250.00
8" engraved, without stand.   1995   175.00 - 225.00

WATERFORD CRYSTAL CARRIAGE CLOCK
7-1/4" x 5-1/2", on base.   1996   200.00 - 240.00

WATERFORD CRYSTAL ENGLISH BISCUIT JAR
Engraveable logo, with walnut stand.   1995   250.00 - 300.00
Engraveable logo, without stand.   1995   200.00 - 240.00

WATERFORD CRYSTAL METROPOLITAN CLOCK
6-1/8" x 6-5/8", on base.   2000   225.00 - 275.00

WATERFORD CRYSTAL TRAY
Tenderfoot emblem etched on 8" diameter tray.   1992   100.00 - 125.00

WATERFORD STATUETTE, TOMMY TENDERFOOT
6" tall.   1997   140.00 - 160.00

WATERFORD UNIVERSAL EMBLEM PAPERWEIGHT
Tenderfoot emblem on dome, 3-1/2" around.   1996   50.00 - 75.00

WEATHER TRIO DESK SET
Thermometer, barometer and humidity gauge arranged vertically, horizontal area for various emblems.   1985   65.00 - 75.00

CALENDARS

Calendars in the early years of scouting were of a variety of shapes, sizes, and formats. Norman Rockwell designed the calendars until 1976, and since then they have been by Joseph Csatari. The prices are for the largest format, usually 14" x 20", with just the graphic design. Calendars with full year or partial year pads command a premium over just the image. Brown & Bigelow also made several smaller designs, 10 x 14" with removable month pads and a 6" x 8" with a color cover, and month sheets below on separate pages, with additional images and program helps. These smaller ones are somewhat hard to find complete.

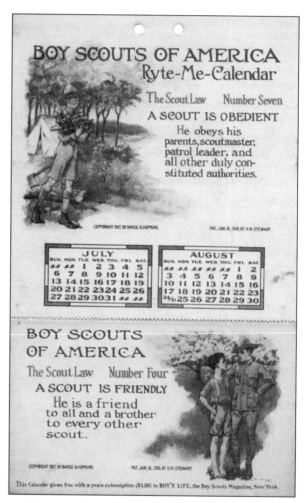

1917, BOY SCOUT RYTE-ME-CALENDAR
Detachable postcards.   1917   50.00 - 75.00

1918, RESCUE CARRY
Merit badge.

1918   150.00 - 200.00

1918, THE DAILY GOOD TURN
Scout w/ suitcase, helping elderly man.
Rockwell, N.

1918   50.00 - 75.00

1925, A GOOD SCOUT
Two dogs, scout bandaging smaller dog's leg.
Rockwell, N.

1925   50.00 - 75.00

1926, A GOOD TURN
Scout seated on floor reading to old sailor.
Rockwell, N.

1926   50.00 - 75.00

1927, GOOD FRIENDS
Scout kneeling, feeding litter of puppies.
Rockwell, N.

1927   50.00 - 75.00

1929, SPIRIT OF AMERICA
Boy Scout profile left. Rockwell, N.

1929   50.00 - 75.00

1931, SCOUT MEMORIES
Dan Beard telling story to listening scout.
Rockwell, N.

1931   40.00 - 60.00

1932, A SCOUT IS LOYAL
Colonial patriot w/ outstretched hand, scout
striding left. Rockwell, N.

1932   40.00 - 60.00

1933, AN ARMY OF FRIENDSHIP
Array of seven international scouts facing
forward, saluting. Rockwell, N.

1933   40.00 - 60.00

1934, CARRY ON
Old prospector pointing way to scout and dog.
Rockwell, N.

1934   40.00 - 60.00

1935, ON TO WASHINGTON
1935 National Jamboree, scout striding before
capitol and eagle in flight. Rockwell, N.

1935   40.00 - 60.00

1936, THE CAMPFIRE STORY
Scout leader holding headdress, four scouts
and dog around. Rockwell, N.

1936   40.00 - 60.00

1937, SCOUTS OF MANY TRAILS
Old Salt w/ globe seated at table w/ Sea Scout
and Boy Scout. Rockwell, N.

1937   40.00 - 60.00

1938, AMERICA BUILDS FOR TOMORROW
Boy Scouts builds bird house w/ two Cubs and
Den Mother. Rockwell, N.

1938   40.00 - 60.00

1939, THE SCOUTING TRAIL
Cub, Boy Scout, and Sea Explorer advancing
left. In background, profiles of historical
explorers. Rockwell, N.

1939   40.00 - 60.00

1940, A SCOUT IS REVERENT
Scout and old man kneeling in pew. Rockwell,
N.

1940   30.00 - 50.00

1942, A SCOUT IS LOYAL
First-Class Scout striding forward holding
campaign hat, Lincoln and Washington in
background. Rockwell, N.

1942   30.00 - 50.00

1943, A SCOUT IS FRIENDLY
Patrol Leader helping immigrant family read.
Rockwell, N.

1943   30.00 - 50.00

1944, WE, TOO, HAVE A JOB TO DO
Facing scout in campaign hat, saluting, flag in
background. Rockwell, N.

1944   30.00 - 50.00

*The 1945 calendar by Norman Rockwell titled "I Will
Do My Best." This is just the front cover from a 6" x
8" calendar. Worth about 1/3 of the price listed for the
largest size.*

1945, I WILL DO MY BEST
First-Class Scout holding campaign hat, giving
scout sign, before background of the oath.
Rockwell, N.

1945   30.00 - 50.00

1946, A GUIDING HAND
Boy Scout teaching Cub Scout a knot.
Rockwell, N.

1946   30.00 - 50.00

1947, ALL TOGETHER
Scout on high outcrop helps another up to the 1947   30.00 - 50.00
top. Rockwell, N.

1948, MEN OF TOMORROW
Patrol portaging two canoes, cub seated in   1948   30.00 - 50.00
corner watching. Rockwell, N.

1949, FRIEND IN NEED
Boy Scout patches dog's leg, held by Cub   1949   30.00 - 50.00
Scout. Rockwell, N.

1950, OUR HERITAGE
Boy and Cub Scout striding, looking upward at 1950   25.00 - 40.00
Washington kneeling in prayer left. Rockwell,
N.

1951, FORWARD AMERICA
Explorer, Cub Scout, Boy Scout, Air Scout, and 1951   25.00 - 40.00
Sea Scout all striding left. Rockwell, N.

1952, THE ADVENTURE TRAIL
Boy Scout as den chief showing arrowheads to 1952   25.00 - 40.00
two intrigued Cub Scouts, all under a tree.
Rockwell, N.

1953, ON MY HONOR
Cub Scout at attention, Boy Scout and Explorer 1953   25.00 - 40.00
giving scout sign, against background of
scout oath and Liberty Bell. Rockwell, N.

1954, A SCOUT IS REVERENT
Cub, Explorer, and Boy Scout seated in church 1954   25.00 - 40.00
pews. Rockwell, N.

1955, THE RIGHT WAY
Explorer looks on as Boy Scout shows bird   1955   25.00 - 40.00
house to two Cub Scouts. Rockwell, N.

1956, THE SCOUTMASTER
Adult standing by campfire as scouts sleep in 1956   30.00 - 50.00
tents in background. Rockwell, N.

1957, HIGH ADVENTURE
Group of Explorers along Philmont trail, Tooth 1957   25.00 - 40.00
of Time in distance. Rockwell, N.

1958, MIGHTY PROUD
Explorer and mother sharpen up Tenderfoot   1958   25.00 - 40.00
uniform on ex-Cub Scout. Rockwell, N.

1959, TOMORROW'S LEADER
Boy Scout w/ knapsack and compass striding,   1959   25.00 - 40.00
looking right, large First-Class badge and
montage of merit badges in background.
Rockwell, N.

1960, EVER ONWARD
1910 Scout passing Scout Oath Scroll to 1960   1960   25.00 - 40.00
Eagle Scout and Cub Scout. Rockwell, N.

1961, HOMECOMING
Dad, Cub Scout greet Boy Scout w/ backpack   1961   20.00 - 30.00
and duffel bag. Rockwell, N.

1962, POINTING THE WAY
Scoutmaster w/ compass directing three   1962   20.00 - 30.00
scouts. Rockwell, N.

1963, A GOOD SIGN ALL OVER THE WORLD
Scottish Scout and Boy Scout dancing jig, four 1963   20.00 - 30.00
others around, large globe and scout sign in
background. Rockwell, N.

1964, TO KEEP MYSELF PHYSICALLY STRONG
Cub Scout measuring Boy Scout's chest.   1964   20.00 - 30.00
Rockwell, N.

1965, A GREAT MOMENT
Mother pins Eagle Medal on son's chest, dad   1965   20.00 - 30.00
and scoutmaster look on. Rockwell, N.

1966, GROWTH OF A LEADER
Scoutmaster, Explorer, Boy Scout, and Cub   1966   20.00 - 30.00
Scout in profile left, flag in background.
Rockwell, N.

1967, BREAKTHROUGH FOR FREEDOM
Six international scouts walking forward w/   1967   20.00 - 30.00
arms linked. Rockwell, N.

1969, BEHIND THE EASEL
Scouts look on as Rockwell paints a scene.   1969   30.00 - 40.00
Rockwell, N.

1970, COME AND GET IT!
Scouts camping and cooking at lakeside.   1970   20.00 - 30.00
Rockwell, N.

1971, AMERICA'S MANPOWER BEGINS WITH BOYPOWER
Two Cubs, Den Mother, Boy Scout, and   1971   10.00 - 15.00
Explorer, back row of adult leaders. Rockwell,
N.

1972, CAN'T WAIT
Cub Scout dressing in very loose-fitting Boy   1972   10.00 - 15.00
Scout uniform. Rockwell, N.

1973, FROM CONCORD TO TRANQUILITY
Cub Scout, Boy Scouts, Explorer, Astronaut,   1973   10.00 - 15.00
and Colonial Patriot all salute flag in
background. Rockwell, N.

1974, WE THANK THEE, O' LORD
Patrol at camp, cook by meal, all bowed in   1974   10.00 - 15.00
grace. Rockwell, N.

1975, SO MUCH CONCERN
Three scouts and explorer plant sapling,   1975   5.00 - 10.00
Rockwell, N.

1976, THE SPIRIT OF 1976
Cub Scout, Boy Scout & Explorer as drummer   1976   10.00 - 15.00
and flag bearer. Rockwell, N.

1977, THE NEW SPIRIT
Cub, two Scouts and Explorer ringing bell.   1977   7.50 - 12.50
Csatari, J.

1978, SCOUTING THROUGH THE YEARS
Grandfather showing Cub and Scout   1978   7.50 - 12.50
collectibles. Csatari, J.

The 8" x 14-1/2" calendar, with monthly pads and program ideas.

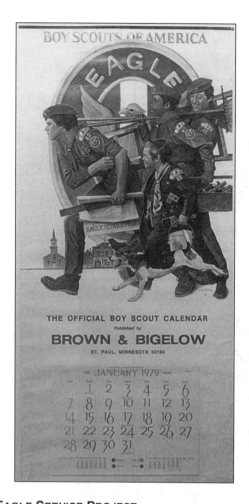

1985, THE SPIRIT LIVES ON, 1910-1985
Baden-Powell and 1910 scout look out over   1985   7.50 - 12.50
   1985 scouts starting friction fire. Csatari, J.

1986, IT'S A BOY'S LIFE
Scouts reading Boys' Life on a camping trip.   1986   7.50 - 12.50
   Csatari, J.

1987, VALUES THAT LAST A LIFETIME
Scouts with backpacks handing Tenderfoot   1987   7.50 - 12.50
   emblem to Webelo. Advancement badges.
   Csatari, J.

1988, WINTER CAMPING SCENE
Scouts in a snow scene. Csatari, J.   1988   7.50 - 12.50

1989, YOU CAN DO IT
Webelos Den Leader, Den Chief and Cub   1989   7.50 - 12.50
   Scouts at a meeting. Csatari, J.

1990, THE SCOUTMASTER
Scoutmaster standing before Tenderfoot   1990   7.50 - 12.50
   emblem, scenes in background. Csatari, J.

1991, SCOUTING FOR ALL SEASONS
Dual views of summer and winter hiking.   1991   7.50 - 12.50
   Csatari, J.

1992, FLORIDA SEA BASE
Montage of activities at the Sea Base. Csatari, 1992   7.50 - 12.50
   J.

1993, A GOOD TURN
Needy family and Scouts with scouting-for-   1993   7.50 - 12.50
   food bags. Csatari, J.

1994, A SCOUT IS REVERENT
Scouts admiring church stained glass window. 1994   7.50 - 12.50
   Csatari, J.

1995, CHARACTER COUNTS
Cubs and Scouts giving sign, Statue of Liberty 1995   7.50 - 12.50
   and flag in background. Csatari, J.

1996, PASS IT ON
Dan Beard and Baden-Powell in background,   1996   7.50 - 12.50
   three generations of the BSA president's
   family. Csatari, J.

1997, SCOUTING VALUES
Cub and three Scouts look at photo album,   1997   7.50 - 12.50
   family scenes in background. Csatari, J.

1998, URBAN GOOD TURN
Scout Troop helping spruce up lady's city   1998   7.50 - 12.50
   house. Csatari, J.

2000, OUT OF THE PAST, INTO THE FUTURE
Seton, Beard, Roosevelt, Phillips, and current 2000   7.50 - 12.50
   scouts; 1910 Society. Csatari, J.

1979, EAGLE SERVICE PROJECT
Cub and three Scouts off to work on a project. 1979   7.50 - 12.50
   Eagle Badge. Csatari, J.

1980, THE REUNION
Cub Pack's 35th Anniversary. Men with photos 1980   7.50 - 12.50
   as a boy. Csatari, J.

1981, AFTER HOURS
Scoutmaster teaching first aid at a home.   1981   7.50 - 12.50
   Csatari, J.

1982, THE PATROL LEADER
Patrol leader with a backpack demonstration.   1982   7.50 - 12.50
   Csatari, J.

1983, FAMILY CAMPING
Family off to a family summer camp. Csatari, J. 1983   7.50 - 12.50

1984, THANK YOU, SCOUT VOLUNTEERS
Scout standing before troop committee.   1984   7.50 - 12.50
   Csatari, J.

PINBACK BUTTONS

1ST BAR NONE
FDL outline, 5/8" fold tab.   1950-1960   4.00 - 6.00

66TH NATIONAL ENCAMPMENT G.A.R.
Scout facing in campaign hat.   1931   75.00 - 125.00

ANNIVERSARY WEEK, FEB. 7-13
Scout bust facing, 7/8".   1930   15.00 - 25.00

BE PREPARED
On red-white-blue background, 1/2".   1950-1965   5.00 - 7.50

BEN ALEXANDER SAYS
Scott of the Scouts, a Rayart Serial Play,   1915-1925   20.00 - 25.00
  Scout saluting, 7/8".

BETTER UNIFORMING
Count on me, FDL, 1-3/16".   1972   2.00 - 3.00
Try it - you'll like it, FDL, 1-3/16".   1972   2.00 - 3.00

BOSTON GARDEN SCOUT CAPADES
Changeable image, 2-1/2".   1960   10.00 - 15.00

BOY SCOUT GUIDE
First-Class emblem, 1-3/4".   1935-1945   10.00 - 15.00

BOY SCOUT HOSIERY
Scout kneeling with staff looking right, 3/4".   1915-1920   20.00 - 25.00

BOY SCOUT JAMBOREE
  1-1/4".   1953   3.00 - 5.00
On red-white-blue background, 1-3/4".   1950   10.00 - 15.00
On red-white-blue background,   1950   10.00 - 15.00
  ribbons below, 1-1/4".

BOY SCOUT ROUND UP
First-Class, bronco rider, 1-1/4"   1928   20.00 - 30.00
Second-Class, bronco rider, 1-1/4"   1928   20.00 - 30.00

BOY SCOUT WEEK
June 8-14, Scout standing, saluting, 7/8".   1915-1925   20.00 - 30.00

BOY SCOUT
Scout standing with Morse signal flags,   1915-1925   25.00 - 35.00
  1-1/8" shield-shaped fold tab.

BOY SCOUTS ANNIVERSARY, 1921
Ribbon below, 1-1/4".   1921   25.00 - 35.00

BOY SCOUTS OF AMERICA 100% DUTY
Tenderfoot emblem, 7/8".   1940   5.00 - 10.00

BOY SCOUTS OF AMERICA 100% DUTY
100% duty one month,   1940   5.00 - 10.00
  Tenderfoot emblem, 7/8".

BOY SCOUTS OF AMERICA 25TH ANNIVERSARY. 1910-1935
Scout bugling, Washington D.C.   1935   40.00 - 60.00
  view in distance, 1-1/4".

BOY SCOUTS OF AMERICA, 1936
Half-length view of scout standing right,   1936   15.00 - 20.00
  with campaign hat, 1-1/4".

BOY SCOUTS OF AMERICA
Red-white-blue background, 1-1/4".   1950-1960   3.00 - 5.00
Red-white-blue background, 1-3/4".   1950-1960   7.50 - 10.00

BOYS' LIFE FISH DERBY
Warden, 1-1/2" star-shaped fold tab.   1940-1955   7.50 - 10.00

BRANDED 1000 NEW SCOUTS
Cowboy on horse w/ lasso.   1935   20.00 - 30.00

BSA EXPO

1968, I'm on the go!, Road Runner, 2".	1968	3.00 - 5.00

BSA

Aide, 2-1/2".	1960	3.00 - 5.00
Campaign worker, Tenderfoot emblem in ctr, red-white-blue background, 7/8" w/ fold tab.	1960-1965	2.00 - 4.00
Campaign worker, Tenderfoot emblem in ctr, red-white-blue background, 7/8".	1950-1965	5.00 - 7.50
Clear with slide in name slot, 2-1/2".	1960	3.00 - 5.00
Committee, 2-1/2".	1960	3.00 - 5.00
Director, 2-1/2".	1960	3.00 - 5.00
Friend of Scouting, Tenderfoot emblem in ctr, red-white-blue background, 7/8" w/ fold tab.	1960-1965	2.00 - 4.00
I Gave (3 letter thicknesses), Tenderfoot emblem above, red-white-blue background, 7/8".	1950-1965	5.00 - 7.50
I'll Be Invested, Tenderfoot emblem above, red-white-blue background, 7/8".	1950-1965	5.00 - 7.50
I've Invested in Scouting, Tenderfoot emblem below, red-white-blue background, 7/8".	1950-1965	5.00 - 7.50
Judge, 2-1/2".	1960	3.00 - 5.00
Official, 2-1/2".	1960	3.00 - 5.00
Orderly, 2-1/2".	1960	3.00 - 5.00
Participant, 2-1/2".	1960	3.00 - 5.00
Pledged to Be First-Class Scout, First-Class emblem in ctr, red-white-blue background, 7/8" w/ fold tab.	1960-1965	2.00 - 4.00
Reception, 2-1/2".	1960	3.00 - 5.00
Support Scouting, Tenderfoot emblem in ctr, red-white-blue background, 7/8".	1950-1965	5.00 - 7.50
Usher, 2-1/2".	1960	3.00 - 5.00
We're Backing Boy Scouts, Tenderfoot emblem in ctr, red-white-blue background, 7/8" w/ fold tab.	1960-1965	2.00 - 4.00
We're Backing Boy Scouts, Tenderfoot emblem in ctr, red-white-blue background, 7/8".	1950-1965	5.00 - 7.50
White space for name to be written, 2-1/2"	1960	3.00 - 5.00

BUCKS COUNTY COUNCIL

Scouting Booster, 2-1/4".	1936	10.00 - 15.00

CAMDEN COUNTY BOY SCOUTS

Scout saluting, 7/8".	1920	20.00 - 30.00

CAMP BRERETON

St. Louis Council, 2".	1942	10.00 - 15.00
St. Louis Council, 2".	1955	7.50 - 10.00

CAMP KI-SHAU-WAU

First-Class emblem, 1".	1940-1950	10.00 - 15.00

CAMP MIGRATION OF '37

B.S.A. and Arrowhead, 1-1/4".	1937	15.00 - 20.00

CAMP RUSH OF '36

B.S.A. and nugget, 1-1/4".	1936	15.00 - 20.00
Wagon Boss, B.S.A. and nugget, 1-1/4".	1936	20.00 - 30.00

CATCH THE SCOUTING SPIRIT

	1985	1.00 - 2.00

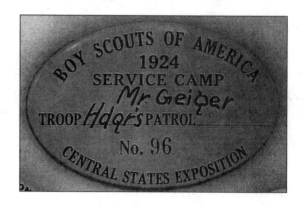

CENTRAL STATES EXPOSITION

Scout Service, 2-3/4" x 1-3/4" oval.	1924	75.00 - 125.00
Scout Services, 2-3/4" x 1-3/4" oval.	1923	75.00 - 125.00

CHICAGO BOY SCOUT CAMPS

Indian head I, Wrangler, 1-1/4" with top bar, fold tab.	1950-1960	5.00 - 7.50
Paul Bunyan's Crew, crew boss, 1-1/4".	1935	15.00 - 25.00
Paul Bunyan's Crew, Paul and the blue ox, 1-1/4".	1935	15.00 - 25.00

CHICAGO SCOUT CAMPS

I'm Going to Camp, pine tree, 7/8".	1933	20.00 - 30.00

COURT OF HONOR, DECATUR AREA No. 121

Advancement, 1-1/4".	1940-1946	10.00 - 15.00

DAD SCOUT
Dan Beard seated talking with Scout, 1-1/2"   1935-1945   20.00 - 30.00

FIRE BRIGADE
Fireman's helmet, 1".   1952-1953   7.50 - 10.00

GIVE
Boy Scouts of America, Tenderfoot emblem,   1950-1955   5.00 - 7.50
  1-1/4".

GO TO SCOUT CAMP
Silhouette of two scouts at campfire, scout   1940-1950   10.00 - 15.00
  facing as ghost image above, 1-1/4".

GOLDEN JUBILEE SCOUT FAIR
May 18-19, 1969, 1".   1968   2.00 - 3.00

GOOD TURNS FOR GOODWILL
Good Willy character,   1975   2.00 - 4.00
  Zane Trace Council, 2-1/2".

HEADING FOR THE SCOUTING EXPOSITION
Cartoon Indian boy, May 17-19, 1956, 2-1/4".   1956   5.00 - 7.50

I AM A SCOUTER
Tenderfoot badge, on red-white-blue, 7/8".   1940-1946   5.00 - 7.50

I GAVE
Full-length scout walking forward,   1955-1965   5.00 - 7.50
  1/2" x 1-1/2", fold tab.
Tenderfoot emblem in circle, 7/8", fold tab.   1965-1975   3.00 - 4.00
Tenderfoot emblem, 3/4" x 1", fold tab.   1965-1975   2.00 - 3.00

I PASSED THE BUCK
Liberty Head Dollar, 1-1/4".   1957   12.50 - 17.50

I ROPED ONE
Cowboy on horse w/ lasso, 1-1/4".   1935   10.00 - 20.00

I SWING
Troop 1, Lewisboro (NY), 2".   1985   5.00 - 7.50

I WILL BE AT THE SCOUT CAMP THIS SUMMER
1-1/4".   1930-1940   7.50 - 12.50

I'LL BE INVESTED
at Scout Camps, 7/8".   1935   10.00 - 20.00
Boy Scouts of America, Tenderfoot emblem,   1940-1946   5.00 - 10.00
  1-1/4"
The Scout Circus, 7/8".   1935   7.50 - 12.50

I'M A '49ER, B.S.A.
7/8".   1949   10.00 - 15.00

I'M A CAMPER
Scout by tent and campfire, 7/8".   1940-1946   5.00 - 7.50
Scout by tent and campfire, 1-1/4".   1940-1946   5.00 - 10.00

I'M A CLEAN WATER SCOUT
7/8".   1970   3.00 - 5.00

I'M SELLING SCOUTING
Cub, Explorer, Boy Scout, 1-1/4" x 1-3/4",   1950-1965   5.00 - 7.50
  fold tab.

I'VE GOT MINE FOR '49
S.L.C., B.S.A., Tenderfoot emblem, 7/8".   1949   5.00 - 7.50

IVER JOHNSON BOY SCOUT BICYCLE
7/8".   1915-1925 40.00 - 60.00

LIBERTY BELL
BSA Pledged, 3/4" x 1", fold tab.   1950-1960 5.00 - 7.50
BSA, I'm Joining, 3/4" x 1", fold tab.   1950-1960 5.00 - 7.50
I Recruited One, BSA, 3/4" x 1", fold tab.   1950-1960 5.00 - 7.50

LINEN CLAD SCOUT STOCKING
7/8".   1915-1920 20.00 - 30.00

MAVERICK
Bucking calf, BSA as brand, three background   1935   15.00 - 25.00
  color varieties, 1-1/4".

MEMORIAL AUDITORIUM
Changeable image, 2-1/2".   1957   10.00 - 15.00

MERIT BADGE EXPOSITION
Participant, 1-1/4".   1940-1950 5.00 - 10.00

NATIONAL JAMBOREE, 1935
Scout on horseback.   1935   25.00 - 40.00
Scout w/ bugle, ribbons below.   1935   35.00 - 50.00
Show Me, Scout on horseback, capitol and   1935   35.00 - 50.00
  Washington Monument. 1-1/4".

NATIONAL JAMBOREE, 1937
I'm Going, Jamboree logo.   1937   15.00 - 25.00

NATIONAL JAMBOREE, 1950
Valley Forge, red-white-blue background,   1950   15.00 - 25.00
  1-1/4".
Valley Forge.   1950   20.00 - 30.00

NATIONAL JAMBOREE, 1953
I'm Going, Jamboree logo.   1953   20.00 - 30.00
On to the Pacific, Tenderfoot emblem, 1-1/4". 1953   20.00 - 30.00

NATIONAL JAMBOREE, 1957
Boy Scouts Jamboree, white background,   1957   15.00 - 25.00
  1-3/4".

NATIONAL JAMBOREE, 1973
Fishing permit.   1973   10.00 - 15.00
Jamboree '73, B.S.A., 1".   1973   5.00 - 7.50

NATIONAL JAMBOREE, 1977
Orienteering.   1977   2.00 - 3.00

NATIONAL JAMBOREE, 1981
Archery.   1981   2.00 - 3.00
Rifle Shooting.   1981   2.00 - 3.00

NORTH SHORE AREA
Boy Scout Monthly Paper Collection, 1-3/4".   1941-1945 10.00 - 15.00

OWASIPPEE LODGE
Camp Promotion Information Center, 2-1/8".   1966   7.50 - 10.00

PHILMONT TRAINING CENTER
Three color varieties, 1-1/4".   1955-1990 2.00 - 3.00

PLEDGED TO BE
First-Class for Scout Circus, First-Class   1935-1940 10.00 - 15.00
  emblem, two background color varieties,
  1-1/4".
First-Class Scout, badge on red-white-blue,   1940-1946 3.00 - 5.00
  7/8".
Second-Class for Scout Circus, First-Class   1935-1940 10.00 - 15.00
  emblem, two background color varieties,
  1-1/4".
Second-Class Scout, badge on red-white-blue,   1940-1946 3.00 - 5.00
  7/8".
Tenderfoot Scout, badge on red-white-blue,   1940-1946 3.00 - 5.00
  7/8".

PLEDGED TO PASS
Merit Badge Tests for the Scout Circus,   1935-1940 10.00 - 15.00
  First-Class emblem, two background color
  varieties, 1-1/4".
Merit Badge Tests for the Scout Rodeo,   1935-1940 10.00 - 15.00
  First-Class emblem, two background color
  varieties, 1-1/4".
Merit Badge Tests, Tenderfoot badge on   1940-1946 3.00 - 5.00
  red-white-blue, 7/8".

PRESIDENT W.W. HEAD ACORN AWARD
7/8".   1920-1930 10.00 - 15.00

PRESIDENTIAL INAUGURATION, BOY SCOUT USHER
Brass tag, ribbon below.   1961   75.00 - 100.00
Brass tag, ribbon below.   1965   75.00 - 100.00

PROJECT S.O.A.R.
1-3/4".   1971   2.00 - 4.00

RAINBOW COUNCIL CAMP DEVELOPMENT CAMPAIGN
Scout facing in overseas cap, 2-1/4".   1960-1970   5.00 - 7.50

RAISE A BILLION $
Changeable image, 2-1/2".   1969   10.00 - 15.00

REGION SEVEN CAMP CONFERENCE
Aurora, IL,. Jan. 22-23, 1924, 2-1/8".   1924   75.00 - 125.00

REGION SEVEN, B.S.A.
Scout Signaling, Map w/ WI, IL, IN, MI,   1925   75.00 - 125.00
2" x 2-3/4" vertical oval.

ROOSEVELT PILGRIMAGE

12th, 1-1/4".	1931	20.00 - 30.00
13th, 1-1/4".	1932	20.00 - 30.00
14th, 1-1/4".	1933	20.00 - 30.00
15th, 1-1/4".	1934	20.00 - 30.00
16th, 1-1/4".	1935	20.00 - 30.00
17th, 1-1/4".	1936	20.00 - 30.00
18th, 1-1/4".	1937	10.00 - 15.00
19th, 1-1/4".	1938	20.00 - 30.00
20th, 1-1/4".	1939	20.00 - 30.00
21st, 1-1/4".	1940	20.00 - 30.00
22nd, 1-1/4".	1941	20.00 - 30.00
23rd, 1-1/4".	1942	20.00 - 30.00
24th, 1-1/4".	1943	20.00 - 30.00
25th, 1-1/4".	1944	20.00 - 30.00
26th, 1-1/4".	1945	20.00 - 30.00
27th, 1-1/4".	1946	20.00 - 30.00
28th, 1-1/4".	1947	20.00 - 30.00

ROUND-UP BSA

Cowhand, 1-1/2" star-shaped fold tab.	1940-1955	7.50 - 10.00
I Roped One, 1-1/2" star-shaped fold tab.	1940-1955	7.50 - 10.00
Maverick, 1-1/2" star-shaped fold tab.	1940-1955	7.50 - 10.00
Rancher, 1-1/2" star-shaped fold tab.	1940-1955	7.50 - 10.00
Range Rider, 1-1/2" star-shaped fold tab.	1940-1955	7.50 - 10.00

ROUND-UP
Recruiter, Tenderfoot emblem, 7/8".   1940-1950   7.50 - 10.00

ROUND-UP, 1948
Cowboy on bucking bronco, 1-1/4".   1948   10.00 - 15.00

ROUND-UP, 1951
Cowboy on bucking bronco, 1-1/4".   1951   10.00 - 15.00

SCHUYLKILL COUNTY 6TH ANNUAL BOY SCOUT MEET
September 3, 1928, Scouts signaling as on   1928   75.00 - 125.00
handbook cover, 1-3/4", multicolored.

SCOUT AIR DERBY

First-Class, five planes in formation in clouds, 1-1/4".	1945-1955	25.00 - 35.00
Parachute Jump, 1-1/4".	1945-1955	25.00 - 35.00
Second-Class, racing plane and finish tower, 1-1/4".	1945-1955	25.00 - 35.00
Solo Flight, plane in clouds, 1-1/4".	1945-1955	25.00 - 35.00
Two merit badges, helicopter, 1-1/4".	1945-1955	25.00 - 35.00

SCOUT AIR RACE
First-Class, five planes in formation in clouds,   1945-1955   25.00 - 35.00
1-1/4".

SCOUT CIRCUS
Official, clown, 1-3/4".   1945-1955   10.00 - 15.00

SCOUT CIRCUS, COTTON BOWL
Clown, May 18, 1951, 1-1/4".   1951   10.00 - 15.00

SCOUT FACING

I'll Be Invested at the Scout Circus, 1-1/4".	1930-1940	10.00 - 15.00
Recruit Boy Scouts, 3/4".	1930-1940	10.00 - 15.00
Wearing campaign hat, on red-white-blue background, 7/8".	1940-1946	3.00 - 5.00
Wearing campaign hat, on blue background, 7/8".	1923-1930	7.50 - 12.50
Wearing campaign hat, on blue background, Boy Scouts of America 1924 legend, 7/8".	1924	10.00 - 15.00
Wearing campaign hat, on blue background, Boy Scouts of America 1925 legend, 7/8".	1925	20.00 - 30.00
Wearing campaign hat, on blue background, Boy Scouts of America 1926 legend, 7/8".	1926	20.00 - 30.00
Wearing campaign hat, on blue background, Boy Scouts of America legend, 7/8".	1923-1930	7.50 - 12.50
Wearing campaign hat, on blue background, Do a Good Turn Daily legend, 7/8".	1923-1930	7.50 - 12.50
Wearing campaign hat, red-white-blue background, 1-1/4".	1940-1946	10.00 - 15.00
Wearing overseas cap, on red-white-blue background, 7/8".	1955	5.00 - 7.50

SCOUT POLICE

Two ribbons below, 7/8".	1930-1945	20.00 - 30.00

SCOUT PROFILE LEFT

On dark blue background, 7/8".	1940-1946	5.00 - 7.50
On dark blue background, 1-1/4"	1940-1946	5.00 - 10.00

SCOUT SMILING

Anniversary Week, Feb. 7-13, 7/8".	1920-1930	10.00 - 15.00
Davis Scout Contest, 7/8".	1920-1930	10.00 - 15.00

SCOUT-O-RAMA

Investiture Scout, Tenderfoot emblem, 7/8".	1948	7.50 - 12.50

SCOUTS

Half length figure facing, 11/16"	1930-1945	12.50 - 20.00

TENDERFOOT BADGE

On red-white-blue background, 3/4".	1940-1946	3.00 - 5.00
On blue background, 5/8".	1940-1946	5.00 - 7.50

TENDERFOOT EMBLEM AND GIRL SCOUT EMBLEM

Feather between, 1".	1945	7.50 - 10.00

THE BOY SCOUTS FLAG

U.S. Flag, 3/4".	1915-1925	20.00 - 30.00

TROOP 31, HOLLYWOOD

Historic Trails, covered wagon, 7/8".	1968	5.00 - 7.50

TROOP ACHIEVEMENT CAMPAIGN

Advancement Coup, feather, 7/8".	1930-1935	10.00 - 15.00
Membership Coup, feather, 7/8".	1930-1935	20.00 - 30.00

WALI-GA-ZHU

Blue Earth, First-Class emblem, 1-1/2".	1935	15.00 - 25.00

WE HELPED BUILD OUR CAMPS

Camp cabin and sign, 1-1/4".	1940-1950	10.00 - 15.00

MEDALLIONS

Medallions (tokens) saw their initial use in 1910 with the Excelsior Shoe issues (great advertising!). Groups have used a small pocket piece for various events ever since. They have been extensively cataloged by Rudy Dioszegi in his book *Scouting Exonumia Worldwide*, second edition. 1993. The references in this listing come from Dioszegi's book.

EXCELSIOR SHOE CO.

Description	Year	Ref	Price
Inverted 1st quote, two reins, SCOUT, 12 mm date, Co. four stars. 33 mm, brass.	1910	Dio.1910.1A1	8.00 - 15.00
Inverted 1st quote, two reins, SCOUT, 12 mm date, Co. four stars. 33mm, brass.	1910	Dio.1910.1A1	8.00 - 15.00
Inverted 1st quote, two reins, SCOUT, 14 mm date, Co. 12 mm date, Co. four stars. 33 mm, brass.	1910	Dio.1910.1A2	15.00 - 25.00
Inverted 1st quote, three reins, SCOUTS, 14 mm date, Co. 13 mm date, Co. four stars. 33 mm, brass.	1910	Dio.1910.1B1	8.00 - 15.00
Inverted 1st quote, three reins, SCOUTS, 14 mm date, Co. 13 mm date, four stars. 33 mm, brass.	1910	Dio.1910.1B2	8.00 - 15.00
Inverted 1st quotes, three reins, SCOUTS, 15 mm date, four stars. 33 mm, brass.	1910	Dio.1910.1B3	15.00 - 25.00
Inverted 1st quotes, three reins, SCOUTS, 12 mm date, four stars. 33 mm, brass.	1910	Dio.1910.1B4	8.00 - 15.00
Reversed 1st quotes, three reins, SCOUTS, 14 mm date, Co. five stars. 33 mm, brass.	1910	Dio.1910.1C	8.00 - 15.00
Normal quotes, three reins, SCOUTS, 13 mm date, Co. five stars. 33 mm, brass.	1910	Dio.1910.1D	15.00 - 25.00
Reversed 1st quote, three reins, SCOUTS, 13 mm date, Co. five stars. 33 mm, brass.	1910	Dio.1910.1E	10.00 - 17.50
Reversed 1st quote, three reins, SCOUTS, 13 mm date, Co. five stars. 33 mm, brass, thin planchet.	1910	Dio.1910.1E1	10.00 - 17.00
Inverted 1st quote, three reins, SCOUTS, 12 mm date, Co. five stars. 33 mm, brass.	1910	Dio.1910.1F	8.00 - 15.00
Inverted 1st quote, three reins, SCOUTS, 14 mm date, Co. five stars. 33 mm, brass.	1910	Dio.1910.1G	10.00 - 17.50
Inverted 1st quote, four stars, three reins, SCOUT, 13 mm date. 33 mm, brass.	1910	Dio.1910.2A	15.00 - 25.00
Inverted 1st quote, four stars, three reins, SCOUTS, 13 mm date. 33 mm, brass.	1910	Dio.1910.2A1	8.00 - 15.00
Normal quotes, four stars, two reins, SCOUTS, 13 mm date. 33 mm, brass.	1910	Dio.1910.2B	8.00 - 15.00
Normal quotes, four stars, two reins, SCOUTS, 15 mm date. 33 mm, brass.	1910	Dio.1910.2B1	8.00 - 15.00
Normal quotes, four stars, two reins, SCOUTS, 15 mm date. 33 mm, copper.	1910	Dio.1910.2B2	15.00 - 25.00
Normal quotes, four stars, three reins, SCOUTS, 15 mm date. 33 mm, copper.	1910	Dio.1910.2C	8.00 - 15.00
Reversed 1st quote, five stars, three reins, SCOUTS, 13 mm date. 33 mm, brass.	1910	Dio.1910.2D	8.00 - 15.00
Normal quotes, four stars, three reins, SCOUTS, 13 mm date. 33 mm, brass.	1910	Dio.1910.2E	8.00 - 15.00
Normal quotes, four stars, two reins, SCOUTS, 13 mm date, no maker's name. 33 mm, brass.	1910	Dio.1910.2E1	8.00 - 15.00
Inverted 1st quote, 4 stars, 2 reins, SCOUTS, 13 mm date. No reins on right side from hand to horse. 33 mm, brass.	1910	Dio.1910.2F	10.00 - 17.50
Inverted 1st quote, four stars, two reins, SCOUTS, 13 mm date. 33 mm, brass.	1910	Dio.1910.2F1	10.00 - 17.50
Normal quotes, five stars, three reins, SCOUTS, 13 mm date. 33 mm, copper.	1910	Dio.1910.2G	10.00 - 17.50
Normal quotes, five stars, three reins, SCOUTS, 13 mm date, no maker's name. 33 mm, brass.	1910	Dio.1910.2H	15.00 - 25.00
Inverted 1st quote, five stars, three reins, SCOUTS, 13 mm date. 33 mm, copper.	1910	Dio.1910.2I	15.00 - 25.00
Inverted 1st quote, five stars, two reins, SCOUT, 12 mm date. 33 mm, brass.	1910	Dio.1910.2J	15.00 - 25.00
Normal quote, four stars, SCOUT, 13 mm date. 33 mm, brass.	1910	Dio.1910.2K	10.00 - 17.50
Normal quotes, two star, w/ per; 15 mm maker. 33 mm, brass.	1910	Dio.1910.3A	8.00 - 15.00
Normal quotes, two star, w/ per;. 15 mm maker. Co. as ligature. 33 mm, brass.	1910	Dio.1910.3A1	15.00 - 25.00
Normal quotes, two star, w/ per; 15 mm maker. Co. as ligature. 33 mm, sterling silver.	1910	Dio.1910.3B	8.00 - 15.00
Normal quotes, two stars, w/ per; 18 mm name. 33 mm, brass.	1910	Dio.1910.3C	8.00 - 15.00
Normal quotes, two stars, w/o per; 18 mm name. 33 mm, brass.	1910	Dio.1910.3C1	8.00 - 15.00
Normal quotes, two star, w/o per., 18 mm name. 33 mm, brass.	1910	Dio.1910.3C2	8.00 - 15.00
Inverted 1st quote, two star, w/o per., 18 mm name. 33 mm, brass.	1910	Dio.1910.3D	8.00 - 15.00
Inverted 2nd quote, 21mm name. 33 mm, brass.	1910	Dio.1910.3E	8.00 - 15.00
Inverted 2nd quote, two stars, w/o per., 18 mm name. 33 mm, brass.	1910	Dio.1910.3E1	8.00 - 15.00
Normal quote, w/o per., 18 mm name. 33 mm, brass.	1910	Dio.1910.3F	35.00 - 50.00
Normal quote, w/o per., no name. 33 mm, copper.	1910	Dio.1910.3G	10.00 - 17.50
Normal quote, two star, w/o per., 18 mm name. 33 mm, copper.	1910	Dio.1910.3G1	15.00 - 25.00
Inverted 1st quote, no name. 33 mm, copper.	1910	Dio.1910.3H	0.00 - 0.00
Reversed 1st quote, no maker's name. 33 mm, brass.	1910	Dio.1910.3I	15.00 - 25.00
Inverted 1st quote, three stars, w/o per., 18 mm name. 33 mm, brass.	1910	Dio.1910.3J	15.00 - 25.00
Inverted 1st quote, three stars, w/o per., 14 mm maker. 33 mm, brass.	1910	Dio.1910.3K	15.00 - 25.00

Normal quotes, two star, w/ per., 16 mm maker. 33 mm, brass.	1910	Dio.1910.3L	10.00 - 17.50
Inverted 2nd quote, two stars, w/o per., 15 mm maker. 33 mm, brass.	1910	Dio.1910.3M	10.00 - 17.50
Inverted 2nd quote, three stars, w/o per., 18 mm maker. 33 mm, brass.	1910	Dio.1910.3N	10.00 - 17.50
No quotes, w/ per., 14 mm maker. 33 mm, brass.	1910	Dio.1910.3O	15.00 - 25.00
No quotes, two star, w/o per., 14 mm maker. 33 mm, brass.	1910	Dio.1910.3O1	15.00 - 25.00
Inverted 2nd quote, three star, w/o per., 14 mm maker. No reins from hand to horse. 33 mm, brass.	1910	Dio.1910.3P	15.00 - 25.00
Indian Scout, maker as Whitehead & Hoag. 33 mm, brass.	1910	Dio.1910.4A	15.00 - 25.00
Indian Scout, maker as Schwaab. 33 mm, brass.	1910	Dio.1910.4B	15.00 - 25.00
Normal quotes, five stars, three reins, no date, SCOUTS, maker: SCHWAAB MILWAUKEE in straight line. 33 mm, brass.	1910	Dio.1910.5A	10.00 - 17.50
Same as 5a but 33 mm and made of copper.	1910	Dio.1910.5B	15.00 - 25.00
Same as 5a but 33 mm and made of nickel.	1910	Dio.1910.5C	20.00 - 30.00
Legend reads: The Original Boy Scouts Army Shoe - Munson Last. Normal quotes, 5 stars, 3 reins. Reverse is seal, 33 mm, brass.	1910	Dio.1910.6A	10.00 - 17.50
Legend reads: The Original Boy Scouts Army Shoe - Munson Last. Normal quotes, 5 stars, 3 reins. Reverse is seal, 33 mm, gilt brass.	1910	Dio.1910.6B	15.00 - 25.00
Obverse same as Type 3 but w/ grass clumps under horse. No beading on rim. 33 mm, brass.	1910	Dio.1910.7A	8.00 - 15.00
Obverse same as Type 3 but w/ grass clumps under horse. Beading on obverse rim. 33 mm, brass.	1910	Dio.1910.7B	10.00 - 17.50
Obverse same as Type 6, reverse same as Type 2. 33 mm, brass.	1910	Dio.1910.8	15.00 - 25.00
Obverse same as Type 2, less date, reverse same as Type 4. 33 mm, brass.	1910	Dio.1910.9	15.00 - 25.00

BOY SCOUT STANDING W/ STAFF. HOLED.

32 mm, bronze.	1913	Dio.1913.1	25.00 - 40.00

EVERY SCOUT TO SAVE A SOLDIER/WEAPONS FOR LIBERTY

Kneeling Scout holds sword to standing and flag-draped Liberty. 28 mm, gold, uniface.	1917	Dio.1917.1A	1,500. - 2,000.
Kneeling Scout holds sword to standing and flag-draped Liberty. 28 mm, silver, uniface.	1917	Dio.1917.1B	750.00 - 1,000.
Kneeling Scout holds sword to standing and flag-draped Liberty. 28 mm, bronze, uniface.	1917	Dio.1917.1C	250.00 - 400.00

ROTARY CLUB, MORRIS IL. GOOD TURN TOKEN.
LINCOLN BUST RIGHT.

31 mm, copper.	1920	Dio.1920.1	30.00 - 50.00

BOY SCOUTS, NIAGARA FALLS NY

32 mm, aluminum.	1923	Dio.1923.1	30.00 - 50.00

MILWAUKEE BOY SCOUTS FATHER AND SON BANQUET

32 mm, bronze, four finishes.	1924	Dio.1924.1A-D	30.00 - 50.00
32 mm, copper, two finishes.	1924	Dio.1924.1E-F	30.00 - 50.00
32 mm, brass, two finishes.	1924	Dio.1924.1G-I	30.00 - 50.00
32 mm, oriode.	1924	Dio.1924.1J	60.00 - 80.00
32 mm, aluminum.	1924	Dio.1924.1K	60.00 - 80.00
32 mm, copper-nickel.	1924	Dio.1924.1L	60.00 - 80.00
32 mm, lead.	1924	Dio.1924.1M	60.00 - 80.00

BOY SCOUTS OF DALLAS, TX.
SERVICE AT THE CONFEDERATE REUNION.

36 mm, aluminum.	1925	Dio.1925.1	100.00 - 150.00

ABRAHAM LINCOLN COUNCIL, IL. LINCOLN TRAIL HIKE.

31 mm, bronze.	1926	Dio.1926.1	30.00 - 50.00

CAMP GIFFORD, OMAHA AND COVERED WAGON COUNCILS

Good for 1 cent in trade. 20 mm, aluminum.	1926	Dio.1926.2	20.00 - 30.00
Good for 5 cents in trade. 20 mm, aluminum.	1926	Dio.1926.3	20.00 - 30.00

KANSAS CITY, MO, FIRST NATIONAL CAMPOREE, HONOR CAMPER.

30 mm, brass.	1933	Dio.1933.01	60.00 - 80.00

SALT LAKE COUNCIL, DO A GOOD TURN DAILY.
STEER'S SKULL.

26 mm, brass.	1935	Dio.1935.01	30.00 - 50.00

OWASIPPI SCOUT CAMPS, CHICAGO COUNCIL

GF 1 cent in merchandise. 18 mm, aluminum.	1936	Dio.1936.01	0.00 - 0.00
GF 5 cents in merchandise. 20 mm, aluminum.	1936	Dio.1936.02	0.00 - 0.00
GF 10 cents in merchandise. 22 mm, aluminum.	1936	Dio.1936.03	0.00 - 0.00
GF 25 cents in merchandise. 26 mm, aluminum.	1936	Dio.1936.04	0.00 - 0.00
GF 5 cents in merchandise. 20 mm, brass.	1936	Dio.1936.05	0.00 - 0.00

PIASE BIRD COUNCIL, NATIONAL SCOUT JAMBOREE

25 mm, brass.	1937	Dio.1937.01	20.00 - 30.00

TROOP 2, WILKINSBURG, PA 25TH ANNIVERSARY.

36 mm, white metal.	1937	Dio.1937.02	30.00 - 50.00

MANITOWOC COUNTY COUNCIL, NATIONAL SCOUT JAMBOREE, ENCASED CENT

35 mm, aluminum.	1937	Dio.1937.03	5.00 - 10.00

SILVER LAKE SCOUT BOOSTER, 1937, ENCASED CENT

34 mm, aluminum.	1937	Dio.1937.04	5.00 - 10.00

TROOP 87, STROUDSBURG, PA. MONROE COUNTY, THE PLAYGROUND OF AMERICA

58 mm, white metal.	1937	Dio.1937.05	10.00 - 17.50

GIFFORD RUNYON, TROOP 17, ANDERSON IN

25 mm.	1937	Dio.1937.06	15.00 - 25.00

NASSAU COUNTY COUNCIL, NATIONAL SCOUT JAMBOREE

22 mm, copper.	1937	Dio.1937.07	20.00 - 30.00

SACHEM COUNCIL, WALTHAM, WATCH FACE, 1937 JAMBOREE

40 mm.	1937	Dio.1937.08	25.00 -3 0.00

WORLD'S FAIR GREETINGS, SCOUT SALUTING W/ TRILON AND PERISPHER IN BACKGROUND

Elongated Lincoln cent, Indian cent, large cent, two-cent piece, and various foreign coins and tokens.	1939	Dio.1939.01a-1f	20.00 - 35.00
Elongated 1940 Lincoln cent.	1940	Dio.1940.01	20.00 - 35.00

BOYCE MEMORIAL, OTTAWA, IL, STARVED ROCK COUNCIL

39 mm, brass.	1941	Dio.1941.01	10.00 - 17.50

TREASURE ISLAND ADVENTURE, DISTRICT 9

28 mm, brass.	1946	Dio.1946.01	20.00 - 30.00

TREASURE ISLAND ADVENTURE, DISTRICT 8

28 mm, brass.	1946	Dio.1946.02	20.00 - 30.00

TREASURE ISLAND ADVENTURE, DISTRICT 4

28 mm, brass.	1946	Dio.1946.03	20.00 - 30.00

SAUK PAUL BUNYAN DAYS

65 mm, aluminum.	1949	Dio.1949.01	15.00 - 25.00

MYSTERIOUS ISLAND, DISTRICT 8

30 mm, brass.	1949	Dio.1949.02	15.00 - 25.00

REGION 9, B.S.A. ENCASED BUFFALO NICKEL

39 mm, aluminum.	1949	Dio.1949.03	50.00 - 80.00

NATIONAL JAMBOREE, VALLEY FORGE, OFFICIAL MEDAL

Washington kneeling. Reverse w/ "Hallowed ground" text. 36 mm, bronze.	1950	Dio.1950.01	5.00 - 10.00

NATIONAL SCOUT JAMBOREE, TEXAS TRADERS, CONCHO VALLEY COUNCIL

Washington kneeling, Texas map and bronco rider. 32 mm, aluminum.	1950	Dio.1950.02	15.00 - 25.00

NATIONAL SCOUT JAMBOREE, BAY SHORE COUNCIL, GENERAL ELECTRIC RIVER WORKS, LYNN, MA

48 mm, copper painted red.	1950	Dio.1950.03	15.00 - 25.00

NATIONAL JAMBOREE, CLEVELAND COUNCIL, FIRESTONE TIRE COMPANY

65 mm, steel, 2 large holes.	1950	Dio.1950.04	15.00 - 25.00

NATIONAL SCOUT JAMBOREE, BRUDER DAIRY, CLEVELAND OH

Good luck piece. 32 mm, aluminum.	1950	Dio.1950.05	10.00 - 17.50

NATIONAL SCOUT JAMBOREE, CAMDEN COUNTY COUNCIL, NJ

Hires Root Beer. 30 mm, aluminum.	1950	Dio.1950.07	10.00 - 17.50

NATIONAL SCOUT JAMBOREE. WASHINGTON KNEELING, SCOUT BADGE REVERSE.

25 mm, bronze.	1950	Dio.1950.07	10.00 - 17.50

NATIONAL SCOUT JAMBOREE, TROOP 33, PLEASANT VALLEY, NY.

38 mm, bronze.	1950	Dio.1950.09	15.00 - 25.00

NATIONAL SCOUT JAMBOREE, BADGER COUNCIL, KEWASKUM, WI

Lucky Wamoum. 40 mm, aluminum.	1950	Dio.1950.12	10.00 - 17.50

ALPHA PHI OMEGA, 25TH ANNIVERSARY NATIONAL CONVENTION

28 mm, silver.	1950	Dio.1950.06	15.00 - 25.00

DODGE CITY LAND RUSH, DISTRICT 4, DETROIT, MI

33 mm, aluminum.	1950	Dio.1950.10	15.00 - 25.00

FREEDOM FOUNDATION GET OUT THE VOTE CAMPAIGN

32 mm, silvered plastic.	1952	Dio.1952.01a	2.00 - 5.00
32 mm, golden plastic.	1952	Dio.1952.01b	15.00 - 25.00

Karl Gruppe designed this medal issued by the Society of Medalists to honor scouting.

YOUTH OF THE SCOUTING WORLD, SOCIETY OF MEDALLISTS ISSUE #46
Eagle breaking chains. Reverse   1952   Dio.1952.02a   150.00 - 200.00
Scouts signaling and receiving.
72 mm, silver.
Eagle breaking chains. Reverse   1952   Dio.1952.02b   75.00 - 100.00
Scouts signaling and receiving.
72 mm, bronze.

TROOP 75 BOY SCOUT FAIR
22 mm, copper.   1952   Dio.1952.03   10.00 - 17.50

NATIONAL SCOUT JAMBOREE, OFFICIAL MEDAL. COVERED WAGON, "FORWARD ON LIBERTY'S TEAM" LEGEND.
36 mm, bronze.   1953   Dio.1953.01   10.00 - 17.50

NATIONAL SCOUT JAMBOREE, REGION 4, OHIO SESQUICENTENNIAL
33 mm, aluminum.   1953   Dio.1953.02   15.00 - 25.00

NATIONAL SCOUT JAMBOREE, PLYMOUTH AUTO
31 mm, bronze.   1953   Dio.1953.03   15.00 - 25.00

BOY SCOUT JAMBOREE, LOS ANGELES, CA
Bronco rider. 44 mm, aluminum. 1953   Dio.1953.04   15.00 - 25.00

NATIONAL SCOUT JAMBOREE, AKRON AREA COUNCIL, OH
33 mm, bronze.   1953   Dio.1953.05   15.00 - 25.00

CHURCH OF JESUS CHRIST OF LATER DAY SAINTS, 40TH ANNIVERSARY IN SCOUTING
Eagle and Silver Award   1953   Dio.1953.06   20.00 - 30.00
recognition. 30 mm, pewter.

HARVEY S. FIRESTONE AWARD. SCOUT W/ SAPLING, TOWN VIEW IN BACKGROUND.
89 mm, bronze.   1953   Dio.1953.07   60.00 - 80.00

CIRCLE B ROUND-UP
36 mm, bronze.   1953   Dio.1953.08   15.00 - 25.00

NATIONAL SCOUT JAMBOREE, TROOP 21, QUIVERA COUNCIL, WICHITA, KS
70 mm, painted aluminum.   1953   Dio.1953.09   10.00 - 15.00

DOUGLAS AIRCRAFT, TENDERFOOT EMBLEM
51 mm, aluminum, 9 mm thick. 1953   Dio.1953.10   15.00 - 25.00

BSA FALL ROUND-UP. CABIN. REVERSE EAGLE'S NEST.
37 mm, bronze.   1954   Dio.1954.01   15.00 - 25.00

SCOUTING EXPOSITION, TROOP 108
40 mm, steel.   1954   Dio.1954.02   15.00 - 25.00

SCOUTS OF GREENVILLE, SC. 9TH ANNUAL CAMPOREE
16 mm, bronze.   1955   Dio.1955.01   15.00 - 25.00

SAN GABRIEL VALLEY COUNCIL, CA. I JOINED 1955; CIRCUS, MAY 21
32 mm, aluminum.   1955   Dio.1955.02   15.00 - 25.00

DETROIT AREA COUNCIL, MI. GOVERNOR'S RECOGNITION DAY
1955   Dio.1955.03   15.00 - 25.00

JOHN R. DONNELL AWARD, REGION 4
Silvered medal set into lucite   1956   Dio.1956.03   20.00 - 30.00
block.

NATIONAL SCOUT JAMBOREE, VALLEY FORGE, PA. OFFICIAL MEDAL
Washington kneeling, "Hallowed 1957   Dio.1957.01   8.00 - 15.00
Ground" text. 37 mm, bronze.

NATIONAL SCOUT JAMBOREE, SCOUT TOWER AT VALLEY FORGE
32 mm, bronze.   1957   Dio.1957.02   10.00 - 17.50

NATIONAL SCOUT JAMBOREE, LUCKY PENNY
74 mm, copper-plated pot   1957   Dio.1957.03   15.00 - 25.00
metal.

GREATER CLEVELAND COUNCIL, OH. BADEN-POWELL CENTENNIAL ROUND-UP.
36 mm, golden brass.   1957   Dio.1957.04   8.00 - 15.00

NATIONAL SCOUT JAMBOREE, DIFFERENT DIE THAN OFFICIAL MEDAL, UNIFACE
39 mm, nickel.   1957   Dio.1957.05   10.00 - 17.50

NATIONAL SCOUT JAMBOREE, LUCKY NICKEL
74 mm, nickel-plated pot metal. 1957   Dio.1957.06   15.00 - 25.00

NATIONAL SCOUT JAMBOREE, PENNSYLVANIA RAILROAD GOOD LUCK PIECE
34 mm, aluminum.   1957   Dio.1957.07   20.00 - 30.00

SAFETY GOOD TURN. SET IN LUCITE.
47 mm, green enameled steel.   1958   Dio.1958.01   20.00 - 30.00

SAFETY GOOD TURN. SET INTO LUCITE.
50 mm, black enameled steel.   1958   Dio.1958.03   20.00 - 30.00

TROOP 12, BURBANK, CA.
  HAWAIIAN ADVENTURE SOUVENIR.
33 mm, bronze.   1958   Dio.1958.02   15.00 - 25.00

CIRCLE 10, BSA
32 mm, white plastic.   1959   Dio.1959.01   10.00 - 15.00

NASSAU CAMPOREE, '59 (NASSAU COUNTY COUNCIL, NY?)
43 mm, aluminum.   1959   Dio.1959.02   15.00 - 25.00

NATIONAL SCOUT JAMBOREE, TROOP 126, KEWAUNEE, WI
35 mm, aluminum.   1960   Dio.1960.10   10.00 - 17.50

50TH ANNIVERSARY OF BSA FOUNDING, WASHINGTON D.C.
  SCOUT STATUE AND FIRST-CLASS BADGE
39 mm, silver.   1960   Dio.1960.11   20.00 - 30.00

ROCKY MOUNTAIN COUNCIL, CO, SCOUT OLYMPICS
105 mm, cast pot metal.   1960   Dio.1960.12   10.00 - 17.50

BSA 50TH ANNIVERSARY OFFICIAL TOKEN
For God and Country design.   1960   Dio.1960.01a   2.00 - 5.00
  Reverse w/ Scout Oath.
  26 mm, bronze.
For God and Country design.   1960   Dio.1960.01b-c   20.00 - 30.00
  Reverse w/ Scout Oath.
  26 mm, gilt bronze.
For God and Country design.   1960   Dio.1960.01d   3.00 - 8.00
  Reverse w/ Scout Oath.
  26 mm, chrome-plated, holed.

BSA 50TH ANNIVERSARY MEDAL
For God and Country legend.   1960   Dio.1960.02a-b   10.00 - 17.50
  Reverse w/ Scout Oath on
  plaque within wreath. 63 mm,
  bronze.

BSA, UNOFFICIAL 50TH ANNIVERSARY MEDAL
Scout standing. Reverse   1960   Dio.1960.03a   25.00 - 35.00
  First-Class badge in rays.
  30 mm, silver. 7,500 minted
  and distributed in numbered
  envelopes.
Scout standing. Reverse   1960   Dio.1960.03b   250.00 - 350.00
  First-Class badge in rays.
  30 mm, gold. 50 minted
  and distributed in numbered
  envelopes.

NATIONAL SCOUT JAMBOREE, OFFICIAL MEDAL
36 mm, bronze.   1960   Dio.1960.04   3.00 - 8.00
38 mm, bronze.   1985   Dio.1985.01   3.00 - 5.00

NATIONAL SCOUT JAMBOREE, TROOP 107, ERIE PA
Copper.   1960   Dio.1960.05   15.00 - 25.00

BOY SCOUTS OF AMERICA, 1960. ENCASED CENT.
33 mm, aluminum.   1960   Dio.1960.06   2.00 - 5.00

NATIONAL SCOUT JAMBOREE,
  TOM CHARLIER, KEWAUNEE, WI. ENCASED CENT.
33 mm, aluminum.   1960   Dio.1960.07   2.00 - 5.00

OA AREA 7F CONFERENCE. SCOUT BADGE AND ARROW.
90 mm, bronze.   1960   Dio.1960.08   15.00 - 25.00

NATIONAL SCOUT JAMBOREE,
  PIASA BIRD COUNCIL, ALTON, IL
51 mm x 35 mm oval, copper.   1960   Dio.1960.09   15.00 - 25.00

REGION ELEVEN, EXPLORING CONFERENCE,
  REED COLLEGE, PORTLAND, OR
28 mm, bronze.   1961   Dio.1961.01   15.00 - 25.00

GREATER NEW YORK COUNCIL SCOUTING EXPOSITION
26 mm x 18 mm oval, bronze.   1961   Dio.1961.02   15.00 - 25.00

CAMP SEQUASSEN, QUINNIPIAC COUNCIL,
  INTERNATIONAL CAMPOREE.
36 mm, bronze.   1962   Dio.1962.01   10.00 - 17.50

CAMP SALMEM, SLIDELL, LA.
  NEW ORLEANS AREA COUNCIL.
38 mm, bronze.   1963   Dio.1963.01a   5.00 - 10.00
39 mm, antiqued silver.   1963   Dio.1963.01b   10.00 - 17.50
39 mm, .999 fine silver.   1963   Dio.1963.01c   50.00 - 70.00

TENDERFOOT EMBLEM STAMPED INTO LINCOLN CENT
Copper. Done much later.   1963   Dio.1963.02   0.50 - 1.00

NATIONAL SCOUT JAMBOREE,
  VALLEY FORGE, OFFICIAL MEDAL
Washington kneeling. Reverse   1964   Dio.1964.01a   3.00 - 8.00
  w/ Liberty Bell, log cabin, and
  arch. 36 mm, oxidized bronze.
36 mm, oxidized silver.   1964   Dio.1964.01b   5.00 - 10.00

NATIONAL SCOUT JAMBOREE, CONTINENTAL DOLLAR COPY
39 mm, aluminum.   1964   Dio.1964.02   2.00 - 5.00

NATIONAL SCOUT JAMBOREE,
  REGION XI, BUNKER HILL CO. KELLOGG, ID
57 mm, cast pot metal.   1964   Dio.1964.03   8.00 - 15.00

WONDERFUL WORLD OF SCOUTING, NY WORLD'S FAIR
35 mm, bronze.   1964   Dio.1964.04   2.00 - 5.00

AMF EXPLORER FITNESS PROGRAM
I played Dick Weber.   1964   Dio.1964.05   2.00 - 5.00
  39 mm, oxidized bronze.
I beat Dick Weber.   1964   Dio.1964.06   5.00 - 10.00
  39 mm, oxidized bronze.
I played Ben Hogan.   1964   Dio.1964.07   2.00 - 5.00
  39 mm, oxidized bronze.
I beat Ben Hogan.   1964   Dio.1964.08   5.00 - 10.00
  39 mm, oxidized bronze.
I qualified for Swim Tests.   1964   Dio.1964.09   2.00 - 5.00
  39 mm, oxidized bronze.
I passed the Fitness Tests.   1964   Dio.1964.10   2.00 - 5.00
  39 mm, oxidized bronze.

NATIONAL SCOUT JAMBOREE, BSA, KEWAUNEE, WI
Encased cent. 36 mm,   1964   Dio.1964.11   2.00 - 5.00
  aluminum.

NATIONAL SCOUT JAMBOREE, VALLEY FORGE.
  PATCH DESIGN ENAMELLED, SET INTO LUCITE.
Staff Service.   1964   Dio.1964.13   15.00 - 25.00

NATIONAL ELECTED EXPLORER DELEGATE CONFERENCE
36 mm, oxidized silvered   1964   Dio.1964.14   8.00 - 15.00
  bronze.

STRENGTHENING AMERICA'S HERITAGE.
  SCOUT SIGN PARTIALLY ENCIRCLED BY STARS.
Scout Oath on reverse.   1964   Dio.1964.15   8.00 - 15.00
  65 mm, bronze.

CIRCLE TEN COUNCIL, TX, SCOUT CIRCUS
36 mm, aluminum.   1965   Dio.1965.01   8.00 - 15.00

XII WORLD JAMBOREE, IDAHO, U.S.A.
Scout sign between two   1967   Dio.1967.01   3.00 - 5.00
  hemispheres. 35 mm, bronze.
Six Scouts marching.   1967   Dio.1967.02a   8.00 - 15.00
  39 mm, bronze.
Six Scouts marching. 39 mm,   1967   Dio.1967.02b   8.00 - 15.00
  oxidized bronze.
Six Scouts marching. 39 mm,   1967   Dio.1967.02c   10.00 - 17.50
  oxidized silvered bronze.

Six Scouts marching. 39 mm, 1967   Dio.1967.02d   20.00 - 30.00
.999 fine silver.

Region Eleven Friendship Medal. 1967   Dio.1967.03   8.00 - 15.00
35 mm, white metal.

XII WORLD JAMBOREE, I AM INDIAN TEA
White plastic.   1967   Dio.1967.04   8.00 - 15.00

**XII WORLD JAMBOREE, TRANS-ATLANTIC COUNCIL,
BSA, HEIDELBERG, GERMANY**
36 mm, bronze.   1967   Dio.1967.05   10.00 - 15.00

**CAMP ALEXANDER, COLORADO SPRINGS, CO.
JULY 1967, ONE FARE.**
24 mm, brass.   1967   Dio.1967.06   2.00 - 5.00

NASSAU COUNTY COUNCIL, NY. TEDDY ROOSEVELT FACE.
45 mm, bronzed pot metal,   1967   Dio.1967.07   10.00 - 17.50
uniface.

**BSA NATIONAL MEETING, PITTSBURGH, PA.
U.S. STEEL CO. LOGO.**
51 mm, steel.   1967   Dio.1967.09   2.00 - 5.00

PIKE'S PEAK COUNCIL, CO. REGION 8 ANNUAL MEETING.
Elongated cent.   1967   Dio.1967.10   3.00 - 8.00
Elongated dime.   1967   Dio.1967.11   8.00 - 15.00
Set of elongated cent, nickel,   1967   Dio.1967.12   50.00 - 70.00
dime, quarter, and half dollar.

NOAC, MAKA INA LODGE #350. ARROW HEAD.
44 mm x 35 mm uniface, nickel. 1967   Dio.1967.14   5.00 - 10.00

BSA, OFFICIAL POCKET PIECE. SCOUT LAW, SCOUT OATH.
39 mm, bronze.   1968   Dio.1968.01   2.00 - 5.00

BSA, PEDRO, GOOD LUCK
38 mm, bronze.   1968   Dio.1968.02   2.00 - 5.00

LOS ANGELES AREA COUNCIL, CA. SCOUT-O-RAMA.
39 mm, aluminum.   1968   Dio.1968.03   5.00 - 10.00

LEWIS-CLARK TRAIL PROJECT
35 mm, bronze.   1968   Dio.1968.09   15.00 - 25.00

**CHIEF GREEN'S 20TH ANNIVERSARY IN SCOUTING,
GREATER CLEVELAND COUNCIL.**
32 mm, aluminum.   1968   Dio.1968.10   10.00 - 17.50

**NATIONAL SCOUT JAMBOREE, OFFICIAL MEDAL.
DEER, MAP OF IDAHO REVERSE.**
34 mm, bronze.   1969   Dio.1969.01a   2.00 - 5.00
34 mm, oxidized silvered bronze. 1969   Dio.1969.01b   3.00 - 8.00

**NATIONAL SCOUT JAMBOREE,
TROOP 10, PENINSULA COUNCIL, VA**
39 mm, aluminum, golden color. 1969   Dio.1969.03   8.00 - 15.00

**NATIONAL SCOUT JAMBOREE,
TROOP 70, MOUNT RAINIER COUNCIL, WA**
34 mm, bronze.   1969   Dio.1969.04   8.00 - 15.00

NATIONAL SCOUT JAMBOREE, GREAT NORTHERN RAILWAY
34 mm, bronze.   1969   Dio.1969.05   5.00 - 10.00

NATIONAL SCOUT JAMBOREE, KAISER ALUMINUM CO.
39 mm, aluminum.   1969   Dio.1969.06   10.00 - 17.50

**NATIONAL SCOUT JAMBOREE,
WASHINGTON WHEAT GROWERS ASSOC.**
36 mm, aluminum.   1969   Dio.1969.07   8.00 - 15.00

**NATIONAL SCOUT JAMBOREE,
TROOP 13, RIVERSIDE COUNTY COUNCIL, CA**
34 mm, cast pot metal.   1969   Dio.1969.08   10.00 - 17.50
49 mm, cast pot metal.   1969   Dio.1969.09   10.00 - 17.50

CALUMET COUNCIL, IL-IN. PEACE PIPE ON SCOUT BADGE.
39 mm, thin aluminum.   1969   Dio.1969.10   8.00 - 15.00

**NATIONAL CAPITAL AREA COUNCIL,
ADMIRAL ARLEIGH BURKE. SCOUTER OF THE YEAR.**
39 mm, bronze.   1969   Dio.1969.11a   15.00 - 25.00
39 mm, proof bronze.   1969   Dio.1969.11b   10.00 - 17.50
39 mm, .925 silver.   1969   Dio.1969.11c   20.00 - 30.00
39 mm, 18 kt. gold.   1969   Dio.1969.11d   350.00 - 500.00

PIKE'S PEAK COUNCIL, CO. BOY POWER AWARD
39 mm, aluminum, golden color. 1969   Dio.1969.12a   10.00 - 17.50
39 mm, oxidized copper-nickel. 1969   Dio.1969.12b   15.00 - 25.00

NATIONAL SCOUT JAMBOREE, CLEVE COEUR COUNCIL, IL
30 mm, golden plastic.   1969   Dio.1969.17   3.00 - 8.00

**ALPHA PHI OMEGA, 45TH ANNIVERSARY
NATIONAL CONVENTION**
39 mm, aluminum.   1970   Dio.1970.06a   5.00 - 10.00
39 mm, .999 fine silver.   1970   Dio.1970.06b   8.00 - 15.00

**13TH WORLD JAMBOREE, ASAGAI HEIGHTS,
NIPPON, U.S. CONTINGENT**
32 mm, bronze.   1971   Dio.1971.01a   1.00 - 3.00
32 mm, .925 silver.   1971   Dio.1971.01b   20.00 - 30.00

13TH WORLD JAMBOREE, WASHINGTON TRAIL COUNCIL, PA
35 mm, aluminum.   1971   Dio.1971.02   3.00 - 8.00

13TH WORLD JAMBOREE, NEW ORLEANS COUNCIL, LA
39 mm, aluminum.   1971   Dio.1971.03a   8.00 - 15.00
39 mm, aluminum,   1971   Dio.1971.03b   2.00 - 5.00
colored purple.
39 mm, aluminum, colored   1971   Dio.1971.03c   2.00 - 5.00
purple, reverse rotated.
39 mm, bronze.   1971   Dio.1971.03d   10.00 - 17.50
39 mm, aluminum, colored blue. 1971   Dio.1971.03e   3.00 - 8.00

**13TH WORLD JAMBOREE,
PHILADELPHIA AND LANCASTER COUNCILS, PA**
39 mm, aluminum.   1971   Dio.1971.04   5.00 - 10.00

**13TH WORLD JAMBOREE,
BADEN-POWELL ELONGATED CENT.**
Copper.   1971   Dio.1971.05a   1.00 - 3.00

13TH WORLD JAMBOREE, BADEN-POWELL ELONGATED DIME.
Copper-nickel, clad.   1971   Dio.1971.05b   1.00 - 3.00

BOYPOWER/MANPOWER, SCOUT OATH
38 mm, silvered bronze.   1971   Dio.1971.06a   5.00 - 10.00
38 mm, bronze.   1971   Dio.1971.06b   2.00 - 5.00

BOYPOWER/MANPOWER. PROJECT SOAR
38 mm, bronze.   1971   Dio.1971.07   5.00 - 10.00

REYNOLDS ALUMINUM COMPANY RECYCLING PROJECT
41 mm, olive-colored rubber w/ 1971   Dio.1971.08   5.00 - 10.00
magnet inside.

**LANCASTER COUNTY COUNCIL
JAMBOREE PARTICIPATION AWARD**
41 mm, aluminum.   1971   Dio.1971.12   1.00 - 2.00

REGION III ANNUAL MEETING, PITTSBURGH, PA
52 mm, steel.   1971   Dio.1971.13   5.00 - 10.00

**LOST LAKE SCOUT RESERVATION,
CLINTON VALLEY COUNCIL, MI**
33 mm, bronze.   1971   Dio.1971.14   8.00 - 15.00

13TH WORLD JAMBOREE, TROOP 412, OHIO
37 mm x 26 mm, bronze,   1971   Dio.1971.15   10.00 - 17.50
uniface.

SALVATION ARMY,
  NEW ORLEANS AREA COUNCIL SCOUT GOOD TURN

39 mm, aluminum.	1971	Dio.1971.16a	2.00 - 5.00
39 mm, aluminum, golden color.	1971	Dio.1971.16b	2.00 - 5.00

SPIRIT OF SCOUTING, FRANKLIN MINT

A Scout is Trustworthy. 39 mm, .925 silver.	1972	Dio.1972.01	15.00 - 25.00
A Scout is Loyal. 39 mm, .925 silver.	1972	Dio.1972.02	15.00 - 25.00
A Scout is Helpful. 39 mm, .925 silver.	1972	Dio.1972.03	15.00 - 25.00
A Scout is Friendly. 39 mm, .925 silver.	1972	Dio.1972.04	15.00 - 25.00
A Scout is Courteous. 39 mm, .925 silver.	1972	Dio.1972.05	15.00 - 25.00
A Scout is Kind. 39 mm, .925 silver.	1972	Dio.1972.06	15.00 - 25.00
A Scout is Obedient. 39 mm, .925 silver.	1972	Dio.1972.07	15.00 - 25.00
A Scout is Cheerful. 39 mm, .925 silver.	1972	Dio.1972.08	15.00 - 25.00
A Scout is Thrifty. 39 mm, .925 silver.	1972	Dio.1972.09	15.00 - 25.00
A Scout is Brave. 39 mm, .925 silver.	1972	Dio.1972.10	15.00 - 25.00
A Scout is Clean. 39 mm, .925 silver.	1972	Dio.1972.11	15.00 - 25.00
A Scout is Reverent. 39 mm, .925 silver.	1972	Dio.1972.12	15.00 - 25.00

BLACKHAWK COUNCIL, IL, U.S. GRANT SESQUICENTENNIAL

44 mm, bronze.	1972	Dio.1972.14	8.00 - 15.00

SALVATION ARMY, NEW ORLEANS AREA COUNCIL, LA.
  SCOUT GOOD TURN.

39 mm, aluminum.	1972	Dio.1972.19a	2.00 - 5.00
39 mm, aluminum, golden color.	1972	Dio.1972.19b	2.00 - 5.00

BOYPOWER/MANPOWER. ELONGATED CENT.

Copper.	1972	Dio.1972.20	2.00 - 5.00

8TH NATIONAL SCOUT JAMBOREE.
  FARRAGUT ID, MORAINE, PA. OFFICIAL MEDAL.

39 mm, bronze.	1973	Dio.1973.01a	2.00 - 5.00
39 mm, oxidized silvered bronze.	1973	Dio.1973.01b	3.00 - 8.00

1937 JAMBOREE/LINCOLN MEMORIAL

Restrike. 39 mm, bronze.	1973	Dio.1973.02	1.00 - 2.00

1950 JAMBOREE MEDAL,
  LARGE KNEELING GEORGE WASHINGTON

Restrike. 39 mm, bronze.	1973	Dio.1973.03	1.00 - 2.00

1953 JAMBOREE MEDAL. MAP OF CALIFORNIA.

Restrike. 39 mm, bronze.	1973	Dio.1973.04	1.00 - 2.00

1957 JAMBOREE MEDAL

Restrike. 39 mm, bronze.	1973	Dio.1973.05	1.00 - 2.00

1960 JAMBOREE MEDAL

Restrike. 39 mm, bronze.	1973	Dio.1973.06	1.00 - 2.00

1964 JAMBOREE MEDAL

Restrike. 39 mm, bronze.	1973	Dio.1973.07	1.00 - 2.00

1969 JAMBOREE MEDAL

Restrike. 39 mm, bronze.	1973	Dio.1973.08	1.00 - 2.00

1973 NATIONAL JAMBOREE, LONGS PEAK COUNCIL,
  CHEYENNE, WY, TROOP 101

39 mm, bronze.	1973	Dio.1973.10a	5.00 - 10.00
39 mm, .999 fine silver.	1973	Dio.1973.10b	20.00 - 30.00

1973 NATIONAL JAMBOREE EAST. TROOP 44, BROOKLYN CT

47 mm, lead.	1973	Dio.1973.11	5.00 - 10.00

1973 NATIONAL JAMBOREE, LONGS PEAK COUNCIL, WY,
  TROOP 3

39 mm, aluminum.	1973	Dio.1973.12	8.00 - 15.00

BICENTENNIAL PROGRAM, GIFT

39 mm, bronze.	1973	Dio.1973.13	2.00 - 5.00

NORMAN ROCKWELL'S FONDEST MEMORIES, FRANKLIN MINT

The Big Parade. Two Scouts holding American flag, 50 mm x 64 mm, .925 silver.	1973	Dio.1973.15	25.00 - 40.00

SALVATION ARMY, NEW ORLEANS AREA COUNCIL.
  SCOUT GOOD TURN.

40 mm, aluminum.	1973	Dio.1973.17a	2.00 - 5.00
40 mm, aluminum, golden color.	1973	Dio.1973.17b	2.00 - 5.00

TUSCARORA COUNCIL, NC, 50TH ANNIVERSARY

34 mm, copper-nickel.	1973	Dio.1973.18	10.00 - 17.50

1973 JAMBOREE EAST. PIASA BIRD COUNCIL,
  WINCHESTER WESTERN.

28 mm, bronze.	1973	Dio.1973.19	5.00 - 10.00

1973 JAMBOREE EAST. TROOP 353, RALEIGH, NC.

34 mm, brass.	1973	Dio.1973.20	8.00 - 15.00

ROCKLAND COUNTY COUNCIL, NY. 50TH ANNIVERSARY.
  DANIEL CARTER BEARD.

51 mm, bronze.	1974	Dio.1974.01a	10.00 - 17.50
51 mm, .925 silver, gilt.	1974	Dio.1974.01b	35.00 - 50.00
51 mm, .925 silver.	1974	Dio.1974.01c	20.00 - 30.00

SCOUT OATH SERIES, WITTNAUER MINT

The Scout Oath. 40 mm, silver.	1974	Dio.1974.01a	15.00 - 25.00
The Scout Oath. 40 mm, bronze, proof.	1974	Dio.1974.01b	10.00 - 15.00
On My Honor 40 mm, silver.	1974	Dio.1974.02a	15.00 - 25.00
On My Honor. 40 mm, bronze, proof.	1974	Dio.1974.02b	10.00 - 15.00
I Will Do My Best. 40 mm, silver.	1974	Dio.1974.03a	15.00 - 25.00
I Will Do My Best. 40 mm, bronze, proof.	1974	Dio.1974.03b	10.00 - 15.00
To Do My Duty to God. 40 mm, silver.	1974	Dio.1974.04a	15.00 - 25.00
To Do My Duty to God. 40 mm, bronze, proof.	1974	Dio.1974.04b	10.00 - 15.00
And My Country. 40 mm, silver.	1974	Dio.1974.05a	15.00 - 25.00
And My Country. 40 mm, bronze, proof.	1974	Dio.1974.05b	10.00 - 15.00
To Obey the Scout Law. 40 mm, silver.	1974	Dio.1974.06a	15.00 - 25.00
To Obey the Scout Law. 40 mm, bronze, proof.	1974	Dio.1974.06b	10.00 - 15.00
To Help Other People at all Times. 40 mm, silver.	1974	Dio.1974.07a	15.00 - 25.00
To Help Other People at all Times. 40 mm, bronze, proof.	1974	Dio.1974.07b	10.00 - 15.00
To Keep Myself Physically Strong. 40 mm, silver.	1974	Dio.1974.08a	15.00 - 25.00
To Keep Myself Physically Strong. 40 mm, bronze, proof.	1974	Dio.1974.08b	10.00 - 15.00
Mentally Awake. 40 mm, silver.	1974	Dio.1974.09a	15.00 - 25.00
Mentally Awake. 40 mm, bronze, proof.	1974	Dio.1974.09b	10.00 - 15.00
And Morally Straight. 40 mm, silver.	1974	Dio.1974.10a	15.00 - 25.00
And Morally Straight. 40 mm, bronze, proof.	1974	Dio.1974.10b	10.00 - 15.00
Be Prepared. 40 mm, silver.	1974	Dio.1974.11a	15.00 - 25.00
Be Prepared. 40 mm, bronze, proof.	1974	Dio.1974.11b	10.00 - 15.00
Do A Good Turn Daily. 40 mm, silver.	1974	Dio.1974.12a	15.00 - 25.00
Do A Good Turn Daily. 40 mm, bronze, proof.	1974	Dio.1974.12b	10.00 - 15.00

TROOP 44, BROOKLYN, CT. 25TH ANNIVERSARY.

39 mm, bronze.	1974	Dio.1974.14	5.00 - 10.00

BICENTENNIAL. BE PREPARED FOR LIFE.

39 mm, bronze.	1974	Dio.1974.15	2.00 - 50.00

TACONIC DISTRICT, WASHINGTON IRVING COUNCIL, NY. KLONDIKE DERBY.

47 mm, aluminum.	1974	Dio.1974.16	8.00 - 15.00

NATIONAL CAPITAL AREA COUNCIL. GERALD R. FORD, SCOUTER OF THE YEAR.

40 mm, proof bronze.	1974	Dio.1974.17a	15.00 - 25.00
40 mm, proof silver.	1974	Dio.1974.17b	25.00 - 40.00
40 mm, proof 18kt. gold.	1974	Dio.1974.17c	350.00 - 500.00

SALVATION ARMY, NEW ORLEANS AREA COUNCIL, LA. SCOUT GOOD TURN.

39 mm, aluminum.	1974	Dio.1974.18a	2.00 - 5.00
39 mm, aluminum, golden color.	1974	Dio.1974.18b	2.00 - 5.00

14TH WORLD JAMBOREE, TROOP 3-1, LA-TX

40 mm, aluminum, purple color.	1975	Dio.1975.01a	2.00 - 5.00
40 mm, aluminum.	1975	Dio.1975.01b	2.00 - 5.00

BICENTENNIAL, HERITAGE '76

40 mm, bronze.	1975	Dio.1975.02	2.00 - 5.00

BICENTENNIAL, HORIZONS '76

40 mm, bronze.	1975	Dio.1975.03	2.00 - 5.00

BICENTENNIAL, FESTIVAL U.S.A.

40 mm, bronze.	1975	Dio.1975.04	2.00 - 5.00

14TH WORLD JAMBOREE. SCOUTING/ U.S.A., SCOUT LAW.

31 mm, copper-nickel.	1975	Dio.1975.05	3.00 - 8.00

NORDJAMB '75 , YOU MAKE THE DIFFERENCE

22 mm, brass.	1975	Dio.1975.06	3.00 - 8.00

NORDJAMB '75/NEW ORLEANS AREA COUNCIL POW WOW

39 mm, aluminum, golden color.	1975	Dio.1975.07a	2.00 - 5.00
39 mm, aluminum.	1975	Dio.1975.07b	2.00 - 5.00
39 mm, aluminum, purple color.	1975	Dio.1975.07c	2.00 - 5.00
39 mm, aluminum, orange color.	1975	Dio.1975.07d	2.00 - 5.00

BI-CENT-O-RAMA. TROOP 76

50 mm, pot metal, uniface.	1975	Dio.1975.08	5.00 - 10.00

ARCH MONSON, JR. PRESIDENT, BOY SCOUTS OF AMERICA. GREETINGS.

40 mm, aluminum.	1975	Dio.1975.10	3.00 - 8.00

OA, NE REGION SECTION 4A

51 mm x 39 mm, brass, uniface.	1975	Dio.1975.11	5.00 - 10.00

BUFFALO TRAIL COUNCIL, TX. AMERICA'S BICENTENNIAL.

39 mm, oxidized bronze.	1976	Dio.1976.01a	8.00 - 15.00
39 mm, oxidized brass.	1976	Dio.1976.01b	8.00 - 15.00
39 mm, .925 silver.	1976	Dio.1976.01c	25.00 - 40.00

CONCHO VALLEY COUNCIL, TX. AMERICA'S BICENTENNIAL.

35 mm, copper-nickel.	1976	Dio.1976.02	8.00 - 15.00

LANCASTER, PA. SCOUT SHOW

40 mm, aluminum.	1976	Dio.1976.03	5.00 - 10.00

LONG RIVERS COUNCIL, BICENTENNIAL ENCAMPMENT

35 mm, bronze.	1976	Dio.1976.04	5.00 - 10.00

BSA, NATIONAL ISSUE. BICENTENNIAL.

64 mm, bronze.	1976	Dio.1976.05	8.00 - 15.00

ARROWHEAD DISTRICT, COLUMBUS, OH. BICENTENNIAL CAMPORAL.

38 mm, tan plastic w/ red lettering.	1976	Dio.1976.06	2.00 - 5.00

NORTHWEST SUBURBAN COUNCIL, IL, 50TH ANNIVERSARY

43 mm, pewter, uniface. Exists plain, as a bolo, or mounted on a block.	1976	Dio.1976.07	8.00 - 15.00

NATIONAL SCOUT JAMBOREE, OFFICIAL MEDAL. MORAINE STATE PARK, PA.

39 mm, bronze.	1977	Dio.1977.01a	2.00 - 5.00
39 mm, oxidized copper-nickel.	1977	Dio.1977.01b	3.00 - 8.00

BLACKHAWK AREA COUNCIL, IL-WI

49 mm, stainless steel.	1977	Dio.1977.02a	5.00 - 10.00
49 mm, copper.	1977	Dio.1977.02b	15.00 - 25.00

NATIONAL SCOUT JAMBOREE AZIMUTH TRAIL

33 mm, green plastic, white letters.	1977	Dio.1977.03	2.00 - 5.00

NATIONAL SCOUT JAMBOREE. WE FOUND IT.
33 mm, red plastic, white letters. 1977   Dio.1977.04   2.00 - 5.00

NORTHEAST REGION PONTOON PASS,
GEORGE CUHAJ PERSONAL TOKEN
38 mm, green plastic,   1977   Dio.1977.07   2.00 - 5.00
white lettering.

ORDER OF THE ARROW, BSA
43 mm, pewter, uniface. Set into 1977   Dio.1977.20   8.00 - 15.00
a larger medal or plaque.
German in origin.

LANCASTER-LEGANON COUNCIL. LONG PARK, JUNE 1978.
33 mm, aluminum.   1978   Dio.1978.01a   3.00 - 8.00
33 mm, bronze.   1978   Dio.1978.01b   5.00 - 10.00

GENERAL GREEN COUNCIL, NC. 1978 IRISH JAMBOREE.
Copper.   1978   Dio.1978.02   3.00 - 8.00

NATIONAL ORDER OF THE ARROW CONFERENCE. FT.
COLLINS, CO. FOUNDERS DAY AWARD.
32 mm, brass.   1979   Dio.1979.01   5.00 - 10.00

I DELIVERED THE PROMISE, 1979. SCOUT BADGE.
36 mm, aluminum.   1979   Dio.1979.02   3.00 - 8.00

SUANHACKY LODGE #49. GOLDEN ANNIVERSARY BANQUET.
42 mm, red plastic, gold   1979   Dio.1979.03   1.00 - 3.00
lettering.

NATIONAL COUNCIL MEETING, NEW ORLEANS, LA
40 mm, aluminum.   1980   Dio.1980.01   3.00 - 8.00

SUANHACKY LODGE #49. LODGE BANQUET.
42 mm, white plastic,   1980   Dio.1980.03   1.00 - 3.00
red lettering.

SUANHACKY LODGE #49. 50TH ANNIVERSARY ORDEAL,
CAMP KERNOCHAN.
42 mm, black plastic, gold   1980   Dio.1980.04   1.00 - 3.00
lettering.

LANCASTER-LEBANON COUNCIL. LONG'S PARK.
SHOWMAN SAM.
36 mm, aluminum.   1980   Dio.1980.05   3.00 - 8.00

EAGLE TROOP 31, LOS ALTOS, CA. GOOD FOR $1 IN TRADE.
32 mm, brass.   1980   Dio.1980.06   3.00 - 8.00

1981 NATIONAL SCOUT JAMBOREE, OFFICIAL MEDAL, FT.
A.P. HILL, VA.
40 mm, copper-nickel,   1981   Dio.1981.01   2.00 - 5.00
reeded edge.

1981 NATIONAL SCOUT JAMBOREE, OFFICIAL MEDAL
40 mm, copper-nickel, reeded 1981   Dio.1981.01b   5.00 - 10.00
edge. Set into a lucite block.

1937 JAMBOREE MEDAL. RESTRIKE.
40 mm, copper-nickel,   1981   Dio.1981.02   1.00 - 2.00
reeded edge.

1950 JAMBOREE MEDAL. RESTRIKE.
40 mm, copper-nickel,   1981   Dio.1981.03   1.00 - 2.00
reeded edge.

1953 JAMBOREE MEDAL. RESTRIKE.
40 mm, copper-nickel,   1981   Dio.1981.04   1.00 - 2.00
reeded edge.

1957 JAMBOREE MEDAL. RESTRIKE.
40 mm, copper-nickel,   1981   Dio.1981.05   1.00 - 2.00
reeded edge.

1960 JAMBOREE MEDAL. RESTRIKE.
40 mm, copper-nickel,   1981   Dio.1981.07   1.00 - 2.00
reeded edge.

1964 JAMBOREE MEDAL. RESTRIKE.
40 mm, copper-nickel,   1981   Dio.1981.08   1.00 - 2.00
reeded edge.

1969 JAMBOREE MEDAL. RESTRIKE.
40 mm, copper-nickel,   1981   Dio.1981.09   1.00 - 2.00
reeded edge.

1973 JAMBOREE MEDAL. RESTRIKE.
40 mm, copper-nickel,   1981   Dio.1981.10   1.00 - 2.00
reeded edge.

1977 JAMBOREE MEDAL. RESTRIKE.
40 mm, copper-nickel,   1981   Dio.1981.10   1.00 - 2.00
reeded edge.

NATIONAL JAMBOREE. JOHNNY APPLESEED AREA COUNCIL,
OH.
33 mm, brass.   1981   Dio.1981.11   3.00 - 8.00

NATIONAL JAMBOREE. COIN COLLECTING MERIT BADGE
MIDWAY BOOTH. ELONGATED CENT.
Copper.   1981   Dio.1981.12   1.00 - 2.00

NATIONAL JAMBOREE. COIN COLLECTING MERIT BADGE
MIDWAY BOOTH. ELONGATED.
Issued on nickel, dime, quarter, 1981   Dio.1981.12b-h   5.00 - 10.00
half dollar, and SBA dollar.
Clean design and cancelled die.

NATIONAL JAMBOREE, INLAND EMPIRE COUNCIL, CA.
TROOP 701-702.
34 mm, brass.   1981   Dio.1981.13   5.00 - 10.00

NATIONAL JAMBOREE. SANTA CLARA COUNTY, CA.
SILICON CHIP ATTACHED TO CENTER OF DISC.
32 mm, aluminum.   1981   Dio.1981.14   5.00 - 10.00

NATIONAL JAMBOREE. GEORGE H. LANIER COUNCIL,
AL-GA.
59 mm, aluminum, cast, uniface. 1981   Dio.1981.15   8.00 - 15.00

ORDER OF THE ARROW, BSA
Founders of the Order.   1981   Dio.1981.16a   2.00 - 8.00
  40 mm, oxidized bronze.
Founders of the Order.   1981   Dio.1981.16b   20.00 - 30.00
  40 mm, .925 silver.
Treasure Island.   1981   Dio.1981.17a   3.00 - 8.00
  40 mm, oxidized bronze.
Treasure Island.   1981   Dio.1981.17b   20.00 - 30.00
  40 mm, .925 silver.
Early Ceremony.   1981   Dio.1981.18a   3.00 - 8.00
  40 mm, oxidized bronze.
Early Ceremony.   1981   Dio.1981.18b   20.00 - 30.00
  40 mm, .925 silver.
The Ordeal.   1981   Dio.1981.19a   3.00 - 8.00
  40 mm, oxidized bronze.
The Ordeal. 40 mm, .925 silver. 1981   Dio.1981.19b   20.00 - 30.00
OA Fireplace, Brotherhood Barn. 1981   Dio.1981.20a   3.00 - 8.00
  40 mm, oxidized bronze.
OA Fireplace, Brotherhood Barn. 1981   Dio.1981.20b   20.00 - 30.00
  40 mm, .925 silver.

SUANHACKY LODGE #49. JOHANNES KNOOPS, LODGE CHIEF
PERSONAL TOKEN.
42 mm, white plastic,   1981   Dio.1981.21   2.00 - 5.00
red lettering.

NATIONAL JAMBOREE,
SCUBAPRO SNORKEL SWIMMING AWARD
31 mm, bronze.   1981   Dio.1981.22   3.00 - 8.00

NATIONAL JAMBOREE. ORANGE COUNCIL, CA, TROOP 5.
37 mm, orange plastic,   1981   Dio.1981.23   3.00 - 8.00
raised lettering.

Patrol of Eagle Scouts on their way to the 1947 World Jamboree visit the Statue of Liberty.

ROBERT A. JOHNSON PERSONAL TOKEN
28 mm, green plastic, gold   1981   Dio.1981.24   1.00 - 3.00
   lettering.

NATIONAL JAMBOREE, DISPLAYS & EXHIBITS
50 mm x 26 mm,   1981   Dio.1981.25   5.00 - 10.00
   aluminum, uniface.

NATIONAL JAMBOREE. INLAND EMPIRE COUNCIL, CA. TROOP 700-701.
34 mm, brass.   1981   Dio.1981.26   5.00 - 10.00

NATIONAL JAMBOREE, EAST CENTRAL REGION. THANKS PLAQUE.
74 mm x 50 mm, bronze,   1981   Dio.1981.28   10.00 - 17.50
   uniface. Set into a lucite block.

NATIONAL CAPITAL AREA COUNCIL, RONALD REAGAN, SCOUTER OF THE YEAR
36 mm, proof bronze.   1982   Dio.1982.01   15.00 - 20.00

SCOUTING, 75TH ANNIVERSARY. MD. ATCA.
28 mm, white plastic,   1982   Dio.1982.03   1.00 - 3.00
   green lettering.

JOHNNY APPLESEED COUNCIL, OA. CATCH THAT PEPSI SPIRIT.
Scout Badge.   1982   Dio.1982.10   8.00 - 15.00
   38 mm, bronze, cast.
Large Tenderfoot Badge.   1982   Dio.1982.11   8.00 - 15.00
   38 mm, bronze, cast.
Large Second-Class Badge.   1982   Dio.1982.12   8.00 - 15.00
   38 mm, bronze, cast.
Large Star Badge.   1982   Dio.1982.13   8.00 - 15.00
   38 mm, bronze, cast.
Large Life Badge.   1982   Dio.1982.15   8.00 - 15.00
   38 mm, bronze, cast.
Small Tenderfoot Badge.   1982   Dio.1982.15   8.00 - 15.00
   38 mm, bronze, cast.
Eagle Scout Award.   1982   Dio.1982.16   8.00 - 15.00
   38 mm, bronze, cast.
Small Second-Class Award.   1982   Dio.1982.17   8.00 - 15.00
   38 mm, bronze, cast.
Small First-Class Badge.   1982   Dio.1982.18   8.00 - 15.00
   38 mm, bronze, cast.
Small Star Badge.   1982   Dio.1982.19   8.00 - 15.00
   38 mm, bronze, cast.

FIRST-CLASS BADGE COUNTERSTRUCK ON LINCOLN CENT
Copper.   1982   Dio.1982.20   1.00 - 2.00

75TH ANNIVERSARY OF SCOUTING. ST. GEORGE. ENAMELLED.
50 mm, brass.   1982   Dio.1982.22   3.00 - 8.00

ORDER OF THE ARROW
Ordeal, Brotherhood, Vigil.   1983   Dio.1983.01a   3.00 - 8.00
   40 mm, oxidized bronze.
Ordeal, Brotherhood, Vigil.   1983   Dio.1983.01b   20.00 - 30.00
   40 mm, .925 silver.
Lenni Lenape.   1983   Dio.1983.02a   3.00 - 8.00
   40 mm, oxidized bronze.
Lenni Lenape.   1983   Dio.1983.02b   20.00 - 30.00
   40 mm, .925 silver.
Carroll A. Edson.   1983   Dio.1983.03a   3.00 - 5.00
   40 mm, oxidized bronze.
Carroll A. Edson.   1983   Dio.1983.03b   20.00 - 30.00
   40 mm, .925 silver.
Dr. E. Urner Goodman.   1983   Dio.1983.04a   3.00 - 8.00
   40 mm, oxidized bronze.
Dr. E. Urner Goodman.   1983   Dio.1983.04b   20.00 - 30.00
   40 mm, .925 silver.
The Legend.   1983   Dio.1983.05a   3.00 - 5.00
   40 mm, oxidized bronze.
The Legend. 40 mm, .925 silver. 1983   Dio.1983.05b   20.00 - 30.00

BOB JOHNSON, SCOUTS ON TOKENS SOCIETY #1
29 mm, green plastic, gold   1983   Dio.1983.09   1.00 - 2.00
   lettering.
42 mm, white plastic,   1983   Dio.1983.06   1.00 - 2.00
   green lettering.

NOAC 1983, SE REGION, SECTION 7
29 mm, red plastic,   1983   Dio.1983.07   3.00 - 5.00
   gold lettering.

SCOUTING, 1907-1983, MATCA, 16 YEARS
28 mm, white plastic,   1983   Dio.1983.08   1.00 - 2.00
   green lettering.

XV WORLD JAMBOREE, TROOP 605
Elongate cent, copper.   1983   Dio.1983.10   1.00 - 3.00

SUANHACKY LODGE #49. NOAC DELEGATE.
42 mm, white plastic,   1983   Dio.1983.11   1.00 - 3.00
   red lettering.

GREATER NEW YORK COUNCILS, NY. KEY TO SCOUTING.
55 mm x 85 mm,   1983   Dio.1983.12   5.00 - 10.00
   cast pewter, uniface.

SCOUTS ON TOKENS SOCIETY, 1ST ANNIVERSARY
29 mm, white plastic,   1984   Dio.1984.01   1.00 - 2.00
   green lettering.

SCOUTS ON TOKENS SOCIETY, SCOUTING 1984
29 mm, white plastic,   1984   Dio.1984.02   1.00 - 2.00
   green lettering.

LDS SCOUT ENCAMPMENT, FARRAGUT STATE PARK, ID
Elongate cent, copper.   1984   Dio.1984.03   2.00 - 4.00

NATIONAL SCOUT JAMBOREE, OFFICIAL MEDAL
36 mm, bronze.   1960   Dio.1960.04   3.00 - 8.00
38 mm, bronze.   1985   Dio.1985.01   3.00 - 5.00

FOOTSTEPS OF THE FOUNDER. WORLD SCOUTING 75TH ANNIVERSARY.
37 mm, cast pewter, uniface.   1985   Dio.1985.02   3.00 - 5.00
   Often encountered as a bolo.

NATIONAL JAMBOREE, DANIEL WEBSTER COUNCIL, NH
40 mm, bronze.   1985   Dio.1985.03   3.00 - 5.00

NATIONAL JAMBOREE, COIN COLLECTING MERIT BADGE BOOTH. GEORGE CUHAJ PERSONAL TOKEN.
42 mm, green plastic,   1985   Dio.1985.05   1.00 - 3.00
   gold letting.

NATIONAL JAMBOREE, PIASA BIRD COUNCIL, IL
27 mm, brass.   1985   Dio.1985.06   5.00 - 10.00

TENDERFOOT BADGE
38 mm, cast pewter,   1985   Dio.1985.07   3.00 - 7.50
   high relief, uniface.
   Usually found as a bolo.

CATCH THE SCOUTING SPIRIT
38 mm, cast pewter, uniface.   1985   Dio.1985.08   3.00 - 7.50
   Usually found as a bolo.

SOAR FOR THE BETTER LIFE
38 mm, cast pewter, uniface.   1985   Dio.1985.09   3.00 - 5.00
   Usually found as a bolo.

DIAMOND JUBILEE, 75TH DIAMOND LOGO
38 mm, cast pewter, uniface.   1985   Dio.1985.10   2.00 - 5.00
   Usually found as a bolo.

CAMP SUNNEN, CAHOKIA MOUND COUNCIL
38 mm, cast pewter, uniface.   1985   Dio.1985.11   2.00 - 5.00
   Usually found as a bolo.

75TH ANNIVERSARY DIAMOND LOGO, REVERSE A PLAIN WREATH AND SPACE FOR ENGRAVED PLAQUE.

76 mm, bronze.	1985	Dio.1985.12	2.00 - 5.00

NATIONAL JAMBOREE, SOUTH CENTRAL REGION

Youth Staff. 38 mm, cast pewter, uniface. Usually found as a bolo.	1985	Dio.1985.13	5.00 - 10.00
Adult Staff. 38 mm, cast pewter, uniface. Usually found as a bolo.	1985	Dio.1985.14	5.00 - 10.00
Youth Leader. 38 mm, cast pewter, uniface. Usually found as a bolo.	1985	Dio.1985.15	5.00 - 10.00
Adult Leader. 38 mm, cast pewter, uniface. Usually found as a bolo.	1985	Dio.1985.16	5.00 - 10.00

NATIONAL JAMBOREE, ORANGE COUNTY, CA. TROOPS 867-868.

33 mm, pewter.	1985	Dio.1985.17	2.00 - 5.00

NATIONAL JAMBOREE, WEST CENTRAL FLORIDA COUNCIL, TROOP 15. TUIT.

39 mm, tan plastic, red lettering.	1985	Dio.1985.18	2.00 - 5.00

NATIONAL SCOUT JAMBOREE, FAIRFIELD COUNTY COUNCIL, CT. TROOP 402.

38 mm, copper.	1985	Dio.1985.19a	5.00 - 7.50
38 mm, copper-nickel.	1985	Dio.1985.19b	2.00 - 5.00
38 mm, copper, 1/2" thick.	1985	Dio.1985.19c	20.00 - 30.00

SAN BERNADINO COIN CLUB. CA. SALUTES SCOUTING, 22ND ANNUAL COIN SHOW.

32 mm, aluminum.	1985	Dio.1985.20	2.00 - 5.00

LOS ALTOS EAGLE TROOP 31. GOOD FOR $1 IN TRADE. SALUTES 75TH ANNIVERSARY.

32 mm, brass.	1985	Dio.1985.21	3.00 - 5.00

75TH ANNIVERSARY, NATIONAL MEDAL. PRIDE IN THE PAST, FOOTSTEPS OF THE FUTURE.

38 mm, bronze.	1985	Dio.1985.22	3.00 - 5.00

NATIONAL JAMBOREE, DISPLAYS AND EXHIBITS

50 mm x 26 mm, aluminum.	1985	Dio.1985.23	3.00 - 5.00
50 mm x 26 mm, aluminum.	1989	Dio.1989.06	3.00 - 8.00

BOY SCOUT SALUTING, DIAMOND JUBILEE LOGO. ENGRAVED BY FRANK GASPARO.

	1985	Dio.1985.24	5.00 - 10.00

NATIONAL JAMBOREE. JAMBOREE EMBLEM ELONGATED.

Cent, copper.	1985	Dio.1985.25	1.00 - 2.00

95TH ANA CONVENTION. MILWAUKEE, COIN COLLECTING MERIT BADGE CLINIC.

Encased cent in horseshoe case.	1986	Dio.1986.01	2.00 - 5.00

ORANGE COUNTY COUNCIL, CA. SCOUT SERVICE CENTER DEDICATION.

38 mm, bronze.	1986	Dio.1986.02	7.50 - 10.00

CAMP TUSCARORA, SUSQUENANGO COUNCIL, NY. ROBERT J. MOPPERT, ROTARY.

40 mm, .999 fine silver.	1986	Dio.1986.03a	20.00 - 30.00
409 mm, oxidized bronze.	1986	Dio.1986.03b	8.00 - 15.00
40 mm, proof bronze.	1986	Dio.1986.03c	5.00 - 10.00
40 mm, aluminum.	1986	Dio.1986.03d	2.00 - 5.00

TROOP 51, 25TH ANNIVERSARY

34 mm, bronze.	1986	Dio.1986.04	2.00 - 5.00

BALTIMORE AREA COUNCIL, MD. ELONGATED CENT.

Copper.	1986	Dio.1986.05	1.00 - 2.00

EL-KU-TA LODGE #520. UT. ELONGATED CENT

Copper.	1986	Dio.1986.06	1.00 - 2.00

WOOD BADGE ELONGATED CENT

Copper.	1986	Dio.1986.07	1.00 - 2.00

BADGE POWELL ON ELONGATED CENT

Copper.	1986	Dio.1986.09	1.00 - 2.00

PIASA BIRD COUNCIL

32 mm, bronze.	1988	Dio.1988.01	2.00 - 5.00

NATIONAL COUNCIL MEETING, SAN DIEGO, CA

28 mm, aluminum.	1988	Dio.1988.02	3.00 - 8.00

NOAC. FOUNDER'S DAY AWARD. KINDLE THE FLAME FROM WITHIN.

39 mm, aluminum.	1988	Dio.1988.03	3.00 - 8.00

AH TIC LODGE 50TH ANNIVERSARY. ALPHA SINTERED METALS, RIDGEWAY, PA.

36 mm, steel.	1988	Dio.1988.04	2.00 - 5.00

PHILMONT 50TH ANNIVERSARY. PHILMONT GRACE REVERSE.

32 mm, bronze.	1988	Dio.1988.05	2.00 - 5.00

GREAT SALT LAKE COUNCIL, UT. INTERNATIONAL JAMBORAL.

38 mm, brass, uniface.	1988	Dio.1988.06	2.00 - 5.00

NATIONAL SCOUT JAMBOREE, OFFICIAL MEDAL. SPACE SHUTTLE AND SAY NO TO DRUGS

38 mm, bronze.	1989	Dio.1989.01	3.00 - 5.00

NATIONAL JAMBOREE. BSA HIGH ADVENTURE.

Elongated cent, copper.	1989	Dio.1989.02	1.00 - 2.00

NATIONAL JAMBOREE. TROOP 817.

37 mm, black plastic, raised letters.	1989	Dio.1989.03	3.00 - 8.00

NATIONAL TOP HANDS CONFERENCE, ORLANDO, FL. HIGH ADVENTURE

Elongate Cent, copper.	1989	Dio.1989.04	1.00 - 2.00

BLACKHAWK AREA COUNCIL. 1989 CAMPOREE.

39 mm, aluminum, uniface.	1989	Dio.1989.05	2.00 - 4.00

NATIONAL JAMBOREE, DISPLAYS AND EXHIBITS

50 mm x 26 mm, aluminum.	1985	Dio.1985.23	3.00 - 5.00
50 mm x 26 mm, aluminum.	1989	Dio.1989.06	3.00 - 8.00

FLORIDA SEA BASE. HIGH ADVENTURE.

Elongated cent, copper.	1989	Dio.1989.07	1.00 - 2.00

FLORIDA SEA BASE. 10TH ANNIVERSARY.

29 mm, .999 fine silver.	1990	Dio.1990.01	20.00 - 30.00

ROBERT E. LEE COUNCIL, VA. APPALACHIAN TRAIL ELONGATED CENT.

Copper.	1990	Dio.1990.01	1.00 - 2.00

SCOUT OATH ELONGATED CENT

Copper	1990	Dio.1990.02	1.00 - 2.00

SCOUT LAW ELONGATED CENT

Copper.	1990	Dio.1990.03	1.00 - 2.00

SCOUT MOTTO AND SLOGAN ELONGATED CENT

Copper.	1990	Dio.1990.04	1.00 - 2.00

NOAC '90. CEREMONY COMPETITION AWARD BENEFACTOR.

Cast bronze.	1990	Dio.1990.05	100.00 - 150.00

NOAC '90. GEORGE CUHAJ PERSONAL TOKEN & VIGIL NAME.

42 mm, white plastic, red lettering.	1990	Dio.1990.06	2.00 - 5.00

WOOD BADGE BEADS ELONGATED CENT
Copper.   1990   Dio.1990.07   1.00 - 2.00

GREAT SALT LAKE COUNCIL, UT. HERITAGE JAMBORAL.
22 mm, gilt brass.   1990   Dio.1990.08   3.00 - 8.00
38 mm, oxidized brass.   1990   Dio.1990.11   2.00 - 5.00

NOAC '90. FOUNDER'S DAY MEDAL.
  INSPIRED TO LEAD, DEDICATED TO SERVE.
39 mm, aluminum.   1990   Dio.1990.09   3.00 - 8.00

JACK KOHLER CAMPERSHIP ASSOCIATION,
  OUTSTANDING SCOUTER AWARD OF EXCELLENCE
57 mm, cast bronze, artist proof. 1990   Dio.1990.10   100.00 - 150.00

BADEN-POWELL ELONGATED CENT
Copper.   1990   Dio.1990.12   1.00 - 2.00

WOODBADGE WORDS ELONGATED CENT
Copper.   1990   Dio.1990.13   1.00 - 2.00

WOOD BADGE AXE AND LOG ELONGATED CENT
Copper.   1990   Dio.1990.14   1.00 - 2.00

MOTTO AND SLOGAN ELONGATED CENT. RR MAKER.
Copper.   1990   Dio.1990.15   1.00 - 2.00

ROBERT E. LEE COUNCIL, VA. APPALACHIAN TRAIL
  ELONGATED NICKEL, DIME, QUARTER, AND SBA DOLLAR
                                           1991   Dio.1991.02-05   5.00 - 7.50

NATIONAL TOP HANDS, NASHVILLE TN. PHILMONT
  ARROWHEAD PATCH ON ELONGATED CENT.
Copper.   1991   Dio.1991.06   1.00 - 2.00

NATIONAL TOP HANDS, NASHVILLE, TN.
  FLORIDA SEA BASE DESIGN ON ELONGATED CENT.
Copper.   1991   Dio.1991.07   1.00 - 2.00

NATIONAL TOP HANDS, NASHVILLE, TN.
  C.L. SOMMERS DESIGN ON ELONGATED CENT.
Copper.   1991   Dio.1991.08   1.00 - 2.00

BSA HIGH ADVENTURE OUTDOOR PROGRAM SEMINAR,
  DALLAS TX
Elongated cent, copper.   1991   Dio.1991.09   1.00 - 2.00

NATIONAL TOP HANDS CONFERENCE, FB MAKER
Elongated cent, copper.   1992   Dio.1992.01   1.00 - 2.00

WEST MICHIGAN SHORE COUNCIL, MI. SCOUTING RALLY.
Elongated cent, copper.   1992   Dio.1992.02   1.00 - 2.00

GREAT SALT LAKE COUNCIL, UT. JAMBORAL.
22 mm, gilt brass.   1992   Dio.1992.03   3.00 - 8.00
22 mm, gilt brass.   1992   Dio.1992.04   3.00 - 8.00

BOY SCOUT. MOTTO AND SLOGAN MEDAL.
37 mm, bronze.   1992   Dio.1992.07   1.00 - 2.00

NOAC '92. NATIONAL CEREMONY EVENTS STAFF MEDAL.
Cast bronze.   1992   Dio.1992.08   100.00 - 150.00

ISTROUMA AREA COUNCIL. MANCHAC DISTRICT. CAMPOREE.
20 mm, aluminum, yellow color. 1992   Dio.1992.10   2.00 - 3.00

GREAT SALT LAKE COUNCIL, UT. HERITAGE MEDAL.
  CP AND UP RAILROADS.
38 mm, .999 fine silver.   1993   Dio.1993.01a   20.00 - 30.00
38 mm, 24kt. plated   1993   Dio.1993.01b   30.00 - 40.00
  .999 fine silver.

NATIONAL JAMBOREE, OFFICIAL MEDAL. A BRIDGE TO THE
  FUTURE. A SCOUT IS BRAVE, HE SAYS NO TO DRUGS.
.38 mm, bronze.   1993   Dio.1993.03   3.00 - 8.00

NATIONAL JAMBOREE, COIN COLLECTING MERIT BADGE
  BOOTH
George Cuhaj personal token. 41 1993   Dio.1993.04   1.00 - 2.00
  mm, red plastic, gold lettering.
Larry Baber personal token.   1993   Dio.1993.05   1.00 - 2.00
  Green plastic, gold lettering.
Thorton Ridder personal token.   1993   Dio.1993.06   1.00 - 2.00
  Green plastic, gold lettering.
Geoffrey Allred personal token. 1993   Dio.1993.07   1.00 - 2.00
  Blue plastic, gold lettering.
J.R. Luten personal token.   1993   Dio.1993.5   1.00 - 2.00
  Black plastic, gold lettering.

NATIONAL JAMBOREE, LOGO ELONGATED CENT
Copper.   1993   Dio.1993.08   1.00 - 2.00

NATIONAL JAMBOREE. LDS
  80TH ANNIVERSARY IN SCOUTING.
39 mm, aluminum.   1993   Dio.1993.09   2.00 - 5.00

NATIONAL JAMBOREE, FLORIDA SEA BASE DOBLOON
38 mm, aluminum, gold color. 1993   Dio.1993.10   1.00 - 2.00

NATIONAL JAMBOREE. TROOP 414
Elongated cent, copper.   1993   Dio.1993.11   1.00 - 2.00

NATIONAL JAMBOREE, PONY EXPRESS COUNCIL, MO-KS
Elongated cent, copper.   1993   Dio.1993.12   1.00 - 2.00

NATIONAL JAMBOREE. CENTRAL REGION, SUB-CAMP 2.
  INITIATIVE GAMES.
28 mm, white plastic,   1993   Dio.1993.13   2.00 - 5.00
  green lettering.

NATIONAL JAMBOREE. CENTRAL REGION, SUB-CAMP 3.
  INITIATIVE GAMES.
28 mm, white plastic, red   1993   Dio.1993.14   2.00 - 5.00
  lettering.

NATIONAL JAMBOREE. CENTRAL REGION, SUB-CAMP 4.
  INITIATIVE GAMES.
28 mm, white plastic,   1993   Dio.1993.15   2.00 - 5.00
  green lettering.

NORTHEAST REGION, WILLIAM D. BOYCE, PIONEER
Portrait of Boyce. 38 mm,   1994   Dio.1994.04   7.50 - 10.00
  antique bronze, uniface.

UTAH HERITAGE, MINING
                                 1994   Dio.1994.05   10.00 - 15.00

NORTHEAST REGION, ERNEST THOMPSON SETON
Portrait of Seton. 38 mm,   1995   Dio.1995.01   7.50 - 10.00
  antique bronze, uniface.

UTAH HERITAGE, RANCHING
                                 1995   Dio.1995.02   10.00 - 15.00

EL-KU-TA, LODGE 520, ELONGATED CENT.
  LODGE FLAP DESIGN.
                                 1995   Dio.1995.03   2.00 - 3.00

NORTHEAST REGION, DANIEL CARTER BEARD
Portrait of Beard. 38 mm,   1996   Dio.1996.01   7.50 - 10.00
  antique bronze, uniface.

UTAH HERITAGE, ELK
                                 1996   Dio.1996.03   10.00 - 15.00

UTAH HERITAGE, EAGLE
                                 1996   Dio.1996.04   10.00 - 15.00

NATIONAL JAMBOREE, OFFICIAL MEDAL,
  BE PREPARED FOR THE 21ST CENTURY
Dates of the jamboree in ctr. on 1997   Dio.1997.01   4.00 - 6.00
  reverse. 38 mm, antique finish
  and polished copper-nickel.

Scouts of Wauwatosa, WI, attending Indian Mound Scout Reservation in 1928—quite handsome in full uniforms!

NATIONAL JAMBOREE, LDS CHURCH
84 YEARS OF PARTNERSHIP

Jamboree Logo and LDS Emblem. 38 mm, brown aluminumn.	1997	Dio.1997.02	2.00 - 4.00
Jamboree Emblem modified, Old and New Coin Collecting Merit Badges. 38 mm, .999 silver (ounce); 20 made.	1997	Dio.1997.03a	75.00 - 100.00
Jamboree Emblem modified, Old and New Coin Collecting Merit Badges. 38 mm, aluminum, reeded edge.	1997	Dio.1997.03b	2.00 - 3.00

NATIONAL JAMBOREE, HIGH ADVENTURE

Sommers, Philmont, Florida Sea Base logos. 38 mm, aluminum.	1997	Dio.1997.04	2.00 - 3.00

NATIONAL JAMBOREE, PONTIAC-GMC LEGEND

37 mm, pewter.	1997	Dio.1997.05	3.00 - 5.00

NATIONAL JAMBOREE, HIGH ADVENTURE ELONGATED CENT

Jamboree logo.	1997	Dio.1997.06	1.00 - 2.00

NATIONAL JAMBOREE, METALWORK, MERIT BADGE

Eagle Stamp, NJ 97 flanking. 37 mm, aluminum, handstamped.	1997	Dio.1997.07	4.00 - 5.00

NATIONAL JAMBOREE, FDL STAMPED OUT IN DISC,
97 JAMBOREE ENGRAVED W/ HANDTOOL

44 mm, steel; 60 made.	1997	Dio.1997.08	5.00 - 7.50

PETERS SHOE CO. ST. LOUIS, MO.
DIAMOND BRAND OF SHOES. SCOUT STRIDING W/ STAFF.

32 mm, bronze.	1920-1920	Dio.U.2	25.00 - 35.00

CIVIC GOOD TURN. TENDERFOOT BADGE.

29 mm, silvered brass.	1920	Dio.U.3	15.00 - 25.00

BSA. OFFICIAL. TENDERFOOT BADGE WITHIN WREATH.

Reverse black for engraving. 76 mm, bronze.	1960	Dio.U.09	1.00 - 2.00
Reverse w/ PRESENTED TO legend. 67 mm, bronze.	1960	Dio.U.10	1.00 - 2.00
Recognition for service legend, reverse Scout Oath. 68 mm, bronze.	1960	Dio.U.11	1.00 - 2.00

5TH ANNUAL BSA VACATION TRAINING CAMP.
CATALINA ISLAND, CA.

33 mm, aluminum.	1960	Dio.U.12	15.00 - 20.00

POSTCARDS & GREETING CARDS

Postcards have been national supply items since 1912. Two of the more handsome issues are the 1915 set for the points of the Scout Law and the 1920s series for Christmas. In the 1950s a humorous group was made for camps, and finally in the 1960s a humorous selection of note cards was produced. Most camps have cards, and only a small selection are noted here. Real photo cards are more desirable than printed cards.

1937 BOY SCOUT JAMBOREE, HOWARD CHANDLER CHRISTY
PAINTING

Scout w/ Franklin, Madison, Washington, and Hamilton in background.	1937	10.00 - 15.00

1950 NATIONAL JAMBOREE

Headquarters' Flag area.	1950	2.00 - 4.00
Official card.	1950	5.00 - 7.50
Scout Troop marching on road.	1950	2.00 - 4.00

1953 NATIONAL JAMBOREE

Official card.	1953	5.00 - 7.50

1957 NATIONAL JAMBOREE

Official card.	1957	3.00 - 5.00

1960 NATIONAL JAMBOREE

Official card.	1960	3.00 - 5.00

1964 NATIONAL JAMBOREE

Official card.	1964	3.00 - 5.00

1967 WORLD JAMBOREE, IDAHO

McDonald's Salute to Scouting.	1967	1.50 - 2.00

1969 NATIONAL JAMBOREE

Boys' Life Exhibit.	1969	1.00 - 2.00
Official card.	1969	2.00 - 3.00

1973 NATIONAL JAMBOREE

Jamboree East.	1973	1.00 - 2.00
Jamboree West.	1973	1.00 - 2.00

1977 NATIONAL JAMBOREE

Official card.	1977	1.00 - 2.00

1981 NATIONAL JAMBOREE

Official card.	1981	1.00 - 2.00

1985 NATIONAL JAMBOREE

Boy Scout stamp, 22 cents. Yellow-orange card.	1985	1.00 - 1.50
Boy Scout stamp, 22 cents. Green card.	1985	1.00 - 1.50
Official card.	1985	0.50 - 1.00
SOSSI logo.	1985	1.00 - 1.50

1989 NATIONAL JAMBOREE

Space Shuttle Atlantis launching in sky background.	1989	1.00 - 1.50
Space Shuttle on launch pad.	1989	1.00 - 1.50

1993 NATIONAL JAMBOREE

Jamboree emblem.	1993	0.50 - 1.00
Jamboree emblem.	1993	1.00 - 1.50

1997 NATIONAL JAMBOREE

Jamboree emblem.	1997	0.50 - 1.00

38TH ANNIVERSARY, BOY SCOUT WEEK

Cub, Sea Scout, Air Scout, Explorer and Boy Scout.	1948	5.00 - 7.50

Set of ten photos in a card folder sold at Camp Burton, Allaire, NJ, in 1931.

NATURE TRAIL
CAMP BURTON AT ALLAIRE
MONMOUTH COUNCIL BOY SCOUTS

CHAPEL
CAMP BURTON AT ALLAIRE
MONMOUTH COUNCIL BOY SCOUTS

TENTS - CAMP BURTON AT ALLAIRE
MONMOUTH COUNCIL BOY SCOUTS

EXECUTIVE STAFF
MONMOUTH COUNCIL BOY SCOUTS

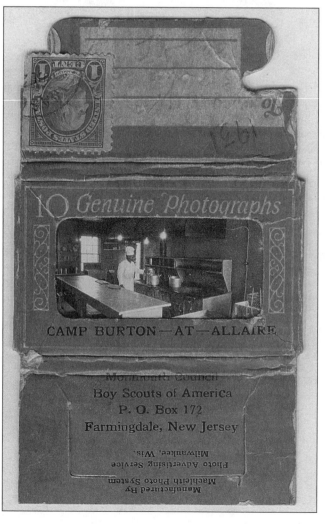

10 Genuine Photographs

CAMP BURTON —AT— ALLAIRE

Monmouth Council
Boy Scouts of America
P. O. Box 172
Farmingdale, New Jersey

Photo Advertising Service
Milwaukee, Wis.

Manufactured By
Mechleith Photo System

OLD SWIMMING HOLE
CAMP BURTON AT ALLAIRE
MONMOUTH COUNCIL BOY SCOUTS

HEADQUARTERS
CAMP BURTON AT ALLAIRE
MONMOUTH COUNCIL BOY SCOUTS

RODY, THE RANGER
CAMP BURTON AT ALLAIRE-MONMOUTH COUNCIL BOY SCOUTS

MR. ARTHUR BRISBANE
CAMP BURTON AT ALLAIRE
MONMOUTH COUNCIL BOY SCOUTS

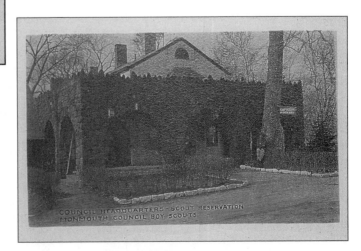

COUNCIL HEADQUARTERS-SCOUT RESERVATION
MONMOUTH COUNCIL BOY SCOUTS

ALPINE SCOUT CAMP, ALPINE, NJ. GNYC

Ohrbach Scout Arena.	1970	1.00 - 1.50
Trading post interior.	1970	1.00 - 1.50

BOY SCOUT MEMORIAL OF W.D. BOYCE

	1960	2.50 - 5.00

BOYS' LIFE ADVERTISING

Santa at chimney rooftop.	1915-1925	10.00 - 15.00

BOYCE IN LONDON FOG

	1984	0.50 - 1.00

BROAD CREEK MEMORIAL SCOUT CAMPS

Patrol with wagon.	1955	2.50 - 5.00
Troop hiking with packs.	1955	2.50 - 5.00

BROOKLYN SCOUT CAMP TRADING POST

(Ten Mile River Scout Camps).	1934	10.00 - 15.00

BROOKLYN SCOUT CAMPS, TUSTEN, NY

(Ten Mile River Scout Camps).	1934	10.00 - 15.00

CAMP BEDFORD, ADIRONDACK COUNCIL, NY

Lake and lodge scene.	1942	5.00 - 7.50

CAMP BURTON AT ALLAIRE, MONMOUTH COUNCIL, NJ

Ten 1-3/4" x 2-3/4" photographic views in mailing folder.	1931	20.00 - 25.00

CAMP MANNING

Mess call.	1926	10.00 - 12.50

CHILD WELFARE EXHIBIT, COLISEUM, CHICAGO, IL

Scout standing in uniform w/ stave.	1911	25.00 - 35.00

CHIPPEWA VALLEY COUNCIL, WI

Council Map and Scout's portrait.	1955	7.50 - 12.50

CHRISTMAS

Eight scouts hiking along ridge, pine tree at left.	1970-1975	3.00 - 5.00
Profile left, in campaign hat and neckerchief, red tenderfoot emblem.	1915-1925	15.00 - 25.00
Rural town view, First-Class emblem to right, two-line text.	1920-1940	15.00 - 25.00
Scout bugling in red circle, Be Prepared and four-line text, First-Class emblem.	1915-1925	15.00 - 25.00
Scout in beret dressing Santa, Cub wearing beard.	1970-1975	3.00 - 5.00
Scout leader striding w/ notecard, Be Prepared and four-line text, First-Class emblem.	1915-1925	15.00 - 25.00
Scout rolling large snowball.	1915-1925	15.00 - 25.00
Scout Saluting, two wreaths flanking, folds in half.	1915-1925	15.00 - 25.00
Scout signaling in red circle, Be Prepared and three-line text, First-Class emblem.	1915-1925	15.00 - 25.00
Scout standing, saluting in red circle, Be Prepared and four-line text. First-Class emblem.	1915-1925	15.00 - 25.00
Scout standing, signaling, pine trees in background, First-Class emblem and five-line text.	1920-1940	15.00 - 25.00
Scout striding in doorway of log cabin, First-Class emblem.	1915-1925	15.00 - 25.00
Silhouette of scout bugling and camp scene in pine trees, First-Class emblem.	1915-1925	15.00 - 25.00
Star above pine forest scene, First-Class emblem in shield, four-line text.	1920-1940	15.00 - 25.00

Three scouts in forest walking in snow left, four-line saying and First-Class emblem.   1920-1940   15.00 - 25.00

Two scouts carrying tree to log cabin, ive-line text, First-Class emblem.   1920-1940   15.00 - 25.00

COMMERCIAL COLORTYPE CO. CHICAGO.
SEPIA TONE, BLUE SKY.
Boy Scout Work at a Redpath - Brockway Chautauqua.   1913   15.00 - 20.00

COMMERCIAL COLORTYPE CO. CHICAGO. SEPIA TONE.
A Lean-to built in five minutes.	1913	15.00 - 20.00
A Letter from Home.	1913	15.00 - 20.00
A Signal Station.	1913	15.00 - 20.00
Basket Carry.	1913	15.00 - 20.00
Carrying the Patient Improved Litter.	1913	15.00 - 20.00
Handling the Patient.	1913	15.00 - 20.00
Kindness to Animals.	1913	15.00 - 20.00
Making Fire by Friction.	1913	15.00 - 20.00
On Parade - A Prize Group of Boy Scouts.	1913	15.00 - 20.00
Sylvester Method - Reviving the Suffocated.	1913	15.00 - 20.00
Typical Scout.	1913	15.00 - 20.00
Typical Scouting Scene.	1913	15.00 - 20.00

GOVERNMENT POSTCARD
PRINTED W/ MERIT BADGE APPOINTMENT INFORMATION
1930-1940   5.00 - 7.50

HEADQUARTERS, BSA, HILL TOP PARK, BALTIMORE, MD
1912   15.00 - 25.00

CANOE SAILING AT I. M. R.

INDIAN MOUND RESERVATION
Canoe sailing.	1949	5.00 - 7.50
Swim area 'buddy check.'	1948	2.50 - 5.00

INSTRUCTION IN KNOT TYING
Ten scouts, four tents and two bicycles in background.   1923   10.00 - 15.00

JOHNSTON HISTORICAL MUSEUM
Baden-Powell at desk.	1975	1.00 - 2.00
Central exhibition area.	1975	1.00 - 2.00

JOHNSTON NATIONAL SCOUT MUSEUM
Baden-Powell wax figure.	1965	1.00 - 2.00
Interior view, large globe.	1965	1.00 - 2.00

MERCURY ASTRONAUTS ON RECORD POSTCARDS
Alan B. Shepard.	1962	10.00 - 15.00
BSA President Ellsworth H. Augustus.	1962	10.00 - 15.00
Chief Scout Executive Joseph A. Brunton.	1962	10.00 - 15.00
John Glenn.	1962	10.00 - 15.00
Virgil "Gus" Grissom.	1962	10.00 - 15.00

MESSAGE FROM GREEN BAR BILL
1937 World Jamboree, envelope and enclosure.   1937   30.00 - 40.00

MILWAUKEE COUNTY COUNCIL
Scout Service Center architect's illustration.   1970   2.50 - 5.00

NATIONAL HEADQUARTERS, NORTH BRUNSWICK, NJ
Exterior view.	1965	1.00 - 2.00
MacKenzie statue close-up.	1965	1.00 - 2.00
MacKenzie statue and reflecting pool.	1960	3.00 - 4.00

NATIONAL SCOUTING MUSEUM, MURRAY, KY
Exterior view.	1987	0.50 - 1.00
Jamboree poster, 1937.	1987	0.50 - 1.00
Patch design.	1987	0.50 - 1.00
Patrol Theater.	1987	0.50 - 1.00
Robotic Baden-Powell.	1987	0.50 - 1.00
Rockwell's calendar paintings.	1987	0.50 - 1.00
Troop visits Teddy Roosevelt.	1987	0.50 - 1.00
World War I era uniform and stuff.	1987	0.50 - 1.00

NATIONAL SUPPLY CARTOON SET, NO. 3056
Chow's fine, eating like a horse.	1947	3.00 - 5.00
Had a swell time here and will be home soon.	1947	3.00 - 5.00
Just arrived.	1947	3.00 - 5.00
Learn something every day.	1947	3.00 - 5.00
No trouble getting up here.	1947	3.00 - 5.00
Our nightlife.	1947	3.00 - 5.00
Snapshot of the gang.	1947	3.00 - 5.00
This is the life (diving).	1947	3.00 - 5.00
This is the life (fishing).	1947	3.00 - 5.00
Will write later.	1947	3.00 - 5.00

NATIONAL SUPPLY CARTOON SET, NO. 3067
Craft lodge.	1956	2.00 - 3.00
Food's fine.	1956	2.00 - 3.00
Had a swell time and I'm coming home.	1956	2.00 - 3.00
He says there's a bear in those woods.	1956	2.00 - 3.00
Hello! I just arrived!	1956	2.00 - 3.00
Hi - I've decided to buy that compass!	1956	2.00 - 3.00
I was going to mail you more scout photos, but.	1956	2.00 - 3.00
OK Fred, here's the lake!	1956	2.00 - 3.00
Sure is peaceful here!	1956	2.00 - 3.00

NATIONAL SUPPLY CARTOON SET, NO. 3067A
Arrived OK, got a wonderful reception.	1958	2.00 - 3.00
Camp snapshot, have a lot more to show you.	1958	2.00 - 3.00
Every day is full of surprises!	1958	2.00 - 3.00
The food here is "fit for a king."	1958	2.00 - 3.00
I never had it so good!	1958	2.00 - 3.00
In the afternoon, we go for a long leisurely hike!	1958	2.00 - 3.00
Made friends quickly, lots of help.	1958	2.00 - 3.00
Our night life and don't miss the who-dun-its.	1958	2.00 - 3.00
Too much to do to write!	1958	2.00 - 3.00
Unexpected visitors, will finish writing later!	1958	2.00 - 3.00

NATIONAL SUPPLY, ROCKWELL PAINTINGS
A Scout is helpful.	1993	1.00 - 1.50
A Scout is loyal.	1993	1.00 - 1.50
Breakthrough for freedom.	1993	1.00 - 1.50
Can't wait.	1993	1.00 - 1.50
Forward America.	1993	1.00 - 1.50
Growth of a leader.	1993	1.00 - 1.50
I will do my best.	1993	1.00 - 1.50
On my honor.	1993	1.00 - 1.50
Our heritage.	1993	1.00 - 1.50
The right way.	1993	1.00 - 1.50
So much concern.	1993	1.00 - 1.50
We, too, have a job to do.	1993	1.00 - 1.50

1990s National Supply postcards of Rockwell paintings.

NATIONAL SUPPLY

Be a Boy Scout, blue and red recruiting card.	1985	0.25 - 0.50
Cub Scout, Explorer and Boy Scout advancing right.	1955	1.00 - 2.00
Scout saluting, red-white-blue ribbon below.	1959	2.00 - 4.00
Scouts seated on lake dock, some swimming.	1975	1.00 - 1.50
Six scouts swimming.	1975	1.00 - 1.50

NORTHWOODS CAMP, LAKE TOMAHAWK, WI.
MILWAUKEE COUNTY COUNCIL

Canoe at pier. Real photo postcard.	1929	15.00 - 20.00
Five scouts on horseback. Real photo postcard.	1929	15.00 - 20.00
Lake dock scene. Real photo postcard.	1929	15.00 - 20.00
Large group learning skill in wooded area. Real photo postcard.	1929	15.00 - 20.00
Patrol learning skill in open area. Real photo postcard.	1929	15.00 - 20.00

OFFICIAL SCOUT POST CARDS

01. Nautical Scouts Signaling.	1916	10.00 - 15.00
02. A Scout is Thrifty.	1916	15.00 - 25.00
03. Full Ranks on Sunday.	1916	10.00 - 15.00
04. A Crew of Nautical Scouts.	1916	10.00 - 15.00
05. Good Woodcraft.	1916	10.00 - 15.00
06. Sending Semaphore Signals.	1916	10.00 - 15.00
07. Weaving a Tent Mattress.	1916	10.00 - 15.00
08. Genuine First Aid.	1916	15.00 - 25.00
09. The Lodge by the Lake.	1916	10.00 - 15.00
10. Bicycle Patrol Awaiting Orders.	1916	10.00 - 15.00
11. Respect to the Flag; Morning Colors.	1916	10.00 - 15.00
12. Scout Build Bridges.	1916	10.00 - 15.00
13. Scout Fire Rescue Squad.	1916	10.00 - 15.00
14. Wheelbarrow Race at Scout Rally.	1916	10.00 - 15.00
15. How to Throw a Rope.	1916	10.00 - 15.00
16. Erecting Camp Wireless.	1916	10.00 - 15.00
17. Doing a Neighbor a Good Turn.	1916	10.00 - 15.00
18. Scouts Learn Archery.	1916	10.00 - 15.00
19. This is the Life.	1916	10.00 - 15.00
20. Scouts Study as well as Play.	1916	10.00 - 15.00
21. Scouts Assisting Forestry Commission.	1916	10.00 - 15.00
22. Decoration Day Duties.	1916	10.00 - 15.00
23. A Field Wireless Outfit.	1916	10.00 - 20.00
24. Morning Camp Inspection.	1916	10.00 - 15.00
25. Each Respects the Other.	1916	10.00 - 15.00
26. A Prize Crop.	1916	10.00 - 15.00
27. Outdoor Church at Camp.	1916	10.00 - 15.00
28. Scout Tilting Contest.	1916	10.00 - 15.00
29. A Business-like Wireless Station.	1916	10.00 - 15.00
30. Instruction in Knot Tying.	1916	10.00 - 15.00

OWASIPPE SCOUT CAMPS

White river canoe trip.	1957	2.50 - 5.00

OWASIPPE SCOUT RESERVATION

Patrol camp site.	1965	2.50 - 5.00
Patrol cooking scene along lake front.	1965	2.50 - 5.00

PHILMONT

Apache Springs Camp.	1975	1.00 - 1.50
Baldy Mountain, view from Wilson Mesa.	1975	1.00 - 1.50
Baldy Mountain.	1975	1.00 - 1.50
Camping Headquarters, b/w, full frame.	1954	7.50 - 10.00
Clear Creek Mountain, b/w, w/ white border.	1954	7.50 - 10.00
Explorers panning for gold.	1975	1.00 - 1.50
Gateway to High Adventure, Maguire Foundation.	1975	1.00 - 1.50
Horse Headquarters, b/w, w/ white edge.	1954	7.50 - 10.00
I want to go back.	1980	1.00 - 1.50
Philmont Buffalo.	1975	1.00 - 1.50
Philmont Grace and Tooth of Time.	1975	1.00 - 1.50
Ponil Base Camp, b/w, w/ white edge.	1954	7.50 - 10.00
Rayado, b/w, w/ white edge.	1954	7.50 - 10.00
Scouting, Road to Manhood statue.	1975	1.00 - 1.50
Seton Museum	1975	1.00 - 1.50

210

Philmont Scout Ranch
views 1950s (left) and
1960s (above).

The Stockade, b/w, full frame.	1954	7.50 - 10.00
Summer dawn on Baldy.	1975	1.00 - 1.50
Tooth of Time, horizontal view.	1975	1.00 - 1.50
Tooth of Time, vertical view through trees.	1975	1.00 - 1.50
Tooth of Time, view from Crater Lake.	1975	1.00 - 1.50
Villa Philmonte exterior.	1975	1.00 - 1.50
Villa Philmonte Trophy Room.	1975	1.00 - 1.50
Woodbadge Lodge, b/w, full frame.	1954	7.50 - 10.00

REXCRAFT OFFICIAL BUGLE POSTCARD

Bugle and jobbers listing.	1928	7.50 - 12.50
Bugle, box and bag.	1928	10.00 - 15.00

SCHIFF SCOUT RESERVATION

East Hall.	1970	1.50 - 2.00
Manor House.	1970	1.50 - 2.00
Woodbadge Totem sun dial.	1970	1.50 - 2.00

SCOUT EXHIBIT, NEW YORK WORLD'S FAIR

Indian Dances.	1964-1965	5.00 - 7.50
Scout helping family at location map.	1964-1965	5.00 - 7.50
Scouts by Globe.	1964-1965	5.00 - 7.50
Scouts w/ wheelchairs.	1964-1965	5.00 - 7.50
Scouts with flags at Unisphere.	1964-1965	5.00 - 7.50
Scouts with flags at U.S. Pavilion.	1964-1965	5.00 - 7.50
Set of six in packet.	1964-1965	30.00 - 45.00

SCOUT GUM CO.

01. Bugle Calls.	1916	10.00 - 15.00
02. Swimming.	1916	10.00 - 15.00
03. Building fire w/o matches.	1916	10.00 - 15.00
04. Blazing a trail.	1916	10.00 - 15.00
05. Signaling.	1916	10.00 - 15.00
06. Hiding a trail.	1916	10.00 - 15.00
07. Vaulting a stream.	1916	10.00 - 15.00
08. Loading a canoe.	1916	10.00 - 15.00
09. Toting.	1916	10.00 - 15.00
10. First aid.	1916	10.00 - 15.00
11. Flag salute.	1916	10.00 - 15.00
12. The camp fire.	1916	10.00 - 15.00

SCOUT LAW SERIES, © BARSE & HOPKINS

01. Trustworthy.	1917	15.00 - 25.00
02. Loyal.	1917	15.00 - 25.00
03. Helpful.	1917	15.00 - 25.00
04. Friendly.	1917	15.00 - 25.00
05. Courteous.	1917	15.00 - 25.00
06. Kind.	1917	15.00 - 25.00
07. Obedient.	1917	15.00 - 25.00
08. Cheerful.	1917	15.00 - 25.00
09. Thrifty.	1917	15.00 - 25.00
10. Brave.	1917	10.00 - 15.00
11. Clean.	1917	15.00 - 25.00
12. Reverent.	1917	15.00 - 25.00

SCOUT LAW SERIES, DRAWN BY S.H.W.

01. Trustworthy.	1912	15.00 - 25.00
02. Loyal.	1912	15.00 - 25.00
03. Helpful.	1912	15.00 - 25.00
04. Friendly.	1912	15.00 - 25.00
05. Courteous.	1912	15.00 - 25.00
06. Kind.	1912	15.00 - 25.00
07. Obedient.	1912	15.00 - 25.00
08. Cheerful.	1912	15.00 - 25.00
09. Thrifty.	1912	15.00 - 25.00
10. Brave.	1912	15.00 - 25.00
11. Clean.	1912	15.00 - 25.00
12. Reverent.	1912	15.00 - 25.00

SCOUT LAW, © BARSE & HOPKINS

Full Scout Law on single card.	1917	15.00 - 25.00

SCOUT OATH, © BARSE & HOPKINS

Full oath on single card.	1917	15.00 - 25.00

SCOUTING - GATEWAY TO ADVENTURE

Adirondack rappelling scene.	1994	0.50 - 1.00
Unit recruiting back.		

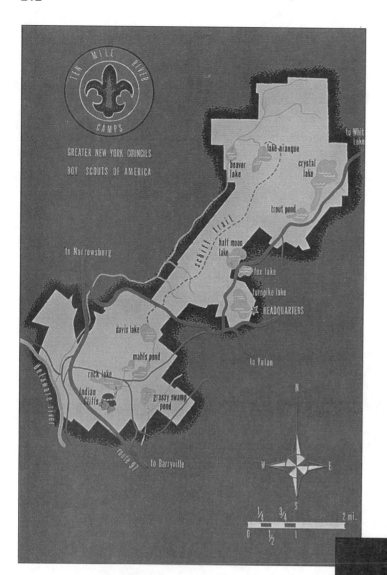

Ten Mile River postcards of the 1950s.

SCOUTS OF THE WORLD

Boxed set of 111 cards in color.	1968	30.00 - 50.00
Boxed set of 68 cards in color.	1968	50.00 - 75.00

STATUE OF BLACK HAWK W/ SCOUTS

	1958	5.00 - 7.50

T.P. & CO. NY, SET OF 30 VIEWS OF SCOUTING ACTIVITIES, NUMBERED.

Series No. 252, Official Boy Scout Post Card. Each.	1917	15.00 - 25.00

T.P. & CO. NY, SET OF 30 VIEWS OF SCOUTING ACTIVITIES, NUMBERED. DEER HEAD LOGO.

Series No. 252. Nat. Head, author. BSA. Each.	1915	10.00 - 15.00

TEN MILE RIVER SCOUT CAMPS, GNYC

Archery line.	1970	1.00 - 1.50
Camp Keowa Catholic Chapel.	1970	1.00 - 1.50
Camp Keowa Waterfront.	1974	1.00 - 1.50
Campsite scene.	1970	1.00 - 1.50
Canoeing on the Delaware River.	1970	1.00 - 1.50
Down the Delaware, four canoes.	1975	1.00 - 1.50
Family camp cabin.	1971	1.00 - 1.50
Indian Cliffs and Delaware River view.	1970	1.00 - 1.50
Lake sunset.	1970	1.00 - 1.50
Off on the trail - horseback riding.	1970	1.00 - 1.50
Ready for a horse ride.	1970	1.00 - 1.50
Rifle and shotgun range.	1970	1.00 - 1.50
Scout reviving OA Legend.	1970	1.00 - 1.50
Six Views fold-out, map and message area.	1965	5.00 - 7.50
Stone arch bridge.	1970	1.00 - 1.50
Sunfish sailing boats on one of the seven lakes.	1970	1.00 - 1.50
Swimming in one of the seven lakes.	1975	1.00 - 1.50
Troop 216 at TMR.	1965	5.00 - 7.50
Waterfront, E-shaped pier.	1970	1.00 - 1.50

TEN MILE RIVER, CAMP MAN

A Camp Fire.	1940-1955	10.00 - 15.00
Canoeing on Crystal Lake.	1940-1955	10.00 - 15.00
Sea Scouts sailing on Crystal Lake.	1940-1955	10.00 - 15.00

THE BOY SCOUT TREE

Giant Redwood and scout troop.	1935	5.00 - 7.50

THE SCOUT LAW, © BSA

	1913	15.00 - 25.00

THE SCOUT OATH, © BSA

	1913	15.00 - 20.00

W.D. BOYCE MEMORIAL, OTTAWA, IL

Boyce, Scout, Big Ben, and Ottawa Memorial.	1985	0.50 - 1.00

WE, TOO, HAVE A JOB TO DO

Liberty Advancing, Boy Scout and Sea Scout following.	1943	5.00 - 7.50

WORLD JAMBOREE, IDAHO

U.S. government postcard, first-day cancel.	1967	2.00 - 3.00

1969 Greater NY Councils
recruiting cards of Yankees
and Mets. The Seaver card is
valued at $135.00 - $450.00.
Others $20.00 - $60.00.
Tommy Agee
Bud Harrelson
Cleon Jones
Bobby Murcer
Art Shamsky
Mel Stottlemyre
Ron Swoboda

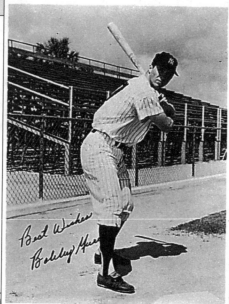

Atlanta Council

1992	Jeff Treadway	$3.00
1993	Dale Murphy	$15.00
1994	Deion Sanders	$8.00
1995	Gregory McMichael	$3.00
1996	Ryan Klesko	$5.00
1997	Jeff Blanser	$3.00
1998	Greg Maddux	$15.00
1999	John Rocker	$5.00

NASSAU County Council
Duke Snider, Mets $45.00-150.00

SEALS & STICKERS

B.S.A. 16TH ANNIVERSARY
Scout standing on rock, pointing right,   1926   20.00 - 25.00
  patrol below looking at landscape.

B.S.A. 17TH ANNIVERSARY
Scout bandaging girl's arm.   1927   20.00 - 25.00

B.S.A. 18TH ANNIVERSARY
Scout striding w/ Indian looking left   1928   20.00 - 25.00
  and aviator right.

B.S.A. 21ST ANNIVERSARY
Scout striding left.   1931   15.00 - 20.00

B.S.A. 21ST ANNUAL MEETING
Memphis TN, Scout striding right with dog.   1931   15.00 - 20.00

B.S.A. 24TH ANNIVERSARY
Boy Scout Week, Tenderfoot emblem,   1934   10.00 - 15.00
  blue and red.

B.S.A. 38TH ANNIVERSARY
The Scout Citizen at work, Cub, Sea, Air,   1948   10.00 - 15.00
  Explorer and Boy Scouts standing, flag at left,
  Boy Scout Week at bottom.

B.S.A. 19TH ANNIVERSARY
Scout seated by campfire, pioneer dream   1929   20.00 - 25.00
  scene above.

B.S.A. 40TH ANNIVERSARY CRUSADE
Strengthen the Arm of Liberty seal, 2" x 2-7/8". 1950   5.00 - 7.50

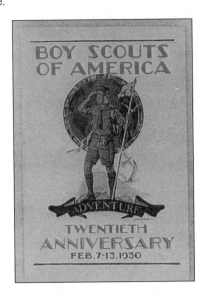

B.S.A. 50TH ANNIVERSARY
Foil seal, 1-1/4".   1960   1.00 - 1.25

BOY SCOUT STAMPS, B.S.A.
Head shot of Boy Scout, sheet of 100 stamps. 1955   10.00 - 12.50

BOY SCOUT WEEK

Scout seated with book, Washington image in background.	1932	10.00 - 15.00
Scout standing looking left, with globe in background.	1930	10.00 - 15.00
Scout standing with stag, eagle on black background.	1936	10.00 - 15.00
Uncle Sam brushing shoulders of youth in suit, Scout camp scene below.	1944	10.00 - 15.00

BOYS' LIFE WEEK

December 10-16th, better reading for boys.	1936	5.00 - 7.50
December 1-7th, Scout at workbench with wood horse.	1934	5.00 - 7.50
December 9-16th, better reading for Boys.	1935	5.00 - 7.50

EVERY TROOP A CAMPING TROOP

Two tends along lake, black and green.	1950	5.00 - 7.50

GREATER NEW YORK COUNCILS, QUEENS, SOUTH DISTRICT

Camp promotions sticker.	1991	1.00 - 1.50

GREATER NEW YORK COUNCILS

Sustaining member sticker.	1983	1.00 - 1.50
Sustaining member sticker.	1991	1.00 - 1.50

HISTORIC TRAILS AWARD WATER DECAL

	1970	2.00 - 3.00

NATIONAL JAMBOREE WATER DECAL

Washington kneeling left.	1964	5.00 - 7.50
Washington kneeling left.	1957	5.00 - 7.50

NATIONAL JAMBOREE, 1935

Capitol dome and scout facing.	1935	20.00 - 30.00
On to Washington, Scout advancing right and eagle, 1-3/4" x 2-3/4".	1935	20.00 - 25.00

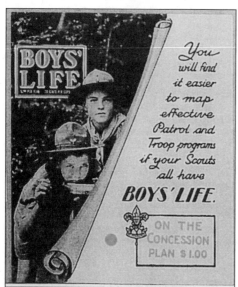

BOYS' LIFE

Easier, effective patrol and troop program, two scouts at left.	1930	5.00 - 7.50

EVERY BOY IN CAMP

Camp fire scene.	1928	7.50 - 10.00

EVERY SCOUT IN CAMP

Scout bugler standing right, two tents left, black and green.	1950	5.00 - 7.50
Scout bugler standing right, two tents left, black and red.	1950	5.00 - 7.50

NATIONAL JAMBOREE, 1937

On to the Jamboree, 1937, Washington Monument and First-Class emblem, blue sky, dark blue trees.	1937	15.00 - 20.00
On to the Jamboree, 1937, Washington Monument and First-Class emblem, r-w-b banner at bottom.	1937	15.00 - 20.00
On to the Jamboree, 1937, Washington Monument, First-Class emblem in r-w-b poster insert, tents below.	1937	15.00 - 20.00
On to the Jamboree, Washington Monument.	1937	15.00 - 20.00

NEW YORK WORLD'S FAIR AND GOLDEN GATE EXPOSITION
Boy Scout camp, 1-3/4" x 2-1/2".   1939   25.00 - 35.00

PHILMONT SCOUT RANCH
Pendant shape, green lettering.   1950   5.00 - 7.50

SAVE OUR NATURAL RESOURCES, PROJECT SOAR
Sheet of eight stamps.   1971   2.00 - 3.00

SCHIFF SCOUT RESERVATION WATER DECAL
                                        1970   5.00 - 7.50

SCOUT ANNIVERSARY WEEK
February 8 to 14, two Scouts standing. 1940   5.00 - 7.50

SCOUTS, TOO, HAVE A JOB TO DO
Liberty advancing right, with navy and army   1942   10.00 - 15.00
   troops, Scouting Needs Leaders at top.
Liberty advancing right, with navy and army   1942   10.00 - 15.00
   troops, Scouting Needs Money at top.
Liberty advancing right, with navy and army   1942   10.00 - 15.00
   troops, Scouts, too, have a job to do at top.

SUSTAINING MEMBER WINDOW STICKER
                                        1980   2.00 - 3.00

TENDERFOOT EMBLEM
Sheet of 8.   1985   0.50 - 1.00

TENDERFOOT EMBLEM,
   ON RED-WHITE-BLUE SQUARE, WATER DECAL
                                        1972   2.00 - 3.00

TENDERFOOT EMBLEM, OUTLINE, WATER DECAL
                                        1975   1.00 - 2.00

THE SCOUT CITIZEN AT WORK
Cub, Sea, Air, Explorer and Boy Scouts   1948   10.00 - 15.00
   standing, flag at left, Scouting is for All Boys
   at bottom.

W.D. BOYCE, BSA, LSA, SEAL
                                        1985   0.50 - 1.00

WORLD JAMBOREE, IDAHO
Jamboree emblem, sheet of 50 seals   1967   10.00 - 15.00

SCOUT SERVICE CAMP, NEW YORK WORLD'S FAIR
Blue-orange 3" circle.   1940   20.00 - 30.00

WORLD WAR SERVICE AWARDS

To assist in the effort on the home front in both World Wars, the Boy Scouts sold bonds for which the U.S. Department of the Treasury awarded a series of medals for each of the five bonds drives (and bars for selling in more than one drive). For the Third Liberty Loan Campaign the scouts were honored with a patriotic poster and an additional medal incentive. Finally, for selling War Savings Stamps, scouts were awarded an Ace medal which featured the torch of the Statue of Liberty.

For World War II efforts scouts were awarded an Eisenhower Waste Paper Campaign medal and two varieties of the MacArthur Garden Medal.

CITY OF ENGLEWOOD, NJ
For War Service.   1918   250.00 - 300.00

EISENHOWER WASTE PAPER CAMPAIGN
Certificate of Participation.   1942-1945   20.00 - 30.00
Plastic pendant from red-white-red ribbon bar. 1942-1945   15.00 - 25.00

FOR PATRIOTIC SERVICE
Scout planting, crossed flags below.   1917   50.00 - 75.00

Green ribbon.

Red ribbon.

MACARTHUR GARDEN MEDAL
Green ribbon, BSA name incuse on reverse. 1942-1945   40.00 - 50.00
Red ribbon, BSA name on front.   1942-1945   40.00 - 50.00

PHILADELPHIA COUNCIL
Scout standing, signaling with blue enamel   1917-1918 150.00 - 200.00
 flags.
Scout standing, signaling with red enamel   1917-1918 150.00 - 200.00
 flags.
Scout standing, signaling with white enamel 1917-1918 150.00 - 200.00
 flags.

STRENGTHEN THE ARM OF LIBERTY
Sebastian porcelain.   1917   150.00 - 225.00

STRENGTHEN THE ARM OF LIBERTY POSTER
Original.   1917   150.00 - 225.00

TREASURY LIBERTY LOAN MEDAL
1917 June pendant on blue ribbon.   1917   35.00 - 50.00
1917 June pendant w/ one bar.   1917   40.00 - 60.00
1917 June pendant w/ two bars.   1917   50.00 - 70.00
1917 June pendant w/ three bars.   1917   60.00 - 80.00
1917 June pendant w/ four bars.   1917   100.00 - 125.00

1917 October pendant on blue ribbon.	1917	35.00 - 50.00
1917 October pendant w/ one bar.	1917	40.00 - 60.00
1917 October pendant w/ two bars.	1917	50.00 - 70.00
1917 October pendant w/ three bars.	1917	60.00 - 80.00
1918 April pendant on blue ribbon.	1918	35.00 - 50.00
1918 April pendant w/ one bar.	1918	40.00 - 60.00
1918 April pendant w/ two bars.	1918	50.00 - 70.00
1918 October pendant on blue ribbon.	1918	35.00 - 50.00
1918 October pendant w/ one bar.	1918	40.00 - 60.00
1919 May pendant on blue ribbon.	1919	35.00 - 50.00

U.S. GOVERNMENT BONDS

Manual for the BSA.	1918	20.00 - 30.00

WAR PRODUCTION BOARD, WASTE PAPER AWARD

1000 above eagle.	1917-1919	20.00 - 30.00

WAR SAVINGS STAMPS ACE AWARD

Statue of Liberty Torch on red-white-blue satin ribbon, copper pendant and pin bar, w/ bronze palm on ribbon.	1917-1919	75.00 - 100.00
Statue of Liberty Torch on red-white-blue satin ribbon, copper pendant and pin bar, w/ bronze and silver palm.	1917-1919	150.00 - 200.00
Statue of Liberty Torch on red-white-blue satin ribbon, copper pendant and pin bar, w/ silver palm on ribbon.	1917-1919	100.00 - 125.00
Statue of Liberty Torch on red-white-blue satin ribbon, copper pendant and pin bar, w/ gold palm on ribbon.	1917-1919	500.00 - 750.00
Statue of Liberty Torch on red-white-blue satin ribbon, copper pendant and pin bar.	1917-1919	60.00 - 80.00

EVERY SCOUT TO SAVE A SOLDIER/ WEAPONS FOR LIBERTY

Kneeling Scout holds sword to standing and flag-draped Liberty. 28 mm, gold, uniface.	1917	Dio.1917.1A	1,500. - 2,000.
Kneeling Scout holds sword to standing and flag-draped Liberty. 28 mm, silver, uniface.	1917	Dio.1917.1B	750.00 - 1,000.
Kneeling Scout holds sword to standing and flag-draped Liberty. 28 mm, bronze, uniface.	1917	Dio.1917.1C	250.00 - 400.00

Brooklyn Council newspaper drive, WWII.

220

WWI poster. Actual size 20 x 30". Two smaller reproductions exist, as do modern postcards.

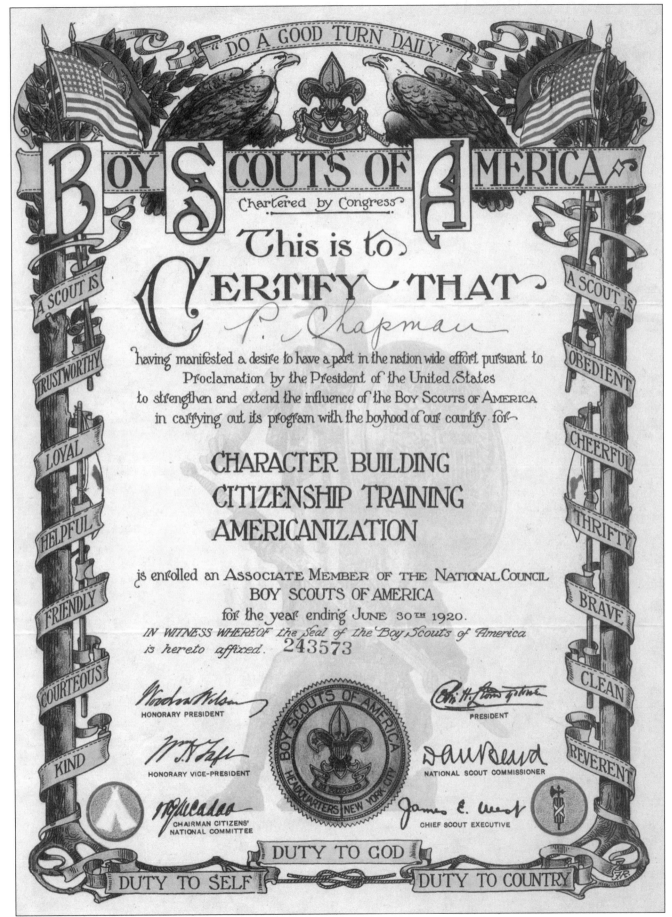

Associate member certificates were available for $1.00 originally. They now command $75.00-125.00.

WORLD JAMBOREE U.S. CONTIGENT

Both National and World Jamborees are unforgettable life-time experiences for all who attend. The First National Scout Jamboree in the U.S. was planned for 1935 to honor the 25th Anniversary of the movement; however, an outbreak of polio caused it to be postponed until 1937. After World War II, jamborees resumed in 1950, 1953, 1957, 1960, 1964, 1969, 1973, 1977, 1981, 1985, 1989, 1993, and 1997. The break in the sequence is to have them avoid World Jamboree years and to fall on successive 25th anniversaries. They have been held around the country, but since 1981, all have been at Fort A.P. Hill, Bowling Green, VA. World Jamborees have been held since 1920, with each national scouting organization sending troops of scouts as representatives.

Chief executive scout James E. West at the 1929 World Jamboree.

CONTINGENT BACK PATCH

Statue of Liberty on inverted triangle. Rolled edge, shield shape, 145 x 152 mm.	1971	20.00 - 30.00
Bicentennial Logo in center, 102 x 122 mm.	1975	15.00 - 25.00
U.S. Flag flying over mountains. 105 x 119 mm.	1983	15.00 - 25.00
Eagle head above flag. FDL at r. 150 mm, round.	1987	15.00 - 20.00
Legend in flying flag design. 100 x 76 mm.	1995	15.00 - 20.00

CONTINGENT JACKET PATCH

Statue of Liberty on inverted triangle. Rolled edge, shield shape, 86 x 90 mm.	1971	15.00 - 20.00

CONTINGENT MEDAL

First Class emblem on globe, text on back.	1920	1,000. - 1,250.
First Class emblem (small) above two hemispheres, named on back.	1924	2,250. - 2,750.
First Class emblem (large) above two hemispheres.	1929	350.00 - 450.00
First Class emblem (large) above two hemispheres.	1933	400.00 - 600.00

Scouts at the 1929 World Jamboree.

CONTINGENT POCKET PATCH

Eagle above shield, Boy Scouts of America around. Openwork shield. 77 mm. 1920 and 1924 used the same patch.	1920	350.00 - 450.00
Eagle above shield, Boy Scouts of America around. Solid. 54 mm.	1929	175.00 - 250.00
Eagle above shield, Boy Scouts of America around. Solid. 52 mm.	1933	175.00 - 225.00
Eagle above shield, Boy Scouts of America around cut edge. Solid. 77 mm.	1947	80.00 - 120.00
Eagle above shield, Boy Scouts of America around, cut edge. Solid. 78 mm.	1951	40.00 - 60.00
Eagle above shield, Boy Scouts of America around, rolled edge. Solid. 78 mm.	1955	20.00 - 30.00
Boy Scouts of America in blue area of shield, Eagle in flight over stripes. Rolled edge, shield shape, 68 x 87 mm.	1957	20.00 - 30.00
Boy Scouts of America in blue area of shield, Eagle in flight over stripes. Rolled edge, shield shape, 70 x 88 mm.	1959	20.00 - 30.00
Boy Scouts of America in blue area of shield, Eagle in flight over stripes. Rolled edge, shield shape, 70 x 88 mm.	1963	20.00 - 30.00
Statue of Liberty on inverted triangle. Rolled edge, shield shape, 56 x 60 mm.	1971	10.00 - 15.00
Bicentennial Logo in center, 78 x 90 mm.	1975	10.00 - 15.00
U.S. Flag flying over mountains. 77 x 89 mm.	1983	10.00 - 15.00
Eagle head abovve flag. FDL at r. 80 mm, round.	1987	10.00 - 15.00
Tenderfoot emblem in ctr. of curved top shield shape. 80 x 80 mm.	1991	10.00 - 15.00
Legend in flying flag design. 98 x 74 mm.	1995	10.00 - 15.00
Eagle head below red-whte-blue ribbon. 96 x 75 mm.	1999	10.00 - 15.00

CONTINGENT SHOULDER RIBBON

USA on blue, unit number on red. Silkscreened felt. (Worn while at '37 National Jamboree).	1937	150.00 - 200.00
WJ and globe on blue, unit number on red. Silkscreened felt.	1937	150.00 - 200.00

CONTINGENT BACK PATCH

Tenderfoot emblem in ctr. of curved top shield shape. 130 x 130 mm.	1991	15.00 - 20.00

William P. Curtis of Michigan returning from the 1929 World Jamboree.

Staff members at the 1964 National Jamboree at Valley Forge, PA.

Williard Scott interviews The Jamboree Today *editor at the 1989 National Jamboree.*

The National Scout Jamboree is usually a once-in-a-lifetime experience for a scout as a youth. Neckerchiefs are one of the popular collectibles, in addition to patches, baggage tags, rings, and food tickets. The same general design elements are used for the event.

Artistic graphics illustrated contemporary uniforms and events before photographic images became cost-effective. Storefront posters commonly announced scouting events. Program covers were great promotional items and fond remembrances of an event. Pen ink blotters were commonplace, and a constant scouting reminder.

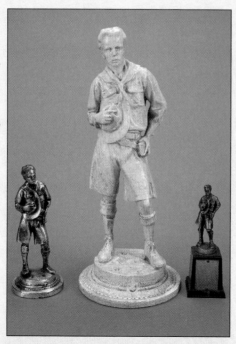

The R. Tait McKenzie statue is probably the most familiar scouting sculpture. Created in 1914 by the University of Pennsylvania professor for the Philadelphia Council, in a 17-inch size, it was made available in plaster reproductions colored in ivory or bronze through the National Supply Catalog. For the 25th Anniversary, a life-size statue was produced, and that has now been duplicated at more than 75 locations. In the 1930s, the plaster version was replaced by 12-inch white-metal castings plated in a silver or bronze wash. In the 1950s, a four-inch version was introduced. The 17-inch version made a re-appearance as a special award in the 1990s in a green patina.

Jeanne Stevens-Sollman, an award-winning sculptor in Bellefonte, PA, has added two scout themes to her line of rabbit personalities: a Scout Rabbit giving the scout sign, and a Cooking Rabbit with bacon and eggs.

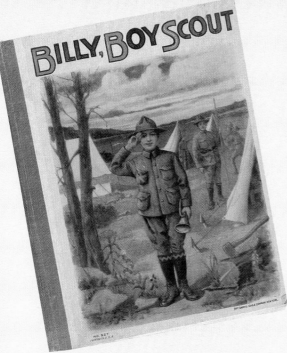

Billy, Boy Scout is just one of the hundreds of fiction books which have long been a popular way to get youth to read. This particular book is for an age group younger than 11, but it has some great illustrations to augment the story.

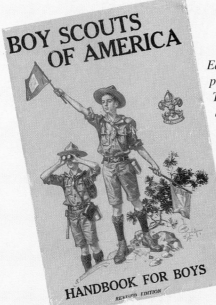

Early scout handbooks had paper printed covers backed onto cloth. This caused the cover and spine design to quickly chip, and particularly nice examples are hard to find.

The first official Boy Scout camera is from 1928, although the copyright dates are much earlier. The green bellows were replaced with black bellows within two years. The carrying case has a slit in the back for a belt to pass through.

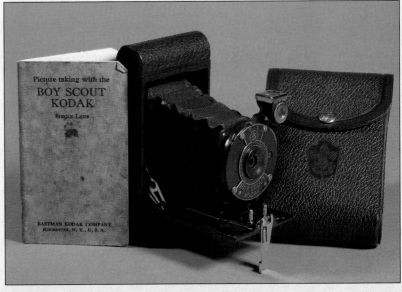

These are the merit-badge sash and uniform shirt of William Spengler. The merit-badge sash includes the rank patches and on the back, the 1935 and 1937 National Jamboree Pocket Patches, a Camp Gardner Dam patch and award arrows, Assistant Patrol Leader, Patrol Leader and a Senior Scout Patrol Leader Chevron. The red-arch patch is the troop shoulder patch for the 1935 National Jamboree. (That event was canceled due to a polio outbreak). His shirt includes the 1937 World Jamboree patch, Eagle medal, contest medal, and attendance bars.

Patrol designations followed the British system of colored ribbons until 1925, when a silk-screened design on a felt square was introduced. Embroidered designs on red felt were introduced by 1928, and later the BSA designation was added. Twill replaced the felt in 1953, and in 1972 colored designs were introduced. The eagle on blue is a late 1920s issue of private manfacture.

These pre-1921 cards are three or four pages, with a celluloid cover and either a rivet in the corner or two rings. From 1920 through 1942, they were tri-fold with various graphic changes. In the mid-1940s, the bi-fold card was introduced and by the 1950s, a single-sheet card was introduced.

230

The Medal of Merit, at left, is awarded for saving another's life using scouting skills. The Honor Medal, right, is awarded for saving a life with risk to one's own. Un-awarded copies are available, but it is very uncommon to have a medal and citation available for collectors.

Scouts of many faiths can earn a religious award. Some faiths have one, while others have various awards depending on age group. The Roman Catholic medals illustrated are for Tiger Cubs, Cub Scouts, Boy Scouts, and Explorers.

Early contest medals were on a red-white-blue ribbon, and also came with a drape in the back. These were simplified to just a ribbon, and then later, a plain blue ribbon. In the 1950s, the individual event medals were changed to a tenderfoot emblem on a pendant hanging from a red-white ribbon. Many dye varieties exist.

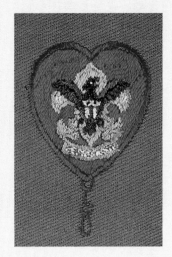

The eagle patch, above, is of the cut-edge khaki variety.

First Class Patrol Leader, at left, was a combination badge designation. A silver background replaces the standard gold. For the First Class Scribe, the scribe's quills were added to the large cloth design. An early Life Scout badge, at right, has the knot in red.

Early First Class (above) and Star Scout Ranks (below), come in both short and tall crown varieties. The tall crowns have a center line dividing the crown.

The first life-size statue was made for the Philadelphia Council Office in 1935 for Scouting's 25th Anniversary. Since that time, examples have been made for other council offices, the national office, and several camps.

James E. West

Scoutmaster's Key

Eagle Scout

Silver Beaver

Honor Medal

Cub Leader Training

Medal of Merit on tan

Medal of Merit on khaki

The youth ranks, honor medals, and adult training and service awards are represented on the every-day uniform by knot patches which are worn over the left pocket. They come with a colored background—blue and yellow for the cub program, dark green for the explorer program, and khaki or tan for the scout program. Other background colors include white, red, and gray.

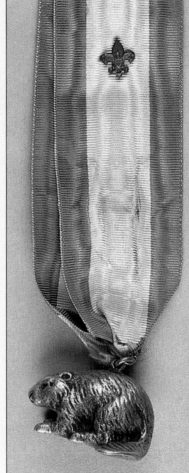

The Silver Beaver Award is the highest award which a council can present to an adult volunteer. This is the first pendant variety, of a very large beaver. The neck ribbon is of the second variety, with a small tenderfoot emblem on the white band. This particular example was awarded in 1939.

The first design of the Explorer Silver Award was the program's Compass-Anchor-Wings design hanging from an orange-red ribbon.

The Air Scout program's Ace Award has a four-prop plane wing below Eagle Wings, on a compass bordered pendant.

The Explorer Scout Ranger Award features a powder horn on a compass border.

There have been six manufacturers of the Eagle Scout Award since 1911 and more than 100 documented varieties in style of pendant ribbons or brooch. Examples include a Degist and Clust, Robbins and Custom Fine Jewlery.

The second variety of the Explorer Silver Award has an eagle in flight above a tenderfoot emblem with in a compass.

In the 1998 revision of the Explorer program into Venturing, new medals were introduced for the Silver, Ranger, and G.O.L.D. Award.

Early shoulder patches were a red embroidery on khaki cloth, and usually only worn by the professional staff or council and district personnel. Separate community name strip and state abbreviation are the commonly found examples; much scarcer are single line half strips combining community and state. A later development was the council name and state together.

Early adult position patches were a large first class badge worn on the shirt sleeve. This patch is for Assistant Scoutmaster

Adult position patches come in many material and embroidery varieties. Adult office positions such as chaplain, physician, commissioner and national staff are represented, along with veteran tenure. The earliest patches have many wreath varieties; the later patches have cut edges or rolled edges, as well as gauze back or plastic-back varieties.

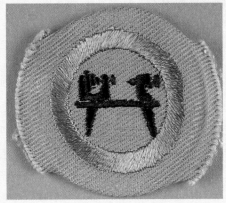
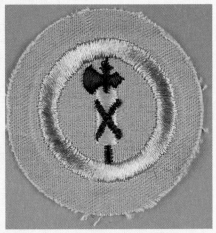

The earliest merit badges were full square, with a rough-cut edge. Some exist with a black pattern on the back of the material, often incorporating part or all of the national office logo. Wide crimp tan cloth badges were instituted to assist in the sewing of the badge to the sash in a circle. Due to a material shortage during World War II, a variety with a fine twill was used. This was followed by a narrow crimp on tan. In the 1950s, the uniform was changed to khaki green, and narrow crimp badges were introduced.

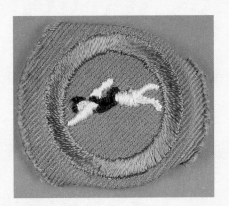
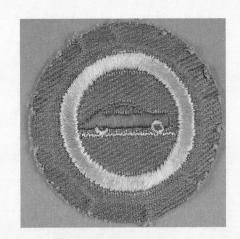

With technology changes, the cut-cloth designs were replaced by a rolled edge. And in the 1960s, many badges became fully embroidered. With the 1972 change in the advancement program, the required badges for Eagle Scout incorporated a silver (white) border, while non-required badges kept the green border. As the required badges changed, so did the border color—thus, some exist both ways. Cloth backing, clear, or bluish plastic backing are some of the additional collectible varieties. In 1993, a change was made in about 30 of the badges into a computer stitched, larger design, which has since been discontinued. These computer-designed badges came individually packed, and are distinguished by a brown ring between the badge design and outer green rolled edge.

This 1920s Milton Bradley Co. board game featured great graphics and was wholesome entertainment for the time.

Laminate plaques have been popular since the late 1930s. They were first made available with photos of popular scouting figures, and then with cub and scout ranks. The 1950s and 1960s saw their use expand into appreciation awards for service and contributors.

On the scout campaign hat a, youth could wear a large rank pin in brass, or in the 1920s as a patrol leader, a silvered rank pin. Senior Patrol Leaders and their assistants, as well as Junior Assistant Scoutmasters also had hat pins for their rank. For uniform wear, smaller rank pins were available. In the 1920s, 1 inch or so pins made an appearance for use on the coats worn by adult scout leaders and the professional staff. These coats lasted until 1970 with a number of changes, and the pins also change with the size of the emblem, the type of coloring (enameling or cloisonné) and the type of attachment (screw back, pin back or clutch back). Similar but smaller pins were available for civilian wear.

Boy leadership positions include Assistant Patrol Leader, Patrol Leader, Senior Patrol Leader, Junior Assistant Scoutmaster, Scribe, Librarian, and many others. The developments of these patches include: cut cloth tan or khaki, cut edge khaki with fine or coarse twill, and rolled edge. In addition, backing materials include gauze, glue and gauze, and finally, plastic.

A high point for most scouts is attendance at a National High Adventure Base. The photos above were taken at Philmont, in New Mexico. The photos below are from the Sea Base in Florida. (Photos are courtesy of Phil E. Davis)

These photos were taken at the Northern Tier Wilderness Canoe Base (C.H. Sommers), Ely, Minnesota and feature both summer and winter events. (Photos courtesy of Phil E. Davis)

President George Bush spoke at an arena show during the 1985 National Scout Jamboree. William "Green Bar Bill" Hillcourt, in the photo to left, wrote the 1929 Patrol Leader Handbook and the Scout Handbook of 1989. He was a popular Jamboree figure. (Photos courtesy of the Jamboree Photo Pool)

World Jamborees are great events for scouts to attend.

Pin-back buttons include some great graphics. The blue backgrounds were introduced in the 1920s, while the red-white-blue backgrounds were popular in the 1940s.

Handbooks are what every scout needed and should have used well. The earliest cover in this group is from 1920 (middle row, left). The others represent the major cover designs through 1997.

NATIONAL JAMBOREE ITEMS

1935 NATIONAL JAMBOREE

Identification card.	1935	15.00 - 25.00
Neckerchief, boy's, blue, 4" insignia, full square.	1935	100.00 - 150.00
Neckerchief, boy's, red, 4" insignia, full square.	1935	100.00 - 150.00
Neckerchief, leader, blue, 2" insignia, full square.	1935	100.00 - 150.00
Neckerchief, leader, red, 2" insignia, full square.	1935	100.00 - 150.00
Neckerchief, staff, purple, 2" insignia, full square.	1935	200.00 - 250.00
Pennant, felt, 10-1/2" x 28-3/4".	1935	100.00 - 125.00
Pocket patch, felt copy, yellow inner and purple-yellow outer circle, red lettering.	1935	3.00 - 5.00
Pocket patch, felt, blue inner and purple-gold outer circle, dark red lettering.	1935	100.00 - 150.00
Pocket patch, felt, blue inner circle, purple-gold outer circle, red lettering.	1935	125.00 - 150.00

Region shoulder patch, felt.	1935	200.00 - 250.00
Ring, silver.	1935	75.00 - 100.00
Troop flag.	1935	750.00 - 1,000.

1937 NATIONAL JAMBOREE

Contest medal, red-white-blue ribbon.	1937	250.00 - 350.00
Identification card w/ RR pass.	1937	15.00 - 25.00
Identification card.	1937	7.50 - 15.00

Neckerchief, boy's, two blue or red emblems, full square.	1937	90.00 - 120.00
Neckerchief, leader's, blue emblem w/ red border, or red emblem w/ blue border. Full square.	1937	150.00 - 200.00
Newspaper, full set, hardbound.	1937	60.00 - 90.00
Pennant, felt, 11-1/2" x 29".	1937	90.00 - 120.00
Pocket patch, felt.	1937	60.00 - 90.00

Region ribbon identification.	1937	100.00 - 140.00
Stationery, envelope and letter sheet.	1937	5.00 - 7.50
Troop flag.	1937	750.00 - 1,000.

1957 NATIONAL JAMBOREE

Baggage tag.	1957	5.00 - 10.00
Contest medal, red-white-blue ribbon.	1957	100.00 - 150.00
Jacket patch, twill.	1957	40.00 - 65.00
Leather patch.	1957	30.00 - 45.00
Neckerchief, white cotton; thin, medium or thick letters.	1957	15.00 - 25.00
Newspaper (full set).	1957	10.00 - 15.00
Pocket patch, twill.	1957	15.00 - 20.00
Sardines in can.	1957	15.00 - 25.00
Stationery, envelope and letter sheet.	1957	3.00 - 5.00
Tie, silk screen on maroon.	1957	75.00 - 100.00
Troop flag.	1957	300.00 - 400.00

1950 NATIONAL JAMBOREE

Identification card.	1950	10.00 - 15.00
Neckerchief, rayon-silk material.	1950	30.00 - 50.00
Neckerchief, cotton, black or brown spur.	1950	25.00 - 40.00
Pennant, blue felt, 11-1/2" x 29".	1950	20.00 - 30.00
Pocket patch, canvas, fine or coarse weave.	1950	30.00 - 40.00
Pocket patch, twill.	1950	25.00 - 40.00
Ring, silver.	1950	30.00 - 40.00
Stationery, envelope and letter sheet.	1950	4.00 - 7.50
Troop flag.	1950	300.00 - 400.00

1960 NATIONAL JAMBOREE

Area competition medal, gilt.	1960	50.00 - 75.00
Baggage tag.	1960	7.50 - 12.50
Competition medal, gilt silvered, or bronze.	1960	150.00 - 175.00
Golden Rule marble, blue.	1960	7.50 - 10.00
Jacket patch, twill.	1960	25.00 - 35.00
Neckerchief, white cotton.	1960	15.00 - 25.00
Newspaper (full set).	1960	5.00 - 10.00
Pennant, blue felt, 11" x 29-1/2".	1960	15.00 - 20.00
Pocket patch, twill.	1960	12.50 - 17.50

1953 NATIONAL JAMBOREE

Identification card.	1953	7.50 - 10.00
Jacket patch, twill.	1953	50.00 - 75.00
Neckerchief, white cotton.	1953	20.00 - 30.00
Pennant, blue felt, 11" x 28-3/4".	1953	20.00 - 25.00
Pocket patch, twill.	1953	20.00 - 30.00
Ring, silver.	1953	20.00 - 30.00
Troop flag.	1953	300.00 - 400.00

Sardines in can.	1960	15.00 - 25.00
Stationery, envelope and letter sheet.	1960	3.00 - 5.00
Troop flag.	1960	300.00 - 400.00

1964 NATIONAL JAMBOREE

Baggage tag.	1964	2.00 - 3.00
Jacket patch, twill.	1964	15.00 - 20.00
Leather patch.	1964	15.00 - 20.00
Neckerchief, white cotton; thin, medium or thick letters.	1964	10.00 - 15.00
Newspaper (full set).	1964	5.00 - 10.00
Pocket patch, cloth back.	1964	10.00 - 20.00
Sardine can.	1964	5.00 - 7.50
Troop flag.	1964	300.00 - 400.00

1969 NATIONAL JAMBOREE

Jacket patch.	1969	10.00 - 15.00
Leather patch.	1969	12.50 - 17.50
Neckerchief, green and brown on yellow.	1969	10.00 - 15.00
Neckerchief, souvenir, red and blue on white cotton. Printed envelope.	1969	5.00 - 7.50
Pennant, 11-1/2" x 28-1/2"	1969	17.50 - 25.00
Pocket patch, open or solid bough.	1969	10.00 - 12.50
Stationery, envelope and letter sheet.	1969	3.00 - 5.00
Troop flag.	1969	300.00 - 400.00
Zippo knife.	1969	10.00 - 15.00

1973 NATIONAL JAMBOREE

Baggage tag.	1973	1.00 - 3.00
Jacket patch, clear or green plastic back.	1973	7.50 - 10.00
Jacket patch, white or yellow woven back.	1973	7.50 - 10.00
Leather patch.	1973	7.50 - 10.00
Neckerchief.	1973	5.00 - 10.00
Pocket patch, twill, clear or green plastic back.	1973	3.00 - 5.00
Pocket patch, twill, white or yellow woven back.	1973	5.00 - 7.50

Sardine can.	1973	5.00 - 7.50
Stationery, envelope and letter sheet.	1973	3.00 - 5.00
Troop flag.	1973	300.00 - 400.00

1977 NATIONAL JAMBOREE

Baggage tag.	1977	1.00 - 3.00
Jacket patch, twill.	1977	5.00 - 7.50
Leather patch.	1977	10.00 - 12.50
Neckerchief, white cotton poly, m/c silk screen.	1977	5.00 - 10.00
Newspaper (full set).	1977	5.00 - 7.50
Pocket patch, twill.	1977	3.00 - 5.00

Sardines in can.	1977	7.50 - 10.00
Troop flag.	1977	300.00 - 400.00

1981 NATIONAL JAMBOREE

Baggage tag.	1981	1.00 - 2.00
Jacket patch.	1981	5.00 - 7.50
Leather patch.	1981	4.00 - 6.00

Neckerchief.	1981	4.00 - 6.00
Pocket patch.	1981	4.00 - 6.00
Troop flag.	1981	300.00 - 400.00

1985 NATIONAL JAMBOREE

Baggage tag.	1985	0.50 - 1.00
Jacket patch.	1985	7.50 - 10.00
Leather patch.	1985	5.00 - 7.50
Neckerchief.	1985	4.00 - 6.00
Newspaper (full set).	1985	5.00 - 7.50
Pennant, 9 x 18".	1985	10.00 - 15.00
Pocket patch.	1985	4.50 - 6.50
Stationery, envelope and letter sheet.	1985	1.00 - 2.00
Troop flag.	1985	300.00 - 400.00

1997 NATIONAL JAMBOREE

Jacket patch, fuzzy.	1997	7.50 - 10.00
Jacket patch, twill.	1997	20.00 - 30.00
Neckerchief.	1987	4.00 - 6.00
Newspaper (full set).	1997	5.00 - 7.50
Pocket patch.	1997	4.00 - 6.00
Troop flag.		250.00 - 350.00

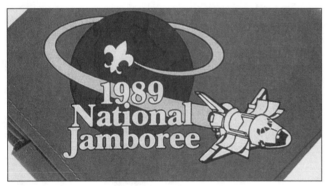

1989 NATIONAL JAMBOREE

Baggage tag.	1989	0.50 - 1.00
Jacket patch.	1989	7.50 - 10.00
Neckerchief.	1989	4.00 - 6.00
Newspaper (full set).	1989	5.00 - 7.50
Pocket patch.	1989	5.00 - 7.50
Stationery, envelope and letter sheet.	1989	0.50 - 1.00
Troop flag.	1989	300.00 - 400.00

1985 Plate Printer's Union commemorative engraving.

1993 NATIONAL JAMBOREE

Baggage tag.	1993	0.50 - 1.00
Jacket patch.	1993	7.50 - 10.00
Neckerchief.	1993	4.00 - 6.00
Pocket patch.	1993	4.00 - 6.00
Troop flag.	1993	250.00 - 350.00

SCOUT SERVICE CORPS

CHICAGO'S CENTURY OF PROGRESS FAIR
Service Unit, pocket patch.	1933	200.00 - 250.00
Service Unit, neckerchief.	1933	150.00 - 200.00

GETTYSBURG, 50TH ANNIVERSARY REUNION
Scout Service Medal.	1913	1,000. - 1,250.
Scout Service Patch.	1913	2,500. - 3,000.

INTERNATIONAL EUCHARISTIC CONGRESS, PHILADELPHIA, PA
Scout Service Corps, pocket patch.	1976	50.00 - 75.00
Scout Service Corps, neckerchief.	1976	40.00 - 50.00

NEW YORK WORLD'S FAIR
Service Camp patch.	1939	40.00 - 50.00
Service Camp, neckerchief slide, blue-orange Turk's head.	1939	30.00 - 40.00
Service Camp, patch.	1940	40.00 - 50.00
Service Camp, neckerchief.	1939	40.00 - 50.00
Service Camp, neckerchief.	1940	40.00 - 50.00
Service Corps, metal neckerchief slide.	1964-1965	15.00 - 20.00
Service Corps, pocket patch.	1964-1965	20.00 - 25.00
Service Corps, neckerchief.	1964-1965	40.00 - 50.00

SEATTLE WORLD'S FAIR
Service Scouts, neckerchief.	1962	100.00 - 150.00
Service Scouts, patch.	1962	100.00 - 125.00

Linen patch and red cross armband worn by a Service Scout at the Gettysburg veterans' 50th anniversary reunion.

Troop at the 1963 National Jamboree, Irvine, CA.

VARSITY SCOUTS

RANK BADGES

ACTIVITY PINS

Backpacking.	1989	2.00 - 3.00
Basketball.	1989	2.00 - 3.00
Bowling.	1989	2.00 - 3.00
Canoe camping.	1989	2.00 - 3.00
Caving.	1989	2.00 - 3.00
Cross-country skiing.	1989	2.00 - 3.00
Cycling.	1989	2.00 - 3.00
Discovering adventure.	1989	2.00 - 3.00
Fishing.	1989	2.00 - 3.00
Freestyle biking.	1989	2.00 - 3.00
Frontiersman.	1989	2.00 - 3.00
Mechanics.	1989	2.00 - 3.00
Orienteering.	1989	2.00 - 3.00
Rock climbing and rappelling.	1989	2.00 - 3.00
Roller hockey.	1989	2.00 - 3.00
Shooting sports.	1989	2.00 - 3.00
Snow camping.	1989	2.00 - 3.00
Soccer.	1989	2.00 - 3.00
Softball.	1989	2.00 - 3.00
Survival.	1989	2.00 - 3.00
Swimming.	1989	2.00 - 3.00
Tennis.	1989	2.00 - 3.00
Triathlon.	1989	2.00 - 3.00
Volleyball.	1989	2.00 - 3.00
Water-skiing.	1989	2.00 - 3.00
Whitewater canoeing.	1989	2.00 - 3.00

V LARGE CHENILLE BROWN WITH WHITE BORDER

	1989	5.00 - 7.50

VS LARGE CHENILLE BROWN WITH WHITE BORDER

	1980-1989	5.00 - 7.50

POSITION BADGES

PROGRAM MANAGER

Title above Tenderfoot emblem, tan rolled edge.	1989	1.00 - 1.50

SQUAD LEADER

Title around VS logo.	1984-1989	5.00 - 7.50
Title above Tenderfoot emblem, tan rolled edge.	1989	1.00 - 1.50

TEAM CAPTAIN

Title around VS logo.	1984-1989	5.00 - 7.50

TEAM CO-CAPTAIN

Title around VS logo.	1984-1989	5.00 - 7.50

VARSITY LETTER BAR

One bar with white border.	1980-1989	5.00 - 7.50
Single bar without border.	1980-1989	5.00 - 7.50
Three bars with white border.	1980-1989	5.00 - 7.50
Three bars without border.	1980-1989	5.00 - 7.50
Two bars with white border.	1980-1989	5.00 - 7.50
Two bars without border.	1980-1989	5.00 - 7.50

VARSITY TEAM CAPTAIN

Title above Tenderfoot emblem, tan rolled edge.	1989	1.00 - 1.50

VARSITY TEAM CO-CAPTAIN

Title above Tenderfoot emblem, tan rolled edge.	1989	1.00 - 1.50

UNIFORMS

BASEBALL STYLE MESH CAP

V/S logo on one-size-fits-all cap.	1985	5.00 - 7.50

HAT

Orange and brown mesh baseball cap, VS logo.	1984-1998	10.00 - 15.00

JACKET

Orange, cotton.	1979	30.00 - 40.00
Orange, nylon.	1979	30.00 - 40.00

ORANGE JACKET, VS LOGO ON RIGHT BREAST

	1984-1998	20.00 - 25.00

PULL-OVER SHORT SLEEVE SHIRT. VS LOGO ON RIGHT BREAST

	1984	10.00 - 15.00

SHIRT

Beige pull-over, brown trim. Tenderfoot emblem and VARSITY.	1979	10.00 - 15.00
Beige pull-over, brown trim. VS logo.	1979	10.00 - 15.00

SHOULDER LOOPS

Orange.	1985	1.00 - 1.50

POSITION BADGES - ADULT

ASSISTANT TEAM COACH

Title around VS logo.	1984-1989	5.00 - 7.50
Title above Tenderfoot emblem, tan rolled edge.	1989	1.00 - 1.50

COMMITTEE CHAIRMAN

Title around VS logo.	1984-1989	5.00 - 7.50

TEAM COACH

Title around VS logo.	1984-1989	5.00 - 7.50
Title above Tenderfoot emblem, tan rolled edge.	1989	1.00 - 1.50

TEAM COMMITTEE

Title around VS logo.	1984-1989	5.00 - 7.50
Title above Tenderfoot emblem, tan rolled edge.	1989	1.00 - 1.50

TEAM COMMITTEE CHAIRMAN

Title above Tenderfoot emblem, tan rolled edge.	1989	1.00 - 1.50

VARSITY HUDDLE COMMISSIONER

Tenderfoot Emblem within wreath on blaze twill.	1989	1.00 - 1.50

VARSITY HUDDLE STAFF

Tenderfoot Emblem within wreath on blaze twill.	1989	1.00 - 1.50

HANDBOOKS

VARSITY SCOUT HANDBOOK
First edition, three printings.   1978-1980   10.00 - 15.00
Second edition, two printings.   1984-1985   10.00 - 15.00

HANDBOOKS - LEADERS

LEADERS GUIDEBOOK OF VARSITY SCOUTING
Two editions.   1978-1980   15.00 - 20.00

VARSITY SCOUT LEADER GUIDEBOOK
Fourth edition, three printings.   1991-1997   5.00 - 7.50
One edition.   1984   10.00 - 15.00

RESOURCE BOOKS

ACTIVITY PAMPHLET
Backpacking.   1989   2.50 - 4.00
Basketball.   1989   2.50 - 4.00
Bowling.   1989   2.50 - 4.00
Canoe camping.   1989   2.50 - 4.00
Caving.   1989   2.50 - 4.00
Cross-country skiing.   1989   2.50 - 4.00
Cycling.   1989   2.50 - 4.00
Discovering adventure.   1989   2.50 - 4.00
Fishing.   1989   2.50 - 4.00
Freestyle biking.   1989   2.50 - 4.00
Frontiersman.   1989   2.50 - 4.00
Mechanics.   1989   2.50 - 4.00
Orienteering.   1989   2.50 - 4.00
Rock climbing and rappelling.   1989   2.50 - 4.00
Roller hockey.   1989   2.50 - 4.00
Shooting sports.   1989   2.50 - 4.00
Snow camping.   1989   2.50 - 4.00
Soccer.   1989   2.50 - 4.00
Softball.   1989   2.50 - 4.00
Survival.   1989   2.50 - 4.00
Swimming.   1989   2.50 - 4.00
Tennis.   1989   2.50 - 4.00
Triathlon.   1989   2.50 - 4.00
Volleyball.   1989   2.50 - 4.00
Water-skiing.   1989   2.50 - 4.00
Whitewater canoeing.   1989   2.50 - 4.00

TEAM FINANCIAL RECORD BOOK
Sailing cover, 8-1/2" x 11".   1985   5.00 - 7.50

TEAM RECORD BOOK
Five scouts in various activities cover, 8-1/2" x 11".   1985   5.00 - 7.50

VARSITY SCOUT GAME PLAN
Volume 1.   1984   7.50 - 10.00
Volume 2.   1984   7.50 - 10.00
Volume 3.   1984   7.50 - 10.00

VARSITY SCOUT LEADER HUDDLE
Planning Guide.   1984   15.00 - 20.00
Supplement 1.   1984   5.00 - 7.50
Supplement 2.   1984   5.00 - 7.50

LONE SCOUTS OF AMERICA

The Lone Scouts of America was a program developed in 1915 by William D. Boyce and was run out of his Chicago offices until 1925 when the Boy Scouts of America incorporated the program's goals and objectives into their own. The distinctive Native American themes and logo gained the imagination of youth in rural America where groups of one to ten could gather after school for projects. The advancement program was reinforced by a weekly newspaper, which was mailed to all members (by 1925 it was a monthly), that provided opportunity to highlight activities by the rural groups.

This section is referenced to Mitch Reis's book *The History of the Lone Scouts through Memorabilia*.

RANK BADGES

FIRST DEGREE
Indian Brave standing right w/ arms extended, 5/8" bronze shield, pinback or lapel clasp. — 1916-1928 — MR.2.1 — 50.00 - 75.00

FOURTH-SIXTH DEGREE, TOTEM POLE LODGE
LSA on scroll, head and hands above, gilt bronze and enamel. — 1916-1928 — MR.5.1 — 75.00 - 125.00

MEMBERSHIP PIN
Circle on arrowhead, gilt bronze, red LSA monogram at center, blue background, 3/4". — 1921-1935 — 25.00 - 40.00

Circle on arrowhead, silver, red LSA monogram at center, blue background, 3/4". — 1921-1935 — 25.00 - 40.00

Celluloid, 7/8". — 1915-1916 — MR.1.1 — 15.00 - 25.00

Arrowhead in circle, "Lone Scout / Do a Useful Thing Each Day" on arrowhead, 3/4" bronze. — 1916-1921 — MR.1.2 — 25.00 - 35.00

Circle on arrowhead, LSA monogram at center, 3/4" bronze. — 1921-1935 — MR.1.3 — 10.00 - 15.00

SAGAMORE LODGE
Indian on horseback left within wreath, gilt bronze and enamel. — 1917-1928 — MR.5.1 — 100.00 - 140.00

SECOND DEGREE
Campfire within triangle on shield, 11/16", bronze. — 1916-1928 — MR.3.1 — 75.00 - 100.00

THIRD DEGREE
Eagle in flight on shield, 5/8", nickel silver. — 1916-1928 — MR.4.1 — 75.00 - 100.00

AWARD MEDALS

MERIT AWARD, FIRST PRIZE
Gilt pendant on red-blue ribbon. — 1916-1930 — 250.00 - 400.00

MERIT AWARD, SECOND PRIZE
Silvered pendant on red-blue ribbon. — 1916-1930 — 250.00 - 400.00

MERIT AWARD, THIRD AWARD, LITERARY ACHIEVEMENT
Bronze pendant on red-blue ribbon. — 1925-1930 — 250.00 - 400.00

MERIT AWARD, THIRD PRIZE
Bronze pendant on red-blue ribbon. — 1916-1925 — 250.00 - 400.00

POSITION BADGES

LSD AND BSA IN RED CIRCLE. STANDING INDIAN LEFT.
Tan cut edge. — 1927-1933 — 40.00 - 60.00

LSS AND BSA IN RED CIRCLE. STANDING INDIAN LEFT.
Tan cut edge. — 1933-1979 — 30.00 - 50.00

LONE SCOUT BSA AND STANDING INDIAN
Khaki cloth, red rolled edge border. — 1980-1982 — 3.00 - 5.00
Tan cloth, red rolled edge border. — 1982-1989 — 3.00 - 5.00
Tan cloth, black rolled edge border. — 1985 — 3.00 - 5.00
Tan cloth, tan cut edge border. — 1990 — 3.00 - 5.00

POSITION BADGES - ADULT

TRIBE CAPTAIN
Indian bust left w/ headdress, on shield. — 1917-1920 — 100.00 - 150.00

TRIBE CHIEF
TRIBE CHIEF and LSA monogram below Indian bust left. — 1921-1928 — 100.00 - 150.00

HANDBOOKS

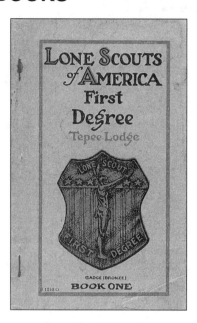

**LONE SCOUTS OF AMERICA.
THE FIRST, OR LONE, SCOUT DEGREE.**
Four varieties, Indian striding   1915-1918   MR.1.1-4   10.00 - 15.00
right w/ arms outstretched.

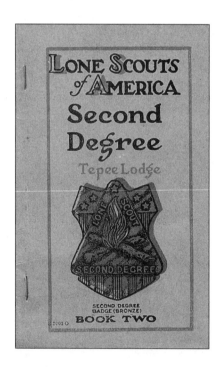

**LONE SCOUTS OF AMERICA.
THE SECOND, OR WOODCRAFT, DEGREE.**
1916-1918   MR.1.5   15.00 - 20.00

LONE SCOUTS OF AMERICA. TEEPEE LODGE TESTS.
Magazine size.   1916-1918   MR.1.6   15.00 - 20.00

**LONE SCOUTS OF AMERICA. TEEPEE LODGE BOOK,
FIRST, SECOND, AND THIRD DEGREE.**
1918-1920   MR.2.1   20.00 - 30.00

**LONE SCOUTS OF AMERICA. TOTEM POLE LODGE BOOK,
FOURTH, FIFTH, AND SIXTH DEGREE.**
1918-1920   MR.2.2   20.00 - 30.00

**LONE SCOUTS OF AMERICA.
SAGAMORE LODGE (SEVENTH DEGREE).**
Lone Scout Record Book.   1918-1920   MR.2.3   20.00 - 30.00

LONE SCOUTS OF AMERICA. FIRST DEGREE, TEEPEE LODGE.
1920-1930   MR.3.1   20.00 - 30.00

**LONE SCOUTS OF AMERICA.
SECOND DEGREE, TEEPEE LODGE.**
1920-1930   MR.3.2   20.00 - 30.00

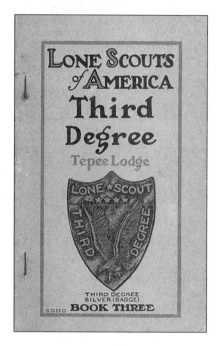

LONE SCOUTS OF AMERICA. THIRD DEGREE, TEEPEE LODGE.
Varieties on pg. 39 w/ Boyce, or   1920-1930   MR.3.3   20.00 - 30.00
West (post-1925), as Chief
Totem.

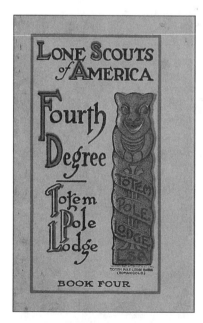

**LONE SCOUTS OF AMERICA.
FOURTH DEGREE, TOTEM POLE LODGE.**
Variety on pg. 48 w/ LSA address   1920-1930   MR.3.4   20.00 - 30.00
at Dearborn Street, or post-
1925 w/ BSA at that address.

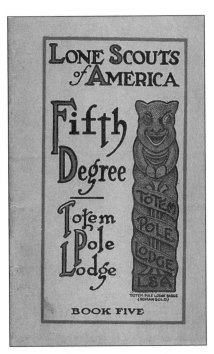

LONE SCOUTS OF AMERICA.
FIFTH DEGREE, TOTEM POLE LODGE.
Variety w/ or w/o BSA paper   1920-1930   MR.3.5   20.00 - 30.00
street address label (post-
1925)

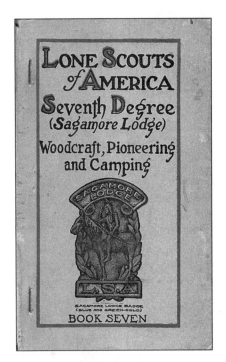

LONE SCOUTS OF AMERICA.
SEVENTH DEGREE (SAGAMORE LODGE).
Woodcraft, Pioneering, and   1920-1930   MR.3.7   20.00 - 30.00
Camping, varieties w/ or w/o
BSA address (post-1925).

LONE SCOUTS OF AMERICA, HANDBOOK
Indian standing right w/ arms   1920-1921   MR.4.1   30.00 - 50.00
outstretched.

OFFICIAL HANDBOOK OF THE LONE SCOUTS OF AMERICA
Two Indians flanking title,   1921-1925   MR.4.2   30.00 - 50.00
drawings in four corners. Pg.
22 date is 1921, two varieties.

Two Indians standing, flanking   1925-1927   MR.4.3-4   30.00 - 50.00
title, drawings in four corners.
Pg. 22 date is 1925, two
varieties.

PINS

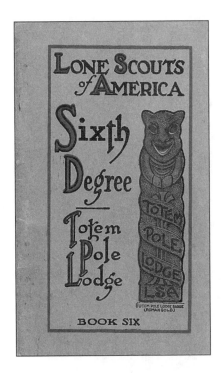

LSA WITHIN CIRCLE
Bronze.   1917-1921   40.00 - 60.00

LONE SCOUTS OF AMERICA.
SIXTH DEGREE, TOTEM POLE LODGE.
Variety w/ or w/o BSA address   1920-1930   MR.3.6   20.00 - 30.00
(post-1925) inside front cover.

POSTCARDS & GREETING CARDS

1918 LONE SCOUT MAGAZINE COVER	1918	100.00 - 150.00
Four-paragraph verse, MAC, FIDO, SLIPPERY FRITZ, AND JAKE	1918-1920	250.00 - 300.00

MISCELLANEOUS STUFF

BOOSTER BUTTON
LSA enameled within golden wreath, 5/8".	1920-1930	200.00 - 250.00

FLAG
LSA in circle in red, on blue felt.	1918-1920	250.00 - 300.00

KEY CHAIN
Indian on horseback left, within inverted triangle, LSA on shield, DAUTED below, bronze or silvered.	1917-1921	150.00 - 200.00

LONE SCOUT RING
LS and XVII on arrowhead on top, eagles at sides, for the 17th Club.	1917	150.00 - 200.00

LONE SCOUT, OFFICIAL MAGAZINE
Weekly 10/15-12/1920, then monthly to 4/1924, any single issue.	1915-1924	10.00 - 15.00

LSA HELPING TO WIN THE WAR
1-5/16" bronze pin, scenes of planes above fields and glass preserves.	1918	200.00 - 250.00

LSA MONOGRAM
Red felt on blue circle.	1922-1927	100.00 - 150.00
Red felt.	1922-1927	100.00 - 150.00

LSC ENAMELED, W/ GOLD QUILL IN INKWELL
Pinback.	1919-1930	250.00 - 300.00

MEMBERSHIP CARD
Four varieties.	1915-1924	10.00 - 15.00

RING
LSD and BSA w/ Indian standing left on round top, shields w/ First Class emblem at sides.	1927-1930	300.00 - 350.00
LSD and BSA w/ Indian standing left in oval top, knots at sides, gold filled.	1930-1938	200.00 - 250.00
LSD and BSA w/ Indian standing left in oval top, knots at sides, silver.	1930-1941	200.00 - 250.00

SERVICE BAR
LSA on 1" x 5/16" bronze bar, for six month membership.	1919-1926	75.00 - 100.00
LSA on 1" x 5/16" gilt bar, for two year membership.	1919-1926	100.00 - 150.00
LSA on 1" x 5/16" silvered bar, for one year membership.	1919-1926	75.00 - 100.00

SWEATER
LSA monogram in red on blue circle.	1917-1921	250.00 - 350.00

WATCH FOB
Indian on horseback within inverted triangle, LSA on shield, DAUTED below, bronze or silvered pendant on leather strap.	1917-1921	200.00 - 250.00

SEA SCOUTING

RANK BADGES

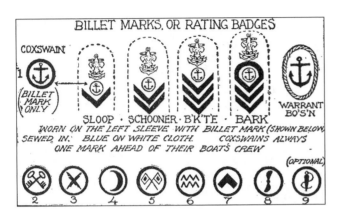

BILLET MARKS

Cook, crescent.	1915-1918	150.00 - 200.00
Crew Leader, anchor.	1915-1918	150.00 - 200.00
Handyman, square.	1915-1918	150.00 - 200.00
Sailmake, awl.	1915-1918	150.00 - 200.00
Shipsmith, propeller.	1915-1918	150.00 - 200.00
Signalman, crossed flags.	1915-1918	150.00 - 200.00
Steward, crossed keys.	1915-1918	150.00 - 200.00
Waterman, pair of waves.	1915-1918	150.00 - 200.00
Yeoman, crossed quills.	1915-1918	150.00 - 200.00

EAGLE SCOUT

Black felt cloth, scroll border within oval, no knot beneath.	1924-1932	300.00 - 400.00
Blue felt, no wording.	1924-1932	500.00 - 600.00
Cut edge white twill cloth, scroll border within oval, no knot beneath.	1924-1932	300.00 - 400.00
White twill, no wording.	1924-1932	500.00 - 600.00
White twill cloth, complete lettering around, cotton or silk threads.	1932-1955	200.00 - 300.00
Black felt cloth, complete lettering around, cotton or silk thread.	1933-1955	300.00 - 400.00
Blue felt, full wording in cotton thread.	1933-1955	300.00 - 400.00
Blue felt, full wording in silk thread.	1933-1955	200.00 - 300.00
White twill, full wording in cotton thread.	1933-1955	300.00 - 400.00
White twill, full wording in silk thread.	1933-1955	300.00 - 400.00

LIFE SCOUT

Blue felt, knot under heart, gold-lettered motto.	1925-1942	500.00 - 600.00
White twill, knot under heart, gold-lettered motto.	1925-1942	150.00 - 200.00
White twill, knot in heart, white-lettered motto.	1942-1950	100.00 - 150.00
Blue felt, two red stripes.	1950-1956	100.00 - 150.00
White twill, two red stripes.	1950-1956	100.00 - 150.00

STAR SCOUT

Blue felt, double knot below.	1925-1942	150.00 - 200.00
Blue felt, single knot below.	1925-1942	150.00 - 200.00
White twill, double knot below	1925-1942	500.00 - 600.00
White twill, single knot below.	1925-1942	500.00 - 600.00
Blue felt, two red lines in shield.	1942-1954	100.00 - 150.00
White twill, two red lines in shield.	1942-1954	100.00 - 150.00

Sea Scout Apprentice, Ordinary, and Able patches.

SEA SCOUT ABLE

Anchor behind First Class emblem, three bars below.	1924	10.00 - 15.00

SEA SCOUT APPRENTICE

Anchor behind First Class emblem, one bar below.	1924	15.00 - 25.00
Anchor behind First Class emblem, one bar below.	1924-1949	15.00 - 25.00

SEA SCOUT ORDINARY

Anchor behind First Class emblem, two bars below.	1924	25.00 - 40.00

RANK MEDALS

LIFE SCOUT

Blue felt, knot in heart, white-lettered motto.	1942-1950	75.00 - 100.00

QUARTERMASTER AWARD MEDAL

Anchor behind First Class emblem on compass and ship's wheel, blue ribbon w/ diagonal stripe.	1931-1937	500.00 - 750.00
Anchor behind First Class emblem on compass and ship's wheel, blue ribbon, enamel on silver pendant.	1937-1969	175.00 - 200.00
Anchor behind First Class emblem on compass and ship's wheel, blue ribbon, enamel on rhodium pendant.	1969	50.00 - 75.00

POSITION BADGES

SEA SCOUT BOATSWAIN

Anchor behind First Class emblem, three felt chevrons.	1918-1949	5.00 - 10.00
Anchor behind First Class emblem, three twill chevrons.	1918-1949	20.00 - 30.00

SEA SCOUT BOATSWAIN'S MATE

Anchor behind First Class emblem, two felt chevrons.	1918-1949	20.00 - 30.00
Anchor behind First Class emblem, two twill chevrons.	1918-1949	20.00 - 30.00

SEA SCOUT BUGLER

Bugle.	1941-1949	10.00 - 15.00

SEA SCOUT COXWAIN

Anchor behind First Class emblem, one felt chevron.	1918-1949	20.00 - 30.00
Anchor behind First Class emblem, one twill chevron.	1918-1949	20.00 - 30.00

SEA SCOUT YEOMAN

Crossed quills.	1941-1949	10.00 - 15.00

POSITION BADGES - ADULT

COMMITTEE CHAIRMAN

Anchor behind First Class emblem in diamond rope border.	1941-1949	15.00 - 25.00

COMMITTEEMAN

Anchor behind First Class emblem in oval rope border.	1941-1949	15.00 - 25.00

LOCAL OFFICER RATING STRIP

Two stars.	1941-1949	5.00 - 10.00

MATE

Anchor behind First Class emblem, one stripe below.	1918-1941	30.00 - 50.00
Star patch to be added to Universal emblem.	1941-1949	15.00 - 25.00

OFFICER INSIGNIA

Bark. Circle with two thick and one thin bars below SEA SCOUTS B.S.A.	1915-1920	2,000. - 2,500.
Barkentine. Circle with two bars below SEA SCOUTS B.S.A.	1915-1920	2,000.- 2,500.
Chief Seascout. Circle with two stars on one very wide bar below SEA SCOUTS B.S.A.	1915-1920	4,000. - 5,000.
Commodore. Circle with one very wide bar below SEA SCOUTS B.S.A.	1915-1920	4,000. - 5,000.
Fleet Portmaster. Circle with star on one very wide bar below SEA SCOUTS B.S.A.	1915-1920	4,000. - 5,000.
Portmaster. Circle with four bars below SEA SCOUTS B.S.A.	1915-1920	4,000. - 5,000.
Schooner. Circle with one thin and one thick bar below SEA SCOUTS B.S.A.	1915-1920	2,000. - 2,500.
Ship. Circle with three bars below SEA SCOUTS B.S.A.	1915-1920	2,000. - 2,500.
Sloop. Circle with single bar below SEA SCOUTS B.S.A.	1915-1920	2,000. - 2,500.

REGIONAL / NATIONAL OFFICER RATING STRIP

Four stars.	1941-1949	5.00 - 10.00

SEA SCOUT UNIVERSAL EMBLEM

Anchor behind First Class emblem.	1941-1949	10.00 - 15.00

SHIP COMMITTEE

Anchor behind First Class emblem, all within rope oval, 1-1/2 stripes below.	1918-1941	30.00 - 50.00

SHIP COMMITTEE CHAIRMAN

Anchor behind First Class emblem, all within rope diamond, 1-1/2 stripes below.	1918-1941	30.00 - 50.00

SHIP OFFICER RATING STRIP

One star.	1941-1949	5.00 - 10.00

SKIPPER

Anchor behind First Class emblem, 1-1/2 stripes below.	1918-1941	30.00 - 50.00
Star and bar patch to be added to Universal emblem.	1941-1949	15.00 - 25.00

HANDBOOKS

SEA SCOUTING AND SEAMANSHIP FOR BOYS. BADEN-POWELL, WARRINGTON

The English Sea Scout Manual used in the U.S.	1911	500.00 - 650.00

CRUISING FOR SEA SCOUTS. CAREY, A.A.

Three printings.	1912-1914	25.00 - 40.00

NAUTICAL SCOUTING FOR BOY SCOUTS OF AMERICA

	1915	20.00 - 30.00

THE SEA SCOUT MANUAL

BOY SCOUTS OF AMERICA

THE SEA SCOUT MANUAL

J.A. Wilder, editor, five printings.	1919-1923	150.00 - 250.00
Capt. Felix Riesenberg, editor, fourteen printings.	1925-1938	40.00 - 75.00
Carl Langenbacher, ten printings, 698 pgs. + 10-pg. preface.	1939-1949	40.00 - 60.00

SEA EXPLORER MANUAL

Revised edition, 640 pgs + 4-pg. forward, 4-5/8" x 7".	1950-1963	10.00 - 25.00

SEA EXPLORING MANUAL

442 pgs., 5-3/8" x 8".	1966-1976	7.50 - 15.00

HANDBOOKS - LEADERS

HANDBOOK FOR CREW LEADERS

First edition, two printings.	1941-1942	15.00 - 25.00
Second edition, one printing.	1946	25.00 - 35.00

HANDBOOK FOR SKIPPERS

W.C. Menninger, first edition, three printings, 280 pgs.	1932-1936	75.00 - 100.00
Second edition, five printings, 400-440 pgs. (fifth is 314 pgs).	1939-1947	50.00 - 75.00
Third edition, 224 pgs.	1971	10.00 - 20.00

UNIFORMS

CAP

Khaki, Sea Scout emblem, blue, Bark.	1912-1924	75.00 - 125.00
Khaki, Sea Scout emblem, one blue band, Barkentine.	1912-1924	75.00 - 125.00
Khaki, Sea Scout emblem, one white band, schooner.	1912-1924	75.00 - 125.00
Khaki, Sea Scout emblem, sloop.	1912-1924	75.00 - 125.00
Khaki, Sea Scout emblem, white, ship.	1912-1924	40.00 - 75.00
White.	1924-1953	15.00 - 25.00
White.	1953-1969	10.00 - 15.00

COMMUNITY STRIP

Blue on white twill or white on blue felt.	1924	3.00 - 5.00

FLAGSHIP FLEET RATING

Anchor behind First Class emblem at ctr., red and blue fully embroidered background patch.	1941-1947	10.00 - 15.00

FLAGSHIP FLOTILLA RATING

Anchor behind First Class emblem at ctr., red and blue fully embroidered background patch.	1941-1947	10.00 - 15.00

FLAGSHIP SQUADRON RATING

Anchor behind First Class emblem at ctr., red and blue fully embroidered background patch.	1941-1947	10.00 - 15.00

JUMPER

Khaki with navy blue collar, pocket flaps and wrist bands.	1912-1924	200.00 - 300.00
Blue with BSA National Council, New York City label.	1924-1953	50.00 - 75.00
White with BSA National Council, New York City label.	1924-1953	50.00 - 75.00
Blue with BSA National Council label.	1953-1969	50.00 - 75.00
White with BSA National Council label.	1953-1969	50.00 - 75.00

LONG CRUISE

Red or white arc patch.	1924	10.00 - 15.00
Sailing ship in circle.	1924	5.00 - 10.00

NATIONAL FLEET RATING

Anchor behind First Class emblem at ctr., blue fully embroidered patch.	1939-1940	10.00 - 15.00

PANTS

Khaki.	1912-1924	400.00 - 500.00
Blue with BSA National Council, New York City label.	1924-1953	50.00 - 75.00
White with BSA National Council, New York City label.	1924-1953	50.00 - 75.00
Blue with BSA National Council label.	1953-1969	50.00 - 75.00
White with BSA National Council label.	1953-1969	50.00 - 75.00

REGIONAL FLOTILLA RATING

Anchor behind First Class emblem at ctr., blue fully embroidered patch.	1939-1940	10.00 - 15.00

SHIRT STRIP

Sea Scouts B.S.A. in blue on white.	1924-1949	7.50 - 10.00
Sea Scouts B.S.A. in white on blue.	1924-1949	7.50 - 10.00

STATE STRIP

Blue on white twill or white on blue felt.	1924	15.00 - 20.00

SWEATER PATCH

BSA in FDL on anchor, SEA SCOUTS around, white on blue felt.	1918-1924	75.00 - 125.00
Sea Scout emblem in blue felt circle.	1924-1941	60.00 - 100.00

UNIFORMS - ADULT

BLAZER, BULLION-EMBROIDERED PROGRAM EMBLEM

First Class emblem on anchor.	1971	15.00 - 20.00

UNIFORM SQUARE KNOTS

RIBBON BAR

Quartermaster Award. Blue. 1 3/8 x 1/4.	1934-1946	200.00 - 250.00

RECOGNITIONS - ADULT

SKIPPER'S KEY TRAINING AWARD

First-Class emblem on anchor on training award key pendant, 10 kt. GF, solid blue ribbon.	1941	75.00 - 100.00
First-Class emblem on anchor on training award key pendant, 10 kt. GF, blue-white ribbon.	1941	50.00 - 75.00

RESOURCE BOOKS

SERVICE LIBRARY - SERIES E

The Sea Scout Patrol.	1930	10.00 - 15.00
What Sea Scouts Do.	1930	10.00 - 15.00
Aids for Sea Scout Leaders.	1931	10.00 - 15.00
How to Organize a Sea Scout Ship.	1931	10.00 - 15.00
The Sea Scout Patrol and How it Holds Scouts in the Troop.	1931	10.00 - 15.00
Sea Scouts Afloat.	1931	10.00 - 15.00
The Sea Scout Patrol in a Troop-A Scoutmaster's Opportunity.	1939	10.00 - 15.00

UNIT EQUIPMENT

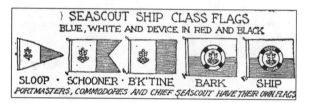

FLAG

Rectangular flag, Sea Scout emblem at left end. Barkentine.	1912-1924	200.00 - 300.00
Rectangular flag, Sea Scout emblem within white life ring with additional ornamentation. Ship.	1912-1924	200.00 - 300.00
Rectangular flag, Sea Scout emblem within white life ring. Bark.	1912-1924	200.00 - 300.00
Rectangular flag, 'swallow tail ends', Sea Scout emblem at left end. Schooner.	1912-1924	200.00 - 300.00
Triangular pennant, Sea Scout emblem at wide end. Sloop.	1912-1924	200.00 - 300.00

KNIVES

ULSTER KNIFE CO.

Sea Scout emblem in shield-shaped shield, 4-1/8" bone handle, sheep foot and marlin spike.	1936-1940	U.7	150.00 - 200.00

PINBACK BUTTONS

SEA SCOUT FACING

On red-white-blue background, 3/4".	1960-1965	15.00 - 25.00

MEDALLIONS

SEA SCOUTING 75TH ANNIVERSARY

Cast pewter, uniface.	1987	Dio.1987.1	10.00 - 15.00

Sea scout signaling.

Sea scout region officials.

SEA EXPLORING

RANK BADGES

QUARTERMASTER AWARD PATCH
Anchor behind First Class emblem on   1966   10.00 - 15.00
  compass and ship's wheel.

RANK MEDALS

QUARTERMASTER AWARD MEDAL
Anchor behind First Class emblem   1996-1998 150.00 - 200.00
  on compass and ship's wheel as pendant,
  openwork knot bar on blue ribbon.
Anchor behind First Class emblem   1998   75.00 - 100.00
  on compass and ship's wheel as pendant,
  solid knot bar on blue ribbon.

POSITION BADGES - ADULT

LOCAL CHAIRMAN
Anchor behind First Class emblem within   1949   10.00 - 15.00
  rope diamond, two stars below.

LOCAL COMMITTEE MEMBER
Anchor behind First Class emblem within   1949   10.00 - 15.00
  rope oval, two stars below.

LOCAL COUNCIL STAFF
Anchor behind First Class emblem,   1949   10.00 - 15.00
  two stars below.

NATIONAL PROFESSIONAL STAFF
Anchor behind First Class emblem,   1949   10.00 - 15.00
  four stars below.

REGIONAL / NATIONAL CHAIRMAN
Anchor behind First Class emblem   1949   20.00 - 30.00
  within rope diamond, four stars below.

REGIONAL/NATIONAL COMMITTEE MEMBER
Anchor behind First Class emblem   1949   10.00 - 15.00
  within rope oval, four stars below.

SEA EXPLORER SKIPPER
Anchor behind First Class emblem,   1949   5.00 - 10.00
  star and bar below.

SEAMAN / MATE
Anchor behind First Class emblem, one star   1949   5.00 - 10.00
  below.

SHIP COMMITTEE CHAIRMAN
Anchor behind First Class emblem   1949   10.00 - 15.00
  within rope diamond, one star below.

SHIP COMMITTEE MEMBER
Anchor behind First Class emblem   1949   10.00 - 15.00
  within rope oval, one star below.

HANDBOOKS - LEADERS

HANDBOOK FOR SKIPPERS
Fourth edition.   2000   10.00 - 15.00

PETTY OFFICERS HANDBOOK
Third edition.   2000   10.00 - 15.00

UNIFORMS

QUALIFIED SEAMAN PIN
   1960   10.00 - 15.00

SEA EXPLORER MEDALLION
Anchor behind First Class emblem   1949   5.00 - 10.00
  on cut edge blue felt.
Anchor behind First Class emblem   1949   5.00 - 10.00
  on rolled edge blue twill.
Anchor behind First Class emblem   1949   5.00 - 10.00
  on rolled edge white twill.

SHIRT STRIP
Sea Explorers B.S.A. in blue on white.   1949   5.00 - 7.50
Sea Explorers B.S.A. in white on blue.   1949   5.00 - 7.50

SMALL-BOAT HANDLER PIN
   1960   10.00 - 15.00

UNIT NUMERALS
Solid embroidery, white on blue, blue on   1960   2.50 - 5.00
  white, black on white, 0, 1, 2, 3, 4, 5, 6, 7, 8.

RECOGNITIONS - ADULT

SEA BADGE PIN
Trident behind Sea Scout emblem.   1970   20.00 - 30.00
Trident within wreath.   1970   20.00 - 30.00

RESOURCE BOOKS

ADVANCED SEAMANSHIP
Instructor's Guide.   1966   5.00 - 10.00
Workbook.   1966   5.00 - 10.00

SAFE-BOATING
Instructor's Guide.   1966   5.00 - 10.00
Workbook.   1966   5.00 - 10.00

UNIT EQUIPMENT

SHIP FLAG
Wool, red top, blue bottom,   1950-1970 35.00 - 50.00
  Sea Scout emblem in ctr.
Nylon, blue, white Sea Scout emblem in ctr.   1971   50.00 - 75.00

ROVER SCOUTING

UNIFORMS

ROVER SCOUT ON CIRCLE BELOW **TENDERFOOT BADGE**

Squat crown, cut edge.	1935-1954	75.00 - 100.00
Tall crown w/ctr. line, cut edge.	1935-1954	250.00 - 300.00
Tan, cut cloth.	1935-1954	200.00 - 300.00

SENIOR SCOUT OUTFIT

POSITION BADGES

SENIOR SCOUT OUTFIT ASSISTANT CREW LEADER
One bar behind white universal emblem,   1945-1949   50.00 - 75.00
   cut edge blue twill.

SENIOR SCOUT OUTFIT CREW LEADER
Two bars behind white universal emblem,   1945-1949   50.00 - 75.00
   cut edge blue twill.

SENIOR SCOUT OUTFIT DEPUTY SENIOR CREW LEADER
2-1/2" bars behind white universal emblem,   1945-1949   20.00 - 30.00
   cut edge blue twill.

SENIOR SCOUT OUTFIT SENIOR CREW LEADER
Three bars behind white universal emblem,   1935-1949   50.00 - 75.00
   cut edge blue twill.

SENIOR SCOUT OUTFIT UNIVERSAL EMBLEM
White C.A.W. on gold FDL, white border on   1945-1949   15.00 - 20.00
   blue cut edge twill.

SENIOR SCOUTING

RANK BADGES

EXPLORER FIRST HONORS
Two green bars on tan cut cloth.   1935-1949   50.00 - 75.00

EXPLORER SECOND HONORS
Three green bars on tan cut cloth.   1935-1949   50.00 - 75.00

SENIOR SCOUT TITLE

Artisan, on explorer green twill.	1935-1949	30.00 - 45.00
Artisan, on scout green twill.	1935-1949	15.00 - 25.00
Artisan, on sea scout blue felt.	1935-1949	40.00 - 60.00
Artisan, on sea scout blue felt.	1935-1949	40.00 - 60.00
Artist, on explorer green twill.	1935-1949	30.00 - 45.00
Artist, on scout green twill.	1935-1949	15.00 - 25.00
Artist, on sea scout blue felt.	1935-1949	40.00 - 60.00
Citizen, on explorer green twill.	1935-1949	30.00 - 45.00
Citizen, on scout green twill.	1935-1949	15.00 - 25.00
Citizen, on sea scout blue felt.	1935-1949	40.00 - 60.00
Conservationist, on explorer green twill.	1935-1949	30.00 - 45.00
Conservationist, on scout green twill.	1935-1949	15.00 - 25.00
Conservationist, on sea scout blue felt.	1935-1949	40.00 - 60.00
Craftsman, on explorer green twill.	1935-1949	30.00 - 45.00
Craftsman, on scout green twill.	1935-1949	15.00 - 25.00
Craftsman, on sea scout blue felt.	1935-1949	40.00 - 60.00
Journalist, on explorer green twill.	1935-1949	30.00 - 45.00
Journalist, on scout green twill.	1935-1949	15.00 - 25.00
Journalist, on sea scout blue felt.	1935-1949	40.00 - 60.00
Naturalist, on explorer green twill.	1935-1949	30.00 - 45.00
Naturalist, on scout green twill.	1935-1949	15.00 - 25.00
Naturalist, on sea scout blue felt.	1935-1949	40.00 - 60.00
Radioman, on explorer green twill.	1935-1949	30.00 - 45.00
Radioman, on scout green twill.	1935-1949	15.00 - 25.00
Radioman, on sea scout blue felt.	1935-1949	40.00 - 60.00
Seaman, on explorer green twill.	1935-1949	30.00 - 45.00
Seaman, on scout green twill.	1935-1949	15.00 - 25.00
Seaman, on sea scout blue felt.	1935-1949	40.00 - 60.00
Sportsman, on explorer green twill.	1935-1949	30.00 - 45.00
Sportsman, on scout green twill.	1935-1949	15.00 - 25.00
Sportsman, on sea scout blue felt.	1935-1949	40.00 - 60.00
Woodsman, on explorer green twill.	1935-1949	30.00 - 45.00
Woodsman, on scout green twill.	1935-1949	15.00 - 25.00
Woodsman, on sea scout blue felt.	1935-1949	40.00 - 60.00
Dairyman, on explorer green twill.	1942-1949	30.00 - 45.00
Dairyman, on scout green twill.	1942-1949	15.00 - 25.00
Farm manager, on explorer green twill.	1942-1949	30.00 - 45.00
Farm manager, on scout green twill.	1942-1949	15.00 - 25.00
Gardener, on explorer green twill.	1942-1949	30.00 - 45.00
Gardener, on scout green twill.	1942-1949	15.00 - 25.00
Livestockman, on explorer green twill.	1942-1949	30.00 - 45.00
Livestockman, on scout green twill.	1942-1949	15.00 - 25.00
Poultryman, on explorer green twill.	1942-1949	30.00 - 45.00
Poultryman, on scout green twill.	1942-1949	15.00 - 25.00
Airman, on air scout blue twill.	1943-1949	150.00 - 200.00

UNIVERSAL EXPLORER MEDALLION
BSA at top, EXPLORER SCOUT legend below,   1935-1949   10.00 - 15.00
  Tenderfoot emblem at ctr. Senior Scout titles
  added around this central badge.

RANK & POSITION BADGES

EXPLORER PATROL LEADER
One green chevron on tan cut cloth.   1935-1949   50.00 - 75.00

EXPLORER PATROL LEADER W/ FIRST HONORS
Two green chevrons on tan cut cloth.   1935-1949   50.00 - 75.00

EXPLORER PATROL LEADER W/ SECOND HONORS
Three green chevrons on tan cut cloth.   1935-1949   50.00 - 75.00

POSITION BADGES - ADULT

ADVISOR
BOY SCOUTS OF AMERICA EXPLORERS   1935-1949   25.00 - 35.00
  legend, 8-pointed star behind First Class
  emblem, white on green twill, cut edge.

ASSISTANT ADVISOR
BOY SCOUTS OF AMERICA EXPLORERS   1935-1949   20.00 - 30.00
  legend, 8-pointed star behind First Class
  emblem, gold on green twill, cut edge.

HANDBOOKS

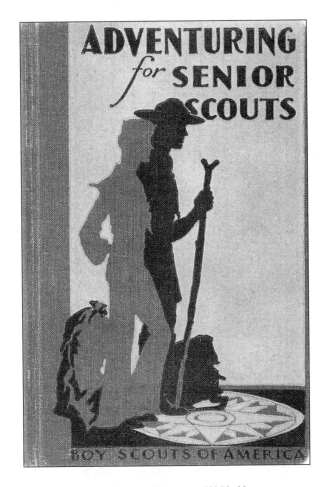

ADVENTURING FOR SENIOR SCOUTS, W.H. HURT, ED.

Hardcover w/ Senior and Sea Scout, proof edition and all printings.	1938-1939	25.00 - 40.00
Hardcover w/ Senior and Sea Scout, revised second printing in 1944 w/ red cover.	1942-1944	25.00 - 40.00
Tan cover w/ Senior, Sea Scout, and Air Scout.	1945-1946	25.00 - 40.00

RESOURCE BOOKS

HINTS ON SENIOR SCOUT LEADERSHIP
1947 edition.	10.00 - 15.00
1948 edition.	10.00 - 15.00
1949 edition.	10.00 - 15.00

SENIOR SCOUTING GUIDEBOOK
1942 edition.	15.00 - 25.00
1946 edition, Dec. printing.	10.00 - 15.00
1946 edition, Jan. printing.	10.00 - 15.00

SENIOR SCOUTING PROGRAM NOTEBOOK
1945 edition.	10.00 - 15.00
1946 edition.	7.50 - 10.00
1947 edition.	7.50 - 10.00
1948 edition.	7.50 - 10.00
1949-50 edition.	7.50 - 10.00

THE GUIDE BOOK OF SENIOR SCOUTING
1935 printing.	25.00 - 35.00
1937 printing.	20.00 - 30.00
1938 printing.	20.00 - 30.00
1941 printing.	20.00 - 30.00

THE SENIOR PROGRAM GUIDE BOOK
1935 printing.	25.00 - 35.00

UNIFORMS

SENIOR SCOUT HAT PATCH
White C.A.W. on gold outline FDL, red twill.	1935-1949	10.00 - 15.00

UNIVERSAL SENIOR SCOUT EMBLEM
SENIOR SCOUT around Tenderfoot emblem, red twill, gold border, cut edge.	1935	50.00 - 75.00

MISCELLANEOUS STUFF

SENIOR SCOUT UNIT LOCAL STANDARD PATCH
Fully embroidered, red-blue background.	1935-1949	10.00 - 15.00

SENIOR SCOUT UNIT NATIONAL STANDARD PATCH
Fully embroidered, red-blue background.	1935-1949	10.00 - 15.00

SENIOR SCOUT UNIT REGIONAL STANDARD PATCH
Fully embroidered, red-blue background.	1935-1949	10.00 - 15.00

EMERGENCY SERVICE CORPS & EXPLORING

POSITION BADGES

EMERGENCY SERVICE APPRENTICE

Lightning bolt on First Class emblem all on red felt.	1941-1949	20.00 - 30.00

EMERGENCY SERVICE CORPS

Lightning bolt and life ring on FDL, EMERGENCY SERVICE CORPS legend, red felt, black legend.	1941-1948	20.00 - 30.00

EMERGENCY SERVICE EXPLORER

Lightning bolt and life ring on FDL, EMERGENCY SERVICE EXPLORER legend, red felt, black legend.	1949-1957	15.00 - 20.00

UNIFORMS

EMERGENCY SERVICE ARMBAND

On khaki cloth.	1939-1948	20.00 - 30.00
On red felt.	1939-1948	20.00 - 30.00
Oval red twill patch, elastic strap.	1939-1948	20.00 - 30.00

Apprentice emblem on oval red twill patch, elastic armband.	1941-1948	10.00 - 15.00
Apprentice emblem on red felt armband.	1941-1948	20.00 - 25.00
Explorer emblem on oval red twill patch on elastic armband.	1949-1957	10.00 - 15.00
Explorer emblem, black legend on red twill armband.	1949-1957	15.00 - 20.00

EMERGENCY SERVICE IN TRAINING ARMBAND

Lightning bolt through BSA on red twill patch, elastic armband.	1949-1957	10.00 - 15.00

EMERGENCY SERVICE IN TRAINING ARMBAND

Lightning bolt through BSA on red twill.	1949-1957	10.00 - 15.00

EMERGENCY SERVICE READY ARMBAND

Circle-V emblem on oval patch, elastic armband.	1958-1969	10.00 - 15.00

EMERGENCY SERVICE, LARGE E ARMBAND

Large E in oval patch, elastic armband.	1969	5.00 - 10.00

RESOURCE BOOKS

EMERGENCY PREPAREDNESS, BSA

A Guide for Leaders.	1964	10.00 - 15.00
	1971	5.00 - 7.50
	1985	5.00 - 7.50

EMERGENCY SERVICE TRAINING PLAN

	1940	10.00 - 15.00
	1941	10.00 - 15.00

FIRE / EMERGENCY SERVICES

	5.00 - 7.50

SCOUT EMERGENCY

First Aid Unit.	1924	25.00 - 35.00
First Aid Unit.	1925	25.00 - 35.00
First Aid Unit.	1925	25.00 - 35.00

SCOUT EMERGENCY UNITS

	1926	15.00 - 25.00
	1930	15.00 - 25.00

SIGNAL EMERGENCY UNITS

	1919	20.00 - 30.00

TRAINING FOR MOBILIZATION, COUNCIL, DISTRICT & TROOP

	1940	10.00 - 15.00

Explorer Scouts act as honor guard at the Inauguration Parade for Lyndon B. Johnson and Hubert Humphrey, January 20, 1965.

AIR SCOUTING

RANK BADGES

TENDERFOOT AIR SCOUT CANDIDATE
Twin-blade prop. in blue on tan
or khaki cut twill.   1942-1949   50.00 - 75.00

SECOND CLASS AIR SCOUT CANDIDATE
Triple-blade prop. in blue on tan
or khaki cut twill.   1942-1949   75.00 - 100.00

FIRST CLASS AIR SCOUT CANDIDATE
Four-blade prop. in blue on tan
or khaki cut twill.   1942-1949   75.00 - 100.00

AIR SCOUT APPRENTICE
Single-engine plane w/ AIR SCOUT
and FDL below.   1942-1949   50.00 - 75.00

AIR SCOUT OBSERVER
Twin-engine plane w/ AIR SCOUT
and FDL below.   1942-1949   50.00 - 75.00

AIR SCOUT CRAFTSMAN
Tri-motor plane w/ AIR SCOUT and FDL below. 1942-1949   50.00 - 75.00

AIR SCOUT ACE
Four-motor plane w/ AIR SCOUT
and FDL below.   1942-1949   50.00 - 75.00

Observer   Craftsman   Ace

SPECIALIST RATING
Ace Airman.	1947-1949	10.00 - 15.00
Ace Builder.	1947-1949	10.00 - 15.00
Ace Communicator.	1947-1949	10.00 - 15.00
Ace Mechanic.	1947-1949	10.00 - 15.00
Ace Navigator.	1947-1949	10.00 - 15.00
Ace Outdoorsman.	1947-1949	10.00 - 15.00
Craftsman Airman.	1947-1949	10.00 - 15.00
Craftsman Builder.	1947-1949	10.00 - 15.00
Craftsman Communicator.	1947-1949	10.00 - 15.00
Craftsman Mechanic.	1947-1949	10.00 - 15.00
Craftsman Navigator.	1947-1949	10.00 - 15.00
Craftsman Outdoorsman.	1947-1949	10.00 - 15.00
Observer Airman.	1947-1949	10.00 - 15.00
Observer Builder.	1947-1949	10.00 - 15.00
Observer Communicator.	1947-1949	10.00 - 15.00
Observer Mechanic.	1947-1949	10.00 - 15.00
Observer Navigator.	1947-1949	10.00 - 15.00
Observer Outdoorsman.	1947-1949	10.00 - 15.00

MERIT BADGES

AERODYNAMICS
Blue border and background.   1942-1952   75.00 - 150.00

AERONAUTICS
Blue border and background.   1942-1952   75.00 - 150.00

AIRPLANE DESIGN
Blue border and background.   1942-1952   75.00 - 150.00

AIRPLANE STRUCTURE
Blue border and background.   1942-1952   75.00 - 150.00

RANK MEDALS

AIR SCOUT ACE
Wings upstretched from four-motor plane,   1942-1949   1,250. - 1,500.
  Tenderfoot emblem at bottom, compass as
  frame, wide blue ribbon w/ thin red edging.

POSITION BADGES

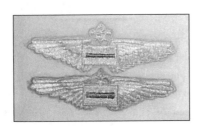

AIR SCOUT ASSISTANT FLIGHT PILOT
Tenderfoot emblem above blue rectangle   1942-1949   50.00 - 75.00
  w/ one gold bar, gold wings at sides.
Tenderfoot emblem above rectangle   1942-1949   50.00 - 75.00
  w/ one blue bar, gold wings at sides.

AIR SCOUT ASSISTANT SQUADRON PILOT
Tenderfoot emblem above blue rectangle   1942-1949   50.00 - 75.00
  w/ 2-1/2 blue bars, gold wings at sides.
Tenderfoot emblem above rectangle   1942-1949   50.00 - 75.00
  w/ 2-1/2 blue bars, gold wings at sides.

AIR SCOUT FLIGHT PILOT
Tenderfoot emblem above blue rectangle   1942-1949   50.00 - 75.00
  w/ 2 silver bars, silver wings at sides.
Tenderfoot emblem above rectangle   1942-1949   50.00 - 75.00
  w/ 2 blue bars, gold wings at sides.

AIR SCOUT SCRIBE
Crossed blue quills on light blue cut twill. 1942-1949   100.00 - 150.00

AIR SCOUT SQUADRON PILOT
Tenderfoot emblem above blue rectangle   1942-1949   50.00 - 75.00
  w/ 2-1/2 silver bars, silver wings at sides.
Tenderfoot emblem above rectangle   1942-1949   50.00 - 75.00
  w/ 2-1/2 blue bars, silver wings at sides.

AIR SCOUT UNIVERSAL MEDALLION
Universal emblem within light blue twill,   1942-1949   40.00 - 50.00
  dark blue rolled edge border.

AIR SCOUT UNIVERSAL WINGS (TYPE 1)
Tenderfoot emblem w/ silver wings.   1942-1949   75.00 - 100.00

POSITION BADGES - ADULT

AIR SCOUT ASSISTANT SQUADRON LEADER

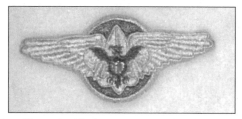

Tenderfoot emblem w/ gold wings,   1942-1949   40.00 - 50.00
  small circle behind at ctr.

AIR SCOUT SQUADRON LEADER
Tenderfoot emblem w/ silver wings,   1942-1949   40.00 - 50.00
  small circle behind at ctr.

HANDBOOKS

AIR SCOUT MANUAL
H.W. Hunt, Lorne W. Barclay, editors,   1942   50.00 - 75.00
  two pre-proof editions.
H.W. Hunt, Lorne W. Barclay, editors,   1942-1943   40.00 - 60.00
  six printings.

AIR EXPLORER MANUAL
Ted S. Holstein, editor, proof edition   1951-1958   20.00 - 40.00
  and five printings.

UNIFORMS

AIR SCOUT HAT PATCH
Gold Tenderfoot emblem on silver wings.   1942-1949   25.00 - 40.00

BELT
Dark blue web, buckle w/First Class emblem.   1942-1949   50.00 - 75.00

COMMUNITY STRIP
Dark blue embroidery on light blue twill.   1942-1949   50.00 - 75.00

MERIT BADGE SASH
Wide light blue (three across).   1946-1957   100.00 - 150.00

PANTS
Light blue, long.   1942-1949   150.00 - 200.00

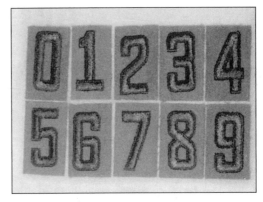

SHIRT

Light blue, long sleeve. AIR SCOUTS B.S.A. pocket strip.	1942-1949	150.00 - 200.00
Light blue, long sleeve. AIR EXPLORER B.S.A. pocket strip.	1949-1966	200.00 - 250.00

SQUADRON NUMERALS

Royal blue embroidery on light blue felt, 0, 1, 2, 3, 4, 5, 6, 7, 8.	1942-1949	10.00 - 15.00

STATE STRIP

Dark blue embroidery on light blue twill.	1942-1949	50.00 - 75.00

TIE

Dark blue.	1945-1966	50.00 - 75.00

Charles Atlas signs up as a fitness merit badge councelor.

AIR EXPLORING

RANK BADGES

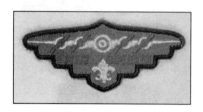

AIR EXPLORER ACE
Four-motor plane, AIR EXPLORER and FDL below.	1949-1954	30.00 - 50.00

AIR EXPLORER APPRENTICE
Single-engine plane, AIR EXPLORER and FDL below.	1949-1954	30.00 - 50.00
Single-engine plane above FDL.	1954-1966	10.00 - 15.00

AIR EXPLORER CRAFTSMAN
Tri-motor plane, AIR EXPLORER and FDL below.	1949-1954	30.00 - 50.00
Tri-motor plane above FDL.	1954-1966	10.00 - 15.00

AIR EXPLORER OBSERVER
Twin-engine plane, AIR EXPLORER and FDL below.	1949-1954	30.00 - 50.00
Twin-engine plane above FDL.	1954-1966	10.00 - 15.00

PIN
Advanced Aeronautics and wings with Circle V at ctr.	1959-1966	15.00 - 20.00
Basic Aeronautics and wings with Circle V at ctr.	1959-1966	15.00 - 20.00

SKILLS RATING
Construction.	1954-1966	10.00 - 15.00
Mechanics.	1954-1966	10.00 - 15.00
Weather.	1954-1966	10.00 - 15.00

RANK MEDALS

AIR EXPLORER ACE MEDAL
Wings upstretched, four-motor plane and Tenderfoot emblem below, compass in back, red-blue-red ribbon of equal widths.	1949-1954	1,200. - 1,500.

POSITION BADGES

AIR EXPLORER DEPUTY SENIOR CREW LEADER
Tenderfoot emblem above three blue bars within rectangle, gold wings.	1949-1966	25.00 - 40.00

AIR EXPLORER SECRETARY
Tenderfoot emblem above crossed
  blue quills within rectangle, gold wings.   1949-1966   25.00 - 40.00

AIR EXPLORER SENIOR CREW LEADER
Tenderfoot emblem above three   1949-1966   25.00 - 40.00
  blue bars within rectangle, silver wings,
  blue circle at ctr. back.

AIR EXPLORING UNIVERSAL EMBLEM
E and FDL at ctr. of wings,   1969   5.00 - 10.00
  on blue twill rectangle.

AIRPORT MANAGEMENT
E and FDL at ctr. of wings, title below,   1969   5.00 - 10.00
  on blue twill rectangle.

FLIGHT ATTENDANT
E and FDL at ctr. of wings, title below,   1969   5.00 - 10.00
  on blue twill rectangle.

GROUND SUPPORT
E and FDL at ctr. of wings, title below,   1969   5.00 - 10.00
  on blue twill rectangle.

MECHANIC
E and FDL at ctr. of wings, title below,   1969   5.00 - 10.00
  on blue twill rectangle.

PRIVATE PILOT
E and FDL at ctr. of wings, title below,   1969   5.00 - 10.00
  on blue twill rectangle.

STUDENT PILOT
E and FDL at ctr. of wings, title below,   1969   5.00 - 10.00
  on blue twill rectangle.

UNIFORMS

AIR EXPLORER JACKET PATCH
Tenderfoot emblem at ctr. of wings   1969   15.00 - 25.00
  on blue twill.

AIR EXPLORER UNIVERSAL WINGS
Tenderfoot emblem at ctr. of   1949-1966   15.00 - 20.00
  extended silver wings, wings dip at ctr.

Troop from St. Joseph, Missouri scouts from the 1940s.

EXPLORER SCOUT PROGRAM

The Explorer Scout Program was an outgrowth of the Senior Scout program in 1935. The logo was the tenderfoot emblem on a compass background. In 1949 with the change in the Senior Scout program, the name changed to simply Explorers, and the Compass-Anchor-Wings logo was adopted. At this time also there was a change in the advancement program. In 1959 the program name was changed to Exploring, and the Circle-V logo was adopted. In 1965 the special advancement program ended. In 1969 the program allowed girls as participates, and in 1971 full membership. Also in 1971, the upper age of the program was raised from 17 to 20. The program logo gradually changed to a large letter E, at first with a small Circle-V at the bottom, then in 1982 or so, that was replaced with a fleur-de-lis. In 1990 it was changed again to a fleur-de-lis and an extended line under the E. In 1998 the traditional exploring program was changed to the Venturing Program. The "Career Awareness" explorers became participants in the Learning for Live program. They are not members of the BSA.

Explorer officers meet with President John F. Kennedy.

RANK BADGES

EXPLORER SCOUT APPRENTICE
Tenderfoot emblem at top of empty compass,   1944-1949   40.00 - 60.00
EXPLORER SCOUT below, dark green twill.

EXPLORER SCOUT FRONTIERSMAN
Tenderfoot emblem at top of compass   1935-1949   40.00 - 60.00
w/ teepee within, EXPLORER SCOUT below,
dark green twill.

EXPLORER SCOUT RANGER AWARD
Tenderfoot emblem at top of compass   1944-1949   150.00 - 200.00
w/ powder horn within, EXPLORER SCOUT
below, dark green twill.

EXPLORER SCOUT WOODSMAN
Tenderfoot emblem at top of compass   1944-1949   40.00 - 60.00
w/ pine tree within, EXPLORER SCOUT
below, dark green twill.

EXPLORER SILVER AWARD
Silver C.A.W and white FDL, dark green twill.   1944-1958   75.00 - 100.00

EXPLORING UNIVERSAL EMBLEM
EXPLORER SCOUT and BSA around compass   1935-1949   10.00 - 15.00
w/ 8-pointed star behind Tenderfoot emblem,
dark green twill.

EXPLORER BRONZE AWARD
Bronze C.A.W and white FDL on blue twill.   1949-1958   15.00 - 25.00
Bronze C.A.W and white FDL on dark green   1949-1958   15.00 - 25.00
twill.

EXPLORER GOLD AWARD
Gold C.A.W and white FDL on blue twill.   1949-1958   15.00 - 25.00
Gold C.A.W and white FDL on dark green twill. 1949-1958   15.00 - 25.00

EXPLORER SILVER AWARD
Eagle in flight left on compass, red-white-blue 1949-1958   60.00 - 80.00
background.
Silver C.A.W and white FDL on blue twill.   1949-1958   50.00 - 75.00

SKILLS RATING STRIP
Aviation.	1949-1958	10.00 - 15.00
Communications.	1949-1958	10.00 - 15.00
Craft.	1949-1958	10.00 - 15.00
Emergency.	1949-1958	10.00 - 15.00
Navigation.	1949-1958	10.00 - 15.00
Outdoor.	1949-1958	10.00 - 15.00
Physical Fitness.	1949-1958	10.00 - 15.00
Seamanship.	1949-1958	10.00 - 15.00
Vocational Exploration.	1949-1958	10.00 - 15.00

STAR SCOUT
Dark green C/E, coarse twill.   1958-1969   20.00 - 30.00

RANK MEDALS

EXPLORER SCOUT RANGER MEDAL
Powderhorn in ctr. of compass, Tenderfoot emblem above, green-white-green ribbon.   1944-1949   700.00 - 900.00

BRONZE AWARD
Bronze C.A.W. pendant on red-orange ribbon.   1949-1959   200.00 - 250.00

GOLD AWARD
Gold C.A.W. pendant on red-orange ribbon.   1949-1959   400.00 - 500.00

SILVER AWARD, TYPE I
Silver C.A.W. pendant on red-orange ribbon.   1949-1959   1,000.- 1,400.

SILVER AWARD, TYPE II
Eagle in flight left on compass, Tenderfoot emblem below, white ribbon w/thin red-white-blue stripe.   1954-1959   200.00 - 275.00

AWARD MEDALS

CONTEST MEDAL

Bronze C.A.W. within wreath, red-blue ribbon.	1949-1958	75.00 - 100.00
Gold C.A.W. within wreath, red-blue ribbon.	1949-1958	75.00 - 100.00
Silver C.A.W. within wreath, red-blue ribbon.	1949-1958	75.00 - 100.00

POSITION BADGES

EXPLORER ASSISTANT CREW LEADER
One white bar behind white C.A.W. and gold   1944-1960   10.00 - 15.00
  FDL, cut edge blue twill.

EXPLORER CREW LEADER
Two white bars behind white C.A.W. and gold 1944-1960   10.00 - 15.00
  FDL, cut edge green twill w/ border.

EXPLORER DEPUTY SENIOR CREW LEADER
Three white bars behind white C.A.W. and gold 1944-1960   25.00 - 40.00
  FDL, cut edge dark green twill w/ border.

EXPLORER POST SECRETARY
Crossed quills behind white C.A.W. with gold   1944-1960   40.00 - 60.00
  FDL, cut edge dark green twill w/ border.

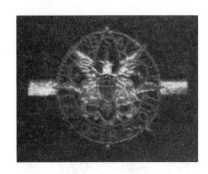

EXPLORER SCOUT ASSISTANT CREW LEADER
One bar behind Explorer Scout emblem, gold   1935-1949   40.00 - 60.00
  on green cut cloth twill.

EXPLORER SCOUT CREW LEADER
Two bars behind Explorer Scout emblem, gold 1935-1949   40.00 - 60.00
  on green cut cloth twill.

EXPLORER SCOUT POST ASSISTANT GUIDE
2-1/2 bars behind Explorer Scout emblem,   1935-1949   40.00 - 60.00
  gold on green cut cloth twill.

EXPLORER SCOUT POST GUIDE
Three bars behind Explorer Scout emblem,   1935-1949   40.00 - 60.00
  gold on green cut cloth twill.

EXPLORER SCOUT POST SECRETARY
Crossed quills behind Explorer Scout emblem, 1935-1949   50.00 - 75.00
  gold on green cut cloth twill.

EXPLORER ASSISTANT CREW LEADER
One white bar behind white C.A.W. and gold   1949-1958   10.00 - 15.00
  FDL, cut edge green twill.

EXPLORER CREW LEADER

Two white bars behind white C.A.W. and gold FDL, cut edge blue twill.	1949-1958	10.00 - 15.00
Two white bars behind white C.A.W. and gold FDL, cut edge green twill.	1949-1958	10.00 - 15.00

EXPLORER DEPUTY SENIOR CREW LEADER

Three white bars behind white C.A.W. and gold FDL, cut edge blue twill.	1949-1958	25.00 - 40.00

EXPLORER POST SECRETARY

Crossed quills behind white C.A.W. w/ gold FDL, cut edge blue twill.	1949-1958	40.00 - 60.00
Crossed quills behind white C.A.W. w/ gold FDL, cut edge dark green twill.	1949-1958	40.00 - 60.00

EXPLORER SENIOR CREW LEADER

White C.A.W. and gold FDL, cut edge blue twill.	1949-1958	25.00 - 40.00
White C.A.W. and gold FDL, cut edge dark green twill.	1949-1958	25.00 - 40.00

POSITION BADGES - ADULT

EXPLORER POST ASSISTANT ADVISOR

Gold C.A.W. and FDL on blue twill.	1944-1960	15.00 - 25.00
Gold C.A.W. and FDL on dark green twill.	1949-1958	10.00 - 15.00

EXPLORER SCOUT ADVISOR

BOY SCOUTS OF AMERICA and EXPLORERS legend around First Class emblem on 8-pointed star, white on dark green twill.	1935-1949	20.00 - 30.00

EXPLORER SCOUT ASSISTANT ADVISOR

BOY SCOUTS OF AMERICA and EXPLORERS legend around First Class emblem on 8-pointed star, gold on dark green twill.	1935-1949	20.00 - 30.00

EXPLORER POST ADVISOR

White C.A.W. and FDL on blue twill.	1949-1958	10.00 - 15.00
White C.A.W. and FDL on dark green twill.	1949-1958	10.00 - 15.00

A Region 7 executive and four happy Explorers celebrate receiving Eagle or Silver Awards. Note the placement on the sleeve of the Universal Emblem, a National Standard Post Award, the Emergency Service Patch, and rating strips.

HANDBOOKS

EXPLORER SCOUT MANUAL
Carl D. Lane, 382 pgs, two printings.   1946-1947   15.00 - 25.00

EXPLORER MANUAL
Ted S. Holstein, editor, 330 pgs,   1950-1952   10.00 - 20.00
  three printings.
Ted S. Holstein, editor, 380 pgs, 4/54 printing. 1954   10.00 - 15.00
Ted S. Holstein, editor, 386 pgs + 14 pgs, ads, 1954-1958   10.00 - 15.00
  five printings.

EXPLORING
Ted S. Holstein, editor, 317 pgs,   1958-1966   10.00 - 15.00
  three printings.

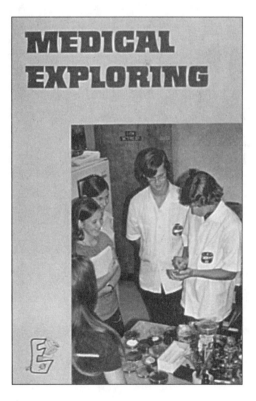

MEDICAL EXPLORING
Two printings.   1973-1980   10.00 - 15.00

UNIFORMS

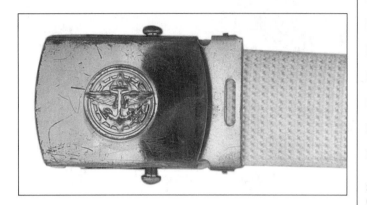

BELT
White web, C-A-W design on brass buckle.	1951-1957	15.00 - 20.00
White web, Circle-V design on brass buckle.	1958-1971	10.00 - 15.00
White web, E design on brass buckle.	1972-1979	10.00 - 15.00

COMMUNITY STRIP, BROWN ON DARK GREEN TWILL
	1949-1958	5.00 - 10.00

COUNCIL STRIP, GREEN AND BROWN.
New York City / Brooklyn.	1945-1955	35.00 - 50.00

EXPLORERS HAT PATCH
Tenderfoot badge on dark green twill.	1949-1958	3.00 - 5.00

EXPLORERS UNIVERSAL BADGE
White C.A.W. in gold outline, FDL on blue twill.	1949-1958	10.00 - 15.00
White C.A.W. in gold outline, FDL on dark green twill.	1949-1958	10.00 - 15.00
White C.A.W. in gold outline, FDL on red twill.	1949-1958	10.00 - 15.00

HAT PATCH
BSA and EXPLORER SCOUT on compass, star behind Tenderfoot emblem.	1935-1949	10.00 - 15.00

MERIT BADGE SASH
Wide, dark green (3 across).	1949-1958	10.00 - 15.00

PANTS
Dark green, long.	1945-1979	15.00 - 25.00
Dark green, short.	1945-1979	15.00 - 25.00

SERVICE STAR
Gold w/ tenure number, screwback on red felt disc.	1947-1955	4.00 - 6.00
Gold star w/ tenure number, clutch back on red plastic disc.	1956	1.00 - 2.00

SHIRT
Dark green, long sleeve, EXPLORER SCOUTS B.S.A. in brown as pocket strip.	1945-1949	40.00 - 60.00
Dark green, long sleeve, EXPLORERS B.S.A. in brown as pocket strip.	1949-1957	30.00 - 50.00
Dark green, short sleeve, EXPLORERS B.S.A. in brown as pocket strip.	1949-1957	30.00 - 50.00
Dark green, long sleeve, EXPLORER in brown as pocket strip.	1958-1979	15.00 - 25.00
Dark green, short sleeve, EXPLORER in brown as pocket strip.	1958-1979	15.00 - 25.00
Dark green, long sleeve, BOY SCOUTS OF AMERICA in brown as pocket strip.	1985-1991	10.00 - 15.00
Dark green, long sleeve, epaulets, EXPLORING BSA as pocket strip.	1994-1998	10.00 - 15.00

STATE STRIP, GREEN AND BROWN
CALIF.	1945-1955	20.00 - 30.00
GA.	1945-1955	20.00 - 30.00
ILL.	1945-1955	20.00 - 30.00
IOWA.	1945-1955	20.00 - 30.00
LA.	1945-1955	25.00 - 35.00
MASS.	1945-1955	20.00 - 30.00
MD.	1945-1955	25.00 - 35.00
MICH.	1945-1955	20.00 - 30.00
MINN.	1945-1955	25.00 - 35.00
MO.	1945-1955	20.00 - 30.00
MONT.	1945-1955	20.00 - 30.00
N.H.	1945-1955	25.00 - 35.00
N.J.	1945-1955	20.00 - 30.00
N.Y.	1945-1955	20.00 - 30.00
OHIO.	1945-1955	20.00 - 30.00
OKLA.	1945-1955	20.00 - 30.00
PA.	1945-1955	20.00 - 30.00
S. DAK.	1945-1955	25.00 - 35.00
TEXAS.	1945-1955	20.00 - 30.00
UTAH.	1945-1955	20.00 - 30.00
WASH.	1945-1955	20.00 - 30.00
WIS.	1945-1955	20.00 - 30.00

TIE
Brown.	1945-1979	10.00 - 15.00
Maroon.	1945-1979	10.00 - 15.00

UNIT NUMERAL
Green twill w/ brown embroidery, 0, 1, 2, 3, 4, 5, 6, 7, 8.	1950-1957	2.00 - 3.00
Brown on green felt, 0, 1, 2, 3, 4, 5, 6, 7, 8.	1935-1949	3.00 - 5.00

UNIFORMS - ADULT

BLAZER, BULLION-EMBROIDERED PROGRAM EMBLEM
Explorer, E.	1971	20.00 - 30.00

HAT OR COLLAR DEVICES

ADVISOR
CAW on blue enamel compass.	1950	60.00 - 80.00
CAW on green enamel.	1950	60.00 - 80.00

ASSISTANT ADVISOR
Gold CAW on blue enamel.	1950	100.00 - 120.00
Gold CAW on green enamel.	1950	60.00 - 80.00

UNIT EQUIPMENT

POST FLAG
Wool, red top, blue bottom, C.A.W. in ctr.	1950-1958	30.00 - 50.00
Cotton, red top, blue bottom, Circle-V emblem in ctr.	1959-1968	20.00 - 30.00
Nylon, blue, white E emblem in ctr.	1969	25.00 - 35.00

KNIVES

CAMILLUS
Exploring E emblem on green handle, 2-1/2", spear, file, and scissors.	1987-1990 E.2		25.00 - 30.00

MEDALLIONS

EXPLORER, "E" YOU MAKE THE DIFFERENCE
Elongated cent, copper.	1992	Dio.1992.9	1.00 - 2.00

PINBACK BUTTONS

NATIONAL JAMBOREE, 1950
Red River Valley Post 22, 2-1/4".	1950	20.00 - 30.00

REGION SEVEN EXPLORER DELEGATE
C.A.W. emblem, 4".	1961	20.00 - 30.00

SEALS & STICKERS

EXPLORERS, B.S.A., HEAD SHOT OF EXPLORER SCOUT
Sheet of 100 stamps.	1955	10.00 - 20.00

MISCELLANEOUS STUFF

EXPLORER UNIT LOCAL STANDARD PATCH
Blue and red, fully embroidered.	1949-1958	5.00 - 10.00

EXPLORER UNIT NATIONAL STANDARD PATCH
Blue and red, fully embroidered.	1949-1958	5.00 - 10.00

EXPLORER UNIT REGIONAL STANDARD PATCH
Blue and red, fully embroidered.	1949-1958	5.00 - 10.00

EXPLORER UNIT STANDARD PATCH
Blue and red, fully embroidered.	1949-1958	5.00 - 10.00

Explorer scouts board a train.

Two Chicago Explorers meet author C.R. Olsen. Note the Eagle and Contest Medals on the center Explorer, and the Eagle and Silver Award Medals on the right Explorer. The OA Sash is a Brotherhood flocked felt variety.

VENTURING

RANK BADGES

BRONZE AWARDS
Arts & Crafts.	1998	10.00 - 15.00
Outdoors.	1998	10.00 - 15.00
Sea Scouting.	1998-2000	10.00 - 15.00
Sea Scouting.	2000	10.00 - 15.00
Sports.	1998	10.00 - 15.00
Youth Ministries.	1998	10.00 - 15.00

VENTURING G.O.L.D.
Venturing logo on gilt pendant suspended from white neck ribbon.	1998	50.00 - 75.00

VENTURING RANGER
Powderhorn on compass, hanging from ribbon bar marked RANGER.	1998	50.00 - 75.00

VENTURING SILVER
Eagle fling left on red-white-blue enamel pendant, handing from ribbon bar named VENTURING.	1998	50.00 - 75.00

POSITION BADGES

PRESIDENT
Mountain and V logo on white.	1998	2.50 - 5.00

SECRETARY
Mountain and V logo on white.	1998	2.50 - 5.00

TREASURER
Mountain and V logo on white.	1998	2.50 - 5.00

VICE PRESIDENT
Mountain and V logo on white.	1998	2.50 - 5.00

POSITION BADGES - ADULT

ADVISOR
Mountain and V logo on red.	1998	2.50 - 5.00

ASSOCIATE ADVISOR
Mountain and V logo on red.	1998	2.50 - 5.00

CREW COMMITTEE
Mountain and V logo on white.	1998	2.50 - 5.00

VENTURING COMMISSIONER
Mountain and V logo.	1998	2.50 - 5.00

VENTURING ROUNDTABLE STAFF
Mountain and V logo.	1998	2.50 - 5.00

HANDBOOKS

SILVER AWARD GUIDEBOOK
First edition.	1998	10.00 - 15.00

THE RANGER GUIDEBOOK
First edition, spiral bound.	1998	10.00 - 15.00

VENTURER HANDBOOK
1999 edition, saddle stitched.		10.00 - 15.00
2000 edition, spiral bound.		10.00 - 15.00

RESOURCE BOOKS

VENTURING LEADER MANUAL	1998	10.00 - 15.00
VENTURING LEADERSHIP SKILLS COURSE	1998	10.00 - 15.00
VENTURING OPERATIONS MANUAL FOR DISTRICTS AND COUNCILS	1998	10.00 - 15.00
VENTURING ROUNDTABLE GUIDE	1998	10.00 - 15.00

UNIFORMS

PANTS
Dark green, long. Venturing label.	1998	15.00 - 25.00
Dark green, short. Venturing label.	1998	15.00 - 25.00

SHIRT
Dark green, short sleve, epaulets, VENTURING BSA as pocket strip.	1998	10.00 - 15.00
Maroon, green and white pull-over. Venturing BSA.	1998	10.00 - 15.00

UNIVERSAL EMBLEM
Mountain and V logo within square patch.	1998	2.50 - 5.00

Troop 17, Gateway District, Queens Council put on some impressive pioneering displays during the many 1980s Queens Day Festivals.

ORDER OF THE ARROW

The Order of the Arrow was founded at the Philadelphia Council summer camp Treasure Island in 1915 by E. Urner Goodman and Carroll A. Edson. It was formed to recognize honor campers. It became an official part of the National Program of the Boy Scouts of America in the 1940s. Within the organization there are Ordeal, Brotherhood, and Vigil Honor members, with a red arrow on white sashes to denote each honor. Each council has a lodge, which acts as part of the council camping committee, and usually each district has a chapter. Lodges have a Lodge Flap, which was developed in the 1950s and worn over the scout's uniform right pocket flap. Lodges are grouped into sections, and sections are grouped into areas. Conferences for sections and areas have their own patches, usually in a circular or other shape, and are worn as temporary uniform insignia. Lodges also have issued neckerchiefs. Lodge items have been cataloged in the *Blue Book*, and only a listing of Lodge names occurs in this book.

National Order of the Arrow Conferences have been held on a national basis since the late 1940s and most recently every two years, usually on a major university campus. Lately more than 5,000 Arrowmen gather at these events for training in lodge administration, ceremonies, or Native American dance. Patches exist for participants and staff, and lately many participating lodges make a special flap.

Eagle Scout Reidan Cruz as Suanhacky Lodge #49's Chief of the Fire, Ten Mile River Scout Camps, G.N.Y.C.

HANDBOOKS

ORDER OF THE ARROW HANDBOOK

1948 edition, paper cover.	200.00 - 300.00
1948 edition, 1948 printing, sash cover.	300.00 - 400.00
1948 edition, hardcover.	400.00 - 600.00
1950 edition, 1950 printing, sash cover.	50.00 - 75.00
1950 edition, 1952 printing, Indian-head cover.	30.00 - 50.00
1961 edition, 1961 printing, classic Indian cover.	15.00 - 25.00
1961 edition, 1964 printing, classic Indian cover.	15.00 - 25.00
1965 edition, 1965 printing, gold cover.	25.00 - 35.00
1965 edition, 1968 printing, classic Indian cover.	10.00 - 15.00
1965 edition, 1966 printing, classic Indian cover.	15.00 - 25.00
1965 edition, 1972 printing, classic Indian cover.	10.00 - 15.00
1965 edition, 1970 printing, classic Indian cover.	10.00 - 15.00
1973 edition, 1973 printing, dancing Indian cover.	10.00 - 15.00
1975 edition, 1975 printing, dancing Indian cover.	10.00 - 15.00
1977 edition, 1977 printing, MGM Indian cover.	7.50 - 10.00
1977 edition, 1979 printing, MGM Indian cover.	7.50 - 10.00
1977 edition, 1981 printing, MGM Indian cover.	5.00 - 7.50
1977 edition, 1983 printing, MGM Indian cover.	5.00 - 7.50
1977 edition, 1985 printing, MGM Indian cover.	5.00 - 7.50
1977 edition, 1987 printing, MGM Indian cover.	5.00 - 7.50
1977 edition, 1986 printing, MGM Indian cover.	5.00 - 7.50
1989 edition, 1989 printing, Indian and scout cover.	2.50 - 5.00
1989 edition, 1990 printing, Indian and scout cover.	2.50 - 5.00

RESOURCE BOOKS

BROTHERHOOD CEREMONY BOOK

1949 edition, 1964 printing.	20.00 - 30.00
1968 edition, 1969 printing.	15.00 - 25.00
1968 edition, 1975 printing.	10.00 - 15.00
1968 edition, 1978 printing.	7.50 - 12.50
1968 edition, 1981 printing.	5.00 - 7.50

GUIDE FOR THE ORDEAL

1981 printing.	2.50 - 5.00

INDIAN RITUAL COSTUMES

1936 printing.	40.00 - 60.00

LOCAL LODGE MANUAL

1936 printing.	35.00 - 50.00
1937 printing.	35.00 - 50.00
1939 printing.	35.00 - 50.00
1942 printing.	35.00 - 50.00

NATIONAL LODGE CONSTITUTION & BY LAWS

1936 printing.	50.00 - 75.00

ORDEAL CEREMONY BOOK

1968 edition, 1980 printing, gray cover.	2.00 - 5.00
1968 edition, 2.75 printing, white.	7.50 - 12.50
1968 edition, 4.78 printing, red.	7.50 - 12.50
1968 edition, 6.69 printing, red and photo cover.	15.00 - 20.00
1980 edition, 1980 printing, gray cover.	2.00 - 5.00
1980 edition, 1990 printing, gray cover.	2.00 - 5.00

SPIRIT OF THE ARROW BOOKLETS

1972/1976 printings.	5.00 - 7.50
1981 printing.	2.50 - 5.00

VIGIL CEREMONY BOOK

1968 edition, 1969 printing.	15.00 - 25.00
1968 edition, 1981 printing, gray.	2.50 - 5.00
1968 edition, 6/78 printing, red.	7.50 - 12.50
1968 edition, 6/73 printing, white.	7.50 - 12.50

POSITION BADGES - ADULT

CHAPTER ADVISER
Tenderfoot emblem and title on light blue background.	1972-1989	2.00 - 3.00

LODGE ADVISER
Tenderfoot emblem and title on light blue background.	1972-1989	2.00 - 3.00

LODGE CHIEF
Tenderfoot emblem and title on light blue background.	1972-1976	150.00 - 200.00

SECTION ADVISOR
Tenderfoot emblem and title on light blue background.	1972-1989	2.00 - 3.00

AWARD MEDALS

NOAC CEREMONY COMPETITION

1990 Award Medal.	200.00 - 400.00
1990 National Ceremony Events Staff.	400.00 - 600.00
1992 Award Medal.	200.00 - 400.00
1992 National Ceremony Events Staff.	400.00 - 600.00
1994 Award Medal.	200.00 - 400.00
1994 National Ceremony Events Staff.	400.00 - 600.00
1996 Award Medal.	125.00 - 175.00
1998 Award Medal.	125.00 - 175.00
2000 Award Medal.	100.00 - 150.00

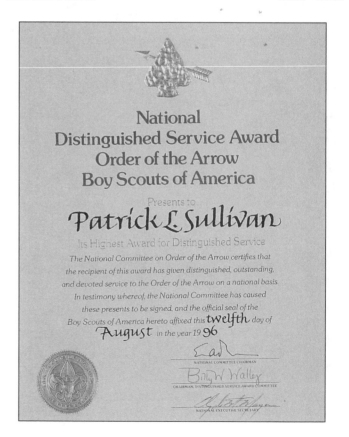

RECOGNITIONS - ADULT

ORDER OF THE ARROW DISTINGUISHED SERVICE AWARD

Arrowhead w/ arrow behind, large silver pendant, green neck ribbon.	1948-1965	600.00 - 800.00
Arrowhead w/ arrow behind, rhodium pendant, white neck ribbon with three red arrows on each side.	1980	50.00 - 75.00
Arrowhead w/ arrow behind, small silver pendant, white neck ribbon with three red arrows on each side.	1966-1980	150.00 - 200.00

MEMBERSHIP CARDS

HORIZONTAL FORMAT, "MGM" INDIAN LOGO IN CENTER AS UNDERPRINT

	1986-1999	2.50 - 5.00

HORIZONTAL FORMAT, "MGM" INDIAN LOGO IN TITLE LINE AT TOP, ARROW AT BOTTOM

	1976-1985	2.50 - 5.00

HORIZONTAL FORMAT, ALL TYPESET, TWO-LINE QUOTE AT BOTTOM.

Three varieties.	1940-1945	15.00 - 25.00

HORIZONTAL FORMAT, ARROWHEAD LOGO

	1998	2.50 - 5.00

HORIZONTAL FORMAT, LARGE INDIAN PROFILE AT LEFT, ARROW AT BOTTOM

	1968-1975	5.00 - 7.50

HORIZONTAL FORMAT, QUIVER AND BUFFALO ON SHIELD

Two varieties.	1945-1950	10.00 - 20.00

HORIZONTAL FORMAT, SMALL INDIAN PROFILE AT UPPER LEFT, ARROW AT TOP POINTS LEFT

	1961-1967	7.50 - 12.50

HORIZONTAL FORMAT, SMALL INDIAN PROFILE AT UPPER LEFT, ARROW AT TOP POINTS RIGHT

	1957-1960	7.50 - 12.50

VERTICAL FORMAT, ALL TYPESET, ARROW AT TOP POINTS RIGHT

	1955-1960	10.00 - 20.00

VERTICAL FORMAT, INDIAN PROFILE LEFT, ARROW AT BOTTOM FACING RIGHT

	1950-1955	10.00 - 20.00

VIGIL CARD

Brass, large Indian profile at left, arrow at bottom	1970-1975	25.00 - 35.00
White plastic, design like certificate, name raised.	1975-1994	10.00 - 15.00
Red plastic, design like certificate, name raised.	1994-1998	7.50 - 12.50
White plastic, large Vigil triangle at upper left.	1998	5.00 - 10.00

CERTIFICATES

HONOR LODGE

		10.00 - 15.00

STANDARD LODGE

		10.00 - 15.00

VIGIL HONOR

Certificate.	1953-1960	30.00 - 50.00
Certificate.	1960-1975	15.00 - 25.00
Certificate.	1975-1990	10.00 - 20.00
Certificate.	1990-2000	5.00 - 10.00

PINBACK BUTTONS

NATIONAL MEETING

Chanute Field, IL. August 1946, Arrow Point, 2-1/2".	1946	25.00 - 35.00

POSTCARDS & GREETING CARDS

1958 NOAC

Nani-Ba Zhu Lodge 321.	1958	3.00 - 5.00

1965 NOAC

Photo of E. Urner Goodman.	1965	3.00 - 5.00

1968 NOAC

Painting of Goodman and Edson.	1968	3.00 - 5.00

RANAHQUA LODGE #4

40th Anniversary.	1956	5.00 - 7.50

EVENT COVERS

07.22.1960	1960 National Jamboree, Camden County Council, Lekau Lodge 77 Cachet.	2.50 - 5.00
08.03.1977	1977 National Jamboree, Troop 266, Tannu Lodge #346, NOAC.	2.50 - 5.00
08.04.1993	1993 National Jamboree, SOSSI OA Service Corps Cachet.	2.50 - 5.00
08.26.1954	39th National Meeting, University of Wyoming, Laramie, Kola Lodge, Longs Peak Council, red.	5.00 - 7.50
08.25.1958	43rd Anniversary Conference, University of Kansas, Lawrence, KS, Sanhican Lodge 2.	5.00 - 7.50
08.25.1958	43rd Anniversary Conference, University of Kansas, Lawrence, KS, red.	5.00 - 7.50
08.21.1961	46th Anniversary Conference, OA, Indiana University, Bloomington, IN, black and red.	5.00 - 7.50
08.13.1981	65th Anniversary Conference, University of Texas, Austin.	5.00 - 7.50
08.14.1986	71st Anniversary Conference, OA, Mt. Pleasant, MI.	5.00 - 7.50
05.25.1957	Area 2-B Conference, Camp Sakawawin, Lodge 287, Branchville, NJ.	5.00 - 7.50
06.12.1959	Area 2-C Conference, Lekau Lodge 77, Camden County Council, red.	5.00 - 7.50
04.11.1959	Area V-E Conference, Camp Kickapoo, Sebooney Okasucca Lodge 260, green, red and brown.	5.00 - 7.50
02.00.1960	BSA 50th Anniversary, Shawanogi Chapter, Shenshawpotoo Lodge 276 Cachet.	2.50 - 5.00
12.30.1958	Miquin Lodge 25th Anniversary, blue, blue and red.	5.00 - 7.50
08.10.1983	NOAC, Rutgers NJ, patch cachet.	5.00 - 7.50
08.13.1981	NOAC, University of Texas, patch cachet.	5.00 - 7.50
08.23.1958	OA Area 2D Conclave, Mahikan Lodge 181, Stratton Mountain Scout Reservation.	5.00 - 7.50
04.04.1987	Scout-o-rama, Wa Hi Nasa Lodge Flap on cancel.	5.00 - 7.50
07.17.1965	SOSSI Liberty Bell Chapter, 50th Anniversary, OA, brave passing down legend, signed by E. Urner Goodman.	75.00 - 100.00
07.17.1965	SOSSI Liberty Bell Chapter, 50th Anniversary, OA, brave passing down legend.	5.00 - 7.50

SEALS & STICKERS

SUANHACKY LODGE #49, QUEENS COUNCIL, OA

Stag head on red circle, water decal.	1973	2.00 - 3.00

NATIONAL OA CONFERENCES

POCKET PATCH

Participant, white CTE on red chenille arrowhead.	1940	150.00 - 200.00
Participant, red on white felt.	1946	150.00 - 200.00
Participant, red silk screen on white.	1948	100.00 - 150.00
Participant, green-silver-red embroidery on white twill.	1950	75.00 - 100.00
Participant, yellow-black-white embroidery on red twill.	1952	75.00 - 100.00
Participant, yellow-blue-red embroidery on white twill.	1954	50.00 - 75.00
Participant, multicolor embroidery on white twill.	1956	50.00 - 75.00
Participant, yellow-red-blue embroidery on white twill w/loop.	1958	40.00 - 60.00
Participant, red-yellow-black embroidery on white twill shield.	1961	40.00 - 60.00

Participant, multicolor fully embroidered arrowhead.	1963	25.00 - 40.00
Participant, multicolor embroidery on gray twill shield.	1965	25.00 - 40.00
Participant, multicolor fully embroidered arrowhead.	1967	25.00 - 40.00
Participant, multicolor fully embroidered emblem.	1969	20.00 - 30.00
Participant, multicolor fully embroidered arrowhead.	1971	20.00 - 30.00
Participant, multicolor embroidery on white twill hexagon.	1973	15.00 - 25.00
Participant.	1975	10.00 - 17.50
Participant.	1977	10.00 - 15.00
Participant.	1979	10.00 - 15.00
Participant.	1981	7.50 - 12.50
Participant.	1983	7.50 - 12.50
Participant.	1986	7.50 - 12.50
Participant.	1988	7.50 - 12.50
Participant.	1990	7.50 - 12.50
Participant.	1992	7.50 - 12.50
Participant.	1994	7.50 - 12.50
Participant.	1996	7.50 - 12.50
Participant.	1998	5.00 - 7.50
Participant.	2000	5.00 - 7.50

POCKET PATCH, STAFF

Participant, red embroidery on white.	1948	150.00 - 200.00
Round.	1979	10.00 - 15.00
Round.	1981	10.00 - 15.00
Round.	1983	10.00 - 15.00
Round.	1986	10.00 - 15.00
Round.	1988	10.00 - 15.00
Round.	1990	10.00 - 15.00
Round.	1992	10.00 - 15.00
Round.	1994	10.00 - 15.00
Round.	1996	10.00 - 15.00
Staff.	1998	10.00 - 15.00
Staff.	2000	10.00 - 15.00

MISCELLANEOUS STUFF

50TH ANNIVERSARY ACHIEVEMENT AWARD
	1965	10.00 - 15.00

60TH ANNIVERSARY BICENTENNIAL AWARD
	1976	7.50 - 10.00

BROTHERHOOD SASH
Red arrow and bars sewn on cotton twill.	1950-1989	10.00 - 15.00
Red Arrow and bars ironed on cotton sash.	1987-1990	10.00 - 15.00

Lodge Totem Pins were available in the 1950s for civilian wear.

LODGE TOTEM LAPEL PINS
Animal totem, arrow w/chain attached. Sterling.	1940-1960	100.00 - 150.00
Animal totem, Vigil triangle on totem, arrow w/chain attached, sterling.	1940-1960	200.00 - 300.00

NATIONAL LEADERSHIP SEMINAR
Participant Patch.	1975-1989	5.00 - 7.50
Staff Patch.	1975-1989	5.00 - 7.50

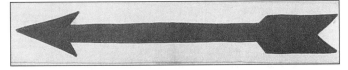

Ordeal sash. Felt on felt.

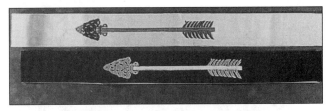

Ordeal Honor Sashes. The red-white is the regular issue and the black-white is a special 1990 75th Anniversary issue.

ORDEAL SASH
Red arrow, solid, on white, wool felt, arrow sewn on.	1922-1948	75.00 - 125.00
Red arrow sewn on cotton twill.	1950-1989	5.00 - 10.00
Red arrow ironed on cotton twill.	1987-1990	8.00 - 10.00
Black cotton, white embroidered arrow, special for 75th Anniversary NOAC.	1990	100.00 - 140.00

POCKET RIBBON DROP
Arrow, silver.	1960-1970	10.00 - 15.00
Arrow, rhodium.	1970	5.00 - 7.50
Golden turtle, 75th Anniversary.	1990	20.00 - 25.00

VIGIL SASH
Red arrow, solid, on white, wool felt, arrow sewn on, large overhanging red triangle added in ctr.	1922-1948	400.00 - 500.00
Red arrow, detail in point and feathers, on white, wool felt, arrow flocked on, red triangle at ctr.	1948-1950	150.00 - 200.00
Red arrow and bars and triangle sewn on cotton twill.	1950-1987	25.00 - 35.00
Red arrow and bars and triangle ironed on cotton twill.	1987-1990	10.00 - 15.00

OA Founders E. Urner Goodman and Carroll A. Edson were popular signers of sashes.

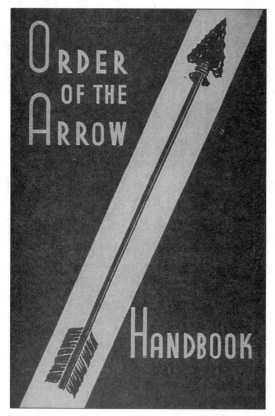

1950.

1952.

1961-72.

1973-79.

OA Handbooks outline the program for the Honor Camper Society.

1977-83.

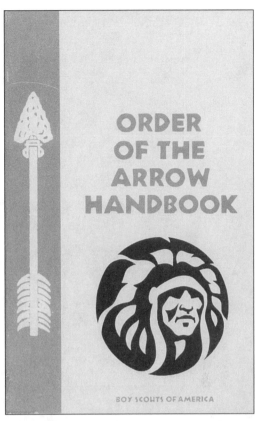

1985-87.

1989.

1990.

Why are these scouts smiling? They have just passed their ordeal without flinching.

EVENT COVERS

1910
1910s   National office or local council return address.   25.00 - 35.00

1920
1920s   National office or local council return address.   15.00 - 25.00
07.00.1920   World Jamboree, BSA Delegation envelope.   40.00 - 50.00
07.00.1920   World Jamboree, BSA hometown news notices.   40.00 - 50.00

1930
08.25.1930   Indianapolis Boy Scouts Welcome Commander R.E. Byrd & Eagle Scout Paul Siple, purple rubber hand stamp cachet.   5.00 - 7.50
1930s   National office or local council return address.   10.00 - 20.00

1932
12.14.1932   Boy Scout Stamp Club of Washington, D.C., Anniv. of Washington's death, purple rubber hand stamp cachet.   5.00 - 7.50

1933
02.08.1933   23rd Anniv., BSA, red and blue hand stamp.   2.50 - 5.00
08.25.1933   Boy Scout Day, Century of Progress Expo. Chicago Council, black hand stamp.   2.50 - 5.00
02.00.1933   BSA Anniversary, green.   2.50 - 5.00
05.07.1933   Centennial of Lincoln as postmaster of New Salem, IL, black cachet.   2.50 - 5.00
05.07.1933   Centennial of Lincoln as postmaster of New Salem, IL, purple hand stamp cachet.   2.50 - 5.00
08.00.1933   World Jamboree, green bar bill envelope and note.   25.00 - 35.00

1935
08.24.1935   FDR's address on the National Jamboree, blue.   5.00 - 7.50
02.08.1935   Troop 1, Schenectady, NY, blue.   5.00 - 7.50

1937
07.00.1937   World Jamboree, Green Bar Bill envelope and note.   25.00 - 35.00

1940
06.15.1940   Boston Sea Scout Division, Annual Fleet Cruise, light blue.   5.00 - 7.50
12.20.1940   Goodwill Tour, Troy, NY to New Orleans, LA via canoe, black on green card.   5.00 - 7.50
1940s   National office or local council return address.   7.50 - 12.50

1941
01.20.1941   Goodwill Tour, Troy, NY to New Orleans, LA via canoe, black on yellow card.   5.00 - 7.50

1945
03.17.1945   BSA Postcard, Cub, Scout and Sea Scout Advancing I.   2.50 - 5.00

1947
05.09.1947   Boy Scout Exposition, Minneapolis, MN, green rubber stamp.   2.50 - 5.00
05.10.1947   Boy Scout Exposition, Minneapolis, MN, green rubber stamp.   2.50 - 5.00
05.09.1947   Boy Scout Exposition, Minneapolis, MN, green and purple hand stamps.   2.50 - 5.00
05.09.1947   Scout Exposition, Minneapolis, MN, green cachet.   2.50 - 5.00

1948
09.25.1948   Saluting Young America, Troop 24, Minneapolis, MN, pink hand stamp.   2.50 - 5.00

1949
05.06.1949   Boy Scout Exposition, Troop 24, Minneapolis, MN, green hand stamp.   2.50 - 5.00

1950
06.30.1950   40th Anniv, FDC, Cachet Craft, L.W. Staehle, brown cachet, pair of stamps.   2.50 - 5.00
06.30.1950   40th Anniv. FDC. C.W. George Cachet. Scout Signaling. Brown and orange. Block of 4.   2.50 - 5.00
06.30.1950   40th Anniv., FDC, Art Craft, block of four.   2.50 - 5.00

Official BSA first day cover for the 40th anniversary.

06.30.1950	40th Anniv., FDC, Art Craft, single stamp.	2.50 - 5.00
06.30.1950	40th Anniv., FDC, Artmaster, black cachet, block of four.	5.00 - 7.50
06.30.1950	40th Anniv., FDC, Artmaster, black cachet, single stamp.	2.50 - 5.00
06.30.1950	40th Anniv., FDC, Artmaster, two scouts with banner, Jamboree logo, single stamp.	2.50 - 5.00
06.30.1950	40th Anniv., FDC, Boy Scout creed card.	2.50 - 5.00
06.30.1950	40th Anniv., FDC, Boy Scout Jamboree, blue and red type, single stamp.	2.50 - 5.00
06.30.1950	40th Anniv., FDC, C.S. Anderson, saluting Scout, blue cachet, single stamp.	2.50 - 5.00
06.30.1950	40th Anniv., FDC, C.S. Anderson, saluting Scout, brown cachet, single stamp.	2.50 - 5.00
06.30.1950	40th Anniv., FDC, C.S. Anderson, saluting Scout, brown cachet, block of four.	2.50 - 5.00
06.30.1950	40th Anniv., FDC, C.S. Anderson, saluting Scout, red cachet, single stamp.	2.50 - 5.00
06.30.1950	40th Anniv., FDC, C.S. Anderson, saluting Scout, red cachet, block of four.	2.50 - 5.00
06.30.1950	40th Anniv., FDC, C.S. Anderson, saluting Scout, red cachet, pair of stamps.	2.50 - 5.00
06.30.1950	40th Anniv., FDC, C.W. George Cachet, scout signaling, brown and orange, pair of stamps.	2.50 - 5.00
06.30.1950	40th Anniv., FDC, C.W. George Cachet, scout signaling, brown and orange, single stamp.	2.50 - 5.00
06.30.1950	40th Anniv., FDC, Cachet Craft, Ken Boll, Scout above Jamboree sign, brown and orange cachet, single stamp.	2.50 - 5.00
06.30.1950	40th Anniv., FDC, Cachet Craft, Ken Boll, Scout above Jamboree sign, brown and orange cachet, block of four.	5.00 - 7.50
06.30.1950	40th Anniv., FDC, Cachet Craft, Ken Boll, Scout above Jamboree sign, brown and orange cachet, pair of stamps.	2.50 - 5.00
06.30.1950	40th Anniv., FDC, cachet craft, Ken Boll, Scout above Jamboree sign, brown and yellow cachet, single stamp.	2.50 - 5.00
06.30.1950	40th Anniv., FDC, Cachet Craft, Ken Boll, Scout, First-Class emblem, eagle, single stamp.	2.50 - 5.00
06.30.1950	40th Anniv., FDC, Cachet Craft, Ken Boll, Scout, First-Class emblem, eagle, block of four.	2.50 - 5.00
06.30.1950	40th Anniv., FDC, Cachet Craft, L.W. Staehle, black cachet, single stamp.	2.50 - 5.00
06.30.1950	40th Anniv., FDC, Cachet Craft, L.W. Staehle, brown cachet, single stamp.	2.50 - 5.00
06.30.1950	40th Anniv., FDC, Fidelity color-craft cachet, saluting scout, flag and eagle, brown and blue, single stamp.	2.50 - 5.00
06.30.1950	40th Anniv., FDC, Fidelity color-craft cachet, saluting scout, flag and eagle, brown and blue, bock of four.	2.50 - 5.00
06.30.1950	40th Anniv., FDC, Fleetwood, block of four.	2.50 - 5.00
06.30.1950	40th Anniv., FDC, Fleetwood, single stamp.	2.50 - 5.00
06.30.1950	40th Anniv., FDC, Fluegel cover, two scouts saluting, flag in background, single stamp.	10.00 - 15.00
06.30.1950	40th Anniv., FDC, HF Cachet, Scout with eagle, gray, block of four.	2.50 - 5.00
06.30.1950	40th Anniv., FDC, HF Cachet, Scout with eagle, gray, single stamp.	2.50 - 5.00
06.30.1950	40th Anniv., FDC, HF Cachet, Scout with eagle, gray, pair of stamps.	2.50 - 5.00
06.30.1950	40th Anniv., FDC, Honoring the B.S.A. Patrol, cooking photo scene, single stamp.	2.50 - 5.00
06.30.1950	40th Anniv., FDC, IOOD Cachet, FDL and scenes within, brown and black, single stamp.	2.50 - 5.00
06.30.1950	40th Anniv., FDC, Kolor Kover cachet, saluting scout, brown and red, single stamp.	2.50 - 5.00

06.30.1950	40th Anniv., FDC, official BSA cover, Explorer, Scout, Cub, single stamp.	2.50 - 5.00
06.30.1950	40th Anniv., FDC, official BSA cover, Explorer, Scout, Cub, block of four.	2.50 - 5.00
06.30.1950	40th Anniv., FDC, official BSA Jamboree envelope, single stamp.	2.50 - 5.00
06.30.1950	40th Anniv., FDC, Pen's Arts Cachet, 40 years of scouting scroll, brown, single stamp.	2.50 - 5.00
06.30.1950	40th Anniv., FDC, Pen's Arts Cachet, Daniel Bear and James E. West portraits, brown, single stamp.	2.50 - 5.00
06.30.1950	40th Anniv., FDC, Pen's Arts Cachet, Scout advancing, uniform parts listed, brown, single stamp.	2.50 - 5.00
06.30.1950	40th Anniv., FDC, Pen's Arts Cachet, Scouts hiking, patrol cooking scenes, brown, single stamp.	2.50 - 5.00
06.30.1950	40th Anniv., FDC, photo of standing scout and bugle, green, single stamp.	2.50 - 5.00
06.30.1950	40th Anniv., FDC, photo of standing scout and bugle, green, block of four.	2.50 - 5.00
06.30.1950	40th Anniv., FDC, Postmaster General Letter.	20.00 - 30.00
06.30.1950	40th Anniv., FDC, Program of FDC Ceremonies, Valley Forge.	20.00 - 30.00
06.30.1950	40th Anniv., FDC, Schacht Cachet, saluting scout standing within frame, yellow/ gold color, block of four.	2.50 - 5.00
06.30.1950	40th Anniv., FDC, Scout waving onward, Washington in background, blue and red, single stamp.	2.50 - 5.00
06.30.1950	40th Anniv., FDC, Scout waving onward, Washington in background, blue and red, block of four.	2.50 - 5.00
06.30.1950	40th Anniv., FDC, Smart Craft, L.W. Staehle, Scout, Washington, Statue of Liberty, flag, single stamp.	2.50 - 5.00
06.30.1950	40th Anniv., FDC, Smart Craft, L.W. Staehle, Scout, Washington, Statue of Liberty, flag, block of four.	2.50 - 5.00
06.30.1950	40th Anniv., FDC, Spartan cachet, Scout saluting, pioneer in background, black and green, single stamp.	2.50 - 5.00
06.30.1950	40th Anniv., FDC, The Aristocrats, Scout standing, Valley Forge scene in background, blue cachet, block of four.	2.50 - 5.00
06.30.1950	40th Anniv., FDC, The Aristocrats, Scout standing, Valley Forge scene in background, blue cachet, single stamp.	2.50 - 5.00
06.30.1950	40th Anniv., FDC, The BSA, Valley Forge, PA, simple type in brown, single stamp.	2.50 - 5.00
06.30.1950	40th Anniv., FDC, Troop 24 Minneapolis, single stamp.	2.50 - 5.00
06.30.1950	40th Anniv., FDC, C.S. Anderson, saluting Scout, blue cachet, block of four.	2.50 - 5.00
06.30.1950	40th Anniv., FDC, B.S.A, First-Class emblem, blue and tan thermography, single stamp.	2.50 - 5.00
10.17.1950	Honoring the BSA, Spartan cachet, green and black.	2.50 - 5.00
1950s	National office or local council return address.	5.00 - 10.00
05.06.1950	Scouting Exposition, San Francisco Area Council, Cow Palace, Troop 121, brown.	2.50 - 5.00
05.05.1950	Scouting Exposition, Staten Island Council, red and blue.	2.50 - 5.00

1951

10.19.1951	Scouting Fair, Valley Forge Council, black.	2.50 - 5.00
05.12.1951	Scout-o-rama, Allegheny Council, light green hand stamp.	2.50 - 5.00
10.19.1951	Valley Forge Council Scouting Fair, black.	2.50 - 5.00

1952

05.03.1952	Scouting Exposition, Cow Palace, San Francisco.	2.50 - 5.00

1953

07.17-23.1953	1953 National Jamboree, BSA Official Jamboree stationery.	2.50 - 5.00
07.17.1953	1953 National Jamboree, Johnny Appleseed, Troop 3 cachet.	2.50 - 5.00
07.18.1953	1953 National Jamboree, North Shore Area Council, rubber stamp cachet.	2.50 - 5.00
07.17.1953	1953 National Jamboree, SOSSI cachet, blue.	5.00 - 7.50
07.17.1953	1953 National Jamboree, SOSSI cachet, brown.	5.00 - 7.50
07.17.1953	1953 National Jamboree, SOSSI cachet, green.	5.00 - 7.50
07.17.1953	1953 National Jamboree, Troop 24, Minneapolis cachet.	2.50 - 5.00
09.29.1953	Johnny Appleseed Area Scout Circus, Troop 3, Shelby, OH, black.	2.50 - 5.00
05.01.1953	Scout-o-rama, Troop 24, Minneapolis, MN, brown.	2.50 - 5.00

1954

08.26.1954	39th National Meeting, University of Wyoming, Laramie, Kola Lodge, Longs Peak Council, red.	5.00 - 7.50
12.11.1954	8th World Jamboree, August 1955, Willard Boyles, secretary, SOSS.	2.50 - 5.00
08.19.1954	Air Explorers, Region 4, training, blue.	2.50 - 5.00
09.26.1954	Johnny Appleseed Area Council, red.	2.50 - 5.00
02.00.1954	Monmouth Council, Conservation Good Turn, green.	2.50 - 5.00
05.15.1954	Scout Fair, Daniel Boon Council, green and brown.	2.50 - 5.00
04.30.1954	Scouting Exposition, Cow Palace, San Francisco, Troop 15, green.	2.50 - 5.00
06.05.1954	Scout-o-rama, Crescent Bay Area Council, Explorer Post 164, Beverly Hills, CA, brown.	2.50 - 5.00
04.30.1954	Scout-o-rama, Troop 72, Humbolt District, Buffalo Area Council, brown and light blue cachet.	2.50 - 5.00
04.30.1954	Scout-o-rama, Troop 72, Humbolt District, Buffalo Area Council, brown and purple cachet.	2.50 - 5.00
05.01.1954	Scout-o-rama, Troop 72, Buffalo Area Council, pink and blue screen-print.	2.50 - 5.00
04.30.1954	Scout-o-rama, Troop 72, Buffalo Area Council, pink and yellow screen-print.	2.50 - 5.00
04.30.1954	Scout-o-rama, Troop 72, Buffalo Area Council, yellow and pink screen-print.	2.50 - 5.00
10.23.1954	Tentoral, Sheepshead Bay District, GNYC, Camp Alpine, brown and green.	2.50 - 5.00

1955

06.11.1955	GNYC 1955 Camporee, Troop 26, Bronx Council, red and blue.	2.50 - 5.00
08.00.1955	Gotlandslagret, Sweden Boy Scout Summer Camp cachet.	7.50 - 10.00
12.00.1955	Monmouth Council, annual recognition banquet, blue.	2.50 - 5.00
02.00.1955	Monmouth Council, Onward for God and My Country, brown.	2.50 - 5.00
04.30.1955	Scout Exposition, Susquenago Council, Troop 36, Binghamton, NY, green.	2.50 - 5.00
05.01.1955	Scout Exposition, Susquenago Council, Troop 36, Binghamton, NY, green.	2.50 - 5.00
04.23.1955	Scout Sportsman Shows, Old Colony Council, Braintree postmark.	2.50 - 5.00
04.23.1955	Scout Sportsman Shows, Old Colony Council, Hingham postmark.	2.50 - 5.00
04.23.1955	Scout Sportsman Shows, Old Colony Council, Norwood postmark.	2.50 - 5.00
03.26.1955	Scouting Exposition, Trenton, NJ, George Washington Council, Troop 30, red and blue.	2.50 - 5.00

06.05.1955	Scout-o-rama, Crescent Bay Area Council, brown and yellow.	2.50 - 5.00
06.04.1955	Scout-o-rama, Crescent Bay Area Council, brown and yellow.	2.50 - 5.00
05.07.1955	Scout-o-rama, Grant Field, Atlanta, GA, Troop 181.	2.50 - 5.00
05.14.1955	Sheepshead Bay District Camporee, GNYC, Camp Alpine, red and blue.	2.50 - 5.00
10.15.1955	Tentoral, Sheepshead Bay District, William H. Pouch Camp, brown and green.	2.50 - 5.00
08.00.1955	World Jamboree, BSA logo cachet.	5.00 - 7.50
08.00.1955	World Jamboree, Buffalo Area Council envelope.	5.00 - 7.50
08.00.1955	World Jamboree, Ken Boll Cachet Craft.	7.50 - 10.00
08.00.1955	World Jamboree, SOSSI cachet.	7.50 - 10.00

1956

07.25.1956	150th Anniv., Lewis & Clark Expedition, Troop 2, Billings, MT, blue.	2.50 - 5.00
05.05.1956	Bird Study Merit Badge, Troop 41, Minneapolis, MN, green and brown.	2.50 - 5.00
04.21.1956	Boy Scout Exposition, San Francisco Council, Cow Palace, Pack 16 and Troop 15, blue hand stamp.	2.50 - 5.00
04.21.1956	Boy Scout Exposition, San Francisco Council, Cow Palace, Pack 16 and Troop 15, blue printed.	2.50 - 5.00
04.15.1956	Eagle Scout and Silver Award Class of 1956, Hunter College, GNYC, Troop 26, Bronx, NY, silver, red and blue.	2.50 - 5.00
10.20.1956	Great North West Round-up, Milwaukee County Council, blue and red.	2.50 - 5.00
04.08.1956	Merit Badge Expo., Troop 3, Shelby, OH, black and blue.	2.50 - 5.00
04.07.1956	Merit Badge Expo., Troop 3, Shelby, OH, red and blue.	2.50 - 5.00
05.19.1956	Scout Fair, Daniel Boone Council, purple and green.	2.50 - 5.00
05.19.1956	Scout Fair, Daniel Boone Council, red and blue.	2.50 - 5.00
04.05.1956	Scout Show, Middlesex Council, Rutgers Field House, blue and red.	2.50 - 5.00
05.05.1956	Scout-a-rade, Camp Development Fund, Troop 18, green.	2.50 - 5.00
09.29.1956	Scouter's Barbecue, GNYC Alpine Scout Camp, Explorer Post 49, Queens, blue, green and red.	2.50 - 5.00
04.07.1956	Scouting's Adventureland, Onondaga Council, Troop 6, purple, blue and light green.	2.50 - 5.00
05.11.1956	Scouting's Big Show, Cincinnati Area Council, Explorer Post 6, blue and red.	2.50 - 5.00
05.18.1956	Scouting's Big Show, Greater Cleveland Council, Troop 15, green.	2.50 - 5.00
06.16.1956	Topex '56, Greater Detroit Chapter #14, American Topical Exposition, blue and red.	2.50 - 5.00

1957

07.11.1957	1957 National Jamboree, Baden-Powell hand-drawn, Jamboree sticker.	2.50 - 5.00
07.12.1957	1957 National Jamboree, large Jamboree logo.	2.50 - 5.00
07.11-23.1957	1957 National Jamboree, official BSA stationery, Boys' Life Philatelic Exhibit rubber stamp added.	2.50 - 5.00
07.12.1957	1957 National Jamboree, SOSSI, G. Washington Chapter cachet.	2.50 - 5.00
07.14.1957	1957 National Jamboree, SOSSI, Liberty Bell Chapter cachet.	2.50 - 5.00
07.14.1957	1957 National Jamboree, Troop 63 cachet.	2.50 - 5.00
05.11.1957	Alhtaha Council, NJ, 40th Anniv., black, red and blue.	2.50 - 5.00

05.11.1957	Alhttaha Council, BSA, 45th Anniv., Paterson, NJ, black on pre-printed BSA cover.	2.50 - 5.00
05.25.1957	Area 2-B, conference, Camp Sakawawin, Lodge 287, Branchville, NJ, red and blue.	5.00 - 7.50
03.30.1957	Baden-Powell Centennial, Lone Tree Council, Scout-o-rama, Troop 1, Haverhill, MA, green.	2.50 - 5.00
03.16.1957	Cambridge Council, MA. Citizens Now Conference, red.	2.50 - 5.00
03.23.1957	Camp Edge 25th Anniv., Atlantic Area Council.	2.50 - 5.00
03.28.1957	Camp Edge, Atlantic Area Council, 25th Anniv., green on yellow/ tan envelope.	2.50 - 5.00
03.28.1957	Choccolocco Council, DeKalb District Camporee, green.	2.50 - 5.00
03.16.1957	Citizens Now Conference, Cambridge Council, red.	2.50 - 5.00
05.03.1957	Clan Gathering Camp-o-ree, Milwaukee County Council, Troop 153.	2.50 - 5.00
03.28.1957	Desoto State Park, DeKalb District, Choccolocco Council.	2.50 - 5.00
05.18.1957	Genesee Council, Armed Forces day, Troop 7, Batavia, NY, blue rubber stamp.	2.50 - 5.00
07.12.1957	Gilwell, Jim Bridger Crew EWB 16.	2.50 - 5.00
05.25.1957	Grand Valley Council, 1957 Jamo-all, Troop 281, red and blue.	2.50 - 5.00
05.26.1957	Green River Scout District Camporee, Renton, WA, green.	2.50 - 5.00
04.06.1957	Johnny Appleseed Area Council Scout-o-rama, Troop 3, Shelby, OH, black.	2.50 - 5.00
07.17.1957	National Jamboree envelope, #10 size, Jamboree cancel.	2.50 - 5.00
07.16.1957	National Jamboree envelope, #6 size, Jamboree cancel.	2.50 - 5.00
03.30.1957	Onondaga Council, Troop 6, Syracuse NY, green, purple and blue.	2.50 - 5.00
05.11.1957	Scout-o-rama, George Washington Council, Troop 30, black.	2.50 - 5.00
05.02.1957	Shenandoah Area Council, Troop 3, 30th Annual Apple Blossom Festival, red, blue and green/ yellow.	2.50 - 5.00
03.10.1957	SOSSI, George Washington Chapter 1st Anniv. meeting, black.	2.50 - 5.00
07.12.1957	SOSSI, II World Congress, H.L. Woodman cachet artist, brown and green on yellow envelope.	2.50 - 5.00
06.29.1957	Ten Mile River Scout Camps, 30th Anniv. GNYC,Explorer Post 631, Bronx, NY, red, blue and green.	2.50 - 5.00
07.04.1957	Troop 63, Payne, Al, 1957 Jamboree trip, brown, blue and purple.	2.50 - 5.00

1958

08.25.1958	43rd. Anniv. conference, University of Kansas, Lawrence, KS, Sanhican Lodge 2.	5.00 - 7.50
08.25.1958	43rd. Anniv. conference, University of Kansas,Lawrence, KS, red.	5.00 - 7.50
02.08.1958	Boy Scout Week, Troop 343, Chickasaw Council, Memphis, TN, yellow and blue.	2.50 - 5.00
05.16.1958	Chicago welcomes Paul A. Siple, national meeting.	2.50 - 5.00
04.01.1958	Middlesex Council, Scout Show, Troop 31, blue and red.	5.00 - 7.50
12.30.1958	Miquin Lodge 25th Anniv., blue, blue and red.	5.00 - 7.50
08.23.1958	OA Area 2D Conclave, Mahikan Lodge 181, Stratton Mountain Scout Reservation.	5.00 - 7.50
02.15.1958	Operation Snowbound, Milwaukee County Council, Troop 153.	2.50 - 5.00
06.06.1958	Scout Camporee, Cayuga County Council, red and blue.	2.50 - 5.00
03.08.1958	Scout-o-rama, Columbia District, Ft. Orange Council, Troop 104, blue and red.	2.50 - 5.00
04.18.1958	Scout-o-rama, Milwaukee, Troop 153.	2.50 - 5.00

03.23.1958	Scouts on Stamps Society, 2nd annual meeting, red and blue.	2.50 - 5.00
05.21.1958	Scouts United Camporee, Troop 153, Milwaukee, WI, blue and yellow.	2.50 - 5.00

1959

06.12.1959	Area 2-C Conference, Lekau Lodge 77,Camden County Council, red.	5.00 - 7.50
04.11.1959	Area V-E Conference, Camp Kickapoo, Sebooney Okasucca Lodge 260, green, red and brown.	5.00 - 7.50
08.26.1959	Conservation Good Turn, green.	2.50 - 5.00
09.26.1959	Daniel Boone Jamborette, Daniel Boone Council, PA, brown and red.	2.50 - 5.00
04.11.1959	Fort Orange Council Scout Craft Exhibition, blue and brown.	5.00 - 7.50
05.31.1959	Lincoln Trail Hike, Lincoln Sesquicentennial, black.	2.50 - 5.00
05.15.1959	Paxton District Camporee, Keystone Area Council, PA, red and blue.	2.50 - 5.00
05.01.1959	Scout-Capades, Buffalo Area Council.	2.50 - 5.00
05.22.1959	Scout-o-rama, San Mateo Council, Troop 160.	2.50 - 5.00
08.15.1959	Troop 116, summer camp.	2.50 - 5.00

1960

07.22.1960	1960 National Jamboree, BSA 50th Anniv. logo in color, in gray square.	2.50 - 5.00
07.22.1960	1960 National Jamboree, Camden County Council, Lekau Lodge 77 cachet.	2.50 - 5.00
07.22.1960	1960 National Jamboree, Canadian Guest Patrol, Malcolm McGregor card.	2.50 - 5.00
07.22.1960	1960 National Jamboree, card with image of Scout giving sign as on 1960 stamp.	2.50 - 5.00
07.22.1960	1960 National Jamboree, Casa Nola Motel cachet.	2.50 - 5.00
07.22.1960	1960 National Jamboree, First-Class emblem, Colorado Springs rubber stamp, legend below.	2.50 - 5.00
07.22.1960	1960 National Jamboree, Fleetwood cachet.	2.50 - 5.00
07.22.1960	1960 National Jamboree, Golden Jamboree in the Golden West.	2.50 - 5.00
07.22.1960	1960 National Jamboree, Inland Empire Council, Troops 77, 78, 79 cachet.	2.50 - 5.00
07.22.1960	1960 National Jamboree, Jamboree logo in purple rubber stamp.	2.50 - 5.00
07.22.1960	1960 National Jamboree, Johnny Appleseed, Troop 3 cachet.	2.50 - 5.00
07.28.1960	1960 National Jamboree, Last Day, Eisenhower Tours Jamboree Site cachet.	2.50 - 5.00
07.22.1960	1960 National Jamboree, North Shore Area Council cachet.	2.50 - 5.00
07.22.1960	1960 National Jamboree, Pony Express Commemorative.	2.50 - 5.00
07.24.1960	1960 National Jamboree, Scout Stamps Collectors Club meeting cachet.	2.50 - 5.00
07.22.1960	1960 National Jamboree, Scout standing on globe cachet.	2.50 - 5.00
07.27.1960	1960 National Jamboree, Tonawandas District cachet.	2.50 - 5.00
07.22.1960	1960 National Jamboree, Tonawandas District cachet.	2.50 - 5.00
07.22.1960	1960 National Jamboree, Troop 1, White River Council.	2.50 - 5.00
07.22.1960	1960 National Jamboree, Troop 58 cachet.	2.50 - 5.00
07.24.1960	1960 National Jamboree, Troop 63 cachet, Heart of Dixie.	2.50 - 5.00
07.22.1960	1960 National Jamboree, Troop 63 cachet.	2.50 - 5.00
07.22.1960	1960 National Jamboree, Troop 77, Watchung Area Council.	2.50 - 5.00
07.22.1960	1960 National Jamboree, USAF Academy Commemorative.	2.50 - 5.00

07.22.1960	1960 National Jamboree, SOSSI, G. Washington Chapter.	2.50 - 5.00
02.08.1960	50th Anniv. Cachet Craft, Ken Boll, First-Class emblem, gold and blue.	2.50 - 5.00
02.08.1960	50th Anniv. Scout handbook cover and laws.	2.50 - 5.00
02.08.1960	50th Anniv., fuzzy green and gold cachet.	2.50 - 5.00
06.11.1960	Akron Scout-o-rama, Post 2401, Wadsworth, OH, blue and red.	2.50 - 5.00
12.28.1960	Alpha-Phi-Omega 35th Anniv. meeting.	2.50 - 5.00
02.08.1960	Boy Scout Week, Andrew Jackson Council, Troop 109, Vicksburg, MS, blue.	2.50 - 5.00
02.11.1960	Boy Scout Week, North Tonawanda, NY., brown and yellow.	2.50 - 5.00
02.09.1960	Boy Scout Week, Troop 86, Anacortes, WA., red, blue and brown.	2.50 - 5.00
02.08.1960	BSA 50th Anniv. Cachet Craft, Ken Boll, large First-Class emblem, block of four.	2.50 - 5.00
02.08.1960	BSA 50th Anniv. Cachet Craft, Ken Boll, large First-Class emblem, single stamp.	2.50 - 5.00
02.08.1960	BSA 50th Anniv. card, enlargement of stamp.	2.50 - 5.00
02.08.1960	BSA 50th Anniv. Cascade Cachet, scout and First-Class emblem, blue, single stamp.	2.50 - 5.00
02.08.1960	BSA 50th Anniv. CCG Cachet, type and BSA Anniv. foil seal, single stamp.	2.50 - 5.00
02.18.1960	BSA 50th Anniv. First Day, Scout Council, Milwaukee County Council, green.	2.50 - 5.00
02.08.1960	BSA 50th Anniv. First-Class emblem and printed anniv. seal, Eisenhower quote, single stamp.	2.50 - 5.00
02.08.1960	BSA 50th Anniv. Fleetwood Cachet, seal, scouts cooking, oath on plaque, card insert, black, block of four.	2.50 - 5.00
02.08.1960	BSA 50th Anniv. Fleetwood Cachet, seal, scouts cooking, oath on plaque, card insert. black, single stamp.	2.50 - 5.00
02.08.1960	BSA 50th Anniv. Fleetwood Cover, Cub, Scout and Explorer, large envelope, cancel with one stamp.	7.50 - 10.00
02.08.1960	BSA 50th Anniv. Fleetwood Cover, Cub, Scout and Explorer, large envelope, cancel with 1950 and 1960 stamps.	7.50 - 10.00
02.08.1960	BSA 50th Anniv. Fleetwood, Masonic Stamp Club Cachet, Daniel Beard, card insert, black, single stamp.	2.50 - 5.00
02.08.1960	BSA 50th Anniv. Fluegel cover, scout saluting within large First-Class emblem, block of four.	10.00 - 15.00
02.08.1960	BSA 50th Anniv. Fluegel cover, scout saluting within large First-Class emblem, single stamp.	10.00 - 15.00
02.08.1960	BSA 50th Anniv. hand-drawn First-Class emblem, single stamp.	2.50 - 5.00
02.08.1960	BSA 50th Anniv. HF Cachet, tan BSA Anniv. seal above crossed flags, block of four.	2.50 - 5.00
02.08.1960	BSA 50th Anniv. HVM Cachet, scene of unknown scout meeting Boyce, card insert, single stamp.	2.50 - 5.00
02.08.1960	BSA 50th Anniv. Kolor Kover Cachet, saluting scout, single stamp.	2.50 - 5.00
03.30.1960	BSA 50th Anniv. Last Day, scout cancel, Milwaukee County Council, purple.	2.50 - 5.00
02.08.1960	BSA 50th Anniv. Mischa card, 1910-1960 BSA poster.	2.50 - 5.00
02.08.1960	BSA 50th Anniv. National Capital Area Council Cachet, capital building on FDL, tan color, single stamp.	2.50 - 5.00
02.08.1960	BSA 50th Anniv. National Capital Area Council Cachet, capital building on FDL, blue color, single stamp.	2.50 - 5.00
02.08.1960	BSA 50th Anniv. plain envelope, single stamp.	1.00 - 2.00
02.08.1960	BSA 50th Anniv. Post 28 Cachet, single stamp.	2.50 - 5.00
02.08.1960	BSA 50th Anniv. postal bulletin with first-day cancel.	5.00 - 7.50
02.08.1960	BSA 50th Anniv. Postmasters of America.	2.50 - 5.00
02.08.1960	BSA 50th Anniv. Shawanogi Chapter, Shenshawpotoo Lodge 276 Cachet, single stamp.	2.50 - 5.00
02.08.1960	BSA 50th Anniv. SOSSI, G. Washington Chapter Cachet, two saluting scouts, Washington head I, brown and red, single stamp.	2.50 - 5.00

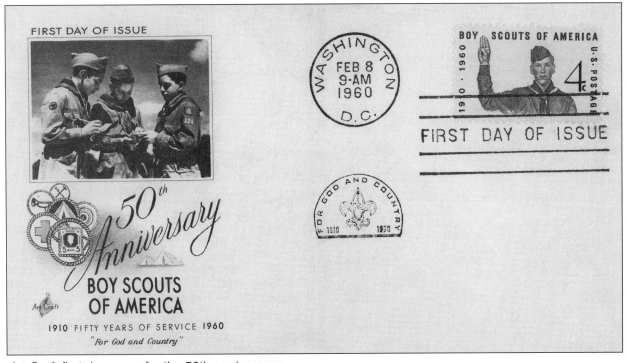

Art Craft first day cover for the 50th anniversary.

02.08.1960	BSA 50th Anniv. SOSSI, Liberty Bell Chapter Cachet, Liberty Bell, card insert, blue, single stamp.	2.50 - 5.00
02.08.1960	BSA 50th Anniv. SOSSI, Old Glory Chapter Cachet, BSA Anniv. logo, blue, single stamp.	2.50 - 5.00
02.08.1960	BSA 50th Anniv. The Aristocrats, Dave Lowry, First-Class emblem above inscription, block of four.	2.50 - 5.00
02.08.1960	BSA 50th Anniv. The Aristocrats, Dave Lowry, First-Class emblem above inscription, single stamp.	2.50 - 5.00
02.08.1960	BSA 50th Anniv. tri-color cachet, First-Class emblem, standing scout, red, green and brown, block of four.	2.50 - 5.00
02.08.1960	BSA 50th Anniv. Troop 1, Unadilla, NY Cachet, colonial scene, blue, single stamp.	2.50 - 5.00
02.08.1960	BSA 50th Anniv. Troop 109 cachet, single stamp.	2.50 - 5.00
02.08.1960	BSA 50th Anniv. Troop 2 cachet, single stamp.	2.50 - 5.00
02.08.1960	BSA 50th Anniv. Troop 24, Minneapolis, single stamp.	2.50 - 5.00
02.08.1960	BSA 50th Anniv. Troop 343, Chickasaw Council cachet, scout giving sign, blue and red, single stamp.	2.50 - 5.00
02.08.1960	BSA 50th Anniv. Troop 63 cachet, Cub, Scout, Explorer saluting, green on orange envelope, single stamp.	2.50 - 5.00
02.00.1960	BSA 50th Anniv. Troop 88, Washington DC Cachet, red, single stamp.	2.50 - 5.00
02.08.1960	BSA 50th Anniv. William Boyce portrait in black and orange, white card insert.	2.50 - 5.00
02.08.1960	BSA 50th Anniv. William Boyce portrait in black, green card insert.	2.50 - 5.00
02.08.1960	BSA 50th Anniv., 5" x 7" card with BSA history.	2.50 - 5.00
02.08.1960	BSA 50th Anniv., 5" x 7" card with law.	2.50 - 5.00
02.08.1960	BSA 50th Anniv., 5" x 7" card with oath.	2.50 - 5.00
02.08.1960	BSA 50th Anniv., Art Craft Cachet, three scouts, block of four.	2.50 - 5.00
02.08.1960	BSA 50th Anniv., Art Craft Cachet, three scouts, single stamp.	2.50 - 5.00
02.08.1960	BSA 50th Anniv., Artmaster Cachet, Cub, Scout and Explorer, block of four.	2.50 - 5.00
02.08.1960	BSA 50th Anniv., Artmaster Cachet, Cub, Scout and Explorer, single stamp.	2.50 - 5.00
02.08.1960	BSA 50th Anniv., Boys' Life cover.	2.50 - 5.00
02.08.1960	BSA 50th Anniv., BSA Anniv. logo, On to Colorado and the Jamboree, single stamp.	2.50 - 5.00
02.08.1960	BSA 50th Anniv., C. George Cachet, 1910 and 1960 scout profiles, brown and orange thermography, single stamp.	2.50 - 5.00
02.08.1960	BSA 50th Anniv., C.S. Anderson Cachet, saluting scout within circle, legend below, blue, single stamp.	2.50 - 5.00
02.08.1960	BSA 50th Anniv., C.S. Anderson Cachet, saluting scout within circle, legend below, black, single stamp.	2.50 - 5.00
02.08.1960	BSA 50th Anniv., C.S. Anderson Cachet, saluting scout within circle, legend below, red, single stamp.	2.50 - 5.00
02.08.1960	BSA 50th Anniv., C.S. Anderson Cachet, saluting scout within circle, legend below, brown, block of four.	2.50 - 5.00
02.08.1960	BSA 50th Anniv., C.S. Anderson Cachet, saluting scout within circle, legend below,. brown, single stamp.	2.50 - 5.00
02.08.1960	BSA 50th Anniv., plain envelope, block of four.	1.00 - 2.00
02.08.1960	Canal Zone R/W, BSA 50th Anniv. Aristocrats cover, Dave Lowry, black.	2.50 - 5.00
02.08.1960	Canal Zone R/W, BSA 50th Anniv. Artmaster cover, block of four.	2.50 - 5.00
02.08.1960	Canal Zone R/W, BSA 50th Anniv. Artmaster cover, pair of stamps.	2.50 - 5.00
02.08.1960	Canal Zone R/W, BSA 50th Anniv. Artmaster cover.	2.50 - 5.00
02.08.1960	Canal Zone R/W, BSA 50th Anniv. Cascade Cachet, First-Class emblem in square.	2.50 - 5.00
02.08.1960	Canal Zone R/W, BSA 50th Anniv. cover with palm and scout striding, multicolor.	2.50 - 5.00
02.08.1960	Canal Zone R/W, BSA 50th Anniv. FDC, cover encircling globe.	2.50 - 5.00
02.08.1960	Canal Zone R/W, BSA 50th Anniv. Fluegel cover.	2.50 - 5.00
02.08.1960	Canal Zone R/W, BSA 50th Anniv. HF cover, 50th Anniv. logo.	2.50 - 5.00
02.08.1960	Canal Zone R/W, BSA 50th Anniv. LSA and BSA, black.	2.50 - 5.00
02.08.1960	Canal Zone R/W, BSA 50th Anniv. Smith cover, Eagle badge, pair of stamps.	2.50 - 5.00
02.08.1960	Canal Zone R/W, BSA 50th Anniv. Smith cover, Eagle badge, single stamp.	2.50 - 5.00
02.08.1960	Canal Zone R/W,. BSA 50th Anniv. Smith cover, Eagle badge, block of four.	2.50 - 5.00
02.08.1960	Canal Zone, BSA 50th, BS Camp at Taboga Island cachet cover, single stamp.	5.00 - 7.50
02.08.1960	Canal Zone, BSA 50th. Artcraft cover, block of four stamps.	7.50 - 10.00
02.08.1960	Canal Zone, BSA 50th. Artcraft cover, single stamp.	2.50 - 5.00
02.08.1960	Canal Zone, BSA 50th. Artmaster cover, single stamp.	2.50 - 5.00
02.08.1960	Canal Zone, BSA 50th. Fleetwood cover, single stamp.	2.50 - 5.00
02.08.1960	Canal Zone, BSA 50th. Fleetwood cover., block of four stamps.	7.50 - 10.00
02.08.1960	Canal Zone, BSA 50th. SC cover, single stamp.	2.50 - 5.00
02.08.1960	Canal Zone, BSA 50th. Smith cover, Eagle Badge, single stamp.	2.50 - 5.00
02.08.1960	Canal Zone, BSA 50th. Troop 87 KC MO Round-up cover, single stamp.	2.50 - 5.00
02.08.1960	Canal Zone, BSA 50th., G. Washington Chapter, SOSSI Cachet cover, single stamp.	2.50 - 5.00
02.12.1960	Choccolocco Council's annual training seminar, Troop 63, green and black on yellow envelope.	2.50 - 5.00
02.13.1960	Cipex 2, Pee Wee Harris Salutes BSA, red and black.	2.50 - 5.00
04.02.1960	Du Page Area Council, Golden Jubilee Exposition.	2.50 - 5.00
06.03.1960	Golden Jubilee Camporee, Charter Oak Council, CT, red and blue.	2.50 - 5.00
07.22.1960	Golden Jubilee Camp-o-ree, Mount Baker Area Council, yellow on gray envelope.	2.50 - 5.00
02.10.1960	James E. West tribute, Troop 1, White River Council, Bloomington, IN, brown.	2.50 - 5.00
06.05.1960	Jubilee Camporee, Buffalo Area Council, brown.	2.50 - 5.00
07.28.1960	Jubilee Camporee, Paxton District, Keystone Area Council, red and blue.	2.50 - 5.00
02.13.1960	Jubilee Scout-o-rama, Tioughnioga Council, NY.	2.50 - 5.00
04.24.1960	Logansport Coin and Stamp Clubs, 50th Anniv., BSA, blue.	2.50 - 5.00
06.18.1960	Loggers Fun Days, benefit to BSA, red.	2.50 - 5.00
11.08.1960	Manhattan Nev. Famous Boy Scout leaders.	5.00 - 7.50
03.06.1965	NASPEX, label, First-Class emblem, brown.	2.50 - 5.00
03.06.1965	NASPEX, Nassau-Suffolk Philatelic Alliance, program, green.	2.50 - 5.00
1960s	National office or local council return address.	5.00 - 10.00
06.04.1960	Scouting Exposition, Alhtaha Council, NJ, black and red, Rosscraft.	2.50 - 5.00

04.23.1960	Scoutlatch, Troop 126, Chief Seattle Council, green on yellow envelope.	2.50 - 5.00
05.07.1960	Scout-o-rama, San Francisco Council, Troop 15. Brown.	2.50 - 5.00
05.20.1960	Scout-o-rama, San Mateo Council, Troop 160, Redwood City, CA, black.	2.50 - 5.00
05.14.1960	Scout-o-rama, Skagit-Island District, Mount Baker Area Council, red and yellow.	2.50 - 5.00
05.07.1960	Scoutpex I, Scout Philatelic Exhibition, Chicago, IL.	2.50 - 5.00
07.06.1960	SOSSI, Old Glory Chapter, BSA 50th Anniv. logo, black.	2.50 - 5.00
02.27.1960	Stanislaus Stamp Club honors BSA, green.	2.50 - 5.00
04.20.1960	Tioughnioga Council, 20th Anniv., blue and red.	2.50 - 5.00
02.16.1960	Troop 1, Unadilla, NY, plain card.	2.50 - 5.00
03.03.1960	Troop 1, Unadilla, NY, scout profile and type, brown and black.	2.50 - 5.00
02.09.1960	Troop 1, Unadilla, NY. 50th Anniv., blue, insert card.	5.00 - 7.50
06.18.1960	Troop 116 Pacoima, CA, summer camp, red and yellow.	2.50 - 5.00
04.27.1960	Troop 62, 25th Anniv., Valley View, PA, multicolored.	2.50 - 5.00
03.16.1960	Troop 88, National Capital Area Council, tan cachet.	2.50 - 5.00
07.22.1960	William Boyce, BSA 50th, with 10¢ Cadillac local post added.	2.50 - 5.00

1961

08.21.1961	46th Anniv. conference, OA, Indiana University, Bloomington, IN, black and red.	5.00 - 7.50
06.10.1961	Adventures in Scouting Camp Veritans, Alhtaha Council, NJ.	2.50 - 5.00
06.14.1961	Flag Day, Troop 86, Anacortes, WA, red, blue and brown.	2.50 - 5.00
01.00.1961	SOSSI, Baden-Powell, green on yellow envelope.	2.50 - 5.00

1962

02.23.1962	Iroquois Troop 62, Brooklyn, NY, 50th Anniv., yellow and brown.	2.50 - 5.00
05.10.1962	Philadelphia Council Scouting in Action Scout Show, SOSSI, Liberty Bell Chapter.	2.50 - 5.00
07.17.1962	Philmont Scout Ranch Expedition, Post 3, St. Louis, MO, black and yellow.	2.50 - 5.00
05.11.1962	Scout-o-rama, SportsAmerica, Cow Palace, Troop 15, brown.	2.50 - 5.00

1963

04.21.1963	GSA 50th Anniv., from Post 88, National Capitol Area Council, blue.	2.50 - 5.00
06.29.1963	Philadelphia Scouts to Boy Scouts of Canada, blue on yellow envelope.	2.50 - 5.00

1964

07.18.1964	1964 National Jamboree, BSA official stationery with Boys' Life Exhibit rubber stamp added.	2.50 - 5.00
07.19.1964	1964 National Jamboree, Pedro Brings Jamboree News postcard.	2.50 - 5.00
07.22.1964	1964 National Jamboree, SOSSI, George Washington Chapter cachet.	2.50 - 5.00
07.17.1964	1964 National Jamboree, SOSSI, Liberty Bell Chapter cachet.	2.50 - 5.00
07.22.1964	1964 National Jamboree, SOSSI, Liberty Bell Chapter cachet.	2.50 - 5.00
07.17.1964	1964 National Jamboree, Troop 44 cachet.	2.50 - 5.00
07.17.1964	National Jamboree Valley Forge, official stationery, black and green.	2.50 - 5.00
04.22.1964	New York World's Fair, First Day cover, FDL, green and black.	2.50 - 5.00
01.09.1964	Tribute to a fallen Scout, John F. Kennedy, Nassau County Council, black.	2.50 - 5.00

1965

07.02.1965	Boy Scout World Bureau, Help give scouting to handicapped boys, black and purple rubber stamp.	2.50 - 5.00
12.00.1965	International Boy Scout Camporee, Nicaragua, ovpt. souv. sheet.	5.00 - 7.50
12.00.1965	International Boy Scout Camporee, Nicaragua, set of ovpt. stamps.	5.00 - 7.50
09.28.1965	NASPEX cachet.	2.50 - 5.00
03.07.1965	NASPEX, First-Class emblem, brown.	2.50 - 5.00
02.06.1965	Ryukyu Islands Boy Scouts, 10th Anniv. Ryukyu District, Far East Council, FDC. Red, blue and green.	2.50 - 5.00
02.06.1965	Ryukyu Islands Boy Scouts, 10th Anniv. The official cover, stamp design and map.	2.50 - 5.00
07.17.1965	SOSSI, Liberty Bell Chapter, 50th Anniv. OA, brave passing down legend, signed by E. Urner Goodman.	75.00 - 100.00
07.17.1965	SOSSI, Liberty Bell Chapter, 50th Anniv. OA, brave passing down legend.	5.00 - 7.50
04.23.1965	SOSSI, Sunset Trails Chapter, light blue.	2.50 - 5.00
05.01.1965	Tioughnioga Council, Cortland, NY, 25th Anniv., blue, green and tan.	2.50 - 5.00
06.07.1965	Troop 2, Logansport, IN, 50th Anniv., blue.	2.50 - 5.00

1966

05.07.1966	Scout-o-rama, Goldenrod District, Mid-America Council, red and blue.	2.50 - 5.00
03.25.1966	SOSSI at Interpex, green.	2.50 - 5.00
03.25.1966	SOSSI, G. Washington Chapter at Interpex, NY, green.	2.50 - 5.00
03.13.1966	SOSSI, George Washington Chapter 10th Anniv., meeting.	2.50 - 5.00
04.29.1966	SOSSI, Theodore Roosevelt Chapter, NASPEX, blue.	2.50 - 5.00
09.17.1966	SOSSI, Sunset Trails Chapter, Suntrapex, blue and red, card insert.	2.50 - 5.00
05.13.1966	Wonderful World of Scouting, SOSSI, Dan Beard Chapter, Cincinnati, OH, brown.	2.50 - 5.00

1967

05.20.1967	Dan Beard Council, Peterloon, 1967, yellow, tan and green, card insert.	2.50 - 5.00
03.18.1967	SOSSI at Interpex, red.	2.50 - 5.00
02.26.1967	SOSSI George Washington Chapter, meeting.	2.50 - 5.00
09.16.1967	SOSSI Sunset Chapter, Suntrapex show cachet.	2.50 - 5.00
06.00.1967	World Jamboree, Idaho, FDC Dahomey, 30f, 70f, and 100f value Soave, sheet.	5.00 - 7.50
06.00.1967	World Jamboree, Idaho, FDC Dahomey, 30f, 70f, and 100f values, cachet as 100f stamp.	5.00 - 7.50
06.00.1967	World Jamboree, Idaho, FDC Gabon, 100f value, cachet as stamp.	5.00 - 7.50
06.00.1967	World Jamboree, Idaho, FDC Gabon, 50f value, cachet as stamp.	5.00 - 7.50
06.00.1967	World Jamboree, Idaho, FDC Mali, 70f, 100f values and seal, thermographed cachet.	5.00 - 7.50
06.00.1967	World Jamboree, Idaho, FDC Mali, 70f, 100f values and seal.	5.00 - 7.50
06.00.1967	World Jamboree, Idaho, FDC Upper Volta, 100f value.	5.00 - 7.50
06.00.1967	World Jamboree, Idaho, FDC Upper Volta, 5f and 20f values.	5.00 - 7.50
06.00.1967	World Jamboree, Idaho, FDC Yemen, set of seven stamps, imperforate.	5.00 - 7.50
06.00.1967	World Jamboree, Idaho, FDC Yemen, set of seven stamps.	5.00 - 7.50
06.00.1967	World Jamboree, Idaho, FDC Yemen, souv. sheet, 20b. imperforate.	5.00 - 7.50
08.01.1967	XII World Jamboree, Idaho, Boy Scout Friendship Around the World, Idaho map.	2.50 - 5.00
08.04.1967	XII World Jamboree, Idaho, official federal postcard, Artcraft cachet.	2.50 - 5.00

Troop 43 cover for the 1967 World Jamboree.

08.04.1967	XII World Jamboree, Idaho, official federal postcard, Artmaster cachet.	2.50 - 5.00
08.04.1967	XII World Jamboree, Idaho, official federal postcard, Brownsea Island blue rubber stamp.	2.50 - 5.00
08.04.1967	XII World Jamboree, Idaho, official federal postcard, Brownsea Island commemorative cachet.	2.50 - 5.00
08.04.1967	XII World Jamboree, Idaho, official federal postcard, Fleetwood cachet.	2.50 - 5.00
08.04.1967	XII World Jamboree, Idaho, official federal postcard, Jamboree Seal affixed.	2.50 - 5.00
08.04.1967	XII World Jamboree, Idaho, official federal postcard, plain.	1.50 - 3.00
08.04.1967	XII World Jamboree, Idaho, official federal postcard, Russian Boy Scouts cachet.	2.50 - 5.00
08.04.1967	XII World Jamboree, Idaho, official federal postcard, Scout saluting, map of Western U.S. cachet.	2.50 - 5.00
08.04.1967	XII World Jamboree, Idaho, official federal postcard, SOSSI, Mohawk Valley Chapter cachet.	2.50 - 5.00
08.04.1967	XII World Jamboree, Idaho, official federal postcard, SOSSI, Liberty Bell Chapter cachet.	2.50 - 5.00
08.04.1967	XII World Jamboree, Idaho, official federal postcard, The Aristocrats Dave Lowry cachet.	2.50 - 5.00
08.04.1967	XII World Jamboree, Idaho, official federal postcard, Troop 43 New Orleans cachet.	2.50 - 5.00
08.04.1967	XII World Jamboree, Idaho, official federal postcard, two scouts clasping hands, black rubber stamp.	2.50 - 5.00
08.04.1967	XII World Jamboree, Idaho, official government postcard with jamboree seal.	2.50 - 5.00
08.04.1967	XII World Jamboree, Idaho, official government postcard, mint.	2.50 - 5.00
08.04.1967	XII World Jamboree, Idaho, official government postcard, SOSSI, Liberty Bell Chapter rubber stamp.	2.50 - 5.00
08.01.1967	XII World Jamboree, Idaho, official picture (of badge) postcard.	2.50 - 5.00
08.01.1967	XII World Jamboree, Idaho, official stationery.	2.50 - 5.00
08.01.1967	XII World Jamboree, Idaho, SOSSI, Liberty Bell Chapter cachet.	2.50 - 5.00

1968

05.04.1968	Scout-o-rama, Goldenrod District, Mid-America Council, brown and green.	2.50 - 5.00
10.26.1968	Yorktown Encampment, Fairfax District.	2.50 - 5.00

1969

08.15.1969	17th Cathoree, Two Rivers.	2.50 - 5.00
07.16.1969	1969 National Jamboree, Allegheny Trails Council, Flag Plaza set with FDC and Jambo cancels, set of 10.	20.00 - 30.00
07.16.1969	1969 National Jamboree, BSA official stationery.	2.50 - 5.00
07.20.1969	1969 National Jamboree, Inland Empire Philatelic Society cachet.	2.50 - 5.00
07.16.1969	1969 National Jamboree, Inland Empire Philatelic Society cachet.	2.50 - 5.00
07.19.1969	1969 National Jamboree, Inland Empire Philatelic Society cachet.	2.50 - 5.00
07.17.1969	1969 National Jamboree, Inland Empire Philatelic Society cachet.	2.50 - 5.00
07.21.1969	1969 National Jamboree, Inland Empire Philatelic Society cachet.	2.50 - 5.00
07.18.1969	1969 National Jamboree, Inland Empire Philatelic Society cachet.	2.50 - 5.00
07.22.1969	1969 National Jamboree, Inland Empire Philatelic Society cachet.	2.50 - 5.00
07.16.1969	1969 National Jamboree, SOSSI cachet, card enclosure.	2.50 - 5.00
05.17.1969	Daniel Boone Jamborette, Daniel Boone Council, PA, red and blue.	2.50 - 5.00
09.27.1969	Monmouth Council Scout County Fair & Camporee.	2.50 - 5.00
07.20.1969	National Scout Jamboree, Visit of Lady Baden-Powell, blue.	2.50 - 5.00
05.03.1969	Scout-o-rama, Goldenrod District, Fremont, NE, red and blue.	2.50 - 5.00
05.17.1969	Squanto Council, 50th Anniv.	2.50 - 5.00
06.00.1969	XII World Jamboree, Idaho, official federal postcard, 1967 and 1969 Jamboree logos cachet.	2.50 - 5.00

1970

02.08.1970	60th Anniv. W.H. Jahne cachet.	2.50 - 5.00
02.08.1970	BSA 60th Anniv. SOSSI, blue.	2.50 - 5.00
04.19.1970	Lakewood Pan American Festival, Knights of Dunamis, Long Beach Chapter, multicolored.	2.50 - 5.00
1970s	National office or local council return address.	2.50 - 5.00
03.22.1970	SOPEX. 60th Anniv. of BSA, yellow, card insert.	2.50 - 5.00
11.20.1970	SOSSI Salutes UN 25th, G. Washington and T. Roosevelt chapters, black and blue.	2.50 - 5.00

1971

08.30.1971	Knights of Dunamis Conference, West Point, NY, Chapter 80.	2.50 - 5.00
04.18.1971	Knights of Dunamis, Pan American Festival, Chapter 80.	2.50 - 5.00
05.21.1971	Scout-o-rama, SOAR, orange and green.	2.50 - 5.00

1972

05.19.1972	NESA Launching, #10 envelope, Eagle badge.	2.50 - 5.00
05.19.1972	NESA Launching, #6 envelope, Eagle badge.	2.50 - 5.00
07.31.1972	Troop 98, Sacramento, CA, visits Hawaii, carved Hawaiian God, brown and blue.	2.50 - 5.00
07.19.1972	Troop 98, Sacramento, CA, visits Hawaii, King Kamehameha, red and blue.	2.50 - 5.00
07.10.1972	Will J. Reid Cub Camp, Knights of Dunamis, Chapter 80.	2.50 - 5.00

1973

08.03.1973	1973 National Jamboree, East, BSA official stationery.	2.50 - 5.00
08.03.1973	1973 National Jamboree, East, official BSA FDC.	2.50 - 5.00
08.03.1973	1973 National Jamboree, East, SOSSI cachet, card enclosure.	2.50 - 5.00
08.03.1973	1973 National Jamboree, East, A and B stickers added to plain envelope.	2.50 - 5.00
08.01.1973	1973 National Jamboree, West and East, Scout tossing coin, canceled 8.3.1973 in PA.	2.50 - 5.00

08.01.1973	1973 National Jamboree, West, BSA official stationery.	2.50 - 5.00
08.03.1973	1973 National Jamboree, West, Inland Empire Philatelic Society cachet.	2.50 - 5.00
08.07.1973	1973 National Jamboree, West, Inland Empire Philatelic Society cachet.	2.50 - 5.00
08.06.1973	1973 National Jamboree, West, Inland Empire Philatelic Society cachet.	2.50 - 5.00
08.04.1973	1973 National Jamboree, West, Inland Empire Philatelic Society cachet.	2.50 - 5.00
08.02.1973	1973 National Jamboree, West, Inland Empire Philatelic Society cachet.	2.50 - 5.00
08.01.1973	1973 National Jamboree, West, Inland Empire Philatelic Society cachet.	2.50 - 5.00
08.05.1973	1973 National Jamboree, West, Inland Empire Philatelic Society cachet.	2.50 - 5.00
08.01.1973	1973 National Jamboree, West, official BSA FDC.	2.50 - 5.00
08.01.1973	1973 National Jamboree, West, SOSSI cachet.	2.50 - 5.00
08.01.1973	1973 National Jamboree, West, SOSSI, Golden Bear Chapter, map cachet.	2.50 - 5.00
04.07.1973	Hancock Council, 50th Anniv., golden.	2.50 - 5.00
08.03.1973	National Scout Jamboree, East, official stationery.	2.50 - 5.00
08.03.1973	National Scout Jamboree, East, SOSSI official cachet, green.	2.50 - 5.00
01.01.1973	Scout memorabilia mailing permit, H.D. Thorsen.	2.50 - 5.00
12.14.1973	Shonto Trek, Knights of Dunamis, Chapter 80.	2.50 - 5.00

1974

02.08.1974	Scout Day, UN. New York, black.	2.50 - 5.00
05.05.1974	Scout-o-Sphere, Baltimore Area Council, purple.	2.50 - 5.00
06.20.1974	Troop 1, Cochituate, MA. 50th Anniv., blue rubber stamp.	2.50 - 5.00

Cover postmarked at both East and West Jamborees.

1975

04.19.1975	Knights of Dunamis, 50th Anniv., gold and blue.	2.50 - 5.00
12.15.1975	Navajo Christmas Trek, Knights of Dunamis.	2.50 - 5.00
09.06.1975	NESA Area Conference, Western Region, UC, Irvine.	2.50 - 5.00
05.24.1975	Scouting Expo, Baltimore Area Council.	2.50 - 5.00
01.18.1975	SOSSI, Golden Bear Chapter, 4th Scout Expo.	2.50 - 5.00
05.17.1975	Tonawandas District Camporee, North Tonawanda, NY, blue.	2.50 - 5.00
05.18.1975	Tonawandas District Camporee, NY	2.50 - 5.00

1976

06.12.1976	Bicentennial Camporee, Tonawandas and Two Nations District, North Tonawanda, NY, red and black.	2.50 - 5.00
06.13.1976	Bicentennial Camporee, Tonawandas and Two Nations District, North Tonawanda, NY, blue and black.	2.50 - 5.00
12.11.1976	Navajo Christmas Trek, Knights of Dunamis.	2.50 - 5.00
07.04.1976	NESA, Long Beach Chapter, trip to Washington, D.C.	2.50 - 5.00
05.00.1976	Project Love, Knights of Dunamis.	2.50 - 5.00
05.21.1976	Putnam Memorial State Park, Redding, CT, Bicentennial Muster.	2.50 - 5.00
07.11.1976	Quinnipiac Council, International Camporee.	2.50 - 5.00
12.11.1976	Scout show cancel, Atlanta Area Council.	2.50 - 5.00
05.08.1976	Scout-o-rama, Occoneechee Council, Durham, N.C.	2.50 - 5.00
05.08.1976	Scout-o-rama, Occoneechee Council, Fayetteville, NC.	2.50 - 5.00
05.08.1976	Scout-o-rama, Occoneechee Council, Raleigh, N.C.	2.50 - 5.00
11.06.1976	SOSSI Pony Express Chapter and Western Traders Assn. Scout Memorabilia Show, green and brown on large yellow card.	5.00 - 7.50
06.11.1976	Tonawandas and Two Nations District, North Tonawanda, NY, green and black.	2.50 - 5.00

1977

08.03.1977	1977 National Jamboree, large red rubber stamp cachet.	2.50 - 5.00
08.03.1977	1977 National Jamboree, North Carolina cards, large 3 in date.	2.50 - 5.00
08.03.1977	1977 National Jamboree, North Carolina cards, small 3 in date.	2.50 - 5.00
08.03.1977	1977 National Jamboree, official BSA stationery.	2.50 - 5.00
08.09.1977	1977 National Jamboree, plain envelope.	1.00 - 2.00
08.08.1977	1977 National Jamboree, plain envelope.	1.00 - 2.00
08.03.1977	1977 National Jamboree, SOSSI, purple cachet.	2.50 - 5.00
08.03.1977	1977 National Jamboree, Troop 266, Tannu Lodge #346, NOAC.	2.50 - 5.00
08.03.1977	1977 National Jamboree, JWO Cachet, Baden-Powell.	2.50 - 5.00
08.03.1977	1977 National Jamboree, SOSSI green Cachet.	2.50 - 5.00
12.10.1977	Atlanta Area Council, Scout show.	2.50 - 5.00
12.10.1977	Atlanta Scout Show, Pedro.	2.50 - 5.00
05.14.1977	Camden County Council, Scout-o-Rama.	2.50 - 5.00
12.17.1977	Navajo Christmas Trek, Knights of Dunamis.	2.50 - 5.00
02.18.1977	Puerto Rico Council, BSA, 50th Anniv., 50 within FDL.	2.50 - 5.00
02.19.1977	Puerto Rico Council, BSA, 50th Anniv., FDL and island map.	2.50 - 5.00
05.14.1977	Scout-o-rama, Occoneechee Council, Durham, NC.	2.50 - 5.00
05.14.1977	Scout-o-rama, Occoneechee Council, Fayetteville, NC.	2.50 - 5.00
05.14.1977	Scout-o-rama, Occoneechee Council, Raleigh, NC.	2.50 - 5.00
11.19.1977	Tidewater Council, Scout Show.	2.50 - 5.00

SOSSI cover for the 1977 National Jamboree.

1978

12.16.1978	Navajo Christmas Trek, Knights of Dunimas.	2.50 - 5.00
08.10.1978	NESA Conference, Nashville, Long Beach chapter.	2.50 - 5.00
05.13.1978	NESA, Knights of Dunamis, Long Beach Chapter, blue.	2.50 - 5.00
09.09.1978	NESA, Western Region Training Conference.	2.50 - 5.00
08.31.1978	Nimham District, Fishkill, NY.	2.50 - 5.00
08.31.1978	Nimham District, NY, Indian, tenderfoot and redman logos.	2.50 - 5.00
08.31.1978	Nimham District, Wooden Flat.	5.00 - 7.50
06.10.1978	Scout-o-rama, Occoneechee Council, SOSSI, Tarheel Chapter.	2.50 - 5.00
11.08.1978	Shenandoah Area Council, 50th Anniv.	2.50 - 5.00

1979

11.10.1979	Atlanta Area Council Scout Show, honors Green Bar Bill.	2.50 - 5.00
06.02.1979	Knights of Dunamis, Long Beach Scout-o-rama.	2.50 - 5.00
11.15.1979	Knights of Dunamis, sword cover.	2.50 - 5.00
12.15.1979	Navajo Christmas Trek, Knights of Dunamis.	2.50 - 5.00
03.31.1979	NESA, Knights of Dunamis, Long Beach Veterans Hospital, black.	2.50 - 5.00
05.19.1979	Occoneechee Council, See-n-do, Raleigh, N.C. G.R. Clark postcard.	2.50 - 5.00
05.19.1979	Occoneechee Council, See-n-do, Raleigh, NC, Molly Pitcher postcard.	2.50 - 5.00
11.10.1979	See-n-do, SOSSI, Tarheel Chapter, Charlotte, N.C.	2.50 - 5.00
01.13.1979	SOSSI, Pony Express and Golden Bear Chapters, Scoutpex.	2.50 - 5.00

1980

10.18.1980	70th Anniv. Motor City Stamp & Cover Club, BSA logo.	2.50 - 5.00
02.20.1980	70th Anniv. of Scouting, Fireside Post seal.	2.50 - 5.00
02.00.1980	BSA 70th Anniversary, postal card limited ed, numbered, image of 1960 stamp.	1.50 - 3.00
02.00.1980	BSA 70th Anniversary, SOSSI, Hampton Roads Chapter #29, card.	1.50 - 3.00

05.17.1980	Chicago Area Council, Camporall '80.	2.50 - 5.00
05.17.1980	Chicago Area Council, Camporall.	2.50 - 5.00
02.15.1980	Cub Pack 14, Long Beach, CA, Knights of Dunamis.	2.50 - 5.00
11.06.1980	Lone Scout 65 Anniv., SOSSI, Tar Heel Chapter, blue and red.	2.50 - 5.00
10.18.1980	Motopex 80, BSA 70th Anniv., red and black.	2.50 - 5.00
10.18.1980	Motopex 80, Cub Scout's 50th Anniv., gold and red.	2.50 - 5.00
1980s	National office or local council return address.	2.50 - 5.00
04.15.1980	NESA, Long Beach, 4th Life-Eagle event, Knights of Dunamis.	2.50 - 5.00
05.10.1980	Occoneechee Council, Raleigh N.C. Scout-o-rama, Cubs, Scouts, Green Bar Bill.	2.50 - 5.00
02.15.1980	Sarapex, Salutes Scouting 70th.	2.50 - 5.00
11.22.1980	Scout Show, Atlanta, Pedro.	2.50 - 5.00
05.17.1980	Scouting 70th Anniv., cancel, Oakhurst, NJ.	2.50 - 5.00
05.17.1980	Scouting the better life, 70th Anniv., Monmouth Council Scout Fair.	2.50 - 5.00
06.07.1980	SOSSI, Daniel Boone Chapter, 70th Anniv. of scouting, blue and red.	2.50 - 5.00
06.07.1980	SOSSI, Daniel Boone Chapter, 70th Anniv. of scouting, green and red.	2.50 - 5.00
06.19.1980	W.D. Boyce Birth Anniversary.	2.50 - 5.00

1981

08.02.1981	1981 National Jamboree, Scout kneeling, lashing, GSC cachet.	2.00 - 3.00
08.01.1981	1981 National Jamboree, Scout kneeling, lashing, GSC cachet.	2.00 - 3.00
08.04.1981	1981 National Jamboree, Scout kneeling, lashing, GSC cachet.	2.00 - 3.00
08.03.1981	1981 National Jamboree, Scout kneeling, lashing, GSC cachet.	2.00 - 3.00
07.31.1981	1981 National Jamboree, Scout kneeling, lashing, GSC cachet.	2.00 - 3.00
07.30.1981	1981 National Jamboree, Scout kneeling, lashing, GSC cachet.	2.00 - 3.00
07.29.1981	1981 National Jamboree, Scout kneeling, lashing, GSC cachet.	2.00 - 3.00

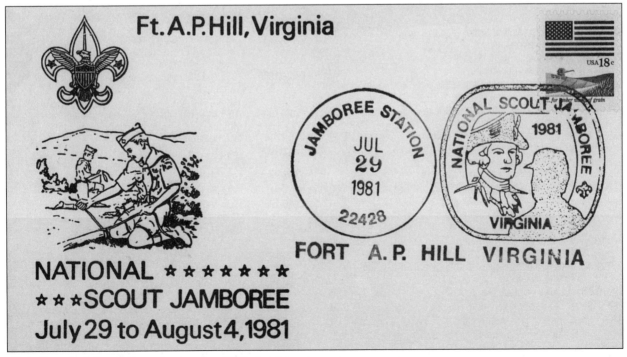

Cuhaj's privately produced cover for 1981 Jamboree.

Date	Description	Price
07.29.1981	1981 National Jamboree, SOSSI, Daniel Boone Chapter, red and blue cachet.	2.50 - 5.00
07.29.1981	1981 National Jamboree, SOSSI, Daniel Boone Chapter, black cachet.	2.50 - 5.00
08.02.1981	1981 National Jamboree, SOSSI, King Karl XVI Gustaf's Jamboree visit.	2.50 - 5.00
07.29.1981	1981 National Jamboree, SOSSI, Liberty Bell Chapter cachet.	2.50 - 5.00
07.29.1981	1981 National Jamboree, SOSSI, official purple cachet, SOSSI logo.	2.50 - 5.00
07.29.1981	1981 National Jamboree, SOSSI, official purple cachet,1981 Jambo logo.	2.50 - 5.00
08.01.1981	1981 National Jamboree, SOSSI, red merit badge booth postcard, Tarheel Chapter.	2.50 - 5.00
07.29.1981	1981 National Jamboree, SOSSI, red merit badge booth postcard, Tarheel Chapter.	2.50 - 5.00
08.04.1981	1981 National Jamboree, SOSSI, red rubber stamp cachet, last day.	2.50 - 5.00
08.13.1981	65th Anniv. Conference, Univ. of Texas, Austin.	5.00 - 7.50
11.07.1981	Atlanta Council Cancel, seal and FMF Local Post added, Troop 350 Kentwood, MI.	5.00 - 7.50
05.17.1981	Camperall, Old Fort Niagara State Park, black and blue.	2.50 - 5.00
05.15.1981	Camperall, Old Fort Niagara State Park.	2.50 - 5.00
05.16.1981	Camperall, Old Fort Niagara State Park.	2.50 - 5.00
11.07.1981	Heritage '81, Atlanta Scout Show, Philatelic Committee.	2.50 - 5.00
11.15.1981	Jojex Honors Scouting.	2.50 - 5.00
05.16.1981	Monmouth Council, BSA, Scouting Expo Cancel.	2.50 - 5.00
07.29.1981	National Scout Jamboree, Gulf Ridge Council, CSP rubber stamp, black.	2.50 - 5.00
07.29.1981	National Scout Jamboree, SOSSI, Baden-Powell character.	2.50 - 5.00
07.29.1981	National Scout Jamboree, SOSSI, Hampton Roads Chapter 29 Cachet, blue and m/c.	2.50 - 5.00
12.10.1981	Navajo Christmas Trek, Knights of Dunamis.	2.50 - 5.00
08.13.1981	NOAC, University of Texas, patch cachet.	5.00 - 7.50
05.02.1981	Occoneechee Council, Scout-o-rama, SOSSI Tarheel Chapter	2.50 - 5.00
08.20.1981	Owasippe Scout Reservation, 70th Anniv., multicolored.	2.50 - 5.00
11.07.1981	Scoutpex II, SOSSI, Pony Express Chapter.	2.50 - 5.00

1982

Date	Description	Price
08.21.1982	4th Latvian Guide and Scout Global Jamboree, Michigan.	2.50 - 5.00
11.21.1982	ASDA National Postage Stamp Show, SOSSI, black and yellow.	2.50 - 5.00
11.18.1982	ASDA National Postage Stamp Show, SOSSI, black and yellow.	2.50 - 5.00
11.20.1982	ASDA National Postage Stamp Show, SOSSI, black and yellow.	2.50 - 5.00
11.20.1982	ASDA National Postage Stamp Show, SOSSI, Colorado silk cachet, Baden-Powell.	2.50 - 5.00
11.19.1982	ASDA National Postage Stamp Show, SOSSI, Colorado silk cachet, Scout and Cub.	2.50 - 5.00
11.20.1982	ASDA National Postage Stamp Show, SOSSI, Colorado silk cachet, Scout and Cub.	2.50 - 5.00
11.19.1982	ASDA National Postage Stamp Show, SOSSI, Colorado silk cachet, three Scouts cooking.	2.50 - 5.00
11.18-21.1982	ASDA National Postage Stamp Show, SOSSI, Colorano silk cachet, Baden-Powell.	2.50 - 5.00
11.18-21.1982	ASDA National Postage Stamp Show, SOSSI, Colorano silk cachet, Scout and Cub.	2.50 - 5.00
11.20.1982	Atlanta Area Council, Scout show.	2.50 - 5.00
11.06.1982	Better life through scouting, Danepex.	2.50 - 5.00
11.20.1982	Bill Allen postcard, autographed.	2.50 - 5.00
03.06.1982	Blackhawk Area Council Scout Show.	2.50 - 5.00
09.12.1982	BSA 75th Anniv. APEX Show cachet.	2.50 - 5.00
06.09.1982	Central Florida Council, 60th, T.D. Scavicek.	2.50 - 5.00

Date	Description	Price
11.07.1982	Four Lakes Council, WI, 70th Anniv., green.	2.50 - 5.00
03.20.1982	GNYC Scout Expo cancel.	2.50 - 5.00
03.20.1982	GNYC Scout Show, SOSSI cover, black cancel.	2.50 - 5.00
03.20.1982	GNYC Scout Show, SOSSI cover, light blue cancel.	2.50 - 5.00
05.15.1982	Monmouth Council, Scout Show, blue.	2.50 - 5.00
05.21.1982	NESA 4th National Conference.	2.50 - 5.00
05.15.1982	Occoneechee S-O-R, 75th Anniv., SOSSI, Tarheel Chapter, red.	2.50 - 5.00
11.13.1982	Rotary Scout Expo., Mecklenburg County Council, Charlotte, NC.	2.50 - 5.00
11.07.1982	Scout, a better life; 75th of BSA, 70th GSA, Danepex, green.	2.50 - 5.00
11.13.1982	SOSSI, Tarheel Chapter, World Scouting salute.	2.50 - 5.00
04.24.1982	Strong on America, Governor Clinton Council Scout Show, gray.	2.50 - 5.00

1983

Date	Description	Price
12.10.1983	16th Annual Navajo Christmas Trek, Knights of Dunamis, brown and yellow.	2.50 - 5.00
12.03.1983	God and Country, 83 Scout Show, Atlanta Area Council, black.	2.50 - 5.00
08.10.1983	NOAC, Rutgers NJ, patch cachet.	5.00 - 7.50
09.27.1983	SOSSI, Tarheel Chapter, Salutes 15th World Jamboree, green.	2.50 - 5.00

1984

Date	Description	Price
11.17.1984	Atlanta Area Council Show, black cachet.	2.50 - 5.00
04.27.1984	Bucks County Council Diamond Jubilee Jamboree, blue and red.	2.50 - 5.00
03.31.1984	GNYC Scout Show, SOSSI cover.	2.50 - 5.00

1985

Date	Description	Price
07.27.1985	1985 National Jamboree, GSC cachet, pen drawing of Scout cooking by stream.	1.00 - 2.00
07.30.1985	1985 National Jamboree, GSC cachet, pen drawing of Scout cooking by stream.	1.00 - 2.00
07.28.1985	1985 National Jamboree, GSC cachet, pen drawing of Scout cooking by stream.	1.00 - 2.00
07.25.1985	1985 National Jamboree, GSC Cachet, pen drawing of Scout cooking by stream.	1.00 - 2.00
07.24.1985	1985 National Jamboree, GSC Cachet, pen drawing of Scout cooking by stream.	1.00 - 2.00
07.29.1985	1985 National Jamboree, GSC Cachet, pen drawing of Scout cooking by stream.	1.00 - 2.00
07.30.1985	1985 National Jamboree, Mann cachet, Scout with banner, Jamboree logo below, blue on yellow envelope.	2.50 - 5.00
07.24.1985	1985 National Jamboree, post card with image of International Youth Year Stamp, green and tan.	1.00 - 2.00
07.24.1985	1985 National Jamboree, post card with image of International Youth Year Stamp, orange and tan.	1.00 - 2.00
07.24.1985	1985 National Jamboree, SOSSI cachet, red and black on blue envelope, Jamboree logo.	2.50 - 5.00
07.24.1985	1985 National Jamboree, SOSSI post card, purple and pink.	1.00 - 2.00
07.28.1985	1985 National Jamboree, SOSSI, meeting cachet.	2.50 - 5.00
07.26.1985	1985 National Jamboree, GSC, cachet, pen drawing of Scout cooking by stream.	1.00 - 2.00
10.00.1985	International Youth Year, Artcraft cachet, block of four.	2.50 - 5.00
10.00.1985	International Youth Year, Colorado 'silk' cachet, block of four.	2.50 - 5.00
10.00.1985	International Youth Year, Fleetwood - BSA Official cover, Rockwell's Tomorrow's Leader painting, single stamp.	2.50 - 5.00
10.00.1985	International Youth Year, Gill Craft cachet, block of four.	2.50 - 5.00

10.00.1985	International Youth Year, Gill Craft cachet, single stamp.	2.50 - 5.00
10.00.1985	International Youth Year, logos of orgs., and Girl, Scout, and youth portraits, block of four.	2.50 - 5.00
10.00.1985	International Youth Year, Postal Commemorative Society, gold-foil image of stamp, single stamp.	2.50 - 5.00
07.30.1985	National Scout Jamboree, SOSSI, black and red cachet on yellow envelope	2.50 - 5.00
07.30.1985	National Scout Jamboree, SOSSI, black and red cachet on blue envelope	2.50 - 5.00
07.24.1985	National Scout Jamboree, SOSSI, black and red cachet on blue envelope.	2.50 - 5.00
07.24.1985	National Scout Jamboree, SOSSI, black and red cachet on yellow envelope.	2.50 - 5.00
07.24.1985	National Scout Jamboree, SOSSI, black and red cachet with long 1910-1985 design on yellow envelope.	2.50 - 5.00
07.24.1985	National Scout Jamboree, SOSSI, Diamond Jubilee logo cachet.	2.50 - 5.00
07.24.1985	National Scout Jamboree, SOSSI, Logo purple cachet.	2.50 - 5.00
07.24.1985	National Scout Jamboree, SOSSI, purple and red official cachet.	2.50 - 5.00
07.24.1985	National Scout Jamboree, SOSSI, red and blue drummers cachet.	2.50 - 5.00
05.18.1985	Quinnipiac Council, 75th Anniv. encampment.	2.50 - 5.00

1986

08.14.1986	71st Anniversary Conference, OA, Mt. Pleasant, MI.	5.00 - 7.50

1987

11.21.1987	Atlanta Area Council, Scout Show.	2.50 - 5.00
08.29.1987	Elk Lick Scout Camp, Calumet International Camporeee.	2.50 - 5.00
10.10.1987	Hickory, NC, Scout World.	2.50 - 5.00
05.02.1987	Monmouth Council Scout Show.	2.50 - 5.00
05.02.1987	Rainbow Council, Scout Show, Joliet, IL.	2.50 - 5.00
10.09.1987	Scouting Rendezvous Station, Raleigh, NC.	2.50 - 5.00
04.04.1987	Scout-o-rama, Wa Hi Nasa Lodge Flap on cancel.	5.00 - 7.50
04.25.1987	SOSSI, Scout Show Station, Slidell, LA.	2.50 - 5.00

1988

05.14.1988	Join In Jamboree, Delaware, OH.	2.50 - 5.00
04.16.1988	Scout Show Station, Kenner, LA.	2.50 - 5.00

1989

08.03.1989	1989 National Jamboree, cancel on BSA Jamboree stationery.	2.50 - 5.00
08.02.1989	1989 National Jamboree, cancel on BSA Jamboree stationery.	2.50 - 5.00
08.04.1989	1989 National Jamboree, cancel on BSA Jamboree stationery.	2.50 - 5.00
08.05.1989	1989 National Jamboree, cancel on BSA Jamboree stationery.	2.50 - 5.00
08.03.1989	1989 National Jamboree, official stationery postmarked.	2.50 - 5.00
08.02.1989	1989 National Jamboree, SOSSI, large cover with 1950, 1960 and 1985 stamps.	5.00 - 7.50
08.02.1989	1989 National Jamboree, SOSSI, meeting notice, single stamp cancel.	2.50 - 5.00
08.02.1989	1989 National Jamboree, SOSSI, small cover, with 1950, 1960 and flag stamps.	5.00 - 7.50
08.04.1989	1989 National Scout Jamboree, official stationery postmarked.	2.50 - 5.00
04.01.1989	GNYC Scout Show, Popeye Cachet.	2.50 - 5.00
08.06.1989	National Scout Jamboree, official stationery postmarked.	2.50 - 5.00
08.02.1989	National Scout Jamboree, official stationery postmarked.	2.50 - 5.00
08.05.1989	National Scout Jamboree, official stationery postmarked.	2.50 - 5.00
08.02.1989	National Scout Jamboree, official stationery postmarked.	2.50 - 5.00
08.02.1989	National Scout Jamboree, SOSSI, patch design and purple cachet.	2.50 - 5.00

1990

1990s	National office or local council return address.	1.00 - 2.50

1993

08.10.1993	1993 National Jamboree, BSA official Jamboree stationery.	2.50 - 5.00
08.04.1993	1993 National Jamboree, BSA postcard, single stamp cancel.	1.00 - 2.00

Official cover for the 1993 Jamboree.

08.04.1993	1993 National Jamboree, Jamboree logo in blue on white envelope.	2.50 - 5.00
08.10.1993	1993 National Jamboree, Jamboree logo in blue on white envelope.	2.50 - 5.00
08.09.1993	1993 National Jamboree, Jamboree logo in blue on white envelope.	2.50 - 5.00
08.07.1993	1993 National Jamboree, Jamboree logo in blue on white envelope.	2.50 - 5.00
08.06.1993	1993 National Jamboree, Jamboree logo in blue on white envelope.	2.50 - 5.00
08.05.1993	1993 National Jamboree, Jamboree logo in blue on white envelope.	2.50 - 5.00
08.08.1993	1993 National Jamboree, Jamboree logo in blue on white envelope.	2.50 - 5.00
08.04.1993	1993 National Jamboree, Jamboree logo in red on yellow envelope.	2.50 - 5.00
08.04.1993	1993 National Jamboree, Jamboree patch image added on as cachet, 1950, 1960. and 1985 stamps.	2.50 - 5.00
08.04.1993	1993 National Jamboree, SOSSI, official cachet, hologram of eagle.	10.00 - 15.00
08.04.1993	1993 National Jamboree, SOSSI, official cachet, hologram of flag.	10.00 - 15.00
08.04.1993	1993 National Jamboree, SOSSI, official cachet, purple on white.	2.50 - 5.00
08.04.1993	1993 National Jamboree, SOSSI, Space Shuttle theme.	2.50 - 5.00
08.04.1993	1993 National Jamboree, SOSSI, Wood Badge theme.	2.50 - 5.00
08.04.1993	1993 National Jamboree, SOSSI, OA Service Corps cachet.	2.50 - 5.00
08.04.1993	1993 National Jamboree, SOSSI, 'silk' cachet.	2.50 - 5.00
08.04.1993	1993 National Jamboree, SOSSI, Smokey the Bear theme.	2.50 - 5.00

Camp Director Charles M. Heistand welcomes President Franklin Roosevelt on his visit to Camp Man, Ten Mile River Scout Reservation in Narrowsburg, NY (1935).

BOY SCOUT STAMPS

3¢ 40th Anniversary	1950	
Mint single		.25
Plate Block of 4		1.00
Full sheet of 50		6.00
4¢ 50th Anniversary	1960	
Mint single		.25
Plate block of 4		1.00
Full sheet of 50		6.00

22¢ 75th Anniversary	1985	
Mint single		.50
Plate block of 4		2.00
Full sheet of 50		13.50
32¢ Part 2 of Centry Series	1997	
Mint single		.50
Full sheet of 15		7.00

1950.

1960.

1997.

1985.

JUVENILE LITERATURE & SERIES BOOKS

AMES, G.D.
Boy Scout Campfires. 1920 3.50 - 7.00

AMES, JOSEPH B.
Clearport Boys, Century. 1925 3.50 - 7.00
The Flying V Mystery, Century. 1928 3.50 - 7.00
The Mounted Troop, Century. 1926 3.50 - 7.00
Mystery of Ram Island, Century. 1918 3.50 - 7.00
The Secret of Spirit Lake, Century. 1927 3.50 - 7.00
Torrance from Texas, Century. 1921 3.50 - 7.00
Under Boy Scout Colors, Century. 1917 3.50 - 7.00

ANNA, C.
From Tenderfoot to Scout, George H. Coran Co. 1911 3.50 - 7.00

BALKIS, MARJORY JUNE
The Adventures of Boy Scouting, Vantage Press, Inc. 1983 3.50 - 7.00

BARBOUR, RALPH HENRY
All Hands Stand By, D. Appleton Century Co. 1942 7.50 - 12.50
The Mystery of the Rubber Boat, D. Appleton Century Co. 1943 7.50 - 12.50

BARCLAY, VERA C.
Danny the Detective, G. P. Putnam's Sons. 1918 3.50 - 7.00

BARR, RONALD W.
Anthology of Lone Scout Verse, Amateur Publications. 1924 25.00 - 35.00

Handsome illustrations popularized scouting books among the public.

BEAR, GILLY
Billy Boy Scout, Chimney Corner Series, Gabriel Sons. 1916 40.00 - 60.00
The Boy Scout ABC Book, Chimney Corner Series, Gabriel Sons. 1916 40.00 - 60.00

BECKER, BOB
Land of the Takatu, Reilly & Lee Co. 1931 3.50 - 7.00

BEEBE, H.
Scouting Serendipities. 1920 3.50 - 7.00

BLAKE, S.
The Honour of the Lions, J.B. Lippincott. 1920 3.50 - 7.00

BOGAN, SAMUEL D.
Let the Coyotes Howl: A Story of Philmont Scout Ranch, G.P. Putnam's Sons. 1946 15.00 - 25.00

BONHAM, FRANK
Mystery in Little Tokyo, E.P. Dutton & Co. 1966 3.50 - 7.00

BOYTON, FR. NEIL, S.J.
Cobra Island. 1922 3.50 - 7.00
Ex-Cub Fitzie. 1950 5.00 - 10.00
On the Sands of Coney. 1925 10.00 - 15.00
Paul in the Scout World. 1930 3.50 - 7.00
Saints for Scouts. 1930 3.50 - 7.00
That Silver Fox Patrol. 1944 3.50 - 7.00

BRERETON, CAPT. F.S.
Tom Stapleton, The Boy Scout, H.M. Caldwell Co. 1920 3.50 - 7.00

BRETT, EDNA PAYSON
A Merry Scout and Other Stories, Rand McNally. 1922 3.50 - 7.00

BROWN, BILL
Down Memory's Lane Together, Privately Printed. 1941 15.00 - 25.00

BURGESS, THORTON W.
The Boy Scouts in a Trapper's Camp, Penn Publishing Co. 1915 5.00 - 10.00
The Boy Scouts of Woodcraft Camp, Penn Publishing Co. 1912 5.00 - 15.00
The Boy Scouts on Lost Trail, Penn Publishing Co. 1914 5.00 - 10.00
The Boy Scouts on Swift River, Penn Publishing Co. 1913 3.50 - 7.00

BURRITT, EDWIN C.
The Boy Scout Crusoes, Fleming H. Revell Co. 1916 3.50 - 7.00

BURT, A.L.
Adventure & Mystery Series for Boys, The Big Opportunity. 1934 3.50 - 7.00

BURTON, CHARLES PIERCE
The Bob's Cave Boys, Henry Holt & Co. 1905 3.50 - 7.00
Bob's Hill Boys in the Everglades, Henry Holt & Co. 1932 3.50 - 7.00
Bob's Hill Boys in Virginia, Henry Holt & Co. 1939 3.50 - 7.00
The Bob's Hill Braves, Henry Holt & Co. 1910 3.50 - 7.00
The Bob's Hill Braves, Henry Holt & Co. 1912 3.50 - 7.00
Bob's Hill Meets the Andes, Henry Holt & Co. 1938 3.50 - 7.00
Bob's Hill on the Air, Henry Holt & Co. 1934 3.50 - 7.00
Bob's Hill Trails, Henry Holt & Co. 1922 3.50 - 7.00
The Boy Scouts of Bob's Hill, Henry Holt & Co. 1912 3.50 - 7.00
Camp Bob's Hill, Henry Holt & Co. 1915 3.50 - 7.00
Raven Patrol of Bob's Hill, Henry Holt & Co. 1917 3.50 - 7.00
The Trail Makers, Henry Holt & Co. 1919 3.50 - 7.00
Treasure Hunters of Bob's Hill, Henry Holt & Co. 1926 3.50 - 7.00

CAREY, A. A.
Boy Scouts at Sea, Little, Brown & Co. 1918 5.00 - 10.00

CARTER, EDWARD CHAMPE
The Lone Scout, Cornhill Co. 1920 5.00 - 10.00

CARTER, HERBERT A.

The Boy Scouts Down in Dixie, or The Strange Secret of Alligator Swamp.	1914	3.50 - 7.50
The Boy Scouts' First Campfire, or Scouting with the Silver Fox Patrol.	1913	3.50 - 7.50
The Boy Scouts in the Blue Ridge, or Marooned Among the Moonshiners.	1913	3.50 - 7.50
The Boy Scouts in the Maine Woods, or The New Test for the Silver Fox Patrol.	1913	3.50 - 7.50
The Boy Scouts in the Rockies, or The Secret of the Hidden Silver Mine.	1913	3.50 - 7.50
The Boy Scouts on Sturgeon Island, or Marooned Among the Gamefish Poachers.	1914	3.50 - 7.50
The Boy Scouts on the Trail, or Scouting through the Big Game Country.	1913	3.50 - 7.50
The Boy Scouts through the Big Timber, or The Search for the Lost Tenderfoot.	1913	3.50 - 7.50

CARTER, RUSSELL G.

Bob Hanson, Scout. Penn Publishing Co.	1921	3.50 - 7.50
Bob Hanson, Tenderfoot. Penn Publishing Co.	1921	3.50 - 7.50
Bob Hanson, Eagle Scout. The Bob Hanson Series. Penn Publishing Co. W/DJ.	1923	15.00 - 20.00
Bob Hanson, Eagle Scout. Penn Publishing Co.	1923	3.50 - 7.50
Bob Hanson, First Class Scout. The Bob Hanson Series. Penn Publishing Co. W/DJ.	1922	15.00 - 20.00
Bob Hanson, First Class Scout. Penn Publishing Co.	1922	3.50 - 7.00
Bob Hanson, Scout. The Bob Hanson Series. Penn Publishing Co. W/DJ.	1921	15.00 - 20.00
Bob Hanson, Tenderfoot. The Bob Hanson Series. Penn Publishing Co. W/DJ.	1921	15.00 - 20.00
Three Points of Honor, Reprint in tan or yellow covers, Grosset & Dunlap.	1926	6.00 - 12.50
Three Points of Honor, Little, Brown & Co.	1926	5.00 - 10.00

CASE, JOHN F.

Banners of Scoutcraft, J.B. Lippincott Co.	1929	5.00 - 10.00

CASE, LAMBERT J.

Approved Boy Scout Plays, W.H. Baker Co.	1931	12.50 - 17.50

CHAFFEE, ALLEN

Lost River, or The Adventurers of Two Boys in the Big Woods, Milton Bradley Co.	1920	15.00 - 20.00
Lost River, or The Adventurers of Two Boys in the Big Woods, reprint, Title changed to Lost! Two Boys Battle with the Elements, McLoughlin Bros.	1930	3.50 - 7.00
Lost River, or The Adventurers of Two Boys in the Big Woods, reprint, Title changed edition, red cover, McLoughlin Bros.	1937	3.50 - 7.00

CHELEY, F.H.

The Boy Scout Trailblazers, Boy Scout Life Series. Barse & Hopkins, Publishers. W/DJ.	1917	15.00 - 20.00
The Boy Scout Trailblazers, Boy Scout Life Series. Barse & Hopkins Publishers.	1917	3.50 - 7.00

CHIMPAN, W.P.

The Boy Scouts at the Battle of Saratoga, or The Story of General Bourgone's Defeat, Reissue of The Boy Scouts, 1909.	1914	7.50 - 15.00

COCHRAN, RICE E.

Be Prepared: The Life and Illusions of a Scoutmaster, Sloane Publishing Co.	1952	10.00 - 15.00
Be Prepared: The Life and Illusions of a Scoutmaster, reprint, Avon paperback edition.	1968	7.50 - 12.50

CODY, H. A.

Rod of the Lone Patrol, Grosset & Dunlap.	1916	3.50 - 7.50

COE, ROLAND

The Little Scouts in Action, McBride & Co.	1944	3.50 - 7.50

CORCORAN, BREWER

The Boy Scouts at Camp Lowell, The Page Co.	1922	3.50 - 7.50
The Boy Scouts of Kendallville, The Page Co.	1918	3.50 - 7.50
The Boy Scouts of the Wolf Patrol, The Page Co.	1918	3.50 - 7.50

CORCORAN, CAPT. A.P.

The Boy Scouts in Africa, Boy Scout Life Series.   1923   15.00 - 20.00
   Barse & Hopkins, Publishers. W/DJ.
The Boy Scouts in Africa, Boy Scout Life Series.   1923   3.50 - 7.50
   Barse & Hopkins Publishers.

CRUMP, IRVING

The Boy Scout Firefighters, Boy Scout Life Series.   1917   15.00 - 20.00
   Barse & Hopkins, Publishers. W/DJ.
The Boy Scout Firefighters, Boy Scout Life Series.   1917   3.50 - 7.50
   Barse & Hopkins Publishers.

DAVIS, RICHARD HARDING

The Boy Scout and Other Stories for Boys,   1917   3.50 - 7.50
   Charles Scribners' Sons.
The Boy Scout and Other Stories for Boys,   1924   3.50 - 7.50
   reprint, Charles Scribners' Sons.
The Boy Scout, Charles Scribners' Sons.   1914   3.50 - 7.50

DIMOCK, A. W.

Be Prepared, or the Boy Scouts in Florida,   1919   3.50 - 7.50
   F.A. Stokes Co.

EASTMAN, CHARLES A.

Indian Scout Talks, Little, Brown & Co.   1914   3.50 - 7.50
Indian Scout Talks, reprint as Indian Scout Craft   1974   3.50 - 7.50
   and Lore, Dover paperback.

EATON, WALTER P.

Boy Scouts at Crater Lake, Boy Scout Series,   1922   3.50 - 7.50
   W.A. Wilde, Publisher.
Boy Scouts at Crater Lake. Boy Scout Series,   1922   15.00 - 20.00
   W.A. Wilde, Publisher. W/DJ.
Boy Scouts at the Grand Canyon, W.A. Wilde,   1932   3.50 - 7.50
   Publisher.
Boy Scouts at the Grand Canyon. Boy Scout Series,   1932   15.00 - 20.00
   W.A. Wilde, Publisher. W/DJ.
Boy Scouts in Death Valley, W.A. Wilde, Publisher.   1939   3.50 - 7.50
Boy Scouts in Death Valley. Boy Scout Series,   1939   15.00 - 20.00
   W.A. Wilde, Publisher. W/DJ.
Boy Scouts in Glacier Park. Boy Scout Series,   1918   15.00 - 20.00
   W.A. Wilde, Publisher. W/DJ.
Boy Scouts in the Dismal Swamp, W.A. Wilde,   1913   3.50 - 7.50
   Publisher.
Boy Scouts in the Dismal Swamp. Boy Scout Series,   1913   15.00 - 20.00
   W.A. Wilde, Publisher. W/DJ.
Boy Scouts in the White Mountains, W.A. Wilde,   1914   3.50 - 7.50
   Publisher.
Boy Scouts in the White Mountains. Boy Scout   1914   15.00 - 20.00
   Series, W.A. Wilde, Publisher. W/DJ.
Boy Scouts of Berkshire, Boy Scout Series,   1912   3.50 - 7.50
   W.A. Wilde, Publisher.
Boy Scouts of Berkshire, Boy Scout Series,   1912   15.00 - 20.00
   W.A. Wilde, Publisher. W/DJ.
Boy Scouts of the Wild Cat Patrol, W.A. Wilde,   1915   3.50 - 7.50
   Publisher.
Boy Scouts of the Wild Cat Patrol. Boy Scout Series,   1915   15.00 - 20.00
   W.A. Wilde, Publisher. W/DJ.
Boy Scouts on Green Mountain Trail, W.A. Wilde,   1929   3.50 - 7.50
   Publisher.
Boy Scouts on Green Mountain Trail. Boy Scout   1929   15.00 - 20.00
   Series, W.A. Wilde, Publisher. W/DJ.
Boy Scouts on Katahdin, W.A. Wilde, Publisher.   1924   3.50 - 7.50
Boy Scouts on Katahdin. Boy Scout Series,   1924   15.00 - 20.00
   W.A. Wilde, Publisher. W/DJ.
Peanut, Cub Reporter, W.A. Wilde, Publisher.   1916   3.50 - 7.50
Peanut, Cub Reporter. Boy Scout Series,   1916   15.00 - 20.00
   W.A. Wilde, Publisher. W/DJ.

EATON, WALTER, P.

Boy Scouts in Glacier Park, W.A. Wilde, Publisher.   1918   3.50 - 7.50

ELDRED, WARREN

St. Dunstan Boy Scouts, Lathrop,   1913   3.50 - 7.50
   Lee & Sheppard Co.

ELLIS, EDWARD S.

The Boy Patrol Around the Council Fire,   1913   5.00 - 10.00
   John C. Winston, Co.
The Boy Patrol Around the Council Fire,   1913   3.50 - 7.50
   Cassell & Co., reprint.
The Boy Patrol Around the Council Fire. The Boy   1913   15.00 - 20.00
   Patrol Series. Cassell & Co. reprint. W/DJ.
The Boy Patrol Around the Council Fire. The Boy   1913   15.00 - 20.00
   Patrol Series. John C. Winston Co. W/DJ.
The Boy Patrol on Guard, John C. Winston Co.   1913   5.00 - 10.00
The Boy Patrol on Guard, Cassell & Co., reprint.   1913   3.50 - 7.50
The Boy Patrol on Guard. The Boy Patrol Series.   1913   15.00 - 20.00
   Cassell & Co. reprint. W/DJ.
The Boy Patrol on Guard. The Boy Patrol Series.   1913   15.00 - 20.00
   John C. Winston Co. W/DJ.

ENGLISH, JAMES W.

Tailbone Patrol, Holiday House, Inc.   1955   5.00 - 10.00
Tops in Troop 10, Macmillan.   1966   5.00 - 10.00

ERNST, CLAYTON

Blind Trails.   1920   5.00 - 10.00

FELSEN, HENRY GREGOR

Anyone for Cub Scouts?, Charles Scribners' Sons.   1954   7.50 - 12.50
Cub Scout at Last, Charles Scribners' Sons.   1952   10.00 - 15.00
Cub Scout at Last, Charles Scribners' Sons,   1952   7.50 - 12.50
   paperback reprint.

FINNEMORE, JOHN

Boy Scouts in the Balkans, Macmillan.   1928   3.50 - 7.50
Boy Scouts with the Russians, Macmillan.   1928   3.50 - 7.50
Brother Scouts, Macmillan.   1928   3.50 - 7.50
The Wolf Patrol. A Tale of Baden-Powell's Boy   1928   3.50 - 7.50
   Scouts, Macmillan.

FITZHUGH, PERCY KEESE

The Adventures of a Boy Scout, Tom Slade Books.   1930   15.00 - 20.00
   Photoplay edition. W/DJ.
The Adventures of a Boy Scout, Photoplay edition   1930   12.50 - 20.00
   of Tom Slade.
Along the Mohawk Trail, Crowell's Scout Book   1912   3.50 - 7.50
   Series. Thomas Y. Crowell Co.
Along the Mohawk Trail. Crowell's Scout Book   1912   15.00 - 20.00
   Series. Thomas Y. Crowell Co. W/DJ.
Boy Scouts in a Lumber Camp. Crowell's Scout   1913   15.00 - 20.00
   Book Series. Thomas Y. Crowell Co. W/DJ.
Boy Scouts in the Maine Woods. Crowell's Scout   1911   15.00 - 20.00
   Book Series. Thomas Y. Crowell Co. W/DJ.
For Uncle Sam Boss, or Boy Scouts at Panama.   1913   15.00 - 20.00
   Crowell's Scout Book Series. Thomas Y. Crowell
   Co. W/DJ.
For Uncle Sam Boss, or, Boy Scouts at Panama,   1913   3.50 - 7.50
   Crowell's Scout Book Series. Thomas Y. Crowell
   Co.
Harvey Willetts, Grosset & Dunlap, Publishers.   1927   3.50 - 7.50
In the Path of LaSalle, or Boy Scouts on the   1914   3.50 - 7.50
   Mississippi, Crowell's Scout Book Series.
   Thomas Y. Crowell Co.
In the Path of LaSalle, or Boy Scouts on the   1914   15.00 - 20.00
   Mississippi. Crowell's Scout Book Series.
   Thomas Y. Crowell Co. W/DJ.
Lefty Leighton, Grosset & Dunlap, Publishers.   1929   3.50 - 7.50
Mark Gilmore Scout of the Air, Grosset & Dunlap,   1930   10.00 - 20.00
   Publishers.
Mark Gilmore Scout of the Air. The Mark Gilmore   1930   15.00 - 20.00
   Books. Grosset & Dunlap, Publishers. W/DJ.
Mark Gilmore Speed Flyer, Grosset & Dunlap,   1931   3.50 - 7.50
   Publishers.

Mark Gilmore Speed Flyer. The Mark Gilmore Books. Grosset & Dunlap, Publishers. W/DJ.	1931	15.00 - 20.00
Mark Gilmore's Lucky Landing, Grosset & Dunlap, Publishers.	1931	3.50 - 7.50
Mark Gilmore's Lucky Landing. The Mark Gilmore Books. Grosset & Dunlap, Publishers. W/DJ.	1931	15.00 - 20.00
Out West with Westy Martin, A four-in-one book, Grosset & Dunlap, Publishers.	1926	5.00 - 15.00
Out West with Westy Martin, a four-in-one book. The Westy Martin Books. Grosset & Dunlap, Publishers. W/DJ.	1926	15.00 - 20.00
The Parachute Jumper: A Tom Slade Story, Grosset & Dunlap, Publishers.	1930	10.00 - 20.00
The Parachute Jumper: A Tom Slade Story, Tom Slade Books. Grosset & Dunlap, Publishers. W/DJ.	1930	15.00 - 20.00
Pee-Wee Harris: Fixer, Grosset & Dunlap, Publishers.	1924	3.50 - 7.50
Pee-Wee Harris Adrift, Grosset & Dunlap, Publishers.	1922	3.50 - 7.50
Pee-Wee Harris Adrift. Pee-Wee Harris Books. Grosset & Dunlap, Publishers. W/DJ.	1922	15.00 - 20.00
Pee-Wee Harris and the Sunken Treasure, Grosset & Dunlap, Publishers.	1927	3.50 - 7.50
Pee-Wee Harris and the Sunken Treasure, Pee-Wee Harris Books. Grosset & Dunlap, Publishers. W/DJ.	1927	15.00 - 20.00
Pee-Wee Harris F.O.B. Bridgeboro, Pee-Wee Harris Books. Grosset & Dunlap, Publishers. W/DJ.	1923	15.00 - 20.00
Pee-Wee Harris F.O.B. Bridgeboro, Grosset & Dunlap, Publishers.	1923	3.50 - 7.50
Pee-Wee Harris in Camp, Grosset & Dunlap, Publishers.	1922	3.50 - 7.50
Pee-Wee Harris in Camp, Pee-Wee Harris Books. Grosset & Dunlap, Publishers. W/DJ.	1922	15.00 - 20.00
Pee-Wee Harris in Darkest Africa, Pee-Wee Harris Books. Grosset & Dunlap, Publishers. W/DJ.	1929	15.00 - 20.00
Pee-Wee Harris in Darkest Africa, Grosset & Dunlap, Publishers.	1929	3.50 - 7.50
Pee-Wee Harris in Luck, Pee-Wee Harris Books. Grosset & Dunlap, Publishers. W/DJ.	1922	15.00 - 20.00
Pee-Wee Harris in Luck, Grosset & Dunlap, Publishers.	1922	3.50 - 7.50
Pee-Wee Harris on the Briny Deep, Grosset & Dunlap, Publishers.	1928	3.50 - 7.50
Pee-Wee Harris on the Briny Deep, Pee-Wee Harris Books. Grosset & Dunlap, Publishers. W/DJ.	1928	15.00 - 20.00
Pee-Wee Harris on the Trail, Whitman reprint.	1922	3.50 - 7.50
Pee-Wee Harris on the Trail, Grosset & Dunlap, Publishers.	1922	3.50 - 7.50
Pee-Wee Harris on the Trail, Pee-Wee Harris Books. Grosset & Dunlap, Publishers. W/DJ.	1922	15.00 - 20.00
Pee-Wee Harris on the Trail. Pee-Wee Harris Books. Whitman Publishing Co. reprint. W/DJ.	1922	15.00 - 20.00
Pee-Wee Harris Turns Detective, Grosset & Dunlap, Publishers.	1930	3.50 - 7.50
Pee-Wee Harris Turns Detective, Pee-Wee Harris Books. Grosset & Dunlap, Publishers. W/DJ.	1930	15.00 - 20.00
Pee-Wee Harris, Grosset & Dunlap, Publishers.	1922	3.50 - 7.50
Pee-Wee Harris, Pee-Wee Harris Books. Grosset & Dunlap, Publishers. W/DJ.	1922	15.00 - 20.00
Pee-Wee Harris: As Good as His Word, Grosset & Dunlap, Publishers.	1925	3.50 - 7.50
Pee-Wee Harris: As Good as His Word, Pee-Wee Harris Books. Grosset & Dunlap, Publishers. W/DJ.	1925	15.00 - 20.00
Pee-Wee Harris: Fixer, Pee-Wee Harris Books. Grosset & Dunlap, Publishers. W/DJ.	1924	15.00 - 20.00
Pee-Wee Harris: Mayor for a Day, Pee-Wee Harris Books. Grosset & Dunlap, Publishers. W/DJ.	1926	15.00 - 20.00
Pee-Wee Harris: Mayor for a Day, Grosset & Dunlap, Publishers.	1926	3.50 - 7.50

Pluck on the Trail, or Boy Scouts in the Rockies, Crowell's Scout Book Series. Thomas Y. Crowell Co. W/DJ.	1912	15.00 - 20.00
Roy Blakeley in the Haunted Camp, Grosset & Dunlap, Publishers.	1922	3.50 - 7.50
Roy Blakeley on the Mohawk Trail, Grosset & Dunlap, Publishers.	1925	3.50 - 7.50
Roy Blakeley Pathfinder, Grosset & Dunlap, Publishers.	1920	3.50 - 7.50
Roy Blakeley Up in the Air, Grosset & Dunlap, Publishers.	1931	10.00 - 20.00
Roy Blakeley, His Story, Grosset & Dunlap, Publishers.	1920	3.50 - 7.50
Roy Blakeley: Lost, Strayed or Stolen, Grosset & Dunlap, Publishers.	1921	3.50 - 7.50
Roy Blakeley's Adventures in Camp, Grosset & Dunlap, Publishers.	1920	3.50 - 7.50
Roy Blakeley's Bee-Line Hike, Grosset & Dunlap, Publishers.	1922	3.50 - 7.50
Roy Blakeley's Camp on Wheels, Grosset & Dunlap, Publishers.	1920	3.50 - 7.50
Roy Blakeley's Elastic Hike, Grosset & Dunlap, Publishers.	1926	3.50 - 7.50
Roy Blakeley's Funny-Bone Hike, Grosset & Dunlap, Publishers.	1922	3.50 - 7.50
Roy Blakeley's Go-As-You-Please Hike, Grosset & Dunlap, Publishers.	1929	3.50 - 7.50
Roy Blakeley's Happy-Go-Lucky Hike, Grosset & Dunlap, Publishers.	1928	3.50 - 7.50
Roy Blakeley's Motor Caravan, Grosset & Dunlap, Publishers.	1921	3.50 - 7.50
Roy Blakeley's Roundabout Hike, Grosset & Dunlap, Publishers.	1926	3.50 - 7.50
Roy Blakeley's Silver Fox Patrol, Grosset & Dunlap, Publishers.	1920	3.50 - 7.50

ROY BLAKELEY
By PERCY KEESE FITZHUGH
APPROVED BY THE BOY SCOUTS OF AMERICA

Roy Blakeley's Tangled Trail, Grosset & Dunlap, Publishers. — 1924 — 3.50 - 7.50

Roy Blakeley's Wild Goose Chase, Grosset & Dunlap, Publishers. — 1930 — 3.50 - 7.50

Roy Blakeley in the Haunted Camp, The Roy Blakeley Books. Grosset & Dunlap, Publishers. W/DJ. — 1922 — 15.00 - 20.00

Roy Blakeley on the Mohawk Trail, The Roy Blakeley Books. Grosset & Dunlap, Publishers. W/DJ. — 1925 — 15.00 - 20.00

Roy Blakeley Pathfinder, The Roy Blakeley Books. Grosset & Dunlap, Publishers. W/DJ. — 1920 — 15.00 - 20.00

Roy Blakeley Up in the Air, The Roy Blakeley Books. Grosset & Dunlap, Publishers. W/DJ. — 1931 — 15.00 - 20.00

Roy Blakeley, His Story, The Roy Blakeley Books. Grosset & Dunlap, Publishers. W/DJ. — 1920 — 15.00 - 20.00

Roy Blakeley: Lost, Strayed or Stolen, The Roy Blakeley Books. Grosset & Dunlap, Publishers. W/DJ. — 1921 — 15.00 - 20.00

Roy Blakeley's Adventures in Camp, The Roy Blakeley Books. Grosset & Dunlap, Publishers. W/DJ. — 1920 — 15.00 - 20.00

Roy Blakeley's Bee-Line Hike, The Roy Blakeley Books. Grosset & Dunlap, Publishers. W/DJ. — 1922 — 15.00 - 20.00

Roy Blakeley's Camp on Wheels, The Roy Blakeley Books. Grosset & Dunlap, Publishers. W/DJ. — 1920 — 15.00 - 20.00

Roy Blakeley's Elastic Hike, The Roy Blakeley Books. Grosset & Dunlap, Publishers. W/DJ. — 1926 — 15.00 - 20.00

Roy Blakeley's Funny-Bone Hike, The Roy Blakeley Books. Grosset & Dunlap, Publishers. W/DJ. — 1922 — 15.00 - 20.00

Roy Blakeley's Go-As-You-Please Hike, The Roy Blakeley Books. Grosset & Dunlap, Publishers. W/DJ. — 1929 — 15.00 - 20.00

Roy Blakeley's Motor Caravan, The Roy Blakeley Books. Grosset & Dunlap, Publishers. W/DJ. — 1928 — 15.00 - 20.00

Roy Blakeley's Roundabout Hike, The Roy Blakeley Books. Grosset & Dunlap, Publishers. W/DJ. — 1926 — 15.00 - 20.00

Roy Blakeley's Silver Fox Patrol, The Roy Blakeley Books. Grosset & Dunlap, Publishers. W/DJ. — 1920 — 15.00 - 20.00

Roy Blakeley's Tangled Trail, The Roy Blakeley Books. Grosset & Dunlap, Publishers. W/DJ. — 1924 — 15.00 - 20.00

Roy Blakeley's Wild Goose Chase, The Roy Blakeley Books. Grosset & Dunlap, Publishers. W/DJ. — 1930 — 15.00 - 20.00

Skinny McCord, Grosset & Dunlap, Publishers. — 1928 — 3.50 - 7.50

Spiffy Henshaw, Grosset & Dunlap, Publishers. — 1929 — 3.50 - 7.50

The Story of Terrible Terry, Grosset & Dunlap, Publishers. — 1930 — 3.50 - 7.50

Tom Slade at Bear Mountain, Tom Slade Books. Grosset & Dunlap, Publishers. W/DJ. — 1925 — 15.00 - 20.00

Tom Slade at Bear Mountain, Grosset & Dunlap, Publishers. — 1925 — 5.00 - 10.00

Tom Slade at Black Lake, Grosset & Dunlap, Publishers. — 1920 — 3.50 - 7.50

Tom Slade at Black Lake, Tom Slade Books. Grosset & Dunlap, Publishers. W/DJ. — 1920 — 15.00 - 20.00

Tom Slade at Haunted Cavern, Grosset & Dunlap, Publishers. — 1929 — 3.50 - 7.50

Tom Slade at Haunted Cavern, Tom Slade Books. Grosset & Dunlap, Publishers. W/DJ. — 1929 — 15.00 - 20.00

Tom Slade at Shadow Island, Grosset & Dunlap, Publishers. — 1927 — 3.50 - 7.50

Tom Slade at Shadow Island, Tom Slade Books. Grosset & Dunlap, Publishers. W/DJ. — 1927 — 15.00 - 20.00

Tom Slade at Temple Camp, Grosset & Dunlap, Publishers. — 1917 — 3.50 - 7.50

Tom Slade at Temple Camp, Tom Slade Books. Grosset & Dunlap, Publishers. W/DJ. — 1917 — 15.00 - 20.00

Tom Slade at Temple Camp, Whitman, reprint. — 1917 — 3.50 - 7.50

Tom Slade at Temple Camp, Tom Slade Books. Whitman Publishing Co. reprint. W/DJ. — 1917 — 15.00 - 20.00

Tom Slade in the North Woods, Tom Slade Books. Grosset & Dunlap, Publishers. W/DJ. — 1927 — 15.00 - 20.00

Tom Slade in the North Woods, Grosset & Dunlap, Publishers. — 1927 — 3.50 - 7.50

Tom Slade on a Transport, Grosset & Dunlap, Publishers. — 1918 — 5.00 - 10.00

Tom Slade on a Transport, Tom Slade Books. Grosset & Dunlap, Publishers. W/DJ. — 1918 — 15.00 - 20.00

Tom Slade on Mystery Trail, Tom Slade Books. Grosset & Dunlap, Publishers. W/DJ. — 1921 — 15.00 - 20.00

Tom Slade on Mystery Trail, Grosset & Dunlap, Publishers. — 1921 — 3.50 - 7.50

Tom Slade on Overlook Mountain, Grosset & Dunlap, Publishers. — 1923 — 3.50 - 7.50

Tom Slade on Overlook Mountain, Tom Slade Books. Grosset & Dunlap, Publishers. W/DJ. — 1923 — 15.00 - 20.00

Tom Slade on the River, Tom Slade Books. Grosset & Dunlap, Publishers. W/DJ. — 1917 — 15.00 - 20.00

Tom Slade on the River, Grosset & Dunlap, Publishers. — 1917 — 3.50 - 7.50

Tom Slade Picks a Winner, Grosset & Dunlap, Publishers. — 1924 — 3.50 - 7.50

Tom Slade Picks a Winner, Tom Slade Books. Grosset & Dunlap, Publishers. W/DJ. — 1924 — 15.00 - 20.00

Tom Slade with the Boys Over There, Grosset & Dunlap, Publishers. — 1918 — 3.50 - 7.50

Tom Slade with the Boys Over There, Tom Slade Books. Grosset & Dunlap, Publishers. W/DJ. — 1918 — 15.00 - 20.00

Tom Slade with the Colors, Tom Slade Books. Grosset & Dunlap, Publishers. W/DJ. — 1918 — 15.00 - 20.00

Tom Slade with the Colors, Grosset & Dunlap, Publishers. — 1918 — 3.50 - 7.50

Tom Slade with the Flying Corps, Tom Slade Books. Grosset & Dunlap, Publishers. W/DJ. — 1919 — 15.00 - 20.00

Tom Slade with the Flying Corps, Grosset & Dunlap, Publishers. — 1919 — 10.00 - 20.00

Tom Slade, Boy Scouts of the Moving Pictures, Grosset & Dunlap, Publishers. — 1915 — 5.00 - 10.00

Tom Slade, Boy Scouts of the Moving Pictures, Tom Slade Books. Grosset & Dunlap, Publishers. W/DJ. — 1915 — 15.00 - 20.00

Tom Slade, Boy Scouts; a reprint of Tom Slade, Boy Scouts of the Moving Pictures. Tom Slade Books. Whitman Publishing Co. reprint. W/DJ.	1915	15.00 - 20.00
Tom Slade, Boy Scouts; reprint of Tom Slade, Boy Scouts of the Moving Pictures, Whitman, reprint.	1915	5.00 - 10.00
Tom Slade, Boy Scouts; reprint of Tom Slade, Boy Scouts of the Moving Pictures, Grosset & Dunlap, Publishers.	1915	5.00 - 10.00
Tom Slade, Boy Scouts; reprint of Tom Slade, Boy Scouts of the Moving Pictures. Tom Slade Books. Grosset & Dunlap, Publishers. W/DJ.	1915	15.00 - 20.00
Tom Slade, Forest Ranger, Grosset & Dunlap, Publishers.	1926	3.50 - 7.50
Tom Slade, Forest Ranger, Tom Slade Books. Grosset & Dunlap, Publishers. W/DJ.	1926	15.00 - 20.00
Tom Slade, Motorcycle Dispatch Bearer, Tom Slade Books. Grosset & Dunlap, Publishers. W/DJ.	1918	15.00 - 20.00
Tom Slade, Motorcycle Dispatch Bearer, Grosset & Dunlap, Publishers.	1918	15.00 - 25.00
Tom Slade's Double Dare, Tom Slade Books. Grosset & Dunlap, Publishers. W/DJ.	1922	15.00 - 20.00
Tom Slade's Double Dare, Grosset & Dunlap, Publishers.	1922	3.50 - 7.50
Westy Martin in the Land of the Purple Sage, The Westy Martin Books. Grosset & Dunlap, Publishers. W/DJ.	1929	15.00 - 20.00
Westy Martin in the Land of the Purple Sage, Grosset & Dunlap, Publishers.	1929	3.50 - 7.50
Westy Martin in the Rockies, Grosset & Dunlap, Publishers.	1924	3.50 - 7.50
Westy Martin in the Rockies, The Westy Martin Books. Grosset & Dunlap, Publishers. W/DJ.	1924	15.00 - 20.00
Westy Martin in the Sierras, Grosset & Dunlap, Publishers.	1931	3.50 - 7.50
Westy Martin in the Sierras, The Westy Martin Books. Grosset & Dunlap, Publishers. W/DJ.	1931	15.00 - 20.00
Westy Martin in the Yellowstone, The Westy Martin Books. Grosset & Dunlap, Publishers. W/DJ.	1924	15.00 - 20.00
Westy Martin in the Yellowstone, Grosset & Dunlap, Publishers.	1924	3.50 - 7.50
Westy Martin on the Mississippi, The Westy Martin Books. Grosset & Dunlap, Publishers. W/DJ.	1930	15.00 - 20.00
Westy Martin on the Mississippi, Grosset & Dunlap, Publishers.	1930	3.50 - 7.50
Westy Martin on the Old Indian Trails, The Westy Martin Books. Grosset & Dunlap, Publishers. W/DJ.	1928	15.00 - 20.00
Westy Martin on the Old Indian Trails, Grosset & Dunlap, Publishers.	1928	3.50 - 7.50
Westy Martin on the Old Santa Fe Trail, The Westy Martin Books. Grosset & Dunlap, Publishers. W/DJ.	1926	15.00 - 20.00
Westy Martin on the Santa Fe Trail, Grosset & Dunlap, Publishers.	1926	3.50 - 7.50
Westy Martin, The Westy Martin Books. Grosset & Dunlap, Publishers. W/DJ.	1924	15.00 - 20.00
Westy Martin, Grosset & Dunlap, Publishers.	1924	3.50 - 7.50
Wigwag Wiegand, Grosset & Dunlap, Publishers.	1929	3.50 - 7.50

FLETCHER, MJR. ARCHIBALD LEE

Boy Scout Pathfinders, or The Strange Hunt for the Beaver Patrol, Boy Scout Series, M.A. Donahue & Co. Publishers. W/DJ.	1913	15.00 - 20.00
Boy Scout Pathfinders, or The Strange Hunt for the Beaver Patrol, M.A. Donahue & Co., Publishers.	1913	5.00 - 15.00
Boy Scout Rivals, or A Leader of the Tenderfoot Patrol, M.A. Donahue & Co., Publishers.	1913	5.00 - 15.00
Boy Scout Rivals, or A Leader of the Tenderfoot Patrol, Boy Scout Series, M.A. Donahue & Co. Publishers. W/DJ.	1913	15.00 - 20.00
Boy Scouts in Alaska, or The Camp on the Glacier, M.A. Donahue & Co., Publishers.	1913	3.50 - 7.50

Boy Scouts in Alaska, or The Camp on the Glacier, Boy Scout Series, M.A. Donahue & Co. Publishers. W/DJ.	1913	15.00 - 20.00
Boy Scouts in Northern Wilds, or The Signal from the Hills, M.A. Donahue & Co., Publishers.	1913	3.50 - 7.50
Boy Scouts in Northern Wilds, or The Signal from the Hills, Boy Scout Series, M.A. Donahue & Co. Publishers. W/DJ.	1913	15.00 - 20.00
Boy Scouts in the Coal Caverns, or The Light in Tunnel Six, M.A. Donahue & Co., Publishers.	1913	3.50 - 7.50
Boy Scouts in the Everglades, or The Island in Lost Channel, M.A. Donahue & Co., Publishers.	1913	3.50 - 7.50
Boy Scouts in the Everglades, or The Island in Lost Channel, Boy Scout Series, M.A. Donahue & Co. Publishers. W/DJ.	1913	15.00 - 20.00
Boy Scouts on a Long Hike, or Two the Rescue in the Black Water Swamps, M.A. Donahue & Co. Publishers.	1913	3.50 - 7.50
Boy Scouts on a Long Hike, or Two the Rescue in the Black Water Swamps. Boy Scout Series, M.A. Donahue & Co. Publishers. W/DJ.	1913	15.00 - 20.00
Boy Scouts on Old Superior, or The Tale of the Pictured Rocks, M.A. Donahue & Co., Publishers.	1913	3.50 - 7.50
Boy Scouts on Old Superior, or The Tale of the Pictured Rocks, Boy Scout Series, M.A. Donahue & Co. Publishers. W/DJ.	1913	15.00 - 20.00
Boy Scouts on the Great Divide, or The Ending of the Trail, M.A. Donahue & Co., Publishers.	1913	3.50 - 7.50
Boy Scouts on the Great Divide, or The Ending of the Trail, Boy Scout Series, M.A. Donahue & Co. Publishers. W/DJ.	1913	15.00 - 20.00
Boy Scouts' Signal Sender, or When Wig Wag Knowledge Paid, M.A. Donahue & Co., Publishers.	1913	3.50 - 7.50
Boy Scouts' Signal Sender, or When Wig Wag Knowledge Paid, Boy Scout Series, M.A. Donahue & Co. Publishers. W/DJ.	1913	15.00 - 20.00
Boy Scouts Test of Courage, or Winning the Merit Badge, Boy Scout Series, M.A. Donahue & Co. Publishers. W/DJ.	1913	15.00 - 20.00
Boy Scouts Test of Courage, or Winning the Merit Badge, M.A. Donahue & Co., Publishers.	1913	3.50 - 7.50
Boy Scout's Woodcraft Lesson, or Proving their Mettle in the Field, Boy Scout Series, M.A. Donahue & Co. Publishers. W/DJ.	1913	15.00 - 20.00
Boy Scout's Woodcraft Lesson, or Proving their Mettle in the Field, M.A. Donahue & Co. Publishers.	1913	3.50 - 7.50
Boy Scouts in the Coal Caverns, or the Light in Tunnel Six, Boy Scout Series, M.A. Donahue & Co. Publishers. W/DJ.	1913	15.00 - 20.00

FRIEND, RUSSELL AND ESTHER

Easy Cub Scout Plays, Baker's Plays.	1948	10.00 - 15.00

GARDNER, LILLIAN SOSKIN

Bill Martin, Cub Scout, From Bobcat to Wolf, Franklin Watts, Inc. reprint of Den Seven title.	1952	5.00 - 10.00
From Bobcat to Wolf: The Story of Den Seven, Pack Four, Franklin Watts, Inc.	1952	5.00 - 10.00

GARFIELD, JAMES B.

Follow My Leader, Viking Press.	1957	5.00 - 10.00
Follow My Leader, Scholastic Book Services paperback.	1957	3.00 - 7.50

GARIS, HOWARD R.

Chad of Knob Hill, The Tale of a Lone Scout, Little, Brown & Co.	1927	3.50 - 7.50

GARTH, JOHN

Boy Scouts on the Trail, Boy Scout Life Series, Barse & Hopkins, Publishers. W/DJ.	1920	15.00 - 20.00

GENDRON, VAL

Behind the Zuni Masks, Longmans, Green & Co.	1958	5.00 - 10.00

Behind the Zuni Masks, Junior Literary Guild Book 1952   3.50 - 7.50
    Club edition.
Behind the Zuni Masks, Junior Literary Guild Book 1962   3.50 - 7.50
    Club edition reprint.

GILMAN, CHARLES L.
The Fox Patrol in the North Woods, The Fox Patrol 1912   15.00 - 20.00
    Series. The Buzza Co. W/DJ.
The Fox Patrol in the North Woods, The Buzza Co. 1912   3.50 - 7.50
The Fox Patrol in the Open, The Fox Patrol Series. 1912   15.00 - 20.00
    The Buzza Co. W/DJ.
The Fox Patrol in the Open, The Buzza Co.   1912   3.50 - 7.50
The Fox Patrol on the River, The Fox Patrol Series. 1912   15.00 - 20.00
    The Buzza Co. W/DJ.
The Fox Patrol on the River, The Buzza Co.   1912   3.50 - 7.50

GORDON, PAUL
The Scout of the Golden Cross, Holt & Co.   1920   3.50 - 7.50

GRATH, JOHN
Boy Scout Life Series. Boy Scouts on the Trail,   1920   3.50 - 7.50
    Barse & Hopkins Publishers.

GUY, ANN
Cub Scout Donny, Abingdon Press.   1958   3.50 - 7.50

HANSON, R. O.
Plays for Boys, Associated Publishers.   1938   10.00 - 15.00

HARE, WALTER BEN
A Country Boy Scout, Dennison.   1916   5.00 - 10.00

HECK, B. H.
Cave-in at Mason's Mine, Scholastic Book Services. 1980   5.00 - 10.00

HENDRICK, EDWARD P.
The 7th Scout, W.A.Wilde Co.   1938   5.00 - 10.00

HEYLIGER, W.
Stan Kent, Captain, Sports and Scouts Series,   1937   15.00 - 20.00
    Saalfield Publishing Co. W/DJ.
Stan Kent, Captain, Sports and Scouts Series,   1937   5.00 - 10.00
    Saalfield Publishing Co.
Stan Kent, Freshman Fullback, Sports and Scouts 1936   15.00 - 20.00
    Series, Saalfield Publishing Co. W/DJ.
Stan Kent, Freshman Fullback, Sports and Scouts 1936   5.00 - 10.00
    Series, Saalfield Publishing Co.
Stan Kent, Varsity Man, Sports and Scouts Series, 1936   15.00 - 20.00
    Saalfield Publishing Co. W/DJ.
Stan Kent, Varsity Man, Sports and Scouts Series, 1936   5.00 - 10.00
    Saalfield Publishing Co.
Three-Finger Joe, Sports and Scouts Series,   1937   15.00 - 20.00
    Saalfield Publishing Co. W/DJ.
Three-Finger Joe, Sports and Scouts Series,   1937   5.00 - 10.00
    Saalfield Publishing Co.
Tommy of Troop Six, Sports and Scouts Series,   1937   15.00 - 20.00
    Saalfield Publishing Co. W/DJ.

HEYLIGER, WILLIAM
Don Strong of the Wolf Patrol, Don Strong Series, 1916   15.00 - 20.00
    D. Appleton & Co. W/DJ.
Don Strong of the Wolf Patrol, D. Appleton & Co. 1916   3.50 - 7.50
Don Strong, American, Don Strong Series,   1920   15.00 - 20.00
    D. Appleton & Co. W/DJ.
Don Strong, American, D. Appleton & Co.   1920   3.50 - 7.50
Don Strong, Patrol Leader, Don Strong Series,   1918   15.00 - 20.00
    D. Appleton & Co. W/DJ.
Don Strong, Patrol Leader, D. Appleton & Co.   1918   5.00 - 15.00
Jerry Hicks and his Gang, Jerry Hicks Series.   1929   15.00 - 20.00
    Grosset & Dunlap, Publishers. W/DJ.
Jerry Hicks and his Gang, Grosset & Dunlap,   1929   3.50 - 7.50
    Publishers.
Jerry Hicks, Explorer, Jerry Hicks Series.   1930   15.00 - 20.00
    Grosset & Dunlap, Publishers. W/DJ.

Jerry Hicks, Explorer, Grosset & Dunlap, Publishers.	1930	3.50 - 7.50
Jerry Hicks, Ghost Hunter, Jerry Hicks Series. Grosset & Dunlap, Publishers. W/DJ.	1929	15.00 - 20.00
Jerry Hicks, Ghost Hunter, Grosset & Dunlap, Publishers.	1929	3.50 - 7.50
SOS Radio Patrol, Dodd-Meed & Co.	1942	3.50 - 7.50
Yours Truly, Jerry Hicks, Jerry Hicks Series. Grosset & Dunlap, Publishers. W/DJ.	1929	15.00 - 20.00
Yours Truly, Jerry Hicks, Grosset & Dunlap, Publishers.	1929	3.50 - 7.50

HOLLAND, RUPERT SARGENT

Blackbeard's Island, The Adventurers of Three Boy Scouts in the Sea Islands, J.B. Lippincott Co.	1916	3.50 - 7.50
The Boy Scouts of Birch-Bark Island, J.B. Lippincott Co.	1911	3.50 - 7.50
The Boy Scouts of Snowshoe Lodge, J.B. Lippincott Co.	1915	3.50 - 7.50
The Sea Scouts of Birch-Bark Island, J.B. Lippincott Co.	1936	3.50 - 7.50

HORNIBROOK, ISABEL K.

A Scout of Today, Houghton & Mifflin Co.	1913	3.50 - 7.50
Coxwain Drake of the Sea Scouts, The Scout Drake Series. Houghton & Mifflin Co. W/DJ.	1920	15.00 - 20.00
Coxwain Drake of the Sea Scouts, Houghton & Mifflin Co.	1920	5.00 - 15.00
Drake and the Adventurers' Cup, The Scout Drake Series. Houghton & Mifflin Co. W/DJ.	1922	15.00 - 20.00
Drake and the Adventurers' Cup, Houghton & Mifflin Co.	1922	3.50 - 7.50
Drake of Troop One, The Scout Drake Series. Houghton & Mifflin Co. W/DJ.	1916	15.00 - 20.00
Drake of Troop One, Houghton & Mifflin Co.	1916	3.50 - 7.50
Lost in the Maine Woods, Houghton & Mifflin Co.	1913	3.50 - 7.50
Scout Drake in Wartime, The Scout Drake Series. Houghton & Mifflin Co. W/DJ.	1918	15.00 - 20.00
Scout Drake in Wartime, Houghton & Mifflin Co.	1918	3.50 - 7.50

HOUSTON, EDWIN JAMES

Our Boy Scouts in Camp, David McKay, Publisher.	1912	3.50 - 7.50

HUNTINGTON, EDWARD

The Forest Pilot, A Story for Boy Scouts, Hearst's International Library Co.	1915	10.00 - 15.00

HYNE, ELIZABETH A. WATSON

Little Brothers to the Scouts, Rand McNally & Co.	1917	3.50 - 7.50

JACKSON, JACQUELINE

The Paleface Redskins, Little, Brown & Co.	1958	3.50 - 7.50
The Paleface Redskins, Little, Brown & Co., reissue.	1968	3.50 - 7.50

JADBERNS, RAYMOND

Three Amateur Scouts, J.B. Lippincott Co.	1920	3.50 - 7.50

JENKINS, MARSHALL

A Freshman Scout at College, D. Appleton & Co.	1917	3.50 - 7.50
The Doins of Troop Five, The Boy Scouts of Troop Five Series. D. Appleton & Co. W/DJ.	1914	15.00 - 20.00
The Doins of Troop Five, D. Appleton & Co.	1914	5.00 - 15.00
The Jackal Patrol of Troop Five, The Boy Scouts of Troop Five Series. D. Appleton & Co. W/DJ.	1915	15.00 - 20.00
The Jackal Patrol of Troop Five, D. Appleton & Co.	1915	3.50 - 7.50
The Norfolk Boy Scouts, D. Appleton & Co.	1916	3.50 - 7.50
Troop Five at Camp, The Boy Scouts of Troop Five Series. D. Appleton & Co. W/DJ.	1914	15.00 - 20.00
Troop Five at Camp, D. Appleton & Co.	1914	3.50 - 7.50

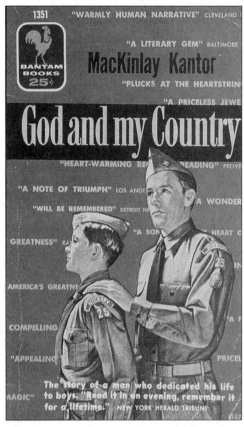

KANTOR, MACKINLEY

Follow Me Boys (Title change after Disney Movie), Grosset & Dunlap.	1956	10.00 - 15.00
Follow Me Boys (Title change after Disney Movie), Temo Books paperback.	1966	7.50 - 12.50
God and My Country, Bantam Books, paperback.	1954	7.50 - 12.50
God and My Country, World Publishing Co.	1954	10.00 - 15.00
God and My Country, Reader's Digest Condensed Books.	1954	2.50 - 5.00

KEABLE, R.

African Scout Stories, Macmillan.	1921	3.50 - 7.50

KEANE, THOMAS J.

Lubbers Afloat, Dodd, Mead & Co.	1932	3.50 - 7.50

KIPLING, RUDYARD

Land and Sea Tales for Scouts and Guides, Macmillan & Co.	1923	5.00 - 10.00
Land and Sea Tales for Scouts and Scout Masters, Sun Dial Press reprint.	1923	5.00 - 10.00
Land and Sea Tales for Scouts and Scout Masters, Doubleday, Page & Co. reprint.	1926	5.00 - 10.00
Land and Sea Tales for Scouts and Scout Masters, Doubleday, Doran & Co., reprint.	1929	5.00 - 10.00

KOHLER, JULILLY H.

Daniel in the Cub Scout Den, Aladdin Books, American Book Co.	1951	5.00 - 10.00
Razzberry Jamboree, Thomas Y. Crowell Co.	1957	3.50 - 7.50

LAMAR, ASHTON

The Aeroplane Boys Series. When Scout Meets Scout; or the Aeroplane Spy, Reilly & Britton.	1912	10.00 - 20.00
When Scout Meets Scout, or the Aeroplane Spy, The Aeroplane Boys Series. Reilly & Britton. W/DJ.	1912	15.00 - 20.00

LAMB, MARRITT

My Scout and Other Poems, W.C. Foote Printing Co.	1916	5.00 - 10.00

LeBretton-Martin, E.

The Boys of the Otter Patrol, J.B. Lippincott Co.	1920	3.50 - 7.50
Otters to the Rescue, J.B. Lippincott Co.	1920	3.50 - 7.50

Lerrigo, Charles Henry

The Boy Scout Treasure Hunters, Barse & Hopkins.	1917	3.50 - 7.50
The Boy Scout Treasure Hunters, Barse Co. reprint.	1917	3.50 - 7.50
The Boy Scout Treasure Hunters, Boy Scout Life Series, Barse & Hopkins, Publishers. W/DJ.	1917	15.00 - 20.00
The Boy Scout Treasure Hunters, Boy Scout Life Series, Barse & Hopkins Publishers.	1917	3.50 - 7.50
Boy Scouts of Round Table Patrol, Barse & Hopkins.	1924	3.50 - 7.50
Boy Scouts of Round Table Patrol, Barse Co. reprint.	1924	3.50 - 7.50
The Boy Scouts of Round Table Patrol, Boy Scout Life Series, Barse & Hopkins, Publishers. W/DJ.	1924	15.00 - 20.00
The Boy Scouts of Round Table Patrol, Boy Scout Life Series, Barse & Hopkins Publishers.	1924	3.50 - 7.50
Boy Scouts on Special Service, Little, Brown & Co.	1922	3.50 - 7.50
The Boy Scouts to the Rescue, Barse & Hopkins.	1920	3.50 - 7.50
The Boy Scouts to the Rescue, Barse Co. reprint.	1920	3.50 - 7.50
Boy Scouts to the Rescue, Boy Scout Life Series, Barse & Hopkins, Publishers. W/DJ.	1920	15.00 - 20.00
Boy Scouts to the Rescue, Boy Scout Life Series, Barse & Hopkins Publishers.	1920	3.50 - 7.50
The Merry Men of Robin Hood Patrol, Barse & Hopkins.	1927	3.50 - 7.50

Lisle, Clifton

A Scout's Honor, Harcourt, Brace and Co.	1921	3.50 - 7.50
Boy Scout Entertainments, Penn Publishing Co.	1918	3.50 - 7.50
Saddle Bags, Penn Publishing Co.	1923	3.50 - 7.50
The Treasure of the Chateau, Penn Publishing Co.	1929	3.50 - 7.50

Lone Scout Classics

Lone Scout Press.	1970	10.00 - 15.00

Lyons, K.

West Point Five, Sports and Scouts Series, Saalfield Publishing Co. W/DJ.	1937	15.00 - 20.00
West Point Five, Sports and Scouts Series, Saalfield Publishing Co.	1937	3.50 - 7.50
West Pointers on the Gridiron, Sports and Scouts Series, Saalfield Publishing Co. W/DJ.	1936	15.00 - 20.00
West Pointers on the Gridiron, Sports and Scouts Series, Saalfield Publishing Co.	1936	5.00 - 10.00
The Winged Four, Sports and Scouts Series, Saalfield Publishing Co. W/DJ.	1937	15.00 - 20.00
The Winged Four, Sports and Scouts Series, Saalfield Publishing Co.	1937	3.50 - 7.50

Lyons, Kennedy

The Vagabond Scouts or The Adventurers of Duncan Dunn, Page & Co.	1931	3.50 - 7.50

Madeline Ö.

Jack of the Circus, Reilly & Lee.	1931	5.00 - 10.00

Martin, Patricia Miles

Calvin and the Cub Scouts, G.P. Putnam's Sons.	1964	5.00 - 10.00
Calvin and the Cub Scouts, Scholastic Book Services paperback.	1971	3.50 - 7.50

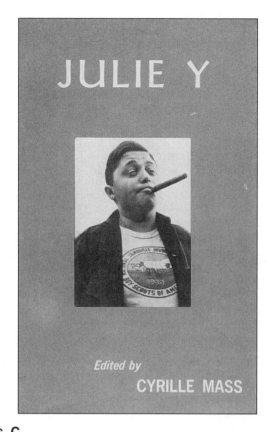

Mass, C.

Julie Y.	1980	10.00 - 15.00

Mathiews, Franklin K.

The Boy Scouts Book of Adventurous Youth, D. Appleton - Century Co.	1931	3.50 - 7.50
The Boy Scouts Book of Campfire Stories, D. Appleton & Co.	1921	3.50 - 7.50
The Boy Scouts Book of Good Turn Stories, Charles Scribners' Sons.	1931	3.50 - 7.50
The Boy Scouts Book of Stories, D. Appleton & Co.	1918	3.50 - 7.50
Boy Scouts Courageous, Barse Co.	1918	3.50 - 7.50
Boy Scouts Courageous, Boy Scout Life Series, Barse & Hopkins Publishers.	1918	3.50 - 7.50
Boy Scouts Courageous, Boy Scout Life Series. Barse & Hopkins, Publishers. W/DJ.	1918	15.00 - 20.00
The Boy Scouts Own Book, D. Appleton & Co.	1929	3.50 - 7.50
Chuckles and Grins, Grosset & Dunlap.	1928	3.50 - 7.50
Coming Through, Grosset & Dunlap.	1927	3.50 - 7.50
Flying High, Grosset & Dunlap.	1930	3.50 - 7.50
Hitting the Trail, Grosset & Dunlap.	1930	3.50 - 7.50
Laugh, Boy Laugh, Grosset & Dunlap.	1930	3.50 - 7.50
The Ransom of Red Chief and Other O. Henry Stories for Boys, Grosset & Dunlap reprint.	1918	3.50 - 7.50
The Ransom of Red Chief and Other O. Henry Stories for Boys, Doubleday, Page & Co.	1918	3.50 - 7.50
Skyward Ho, Grosset & Dunlap.	1930	3.50 - 7.50
Wild Animal Trails, Grosset & Dunlap.	1928	3.50 - 7.50

Matlock

The Old Scoutmaster's Poems.	1937	5.00 - 10.00

McCall, Edith S.

The Buttons and the Boy Scouts, The Button Books, Benefic Press. W/DJ.	1958	15.00 - 20.00
The Buttons and the Boy Scouts, Benefic Press.	1958	3.50 - 7.50

McCarthy, George T.

Scout Adventures, CYO.	1930	10.00 - 15.00

McCormick, Wilfred
Eagle Scout. Bronc Burnett Series.   1952   15.00 - 20.00
   G.P. Putnam's Sons. W/DJ.
Eagle Scout. Bronc Burnett Series.   1952   3.50 - 7.50
   G.P. Putnam's Sons.

McLane, F. Moulton
The Boy Scouts of the Lighthouse Troop, Boy Scout   1917   3.50 - 7.50
   Life Series. Barse & Hopkins Publishers.
The Boy Scouts of the Lighthouse, Boy Scout Life   1917   15.00 - 20.00
   Series. Barse & Hopkins, Publishers. W/DJ.

Michelson, Florence
Whitman Tell-a-Tale Series, Lassie and the Cub   1966   3.00 - 7.50
   Scout, Western Publishing Co.

Nendick, V. R.
Jack Corvit, Patrol Leader, or Always a Scout,   1920   3.50 - 7.50
   J.B. Lippincott Co.

Oakes, Vanya
Hawaiian Treasure, Julian Messner.   1957   10.00 - 15.00

Otis, James
Boy Scouts in a Lumber Camp, Crowell's Scout   1913   3.50 - 7.50
   Book Series. Thomas Y. Crowell Co.
Boy Scouts in the Main Woods, Crowell's Scout   1911   3.50 - 7.50
   Book Series. Thomas Y. Crowell Co.

Palmer, Don
The Boy Scout Explorers at Emerald Valley, The Boy   1955   15.00 - 20.00
   Scout Explorers Series. Cupples & Leon Co.
The Boy Scout Explorers at Headless Hollow, The   1957   15.00 - 20.00
   Boy Scout Explorers Series. Cupples & Leon Co.
The Boy Scout Explorers at Treasure Mountain, The   1955   15.00 - 20.00
   Boy Scout Explorers Series. Cupples & Leon Co.

Park, George F.
Dick Judson, Boy Scout Ranger, McBride & Co.   1916   3.50 - 7.50

Parker, Capt. Thomas D.
The Cruise of the Deep Sea Scouts, W.A. Wilde Co.   1917   3.50 - 7.50

Payson, Lt. Howard
The Boy Scouts and the Army Airship, A.L. Burt Co.,   1911   10.00 - 15.00
   pictorial cover reprint.
The Boy Scouts and the Army Airship, Hurst & Co.   1911   10.00 - 15.00
The Boy Scouts at the Canadian Border, A.L. Burt   1918   5.00 - 10.00
   Co., pictorial cover reprint.
The Boy Scouts at the Canadian Border, Hurst & Co.   1918   3.50 - 7.50
The Boy Scouts at the Panama Canal, A.L. Burt Co.,   1913   5.00 - 10.00
   pictorial cover reprint.
The Boy Scouts at the Panama Canal, Hurst & Co.   1913   3.50 - 7.50
The Boy Scouts at the Panama-Pacific Exposition,   1915   7.50 - 12.50
   Hurst & Co.
The Boy Scouts at the Panama-Pacific Exposition,   1915   10.00 - 15.00
   A.L. Burt Co., pictorial cover reprint.
The Boy Scouts' Badge of Courage, Hurst & Co.   1917   3.50 - 7.50
The Boy Scouts' Badge of Courage, A.L. Burt Co.,   1917   5.00 - 10.00
   pictorial cover reprint.
The Boy Scouts' Campaign for Preparedness,   1916   3.50 - 7.50
   Hurst & Co.
The Boy Scouts' Campaign for Preparedness, A.L.   1916   5.00 - 10.00
   Burt Co., pictorial cover reprint.
The Boy Scouts for Uncle Sam, A.L. Burt Co.,   1912   5.00 - 10.00
   pictorial cover reprint.
The Boy Scouts for Uncle Sam, Hurst & Co.   1912   3.50 - 7.50
The Boy Scouts' Mountain Camp, Hurst & Co.   1912   3.50 - 7.50
The Boy Scouts' Mountain Camp, A.L. Burt Co.,   1912   5.00 - 10.00
   pictorial cover reprint.
The Boy Scouts of the Eagle Patrol, A.L. Burt Co.,   1911   5.00 - 10.00
   pictorial cover reprint.
The Boy Scouts of the Eagle Patrol, Hurst & Co.   1911   3.50 - 7.50
The Boy Scouts on the Belgian Battlefields,   1915   3.50 - 7.50
   Hurst & Co.

The Boy Scouts on the Belgian Battlefields,   1915   5.00 - 10.00
   A.L. Burt Co., pictorial cover reprint.
The Boy Scouts on the Range, A.L. Burt Co.,   1911   5.00 - 10.00
   pictorial cover reprint.
The Boy Scouts on the Range, Hurst & Co.   1911   3.50 - 7.50
The Boy Scouts Under Fire in Mexico, A.L. Burt Co.,   1914   5.00 - 10.00
   pictorial cover reprint.
The Boy Scouts Under Fire in Mexico, Hurst & Co.   1914   3.50 - 7.50
The Boy Scouts Under Sealed Orders, A.L. Burt Co.,   1916   5.00 - 15.00
   pictorial cover reprint.
The Boy Scouts Under Sealed Orders, Hurst & Co.   1916   3.50 - 7.50
The Boy Scouts with the Allies in France, Hurst & Co.   1915   3.50 - 7.50
The Boy Scouts with the Allies in France,   1915   5.00 - 10.00
   A.L. Burt Co., pictorial cover reprint.

Pier, Arthur Stanwood
The Hilltop Troop, Houghton Mifflin Co.   1919   3.50 - 7.50

Puller, Edwin
Biff McCarty, The Eagle Scout, Abingdon Press.   1915   3.50 - 7.50

Quirk, Leslie W.
The Boy Scouts of Black Eagle Patrol, Little, Brown   1915   3.50 - 7.50
   & Co.
The Boy Scouts of Lakeville, The Boy Scout Series.   1920   3.50 - 7.50
   Little, Brown & Co.
The Boy Scouts of Lakeville, Little, Brown & Co.   1920   3.50 - 7.50
The Boy Scouts on Crusade, Little, Brown & Co.   1917   3.50 - 7.50

Ralphson, G. Harvey
The Boy Scout Camera Club, or The Confession of a   1913   3.50 - 7.50
   Photograph, M.A. Donohue & Co.
The Boy Scout Camera Club, or The Confession of a   1913   15.00 - 20.00
   Photograph, The Boy Scout Series. M.A. Donohue
   & Co. W/DJ.
Boy Scout Electricians, or The Hidden Dynamo, The   1913   15.00 - 20.00
   Boy Scout Series. M.A. Donohue & Co. W/DJ.

Boy Scout Electricians, or The Hidden Dynamo, 1913   3.50 - 7.50
M.A. Donohue & Co.

Boy Scouts Beyond the Arctic Circle, or The Lost 1913   3.50 - 7.50
Expedition, M.A. Donohue & Co.

Boy Scouts in a Submarine, or Searching an Ocean 1912   10.00 - 25.00
Floor, The Boy Scout Series. M.A. Donohue & Co.

Boy Scouts in a Submarine, or Searching an Ocean 1912   15.00 - 20.00
Floor, The Boy Scout Series. M.A. Donohue & Co.
W/DJ.

Boy Scouts in an Airship, or The Warning from the 1912   15.00 - 20.00
Sky, The Boy Scout Series. M.A. Donohue & Co.
W/DJ.

Boy Scouts in an Airship, or The Warning from the 1912   10.00 - 25.00
Sky, The Boy Scout Series. M.A. Donohue & Co.

Boy Scouts in Belgium, or Imperiled in a Trap, The 1915   15.00 - 20.00
Boy Scout Series. M.A. Donohue & Co. W/DJ.

Boy Scouts in California, or the Flag on the Cliff, The 1913   15.00 - 20.00
Boy Scout Series. M.A. Donohue & Co. W/DJ.

Boy Scouts in California, or The Flag on the Cliff, 1913   3.50 - 7.50
M.A. Donohue & Co.

Boy Scouts in Death Valley, or The City in the Sky, 1914   3.50 - 7.50
M.A. Donohue & Co.

Boy Scouts in Mexico, or On Guard with Uncle Sam, 1911   15.00 - 20.00
The Boy Scout Series. M.A. Donohue & Co. W/DJ.

Boy Scouts in Southern Waters, or Spaniard's 1915   3.50 - 7.50
Treasure Chest, M.A. Donohue & Co.

Boy Scouts in Southern Waters, or Spaniard's 1913   15.00 - 20.00
Treasure Chest, The Boy Scout Series.
M.A. Donohue & Co.

Boy Scouts in the Canal Zone, or The Plot Against 1911   15.00 - 20.00
Uncle Sam, The Boy Scout Series.
M.A. Donohue & Co. W/DJ.

Boy Scouts in the Canal Zone, or The Plot Against 1911   3.50 - 7.50
Uncle Sam, The Boy Scout Series.
M.A. Donohue & Co.

Boy Scouts in the North Sea, or The Mystery of the 1915   3.50 - 7.50
U-13, M.A. Donohue & Co.

Boy Scouts in the North Sea, or The Mystery of the 1915   15.00 - 20.00
U-13, The Boy Scout Series. M.A. Donohue & Co.
W/DJ.

Boy Scouts in the Northwest, or Fighting Forest 1912   15.00 - 20.00
Fires, The Boy Scout Series. M.A. Donohue & Co.
W/DJ.

Boy Scouts in the Philippines, or The Key to the 1911   3.50 - 7.50
Treaty Box, The Boy Scout Series. M.A. Donohue
& Co.

Boy Scouts in the Philippines, or The Key to the 1911   15.00 - 20.00
Treaty Box, The Boy Scout Series. M.A. Donohue
& Co. W/DJ.

Boy Scouts in the Verdun Attack, or Perils of the 1916   3.50 - 7.50
Black Bear Patrol, M.A. Donohue & Co.

Boy Scouts in the Verdun Attack, or Perils of the 1916   15.00 - 20.00
Black Bear Patrol, The Boy Scout Series.
M.A. Donohue & Co. W/DJ.

Boy Scouts Mysterious Signal, or Perils of the Black 1916   15.00 - 20.00
Bear Patrol, The Boy Scout Series. M.A. Donohue
& Co. W/DJ.

Boy Scouts Mysterious Signal, or Perils of the 1916   3.50 - 7.50
Black-Bear Patrol, M.A. Donohue & Co.

Boy Scouts on Hudson Bay, or The Disappearing 1914   15.00 - 20.00
Fleet, The Boy Scout Series. M.A. Donohue & Co.
W/DJ.

Boy Scouts on Hudson Bay, or The Disappearing 1914   3.50 - 7.50
Fleet, M.A. Donohue & Co.

Boy Scouts on Motorcycles, or With the Flying 1912   10.00 - 25.00
Squadron, The Boy Scout Series.
M.A. Donohue & Co.

Boy Scouts on Motorcycles, or With the Flying 1912   15.00 - 20.00
Squadron, The Boy Scout Series.
M.A. Donohue & Co. W/DJ.

Boy Scouts on the Columbia River, or Adventures in 1912   15.00 - 20.00
a Motor Boat, The Boy Scout Series.
M.A. Donohue & Co. W/DJ.

Boy Scouts on the Columbia River, or Adventures in 1912   3.50 - 7.50
a Motor Boat, The Boy Scout Series.
M.A. Donohue & Co.

Boy Scouts on the Open Plains, or The Roundup Not 1914   3.50 - 7.50
Ordered, M.A. Donohue & Co.

Boy Scouts on the Open Plains, or The Roundup 1914   15.00 - 20.00
Not Ordered, The Boy Scout Series.
M.A. Donohue & Co. W/DJ.

Boy Scouts Under the Kaiser, or The Uhlan's Escape, 1914   15.00 - 20.00
The Boy Scout Series. M.A. Donohue & Co. W/DJ.

Boy Scouts Under the Kaiser, or The Uhlan's Escape, 1916   3.50 - 7.50
M.A. Donohue & Co.

Boy Scouts Under the Kaiser, or the Uhlan's in Peril, 1916   15.00 - 20.00
The Boy Scout Series. M.A. Donohue & Co. W/DJ.

Boy Scouts Under the Kaiser, or The Uhlan's in Peril, 1916   3.50 - 7.50
M.A. Donohue & Co.

Boy Scouts With the Cossacks, or Poland 1916   3.50 - 7.50
Recaptured, M.A. Donohue & Co.

Boy Scouts with the Cossacks, or Poland 1916   15.00 - 20.00
Recaptured, The Boy Scout Series.
M.A. Donohue & Co. W/DJ.

Boy Scouts Beyond the Arctic Circle, or the Lost 1913   15.00 - 20.00
Expedition, The Boy Scout Series.
M.A. Donohue & Co. W/DJ.

Boy Scouts in Belgium, or Imperiled in a Trap, 1915   3.50 - 7.50
M.A. Donohue & Co.

Boy Scouts in Mexico, or On Guard with Uncle Sam, 1911   3.50 - 7.50
The Boy Scout Series. M.A. Donohue & Co.

Boy Scouts in the Northwest, or Fighting Forest 1912   3.50 - 7.50
Fires, The Boy Scout Series. M.A. Donohue & Co.

RAY, ANNA CHAPIN

Buddie at Gray Buttes Camp, The Buddie Books, 1912   15.00 - 20.00
Little, Brown & Co. W/DJ.

Buddie at Gray Buttes Camp, The Buddie Books. 1912   3.50 - 7.50
Little Brown & Co.

Buddie, The Story of a Boy, The Buddie Books, 1911   15.00 - 20.00
Little, Brown & Co. W/DJ.

Buddie, The Story of a Boy, The Buddie Books. 1911   3.50 - 7.50
Little Brown & Co.

The Responsibilities of Buddie, The Buddie Books. 1913   3.50 - 7.50
Little Brown & Co.

The Responsibilities of Buddie, The Buddie Books, 1913   15.00 - 20.00
Little, Brown & Co. W/DJ.

REEVE, ARTHUR B.

The Boy Scouts' Craig Kennedy, Harper & Brothers. 1925   3.50 - 7.50

REYNOLDS, DICKSON AND GERRY

Brother Scouts, Thomas Nelson & Sons. 1952   10.00 - 15.00

RUDD, STEPHEN

The Mystery of the Missing Eyebrows, 1921   3.50 - 7.50
R.H. Gore Publishing Co.

SABIN, EDWIN L.

Pluck on the Trail, or Boy Scouts in the Rockies, 1912   3.50 - 7.50
Crowell's Scout Book Series. Thomas Y. Crowell
Co.

SAVITT, SAM

A Day at the LBJ Ranch, Random House. 1965   10.00 - 15.00

SCHULTZ, JAMES W.

In the Great Apache Forest, The Story of a Lone Boy 1920   3.50 - 7.50
Scout, Houghton-Mifflin Co., green cover.

In the Great Apache Forest, The Story of a Lone Boy 1920   3.50 - 7.50
Scout, Houghton-Mifflin Co., reprint, red cover.

SCOVILLE, SAMUEL, JR.

The Inca Emerald, The Boy Scout Series. 1922   3.50 - 7.50
The Century Co.

The Blue Pearl, The Boy Scout Series. 1920   15.00 - 20.00
The Century Co. W/DJ.

The Blue Pearl, The Boy Scout Series.   1920   3.50 - 7.50
  The Century Co.

Boy Scouts in the Wilderness, The Boy Scout Series. 1919   15.00 - 20.00
  The Century Co. W/DJ.

Boy Scouts in the Wilderness, The Boy Scout Series. 1919   3.50 - 7.50
  The Century Co.

The Inca Emerald. The Boy Scout Series.   1922   15.00 - 20.00
  The Century Co. W/DJ.

The Out-of-Doors Club, Sunday School Times Co.   1919   3.50 - 7.50

The Red Diamond, The Boy Scout Series.   1925   15.00 - 20.00
  The Century Co. W/DJ.

The Red Diamond, The Boy Scout Series.   1925   3.50 - 7.50
  The Century Co.

The Snake Blood Ruby, The Boy Scout Series.   1932   15.00 - 20.00
  The Century Co. W/DJ.

The Snake Blood Ruby, The Boy Scout Series.   1932   3.50 - 7.50
  The Century Co.

SHALER, ROBERT

Boy Scouts and the Prize Pennant, Sterling Boy   1914   3.50 - 7.50
  Scout Books. Hurst & Co., Publishers.

Boy Scouts and the Call to Arms, Sterling Boy Scout 1914   15.00 - 20.00
  Books, Hurst & Co. Publishers. W/DJ.

Boy Scouts and the Call to Arms, Sterling Boy Scout 1914   3.50 - 7.50
  Books. Hurst & Co., Publishers.

Boy Scouts and the Prize Pennant, Sterling Boy   1914   15.00 - 20.00
  Scout Books, Hurst & Co. Publishers. W/DJ.

Boy Scouts and the Prize Pennant, Circling the Globe 1914   15.00 - 20.00
  Series. Arthur Westbrook Co. W/DJ.

Boy Scouts and the Prize Pennant, Circling the Globe 1914   3.50 - 7.50
  Series. Arthur Westbrook Co.

Boy Scouts as County Fair Guides, Circling the Globe 1915   15.00 - 20.00
  Series. Arthur Westbrook Co. W/DJ.

Boy Scouts as County Fair Guides, Circling the Globe 1915   3.50 - 7.50
  Series. Arthur Westbrook Co.

Boy Scouts as County Fair Guides, Sterling Boy   1915   3.50 - 7.50
  Scout Books. Hurst & Co., Publishers.

Boy Scouts as County Fair Guides, Sterling Boy   1915   15.00 - 20.00
  Scout Books, Hurst & Co. Publishers. W/DJ.

Boy Scouts as Forest Fire Fighters, Sterling Boy   1915   3.50 - 7.50
  Scout Books. Hurst & Co., Publishers.

Boy Scouts as Forest Fire Fighters, Circling the   1915   3.50 - 7.50
  Globe Series. Arthur Westbrook Co.

Boy Scouts as Forest Fire Fighters, Sterling Boy   1915   15.00 - 20.00
  Scout Books, Hurst & Co. Publishers. W/DJ.

Boy Scouts as Forest Fire Fighters, Circling the   1915   15.00 - 20.00
  Globe Series. Arthur Westbrook Co. W/DJ.

Boy Scouts at Mobilization Camp, Sterling Boy   1914   15.00 - 20.00
  Scout Books, Hurst & Co. Publishers. W/DJ.

Boy Scouts at Mobilization Camp, Sterling Boy   1914   3.50 - 7.50
  Scout Books. Hurst & Co., Publishers.

Boy Scouts for City Improvement, Circling the Globe 1914   3.50 - 7.50
  Series. Arthur Westbrook Co.

Boy Scouts for City Improvement, Sterling Boy   1914   15.00 - 20.00
  Scout Books, Hurst & Co. Publishers. W/DJ.

Boy Scouts for City Improvement, Hurst & Co.,   1914   3.50 - 7.50
  Publishers.

Boy Scouts for City Improvement, Circling the Globe 1914   15.00 - 20.00
  Series. Arthur Westbrook Co. W/DJ.

Boy Scouts for Home Protection, Sterling Boy Scout   1916   3.50 - 7.50
  Books. Hurst & Co., Publishers.

Boy Scouts for Home Protection, Sterling Boy Scout   1916   15.00 - 20.00
  Books. Hurst & Co. Publishers. W/DJ.

Boy Scouts in the Great Flood, Sterling Boy Scout   1915   3.50 - 7.50
  Books. Hurst & Co., Publishers.

Boy Scouts in the Great Flood, Sterling Boy Scout   1915   15.00 - 20.00
  Books. Hurst & Co. Publishers. W/DJ.

Boy Scouts in the Great Flood, Circling the Globe   1915   3.50 - 7.50
  Series. Arthur Westbrook Co.

Boy Scouts in the Great Flood, Circling the Globe   1915   15.00 - 20.00
  Series. Arthur Westbrook Co.

Boy Scouts of Pioneer Camp, Sterling Boy Scout   1914   15.00 - 20.00
  Books, Hurst & Co. Publishers. W/DJ.

Boy Scouts of Pioneer Camp, Sterling Boy Scout   1914   3.50 - 7.50
  Books. Hurst & Co., Publishers.

Boy Scouts of the Field Hospital, Sterling Boy Scout 1915   3.50 - 7.50
  Books. Hurst & Co., Publishers.

Boy Scouts of the Field Hospital, Sterling Boy Scout 1915   15.00 - 20.00
  Books, Hurst & Co. Publishers. W/DJ.

Boy Scouts of the Flying Squadron, Sterling Boy   1914   10.00 - 20.00
  Scout Books. Hurst & Co., Publishers.

Boy Scouts of the Flying Squadron, Sterling Boy   1914   15.00 - 20.00
  Scout Books, Hurst & Co. Publishers. W/DJ.

Boy Scouts of the Geological Survey, Sterling Boy   1914   3.50 - 7.50
  Scout Books. Hurst & Co., Publishers.

Boy Scouts of the Geological Survey, Sterling Boy   1914   15.00 - 20.00
  Scout Books, Hurst & Co. Publishers. W/DJ.

Boy Scouts of the Life Saving Crew, Sterling Boy   1914   3.50 - 7.50
  Scout Books. Hurst & Co., Publishers.

Boy Scouts of the Life Saving Crew, Sterling Boy   1914   15.00 - 20.00
  Scout Books. Hurst & Co. Publishers. W/DJ.

Boy Scouts of the Naval Reserve, Sterling Boy Scout 1914   15.00 - 20.00
  Books. Hurst & Co. Publishers. W/DJ.

Boy Scouts of the Naval Reserve, Sterling Boy Scout 1914   3.50 - 7.50
  Books. Hurst & Co., Publishers.

Boy Scouts of the Signal Corps, Sterling Boy Scout   1914   3.50 - 7.50
  Books. Hurst & Co., Publishers.

Boy Scouts of the Signal Corps, Sterling Boy Scout   1914   15.00 - 20.00
  Books, Hurst & Co. Publishers. W/DJ.

Boy Scouts on Picket Duty, Sterling Boy Scout   1914   3.50 - 7.50
  Books. Hurst & Co., Publishers.

Boy Scouts on Picket Duty, Sterling Boy Scout   1914   15.00 - 20.00
  Books. Hurst & Co. Publishers. W/DJ.

Boy Scouts on the Roll of Honor, Sterling Boy Scout 1916   15.00 - 20.00
  Books. Hurst & Co. Publishers. W/DJ.

Boy Scouts on the Roll of Honor, Sterling Boy Scout 1916   3.50 - 7.50
  Books. Hurst & Co., Publishers.

Boy Scouts with the Motion Picture Players, Sterling 1916   15.00 - 20.00
  Boy Scout Books, Hurst & Co. Publishers. W/DJ.

Boy Scouts with the Motion Picture Players, Sterling 1916   3.50 - 7.50
  Boy Scout Books. Hurst & Co., Publishers.

Boy Scouts with the Red Cross, Circling the Globe   1915   3.50 - 7.50
  Series. Arthur Westbrook Co.

Boy Scouts with the Red Cross, Circling the Globe   1915   15.00 - 20.00
  Series. Arthur Westbrook Co. W/DJ.

Boy Scouts with the Red Cross, Sterling Boy Scout   1915   3.50 - 7.50
  Books. Hurst & Co., Publishers.

Boy Scouts with the Red Cross, Sterling Boy Scout   1915   15.00 - 20.00
  Books. Hurst & Co. Publishers. W/DJ.

SHERMAN, H.

The Hockey Spare, Sports and Scouts Series,   1937   3.50 - 7.50
  Saalfield Publishing Co.

The Hockey Spare. Sports and Scouts Series,   1937   15.00 - 20.00
  Saalfield Publishing Co. W/DJ.

Last Man Out, Sports and Scouts Series,   1937   15.00 - 20.00
  Saalfield Publishing Co. W/DJ.

Last Man Out, Sports and Scouts Series,   1937   3.50 - 7.50
  Saalfield Publishing Co.

The Winning Point, Sports and Scouts Series,   1936   3.50 - 7.50
  Saalfield Publishing Co.

The Winning Point. Sports and Scouts Series,   1936   15.00 - 20.00
  Saalfield Publishing Co. W/DJ.

SHERMAN, HAROLD, M.

Don Rader, Trail Blazer, Grosset & Dunlap.   1929   3.50 - 7.50

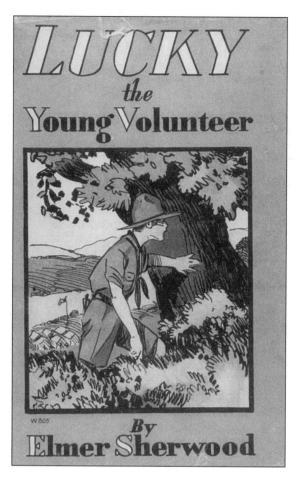

SHERWOOD, ELMER

Lucky and His Friend Steve, Whitman Publishing Co.	1922	3.50 - 7.50
Lucky and His Friend Steve. The Lucky Series. Whitman Publishing Co. W/DJ.	1922	15.00 - 20.00
Lucky and His Travels, Whitman Publishing Co.	1922	3.50 - 7.50
Lucky and His Travels. The Lucky Series. Whitman Publishing Co. W/DJ.	1922	15.00 - 20.00
Lucky Finds a Friend, Whitman Publishing Co.	1920	3.50 - 7.50
Lucky Finds a Friend. The Lucky Series. Whitman Publishing Co. W/DJ.	1920	15.00 - 20.00
Lucky on an Important Mission, Whitman Publishing Co.	1920	3.50 - 7.50
Lucky on an Important Mission. The Lucky Series. Whitman Publishing Co. W/DJ.	1920	15.00 - 20.00
Lucky the Boy Scout, Whitman Publishing Co.	1920	3.50 - 7.50
Lucky the Boy Scout. The Lucky Series. Whitman Publishing Co. W/DJ.	1920	15.00 - 20.00
Lucky the Young Volunteer, The Lucky Series. Whitman Publishing Co.	1920	15.00 - 20.00
Lucky the Young Volunteer, Whitman Publishing Co.	1920	3.50 - 7.50
Lucky, the Boy Scout, The Lucky Series. Whitman Publishing Co. W/DJ.	1916	15.00 - 20.00
Lucky, the Boy Scout, Whitman Publishing Co., reprint.	1916	3.50 - 7.50
Lucky, the Young Navyman, Whitman Publishing Co. reprint.	1917	3.50 - 7.50
Lucky, the Young Navyman, The Lucky Series. Whitman Publishing Co. W/DJ.	1917	15.00 - 20.00
Lucky, the Young Soldier, Whitman Publishing Co., reprint.	1917	3.50 - 7.50
Lucky, the Young Soldier, The Lucky Series. Whitman Publishing Co. W/DJ.	1917	15.00 - 20.00
Ted Marsh and His Friend Steve, The Ted Marsh Series. Whitman Publishing Co. W/DJ.	1920	15.00 - 20.00
Ted Marsh and His Friend Steve, Whitman Publishing Co.	1920	3.50 - 7.50
Ted Marsh and His Great Adventure, Whitman Publishing Co.	1920	3.50 - 7.50
Ted Marsh and His Great Adventure, The Ted Marsh Series. Whitman Publishing Co. W/DJ.	1920	15.00 - 20.00
Ted Marsh on an Important Mission, Whitman Publishing Co.	1920	3.50 - 7.50
Ted Marsh on an Important Mission, The Ted Marsh Series. Whitman Publishing Co. W/DJ.	1920	15.00 - 20.00
Ted Marsh the Boy Scout, The Ted Marsh Series. Whitman Publishing Co. W/DJ.	1920	15.00 - 20.00
Ted Marsh the Boy Scout, Whitman Publishing Co.	1920	3.50 - 7.50
Ted Marsh the Young Volunteer, Whitman Publishing Co.	1920	3.50 - 7.50
Ted Marsh the Young Volunteer. The Ted Marsh Series. Whitman Publishing Co. W/DJ.	1920	15.00 - 20.00

SLOBODKIN, L.

Return to the Apple Tree, Macmillan Co.	1965	5.00 - 10.00
Return to the Apple Tree, Macmillan Co., paperback.	1965	3.50 - 7.50
Space Ship Under the Apple Tree, Macmillan Co.	1952	5.00 - 10.00
Space Ship Under the Apple Tree, Macmillan Co. paperback.	1952	3.50 - 7.50
The Three-Seated Spaceship, Macmillan Co.	1962	10.00 - 15.00
The Three-Seated Spaceship, Macmillan Co. paperback.	1962	3.50 - 7.50

SMEATON, DOUGLAS AND EDWIN BARON

Easy Boy Scout Sketches, Fitzgerald Publishing Co.	1938	10.00 - 15.00

SMITH, L.K.

Corley Takes the Scout Trail, D. Appleton & Co.	1930	3.50 - 7.50
Corley of the Wilderness Trails, Sports and Scouts Series, Saalfield Publishing Co. W/DJ.	1937	15.00 - 20.00
Corley of the Wilderness Trails, Sports and Scouts Series, Saalfield Publishing Co	1937	3.50 - 7.50
Phil Burton, Sleuth, Sports and Scouts Series, Saalfield Publishing Co. W/DJ.	1937	15.00 - 20.00
Phil Burton, Sleuth, Sports and Scouts Series, Saalfield Publishing Co	1937	3.50 - 7.50
Tommy of Troop Six, Sports and Scouts Series, Saalfield Publishing Co	1937	3.50 - 7.50

STANKEVICH, BORIS

Two Green Bars, Doubleday & Co.	1967	3.50 - 7.50

STERLING, DOROTHY

The Cub Scout Mystery, Doubleday & Co., Inc.	1952	5.00 - 10.00

STERLING, GRAY

The Tooth of Time: A Philmont Adventure, Marshall Jones Co.	1955	15.00 - 20.00

STEVENS, C. M.

Uncle Jeremiah at the Panama-Pacific Exposition, Hamming-Whitman Co., Publishers.	1915	10.00 - 20.00

Dan C. Stowe

STOWE, DAN C.
A Scoutmaster Remembers.	1985	10.00 - 15.00

STRONG, P. N.
Behind the Great Smokies.	1920	3.50 - 7.50

STRONG, PASCHAL
Kelly King at Yale Hall, Sports and Scouts Series, Saalfield Publishing Co. W/DJ.	1937	15.00 - 20.00
Kelly King at Yale Hall, Sports and Scouts Series, Saalfield Publishing Co.	1937	3.50 - 7.50

STUART, GORDON
The Boy Scouts of the Air at Cape Peril, The Boy Scouts of the Air Series, Reilly & Britton. W/DJ.	1921	15.00 - 20.00
The Boy Scouts of the Air at Cape Peril, The Boy Scouts of the Air Series, Reilly & Lee Co. W/DJ.	1921	15.00 - 20.00
The Boy Scouts of the Air at Cape Peril, Reilly & Britton or Reilly & Lee Co.	1921	10.00 - 15.00
The Boy Scouts of the Air at Eagle Camp, The Boy Scouts of the Air Series, Reilly & Lee Co. W/DJ.	1912	15.00 - 20.00
The Boy Scouts of the Air at Eagle Camp, The Boy Scouts of the Air Series, Reilly & Britton. W/DJ.	1912	15.00 - 20.00
The Boy Scouts of the Air at Eagle Camp, Reilly & Britton or Reilly & Lee Co.	1912	10.00 - 15.00
The Boy Scouts of the Air at Greenwood School, The Boy Scouts of the Air Series, Reilly & Britton. W/DJ.	1912	15.00 - 20.00
The Boy Scouts of the Air at Greenwood School, The Boy Scouts of the Air Series, Reilly & Lee Co. W/DJ.	1912	15.00 - 20.00
The Boy Scouts of the Air at Greenwood School, Reilly & Britton or Reilly & Lee Co.	1912	10.00 - 15.00
The Boy Scouts of the Air in Belgium, The Boy Scouts of the Air Series, Reilly & Britton. W/DJ.	1915	15.00 - 20.00
The Boy Scouts of the Air in Belgium, The Boy Scouts of the Air Series, Reilly & Lee Co. W/DJ.	1915	15.00 - 20.00
The Boy Scouts of the Air in Belgium, Reilly & Britton or Reilly & Lee Co.	1915	10.00 - 15.00
The Boy Scouts of the Air in Indian Land, The Boy Scouts of the Air Series, Reilly & Lee Co. W/DJ.	1912	15.00 - 20.00
The Boy Scouts of the Air in Indian Land, Reilly & Britton or Reilly & Lee Co.	1912	10.00 - 15.00
The Boy Scouts of the Air in the Lone Star Patrol, The Boy Scouts of the Air Series, Reilly & Lee Co. W/DJ.	1916	15.00 - 20.00
The Boy Scouts of the Air in the Lone Star Patrol, The Boy Scouts of the Air Series, Reilly & Britton. W/DJ.	1916	15.00 - 20.00
The Boy Scouts of the Air in the Lone Star Patrol, Reilly & Britton or Reilly & Lee Co.	1916	10.00 - 15.00
The Boy Scouts of the Air in the Northern Wilds, The Boy Scouts of the Air Series, Reilly & Lee Co. W/DJ.	1912	15.00 - 20.00
The Boy Scouts of the Air in the Northern Wilds, The Boy Scouts of the Air Series, Reilly & Britton. W/DJ.	1912	15.00 - 20.00
The Boy Scouts of the Air in the Northern Wilds, Reilly & Britton or Reilly & Lee Co.	1912	10.00 - 15.00
The Boy Scouts of the Air on Bald Crest, The Boy Scouts of the Air Series, Reilly & Lee Co. W/DJ.	1922	15.00 - 20.00
The Boy Scouts of the Air on Bald Crest, The Boy Scouts of the Air Series, Reilly & Britton. W/DJ.	1922	15.00 - 20.00
The Boy Scouts of the Air on Bald Crest, Reilly & Britton or Reilly & Lee Co.	1922	10.00 - 15.00
The Boy Scouts of the Air on Flathead Mountain, The Boy Scouts of the Air Series, Reilly & Lee Co. W/DJ.	1912	15.00 - 20.00
The Boy Scouts of the Air on Flathead Mountain, The Boy Scouts of the Air Series, Reilly & Britton. W/DJ.	1912	15.00 - 20.00
The Boy Scouts of the Air on Flathead Mountain, Reilly & Britton or Reilly & Lee Co.	1912	10.00 - 15.00
The Boy Scouts of the Air on Lost Island, The Boy Scouts of the Air Series, Reilly & Lee Co. W/DJ.	1917	15.00 - 20.00
The Boy Scouts of the Air on Lost Island, The Boy Scouts of the Air Series, Reilly & Britton. W/DJ.	1917	15.00 - 20.00
The Boy Scouts of the Air on Lost Island, Reilly & Britton or Reilly & Lee Co.	1917	10.00 - 15.00
The Boy Scouts of the Air on The French Front, The Boy Scouts of the Air Series, Reilly & Lee Co. W/DJ.	1918	15.00 - 20.00
The Boy Scouts of the Air on the French Front, The Boy Scouts of the Air Series, Reilly & Britton. W/DJ.	1918	15.00 - 20.00
The Boy Scouts of the Air on the Great Lakes, The Boy Scouts of the Air Series, Reilly & Lee Co. W/DJ.	1912	15.00 - 20.00
The Boy Scouts of the Air on the Great Lakes, The Boy Scouts of the Air Series, Reilly & Britton. W/DJ.	1912	15.00 - 20.00
The Boy Scouts of the Air on the Great Lakes, Reilly & Britton or Reilly & Lee Co.	1912	10.00 - 15.00
The Boy Scouts of the Air on The French Front, Reilly & Britton or Reilly & Lee Co.	1918	10.00 - 15.00
The Boy Scouts of the Air with Pershing, The Boy Scouts of the Air Series, Reilly & Britton. W/DJ.	1919	15.00 - 20.00
The Boy Scouts of the Air with Pershing, The Boy Scouts of the Air Series, Reilly & Lee Co. W/DJ.	1919	15.00 - 20.00
The Boy Scouts of the Air with Pershing, Reilly & Britton or Reilly & Lee Co.	1919	10.00 - 15.00

THE BOY SCOUT SERIES
The Boy Scouts Along the Susquehanna, or The Silver Fox Patrol Caught in a Flood.	1915	3.50 - 7.50
The Boy Scouts on War Trails in Belgium, or Caught Between Hostile Enemies.	1916	3.50 - 7.50

THIESS, LEWIS E.
Flood Mappers Aloft, W.A. Wilde Co.	1937	3.50 - 7.50

THURSTON, IDA TREADWELL
Billy Burns of Troop 5, Gleming H. Revell Co.	1913	3.50 - 7.50
The Scoutmaster of Troop 5, Gleming H. Revell Co.	1912	3.50 - 7.50

TOUSEY, SANFORD

Cub Scout, Ariel.	1952	5.00 - 10.00

TULL, JEWELL BOTHWELL

Rob Riley - The Making of a Boy Scout, Educational Supply Co.	1916	3.50 - 7.50
Winning of the Bronze Cross, Educational Supply Co.	1915	3.50 - 7.50

VICTOR, RALPH

Boy Scouts on the Yukon, Boy Scout Series. A.L. Chatterton Co.	1912	3.50 - 7.50
The Boy Scouts' Motorcycles, Boy Scouts Series, Plate and Peck Co. reprint.	1911	10.00 - 15.00
The Boy Scouts' Air Craft, Boy Scouts Series, A.L. Chatterton. Co.	1912	10.00 - 15.00
The Boy Scouts' Air Craft, Boy Scouts Series, Plate and Peck Co. reprint.	1912	10.00 - 15.00
The Boy Scouts' Air Craft, Boy Scouts Series, Hurst & Co. a still later reprint.	1912	10.00 - 15.00
The Boy Scouts' Air Craft. Boy Scouts Series, Hurst & Co. 3rd reprint. W/DJ.	1912	15.00 - 20.00
The Boy Scouts' Art Craft, Boy Scouts Series, Plate and Peck Co. 2nd reprint. W/DJ.	1911	15.00 - 20.00
The Boy Scouts' Canoe Trip, Boy Scouts Series, A.L. Chatterton Co. W/DJ.	1911	15.00 - 20.00
The Boy Scouts' Canoe Trip, Boy Scouts Series, Plate and Peck Co. reprint.	1911	3.50 - 7.50
The Boy Scouts' Canoe Trip, Boy Scouts Series, Hurst & Co., a still later reprint.	1911	3.50 - 7.50
The Boy Scouts' Canoe Trip, Boy Scouts Series, A.L. Chatterton Co.	1911	3.50 - 7.50
The Boy Scouts' Canoe Trip, Boy Scouts Series, Plate and Peck Co. 2nd reprint. W/DJ.	1911	15.00 - 20.00
The Boy Scouts' Canoe Trip, Boy Scouts Series, Hurst & Co. 3rd reprint. W/DJ.	1911	15.00 - 20.00
Boy Scouts in the Black Hills, Boy Scouts Series, A.L. Chatterton Co. W/DJ.	1913	15.00 - 20.00
Boy Scouts in the Black Hills, Boy Scouts Series, Plate and Peck Co. 2nd reprint. W/DJ.	1913	15.00 - 20.00
Boy Scouts in the Black Hills, Boy Scouts Series, Hurst & Co. 3rd reprint. W/DJ.	1913	15.00 - 20.00
Boy Scouts in the Black Hills, Boy Scouts Series, Plate and Peck Co. reprint.	1913	3.50 - 7.50
Boy Scouts in the Black Hills, Boy Scouts Series, A.L. Chatterton Co.	1913	3.50 - 7.50
Boy Scouts in the Black Hills, Boy Scouts Series, Hurst & Co., a still later reprint.	1913	3.50 - 7.50
The Boy Scouts in the Canadian Rockies, Boy Scouts Series, Plate and Peck Co. reprint.	1911	3.50 - 7.50
The Boy Scouts in the Canadian Rockies, Boy Scouts Series, Hurst & Co. a still later reprint.	1911	3.50 - 7.50
The Boy Scouts in the Canadian Rockies, Boy Scout Series, A.L. Chatterton Co. W/DJ.	1911	15.00 - 20.00
The Boy Scouts in the Canadian Rockies, Boy Scouts Series, A.L. Chatterton Co.	1911	3.50 - 7.50
The Boy Scouts in the Canadian Rockies, Boy Scouts Series, Hurst & Co. 3rd reprint. W/DJ.	1911	15.00 - 20.00
The Boy Scouts in the Canadian Rockies, Boy Scouts Series, Plate and Peck Co. 2nd reprint. W/DJ.	1911	15.00 - 20.00
Boy Scouts in the North Woods, Boy Scouts Series, A.L. Chatterton Co. W/DJ.	1913	15.00 - 20.00
Boy Scouts in the North Woods, Boy Scouts Series, Plate and Peck Co. 2nd reprint. W/DJ.	1913	15.00 - 20.00
The Boy Scouts in the North Woods, Boy Scout Series, Hurst & Co. 3rd reprint. W/DJ.	1913	15.00 - 20.00
Boy Scouts in the North Woods, Boy Scouts Series, Plate and Peck Co. reprint.	1913	3.50 - 7.50
Boy Scouts in the North Woods, Boy Scouts Series, A.L. Chatterton Co.	1913	3.50 - 7.50
Boy Scouts in the North Woods, Boy Scouts Series, Hurst & Co., a still later reprint.	1913	3.50 - 7.50
The Boy Scouts' Motorcycles, Boy Scouts Series, A.L. Chatterton Co.	1911	10.00 - 15.00
The Boy Scouts' Motorcycles, Boy Scouts Series, Hurst & Co. a still later reprint.	1911	10.00 - 15.00
The Boy Scouts' Motorcycles, Boy Scout Series, Plate and Peck Co. 2nd reprint. W/DJ.	1911	15.00 - 20.00
The Boy Scouts' Motorcycles, Boy Scout Series, A.L. Chatterton Co. W/DJ.	1911	15.00 - 20.00
The Boy Scouts' Motorcycles, Boy Scouts Series, Hurst & Co. 3rd reprint. W/DJ.	1911	15.00 - 20.00
Boy Scouts on the Yukon, Boy Scout Series, Hurst & Co. 3rd reprint. W/DJ.	1912	15.00 - 20.00
Boy Scouts on the Yukon, Boy Scout Series, A.L. Chatterton Co. W/DJ.	1912	15.00 - 20.00
Boy Scouts on the Yukon, Boy Scouts Series, Plate and Peck Co. 2nd reprint. W/DJ.	1912	15.00 - 20.00
Boy Scouts on the Yukon, Boy Scouts Series, Plate and Peck Co. reprint.	1912	3.50 - 7.50
Boy Scouts on the Yukon, Boy Scouts Series, Hurst & Co., a still later reprint.	1912	3.50 - 7.50
The Boy Scouts' Patrol, Boy Scouts Series, Plate and Peck Co. reprint.	1911	3.50 - 7.50
The Boy Scouts' Patrol, Boy Scouts Series, A.L. Chatterton Co.	1911	3.50 - 7.50
The Boy Scouts' Patrol, Boy Scout Series, Plate and Peck Co. 2nd reprint. W/DJ.	1911	15.00 - 20.00
The Boy Scouts' Patrol, Boy Scout Series, A.L. Chatterton Co. W/DJ.	1911	15.00 - 20.00
The Boy Scouts' Patrol, Boy Scouts Series, A.L. Chatterton Co. a still later reprint.	1911	10.00 - 15.00
The Boy Scouts' Patrol, Boy Scout Series, Hurst & Co. 3rd reprint. W/DJ.	1911	15.00 - 20.00
The Boy Scouts' Air Craft, Boy Scout Series, A.L. Chatterton Co. W/DJ.	1912	15.00 - 20.00

WALDEN, WALTER

Boy Scouts Afloat, Boy Scout Life Series, Barse & Hopkins Publishers.	1918	3.50 - 7.50
Boy Scouts Afloat, Boy Scout Life Series, Barse & Hopkins, Publishers. W/DJ.	1918	15.00 - 20.00
The Hidden Islands, Small, Maynard & Co.	1918	3.50 - 7.50

WALLACE, DILLON

Troop One of the Labrador, Fleming H. Revell Co.	1920	3.50 - 7.50

WALLACE, MAUDE ORITA

Peanuts and Pennies, A Musical Play for Boys, Raymond A. Hoffman Co.	1927	10.00 - 15.00

WARREN, GEORGE A.

The Banner Boy Scouts Afloat, or The Secret of Cedar Island, Cupples & Leon Co.	1913	3.50 - 7.50
The Banner Boy Scouts Afloat, or The Secret of Cedar Island, World Syndicate Publishing Co. reprint.	1913	3.50 - 7.50
The Banner Boy Scouts Afloat, or The Secret of Cedar Island, Saalfield Publishing Co. reprint.	1913	3.50 - 7.50
The Banner Boy Scouts Afloat, or The Secret of Cedar Island. The Banner Boy Scouts Series. Saalfield Publishing Co. W/DJ.	1913	15.00 - 20.00
The Banner Boy Scouts Afloat, or The Secret of Cedar Island. The Banner Boy Scouts Series. World Syndicate Publishing Co. W/DJ.	1913	15.00 - 20.00
The Banner Boy Scouts Afloat, or The Secret of Cedar Island. The Banner Boy Scouts Series, Cupples & Leon Co. W/DJ.	1913	15.00 - 20.00
The Banner Boy Scouts in the Air, World Syndicate Publishing Co. reprint.	1937	5.00 - 10.00
The Banner Boy Scouts in the Air. The Banner Boy Scouts Series. World Syndicate Publishing Co. W/DJ.	1937	15.00 - 20.00
The Banner Boy Scouts Mystery, World Syndicate Publishing Co. reprint.	1937	3.50 - 7.50
The Banner Boy Scouts Mystery. The Banner Boy Scouts Series. World Syndicate Publishing Co. W/DJ.	1937	15.00 - 20.00
The Banner Boy Scouts on a Tour, or The Mystery of Rattlesnake Mountain, Cupples & Leon Co.	1912	3.50 - 7.50
The Banner Boy Scouts on a Tour, or The Mystery of Rattlesnake Mountain, Saalfield Publishing Co. reprint.	1912	3.50 - 7.50
The Banner Boy Scouts on a Tour, or The Mystery of Rattlesnake Mountain, World Syndicate Publishing Co. reprint.	1912	3.50 - 7.50
The Banner Boy Scouts on a Tour, or The Mystery of Rattlesnake Mountain. The Banner Boy Scouts Series, Cupples & Leon Co. W/DJ.	1912	15.00 - 20.00
The Banner Boy Scouts on a Tour, or The Mystery of Rattlesnake Mountain. The Banner Boy Scouts Series. World Syndicate Publishing Co. W/DJ.	1912	15.00 - 20.00
The Banner Boy Scouts on a Tour, or The Mystery of Rattlesnake Mountain. The Banner Boy Scouts Series. Saalfield Publishing Co. W/DJ.	1912	15.00 - 20.00
The Banner Boy Scouts Snowbound, or a Tour on Skates and Iceboats, Saalfield Publishing Co. reprint.	1916	3.50 - 7.50
The Banner Boy Scouts Snowbound, or A Tour on Skates and Iceboats, Cupples & Leon Co.	1916	3.50 - 7.50
The Banner Boy Scouts Snowbound, or A tour on Skates and Iceboats. The Banner Boy Scouts Series, Cupples & Leon Co. W/DJ.	1916	15.00 - 20.00
The Banner Boy Scouts Snowbound, or a Tour on Skates and Iceboats. The Banner Boy Scouts Series. Saalfield Publishing Co. W/DJ.	1916	15.00 - 20.00
The Banner Boy Scouts, or The Struggle for Leadership, World Syndicate Publishing Co. reprint.	1912	3.50 - 7.50
The Banner Boy Scouts, or The Struggle for Leadership, Cupples & Leon Co.	1912	3.50 - 7.50
The Banner Boy Scouts, or The Struggle for Leadership, Saalfield Publishing Co. reprint.	1912	3.50 - 7.50
The Banner Boy Scouts, or The Struggle for Leadership. The Banner Boy Scouts Series. Saalfield Publishing Co. W/DJ.	1912	15.00 - 20.00
The Banner Boy Scouts, or The Struggle for Leadership. The Banner Boy Scouts Series. World Syndicate Publishing Co. W/DJ.	1912	15.00 - 20.00
The Banner Boy Scouts, or The Struggle for Leadership. The Banner Boy Scouts Series, Cupples & Leon Co. W/DJ.	1912	15.00 - 20.00
The Boy Scouts Snowbound, or A Tour on Skates and Iceboats, World Syndicate Publishing Co. reprint.	1916	3.50 - 7.50
The Boy Scouts Snowbound, or a Tour on Skates and Iceboats. The Banner Boy Scouts Series. World Syndicate Publishing Co. W/DJ.	1916	15.00 - 20.00

WATTS, MABEL

Cub Scout, Giant Books, Rand McNally & Co.	1964	5.00 - 10.00
Cub Scout, A Tip-Top Elf Book reprint.	1964	5.00 - 10.00

WEBSTER, FRANK V.

The Boy Scouts on Lenox, or The Hike Over   1915   10.00 - 17.50
   Big Bear Mountain, Cupples & Leon Co.

WELLMAN, MANLY W.

The Sleuth Patrol, Thomas Nelson & Sons.   1947   3.50 - 7.50

WILSON, JOHN FLEMING

Scouts of the Desert, The Tad Sheldon Series,   1920   3.50 - 7.50
   Macmillan Co., reprint.

Scouts of the Desert. The Tad Sheldon Series,   1920   15.00 - 20.00
   Macmillan Co. reprint. W/DJ.

Tad Sheldon, Boy Scouts, Stories of His Patrol,   1913   3.50 - 7.50
   The Tad Sheldon Series, Sturgis & Walton Co.

Tad Sheldon, Boy Scouts, Stories of His Patrol,   1913   3.50 - 7.50
   The Tad Sheldon Series, Macmillan Co., reprint.

Tad Sheldon's Boy Scouts, Stories of His Patrol. The   1913   15.00 - 20.00
   Tad Sheldon Series. Macmillan Co. reprint. W/DJ.

Tad Sheldon's Boy Scouts, Stories of His Patrol. The   1913   15.00 - 20.00
   Tad Sheldon Series. Sturgis & Walton Co. W/DJ.

Tad Sheldon's Fourth of July, More Stories of His   1913   3.50 - 7.50
   Patrol, The Tad Sheldon Series. Macmillan Co.,
   reprint.

Tad Sheldon's Fourth of July, More Stories of His   1913   3.50 - 7.50
   Patrol, The Tad Sheldon Series, Sturgis & Walton
   Co.

Tad Sheldon's Fourth of July, More Stories of His   1913   15.00 - 20.00
   Patrol. The Tad Sheldon Series, Macmillan Co.
   reprint. W/DJ.

Tad Sheldon's Fourth of July, More Stories of His   1913   15.00 - 20.00
   Patrol. The Tad Sheldon Series, Sturgis & Walton
   Co. W/DJ.

WIRT, MILDRED A.

Dan Carter - Cub Scout, Cupples & Leon.   1949   5.00 - 10.00

Dan Carter and the Cub Honor, Cupples & Leon.   1953   5.00 - 10.00

Dan Carter and the Great Carved Face,   1952   3.50 - 7.50
   Cupples & Leon.

Dan Carter and the Great Carved Face. The Dan   1952   15.00 - 20.00
   Carter Series. Cupples & Leon. W/DJ.

Dan Carter and the Haunted Castle, Cupples & Leon. 1951   5.00 - 10.00

Dan Carter and the Haunted Castle. The Dan Carter   1951   15.00 - 20.00
   Series. Cupples & Leon. W/DJ.

Dan Carter and the Money Box, Cupples & Leon.   1950   3.50 - 7.50

Dan Carter and the River Camp, Cupples & Leon   1949   3.50 - 7.50

Dan Carter and the River Camp. The Dan Carter   1950   15.00 - 20.00
   Series. Cupples & Leon. W/DJ.

WODEHOUSE, P.G.

The Swoop, or How Clarence Saved England,   1979   25.00 - 45.00
   Seabury Press.

WRIGHT, JACK

The Scout Patrol Boys and the Hunting Lodge   1933   3.50 - 7.50
   Mystery, World Syndicate Publishing Co.

The Scout Patrol Boys and the Hunting Lodge   1933   3.50 - 7.50
   Mystery. The Scout Patrol Series. World Syndicate
   Publishing Co.

The Scout Patrol Boys at Circle U Ranch,   1933   3.50 - 7.50
   World Syndicate Publishing Co.

The Scout Patrol Boys at Circle U Ranch. The Scout 1933   3.50 - 7.50
   Patrol Series. World Syndicate Publishing Co.

The Scout Patrol Boys Exploring in Yucatan,   1933   3.50 - 7.50
   World Syndicate Publishing Co.

The Scout Patrol Boys Exploring in Yucatan.   1933   3.50 - 7.50
   The Scout Patrol Series. World Syndicate
   Publishing Co.

The Scout Patrol Boys in the Frozen South,   1933   3.50 - 7.50
   World Syndicate Publishing Co.

The Scout Patrol Boys in the Frozen South.   1933   3.50 - 7.50
   The Scout Patrol Series. World Syndicate
   Publishing Co.

YOUNG LANTERN PRESS EDITORS

Young Reader's Cub Scout Stories.   1930   5.00 - 10.00

Scout troop with staves and drummer.

EVERY BOY'S LIBRARY BOOKS

EVERY BOY'S LIBRARY, BOY SCOUT EDITION.
NO SEAL ON SPINE.

A Midshipman in the Pacific, Brady.	1913	15.00 - 20.00
The Blazed Trail, White.	1913	15.00 - 20.00
Buccaneers and Pirates of Our Coasts, Stockton.	1913	10.00 - 15.00
Cab and Caboose, Monroe.	1913	15.00 - 20.00
The Call of the Wild, London.	1913	20.00 - 30.00
Cattle Ranch to College, Doubleday.	1913	10.00 - 15.00
College Years, Paine.	1913	10.00 - 15.00
Crooked Trails, Remington.	1913	40.00 - 60.00
The Cruise of the Cachelot, Bullen.	1913	10.00 - 15.00
Horseman of the Plains, Althsheler.	1913	10.00 - 15.00
Jeb Hutton, Connolly.	1913	15.00 - 20.00
The Jester of St. Timothy's, Pier.	1913	15.00 - 20.00
Jim Davis, Masefield.	1913	10.00 - 15.00
Pitching in a Pinch, Mathewson.	1913	20.00 - 30.00
The Ranche on the Oxhide, Inman.	1913	10.00 - 15.00
Redney McGaw, McFarland.	1913	15.00 - 20.00
Tecumseh's Young Braves, Tomlinson.	1913	15.00 - 20.00
Three Years Behind the Guns, Tisdale.	1913	15.00 - 30.00
Tom Paulding, Matthews.	1913	15.00 - 20.00
Tom Strong, Washington's Scout, Mason.	1913	15.00 - 20.00
Tommy Remington's Battle, Stevenson.	1913	15.00 - 20.00
Treasure Island, Stevenson.	1913	10.00 - 15.00
Wells Brothers, the Young Cattle Kings, Adams.	1913	10.00 - 15.00
Yankee Ships and Yankee Sailors, Barnes.	1913	15.00 - 20.00
The Cruise of the Cachelot, Bullen.	1914-1930	5.00 - 10.00

EVERY BOY'S LIBRARY, BOY SCOUT EDITION.
NO SEAL ON SPINE. W/DUST JACKET.

A Midshipman in the Pacific, Brady.	1913	25.00 - 35.00
The Blazed Trail, White.	1913	25.00 - 35.00
Buccaneers and Pirates of Our Coasts, Stockton.	1913	20.00 - 30.00
Cab and Caboose, Monroe.	1913	25.00 - 35.00
The Call of the Wild, London.	1913	35.00 - 50.00
Cattle Ranch to College, Doubleday.	1913	20.00 - 30.00
College Years, Paine.	1913	20.00 - 30.00
Crooked Trails, Remington.	1913	60.00 - 90.00
The Cruise of the Cachelot, Bullen.	1913	20.00 - 30.00
Horseman of the Plains, Althsheler.	1913	20.00 - 30.00
Jeb Davis, Masefield.	1913	20.00 - 30.00
Jeb Hutton, Connolly.	1913	25.00 - 35.00
The Jester of St. Timothy's, Pier.	1913	25.00 - 35.00
Pitching in a Pinch, Mathewson.	1913	30.00 - 40.00
The Ranche on the Oxhide, Inman.	1913	20.00 - 30.00
Redney McGaw, McFarland.	1913	25.00 - 35.00
Tecumseh's Young Braves, Tomlinson.	1913	25.00 - 35.00
Three Years Behind the Guns, Tisdale.	1913	25.00 - 35.00
Tom Paulding, Matthews.	1913	25.00 - 35.00
Tom Strong, Washington's Scout, Mason.	1913	25.00 - 35.00
Tommy Remington's Battle, Stevenson.	1913	25.00 - 35.00
Treasure Island, Stevenson.	1913	20.00 - 30.00
Wells Brothers, the Young Cattle Kings, Adams.	1913	20.00 - 30.00
Yankee Ships and Yankee Sailors, Barnes.	1913	25.00 - 35.00

EVERY BOY'S LIBRARY, BOY SCOUT EDITION.
SEAL ON SPINE.

20,000 Leagues Under the Sea, Verne.	1914-1930	10.00 - 15.00
A Gunner Aboard the Yankee, Doubleday.	1914-1930	10.00 - 15.00
A Midshipman in the Pacific, Brady.	1914-1930	10.00 - 15.00
Adventures in Beaver Stream Camp, Dugmore.	1914-1930	10.00 - 15.00
Along the Mohawk Trail, Fitzhugh.	1914-1930	5.00 - 10.00
Animal Heroes, Seton.	1914-1930	5.00 - 10.00

Baby Elton, Quarterback, Quirk.	1914-1930	5.00 - 10.00
Bartley, Freshman Pitcher, Heylinger.	1914-1930	10.00 - 15.00
Be Prepared, The Boy Scouts in Florida, Dimock.	1914-1930	10.00 - 15.00
Billy Topsail with Dr. Luke of the Labrador, Duncan.	1914-1930	10.00 - 15.00
The Biography of a Grizzly, Seton.	1914-1930	5.00 - 10.00
The Blazed Trail, White.	1914-1930	10.00 - 15.00
Boat Building and Boating, Beard.	1914-1930	10.00 - 15.00
The Boy Scouts of Bob's Hill, Burton.	1914-1930	5.00 - 10.00
The Boy Scouts of the Black Eagle Patrol, Quirk.	1914-1930	5.00 - 10.00
The Boy's Book of New Inventions, Maule.	1914-1930	10.00 - 15.00
Brown Wolf, London.	1914-1930	50.00 - 75.00
Buccaneers and Pirates of Our Coasts, Stockton.	1914-1930	5.00 - 10.00
Cab and Caboose, Monroe.	1914-1930	10.00 - 15.00
The Call of the Wild, London.	1914-1930	20.00 - 30.00
Cattle Ranch to College, Doubleday.	1914-1930	5.00 - 10.00
College Years, Paine.	1914-1930	5.00 - 10.00
Crooked Trails, Remington.	1914-1930	50.00 - 75.00
The Cruise of the Dazzler, London.	1914-1930	10.00 - 15.00
Danny Fists, Camp.	1914-1930	20.00 - 30.00
Don Strong of the Wolf Patrol, Heyliger.	1914-1930	5.00 - 10.00
Don Strong, Patrol Leader, Heyliger.	1914-1930	5.00 - 10.00
For the Honor of the School, Barbour.	1914-1930	5.00 - 10.00
The Gaunt Gray Wolf, Wallace.	1914-1930	10.00 - 15.00
Grit-a-Plenty, Wallace.	1914-1930	10.00 - 15.00
The Guns of Europe, Althsheler.	1914-1930	10.00 - 15.00
The Half Back, Barbour.	1914-1930	40.00 - 60.00
Handicraft for Outdoor Boys, Beard.	1914-1930	10.00 - 15.00
Horseman of the Plains, Althsheler.	1914-1930	5.00 - 10.00
Jeb Hutton, Connolly.	1914-1930	10.00 - 15.00
The Jester of St. Timothy's, Pier.	1914-1930	10.00 - 15.00
Jim Davis, Masefield.	1914-1930	5.00 - 10.00
Kidnapped, Stevenson.	1914-1930	5.00 - 10.00
The Last of the Chiefs, Althsheler.	1914-1930	5.00 - 10.00
The Last of the Mohicans, Cooper.	1914-1930	10.00 - 15.00
The Last of the Plainsmen, Grey.	1914-1930	25.00 - 35.00
Lone Bull's Mistake, Schultz.	1914-1930	5.00 - 10.00
The Mutiny of the Flying Spray, Chute.	1914-1930	10.00 - 15.00
Pete, Cow-Puncher, Ames.	1914-1930	20.00 - 30.00
Pitching in a Pinch, Mathewson.	1914-1930	20.00 - 30.00
The Ranche on the Oxhide, Inman.	1914-1930	5.00 - 10.00
The Ransom of Red Chief and Other Stories for Boys, Henry.	1914-1930	25.00 - 35.00
Redney McGaw, McFarland.	1914-1930	10.00 - 15.00
The School Days of Elliot Gray, Jr., Maynard.	1914-1930	10.00 - 15.00
Scouting with Daniel Boone, Tomlinson.	1914-1930	5.00 - 10.00
Scouting with General Funston, Tomlinson.	1914-1930	10.00 - 15.00
Scouting with Kit Carson, Tomlinson.	1914-1930	5.00 - 10.00
Tecumseh's Young Braves, Tomlinson.	1914-1930	10.00 - 15.00
Three Years Behind the Guns, Tisdale.	1914-1930	25.00 - 35.00
Through College on Nothing a Year, Gauss.	1914-1930	10.00 - 15.00
To the Land of the Caribou, Tomlinson.	1914-1930	25.00 - 35.00
Tom Paulding, Matthews.	1914-1930	10.00 - 15.00
Tom Strong, Washington's Scout, Mason.	1914-1930	10.00 - 15.00
Tommy Remington's Battle, Stevenson.	1914-1930	10.00 - 15.00
Treasure Island, Stevenson.	1914-1930	5.00 - 10.00
Under Boy Scout Colors, Ames.	1914-1930	5.00 - 10.00
Ungava Bob, Wallace.	1914-1930	5.00 - 10.00
Wells Brothers, the Young Cattle Kings, Adams.	1914-1930	10.00 - 15.00
Williams of West Point, Johnson.	1914-1930	30.00 - 40.00
The Wireless Man, Collins.	1914-1930	25.00 - 35.00
The Wolf Hunter, Grinnell.	1914-1930	10.00 - 15.00
The Wrecking Master, Paine.	1914-1930	25.00 - 35.00
Yankee Ships and Yankee Sailors, Barnes.	1914-1930	10.00 - 15.00

Handbook for Boys, BSA; 11th printing, 1914. 1914		250.00 - 300.00
Handbook for Boys, BSA; 12th printing, 1915. 1915		250.00 - 300.00
Handbook for Boys, BSA; 13th printing, 1915. 1915		200.00 - 250.00
Handbook for Boys, BSA; 13th printing, reprint, 1915 1915.		200.00 - 250.00
Handbook for Boys, BSA; 14th printing, 1916. 1916		150.00 - 200.00
Handbook for Boys, BSA; 16th printing, 1917. 1917		150.00 - 200.00
Handbook for Boys, BSA;. 19th printing, 1918. 1918		100.00 - 150.00
Handbook for Boys, BSA; 20th printing, 1919. 1919		150.00 - 200.00
Handbook for Boys, BSA; 21st printing, 1919. 1919		150.00 - 200.00
Handbook for Boys, BSA; 22nd printing, 1920. 1920		100.00 - 150.00
Handbook for Boys, BSA; 23rd printing, 1921. 1921		100.00 - 150.00
Handbook for Boys, BSA; 24th printing, 1921. 1921		100.00 - 150.00
Handbook for Boys, BSA; 28th printing, 1923. 1923		100.00 - 150.00

EVERY BOY'S LIBRARY, BOY SCOUT EDITION. SEAL ON SPINE. W/DUST JACKET.

20,000 Leagues Under the Sea, Verne.	1914-1930	20.00 - 30.00
A Gunner Aboard the Yankee, Doubleday.	1914-1930	20.00 - 30.00
A Midshipman in the Pacific, Brady.	1914-1930	20.00 - 30.00
Adventures in Beaver Stream Camp, Dugmore.	1914-1930	20.00 - 30.00
Along the Mohawk Trail, Fitzhugh.	1914-1930	10.00 - 20.00
Animal Heroes, Seton.	1914-1930	10.00 - 20.00
Baby Elton, Quarterback, Quirk.	1914-1930	10.00 - 20.00
Bartley, Freshman Pitcher, Heylinger.	1914-1930	20.00 - 30.00
Be Prepared, The Boy Scouts in Florida, Dimock.	1914-1930	20.00 - 30.00
Billy Topsail with Dr. Luke of the Labrador, Duncan.	1914-1930	20.00 - 30.00
The Biography of a Grizzly, Seton.	1914-1930	10.00 - 20.00
The Blazed Trail, White.	1914-1930	20.00 - 30.00
Boat Building and Boating, Beard.	1914-1930	20.00 - 30.00
The Boy Scouts of Bob's Hill, Burton.	1914-1930	10.00 - 20.00
The Boy Scouts of the Black Eagle Patrol, Quirk.	1914-1930	10.00 - 20.00
The Boy's Book of New Inventions, Maule.	1914-1930	20.00 - 30.00
Brown Wolf, London.	1914-1930	75.00 - 100.00
Buccaneers and Pirates of Our Coasts, Stockton.	1914-1930	10.00 - 20.00
Cab and Caboose, Monroe.	1914-1930	20.00 - 30.00
The Call of the Wild, London.	1914-1930	30.00 - 40.00
Cattle Ranch to College, Doubleday.	1914-1930	10.00 - 20.00
College Years, Paine.	1914-1930	10.00 - 20.00
Crooked Trails, Remington.	1914-1930	75.00 - 100.00
The Cruise of the Dazzler, London.	1914-1930	20.00 - 30.00
Danny Fists, Camp.	1914-1930	30.00 - 40.00
Don Strong of the Wolf Patrol, Heyliger.	1914-1930	10.00 - 20.00
Don Strong, Patrol Leader, Heyliger.	1914-1930	10.00 - 20.00
For the Honor of the School, Barbour.	1914-1930	10.00 - 20.00
The Gaunt Gray Wolf, Wallace.	1914-1930	20.00 - 30.00
Grit-a-Plenty, Wallace.	1914-1930	20.00 - 30.00
The Guns of Europe, Althsheler.	1914-1930	20.00 - 30.00
The Half Back, Barbour.	1914-1930	60.00 - 90.00
Handicraft for Outdoor Boys, Beard.	1914-1930	20.00 - 30.00
Horseman of the Plains, Althsheler.	1914-1930	10.00 - 20.00
Jeb Hutton, Connolly.	1914-1930	20.00 - 30.00
The Jester of St. Timothy's, Pier.	1914-1930	20.00 - 30.00
Jim Davis, Masefield.	1914-1930	10.00 - 20.00
Kidnapped, Stevenson.	1914-1930	10.00 - 20.00
The Last of the Chiefs, Althsheler.	1914-1930	10.00 - 20.00
The Last of the Mohicans, Cooper.	1914-1930	10.00 - 20.00
The Last of the Plainsmen, Grey.	1914-1930	35.00 - 50.00
Lone Bull's Mistake, Schultz.	1914-1930	10.00 - 20.00
The Mutiny of the Flying Spray, Chute.	1914-1930	20.00 - 30.00

Pete, Cow-Puncher, Ames.	1914-1930	30.00 - 40.00
Pitching in a Pinch, Mathewson.	1914-1930	30.00 - 40.00
The Ranche on the Oxhide, Inman.	1914-1930	10.00 - 20.00
The Ransom of Red Chief and Other Stories for Boys, Henry.	1914-1930	35.00 - 50.00
Redney McGraw, McFarland.	1914-1930	20.00 - 30.00
The School Days of Elliot Gray, Jr. Maynard.	1914-1930	20.00 - 30.00
Scouting with Daniel Boone, Tomlinson.	1914-1930	10.00 - 20.00
Scouting with General Funston, Tomlinson.	1914-1930	20.00 - 30.00
Scouting with Kit Carson, Tomlinson.	1914-1930	10.00 - 20.00
Tecumseh's Young Braves, Tomlinson.	1914-1930	20.00 - 30.00
Three Years Behind the Guns, Tisdale.	1914-1930	35.00 - 50.00
Through College on Nothing a Year, Gauss.	1914-1930	20.00 - 30.00
To the Land of the Caribou, Tomlinson.	1914-1930	35.00 - 50.00
Tom Paulding, Matthews.	1914-1930	20.00 - 30.00
Tom Strong, Washington's Scout, Mason.	1914-1930	20.00 - 30.00
Tommy Remington's Battle, Stevenson.	1914-1930	20.00 - 30.00
Treasure Island, Stevenson.	1914-1930	10.00 - 20.00
Under Boy Scout Colors, Ames.	1914-1930	10.00 - 20.00
Ungava Bob, Wallace.	1914-1930	10.00 - 20.00
Wells Brothers, the Young Cattle Kings, Adams.	1914-1930	20.00 - 30.00
Williams of West Point, Johnson.	1914-1930	40.00 - 60.00
The Wireless Man, Collins.	1914-1930	35.00 - 50.00
The Wolf Hunter, Grinnell.	1914-1930	20.00 - 30.00
The Wrecking Master, Paine.	1914-1930	35.00 - 50.00
Yankee Ships and Yankee Sailors, Barnes.	1914-1930	20.00 - 30.00

EVERY BOY'S LIBRARY, BOY SCOUT EDITION. EMBOSSED SEAL ON SPINE.

Along the Mohawk Trail, Fitzhugh.	1930-1945	10.00 - 15.00
Animal Heroes, Seton.	1930-1945	5.00 - 10.00
Baby Elton, Quarterback, Quirk.	1930-1945	10.00 - 15.00
The Biography of a Grizzly, Seton.	1930-1945	5.00 - 10.00
The Boy Scouts of Bob's Hill, Burton.	1930-1945	5.00 - 10.00
The Boy Scouts of the Black Eagle Patrol, Quirk.	1930-1945	5.00 - 10.00
Buccaneers and Pirates of Our Coasts, Stockton.	1930-1945	5.00 - 10.00
The Call of the Wild, London.	1930-1945	30.00 - 50.00
Cattle Ranch to College, Doubleday.	1930-1945	10.00 - 15.00
The Cruise of the Cachelot, Bullen.	1930-1945	5.00 - 10.00
The Cruise of the Dazzler, London.	1930-1945	10.00 - 15.00
Don Strong of the Wolf Patrol, Heyliger.	1930-1945	5.00 - 10.00
Don Strong, Patrol Leader, Heyliger.	1930-1945	5.00 - 10.00
For the Honor of the School, Barbour.	1930-1945	5.00 - 10.00
Grit-a-Plenty, Wallace.	1930-1945	10.00 - 15.00
The Half Back, Barbour.	1930-1945	5.00 - 10.00
Horseman of the Plains, Althsheler.	1930-1945	5.00 - 10.00
Jim Davis, Masefield.	1930-1945	5.00 - 10.00
Kidnapped, Stevenson.	1930-1945	5.00 - 10.00
The Last of the Chiefs, Althsheler.	1930-1945	5.00 - 10.00
The Last of the Mohicans, Cooper.	1930-1945	10.00 - 15.00
The Last of the Plainsmen, Grey.	1930-1945	75.00 - 100.00
Lone Bull's Mistake, Schultz.	1930-1945	5.00 - 10.00
The Ranche on the Oxhide, Inman.	1930-1945	10.00 - 15.00
The Ransom of Red Chief and Other Stories for Boys, Henry.	1930-1945	25.00 - 35.00
The School Days of Elliot Gray, Jr., Maynard.	1930-1945	5.00 - 10.00
Scouting with Daniel Boone, Tomlinson.	1930-1945	5.00 - 10.00
Scouting with Kit Carson, Tomlinson.	1930-1945	5.00 - 10.00
Ungava Bob, Wallace.	1930-1945	5.00 - 10.00
White Fang, London.	1930-1945	75.00 - 100.00

EVERY BOY'S LIBRARY, BOY SCOUT EDITION.
EMBOSSED SEAL ON SPINE. W/ DUST JACKET.

Along the Mohawk Trail, Fitzhugh.	1930-1945	20.00 - 30.00
Animal Heroes, Seton.	1930-1945	10.00 - 20.00
Baby Elton, Quarterback, Quirk.	1930-1945	20.00 - 30.00
The Biography of a Grizzly, Seton.	1930-1945	10.00 - 20.00
The Boy Scouts of Bob's Hill, Burton.	1930-1945	10.00 - 20.00
The Boy Scouts of the Black Eagle Patrol, Quirk.	1930-1945	10.00 - 20.00
Buccaneers and Pirates of Our Coasts, Stockton.	1930-1945	10.00 - 20.00
The Call of the Wild, London.	1930-1945	40.00 - 60.00
Cattle Ranch to College, Doubleday.	1930-1945	20.00 - 30.00
The Cruise of the Cachelot, Bullen.	1930-1945	10.00 - 20.00
The Cruise of the Dazzler, London.	1930-1945	20.00 - 30.00
Don Strong of the Wolf Patrol, Heyliger.	1930-1945	10.00 - 20.00
Don Strong, Patrol Leader, Heyliger.	1930-1945	10.00 - 20.00
For the Honor of the School, Barbour.	1930-1945	10.00 - 20.00
Grit-a-Plenty, Wallace.	1930-1945	20.00 - 30.00
The Half Back, Barbour.	1930-1945	10.00 - 20.00
Horseman of the Plains, Althsheler.	1930-1945	10.00 - 20.00
Jim Davis, Masefield.	1930-1945	10.00 - 20.00
Kidnapped, Stevenson.	1930-1945	10.00 - 20.00
The Last of the Chiefs, Althsheler.	1930-1945	10.00 - 20.00
The Last of the Mohicans, Cooper.	1930-1945	20.00 - 30.00
The Last of the Plainsmen, Grey.	1930-1945	90.00 - 120.00
Lone Bull's Mistake, Schultz.	1930-1945	10.00 - 20.00
The Ranche on the Oxhide, Inman.	1930-1945	20.00 - 30.00
The Ransom of Red Chief and Other Stories for Boys, Henry.	1930-1945	35.00 - 50.00
The School Days of Elliot Gray, Jr., Maynard.	1930-1945	10.00 - 20.00
Scouting with Daniel Boone, Tomlinson.	1930-1945	10.00 - 20.00
Scouting with Kit Carson, Tomlinson.	1930-1945	10.00 - 20.00
Ungava Bob, Wallace.	1930-1945	10.00 - 20.00
White Fang, London.	1930-1945	90.00 - 120.00

The trek cart of Troop 25, Wauatosa, WI, 1928.

Daniel Beard in his famous buckskin outfit. Note the autograph in the upper right hand corner.

BOOKS BY THE U.S. FOUNDERS

Dan Beard at a Silver Buffalo Award dinner.

DANIEL CARTER BEARD

American Boy's Book of Birds and Brownies of the Woods. Lippincott, 1923.	10.00 - 15.00
American Boy's Book of Bugs, Butterflies and Beetles. Lippincott, 1915.	10.00 - 15.00
American Boy's Book of Signs, Signals and Symbols. Lippincott, 1918.	10.00 - 15.00
American Boy's Book of Wild Animals. Lippincott, 1921.	10.00 - 15.00
American Boy's Handbook of Camplore and Woodcraft. Lippincott, 1920.	10.00 - 15.00
American Boy's Handybook: What to Do and How to Do It. Reprint, Nonpareil Book, 1983.	10.00 - 15.00
American Boy's Handybook: What to Do and How to Do It. Scribners, 1882	75.00 - 100.00
Animal Book and Campfire Stories. Moffat, enlarged edition, 1910.	15.00 - 25.00
Animal Book and Campfire Stories. Moffat, 1907.	15.00 - 25.00
Black Wolf Pack. Scribners, 1922.	10.00 - 15.00
Boat Building and Boating. Scribners, 1911.	10.00 - 15.00
Boy Heroes of Today. Brewer, Warren and Putnam, 1932.	10.00 - 15.00
Boy Pioneers of the Buckskin Men. 1911.	10.00 - 15.00
Boy Pioneers: Sons of Daniel Boone. Scribners, 1909.	40.00 - 60.00
The Buckskin Book and Buckskin Calendar. 1911.	20.00 - 30.00
Buckskin Book for Buckskin Men and Boys. Lippincott, 1925.	20.00 - 30.00
Camp Hints for Hike and Bike. U.S. Rubber Co., 1916.	10.00 - 15.00
Dan Beard Talks to Scouts (books and record set.) Garden City, 1940.	50.00 - 75.00
Do It Yourself, Lippincott, 1925.	10.00 - 15.00
Fair Weather Ideas. Scribners, 1904.	20.00 - 25.00
For Playground, Field and Forest: The Outdoor Handybook. Scribners, 1900.	40.00 - 50.00
Handicraft for Outdoor Boys. Grosset and Dunlap, 1913.	10.00 - 15.00
Hardly a Man is Now Alive. Doubleday, 1939.	20.00 - 30.00
How to Make a Totem Bookcase. Lippincott, 1921.	5.00 - 10.00
Jack of All Trades: New Ideas for American Boys. Scribners, 1900.	40.00 - 50.00
Moonlight and Six Feet of Romance. Websterm, 1892.	10.00 - 15.00
Outdoor Games for All Seasons: American Boy's Book of Sports. Scribners, 1906.	40.00 - 50.00
Shelters, Shacks and Shanties. Scribners, 1914.	10.00 - 15.00
Wisdom of the Woods. Lippincott, 1926.	10.00 - 15.00

ERNEST THOMPSON SETON

Animal Heroes. Scribners, 1905.	10.00 - 15.00
Animals: (Selections from Life Histories). The Nature Library. Doubleday, 1926.	10.00 - 15.00
Animals Worth Knowing (Selections from Life Histories) The Little Nature Library. Doubleday, 1928.	10.00 - 15.00
Arctic Prairies. Scribners, 1911.	10.00 - 15.00
Bannertail: The Story of a Grey Squirrel. Scribners, 1922.	10.00 - 15.00
Billy, the Dog that Made Good. Hodder, 1930.	10.00 - 15.00
The Biography of a Grizzly. Century, 1900.	10.00 - 15.00
Biography of a Silver Fox. Century, 1909.	10.00 - 15.00
Biography of an Arctic Fox. Appleton-Century, 1937.	10.00 - 15.00
The Birch Bark Roll combined with Handbook for Boys. Doubleday, Page & Co., 1910.	300.00 - 400.00
The Birch Bark Roll combined with Scouting for Boys. Doubleday, Page & Co.	300.00 - 400.00
The Birch Bark Roll of the Woodcraft Indians. Doubleday, 1908.	150.00 - 200.00
The Birch Bark Roll of the Woodcraft Indians. Doubleday, 1906.	150.00 - 200.00
The Birch Bark Roll: 19th through 30th editions. Doubleday or A.S. Barnes, 1920-1940.	40.00 - 60.00
The Birch Bark Roll: Manual of the Woodcraft Indians. Doubleday, 1915.	40.00 - 60.00
The Birch Bark Roll: The American Boy Scout. Doubleday, Page & Co., 1910.	150.00 - 200.00
The Birch Bark Roll: The Book of Woodcraft and Indian Lore. Doubleday, 1912.	50.00 - 75.00
The Birch Bark Roll: The Book of Woodcraft and Indian Lore. Doubleday, 1915.	50.00 - 75.00
The Birch Bark Roll: Woodcraft Boys, Woodcraft Gild, How to Begin. Woodcraft Headquarters, 1915.	40.00 - 60.00
The Birch Bark Roll: Woodcraft Manual for Boys. Doubleday, 1918.	40.00 - 60.00
The Birch Bark Roll: Woodcraft Manual for Boys. Doubleday, 1917.	40.00 - 60.00
The Birch Bark Roll: Woodcraft Manual for Girls. Doubleday, 1916.	40.00 - 60.00
The Birch Bark Roll: Woodcraft Manual for Girls. Doubleday, 1918.	40.00 - 60.00
Birch Bark Rolls. American Woodcraft, 7 monthly installments in Ladies Home Journal, 1902. Curtis Publishing Co., 1902.	100.00 - 150.00
Birch Bark Rolls. How to Play Indian. Curtis Publishing Co., 1903.	30.00 - 40.00
Birch Bark Rolls. Laws of the Seton Indians. Seton, 1906.	30.00 - 40.00
Birch Bark Rolls. Laws of the Seton Indians. Association Press, 1905.	30.00 - 40.00
Birch Bark Rolls. Laws of the Seton Indians. 1905,	30.00 - 40.00
Birch Bark Rolls. The Red Book, or How to Play Indian. Seton, 1904.	30.00 - 40.00
Birds of Manitoba. Foster, 1892.	20.00 - 30.00
Blazes on the Trail (three pamphlets). Little Peego Press, 1928.	30.00 - 45.00
Brownie Wigwam. Woodcraft League, 1921.	20.00 - 30.00
Buffalo Wind. Private, 1937	200.00 - 300.00
Chink and Other Stories. Hodder, 1927.	10.00 - 15.00
Cute Coyote and Other Stories. Hodder, 1930.	10.00 - 15.00
Fauna of Manitoba. British Assoc. Handbook, 1909.	10.00 - 15.00
Foam the Razorback. Hodder, 1927.	10.00 - 15.00
The Forester's Manual. Doubleday, 1912.	10.00 - 15.00
Gospel of the Redman. Doubleday, 1926.	10.00 - 15.00
Great Historic Animals. Scribners, 1937.	10.00 - 15.00
How Boys Can Form a Band of Indians. Curtis, 1903.	10.00 - 15.00
How to Catch Wolves. Oneida Community, 1884.	40.00 - 50.00
How to Make a Real Indian Teepee. Curtis, 1903.	10.00 - 15.00
Johnny Bear and Other Stories. Hodder, 1927.	10.00 - 15.00
Johnny Bear: Lobo and Other Stories. Scribners, 1935.	10.00 - 15.00
Katug the Snow Child. Blackwell, 1927.	10.00 - 15.00
Krag and Johnny Bear. Scribners, 1902.	15.00 - 20.00
Krag, the Kootenay Ram and Other Stories. University of London Press, 1929.	10.00 - 15.00
The Laws and Honors of the Little Lodge of Woodcraft. Cheyenne, 1919.	25.00 - 35.00

Legend of the White Reindeer. Constable, 1915.	10.00 - 15.00
Library of Pioneering and Woodcraft. Matching set reissue of: Rolf in the Woods, Wild Animal Ways, Two Little Savages, Book of Woodcraft and Indian Lore, Woodland Tales, Wild Animals at Home.	50.00 - 75.00
Lives of Game Animals, four vols. Doubleday, 1925-28.	40.00 - 75.00
Lives of the Hunted. Scribners, 1901.	15.00 - 20.00
Lobo and Other Stories. Hodder, 1927.	10.00 - 15.00
Lobo, Rag, and Vixen. Scribners, 1899.	20.00 - 30.00
Lobo; Bingo; The Pacing Mustang. State, 1930.	10.00 - 15.00
Mainly About Wolves. Methuen, 1937.	10.00 - 15.00
Manual of the Brownies. Woodcraft League, 1922.	20.00 - 30.00
Monarch, the Big Bear of Tallac. Scribners, 1904.	10.00 - 15.00
The Natural History of the Ten Commandments. Scribners, 1907.	10.00 - 15.00
Old Silver Grizzle. Hodder, 1927.	10.00 - 15.00
Pictographs of the Southwest. Cedar Rapids, 1937.	50.00 - 75.00
Preacher of Cedar Mountain. Doubleday, 1917.	10.00 - 15.00
Raggylug and Other Stories. Hodder, 1927.	10.00 - 15.00
The Red Lodge. Private, 1912.	50.00 - 75.00
Rolf in the Woods. Doubleday, 1911.	10.00 - 15.00
Santana, The Hero Dog of France. Phoenix Press, 1945.	150.00 - 200.00
Sign Talk. Doubleday, 1918.	10.00 - 15.00
The Slum Cat. Constable, 1915.	10.00 - 15.00
Studies in Art Anatomy of Animals. MacMillan, 1896.	20.00 - 30.00
The Ten Commandments in the Animal World. Doubleday reprint of Scribners, 1907.	10.00 - 15.00
Trail of an Artist Naturalist. Scribners, 1940.	20.00 - 30.00
Trail of the Sandhill Stag. Scribners, 1899.	20.00 - 30.00
Twelve Pictures of Wild Animals. Scribners, 1901.	25.00 - 35.00
Two Little Savages. Doubleday, 1903.	15.00 - 20.00
War Dance and the Fire-Fly Dance. Doubleday, 1910.	10.00 - 15.00
The Wild Animal Play for Children. Doubleday & Curtis.	10.00 - 15.00
Wild Animal Ways. Doubleday, 1916.	10.00 - 15.00
Wild Animals at Home. Doubleday, 1913.	10.00 - 15.00
Wild Animals I Have Known. Scribners, 1898.	20.00 - 30.00
Woodland Tales. Doubleday, 1921.	20.00 - 30.00
Wood Myth and Fable. Century, 1905.	10.00 - 15.00

James West and Daniel Beard. Note Beard's large National Scout Commissioner patch on his jacket sleeve.

Beginnings of a pioneering project at camp.

SCOUTING FOUNDERS AND FAMOUS PEOPLE

R.S.S. Baden-Powell

General Cigarette card.
Scout Cigarette card.   10.00 - 15.00
Autograph on card.   75.00 - 100.00
Autograph on letter.   100.00 - 150.00
Autograph on photo.   150.00 - 200.00

Ernest T. Seton

Autograph on card.   75.00 - 100.00
Autograph on letter.   100.00 - 150.00
Autograph on photo.   150.00 - 200.00

Daniel C. Beard

Autograph on card.   75.00 - 100.00
Autograph on letter.   100.00 - 150.00
Autograph on photo.   150.00 - 200.00

James C. West

Autograph on card.   20.00 - 30.00
Autograph on letter.   25.00 - 40.00
Autograph on photo.   25.00 - 40.00

Paul Siple (Antarctic Scout)

Autograph on card.   10.00 - 15.00
Autograph on letter.   20.00 - 30.00
Autograph on photo.   25.00 - 35.00

William Hillcourt

Autograph on card.   5.00 - 10.00
Autograph on letter.   10.00 - 15.00
Autograph on photo.   15.00 - 20.00
Autograph in handbook (1979 ed.).   25.00 - 40.00

Colin H. Livingstone

BSA, letter autographed content.   20.00 - 30.00

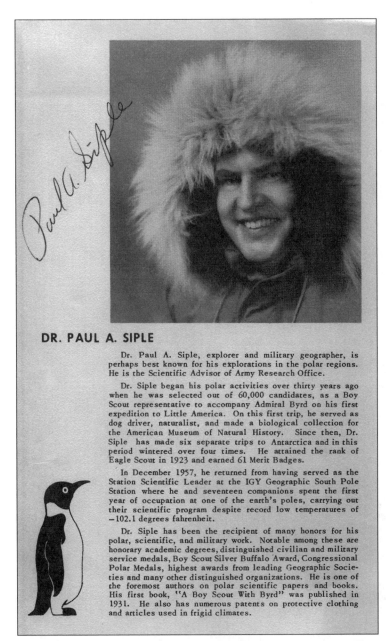

DR. PAUL A. SIPLE

Dr. Paul A. Siple, explorer and military geographer, is perhaps best known for his explorations in the polar regions. He is the Scientific Advisor of Army Research Office.

Dr. Siple began his polar activities over thirty years ago when he was selected out of 60,000 candidates, as a Boy Scout representative to accompany Admiral Byrd on his first expedition to Little America. On this first trip, he served as dog driver, naturalist, and made a biological collection for the American Museum of Natural History. Since then, Dr. Siple has made six separate trips to Antarctica and in this period wintered over four times. He attained the rank of Eagle Scout in 1923 and earned 61 Merit Badges.

In December 1957, he returned from having served as the Station Scientific Leader at the IGY Geographic South Pole Station where he and seventeen companions spent the first year of occupation at one of the earth's poles, carrying out their scientific program despite record low temperatures of −102.1 degrees fahrenheit.

Dr. Siple has been the recipient of many honors for his polar, scientific, and military work. Notable among these are honorary academic degrees, distinguished civilian and military service medals, Boy Scout Silver Buffalo Award, Congressional Polar Medals, highest awards from leading Geographic Societies and many other distinguished organizations. He is one of the foremost authors on polar scientific papers and books. His first book, "A Boy Scout With Byrd" was published in 1931. He also has numerous patents on protective clothing and articles used in frigid climates.

Paul Siple was popular on the speaker circuit for 35 years. This is a page from a 1960 dinner program of Region 10.

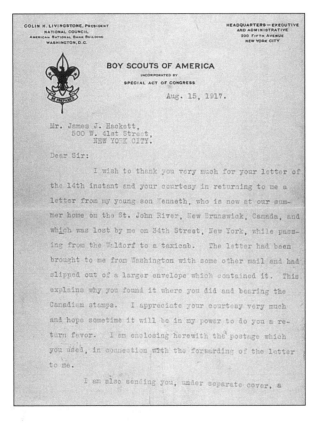

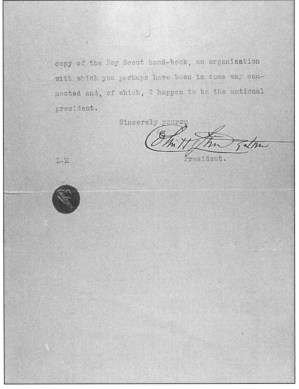

Letter from President Colin Livingstone, 1917.

Programs are great local-interest collectibles. This Madison Square Garden, New York, program includes great photographs and advertisements, value $25.00 - $35.00.

Milwaukee Council program from 1947, $20.00-$30.00.

MAGAZINE SCOUTING ARTICLES

BOYS' LIFE

Any single issue.	1911-1915	40.00 - 60.00
Any single issue.	1916-1920	35.00 - 50.00
Any single issue.	1921-1930	15.00 - 30.00
Any single issue.	1931-1940	8.00 - 15.00
Any single issue.	1941-1950	5.00 - 7.50
Any single issue.	1951-1960	3.00 - 6.00
Any single issue.	1961-1970	2.00 - 3.00
Any single issue.	1971-1997	0.50 - 1.00

LESLIE'S

World War I activities. August 23.	1917	15.00 - 25.00

LIBERTY

August 15, 1936.	(none)	10.00 - 15.00

LIFE

February 5, 1920. The Hero Worshiper by N. Rockwell on cover. (Dog seated at sleeping scout's feet).	1920	20.00 - 25.00

LIFE MAGAZINE

July 24, 1950. National Jamboree article.	1950	15.00 - 20.00

NATIONAL GEOGRAPHIC MAGAZINE

September 1956. Philmont Scout Ranch article.	1956	5.00 - 7.50

SATURDAY EVENING POST

July 23, 1960. National Jamboree article.	1960	7.50 - 10.00
July 23, 1960. Scouts from around the world.	1960	5.00 - 10.00

SCOUT ADMINISTRATOR MAGAZINE

Any single issue.	1925-1935	20.00 - 30.00

SCOUT EXECUTIVE

	1935-1950	5.00 - 10.00

SCOUTING MAGAZINE

Any single issue.	1913-1915	40.00 - 60.00
Any single issue.	1916-1920	30.00 - 50.00
Any single issue.	1921-1930	20.00 - 30.00
Any single issue.	1931-1940	10.00 - 20.00
Any single issue.	1941-1950	7.50 - 10.00
Any single issue.	1951-1960	3.00 - 6.00
Any single issue.	1961-1970	2.00 - 4.00
Any single issue.	1971-1997	0.50 - 1.00

THE WORLD'S WORK

September 1911.	(none)	12.50 - 17.50

TIME

James West on cover.	1937	25.00 - 35.00

The 25th Anniversary prompted many local newspaper articles.

Even today scouting topics make headlines in local newspapers.

JAMES E. WEST

The 1993 Scout Jamboree Book. G.P. Putnam's Sons, 1933.	20.00 - 25.00
The Boy Scout's Book of True Adventure. G.P. Putnam's Sons, 1931.	10.00 - 15.00
The Boys' Book of Honor. F.H. Revell Co., 1934.	10.00 - 15.00
He-Who-Sees-In-The-Dark: The Boys' Story of Frederick Burnham, the American Scout. Brewer, Warren & Putnam, 1932.	10.00 - 15.00
Lone Scout of the Sky: The Story of Charles A. Lindbergh. J.C. Winston Co., 1928.	7.50 - 12.50
Lone Scout of the Sky: The Story of Charles A. Lindbergh. BSA, 1927.	15.00 - 20.00
Lone Scout of the Sky: The Story of Charles A. Lindbergh. Trade edition (orange covers), J.C. Winston, Co., 1928.	7.50 - 12.50
Making the Most of Yourself. D. Appleton-Century Co., 1941.	15.00 - 20.00
The Scout Jamboree Book. G.P. Putnam's Sons, 1930.	15.00 - 20.00
Thirty Years of Service: Tributes to James E. West. Carey Press, 1941.	20.00 - 25.00

WILLIAM HILLCOURT

The 1933 Scout Jamboree Book. G.P. Putnam's Sons, 1933.	10.00 - 15.00
All Out for Scouting - Plan of Action. BSA, 1975.	10.00 - 15.00
Baden Powell - The Two Lives of a Hero. G.P. Putnam's Sons, 1964.	15.00 - 20.00
The Boy Campers. Warren & Putnam, 1931.	10.00 - 15.00
Boy Scout Handbook, 6th edition. BSA, 1959.	10.00 - 15.00
Boy Scout Handbook, 7th edition. BSA, 1965.	5.00 - 10.00
Field Book of Nature Activities and Conservation. G.P. Putnam's Sons, 1961.	10.00 - 15.00
Field Book of Nature Activities and Hobbies. G.P. Putnam's Sons, 1970.	5.00 - 10.00
Field Book of Nature Activities. G.P. Putnam's Sons, 1950.	10.00 - 15.00
Fun with Nature Hobbies. G.P. Putnam's Sons, 1970.	5.00 - 10.00
Golden Book of Camping. Golden Press, 1971.	5.00 - 10.00
Golden Book of Fitness for Boys. Golden Press, 1967.	5.00 - 10.00
Golden Book of Fitness for Girls. Golden Press, 1967.	5.00 - 10.00
Guildebook for Gilwell One Scoutmastership Wood Badge. 1988.	20.00 - 25.00
Handbook for Patrol Leaders, 1st edition. BSA, 1929.	15.00 - 20.00
Handbook for Patrol Leaders, 2nd edition. BSA, 1947.	10.00 - 15.00
Handbook for Patrol Leaders, Golden Jubilee edition. BSA, 1979.	5.00 - 10.00
Handbook for Patrol Leaders, Silver Jubilee edition. BSA, 1935.	15.00 - 25.00
Handbook for Scoutmasters, 4th edition. BSA, 1947.	10.00 - 15.00
Handbook for Scoutmasters, two-volume edition. BSA, 1936-37.	30.00 - 40.00
Norman Rockwell's World of Scouting. H.N. Abrams, 1977.	15.00 - 20.00
Official Boy Scout Handbook, 9th edition. BSA, 1979.	5.00 - 10.00
Official Patrol Leader Handbook, 3rd edition. BSA, 1980.	5.00 - 10.00
Outdoor Things to Do. Golden Press, 1975.	5.00 - 10.00
Scout Field Book. BSA, 1944.	20.00 - 30.00

WILLIAM HILLCOURT, GORDON LYNN PSEUDONYM

Golden Book of Camping and Camp Crafts, A Golden Hobby Book. Golden Press, 1964.	5.00 - 10.00
Golden Book of Camping and Campcrafts. Golden Press, 1959.	5.00 - 10.00

WILLIAM HILLCOURT, R.D. BEZUCHA PSEUDONYM

Golden Anniversary Book of Scouting. Golden Press, 1960.	15.00 - 20.00

WILLIAM HILLCOURT, ROBERT BRENT PSEUDONYM

Golden Book of Chemistry Experiments. Golden Press, 1960.	5.00 - 10.00

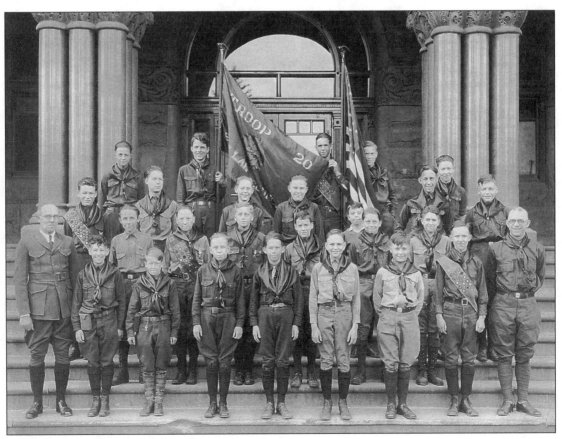

1920s-era troop from Salt Lake City.

COMIC BOOKS

ALLEN R. S.
Who's Minding the Mint? Dell Publishing Co.   1967   5.00 - 7.50

AMERICAN DENTAL ASSOCIATION
The Friendly Cub Scout Casper, His Den   1974   4.00 - 6.00
   and Dentist Fight the Tooth Demons.
   Harvey Publications.

ASSOCIATION OF AMERICAN RAILROADS
Salute to the Boy Scouts.   1960   5.00 - 10.00

BSA
Boy Scout Adventure.   1954   2.00 - 3.50
You Can Be a Scout and a Winner.   1972   3.00 - 5.00

COE, ROLAND
The Little Scouts, #1. July-Sept., 1951.   1951   2.50 - 5.00
   Dell Publishing Co.
The Little Scouts, #2. Oct.-Dec., 1951.   1951   1.50 - 3.00
   Dell Publishing Co.
The Little Scouts, #3. Jan.-March, 1952.   1952   1.50 - 3.00
   Dell Publishing Co.
The Little Scouts, #4. April-June, 1952.   1952   1.50 - 3.00
   Dell Publishing Co.
The Little Scouts, #5. July-Sept., 1952.   1952   1.50 - 3.00
   Dell Publishing Co.
The Little Scouts, #6. Oct.-Dec., 1952.   1952   1.50 - 3.00
   Dell Publishing Co.

CRUMP, IRVING
Scouts to the Rescue, Part 1. Movie Classics.   1937   5.00 - 10.00
Scouts to the Rescue, Part 2. Movie Classics.   1937   5.00 - 10.00

DISNEY, WALT
Donald and Mickey, Cub Scouts, Whitman   1950   15.00 - 20.00
   Publishing Co.
Goofy Scoutmaster.   1962   7.50 - 10.00

FELDSTEIN, ALBERT B.
Mad Special, Spring 1971.   1971   2.50 - 5.00
   E.C. Publications, Inc.

GOLDEN PRESS EDITORS
UFO Encounters. Western Publishing Co.   1978   3.50 - 7.50

HANNA-BARBERA PRODUCTIONS
The Flintstones at the Boy Scout Jamboree,   1964   5.00 - 7.50
   #18. May 1964. K.K. Publications, Inc.
   and Golden Press.

HARVEY PUBLICATIONS, INC.
Casper: Cub Scout of Den Five.   1974   2.00 - 4.00
Devil Kids.   1978   2.50 - 5.00
The Friendly Ghost, Casper and Cub Scout   1974   2.00 - 4.00
   Stories. 1974.
The Friendly Ghost, Casper,   1975   2.50 - 5.00
   Cub Scouts Den O' Fun.
Richie Rich Cash.   1977   1.50 - 3.00
Richie Rich Diamonds.   1979   1.50 - 3.00
Richie Rich Jackpots.   1979   1.50 - 3.00
Richie Rich Profits.   1982   1.50 - 3.00
Richie Rich Success.   1977   1.50 - 3.00
Spooky Spooktown.   1975   2.50 - 5.00

KETCHAM, HANK
Dennis the Menace - the Good Scouts, #138.   1975   2.50 - 5.00
   May 1975.

KIPLING, RUDYARD
Jungle Book #83. Classic Comics.   1940   2.50 - 4.00

McCAY, ROBERT W.
The Life of James E. West, Vol. 1, #2.   1942   7.50 - 12.50
   March 1942. Pioneer Picture Stories,
   quarterly.

SKEATES, STEVE AND REESE, RALPH
The Official Boy Scout Handbook,   1982   1.50 - 3.00
   The City Edition; in Crazy Super Special,
   #85. April 1982. Marvel Magazine.

STENZEL, AL
Your Flag. BSA.   1973   2.50 - 4.00

THE BEST FROM BOYS' LIFE COMICS
April 1958. Gilberton World-Wide Publications.   1958   10.00 - 15.00
January 1958. Gilberton World-Wide   1958   10.00 - 15.00
   Publications.
July 1958. Gilberton World-Wide Publications.   1958   10.00 - 15.00
October 1957. Gilberton World-Wide   1957   10.00 - 15.00
   Publications.
October 1958. Gilberton World-Wide   1958   10.00 - 15.00
   Publications.

SCHIFF SCOUT RESERVATION

BSA 50TH ANNIVERSARY
Pocket patch.   1960   75.00 - 100.00

SCHIFF SCOUT RESERVATION

Square cut khaki cloth, leaf and tent design within circle.	1940-1953	30.00 - 50.00
Cut edge green khaki, leaf and tent design within circle.	1953-1965	25.00 - 30.00
Shield, rolled edge, cloth back.	1965-1972	5.00 - 7.50
Shield, rolled edge, plastic back.	1972-1975	4.00 - 6.00

SHIELD DESIGN

National Conservation Instructor Camp.	1965-1975	15.00 - 20.00
National Conservation Instructor Training Camp.	1965-1975	30.00 - 40.00
National Jr. Leader Instructor Training Camp, two lines.	1965-1972	30.00 - 40.00
National Junior Leader Instruction Camp.	1965-1972	15.00 - 20.00
National Junior Leader Instructor Training Camp, three lines.	1972-1975	30.00 - 40.00

NATIONAL CAMP SCHOOL

AQUATIC SCHOOL

4" red twill cut edge, Tenderfoot emblem in ctr.	10.00 - 15.00

NATIONAL CAMP SCHOOL

Handicrafts.	200.00 - 225.00
Jacket patch, rolled edge khaki.	10.00 - 15.00
Jacket patch, rolled edge tan.	10.00 - 15.00
Pocket patch, cut edge khaki.	10.00 - 15.00
Pocket patch, cut khaki.	30.00 - 40.00
Pocket patch, rolled edge khaki.	7.50 - 10.00
Pocket patch, rolled edge tan.	7.50 - 10.00

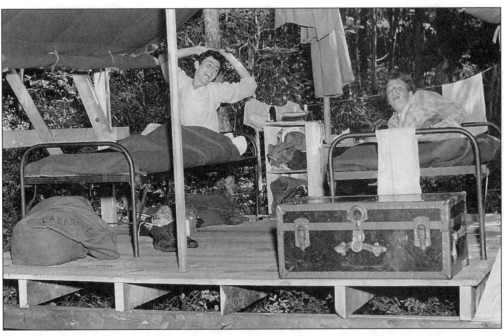

Early morning at summer camp.

REGIONS (12)

REGION 1

Large 1, States of CT, NH, VT, MA, RI, ME, white felt.	30.00 - 40.00
Large 1, States of CT, NH, VT, MA, RI, ME, white twill, cut edge.	15.00 - 25.00
Large 1, States of CT, NH, VT, MA, RI, ME, white twill, rolled edge, Boypower Team.	7.50 - 10.00
Large 1, States of CT, NH, VT, MA, RI, ME, white twill, rolled edge.	10.00 - 15.00
Large 1, States of CT, NH, VT, MA, RI, ME. VT has wavy lines, white felt.	60.00 - 80.00

REGION 2

Dome shaped, Statue of Liberty and NY, NJ names, cut edge.	20.00 - 30.00
Dome shaped, Statue of Liberty and NY, NJ, PR names, cut edge.	15.00 - 25.00
Dome shaped, Statue of Liberty and NY, NJ, PR names, rolled edge.	10.00 - 15.00
Dome shaped, Statue of Liberty and NY, NJ, PR, VI names, rolled edge.	7.50 - 10.00
Oval with large 2, NY and NJ flanking.	75.00 - 125.00
Round 3" blue twill, embroidered 2 and states of NY and NJ.	25.00 - 35.00
Round 3" gray twill, embroidered 2 and states of NY and NJ.	30.00 - 45.00

REGION 3

Band, 1950 jamboree.	100.00 - 150.00
Round 3", scout sign on red twill cut edge.	15.00 - 20.00
Round 3", scout sign on white twill cut edge.	10.00 - 15.00

REGION 4

Red Twill, states of OH, KY, WV, and spacecraft, rolled edge.	7.50 - 10.00
Red Twill, states of OH, KY, WV, green 4.	20.00 - 30.00
Red Twill, states of OH, KY, WV, lime green 4.	17.50 - 25.00
Red Twill, states of OH, KY, WV,. rolled edge.	10.00 - 15.00
Yellow felt, OH, KY and WV states.	100.00 - 140.00

REGION 5

Acorn and large 5 in 3" green felt.	80.00 - 125.00
Green felt circle with yellow V and arrow.	75.00 - 100.00
Shield with V and arrow, R-W-B background, rolled edge.	10.00 - 15.00
Shield with V and arrow. R-W-B background, cut edge.	20.00 - 25.00

REGION 6

White felt, states of NC, SC, GA, FL.	40.00 - 60.00
White twill, states of NC, SC, GA, FL, cut edge.	20.00 - 30.00
White twill, states of NC, SC, GA, FL, rolled edge.	10.00 - 15.00

REGION 7

Shield, large 7 and states WI, MI, IN, IL, cut edge.	15.00 - 20.00
Shield, large 7 and states WI, MI, IN, IL, rolled edge.	10.00 - 15.00

REGION 8

GCW on red felt 4" w/ bronco rider, Great Central West.	100.00 - 130.00
Round 2-7/8" cowboy on beige twill.	75.00 - 100.00
Round 3" bronco and rider on beige twill.	30.00 - 40.00
Round 3" bronco and rider on blue twill.	50.00 - 75.00
Round 3" bronco and rider on flesh twill.	25.00 - 35.00
Tear drop, Bronco rider I.	15.00 - 25.00

REGION 9

Golden 3" felt, bison and 9.	75.00 - 100.00
Round 2" bison and 9 on golden twill.	60.00 - 80.00
Round 2-1/2" bison and 9 on golden twill.	60.00 - 80.00
Star and 9 in shield w/ feathers below.	25.00 - 35.00
Star, 9 and bison in shield w/ feathers below.	20.00 - 25.00
Star, 9 and bison in shield w/ feathers below. Solid embroidery.	7.50 - 12.50

REGION 10

Large faced Paul Bunyan, solid embroidered center, cut edge white twill.	100.00 - 125.00
Paul Bunyan in circle, name below, rolled edge white twill.	10.00 - 15.00
Paul Bunyan in circle, name below, rolled edge white twill.	10.00 - 15.00
Paul Bunyan in circle, Region 10 above, name below, rolled edge white twill.	10.00 - 15.00

REGION 11

Dome shaped, NOR'WESTERS large and ax, cut edge.	40.00 - 60.00
Dome shaped, NOR'WESTERS large and ax, rolled edge.	20.00 - 25.00
Dome shaped, NOR'WESTERS small and ax, rolled edge.	10.00 - 15.00
States OR, WA, ID, MT, listed, red felt.	100.00 - 130.00

REGION 12

Blue felt, 3-1/2" with sunset over water, silk screened, 12 added in design.	120.00 - 140.00
Blue felt, 3-1/2" with sunset over water, silk screened.	125.00 - 150.00
Felt 3" with wagon wheel and state outlines.	90.00 - 120.00
Large 12 and white bull's head on white felt.	130.00 - 160.00
Twill, bull's head on wagon wheel, cut edge.	20.00 - 30.00
Twill, bull's head on wagon wheel, rolled edge.	10.00 - 15.00

Cleveland Scout Show cooking exhibit.

HIGH ADVENTURE BASES

An old car can even enjoy Philmont!

PHILMONT

ARROWHEAD PATCH
Cloth back.	1960-1967	15.00 - 25.00
Plastic back.	1970-1997	10.00 - 15.00

ARROWHEAD PATCH, STAFF
Cloth back.	1960-1967	40.00 - 60.00
Plastic back.	1970-1997	25.00 - 35.00

BSA's 50TH ANNIVERSARY PATCH
	1960	50.00 - 75.00

BULL PATCH
Black felt (men).	1940	5.00 - 7.50
White felt (women).	1940	5.00 - 7.50

BURRO RACE PATCH
White twill.	1970-1975	10.00 - 15.00

CAMP URACCA PATCH
Yellow twill.	1969	30.00 - 50.00

COMMISSARY STAFF PATCH
Brown twill.	1950-1955	50.00 - 75.00

FIELD SPORTS PATCH
Square.	1950-1955	200.00 - 300.00

FIELD SPORTS TOURNAMENT
Rectangle.	1980-1995	10.00 - 15.00

KIT CARSON MEN
Blue twill.	1968	50.00 - 75.00

KIT CARSON TREK
Blue twill.	1974	15.00 - 20.00

NATIONAL EXPLORER ELECTED LEADER
Shield shape.	1956	40.00 - 60.00

NATURE AWARD
Leather Indian head.	1950-1955	50.00 - 75.00

OA INDIAN SEMINAR
	1974	30.00 - 40.00

OA TREK
Pocket patch.	1985	10.00 - 15.00
Pocket patch.	1989	15.00 - 20.00

ORIENTEERING PATCH
Red twill.	1970-1975	17.50 - 22.50

PHILMONT
Tooth of Time belt buckle, bronze.	1960-1998	10.00 - 15.00
Bull in oval belt buckle, bronze.	1970-1998	7.50 - 12.50
Tooth of Time belt buckle, silver.	1970-1998	75.00 - 125.00
30th Anniversary.	1971	40.00 - 50.00
35th Anniversary, light blue twill.	1973-1974	15.00 - 20.00
40th Anniversary.	1981	7.50 - 12.50
50th Anniversary.	1988	2.50 - 5.00

PHILMONT 2" PATCH
P brand, landscape background.	1941-1950	25.00 - 40.00

PHILMONT 2" PATCH SEGMENTS
Camper.	1941-1950	25.00 - 40.00
Conservationist.	1941-1950	30.00 - 50.00
Horseman.	1941-1950	30.00 - 50.00
Mountain Man patch, rifle.	1941-1950	100.00 - 150.00
Naturalist.	1941-1950	30.00 - 50.00
Sportsman.	1941-1950	30.00 - 50.00
Woodman.	1941-1950	30.00 - 50.00

PHILMONT 2" UNIVERSAL PATCH SEGMENT
Staff.	1941-1950	100.00 - 150.00

PHILMONT DIRECTOR PATCH
	1940-1950	300.00 - 400.00

PHILMONT RANGER
Backpatch.	1980-1995	15.00 - 20.00

PHILTURN PATCH
Type I, PT brand, plain background.	1938	225.00 - 275.00
Type II, PT brand, landscape background.	1940	125.00 - 175.00

RAYADO PROGRAM
Gray twill.	1975-1990	10.00 - 15.00

SETON LIBRARY & MUSEUM
Blue twill.	1975-1990	4.00 - 5.00

TRAINING CENTER
Handicraft. Stamped leather skin shape.	(none)	175.00 - 225.00
JLT patch.	1960-1967	40.00 - 60.00
3" round, yellow twill.	1969-1970	10.00 - 12.50
2-3/4" round, yellow twill.	1970-1971	7.50 - 10.00
3" round, orange twill.	1970-1971	4.00 - 5.00
Staff patch.	1970-1971	20.00 - 30.00
National Catholic Conference.	1974-1996	10.00 - 15.00
25th Anniversary, orange twill.	1975	20.00 - 25.00

USA - BICENTENNIAL
Flag over Tooth of Time.	1976	10.00 - 15.00

Tooth of Time at Philmont.

FLORIDA SEA BASE

FLORIDA HIGH ADVENTURE
Bahamas.   3.00 - 5.00
Sailing.   3.00 - 5.00

FLORIDA SEA BASE
Adult patch, 3-1/2" red border.   60.00 - 80.00
Pocket patch, 10th Anniversary.   100.00 - 125.00
Round participant patch, blue.   25.00 - 35.00
Staff patch, 3-1/2" blue border.   100.00 - 130.00
Weekend Course, 3" white border.   50.00 - 60.00

CHARLES H. SOMMERS

CHARLES L. SOMMERS CANOE BASE
Jacket patch.   20.00 - 30.00
Pocket patch, felt.   50.00 - 75.00
w/ loop.   10.00 - 15.00
w/o loop.   10.00 - 15.00

LES VOYAGEURS
Staff.   125.00 - 175.00

REGION TEN BSA WILDERNESS CANOE TRAILS
73 mm round twill.   40.00 - 55.00
78 mm round twill, w/ loop.   25.00 - 35.00

SOMMERS CANOE BASE
Pocket patch.   10.00 - 15.00
Voyageur Historic Trails pocket patch.   10.00 - 15.00

NORTHERN WISCONSIN

EXPLORER CANOE BASE
Three minor varieties.   20.00 - 30.00

NORTHERN WISCONSIN HIGH ADVENTURE
Back patch.   15.00 - 25.00

NORTHERN WISCONSIN HIGH ADVENTURE
Pocket patch.   7.50 - 10.00

NORTHERN WISCONSIN NATIONAL CANOE BASE
Back patch.   25.00 - 35.00
Pocket patch.   10.00 - 15.00
Winter Expedition.   15.00 - 25.00

REGION 7 BASE
Pocket patch, 30th anniversary.   25.00 - 35.00
Pocket patch.   10.00 - 15.00

REGION 7 CANOE BASE
Pocket patch.   10.00 - 15.00

REGION 7 EXPLORER BASE
Pocket patch.   10.00 - 15.00

REGION 7 EXPLORER CANOE BASE
Pocket patch.   10.00 - 15.00

REGION 7 SCOUT LANDING
Cut edge.   60.00 - 80.00

REGION 7 SCOUT LANDING SEGMENTS
Camper.   50.00 - 75.00
Leader.   50.00 - 75.00
Portageur.   100.00 - 150.00
Voyageur.   100.00 - 150.00

LAND BETWEEN THE LAKES
BACK PATCH   17.50 - 22.50

CREW PATCH   10.00 - 15.00

POCKET PATCH   7.50 - 12.50

MAINE

MAINE HIGH ADVENTURE BASE
Back patch.   15.00 - 20.00
Pocket patch, 10th anniversary.   10.00 - 15.00
Pocket patch.   15.00 - 25.00
St. Croix.   80.00 - 100.00

MAINE NATIONAL HIGH ADVENTURE AREA
Back patch.   25.00 - 35.00
Pocket patch.   20.00 - 30.00

MATAGAMON, BSA
Pocket patch.   35.00 - 45.00

Exciting High Adventures continue to be made available to older scouts.

BEAGLE SCOUT

BANK
Snoopy in campaign hat.   (none)   15.00 - 25.00

BANNER
Camp Snoopy, Mall of America.   1994   150.00 - 200.00

BUGLE
Snoopy and Woodstock in campaign hats,   1977   75.00 - 100.00
  sit atop bugle, sounds calls, mint in box.
Snoopy and Woodstock in campaign hats,   1977   15.00 - 20.00
  sit atop bugle, sounds calls.

BULLETIN BOARD
Snoopy and Woodstock in various scenes   1983   50.00 - 75.00
  across U.S. map, one view is as Beagle scout.

COLORFORMS PLAY SET
Snoopy's Beagle Scouts Stand-up Play Set,   1975   30.00 - 50.00
  Lucy and Charlie Brown in overseas caps,
  Snoopy and Woodstock in campaign hats.

GLASS, MCDONALD'S PREMIUM
Glass, Snoopy in campaign hat,   1983   2.50 - 5.00
  Civilization is Overrated.
Plastic, Snoopy in campaign hat,   1983   1.00 - 2.50
  Civilization is Overrated.
Card counter display, Snoopy in campaign hat,   1983   12.50 - 17.50
  Civilization is Overrated.

HALLMARK CARD
Congratulations on your Scouting   1975   4.00 - 7.50
  Achievement, Snoopy presenting badge to
  Woodstock.
Snoopy and Woodstock camping. Thanks!   1980   2.50 - 5.00

HALLMARK GIFT TAG
Snoopy, Woodstock and friends,   1975   2.50 - 5.00
  in campaign hats, rainbow.

HALLMARK NOTEPAPER
Snoopy and Woodstock camping.   1980   10.00 - 15.00
  Congratulations! Boxed set, campfire seal.

LAMP AND NIGHT LIGHT
Snoopy and Woodstock roasting   1974   100.00 - 125.00
  marshmallows, 15-3/4".

MAGNET
Snoopy in campaign hat.   1984   2.50 - 5.00
Woodstock in campaign hat.   1984   2.50 - 5.00

MEMO BOARD
Snoopy as Beagle Scout.   1977   10.00 - 15.00

MINI SNOWFALLS
Snoopy with campaign hat and backpack,   1987   10.00 - 15.00
  Hup, Hup, Hup.

MUSIC BOX
Snoopy in campaign hat and backpack,   1989   75.00 - 100.00
  Beagle Scout, 6-1/2".

NOTE PAD

Stack of Pancakes, Snoopy in campaign hat flipping a pancake.	1970	7.50 - 10.00

PENCIL TOPS

Woodstock in campaign hat.	1980	2.50 - 5.00
Snoopy in campaign hat.	1980	2.50 - 5.00

PINBACK BUTTON

Snoopy with overseas cap, Beagle Scout.	1980	5.00 - 7.50
Snoopy with baseball hat and backpack. Hike it!	1980	2.50 - 5.00
Camp Snoopy, 1st Anniversary, Mall of America, Minneapolis, MN.	1993	5.00 - 7.50

PINS

Snoopy and tenderfoot emblem.	1985	3.00 - 5.00
Snoopy, Woodstock and tenderfoot emblem.	1985	3.00 - 5.00
Snoopy, Woodstock and Cub Scout emblem.	1985	3.00 - 5.00
Snoopy in pinewood derby car, Cub Scout emblem.	1985	3.00 - 5.00
Snoopy and Woodstock, CUB SCOUTS below.	1989	3.00 - 5.00
Snoopy presenting medal to Woodstock. NICE JOB below.	1995	3.00 - 5.00

PLATE BY SCHMID

Snoopy and four birds in campaign hats, hiking, porcelain, 7-1/2". Edition of 20,000, numbered.	1984	35.00 - 50.00

PLUSH TOY

Beagle Scout Outfit, three pieces, 11" Snoopy.	1976	10.00 - 15.00
Beagle Scout Outfit, three pieces, 18" Snoopy.	1976	10.00 - 15.00
Beagle Scout Outfit, four pieces, 9" Woodstock.	1976	15.00 - 20.00
Pup tent, Snoopy, 18".	1978	10.00 - 15.00
Pup tent, Snoopy, 11".	1978	10.00 - 15.00
Sleeping Bag, Rise and Shine, for 18" Snoopy.	1978	10.00 - 15.00
Sleeping Bag, Rise and Shine, for 11" Snoopy.	1978	10.00 - 15.00

SNO-GLOBE

Snoopy and Woodstock toasting marshmallows.	1981	20.00 - 30.00

STACK-UP SNOOPY

Beagle Scout, six pieces, stacks on pole, plastic, 9-1/2" no box.	1980	10.00 - 15.00
Beagle Scout, six pieces, stacks on pole, plastic, 9-1/2" mint in box.	1980	30.00 - 50.00

TROPHY, PLASTIC BASE

Snoopy and Woodstock in campaign hats. Greatest Dad.	(none)	5.00 - 10.00

WESTLAND GIFTWARE, 50TH ANNIVERSARY

Snoopy and Woodstock in campaign hats, Troop 1 banner.	2000	15.00 - 20.00

These listings are referenced to Freddi Karin Margolin's book *"Peanuts™ The Home Collection"* published by Antique Trader Books, a division of Krause Publications, used with permission.

Large Rhode Island rock was a favorite camping location.

COUNCIL LISTINGS

The following section lists alphabetically by state Councils of the Boy Scouts of America which were active in, or since 1972. Why is that important? Well, that is when the National office instituted Council Shoulder Patches (CSP) in multicolored designs. Prior to that time, the council designation was often just a town name or for the professional staff. The patch was red and white, or even earlier, other program color combinations. As council shoulder patches (CSP) are a popular collectible, with an extensive catalog of their own, I will defer you to that reference for listing information. This listing is presented to assist in dating a particular patch to a general time frame. For a full listing of councils since 1910, I refer you to a book by Patrick Geary called *Councils of the BSA, 2000 Edition*.

Council Name	Council #	State	Yr.S	Yr.E
Alabama-Florida	003	AL	1963	
Birmingham Area	002	AL	1915	1996
Black Warrior	006	AL	1922	
Central Alabama	002	AL	1996	
Choccolocco	001	AL	1921	
Mobile Area	004	AL	1927	
Tennessee Valley	659	AL	1934	
Tukabatchee Area	005	AL	1947	
Midnight Sun	696	AK	1960	
Southeast Alaska	608	AK	1955	
Western Alaska	610	AK	1955	
Catalina	011	AZ	1922	
Copper	009	AZ	1962	1977
Desert Trails	029	AZ	1959	1992
Grand Canyon	010	AZ	1993	
Grand Canyon	012	AZ	1944	1993
Theodore Roosevelt	010	AZ	1962	1993
De Soto Area	013	AR	1924	
Eastern Arkansas Area	015	AR	1935	
Ouachita Area	014	AR	1925	
Quapaw Area	018	AR	1927	
Westark Area	016	AR	1937	
Canal Zone	801			1979
Alameda	022	CA	1917	
Buttes Area	647	CA	1924	1992

Council Name	Council #	State	Yr.S	Yr.E
California Inland Empire	045	CA	1973	
Desert Pacific	049	CA	1992	
Forty Niner	052	CA	1957	
Golden Empire	047	CA	1937	
Grayback	024	CA	1952	1974
Great Western	051	CA	1972	1985
Long Beach Area	032	CA	1943	
Los Angeles Area	033	CA	1921	
Los Padres	053	CA	1993	
Marin	035	CA	1923	
Mayfield County	999	CA	1988	
Mission	053	CA	1929	1993
Monterey Bay	025	CA	1934	
Mount Diablo	023	CA	1951	1992
Mount Diablo-Silverado	023	CA	1992	
Mount Larsen Area	036	CA	1924	1992
Mount Whitney Area	054	CA	1929	1992
Old Baldy	043	CA	1922	
Orange County	039	CA	1973	
Pacific Skyline	031	CA		
Piedmont	042	CA	1921	
Redwood	044	CA	1923	1992
Redwood Empire	041	CA	1992	
Riverside County	045	CA	1921	1972
San Diego County	049	CA	1921	1993
San Francisco Bay Area	028	CA	1965	
San Gabriel Valley	040	CA	1951	
San Mateo County	020	CA	1934	1993
Santa Clara County	055	CA	1935	
Santa Lucia Area	056	CA	1939	1993
Sequoia	027	CA	1925	
Silverado Area	038	CA	1923	1992
Sonoma-Mendocino	041	CA	1944	1992
Southern Sierra	030	CA	1966	
Stanford Area	031	CA	1941	1993
Ventura County	057	CA	1921	

Council Name	Council #	State	Yr.S	Yr.E
Verdugo Hills	058	CA	1922	
Western Los Angeles County	051	CA		
Yosemite Area	059	CA	1937	
Denver Area	061	CO	1921	
Longs Peak	062	CO	1929	
Pikes Peak	060	CO	1925	
Rocky Mountain	063	CO	1925	
Western Colorado	064	CO	1942	
Connecticut Rivers	066	CT		
Fairfield County	068	CT	1973	
Greenwich	067	CT	1922	
Housatonic	069	CT	1922	
Indian Trails	073	CT	1971	
Long Rivers	066	CT	1973	
Quinnipiac	074	CT	1935	
Del-Mar-Va	081	DE	1937	
Direct Service	800		1967	
D S Argentina	800			1967
D S Egypt	800			1967
D S Guatemala	800			1967
D S Hong Kong	800			1967
D S Indonesia	800			1967
D S Kenya	800			1967
D S Pakistan	800			1967
D S Panama	800			1967
D S Saudi Arabia	800			1967
D S Singapore	800			1967
D S Venezuela	800			1967
Central Florida	083	FL	1922	
Gulf Coast	773	FL	1939	
Gulf Ridge	086	FL	1939	
Gulf Stream	085	FL	1937	
North Florida	087	FL	1939	
Pinellas Area	089	FL	1935	1978
South Florida	084	FL	1945	

Council Name	Council #	State	Yr.S	Yr.E
Southwest Florida	088	FL	1967	
Sunny Land	724	FL	1926	1995
Suwannee River Area	664	FL	1925	
West Central Florida	089	FL	1978	
Alapha Area	098	GA	1960	
Atlanta Area	092	GA	1921	
Central Georgia	096	GA	1923	
Chattahoochee	091	GA	1964	
Chehaw	097	GA	1985	
Coastal Empire	099	GA	1942	
Flint River	095	GA	1930	
Georgia-Carolina	093	GA	1941	
George H. Lanier	094	GA	1950	1989
Northeast Georgia	101	GA	1935	
Northwest Georgia	100	GA	1934	
Okefenokee Area	758	GA	1926	
Southwest Georgia	097	GA		1985
Transatlantic (Germany)	802		1959	
Aloha	104	HI	1957	
Maui County	102	HI	1941	
Grand Teaton	107	ID	1993	
Idaho Panhandle	110	ID	1929	1992
Lewis-Clark	108	ID	1946	1992
Ore-Ida	106	ID	1935	
Snake River Area	111	ID	1985	
Snake River	111	ID	1924	
Tendoy Area	109	ID	1934	1993
Teaton Peaks	107	ID	1925	1993
Abraham Lincoln	144	IL	1925	
Arrowhead	117	IL	1934	1991
Blackhawk Area	660	IL	1935	
Cahokia Mound	128	IL	1925	1990
Chicago Area	118	IL	1921	
Chief Shabbona	735	IL	1934	1968
Des Plaines Valley	147	IL		

Council Name	Council #	State	Yr.S	Yr.E
Du Page Area	148	IL	1929	1992
Egyptian	120	IL	1941	1994
Illiana	117	IL	1991	
Lincoln Trails	121	IL	1939	
Northeast Illinois	129	IL	1971	
Northwest Suburban	751	IL	1926	
Okaw Valley	116	IL	1965	
Piankeshaw	739	IL	1926	1991
Piasa Bird	112	IL	1930	1990
Prairie	125	IL	1941	1993
Prairielands	117	IL		1991
Rainbow	702	IL	1926	
Saukee Area	141	IL	1935	1993
Thatcher Woods Area	136	IL	1941	1993
Three Fires	127	IL		1968
Trails West	112	IL	1991	
Two Rivers	127	IL	1968	1992
Two Rivers-Dupage Area	127	IL	1992	
W D Boyce	138	IL	1973	
West Suburban	147	IL	1921	1993
Anthony Wayne Area	157	IN	1925	
Buffalo Trace	156	IN	1955	
Calumet	152	IN	1966	
Crossroads Of America	160	IN	1972	
George Rogers Clark Area	143	IN	1927	1993
Hoosier Trails	145	IN	1973	
La Salle	165	IN		1973
Northern Indiana	165	IN	1973	1990
Pioneer Trails	155	IN	1935	1973
Sagamore	162	IN	1973	
Wabash Valley	166	IN	1934	
Hawkeye Area	172	IA	1953	
Illowa	133	IA	1967	
Mid-Iowa	177	IA	1970	
Mississippi Valley	171	IA	1937	1964
Northeast Iowa	178	IA	1935	

Council Name	Council #	State	Yr.S	Yr.E
Prairie Gold Area	179	IA		
Southeast Iowa	171	IA	1969	1993
Winnebago	173	IA	1939	
Far East (Japan)	803		1961	
Coronado Area	192	KS	1939	
Jayhawk Area	197	KS	1929	
Kanza	190	KS	1946	
Kaw	191	KS	1929	1974
Quivira	198	KS	1940	
Santa Fe Trail	194	KS	1946	
Audubon	200	KY	1952	1994
Blue Grass	204	KY	1928	
Four Rivers	207	KY	1940	1994
Lincoln Heritage	205	KY	1993	
Lonesome Pine	203	KY	1934	1979
Many Waters	200	KY	1994	
Old Kentucky Home	205	KY	1953	1993
Shawnee Trails	200	KY		1993
Attakapas	208	LA	1938	
Calcasieu Area	209	LA	1930	
Evangeline Area	212	LA	1924	
Istrouma Area	211	LA	1925	
New Orleans Area	214	LA	1927	
Norwela	215	LA	1923	
Ouachita Valley	213	LA	1925	
Katahdin Area	216	ME	1929	
Pine Tree	218	ME	1933	
Baltimore Area	220	MD	1925	
Mason-Dixon	221	MD	1956	
National Capital Area	082	MD		
Potomac	757	MD	1937	
Algonquin	241	MA	1925	
Annawon	225	MA	1930	
Boston	227	MA	1921	1980
Boston Minuteman	227	MA	1993	

Council Name	Council #	State	Yr.S	Yr.E
Cambridge	229	MA	1919	
Cape Cod & Islands	224	MA	1981	
Great Trails	243	MA	1968	
Greater Boston	227	MA	1980	1993
Greater Lowell	238	MA	1929	
Lone Tree	749	MA	1926	1993
Massachusetts Bay Federation	850	MA	1976	1980
Minuteman	240	MA	1959	1993
Moby Dick	245	MA	1972	
Mohegan	254	MA	1955	
Monadnock	232	MA	1924	1993
Nashua Valley	230	MA	1964	
North Bay	236	MA	1966	1993
North Essex	712	MA	1925	1993
Norumbega	246	MA	1918	
Old Colony	249	MA	1969	
Pioneer Valley	234	MA	1961	
Yankee Clipper	236	MA	1993	
Blue Water	277	MI	1939	
Chief Okemos	271	MI	1932	
Clinton Valley	276	MI	1937	
Detroit Area	262	MI	1926	
Gerald R. Ford	266	MI	1975	
Grand Valley	266	MI	1936	1975
Great Sauk Trail	255	MI		1993
Hiawathaland	261	MI	1945	
Lake Huron Area	265	MI	1971	
Land O'Lakes	269	MI	1971	1993
Land O'Lakes-Wolverine	255	MI	1993	
Scenic Trails	274	MI	1939	
Southwest Michigan	270	MI	1973	
Tall Pine	264	MI	1937	
Timber Trails	275	MI	1944	1975
West Michigan Shores	266	MI	1995	
Wolverine	255	MI	1973	1993
Central Minnesota	296	MN	1926	

Council Name	Council #	State	Yr.S	Yr.E
Gamehaven	299	MN	1925	
Headwaters Area	290	MN	1922	1994
Indianhead	295	MN	1954	
Lake Superior	286	MN	1959	1994
Twin Valley	283	MN	1969	
Viking	283	MN	1951	
Voyageurs Area	286	MN	1994	
Andrew Jackson	303	MS	1937	
Choctaw Area	302	MS	1935	
Delta Area	300	MS	1924	1993
Pine Burr Area	304	MS	1935	
Pushmataha Area	691	MS	1936	
Yocona Area	748	MS	1926	
Great Rivers	653	MO	1951	
Greater St. Louis Area	312	MO	1994	
Heart of America	307	MO	1974	
Mo-Kan Area	306	MO	1929	1994
Ozark Trails	306	MO	1994	
Ozarks	308	MO	1965	1994
Pony Express	311	MO	1932	
St. Louis Area	312	MO	1911	1994
Southeast Missouri	305	MO	1930	1993
Montana	315	MT	1973	
Yellowstone Valley	318	MT	1928	1993
Cornhusker	324	NE	1929	
Mid-America	326	NE	1964	
Overland Trails	322	NE	1954	
Tri Trails	323	NE	1954	1994
Wyo-Braska Area	325	NE	1936	1974
Boulder Dam Area	328	NV	1944	
Nevada Area	329	NV	1929	
Daniel Webster	330	NH	1929	
Aheka	354	NJ	1939	1972
Atlantic Area	331	NJ	1926	1992
Bayonne	332	NJ	1918	1993
Bergen County	350	NJ	1969	

Council Name	Council #	State	Yr.S	Yr.E
Burlington County	690	NJ	1925	
Canden County	335	NJ	1921	
Essex	336	NJ	1975	
George Washington	362	NJ	1937	
Hudson-Hamilton	348	NJ	1968	1993
Hudson Liberty	348	NJ	1993	
Jersey Shore	341	NJ	1991	
Middlesex	344	NJ	1929	1969
Monmouth	347	NJ	1928	
Morris-Sussex Area	343	NJ	1936	
Ocean County	341	NJ	1940	1992
Passaic Valley	353	NJ	1973	
Ridgewood-Glen Rock	359	NJ	1922	
Southern New Jersey	334	NJ	1967	
Tamarack	333	NJ	1935	1985
Thomas Edison	352	NJ	1969	
Union	338	NJ	1928	1980
Watchung Area	358	NJ	1926	
Conquistador	413	NM	1952	
Great Southwest Area	412	NM	1982	
Great Southwest	412	NM	1976	1982
Adirondack	394	NY	1927	
Allegheny Highlands	382	NY	1973	
Baden Powell	381	NY	1975	
Bronx Valley	370	NY	1923	1958
Cayuga County	366	NY	1924	
Chautauqua County	382	NY	1942	1973
Dutchess County	374	NY	1919	1995
Finger Lakes	391	NY	1924	
Five Rivers	375	NY	1990	
General Herkimer	400	NY	1934	
General Sullivan	779	NY	1927	1992
Genesee	667	NY	1925	1994
Governor Clinton	364	NY	1971	1990
Greater New York	640	NY	1936	
G N Y Bronx	642	NY	1915	

Council Name	Council #	State	Yr.S	Yr.E
G N Y Brooklyn	641	NY	1911	
G N Y Manhattan	643	NY	1918	
G N Y Queens	644	NY	1915	
G N Y Staten Island	645	NY	1928	
Greater Niagara Frontier	380	NY	1965	
Hiawatha	373	NY	1969	
Hudson-Delaware	392	NY	1957	1995
Hudson Valley	392	NY	1995	
Iroquois	395	NY	1969	1981
Iroquios Trail	376	NY		
Jefferson Lewis	408	NY	1932	1982
Land of the Oneidas	395	NY	1982	
Lewiston Trail	385	NY	1937	1994
Mohican	378	NY	1927	
Nassau County	386	NY	1916	
Otetiana	397	NY	1943	
Otschodela	393	NY	1927	
Rip Van Winkle	405	NY	1950	
Rockland County	683	NY	1924	1995
St. Lawrence	403	NY	1938	1982
Saratoga County	684	NY	1924	1990
Schenectady County	399	NY	1924	1991
Seaway Valley	403	NY	1982	
Seneca	750	NY	1929	1975
Sir William Johnson	377	NY	1937	1990
Steuben Area	402	NY	1931	1991
Suffolk County	404	NY	1919	
Sullivan Trail	375	NY	1947	1991
Susquenango	368	NY	1925	
Twin Rivers	364	NY	1990	
Upper Mohawk	406	NY	1937	1981
Westchester Putnam	388	NY	1974	
Cape Fear Area	425	NC	1930	
Central North Carolina	416	NC	1937	
Cherokee	417	NC	1923	1994
Daniel Boone	414	NC	1925	

Council Name	Council #	State	Yr.S	Yr.E
East Carolina	426	NC	1932	
General Greene	418	NC	1947	1991
Mecklenburg County	415	NC	1942	
Occoneechee	421	NC	1929	
Old Hickory	427	NC	1942	
Old North State	070	NC	1992	
Piedmont	420	NC	1924	
Tuscarora	424	NC	1923	
Uwharrie	419	NC	1992	1991
Northern Lights	429	ND	1974	
Red River Valley	429	ND	1925	1973
Black Swamp Area	449	OH	1992	
Buckeye	436	OH	1958	
Central Ohio	441	OH	1930	1993
Chief Logan	464	OH	1994	1993
Columbiana	455	OH	1953	1991
Dan Beard	438	OH	1956	
Firelands Area	458	OH	1925	1993
Fort Steuben Area	459	OH	1929	1991
Great Trail	433	OH	1970	
Greater Cleveland	440	OH	1929	
Greater Western Reserve	463	OH	1993	
Harding Area	443	OH	1926	1993
Heart of Ohio	450	OH		
Johnny Appleseed Area	453	OH	1926	1993
Licking County	451	OH	1922	1987
Mahoning Valley	466	OH	1927	1993
Miami Valley	444	OH	1949	
Mound Builder's Area	454	OH	1932	1985
Muskingum Valley	467	OH	1957	
Northeast Ohio	463	OH	1929	1993
Put-Han-Sen Area	449	OH	1930	1991
Scioto Area	457	OH	1931	1993
Shawnee	452	OH	1926	1991
Simon Kenton	441	OH		
Tecumseh	439	OH	1929	

Council Name	Council #	State	Yr.S	Yr.E
Toledo Area	460	OH	1928	
Western Reserve	461	OH	1948	1993
Arbuckle Area	468	OK	1945	
Black Beaver	471	OK	1930	
Cherokee Area Oklahoma	469	OK	1925	
Eastern Oklahoma	478	OK	1948	1983
Great Salt Plains	474	OK	1927	
Indian Nations	488	OK	1957	
Last Frontier	480	OK	1939	
Will Rogers	473	OK	1948	
Cascade Area	493	OR	1926	1992
Cascade Pacific	492	OR	1993	
Columbia Pacific	492	OR	1965	1992
Creater Lake	491	OR	1925	
Modoc Area	494	OR	1936	1993
Oregon Trail	697	OR	1944	
Panama Canal	801			1987
Allegheny Trails	527	PA	1967	1993
Bucks County	777	PA	1927	
Bucktail	509	PA	1930	
Chief Cornplanter	538	PA	1953	
Chester County	539	PA	1919	
Columbia-Montour	504	PA	1931	
East Valley Area	530	PA	1973	1993
Elk Lick	499	PA	1947	1973
Forest Lakes	501	PA	1962	1990
French Creek	532	PA	1972	
Greater Pittsburgh	527	PA	1993	
Hawk Mountain	528	PA	1971	
Juniata Valley	497	PA	1929	
Keystone Area	515	PA	1948	
Lancaster County	519	PA	1924	1970
Lancaster-Lebanon	524	PA	1995	
Lebanon County	650	PA	1924	1970
Minsi Trails	502	PA	1968	
Moraine Trails	500	PA	1973	

Council Name	Council #	State	Yr.S	Yr.E
Northeastern Pennsylvania	501	PA	1990	
Penn Mountains	522	PA	1969	1990
Penn's Woods	508	PA	1970	
Pennsylvania Dutch	524	PA		1995
Philadelphia	525	PA	1914	1996
Susquehanna	553	PA	1974	
Susquehanna Valley Area	533	PA	1927	1974
Valley Forge	507	PA	1936	1996
Washington Trails	511	PA	1944	1972
Westmoreland-Fayette	512	PA	1937	
York Adams Area	544	PA	1931	
Puerto Rico	661			
Narragansett	546	RI	1930	
Blue Ridge	551	SC	1932	
Central South Carolina	553	SC	1929	1978
Coastal Carolina	550	SC	1941	
Indian Waters	553	SC	1978	
Palmetto Area	549	SC	1935	
Pee Dee Area	552	SC	1928	
Black Hills Area	695	SD	1930	
Pheasant	693	SD	1942	1978
Sioux	733	SD	1927	
Cherokee Area	556	TN	1943	
Chickasaw	558	TN	1925	
Great Smoky Mountain	557	TN	1943	
Middle Tennessee	560	TN	1949	
Sequoyah	713	TN	1931	
West Tennessee Area	559	TN	1939	
Adobe Walls	569	TX	1938	1987
Alamo Area	583	TX	1925	
Bay Area	574	TX	1937	
Buffalo Trail	567	TX	1923	
Caddo Area	584	TX	1936	
Capitol Area	564	TX	1934	
Chisholm Trail	561	TX	1926	

Council Name	Council #	State	Yr.S	Yr.E
Circle Ten	571	TX	1928	
Comanche Trail	479	TX	1932	
Concho Valley	741	TX	1926	
East Texas Area	585	TX	1931	
Golden Spread	562	TX	1987	
Gulf Coast Texas	577	TX	1929	
Heart O'Texas	662	TX	1929	
Llano Estacado	562	TX	1939	1987
Longhorn	582	TX	1948	
Netseo Trails	580	TX	1955	
Northwest Texas	587	TX	1937	
Rio Grande	775	TX	1947	
Sam Houston Area	576	TX	1936	
South Plains	694	TX	1925	
Texoma Valley	566	TX	1966	1993
Three Rivers	578	TX	1970	
Yucca	573	TX	1937	
Cache Valley	588	UT	1924	1992
Great Salt Lake	590	UT	1951	
Lake Bonneville	589	UT	1951	1992
Trapper Trails	589	UT	1992	
Utah National Parks	591	UT	1936	
Virgin Islands	410			
Green Mountain	592	VT	1972	
Blue Ridge Mountains	599	VA	1972	
Colonial Virginia	595	VA	1992	
Old Dominion Area	601	VA	1927	1992
Peninsula	595	VA	1929	1992
Robert E. Lee	602	VA	1953	
Shenandoah Area	598	VA	1928	
Stonewall Jackson Area	763	VA	1927	
Tidewater	596	VA	1935	
Blue Mountain	604	WA	1923	
Chief Seattle	609	WA	1954	
Evergreen Area	606	WA	1941	1993

Council Name	Council #	State	Yr.S	Yr.E
Fort Simcoe	614	WA	1954	1992
Grand Columbia	614	WA	1992	
Inland Empire Washington	611	WA	1931	1987
Island Northwest	611	WA	1987	
Mount Baker Area	603	WA	1929	
Mount Rainier	612	WA	1948	1993
North Central Washington	613	WA	1924	1992
Olympic Area	605	WA		1974
Pacific Harbors	612	WA	1993	
Tumwater Area	737	WA	1934	1993
Twin Harbors Area	607	WA	1930	1993
Allohak	618	WV	1990	
Appalachian	701	WV	1956	1991
Buckskin	617	WV	1949	
Central West Virginia	616	WV	1941	1990
Chief Cornstalk	756	WV	1954	1990
Kootaga Area	618	WV	1933	1990
Mountaineer Area	615	WV	1928	
National Trail	619	WV	1966	1991
Ohio River Valley	619	WV	1991	
Tri-State Area	672	WV	1935	
Bay Lakes	635	WI	1973	
Chippewa Valley	637	WI	1928	
Four Lakes	628	WI	1929	
Gateway Area	624	WI	1925	
Milwaukee County	629	WI	1929	
Potawatomi Area	651	WI	1931	
Samoset	627	WI	1930	
Sinnissippi	626	WI	1966	
Southeast Wisconsin	634	WI	1972	
Central Wyoming	638	WY	1929	
Jim Bridger	639	WY	1946	1992

The Author's Vigil, time delayed, a self-portrait. Wischitschanquiwi Mawachpo Bambil Nenajunges Sukachsin Gock Alloquepi Tachpatamauwan Wikwam, which translates to mean "collector."

LODGE LISTINGS

Following is a listing of Order of the Arrow lodges, their council, number, and dates of existence. Lodges issue membership patches called "flaps," which are worn on the right pocket flap of the uniform shirt. They also issue event patches, anniversary patches, and neckerchiefs. These items are cataloged in the "Blue Book," and you should look there for further information.

No.	Lodge Name	Yr.	Council	ST	Notes
001	Unami	1915	Philadelphia	PA	Absorbed 8 in 1924.
002	Trenton	1919	Trenton-Mercer	NJ	Rechartered in 1920s. Changed name.
002	Sanhican	1920s	George Washington	NJ	
003	Pamunkey	1919	Richmond	VA	Rechartered in 1945. Changed name.
003	Nawakwa	1945	Robert E. Lee	VA	
004	Ranachqua	1920	Bronx	NY	
005	Indiandale	1921	Daniel Boone	PA	Changed name in 1920.
005	Minsi	1922	Daniel Boone	PA	Merged 1971 with 125 to form 5.
005	Kittatinny	1971	Hawk Mountain	PA	
006	Umpah	1921	Westmoreland-Fayette	PA	Rechartered in 1939.
006	Wagion	1939	Westmoreland-Fayette	PA	
007	Moqua	1922	Chicago	IL	Merged 1929 with 13, 21, 23, and 25 to form 7.
007	Owasippe	1929	Chicago	IL	From merger of 7, 13, 21, 23, and 25.
008	Unalactigo	1921	Philadephia Camp Biddle	PA	Absorbed into 1 in 1924.
008	Mascoutens	1972	Southeast Wisconsin	WI	From merger of 153 and 524.
009	Cowaw	1922	Raritan	NJ	Merged 1969 with 287 to form 9.
009	Narraticong	1969	Thomas E. Edison	NJ	From merger of 9 and 287.
010	Wawonaissa	1921	Central Union	NJ	Disbanded 1922.
010	Sassacus	1972	Indian Trails	CT	From merger of 297 and 388. Merged 1995 with 59.
010	Tschitani	1995	Connecticut Rivers	CT	From merger with 59.
011	Susquehannock	1922	Keystone Area	PA	
012	Nentico	1922	Baltimore Area	MD	
013	Wakay	1922	Chicago	IL	Merged 1929 with 7, 21, 23, and 25 to form 7.
013	Wiatava	1973	Orange County	CA	From merger of 298 and 430.

No.	Lodge Name	Yr.	Council	ST	Notes
014	Pamrapaugh	1921	Bayonne	NJ	Merged 1993 with 37 to form 14.
014	Mantowagan	1993	Hudson-Liberty	NJ	
015	Chappegat	1923	Siwanoy	NY	Merged 1957 with 47 to form 15.
015	Mide	1957	Hutchinson River	NY	Merged 1973 with 246 to form 15.
015	Ktemaque	1973	Westchester-Putnam	NY	
016	Tonkawampus	1924	Viking	MN	
017	Cuyahoga	1924	Greater Cleveland	OH	Disbanded 1920s. Rechartered 1950s.
018	Wyona	1925	Columbia-Montour	PA	
019	Buffalo	1925	Schenectady County	NY	Changed name in 1920s.
019	Sisilija	1925	Schenectady County	NY	Merged 1991 with 181 to form 19.
019	Ganienkeh	1992	Twin Rivers	NY	
020	Unalachtigo	1925	Del-Mar-Va	DE	Disbanded prior to 1936.
020	Nentego	1957	Del-Mar-Va	DE	
021	Sqechnaxen	1922	Chicago	IL	Changed name in 1920s.
021	Checaugau	1922	Chicago	IL	Merged 1929 with 7, 13, 23, and 25 to form 7.
021	Wulakamike	1973	Crossroads Of America	IN	From merger of 222, 308, and 512.
022	Octoraro	1926	Chester County	PA	
023	Blackhawk	1922	Chicago	IL	Merged 1929 with 7, 13, 21, and 25 to form 7.
023	Wenasa Quenhotan	1973	W.D. Boyce	IL	From merger of 63, 143, and 191.
024	Shu-Shu-Gah	1925?	GNY Brooklyn	NY	
025	Garrison	1922	Chicago	IL	Merged 1929 with 7, 13, 21, and 23 to form 7.
025	Nacha Tindey	1975	West Michigan Shores	MI	From merger of 79 and 401.
026	Blue Ox	1927	Gamehaven	MN	Absorbed 1946 part of 144. Disbanded 1950. Rechartered 1953.
027	Mohawks	1927	Columbia	NY	Disbanded prior to 1936. Absorbed 1944 into 181.
027	Pa-Hin	1976	Northern Lights	ND	From merger of 52, 176, 183, and 371.
028	Mohican	1927	Green	NY	Rechartered 1947 after previously disbanding. Changed name to Half Moon.
028	Half Moon	1927	Rip Van Winkle	NY	
029	Chippewa	1927	Clinton Valley	MI	

No.	Lodge Name	Yr.	Council	ST	Notes
030	Winingus	1927	General Sullivan	PA	Merged 1992 with 186 to form 30.
030	Tkaen Dod	1993	Five Rivers	NY	
031	Chemahgwa	1927	Central Minnesota	MN	Rechartered 1945 after previously disbanding. Changed name to Naguonabe.
031	Naguonabe	1927	Central Minnesota	MN	
032	Kitchawonk	1927	Yonkers	NY	Rechartered 1942 after previously disbanding. Changed name to Tahawus.
032	Tahawus	1927	Yonkers	NY	Absorbed 1955 into 246.
032	Kishkakon	1991	West	IL	From merger 1991 of 94 and 126.
033	Ajapeu	1927	Bucks County	PA	
034	Gonlix	1928	Madison County	NY	Merged 1968 with 500 to form 34.
034	Ko Mosh I Oni	1968	Iroquois	NY	Merged 1981 with 465 to form 34.
034	Ona Yote	1982	Land Of The Oneidas	NY	
035	Wichita	1928	Northwest Texas	TX	
036	Mitigwa	1928	Beaumont Area	TX	Changed name in 1950.
036	Meche	1928	Trinity-Neches	TX	Merged 1970 with 62 to form 578.
037	Achtu	1928	Hudson	NJ	Merged 1969 with 440 to form 37.
037	Elauwit	1969	Hudson-Hamilton	NJ	Merged 1993 with 14 to form 14.
037	Ka-Ti Missi Sipi	1995	Mississippi Valley	IL	From merger 1995 of 80 and 136.
038	Shaubena	1928	Wigwam	IL	Absorbed 45 in 1938. Changed name in 1941.
038	Inali	1928	Prairie	IL	Merged 1994 with 170 to form 38.
038	Konepaka Ketiwa	1994	Illowa	IA	
039	Swatara	1928	Lebanon County	PA	Merged 1972 with 519 to form 39.
039	Wunita Gokhos	1972	Lancaster-Lebanon	PA	
040	Ma-Ka-Ja-Wan	1929	Northest Illinois	IL	Absorbed 248 in 1969 and 215 in 1971.
041	Natokiokan	1929	Du Page Area	IL	Merged 1995 with 106 to form 41.
041	Lawaneu Allanque	1995	Three Fires	IL	
042	Osage	1929	Ozark Area	MO	Merged 1995 with 91 to form 42.
042	Wah-Sha-She	1995	Ozark Trails	MO	
043	Delmont	1929	Valley Forge	PA	
044	Pohopoco	1929	Lehigh County	PA	Merged 1969 with 58 and 476 to form 44.
044	Witauchsoman	1969	Minsi Trails	PA	
045	Pokawachne	1929	Kewanee Area	IL	Absorbed by 38 in 1938.

No.	Lodge Name	Yr.	Council	ST	Notes
045	Tiwahe	1992	Pacific	CA	From merger of 436 and part of 532.
046	Eriez	1929	Washington Trail	PA	Merged 1972 with 251 and 256 to form 46.
046	Langundowi	1972	French Creek	PA	
047	Hanigus	1930	Bronx Valley	NY	Merged 1957 with 15 to form 15.
047	Amangi Nacha	1993	Golden Empire	CA	From merger 1993 of 354, 395, and 485.
048	Wakpominee	1930	Mohican	NY	
049	Suanhacky	1930	GNY Queens	NY	
050	Cherokee	1930	Birmingham Area	AL	
051	Shawnee	1930	Greater St.Louis Area	MO	
052	Chan-O-Wapi	1930	Missouri Valley	ND	Merged 1976 with 176, 183, and 371 to form 27.
052	Moswetuset	1994	Boston Minuteman	MA	From merger 1994 of 195 and 261.
053	Mini Ska	1930	Cedar Valley	MN	Changed name after 1955.
053	Wapaha	1930	Cedar Valley	MN	Merged 1969 with 69 to form 53.
053	Midewiwin	1969	Twin Valley	MN	Changed name in 1975.
053	Wahpekute	1969	Twin Valley	MN	
054	Allemakewink	1930	Morris Sussex Area	NJ	
055	Waukheon	1930	Piankeshaw	IL	Merged 1994 with 92 to form 55.
055	Illini	1994	Prairielands	IL	
056	Okiciyapi	1930	Texoma Valley	TX	Disbanded 1930s. Reorganized 1949. Merged 1994 with 101 to form 101
056	Wapashuwi	1995	Greater Western Reserve	OH	From merger of 114, 368, and 396.
057	Kuwewanik	1931	Allegheny	PA	Merged 1966 with 242 to form 57.
057	Kiasutha	1967	Allegheny Trails	PA	Merged 1993 with 67 to form 57.
057	Enda Lechauhanne	1993	Greater Pittsburgh	PA	
058	Kittatinny	1931	Delaware Valley	PA	Rechartered 1948 after previously disbanding.
058	Ah-Pace	1931	Delaware Valley	PA	Merged 1969 with 44 and 476 to form 44.
058	Ut-In Selica	1994	Mount Diablo-Silverado	CA	From merger of 263 and 468.
059	Wahquimacut	1931	Middlesex	CT	Rechartered 1957 after previously disbanding.
059	Kiehtan	1931	Middlesex County	CT	Merged 1973 with 217, 234, 491, and 558 to form 59.

No.	Lodge Name	Yr.	Council	ST	Notes
059	Eluwak	1973	Long Rivers	CT	Merged 1995 with 10 to form 10.
060	Aina Topa Hutsi	1931	Alamo Area	TX	
061	Shaginappi	1932	Badger	WI	Merged 1974 with 73, 194, 233, 244, and 501 to form 61.
061	Awase	1974	Bay Lakes	WI	
062	Sioux	1932	Sabine Area	TX	Merged 1970 with 36 to form 578.
062	Talligewi	1995	Lincoln Heritage	KY	From merger 1995 of 65 and 123.
063	Potawatomie	1932	Corn Belt	IL	Merged 1973 with 143 and 191 to form 23.
063	Ohlone	1995	Pacific Skyline	CA	From merger 1995 of 207 and 528.
064	Skanondo	1932	Hudson-Delaware	NY	Merged 1995 with 443 and 444.
065	Tseyedin	1932	George Rogers Clark	IN	Merged 1994 with 123 to form 62.
065	Tecumseh	1996	Simon Kenton	OH	From merger of 93, 109, and 350.
066	Yah-Tah-Ney-Si-Kess	1933	Northern New Mexico	NM	Changed name in 1962.
066	Yah-Tah-Hey-Si-Kess	1933	Great Southwest Area	NM	
067	Anicus	1933	East Boroughs	PA	Merged 1973 with 130 to form 67.
067	Tanacharison	1973	East Valley Area	PA	Merged 1993 with 57.
068	Watchung	1933	Watchung Area	NJ	Changed name in 1939.
068	Miquin	1933	Watchung Area	NJ	Absorbed 431 in 1980.
069	Tribe Of Mazasha	1933	Minnesota Valley Area	MN	Changed name in 1944.
069	Mazasha	1933	Minnesota Valley Area	MN	Merged 1969 with 53 to form 53.
070	Tali Taktaki	1933	General Greene	NC	Merged 1992 with 208 to form 70.
070	Keyauwee	1992	Old North State	NC	Merged 1994 with 163 to form 70.
070	Tsoiatsi Tsogali'i	1995	Old North State	NC	
071	Ohowa	1933	Monmouth-Ocean	NJ	Reorganized 1950 after previous lapse. Changed name.
071	Na-Tasi-Hi	1951	Monmouth	NJ	Changed name in 1953.
071	Na-Tsi-Hi	1951	Monmouth	NJ	
072	Tejas	1934	East Texas Area	TX	
073	Ay-Ashe	1934	Manitowoc	WI	Changed name in 1937.
073	Sinawa	1934	Waumegesako	WI	Merged 1974 with 61, 194, 233, 244, and 501 to form 61.
074	Timmeu	1934	Northeast Iowa	IA	
075	Miami	1935	Anthony Wayne Area	IN	Changed name in 1938.
075	Kiskakon	1935	Anthony Wayne Area	IN	Absorbed 1973 half of 142.

No.	Lodge Name	Yr.	Council	ST	Notes
076	Hunnikick	1935	Burlington County	NJ	
077	Lekau	1935	Camden County	NJ	
078	Antelope	1935	Eastern New Mexico	NM	Changed name after 1955.
078	Kwahadi	1935	Conquistador	NM	
079	Jibshe-Wanagan	1935	Grand Valley	MI	Merged 1975 with 401 to form 25.
080	Silver Tomahawk	1935	Southeast Iowa	IA	Merged 1995 with 136 to form 37.
081	Mannaseh	1935	Mississippi Valley	IL	Merged 1966 with 115 to form 81.
081	Taleka	1966	Okaw Valley	IL	
082	Man-A-Hattin	1936	GNY Manhattan	NY	
083	Allogagan	1936	Valley	MA	Absorbed 277 in 1960.
084	Tamarack	1936	Tamarack	NJ	Changed name in 1950.
084	Wakanta	1936	Tamarack	NJ	Disbanded 1986. Absorbed by 178 and 484.
085	Kiondashama	1936	Tampa Bay	FL	Changed name in 1938.
085	Seminole	1936	Gulf Ridge	FL	
086	Wiccopee	1936	Hendrick-Hudson	NY	Merged 1951 with 246 to form 246.
087	Bob White	1936	Georgia-Carolina	GA	
088	Munhacke	1936	Portage Trails	MI	Merged 1973 with 332 to form 88.
088	Allohak	1973	Wolverine	MI	Merged 1994 with 206 to form 88.
088	Manitous	1995	Great Sauk Trail	MI	
089	Kepayshowink	1936	Saginaw Bay Area	MI	Absorbed 214 in 1961. Merged 1972 with 469 to form 89.
089	Mischigonong	1972	Lake Huron Area	MI	
090	Canalino	1936	Mission	CA	Merged 1996 with 304 to form 90.
090	Chumash	1996	Los Padres	CA	
091	Nik-Ka-Ga-Hah	1936	Mo-Kan	MO	Merged 1995 with 42 to form 42.
092	Illini	1936	Arrowhead	IL	Merged 1994 with 55 to form 55.
093	Katinonkwat	1936	Central Ohio	OH	Absorbed 420 in 1987. Merged 1996 with 109 and 350 to form 65.
094	Blackhawk	1936	Piasa Bird	IL	Merged 1990 with 126 to form 32.
094	Tatanka-Anpetu-Wi	1994	Overland Trails	NE	From merger 1994 of 510 and 517.
095	Ty-Ohni	1936	Otetiana	NY	
096	Tesomas	1936	Samoset	WI	Changed name in 1939.
096	Tom Kita Chara	1936	Samoset	WI	
097	Cha-Pa	1936	Southwest Iowa	IA	Merged 1965 with 445 to form 97.
097	Kit-Ke-Hak-O-Kut	1965	Mid-America	NE	

No.	Lodge Name	Yr.	Council	ST	Notes
098	Navajo	1937	Old Baldy	CA	
099	Te Jas	1937	Capitol Area	TX	Changed name in 1940.
099	Tonkawa	1937	Capitol Area	TX	
100	Jonito-Otora	1937	Southeast Missouri	MO	Rechartered 1956 after previously disbanding with a name change.
100	Anpetu-we	1937	Southeast Missouri	MO	Absorbed 240 in 1994. Merged 1995 with 51.
101	Mikanakawa	1937	Circle Ten	TX	Absorbed 209 in 1948. Merged with 56 in 1994.
102	Mirimichi	1937	Mount Whitney	CA	Merged 1994 with 548 to form 195.
103	Juniata	1937	Juniata Valley	PA	Changed name in 1941.
103	Monaken	1937	Juniata Valley	PA	
104	Occoneechee	1937	Occoneechee	NC	
105	Tetonwana	1937	Sioux	SD	Absorbed 460 in 1978.
106	Wiyapunit	1938	Aurora Area	IL	Merged 1968 with 120 to form 106.
106	Kishagamie	1968	Kedeka Area	IL	Merged 1971 with 279 to form 106.
106	Glikhikan	1971	Two Rivers	IL	Merged 1995 with 41 to form 41.
107	Kon-Kon-Tu	1938	South Jersey	NJ	Merged 1967 with 411 to form 107.
107	Apatukwe	1967	Southern New Jersey	NJ	
108	Mesquakie	1938	Wapsipinicon Area	IA	Changed name in 1943.
108	Wakosha	1938	Wapsipinicon Area	IA	Merged 1972 with 473 to form 108.
108	Sac-N-Fox	1972	Winnebago	IA	
109	Shawnee	1938	Scioto Area	OH	Changed name in 1939. Merged 1996 with 93 and 350 to form 65.
109	Scioto	1938	Scioto Area	OH	Changed name in 1950.
109	Shawnee	1938	Scioto Area	OH	
110	Nisaki	1938	Pokagon	IN	Changed name before 1940.
110	Pokagon	1938	Pokagon Trails	IN	Absorbed 122 in 1944. Merged 1965 with 189 to form 110.
110	Michigamea	1965	Calumet	IN	Absorbed 352 in 1972.
111	Wa-Hi-Nasa	1938	Middle Tennessee	TN	
112	Aquehongian	1938	GNY Staten Island	NY	
113	Wihinipa Hinsa	1938	Bay Area	TX	
114	Stigwandish	1938	Northeast Ohio	OH	Merged 1995 with 368 and 396 to form 56.
115	Ellini	1938	Kaskaskia	IL	Changed name in 1938.
115	Cascasquia	1938	Kaskaskia	IL	Merged 1966 with 81 to form 81.

No.	Lodge Name	Yr.	Council	ST	Notes
116	Cherokee	1938	Pee Dee Area	SC	Name not accepted; Lodge 50 had name.
116	Santee	1938	Pee Dee Area	SC	Rechartered 1953 after previously disbanding twice.
117	Croatan	1938	East Carolina	NC	
118	Wahissa	1938	Old Hickory	NC	
119	Toma Chi-Chi	1938	Costal Empire	GA	
120	Chief Shabbona	1938	Chief Shabbona	IL	Changed name in 1963.
120	Ne Con Che Moka	1938	Chief Shabbona	IL	Merged 1968 with 106 to form 106.
120	Gosh Wha Gono	1982	Seaway Valley	NY	From merger of 461 and 357.
121	Wyandota	1938	Harding Area	OH	Merged 1996 with 205 and 513 to form 619.
122	Potawattomi	1938	Potawattomi Trails	IL	Absorbed by 110 in 1944.
123	Zit-Kala-Sha	1938	Old Kentucky Home	KY	Merged 1995 with 65 to form 62.
124	Noquochoke	1938	Massasoit	MA	Merged 1972 with 509 to form 124.
124	Neemat	1972	Moby Dick	MA	
125	Memeu	1938	Appalachian Trail	PA	Merged 1971 with 5 to form 5.
126	Cahokia	1938	Cahokia Mound	IL	Merged 1991 with 94 to form 32.
127	Tahquitz	1938	Riverside County	CA	Merged 1973 with 478 to form 127.
127	Cahuilla	1973	California Inland Empire	CA	Absorbed 380 in 1976.
128	Kickapoo	1938	Wabash Valley	IN	
129	Broad-Winged Hawk	1938	Atlanta Area	GA	Changed name in 1950.
129	Egwa Tawa Dee	1938	Atlanta Area	GA	
130	Sagamore	1938	Monongahela Valley	PA	Merged 1971 with 497 to form 130.
130	Scarouady	1938	Mon-Yough	PA	Merged 1973 with 67 to form 67.
131	Kahagon	1938	Cambridge	MA	
132	Illinek	1938	Abraham Lincoln	IL	
133	Ma-Nu	1938	Last Frontier	OK	
134	Tsali	1938	Daniel Boone	NC	
135	Achunanchi	1938	Choccolocco	AL	
136	Maheengun	1938	Saukee Area	IL	Merged 1995 with 80 to form 37.
137	Coloneh	1938	San Houston	TX	Name corrected in 1950.
137	Colonneh	1938	San Houston Area	TX	
138	Yaqui	1938	Tulsa	OK	Merged 1957 with 154 to form 138.
138	Daw-zu	1957	Indian Nations	OK	Changed name in 1959.

No.	Lodge Name	Yr.	Council	ST	Notes
138	Ta Tsu Hwa	1957	Indian Nations	OK	Absorbed 320 in 1973. Absorbed 328 in 1983.
139	Ah-tic	1938	Bucktail	PA	
140	Blackhawk	1939	Blackhawk Area	IL	Changed name in 1941. Merged 1970 with 227 to form 140.
140	Ma-Ka-Tai-Me-She-Kia-Kiak	1939	Blackhawk Area	IL	
140	Wulapeju	1970	Blackhawk Area	IL	
141	Tatanka	1939	Buffalo Trail	TX	
142	Papakitchie	1939	Pioneer Trails	IN	Half merged 1973 with 182 and 452 to form 573.
143	Kinebo	1939	Starved Rock Area	IL	Changed name in 1950.
143	Nee-Schoock	1939	Starved Rock Area	IL	Merged 1973 with 63 and 191 to form 23.
144	Tsun-Ga'Ni	1939	South Central Minnesota Area	MN	Part absorbed by 26 and 257 in 1946.
145	Nachenum	1939	Mound Builders Area	OH	Merged 1985 with 462 to form 145.
145	Ku-Ni-Eh	1985	Dan Beard	OH	
146	Tichora	1939	Four Lakes	WI	
147	Tamegonit	1939	Heart Of America	MO	Absorbed Tribe of Micosay in 1973.
148	Inola	1939	Will Rogers	OK	Absorbed 283 in 1948.
149	Caddo	1939	Norwela	LA	
150	Nakona	1939	South Plains	TX	
151	Marnoc	1939	Great Trail	OH	
152	Indian Drum	1939	Scenic Trails	MI	
153	Oh-Da-Ko-Ta	1939	Kenosha County	WI	Merged 1972 with 524 to form 8.
154	Checote	1939	Creek Nation	OK	Merged 1957 with 138 to form 138.
155	Nipperine	1939	Northern Kentucky	KY	Rechartered 1953 after previously disbanding. Changed name.
155	Michikinaqua	1939	Northern Kentucky	KY	Absorbed into 462 in 1956.
155	Nisqually	1995	Pacific Harbors	WA	From merger 1995 with 285, 348, and 392.
156	Northwoods Circle	1939	Copper Country Area	MI	Merged 1945 with 198 and 250 to form 156.
156	Ag-Im	1945	Hiawathaland	MI	
157	Delevan	1939	West Suburban	IL	Changed name in 1948.
157	Leekwinai	1939	West Suburban	IL	Merged 1994 with 334 to form 246.
158	Winnepurkit	1939	Bay Shore	MA	Absorbed by 505 in 1965.

No.	Lodge Name	Yr.	Council	ST	Notes
158	Nanepashemet	1993	Yankee Clipper	MA	From merger 1993 with 490, 505, and 539.
159	Ganosote	1939	Buffalo Area	NY	Merged 1966 with 284 to form 159.
159	Ho-De-No-Sau-Nee	1966	Greater Niagara Frontier	NY	
160	Quapaw	1939	Quapaw Area	AR	
161	Ne-Pah-Win	1939	Piedmont Area	VA	Changed name after 1955.
161	Koo Koo Ku Hoo	1939	Piedmont Area	VA	Merged 1972 with 456 to form 161.
161	Tutelo	1972	Blue Ridge Mountains	VA	
162	Mi-Gi-Si O-Paw-Gan	1939	Detroit Area	MI	
163	Tslagi	1939	Cherokee	NC	Changed spelling of name 1987.
163	Tsalagi	1939	Cherokee	NC	Merged 1994 with 70 to form 70.
164	Doog Gni Tuocs	1939	Old Colony	MA	Changed name before 1951.
164	Manomet	1939	Old Colony	MA	Merged 1969 with 518 to form 164.
164	Tisquantum	1969	Old Colony	MA	
165	Chautauqua	1939	Chautauqua	NY	Absorbed 187 in 1942. Merged 1973 with 455 to form 165.
165	Ho-Nan-Ne-Ho-Ont	1973	Allegheny Highlands	NY	Absorbed 547 in 1975.
166	Calcasieu	1939	Calcasieu	LA	Recharted 1952 after previously disbanding. Changed name.
166	Quelqueshoe	1939	Calcasieu	LA	
167	Woapink	1939	Ambraw Wabash	IL	Disbanded 1955 when council divided.
167	Woapink	1957	Lincoln Trails	IL	
168	Unalachtigo	1939	Pioneer Trails	PA	Merged 1973 with 419 to form 168.
168	Kuskitannee	1973	Moraine Trails	PA	
169	Pushmataha	1939	Pushmataha Area	MS	Changed name between 1943 and 1951.
169	Watonala	1939	Pushmataha Area	MS	
170	Khu-Ku-Koo-Huu	1939	Moline Area	IL	Merged 1959 with 504 to form 170.
170	Wisaka	1959	Sac N Fox	IL	Merged 1967 with 313 to form 170.
170	Muc-Kis-Sou	1967	Illowa	IA	Merged 1994 with 38 to form 38.
171	Nasupa Tanka	1939	BlackHills Area	SD	Rechartered 1955 after previously disbanding. Changed name.
171	Crazy Horse	1939	Black Hills Area	SD	Changed name in 1982.
171	Tashunka Witco	1939	Black Hills Area	SD	Changed spelling of name in 1984.
171	Tasunka Witco	1939	Black Hills Area	SD	Changed name in 1988.
171	Crazy Horse	1939	Black Hills Area	SD	

No.	Lodge Name	Yr.	Council	ST	Notes
172	Kiamesha	1940	Susquenango	NY	Changed name prior to 1950.
172	Otahnagon	1940	Susquenango	NY	
173	Ojibwa	1940	Harrison Trails	IN	Merged 1973 with 269 and 425 to form 173.
173	Takachsin	1973	Sagamore	IN	
174	Nagadjiwanang	1940	Gitche Gumee	WI	Absorbed 1959 by 526.
175	Lakota	1940	Northwest Suburban	IL	
176	Minniduta	1940	Red River Valley	ND	Merged 1976 with 52, 183, and 371 to form 27.
177	Victorio	1940	Cochise	AZ	Absorbed by 494 in 1965.
178	Mohican	1940	Robert Treat	NJ	Merged 1976 with 362 and 515 to form 178.
178	Meechgalanne	1976	Essex	NJ	Absorbed part of 84 in 1985.
179	Alabama	1940	Montgomery	AL	Changed name in 1949.
179	Alabamu	1940	Tukabatchee Area	AL	
180	Chickagami	1940	Blue Water	MI	
181	Mahikan	1940	Fort Orange	NY	Merged 1963 with 267 to form 181.
181	Nischa-Nimat	1963	Governor Clinton	NY	Merged 1990 with 268 and 418 to form 181.
181	Ganienkeh	1990	Twin Rivers	NY	Merged 1991 with 19 to form 19.
182	Lone Wolf	1940	St. Joseph Valley	IN	Merged 1952 with 314 to form 182.
182	White Beaver	1952	Tri-Valley	IN	Merged 1972 with part of 142 and 452 to form 573.
183	Chatoka	1940	Great Plains Area	ND	Merged 1976 with 52, 176, and 371 to form 27.
184	Sequoyah	1940	Sequoyah	TN	
185	Atta Kulla Kulla	1940	Blue Ridge	SC	
186	Wakanda	1940	Steuben Area	NY	Merged 1990 with 394 to form 186.
186	Tkaen Dod	1990	Five Rivers	NY	Merged 1993 with 30 to form 30.
187	Sah-Dah-Gey-Ah	1940	Lake Shore	NY	Absorbed by 165 in 1942.
188	Iti Bapishe Iti Hollo	1940	Central North Carolina	NC	
189	Oposa Achomawi	1940	Sauk Trails	IN	Merged 1965 with 110 to form 110.
190	Wisawanik	1940	Arbuckle Area	OK	
191	Kashapiwigamak	1940	Creve Coeur	IL	Merged 1973 with 63 and 143 to form 23.
191	Lowwapaneu	1991	Northeastern Pennsylvania	PA	From merger of 223 and 542 in 1991.
192	Shawnee	1941	Canadian Valley Araea	OK	Absorbed by 133 in 1949.

No.	Lodge Name	Yr.	Council	ST	Notes
193	Choctaw	1941	Choctaw Area	MS	Changed name after 1955.
193	Ashwanchi Kinta	1941	Choctaw Area	MS	
194	Chequah	1941	Nicolet Area	WI	Merged 1974 with 61, 73, 233, 244, and 501 to form 61.
194	Orca	1994	Redwood Empire	CA	From 1994 merger of 262 and 537.
195	Ma-Ta-Cam	1941	Greater Boston	MA	No records exist that 195 ever charted under this name.
195	King Philip	1941	Greater Boston	MA	Absorbed 370 in 1965. Merged 1993 with 261 to form 52.
195	Tah Heetch	1995	Sequoia	CA	From merger of 102 and 548 in 1995.
196	Little Bear	1941	Headwaters Area	MN	Recharted 1953 after previously disbanding. Changed name.
196	Mesabi	1941	Headwaters Area	MN	Merged 1995 with 526 to form 196.
196	Ka'Niss Ma'Ingan	1995	Voyageurs	MN	
197	Waupecan	1941	Rainbow	IL	
198	Ottawa	1941	Iron Range	MI	Merged 1945 with 156 and 250 to form 156.
199	Wahinkto	1941	Concho Valley	TX	
200	Echockotee	1941	North Florida	FL	
201	Kootaga	1941	Kootaga Area	WV	Merged 1990 with 527 to form 618.
201	White Horse	1996	Shawnee Trails	KY	From merger of 367 and 499 in 1996.
202	Chicksa	1941	Yocona Area	MS	
203	Wakazoo	1941	Fruit Belt Area	MI	Merged 1973 with 315 and 373 to form 373.
204	Chattahoochee	1941	Chattahoochee	GA	Absorbed 333 in 1963. Absorbed 273 in 1990.
205	Hilo-Hos-Kula	1941	Firelands Area	OH	Rechartered 1955 after previously disbanding. Changed name.
205	Notowacy	1941	Firelands Area	OH	Inactive 1960–71 then rechartered. Merged 1996 with 121 and 513 to form 619.
206	Teetonkah	1941	Land O Lakes	MI	Merged 1994 with 88 to form 88.
207	Stanford	1941	Stanford Area	CA	Changed name c.1948.
207	Stanford-Oljato	1941	Stanford Area	CA	Merged 1995 with 528 to form 63.
208	Uwharrie	1941	Uwharrie	NC	Merged 1992 with 70 to form 70.
209	Texoma	1941	Red River Valley	TX	Absorbed by 101 in 1947.
210	Blaknik	1941	Logan-Boone-Mingo	WV	Changed name in 1954.
210	Adjudimo	1941	Chief Cornstalk	WV	Merged 1993 with 416 and 475 to form 617.

No.	Lodge Name	Yr.	Council	ST	Notes
211	Pamola	1941	Katahdin	ME	Rechartered 1955 after disbanding in 1951.
212	So-Aka-Gha-Gwa	1941	White River	IN	Merged 1974 with 290 to form 212.
212	Nischa Chuppecat	1974	Hoosier Trails	IN	
213	Thunderbird	1941	Great Salt Plains	OK	Changed name in 1948.
213	Coyote	1941	Great Salt Plains	OK	Changed name after 1955.
213	Ah-Ska	1941	Great Salt Plains	OK	
214	Gimogash	1942	Summer Trails	MI	Changed name after 1947.
214	Tom-Tom	1942	Summer Trails	MI	Changed name back before 1953.
214	Gimogash	1942	Summer Trails	MI	Inactive. Absorbed by 89 in 1961.
215	Noo-Ti-Mis Oh'ke	1942	Oak Plain	IL	Absorbed by 40 in 1972.
216	Metab	1942	Lake Of The Ozarks	MO	Merged 1972 with 426 to form 216.
216	Nampa-Tsi	1972	Great Rivers	MO	
217	Mattatuck	1942	Mattatuck	CT	Merged 1973 with 59, 234, 491, and 558 to form 59.
218	Cuwe	1942	Tall Pine	MI	
219	Calusa	1942	Sunny Land	FL	Disbanded 1956. Rechartered 1961 as 552.
220	Passaconaway	1942	Daniel Webster	NH	
221	Muscogee	1942	Indian Waters	SC	
222	Kikthawenund	1942	Kikthawenund	IN	Merged 1973 with 308 and 512 to form 21.
223	Acahela	1942	Wyoming Valley	PA	Merged 1969 with 316 to form 223.
223	Gischigin	1969	Penn Mountains	PA	Changed name in 1985.
223	Acahela	1969	Penn Mountains	PA	
224	Cowikee	1942	Alabama-Florida	AL	
225	Tamet	1942	Crescent Bay Area	CA	Merged 1972 with 228 to form 566.
226	Potawatomi	1942	State Line	WI	Changed name in 1942.
226	Ka'Katowi Meshe-Ka	1942	State Line	WI	Changed name around 1950.
226	Maunguzet	1942	State Line	WI	Changed name sometime after 1955.
226	Manquzet	1942	State Line	WI	Merged 1965 with 302 to form 226.
226	Chemokemon	1965	Sinnissippi	WI	
227	Wetassa	1942	U.S. Grant	IL	Merged 1970 with 140 to form 140.
228	Walika	1942	San Fernando Valley	CA	Merged 1972 with 225 to form 566.
229	Chippewa	1943	Okefenokee Area	GA	Changed name in 1943.
229	Chawtaw	1943	Okefenokee Area	GA	Changed name around 1950.

No.	Lodge Name	Yr.	Council	ST	Notes
229	Pilthlako	1943	Okefenokee Area	GA	
230	Pelissippi	1943	Great Smokey Mountains	TN	
231	Mikano	1943	Milwaukee County	WI	
232	Akela Wahinapay	1943	Caddo Area	TX	
233	Wa-Zi-Ya-Ta	1943	Valley	WI	Merged 1974 with 61, 73, 194, 244, and 501 to form 61.
234	Keemosahbee	1943	Keemosahbee	CT	Merged 1968 with 471 to form 234.
234	Wihungen	1968	Nathan Hale	CT	Merged 1973 with 59, 217, 491, and 558 to form 59.
235	Ittawamba	1943	West Tennessee Area	TN	
236	Un A Li'yi	1943	Coastal Carolina	SC	
237	Aal-Pa-Tah	1943	Gulf Stream	FL	
238	Meshepeske	1943	Shawnee	OH	Changed name in 1950.
238	Ketchikeniqua	1943	Shawnee	OH	Merged 1994 with 382 to form 449.
239	Suriarco	1943	Suwanee River Area	FL	Changed name in 1948.
239	Semialachee	1943	Suwanee River Area	FL	
240	Ney-A-Ti	1943	Egyptian	IL	Absorbed by 100 in 1994.
241	Tomahawk	1943	Lonesome Pine	KY	Changed name sometime after 1955.
241	Tomahaken		Lonesome Pine	KY	Absorbed by 480 in 1979.
242	Chimalus	1943	Washington Greene	PA	Merged 1967 with 57 to form 57.
243	Mowogo	1943	Northeast Georgia	GA	
244	Day Noomp	1943	Twin Lakes	WI	Merged 1974 with 61, 73, 194, 233, and 501 to form 61.
245	Tulpe	1943	Annawon	MA	
246	Wakoda	1943	Fennimore Cooper	NY	Merged 1951 with 86 to form 246.
246	Apachedotte	1951	Washington Irving	NY	Merged 1955 with 32 to form 246.
246	Horicon	1955	Washington Irving	NY	Merged 1973 with 15 to form 15.
246	Pachsegink	1994	Des Plaines Valley	IL	From merger of 157 and 334 in 1994.
247	Tahgajute	1943	Cayuga County	NY	
248	Wabaningo	1943	Evanston	IL	Absorbed by 40 in 1969.
249	Spe-Le-Yei	1943	Verdugo Hills	CA	
250	Minnewasco	1943	Chippewa Area	MI	Merged 1945 with 156 and 198 to form 156.
251	Hoh-Squa-Sa-Gah-Da	1943	Mercer Country	PA	Merged 1972 with 46 and 256 to form 46.
252	Siwinis	1944	Los Angeles Area	CA	

No.	Lodge Name	Yr.	Council	ST	Notes
253	Tsisqan	1944	Oregon Trail	OR	
254	Comanche	1944	Ouachita Valley	LA	
255	Cornplanter	1944	Warren County	PA	Rechartered about 1954 after possibly disbanding. Changed name about 1954.
255	Chief Cornplanter	1944	Chief Cornplanter	PA	Changed name in 1960.
255	Gyantwachia	1960	Chief Cornplanter	PA	
256	Deer Rock	1944	Colonel Drake	PA	Changed name after 1955.
256	Skanondo Inyan	1944	Colonel Drake	PA	Merged 1972 with 46 and 251 to form 46.
257	Agaming	1944	Indianhead	MN	Absorbed part of 144 in 1946.
258	Shenandoah	1944	Stonewall Jackson Area	VA	
259	Cole Snass Lamatai	1944	Cascade Area	OR	Merged 1994 with 442 to form 442.
260	Sebooney Okasucca	1944	Andrew Jackson	MS	
261	Missituck	1944	Fellsland	MA	Merged 1958 with 447 and 496 to form 261.
261	Taskiagi	1958	Minuteman	MA	Merged 1994 with 195 to form 52.
262	Mow-A-Toc	1944	Redwood Area	CA	Merged 1994 with 537 to form 194.
263	Swegedaigea	1944	Silverado Area	CA	Merged 1993 with 468 to form 58.
264	Attakapas	1944	Attakapas	LA	Changed name in 1949.
264	Osouiga	1944	Attakapas	LA	Changed name in 1952.
264	Ouxouiga	1944	Attakapas	LA	
265	O-Shot-Caw	1944	South Florida	FL	
266	Thunder City	1944	Ore-Ida	ID	Changed name in 1959.
266	In-Mut-Too-Yah-Lat-Lat	1944	Ore-Ida	ID	Merged 1967 with 365 to form 266.
266	Tukarica	1968	Ore-Ida	ID	
267	Mohawk	1944	Uncle San	NY	Merged 1963 with 181 to form 181.
268	Ta-Oun-Ya-Wat-Ha	1944	Saratoga County	NY	Merged 1990 with 181 and 418 to form 181.
269	Akonequa	1944	Meshingomeshia	IN	Changed name around 1950.
269	Me-She-Kin-No-Quah	1944	Meshingomeshia	IN	Merged 1973 with 173 and 425 to form 173.
270	Skyuka	1944	Palmetto Area	SC	
271	Madockawanda	1944	Pine Tree	ME	
272	Wewanoma	1944	Rio Grande	TX	
273	Wehadkee	1944	George H. Lanier	GA	Disbanded 1965. Rechartered 1972. Absorbed by 204 in 1990.

No.	Lodge Name	Yr.	Council	ST	Notes
274	Wangunks	1944	Central Connecticut	CT	Absorbed by 369 in 1978.
275	Monachgeu	1944	William Penn	PA	Rechartered 1954 after previously disbanding. Changed name in 1954.
275	Hopocan	1944	William Penn	PA	Merged 1971 with 347 and 441 to form 275.
275	Nachamawat	1971	Penn's Woods	PA	
276	Shenshawpotoo	1944	Shenandoah Area	VA	
277	Nonotuck	1944	Holyoke Area	MA	Changed name in 1950.
277	Apinakwi Pita	1944	Mount Tom	MA	Absorbed by 83 in 1960.
278	Yo-Se-Mite	1944	Yosemite Area	CA	
279	Nawakwa	1944	Elgin area	IL	Changed name before 1953.
279	Consoke	1944	Fox River Valley	IL	Merged 1971 with 106 to form 106.
280	Wag-O-Shad	1944	Potawatomi	WI	
281	Black Beaver	1945	Black Beaver	OK	Changed name prior to 1960.
281	Sekettummaqua	1945	Black Beaver	OK	
282	Royaneh	1945	San Francisco	CA	Merged 1965 with 375 to form 282.
282	Achewon Nimat	1965	San Francisco Bay Area	CA	
283	Cimeroon	1945	Cimarron Valley Area	OK	Absorbed by 148 in 1948.
284	Tuscarora	1945	Niagara Frontier	NY	Merged 1966 with 159 to form 159.
285	Kcumkum	1945	Twin Harbors Area	WA	Merged 1994 with 348 and 392 to form 155.
286	Iaopogh	1945	Ridgewood-Glen Rock	NJ	
287	Kit-Chee-Ke-Ma	1945	Middlesex	NJ	Changed name in 1948.
287	Sakawawin	1945	Middlesex	NJ	Merged 1970 with 9 to form 9.
288	Washita	1945	Cherokee Area	OK	
289	Papoukewis	1945	Fort Steuben Area	OH	Merged 1993 with 323 to form 36.
290	Wazi Yata	1945	Hoosier Hills Area	IN	Merged 1974 with 212 to form 212.
291	Topa Topa	1945	Ventura County	CA	
292	Tarhe	1945	Tecumseh	OH	
293	Chickamauga	1945	Cherokee Area	TN	Rechartered 1957 after previously disbanding. Changed name.
293	Talidandaganu'	1945	Cherokee Area	TN	
294	Kamargo	1945	General Herkimer	NY	
295	Otena	1945	Comanche Trail	TX	
296	Nayawin Rar	1945	Tuscarora	NC	
297	Uncas	1945	Eastern Connecticut	CT	Merged 1972 with 388 to form 10.

No.	Lodge Name	Yr.	Council	ST	Notes
298	Gorgonia	1945	Orange Empire Area	CA	Changed name about 1948.
298	San Gorgonio	1945	Orange Empire Area	CA	Merged 1972 with 430 to form 13.
299	Nez Perce	1945	Vigilante	MT	Merged 1974 with 300, 361, and 390 to form 300.
300	Peta	1945	North Central Montana	MT	Merged 1974 with 299, 361, and 390 to form 300.
300	Apoxky Aio	1974	Montana	MT	
301	Moskwa	1945	Fort Simcoe Area	WA	Merged 1992 with 335 to form 614.
302	Koshkonong	1945	Indian Trails	WI	Merged 1965 with 226 to form 226.
303	Yowlumne	1945	Southern Sierra	CA	
304	Cayucos	1945	Santa Lucia Area	CA	Rechartered after previously disbanding. Changed name after 1955.
304	Miwok	1945	Santa Lucia Area	CA	Rechartered 1962 after disbanding. Changed name.
304	Chumash	1945	Santa Lucia Area	CA	Merged 1996 with 90 to form 90.
305	Kelcema	1945	Evergreen Area	WA	Merged 1995 with 325 to form 338.
306	Michi-Kina-Kwa	1945	Fort Hamilton	OH	Absorbed by 462 in 1959.
307	Karankawa	1945	Gulf Coast	TX	
308	Wahpinachi	1945	Whitewater Valley	IN	Merged 1973 with 222 and 512 to form 21.
309	Tsutsusid	1945	Wachusett	MA	Merged 1964 with 319 to form 309.
309	Quanopin	1964	Nashua Valley	MA	Merged 1994 with 329 to form 309.
309	Grand Monadnock	1994	Nashua Valley	MA	
310	Kaskanampo	1945	Tennesse Valley	AL	
311	Koo Ben Sho	1945	Idaho Pan Handle	ID	Changed name in 1962.
311	Sel Koo Sho	1945	Idaho Pan Handle	ID	Merged 1994 with 415 to form 311.
311	Es Kaielgu	1994	Inland Northwest	WA	
312	Sinawava	1945	Boulder Dam Area	NV	Disbanded 1950. Changed name when rechartered in 1955.
312	Nebagamon	1945	Boulder Dam Area	NV	
313	Bison	1945	Buffalo Bill	IA	Disbanded 1952. Changed name when rechartered in 1955.
313	Golden Eagle	1945	Buffalo Bill Area	IA	Absorbed 376 in 1959. Merged 1967 with 170 to form 170.
313	Tankiteke	1973	Fairfield County	CT	From merger of 389, 408, and 521 in 1973.
314	Mishawaka	1945	Mishawaka	IN	Merged 1952 with 182 to form 182.
315	Mandoka	1945	Nottawa Trails	MI	Merged 1973 with 203 and 373 to form 373.

No.	Lodge Name	Yr.	Council	ST	Notes
316	Quekolis	1945	Anthracite	PA	Merged 1969 with 223 to form 223.
317	Guneukitschik	1945	Mason-Dixon	MD	
318	Waguli	1945	Northwest Georgia	GA	
319	Watatic	1945	Fitchburg Area	MA	Merged 1964 with 309 to form 309.
320	Oskihoma	1945	Choctaw Area	OK	Changed name in 1956.
320	Oklahoma	1945	Choctaw Area	OK	Changed name in 1966.
320	Oskihoma	1945	Choctaw Area	OK	Absorbed by 138 in 1973.
321	Nani-Ba-Zhu	1945	Kanza	KS	
322	White Fang	1945	Mobile Area	AL	Changed name in 1957.
322	Woa Cholena	1945	Mobile Area	AL	Changed name in 1958.
322	War Eagle	1945	Mobile Area	AL	Changed name.
322	Woa Cholena	1945	Mobile Area	AL	
323	Arrowhead	1945	Nationa Trail	WV	Merged 1993 with 289 to form 36.
324	Thundering Spring	1945	Flint River	GA	Changed name in 1952.
324	Ini-to	1945	Flint River	GA	
325	Quilshan	1945	Mount Baker Area	WA	Merged 1995 with 305 to form 338.
326	Tipisa	1946	Central Florida	FL	
327	Huaco	1946	Heart O'Texas	TX	
328	Ya Ha Klack Go	1946	Muskogee Area	OK	Rechartered after 1955 and after previously disbanding. Changed name.
328	Nanomihistiim	1946	Eastern Oklahoma	OK	Changed name in 1975.
328	Ni-U-Kon-Sha	1946	Eastern Oklahoma	OK	Absorbed by 138 in 1983.
329	Nikiwigi	1946	Monadnock	MA	Merged 1994 with 309 to form 309.
330	Kotso	1946	Chisholm Trail	TX	
331	Klahican	1946	Cape Fear Area	NC	
332	Tecumseh	1946	Wolverine Area	MI	Merged 1973 with 88 to form 88.
333	Hiawassee	1946	West Georgia	GA	Absorbed by 204 in 1963.
333	Wahunsenakah	1996	Colonial Virginia	VA	From merger of 463 and 483 in 1996.
334	Shin-Go-Beek	1946	Thatcher Woods Area	IL	Merged 1994 with 157 to form 246.
335	Ump Quah	1946	North Central Washington	WA	Merged 1992 with 301 to form 614.
336	Wa-La-Moot-Kin	1946	Blue Mountain	WA	
337	Otyokwa	1946	Chippewa Valley	WI	
338	Nisjaw	1946	Three G Counties	AZ	Disbanded 1947. Rechartered 1961 as 551.
338	Sikhis Mox Lamonti	1995	Mount Baker Area	WA	From merger of 305 and 325 in 1995.

No.	Lodge Name	Yr.	Council	ST	Notes
339	Genesee	1946	Genesee	NY	Changed name in 1948.
339	Tana Wis Qua	1946	Genesee	NY	Changed name in 1952.
339	Amo'chk	1946	Genesee	NY	Merged 1994 with 409 to form 339.
339	Ashokwahta	1995	Iroquois Trail	NY	
340	Timuquan	1946	West Central Florida	FL	
341	Chief Lone Wolf	1946	Adobe Walls Area	TX	Merged 1987 with 486 to form 486.
341	Japeechen	1992	Jersey Shore	NJ	From merger with 423 and 535 in 1992.
342	Stanislaus	1946	San-Joaquin-Calaveras	CA	Changed name in 1948.
342	Sumi	1946	Forty-Niner	CA	
343	Wapsu Achtu	1946	Susquehanna Valley	PA	Merged 1975 with 384 to form 343.
343	Woapeu Sisilija	1975	Susquehanna	PA	
344	Golden Tomahawk	1946	Iowa River Valley	IA	Merged 1952 with 467 to form 467.
345	White Panther	1946	Delta Area	MS	Changed name in 1956.
345	Koi Hatachie	1946	Delta Area	MS	Merged 1995 with 406 to form 558.
346	Wiyaka	1946	Nevada Area	NV	Changed name in 1961.
346	Tannu	1946	Nevada Area	NV	
347	Wisawanik	1946	Blair Bedford Area	PA	Changed name in 1946.
347	Wopsononock	1946	Blair Bedford Area	PA	Merged 1971 with 275 and 441 to form 275.
348	Tahoma	1946	Mount Rainier	WA	Merged 1994 with 285 and 392 to form 155.
349	Blue Heron	1946	Tidewater	VA	
350	Maka-Ina	1946	Chief Logan	OH	Merged 1996 with 93 and 109 to form 65.
351	Wisie Hal'a Con	1946	Long Trail	VT	Merged 1973 with 398 to form 351.
351	Ajapeu	1973	Green Mountain	VT	
352	Zhingwak	1946	Twin City	IN	Absorbed by 110 in 1972.
353	Immokalee	1947	Southwest Georgia	GA	
354	Mayi	1947	Golden Empire	CA	Absorbed 511 in 1979. Merged 1993 with 395 and 485 to form 47.
355	Nanuk	1947	Western Alaska	AK	
356	Tatokainyanka	1947	Central Wyoming	WY	
357	Adirondack	1947	Jefferson-Lewis	NY	Merged 1982 with 461 to form 120.
358	Echeconnee	1947	Central Georgia	GA	
359	Aheka	1947	Aheka	NJ	Merged 1974 with 449 to form 359.
359	Aquaninoncke	1974	Passaic Valley	NJ	

No.	Lodge Name	Yr.	Council	ST	Notes
360	Shinnecock	1947	Suffolk County	NY	
361	Wilgus	1947	Western Montana	MT	Merged 1974 with 299, 300, and 390 to form 300.
362	Ken-Etiwa-Pec	1947	Orange Mountain	NJ	Merged 1976 with 178 and 515 to form 178.
363	Shoshoni	1947	Snake River Valley Area	ID	Rechartered 1954 after previously disbanding. Changed name.
363	Ma I Shu	1947	Snake River Area	ID	
364	Loon	1947	Adirondack	NY	
365	Lemonti Lemooto	1947	Mountainview	ID	Merged 1967 with 266 to form 266.
366	Wazhazee	1947	Ouachita Area	AR	
367	Wapiti	1947	Audubon	KY	Absorbed 405 in 1959. Merged 1996 with 499 to form 201.
368	Tapawingo	1947	Western Reserve	OH	Merged 1995 with 114 and 396 to form 56.
369	Chi Sigma	1947	Quinnipiac	CT	Changed name in 1954.
369	Arcoon	1947	Quinnipiac	CT	Absorbed 274 in 1978.
370	Massasoit	1947	Quincy	MA	Rechartered 1959 after previously disbanding. Changed name.
370	Moswetuset	1947	Quincy	MA	Absorbed by 195 in 1965.
371	Thunderbird	1947	Lake Agassiz	ND	Merged 1976 with 52, 176, and 183 to form 27.
372	Mandan	1948	Santa Fe Trail	KS	
373	Carcajou	1948	Southwest Michigan	MI	Merged 1973 with 203 and 315 to form 373.
373	Nacha-Mawat	1973	Southwest Michigan	MI	
374	Gab-Shi-Win-Gi-Ji-Kess	1948	Chief Okemos	MI	
375	Machek N'Gult	1948	Oakland Area	CA	Merged 1965 with 282 to form 282.
376	A-Me-Qua	1948	Mesquakie Area	IA	Absorbed by 313 in 1959.
377	Sipp-O	1948	Buckeye	OH	Absorbed 472 in 1992.
378	Gila	1948	Yucca	TX	
379	Kaweah	1948	Alameda	CA	
380	Ho-Mita-Koda	1948	Redland Area	CA	Rechartered 1955 after previously disbanding. Changed name.
380	A-Tsa	1948	Grayback	CA	Rechartered 1955 after previously disbanding. Absorbed by 127 in 1976.
381	Braves of Decorah	1948	Gateway Area	WI	Changed name in 1995.
381	Ni-Sanak-Tani	1948	Gateway Area	WI	

No.	Lodge Name	Yr.	Council	ST	Notes
382	Eagle Creek	1948	Put-Han-Sen Area	OH	Merged 1994 with 238 to form 449.
383	Tahosa	1948	Denver Area	CO	
384	Tiadaghton	1948	West Branch	PA	Merged 1975 with 343 to form 343.
385	Yustaga	1948	Gulf Coast	FL	
386	Tuckahoe	1948	York Adams Area	PA	
387	Pike's Peak	1948	Pikes Peak	CO	Changed name in 1953.
387	Ha-Kin-Skay-A-Ki	1948	Pikes Peak	CO	
388	Samson Occum	1948	Pequot	CT	Merged 1972 with 297 to form 10.
389	Mauwehu	1948	Mauwehu	CT	Merged 1972 with 408 and 521 to form 313.
390	Nitapokaiyo	1948	Yellowstone Valley	MT	Changed name in 1964.
390	Amangi Mos	1948	Yellowstone Valley	MT	Merged 1974 with 299, 300, and 361 to form 300.
391	Chiriqui	1948	Panama Canal	CZ	Absorbed by 555 in 1987.
392	Tillicum	1948	Tumwater Area	WA	Merged 1994 with 285 and 348 to form 155.
393	Abake-Mi-Sa-Na-Ki	1948	Cape Cod	MA	
394	Seneca	1948	Sullivan Trail	NY	Merged 1990 with 186 to form 186.
395	Tribe of La Porte	1948	Buttres Area	CA	Changed name in 1950.
395	Kowaunkamish	1948	Buttes Area	CA	Merged 1993 with 354 and 485 to form 47.
396	Nea-To-Ka	1948	Mahoning Valley	OH	Rechartered 1953 after previously disbanding. Changed name.
396	Mahoning	1948	Mahoning Valley	OH	Changed name in 1957.
396	Neatoka	1948	Mahoning Valley	OH	Merged 1995 with 114 and 368 to form 56.
397	Chilantakoba	1948	New Orleans	LA	
398	Memphremagog	1948	Green Mountain	VT	Merged 1964 with 493 to form 398.
398	Nianque	1964	Ethan Allen	VT	Merged 1973 with 351 to form 351.
399	A-Booik-Paa-Gun	1948	De Soto Area	AR	
400	Quetzal	1948	Lewis-Clark	ID	Changed name in 1954.
400	Wawookia	1948	Lewis-Clark	ID	Merged 1995 with 311.
401	Nakida-Naou	1948	Timber Trails	MI	Merged 1975 with 79 to form 25.
402	Onteroraus	1948	Otschodela	NY	
403	Red Feather	1948	Wyo-Braska Area	ME	Changed name in 1955.
403	Wiyaka Luta	1948	Wyo-Braska Area	Me	Absorbed by 464 in 1975.
404	Ti'ak	1949	Pine Burr Area	MS	
405	Land of Big Caves	1949	Mammoth Cave	KY	Changed name in 1950.

No.	Lodge Name	Yr.	Council	ST	Notes
405	Walah Elemamekhaki	1949	Mammoth Cave	KY	Absorbed by 367 in 1959.
406	Chickasah	1949	Chickasaw	TN	Merged 1995 with 345 to form 558.
407	Novando Ikeu	1949	Tendoy Area	ID	Merged 1994 with 544 to form 407.
407	Shunkah Mahneetu	1994	Grand Teton	ID	
408	Chief Pomperaug	1949	Pomperaug	CT	Merged 1972 with 389 and 521 to form 313.
409	Tuighaunock	1949	Lewiston Trail	NY	Merged 1994 with 339 to form 339.
410	Aola	1949	Oswego County	NY	Merged 1968 with 516 to form 410.
410	Nischa Nitis	1968	Hiawatha	NY	
411	Unalachtigo	1949	Gloucester-Salem	NJ	Changed spelling in mid 1950s.
411	Unilachtego	1949	Gloucester-Salem	NJ	Merged 1967 with 107 to form 107.
412	Buckskin	1949	Nassau County	NY	
413	Hi'lo Ha Chy'a-la	1949	Eastern Arkansas Area	AR	
414	Musketahquid	1949	Norumbega	MA	
415	Lemolloillahee	1949	Island Empire	WA	Merged 1993 with 311 to form 311.
416	Wolf	1949	South West Virginia	WV	Changed name in 1950s.
416	Hytone	1949	Appalachian	WV	Merged 1993 with 210 and 475 to form 617.
417	Finger Lakes	1949	Finger Lakes	NY	Changed name in 1950s.
417	Ganeodiyo	1949	Finger Lakes	NY	
418	Nick Stoner	1949	Sir William Johnson	NY	Changed name in 1953.
418	Thay-En-Da-Ne-Gea	1949	Sir William Johnson	NY	Merged 1990 with 181 and 268 to form 181.
419	Packanke	1949	Lawrence County	PA	Merged 1973 with 168 to form 168.
420	Kaniengehaga	1949	Licking County	OH	Absorbed by 93 in 1987.
421	Mazama	1949	Crater Lake	OR	Merged 1994 with 437 to form 491.
422	Acorn	1949	South Indiana	IN	Changed name in 1953.
422	Kiondaga	1949	Buffalo Trace	IN	Absorbed part of 167 in 1955.
423	Gitche Gumee	1949	Atlantic Area	NJ	Merged 1992 with 535 to form 341.
424	Amochol	1949	Zane Trace	OH	Changed name after 1952.
424	Netawatamass	1949	Muskingum Valley	OH	Absorbed 448 in 1956. Changed name in 1975.
424	Netawatwees	1949	Muskinggum Valley	OH	
425	Chippewa	1949	Three Rivers	IN	Changed name in 1952.
425	Tipicon	1949	Three Rivers	IN	Merged 1973 with 173 and 269 to form 173.
426	Po-E-Mo	1950	Great Rivers	MO	Merged 1972 with 216 to form 216.

No.	Lodge Name	Yr.	Council	ST	Notes
427	Achewon Netopalis	1949	Greenwich	CT	
428	Loquanne Allangwh	1950	Ne Tse O	TX	
429	Dzie-Hauk Tonga	1950	Jayhawk Area	KS	
430	Ahwahnee	1950	North Orange	CA	Merged 1973 with 298 to form 13.
431	Witauchsundin	1950	Union	NJ	Absorbed by 68 in 1980.
432	Wipala Wiki	1950	Grand Canyon	AZ	Absorbed 503 in 1992.
433	Mi-Ni-Ci-No	1950	Sekan Area	KS	Absorbed by 458 in 1973.
434	Cherokee	1950	Coronado Area	KS	Changed name in 1951.
434	Kidi-Kidish	1950	Coronado Area	KS	
435	Mischa Mokwa	1950	Cumberland	KY	Absorbed by 480 in 1962.
436	Ashie	1950	San Diego County	CA	Merged 1992 with part of 532 to form 45.
437	Makualla	1950	Modoc Area	OR	Merged 1994 with 421 to form 491.
438	Wahpeton	1950	Prairie Gold Area	IA	Merged 1973 with 474 to form 438.
438	Miniconjou	1973	Prairie Gold Area	IA	
439	Miwok	1950	Santa Clara County	CA	Disbanded in 1952. Rechartered in 1964.
440	Chinchewunska	1950	Alexander Hamilton	NJ	Merged 1969 with 37 to form 37.
441	Amadahi	1950	Admiral Robert E. Perry	PA	Merged 1969 with 275 and 347 to form 275.
442	Hyas Chuck Kah Sun Klatawa	1950	Portland Area	OR	Changed name in 1960.
442	Skyloo	1950	Columbia Pacific	OR	Merged 1994 with 259 to form 442.
442	Wauna La-Mon 'Tay	1994	Cascade Pacific	OR	
443	Nooteeming	1950	Dutchess County	NY	Merged 1995 with 64 and 444.
444	Munsi	1950	Rockland County	NY	Merged 1995 with 64 and 443.
445	Pohawk	1950	Covered Wagon	NE	Merged 1964 with 97 to form 97.
446	Cuauhtli	1951	Direct Service	MX	Disbanded 1971. Absorbed by 555.
447	Souhegan	1951	Quannapowitt	MA	Merged 1958 with 261 and 496 to form 261.
448	Wapagoklos	1951	Tomakawk	OH	Absorbed by 424 in 1956.
449	Minisi	1951	Alhtaha	NJ	Merged 1974 with 359 to form 359.
449	Mawat Woakus	1994	Black Swamp Area	OH	From merger of 238 and 382 in 1994.
450	Mitigwa	1951	Mid-Iowa	IA	Absorbed 453 in 1969.
451	Wannalancit	1951	Greater Lowell	MA	
452	She-Sheeb	1951	Pottawattomie	IN	Merged 1972 with half of 142 and 182 to form 573.
453	Winnebago	1951	South Iowa Area	IA	Changed name after 1955.

No.	Lodge Name	Yr.	Council	ST	Notes
453	Bo-Qui	1951	Southern Iowa Area	IA	Absorbed by 450 in 1969.
454	Kamehameha	1951	Kilauea	HI	Merged 1972 with 557 and 565 to form 567.
455	Allegewi	1951	Elk Lick	PA	Merged 1973 with 165 to form 165.
456	Powhatan	1951	Blue Ridge	VA	Merged 1972 with 161 to form 161.
457	Thal-Coo-Zyo	1951	Tri-State Area	WV	
458	Hi-Cha-Ko-Lo	1951	Quivira	KS	
459	Catawba	1951	Mecklenburg County	NC	
460	Iyatonka	1951	Pheasant	SD	Absorbed by 105 in 1978.
461	Manatoanna	1951	St. Lawrence	NY	Merged 1982 with 257 to form 120.
462	Ku-Ni-Eh	1951	Dan Beard	OH	Absorbed 155 in 1956. Absorbed 306 in 1959. Merged 1985 with 145 to form 145.
463	Kecoughtan	1951	Peninsula	VA	Merged 1995 with 483 to form 333.
464	Kola	1951	Longs Peak	CO	Absorbed 403 in 1973.
465	Yahnundasis	1951	Upper Mohawk	NY	Merged 1981 with 34 to form 34.
466	Hungteetsepoppi	1951	Piedmont	CA	
467	Black Crescent	1952	Waubeek Area	IA	Merged 1952 with 344 to form 467.
467	Cho-Gun-Mun-A-Nock	1952	Hawkeye Area	IA	
468	Oo Yum Buli	1952	Mount Diablo	CA	Merged 1993 with 263 to form 58.
469	Tittabawasink	1952	Paul Bunyan	MI	Merged 1972 with 89 to form 89.
470	Amanquemack	1952	National Capital Area	MD	Changed name in 1954.
470	Amangamek-Wipit	1952	National Capital Area	MD	
471	Woapalane	1952	Bristol	CT	Merged 1967 with 234 to form 234.
472	Scaroyadii	1952	Columbiana	OH	Absorbed by 377 in 1992.
473	Aiaouez	1952	Winnebago	IA	Merged 1972 with 108 to form 108.
474	Ta	1952	Sergeant Floyd	IA	Rechartered 1958 after previously disbanding. Changed name.
474	War Eagle	1952	Sergeant Floyd	IA	Merged 1973 with 438 to form 438.
475	Wachu Menetopolis	1952	Buckskin	MV	Merged 1993 with 210 and 416 to form 617.
476	Tunkhannock	1952	Bethlehem Area	PA	Merged 1969 with 44 and 58 to form 44.
477	Ah Wa Ge	1952	Tioughnioga	NY	Merged 1975 with 546 to form 477.
477	Gajuka	1975	Baden-Powell	NY	
478	Wisumahi	1952	Arrowhead Area	CA	Merged 1973 with 127 to form 127.
479	Istrouma	1952	Istrouma Area	LA	Changed name in 1953.

No.	Lodge Name	Yr.	Council	ST	Notes
479	Quinipissa	1952	Istrouma Area	LA	
480	Kawida	1952	Blue Grass	KY	Absorbed 435 in 1962. Absorbed 241 in 1979.
481	Aracoma	1952	Black Warrior	AL	
482	Black Eagle	1952	Transatlantic	GE	
483	Chanco	1952	Old Dominion Area	VA	Merged 1995 with 463 to form 333.
484	Oratam	1952	Bergen	NJ	Absorbed part of 84 in 1985.
485	Tehama	1952	Mount Lassen Area	CA	Merged 1993 with 354 and 395 to form 47.
486	Palo Duro	1952	Llano Estacado	TX	Merged 1987 with 341 to form 486.
486	Nischa Achowalogen	1987	Golden Spread	TX	
487	Taunkacoo	1953	Algonquin	MA	
488	Ta Tanka	1953	San Gabriel Valley	CA	
489	Nishkin Halupa A Pe Lachi	1953	Longhorn	TX	
490	Shingebis	1953	North Essex	MA	Merged 1993 with 505 and 539 to form 158.
491	Tunxis	1953	Tunxis	CT	Merged 1973 with 59, 217 234, and 558 to form 59.
491	Lo La 'Qam Geela	1994	Crater Lake	OR	From merger of 431 and 437 in 1994.
492	Golden Sun	1953	Cornhusker	NE	
493	Kola	1953	Calvin Coolidge	VT	Changed name.
493	Nicaweegee	1953	Calvin Coolidge	VT	Merged 1964 with 398 to form 398.
494	Papago	1953	Catalina	AZ	Absorbed 177 in 1965.
495	Miami	1953	Miami Valley	OH	
496	Menetomi	1953	Sachem	MA	Merged 1958 with 261 and 447 to form 261.
497	Shingis	1953	Yohogania	PA	Merged 1971 with 130 to form 130.
498	Hinode Goya	1953	Far East	JP	Absorbed 538 in 1965. Changed name in 1975.
498	Ikunuhkatsi	1953	Far East	JP	Changed name in 1985.
498	Achpateuny	1953	Far East	JP	
499	White Feather	1953	Four Rivers	KY	Merged 1996 with 367 to form 201.
500	Ona Yote Kaonaga	1953	Fort Stanwix	NY	Merged 1968 with 34 to form 34.
501	Wolverine	1953	Kettle Moraine	WI	Merged 1973 with 61, 73, 194, 233, and 244 to form 61.
502	T'Kope Kwiskwis	1954	Chief Seattle	WA	Absorbed 530 in 1975.
503	Chee Dodge	1954	Grand Canyon	AZ	Absorbed by 432 in 1992.

No.	Lodge Name	Yr.	Council	ST	Notes
504	Saukenuk	1954	Fort Armstrong Area	IL	Merged 1959 with 170 to form 170.
505	Amiskwi	1954	North Bay	MA	Merged 1993 with 490 and 539 to form 158.
506	Yokahu	1954	Puerto Rico	PR	
507	Penain Sew Netami	1954	Berkshire	MA	Merged 1968 with 556 to form 507.
507	Memsochet	1968	Great Trails	MA	
508	Tu-Cubin-Noonie	1954	Utah Nationa Park	UT	
509	Agawam	1954	Cacholot	MA	Merged 1972 with 124 to form 124.
510	Three Arrows	1955	Tri Trails	NE	Merged 1994 with 517 to form 94.
511	Canaku	1955	Tahoe Area	CA	Absorbed by 354 in 1970.
512	Wah-Pe-Kah-Me-Kunk	1955	Delaware County	IN	Merged 1973 with 222 and 308 to form 21.
513	Lou Ott	1955	Johnny Appleseed	OH	Merged 1996 with 121 and 205 to form 619.
514	Choa	1955	Cache Valley	UT	Changed name in 1955.
514	Twoa-Ba-Cha	1955	Cache Valley	UT	Merged 1996 with 529 and 561 to form 535.
515	Oleleu	1955	Eagle Rock	NJ	Merged 1976 with 178 and 362 to form178.
516	Onondaga	1955	Onondaga	NY	Merged 1968 with 410 to form 410.
517	We-U-Shi	1955	Overland Trails	NE	Merged 1994 with 510 to form 94.
518	Tisqauntum	1956	Squanto	MA	Merged 1969 with 164 to form 164.
519	Minqua	1956	Lancaster County	PA	Merged 1972 with 39 to form 39.
520	El-Ku-Ta	1956	Great Salt Lake	UT	
521	Ponus	1956	Alfred W. Dater	CT	Merged 1972 with 389 and 408 to form 313.
522	Wa-Be-Wa-Wa	1957	Toledo Area	OH	Changed name in 1973
522	Tindeuchen	1957	Toledo Area	OH	
523	Kootz	1957	Southeast Alaska	AK	
524	Chippecotton	1957	Racine County	WI	Merged 1972 with 153 to form 8.
525	Pachachoag	1957	Mohegan	MA	Changed name in 1959.
525	Pachachaug	1957	Mohegan	MA	
526	Nahak	1957	Lake Superior	MN	Merged 1995 with 196 to form 196.
527	Buckongehannon	1957	Central West Virginia	WV	Merged 1990 with 201 to form 618.
528	Pomponio	1957	San Mateo County	CA	Merged 1995 with 207 to form 63.
529	Tatanka	1957	Jim Bridger	WY	Merged 1996 with 514 and 561 to form 535.
530	Mox Kar-Po	1957	Olympic Area	WA	Absorbed by 502 in 1975.

No.	Lodge Name	Yr.	Council	ST	Notes
531	Esselen	1957	Monterey Bay Area	CA	
532	Pang	1957	Desert Trails	AZ	Part merged with 436 to form 45 in 1992. Part absorbed by 432 in 1992.
533	Talako	1958	Marin	CA	
534	Wincheck	1958	Narragansett	RI	
535	Schiwa'pew Names	1958	Ocean County	NJ	Merged 1992 with 423 to form 341.
535	Awaxawee Awachia	1996	Trapper Trails	UT	From merger of 514, 529, and 561 in 1996.
536	Tupwee Gudas Gov Youchiquot Soovep	1958	Rocky Mountain	CO	From 1973–93 used abbr. of Tupwee on insignia.
537	Cabrosha	1959	Sonoma Mendocino	CA	Merged 1993 with 262 to form 194.
538	Baluga	1959	Philipine Islands	PI	Absorbed by 498 in 1965.
539	Passaquo	1959	Lone Tree	MA	Merged 1993 with 490 and 505 to form 158.
540	Ahtuhquog	1959	Potomac	MD	
541	Mic-O-Say	1959	Western Colorado	CO	
542	Kiminschi	1960	Mid Valley	PA	Merged 1962 with 543 to form 542.
542	Amad'ahi	1962	Forest Lakes	PA	Merged 1991 with 223 to form 191.
543	Monsey	1960	Dan Beard	PA	Merged 1962 with 542 to form 542.
544	Ha-Wo-Wo-He-Que'-Nah	1960	Teton Peaks	ID	Merged 1994 with 407 to form 407.
545	Alapaha	1960	Alapaha Area	GA	
546	Chi Sigma	1960	Louis Agassiz Fuertes	NY	Merged 1975 with 477 to form 477.
547	Ga-Goh'-Sa	1960	Seneca	NY	Merged 1975 with 165 to form 165.
548	Sha-Cha-Quoi	1961	Sequoia	CA	Merged 1994 with 102 to form 195.
549	Toontuk	1961	Midnight Sun	AK	
550	Menawngihella	1961	Mountaineer Area	WV	
551	Na-Ko-Na	1961	Copper	AZ	Changed name.
551	Saldo	1961	Copper	AZ	Absorbed by 432 in 1977.
552	Eckale Yakanen	1961	Sunny Land	FL	Rechartered 1961 after disbanding in 1955 as 219. Absorbed by 564 in 1995.
553	Paugassett	1961	Housatonic	CT	
554	He-Dia	1962	Maui County	HI	Changed name in 1963
554	Haleakala	1962	Maui County	HI	Changed name in 1964.
554	Maluhia	1962	Maui County	HI	
555	Gamenowinink	1962	Direct Service	TX	Absorbed 446 in 1971 Absorbed 391 in 1987.

No.	Lodge Name	Yr.	Council	ST	Notes
556	Metacomet	1962	Hampshire-Franklin	MA	Merged 1968 with 507 to form 507.
557	Pupukea	1962	Aloha	HI	Merged 1972 with 454 and 565 to form 567.
558	Wipunquoak	1964	Charter Oak	CT	Merged 1973 with 59, 217, 234, and 491 to form 59.
558	Ahoalan-Nachpikin	1995	Chickasaw	YN	From merger of 345 and 406 in 1995.
559	Wachtschu Mawachpo	1964	Westark Area	AR	
560	Eswau Huppeday	1964	Piedmont Area	NC	
561	Oala Ishadalakalish	1966	Lake Bonneville	UT	Merged 1996 with 514 and 529 to form 535.
562	Arawak	1966	Virgin Islands	VI	
563	Atchafalaya	1966	Evangeline Area	LA	
564	Osceola	1968	Southwest Florida	FL	Absorbed 552 in 1995.
565	Achsin	1970	Chamorro	GM	Merged 1973 with 454 and 557 to form 567.
566	Malibu	1972	Great Western	CA	From merger of 225 and 228 in 1972.
567	Mokupuni O Lawelawe	1972	Aloha	HI	From merger of 454, 557, and 565 in 1972. Changed name in 1986.
567	Na Mokupuni O Lawelawe	1972	Aloha	HI	
573	Sakima	1973	LaSalle	IN	From merger of 182, half of 142, and 452 in 1973.
578	Hasinai	1970	Three Rivers	TX	From merger of 36 and 62 in 1970.
614	Tataliya	1992	Grand Columbia	WA	From merger of 301 and 335 in 1992.
617	Chi-Hoota-Wei	1993	Buckskin	WV	From merger of 210, 416, and 475 in 1993.
618	Nendawen	1990	Allohak Area	WV	From merger of 201 and 527 in 1990.
619	Portage	1996	Heart of Ohio	OH	From merger of 121, 205, and 513 in 1996.

GLOSSARY OF COMMONLY USED TERMS

Bar mount: a solid bar onto which the pin is attached (rather than a pin attached directly to device).

BSA: Boy Scouts of America.

B-W-R: Blue-White-Red colors in a patch or ribbon.

C-A-W or C.A.W: Compass-Anchor-Wings combined design of the Explorer Division.

Chenille: fuzzy style of patch, like a school varsity letter.

Cloth back: patch with plain back.

Community Strip: single line arc with town name.

Clutch back: pin or collar device with pin on back and detachable circular squeeze wing.

Crude clasp: safety style pin with only a bent metal fastener; usually found on rank pins.

CSP: Council Shoulder Patch.

Cut edge: patch edge where cloth is just cut.

FDL: Fleur-de-lis; the scout emblem.

Felt: usually a base material which is embroidered with a design.

Flap: a patch in the shape of a button-down pocket flap; worn on the right pocket flap, identifies OA Lodge membership.

Folded pin: plain bent wire.

Full square: a pre-1940 neckerchief which is a large full square of cloth.

Gauze back: patch with gauze material on back.

Green and Brown: Community, State, or Council Strip of brown lettering on green twill (Explorers) (1945–55).

Jacket Patch: a large 6-10" patch made for the back of a jacket.

JSP: Jamboree Council Shoulder Patch.

Khaki and Red: Community, State, or Council Patch with red lettering on khaki twill (1935–1950).

Leather Patch: made for back packs.

LSA: Lone Scouts of America (1915–1925 name).

LSD: Lone Scout Division (post-1925 name, after inclusion into BSA).

LSS: Lone Scout Service (post-1925 name, after inclusion into BSA).

National: The National Council, currently in Irvine, TX; formerly New York City and North Brunswick, NJ.

N/C: neckerchief.

NESA: National Eagle Scout Association.

NOAC: National Order of the Arrow Conference.

NSJ: National Scout Jamboree.

OA: Order of the Arrow.

Plastic back: patch with plastic coating on back.

Pocket Patch: a 2-4" patch usually worn on the right pocket.

Red and White: Community, State, or Council Patch with white lettering on red twill. (1950–1972).

Region: From 1921–1972, the local councils were divided into twelve regional groupings; there are now six.

Rolled edge: patch edge where cloth is embroidered over.

R-W-B: Red-White-Blue colors in a patch or ribbon.

Safety clasp: pin fits into locking housing.

Safety pin clasp: standard style safety pin; usually found on rank pins.

Screw back: pin or collar device with screw post on back and detachable circular, hexagon, or florate.

Solid: a fully-embroidered patch.

State Strip: single line small arc with state name or abbreviation.

Twill: rough or smooth; a cotton base material for a patch with rib-like design which slants left or right.

WJ: World Jamboree.

Yellow and Blue: Community, State, or Council Patch with yellow lettering on blue (Cubs) (1930–1950).

SCOUTING MEMORABILIA DEALERS

The following is a list of dealers who publish fixed price sale list or mail bid/phone auctions of scout memorabilia on a periodic basis. Some dealers charge a subscription fee, others offer their list for free as long as purchases are made. Some are distributed electronically, others by mail. Some offer reference books and storage materials. When requesting sample copies, sending a dollar would be a nice gesture. When requesting information, a self-addressed stamped envelope would be appreciated.

Brush Creek Trading Co.
John Pleasants
P.O. Box 296
Staley, NC 27355-0296
www.oapatch.com

The Carolina Trader
Richard Shields
P.O. Box 769
Monroe, NC 28111-0769
www.thecarolinatrader.com

Looking for Something?
Darrell Wessinger
117 Sandy Bank Drive
Lexington, SC 29072
Darrwess@aol.com

The Scout Patch Auction
Roy More
2484 Dundee
Ann Arbor, MI 48103
www.tpsa.com

Good Ol' Days
Cal Holden
P.O. Box 264
Doylestown, OH 44230
goodolddayscal@aol.com

Grand Teton Scout Museum
Bill Gomm
Shelly, ID 83274

First Class Shop
Robert Burt
RR 7 Box 309, Lot 24
Edinburg, TX 78539
REVLNGBV@aol.com

Heart O'Texas Trader
John Conley Williams
P.O. Box 23374
Waco, TX 76702-3374
www.hottrader.com

Painter's Patch Service
Earle & Delores Painter
P.O. Box 92577
Lakeland, FL 33804-2577
EandDP56@aol.com

Scout Collectors Shop
Jim Clough
P.O. Box 6754
Maryville, TN 37802-6754
TNJIM48@concentric.net

Russell Smart
P.O. Box 16449
Greenville, SC 29606
www.scoutstuff.net

Scout Patch Network
Gene Cobb
P.O. Box 11
Vidalia, LA 71733
genecobb@laribay.net

The Patch Connection
Greg Beachtle
P.O. Box 1248
Summerville, SC 29484-1248
Patchconn@quik.com

Cyber Scout Collectibles
Charlie Gregory
80 Columbia Hill Rd.
Danville, PA 17821-9306
www.cyber-scout.com

The Stevensons
Bea & Jim Stevenson
316 Sage Lane
Euless, TX 76039-7906
www.thestevensons.com

Streamwood
Chris Jensen
P.O. Box 1841
Easley, SC 29641
www.streamwood.net

R.J. Sayers
P.O. Box 629
Brevard, NC 28712

Silverfox Trader
Marty and Derek Wasznicky
12 Emery Rd.
Townsend, MA 01468
www.silverfox@net1plus.com

Scouting Collectible
Doug Bearce
Box 4745
Salem, OR 97302
pearce@prodigy.net

Ozark Philatelics & Collectibles
Kirk Dolan
2600 Grand Ave. Ste. 900
Kansas City, MO 64108
www.kirkdolan.com

Daniel Beard's National Scout Commissioner flag. Courtesy of Troop 1, Flushing, NY.

SCOUTING COLLECTOR ORGANIZATIONS & PUBLICATIONS

Until the beginning of 2001, there were three general publications available, and several more smaller specialized journals. Two of those publications and the collector group which sponsored the separate publications have merged, namely, the American Scouting Traders Association, and the American Scouting Historical Society. The new organization is called the International Scouting Collectors Association (ICTA).

International Scouting Collectors Association Journal
www.scouttrader.org
Treasurer: Doug Krutilek
9025 Alcosta Blvd. #230
San Ramon, CA 94583
Dues $25.00 (US)
    $40.00 (International) $350.00 (Life)

Scout Memorabilia
Lawrence L. Lee Scouting Museum, Daniel Webster
    Council
P.O. Box 1121
Manchester, NH 03105

Specialized Groups:

Scout Sealers
Murray Fried
    25 Gildner St.
    Kitchener, Ontario, N2H 6M4
    Canada

**Scouts on Stamps Society
International (SOSSI)**
C/O Corresponding Secretary
Kenneth Shuker
    22 Cedar Lane
    Cornwell, NY 12518
    www.sossi.org
    Dues $15.00 (US); $28.00 (Foreign, Air)
    Life $250.00 (US) $300 (Foreign)

SCOUTING ON THE INTERNET

Some of these sites are official BSA, others are private, others support the program

www.bsa.scouting.org

www.users.fast.net/~shenning/bsa.html

www.angelfire.com/nm/philpatches/index.html

www.scouter.com

www.tmrmuseum.com

www.macscouter.com

www.mninter.net/~blkeagle/

www.thescoutingway.com

www.digitalscoutpatches.com

www.geocities.com/yosemite/falls/8826

www.gilwell.com

www.oaimages.com

www.mitchreis.com

REFERENCE WORKS

In the past 20 years, collectors have begun to combine their interests and publish specialized guidebooks, many of which are listed below. For specialized information on scouting collectibles, please consider adding to your library some or all of the following books. Many are available from the author directly or your favorite scout memorabilia dealer. (Postage not included in the prices.)

An Aid to Collecting Selected Council Shoulder Patches with Valuation Guide (Franck, Hook, Ellis, Jones) ($25)

Boy Scout of America Uniform Program Strips 1910-1998 Collecting Guide ($22)
Brad Estabrook & Chris Jensen
Streamwood
P.O. Box 1841
Easley, SC 29641

The Blue Book – Standard Order of the Arrow Insignia Catalog, 3rd Ed. ($13)
Bill Topkis
2580 Silver Cloud Court
Park City, UT 84060

The Boy Scouts of America During World War I & II ($15)
Mitch Reis
883 Matianuck Ave.
Windsor, CT 06095

B.S.A. Fruit Salad ($18)
Leonard E. Michaud
168 Cresthill Ave.
Tonawanda, NY 14150

The Camp Book – A Listing of BSA Camps ($18) Minnihan and Sherman
Dave Minnihan
2300 Fairview Rd. #6202
Costa Mesa, CA 92626

Collecting Boy Scout Rank Badges
Paul Myers
P.O. Box 1013
Goshen, IN 46527

Collecting Scouting Literature (Fisk, Bearce) ($18)
Doug Bearce
P.O. Box 4742
Salem, OR 97302

A Comprehensive Guide to the Eagle Scout Award ($25)
Terry Grove
2048 Shady Hill Terrace
Winter Park, FL, 32972

Councils of the BSA
Patrick Geary
1914 Avenue M.
Galveston, TX 77550

First Flaps (Morley, Topkis, Gould)
Bill Topkis
2580 Silver Cloud Court
Park City, UT 84060

Green Khaki Crimped-edge Merit Badges ($8)
Fred Duersch, Jr.
868 North 400 East
Logan, UT 84321

A Guide to Dating and Identifying B.S.A. Badges, Uniforms and Insignia, 3rd Ed. ($23.50)
Mitch Reis
883 Matianuck Ave.
Windsor, CT 06095

The History of the Lone Scouts through Memorabilia ($24)
Mitch Reis
883 Matianuck Ave.
Windsor, CT 06095

Kahunas Katalog of Boy Scouting Handbooks ($25)
Joe Price
559 No. Euclid
Upland, CA 91786

Kahunas Katalog of the Every Boy's Library ($25)
Joe Price
559 No. Euclid
Upland, CA 91786

Kahunas Katalog of Merit Badge Pamphlets ($25)
Joe Price
559 No. Euclid
Upland, CA 91786

Merit Badge Field Guide ($10)
Fred Duersch, Jr.
868 North 400 East
Logan UT 84321

Merit Badge Price Guide ($25)
Chris Jensen
Streamwood
P.O. Box 1841
Easley, SC 29641

National Jamboree Memorabilia Guide Book, 1995 edition (Jensen, Ellis)
Streamwood
P.O. Box 1841
Easley, SC 29641

Official Scout Blades ($20)
Ed Holbrook
Oregon City, OR

Patches and Memorabilia of the Order of the Arrow at National Events, Volumes 1 & 2. ($50)
Ronald G. Aldridg
250 Canyon Oaks Dr.
Argyle, TX 76226

Red & White Council Shoulder Strips, 4th ed. (Hyman & Kutz)
Art Hyman
6311 Rue Sophie
San Antonio, TX 78238

Scouting Exonumia Worldwide ($50)
Rudy J. Dioszegi
3307 126 St.
E. Burnsville, MN 55337

Scouting History through Memorabilia: The Bernie Miller Collection – Volumes 1 & 2. ($50)
Roy More
2484 Dundee
Ann Arbor, MI 48103

Senior Scouting Collectibles ($25)
Jim Clough
P.O. Box 6754
Maryville, TN 37802

Streamwood's Boy Scout Stuff Prices Realized, 1994-2000
Chris Jensen
P.O. Box 1841
Easley, SC 29641

World Jamboree Guide ($20)
Neil W. Larsen
4332 Marigold Ave.
Vadnais Heights, MN 55127

SCOUTING MUSEUMS

There are several types of museums or displays in which scouting items can be seen. One is the local historical society type, in which a case or two of stuff is accumulated together on the history of scouting in that area. A second is at a scout camp or service center where a benefactor has contributed funds for the building, and his material is on display. A camp may have a visitor's center with displays of that camp or council's items. Finally, there is the major facility, where a whole building is devoted to scouting items.

AZ Otis H. Chidester Scout
Museum of Southern Arizona
1937 E. Blacklidge Drive,
Tucson, AZ 85719
520-326-7669 by appointment
www.azscoutmuseum.com

CA Western Museum of Scouting
13115 Washington Boulevard,
Los Angeles, CA 90066

CO Koshare Indian Museum
115 West 18th St.
La Junta, CO 81050
719-384-4411
www.koshare.org

GA Scouting Memorabilia Museum
Atlanta Area Council Office
4th Floor, United Way Building
100 Edgewood Ave. NE
Atlanta, GA 30334
404-577-4810

IL Hillenberg Scout Museum
112 N. Beard St.
Danville, IL 61832
217-442-6678 by appointment
hillnbrg@net66.com

Ottawa Scouting Museum
1100 Canal St.
Ottawa, IL 61350
815-431-9353

KS Central States Scout Museum
815 Broadway
Larned, KS 67550
www.larned.net/~chamber/
tourism/cssm/cssm.htm
April - October 9-9, weekends,
Weekdays till 5, other times by
appointment

KY National Scout Museum
Murray, KY 42071-3316
The museum has closed to the
public, and is in the process of
moving to the National Office in
Irving, TX

MA Bussiere Scout Museum
154 Belmont Rd.
West Harwich, MA 02671

Boston University Library
Scouting Collection

Norman Rockwell Museum at
Stockbridge
Rt. 183,
Stockbridge, MA 01262
413-298-4100
www.nrm.org

Scouting Spirit Museum
64 New Estate Rd.,
Littleton, MA 01460
508-486-4418, by appointment

MI E. Urner Goodman Owaisippe
Museum
Owasippi Scout Reservation
Whitehall, MI 49461

France Scout Museum
12417 State Rd.
Nunica, MI 49448
616-842-2178, by appointment

Washington Historical Scouting
Museum
4772 Woodmire Dr.
Utica, MI 48087

Trailside Museum, Bear Mountain State Park.

Daniel Beard uniform.

MO   H. Roe Bartle Exposition Hall &
     Convention Center
     301 West 13 St.
     Kansas City, MO 64105
     Stuff from the active scouter
       and former mayor.

     National Eagle Scout
       Monument
     39th St. in Hyde Park
     Kansas City, MO 64105

NV   Las Vegas International
       Scouting Museum
     2915 W. Charleston, #4.
     Las Vegas, NV 89102
     www.home.earthlink.net/
       ~olecowboy/museum.htm

NH   Lawrence Lee Scouting
       Museum & Max Silber
       Scouting Library
     Camp Carpenter, RFD 6
     Manchester, NH 03105
     603-625-643(council office),
       Sept-June Saturdays, 10-4;
       July & August, daily, 10-4.
     www.scoutingmusuem.org

NM   Philmont Museum & Seton
       Memorial Library
     Philmont Scout Ranch
     Cimarron, NM 87714
     www.artcom.com/museum/nv/
       mr/87714.htm
     www.etsetoninstitute.org/
       PHILMONT.HTM

NY   Willaim Hillcourt Scout Museum
       and Carson Buck Memorial
       Library
     Camp Woodland
     Kibbie Lake Road
     Constantina, NY 13044
     315-623-9316

     Ten Mile River Scout Museum
     Ten Mile River Scout Camp
     Narrowsburg, NY 12764

     Trailside Museum
       (Dan Beard Stuff)
     Bear Mountain State Park
       Bear Mountain, NY 10911

NC   Long Scout Memory Lodge
       Museum
     Camp John J. Barnhardt
     42830 Cannon Rd.
     New London, NC 28127-9588
     by appointment

OH   Nathan L. Dauby Scout
       Museum
     Greater Cleveland Council,
       Scout Center
     E 22 St. at Woodlawn
     Cleveland, OH 44115

     Frank L. Grubbs Boy Scout
       Museum
     64 High St.
     Glouster, OH 45732
     Weds 1-5, Sat. 9-2,
     or by appointment

OK   Osage County Historical
       Museum
     700 N. Lynn Ave.
     Pawhuska, OK 74056
     918-287-9924
     Daily, 9-5

PA   Atwater-Kent Museum, Norman
       Rockwell Artworks
     15 South 7th St.
       Philadelphia, PA 19106
     www.libertynet.org/iha/tour/
       rock.html

     World of Scouting Musuem
     P.O. Box 2226
     Valley Forge, PA 19482
     610-783-5311
     Fri-Sun, 11-4 Memorial Day-
       Labor Day, Sat-Sun rest of
       year.
     www.worldofscoutingmusuem.org

SC   Palmetto Scout Museum
     420 South Church St.
     Spartanburg, SC 29301
     M-F, 9-5.

TN   Peregrine International
       Museum of Scouting
     6588 Hwy 411 South
     Greenback, TN 37742
     615-856-0244
     April-Oct 10-9, Nov-Mar 10-6

VA   Merrimac Scouting Museum
     15 Woodland St.
     Portsmouth, VA 23702
     757-485-1808, by appointment

     Shenandoah Area Council
       Scout Museum and Training
       Center
     107 Youth Development Court
     Winchester, VA 22602
     540-662-2551
     www.sac-bsa.org/zeb.htm

WI   Heritage Scout Museum
     Milwaukee County Council
       Service Center
     330 So. 84 St.
     Milwaukee, WI 53214

Milwaukee Scout Heritage Museum.

INDEX

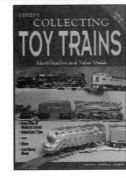

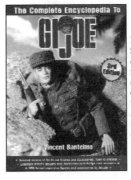